LIVING WITH PERIL

LIVING WITH PERIL

Eisenhower, Kennedy, and Nuclear Weapons

Andreas Wenger

ROWMAN & LITTLEFIELD PUBLISHERS, INC.
Lanham • Boulder • New York • Oxford

ROWMAN & LITTLEFIELD PUBLISHERS, INC.

Published in the United States of America
by Rowman & Littlefield Publishers, Inc.
4720 Boston Way, Lanham, Maryland 20706

12 Hid's Copse Road
Cummor Hill, Oxford OX2 9JJ, England

British Library Cataloguing in Publication Information Available

Library of Congress Cataloging-in-Publication Data

Wenger, Andreas.
    Living with peril : Eisenhower, Kennedy, and nuclear weapons /
Andreas Wenger.
        p.   cm.
    Includes bibliographical references (p.   ) and index.
    ISBN 0-8476-8514-4 (cloth : alk. paper),—ISBN 0-8476-8515-2
(pbk. : alk. paper)
        1. Nuclear weapons—Government policy—United States—History.
2. United States—Foreign relations—1953–1961.   3. United States—
Foreign relations—1961–1963.   4. Nuclear crisis stability.
I. Title.
UA23.W376   1997
355.02′17′0973—dc21   97-2430
                                                                        CIP

ISBN 0-8476-8514-4 (cloth : alk. paper)
ISBN 0-8476-8515-2 (pbk. : alk. paper)

Printed in the United States of America

To my mother and father

It is conceivable that a world of this kind [of mutual atomic plenty] may enjoy a strange stability arising from general understanding that it would be suicidal to "throw the switch." On the other hand it also seems possible that a world so dangerous may not be very calm, and to maintain peace it will be necessary for statesmen to decide against rash action not just once, but every time. In particular, since the coming of such a world will be gradual and since its coming may or may not be correctly estimated in all countries, there is a possibility that one nation or another may be tempted to launch a preventive war "before it is too late," only to find out that the time for such a blow has already passed.

Robert Oppenheimer, chairman, Panel on Armaments
and American Policy, January 1953

Contents

Acknowledgments

In the course of working on this book, I have been extraordinarily fortunate in finding help and assistance from many people and in a variety of ways. The final product has greatly benefited from the comments, suggestions, criticism, and encouragement I have received along the way.

My first and greatest intellectual debt is to Kurt R. Spillmann, whose deep curiosity and wide-ranging historical interests have challenged and inspired me. His constant encouragement has been essential for the conclusion of this book. I also thank Dieter Ruloff for his thoughts on my work.

The Woodrow Wilson School and the Center of International Studies at Princeton University provided a stimulating intellectual environment for the progress of my thinking. I owe a great debt to Wolfgang Danspeckgruber and to the staff of the Woodrow Wilson School as truly indispensable partners in the day-to-day work. Three members of the faculty merit special mention and gratitude. Richard Ullman gave early encouragement and provided opportunities for me to discuss my work within the American academic community. I thank Fred Greenstein for his willingness to share his insights into the workings of the Eisenhower administration. Finally, Aaron Friedberg gave freely of his time and advice, particularly in regard to addressing the concept of national security from a theoretical and a historical perspective.

Others have been of inestimable assistance to me. I thank John Lewis Gaddis of Ohio University, Marc Trachtenberg of the University of Pennsylvania, and Richard Immerman of Temple University for their comments on early manuscripts of the study. While my book has greatly benefited from their suggestions, final responsibility for the historical analysis presented herein is mine alone.

xiii

Many of my friends at Princeton have continued to be a source of good advice and general support. I owe a great debt to Jithendra Jayaratne, Alexander Galetovic, and Barry Pavel. I also want to express my special appreciation to Ted Posner. Without his immeasurable help, this book would be quite different in scope, language, and focus.

This study draws upon numerous archives and their staffs. Librarians and archivists in the John Fitzgerald Kennedy Library, the National Archives, the Library of Congress, and the National Defense University have been unfailingly helpful. Of particular help was Dr. William Burr of the National Security Archive.

I feel lucky to have ended up in the capable hands of Stephen M. Wrinn and Julie Kuzneski at Rowman & Littlefield. They saw my manuscript through to publication with great skill, high standards, and good cheer. I would also like to thank Claude Nicolet and Christoph Münger for their help with the manuscript.

Many organizations and individuals provided financial support to this undertaking. I received a generous grant from the Swiss government, which made it possible to spend an academic year in Princeton. I thank Theodor Winkler, chairman of the Program Committee, and his staff for their continual assistance. The Woodrow Wilson School and the Center of International Studies at Princeton very generously provided further financial assistance. Finally, I want to thank Leo Waldburger, chairman of General Consult Inc., who provided major financial backing for travel in the United States.

My wife Astrid has been my primary source of inspiration and encouragement. With her unflagging faith in me and my project, she helped me to never give up hope that one day the book would be completed. Finally, my deepest obligation is to my parents. They have always offered gladly their assistance and support and they have never failed to be there for me.

Abbreviations

AEC	U.S. Atomic Energy Comission
BMEWS	Ballistic Missile Early Warning System
CEP	Circular Error of Probability
CIA	Central Intelligence Agency
EDC	European Defense Community
ExComm	Executive Committee of the National Security Council (Cuban missile crisis)
FRG	Federal Republic of Germany
FY	Fiscal Year
GDR	German Democratic Republic
ICBM	Intercontinental Ballistic Missile
IRBM	Intermediate Range Ballistic Missile
JCS	Joint Chiefs of Staff
JSOP	Joint Strategic Objectives Plan
LTBT	Limited Test Ban Treaty
MLF	Multilateral Force
MRBM	Mediate Range Ballistic Missile
MSA	Mutual Security Agency
NAC	North Atlantic Council (NATO)
NATO	North Atlantic Treaty Organization
NESC	Net Evaluation Subcommittee
NIE	National Intelligence Estimate
NORAD	North American Air Defense Command
NSAM	National Security Action Memorandum
NSC	National Security Council
NSTL	National Strategic Target List
OAS	Organization of American States
ODM	Office of Defense Mobilization

PACCS	Post-Attack Command and Control System
PAL	Permissive Action Link
SAC	Strategic Air Command
SACEUR	Supreme Allied Commander, Europe (NATO)
SAM	Surface-to-Air Missile
SEATO	Southeast Asia Treaty Organization
SHAPE	Supreme Headquarters, Allied Powers, Europe (NATO)
SIOP	Single Integrated Operational Plan
UN	United Nations
WAPA	Warsaw Pact
WEU	Western European Union
WSEG	Weapons System Evaluation Group

Introduction

The Cold War came to an end without a bang. According to many analysts, nuclear weapons had an important impact on the peaceful transformation from a bipolar superpower rivalry to a more complex multipolar structure. Nuclear weapons, by serving as a constant warning of the dangers of total war, played a crucial stabilizing role in this process. By reminding East and West of mutual vulnerabilities, nuclear weapons locked both sides into fundamentally defensive policies. Nuclear danger forced governments to restrain themselves, and this was the single most important reason why the Cold War never turned hot. Instead, nuclear weapons made the Cold War a "long peace" that ended with the internal collapse of one contestant.[1]

While the observation that nuclear weapons are the great inhibitor of risky policies is almost conventional wisdom, the relevance of this observation has recently been challenged. John Mueller has argued that industrialization has multiplied both the scale and the costs of war—a fact that was so painfully exposed in the catastrophic results of the two world wars of this century. According to the latter thesis, war had become obsolete before the emergence of the nuclear arms race, and a "long peace" would have evolved after 1945 even without nuclear weapons. For this reason, Mueller argues, nuclear weapons were essentially irrelevant in bringing about the remarkable stability of the Cold War international system.[2] If this indeed was the case, why should more nations go down the costly path that leads to deployment of nuclear weapons? Although some contend that Mueller overlooks the impact of the quantum leap in destructive power associated with nuclear weapons, even Mueller's critics must give him credit for reviving the debate over the influence of nuclear weapons on international politics.[3]

Since the early days of the Cold War, strategists have been grappling

1

with the consequences of the first nuclear detonation. The discussion has been shaped by two major streams of thought. One stream of thought recognized the profound impact of the "absolute weapon" on military and political relations among states. Its original spokesman was Bernard Brodie, whose writings emphasized the revolutionary consequences of the nuclear era: Military victory was becoming impossible, and therefore, the most important aim of states was to avoid war.[4] The other stream of thought, at that time represented in the writings of William Liscum Borden, downplayed the significance of nuclear weapons, stressed the comparability of contemporary strategic problems to those of the prenuclear era, and asserted the continuing viability of traditional military principles.[5]

The gradually mounting awareness of mutual vulnerability shifted interest from the military role of nuclear weapons to their political role.[6] Once a state of nuclear stalemate was reached, theory suggested, additional nuclear forces would be of limited military value. Would this mean that the nuclear arms race would end and that the political relevance of nuclear weapons would simply fade into the background? The persistence of the arms race and the perceived political role of nuclear weapons led scholars to ask why stalemate had not diminished the attention paid to nuclear weapons. To answer this question, some scholars looked to bureaucratic politics.[7] This area of specialization, together with new insights into the decision-making process in crisis situations—like the Berlin crises (1958–62) and the Cuban missile crisis—led to increased consideration of psychological factors and to more empirical studies.[8] All of these writings enriched our knowledge of the complexities of nuclear politics. However, fundamental differences remained over the question of the political utility of nuclear weapons.

The later stages of the Cold War saw the refinement of early ideas of the political role of nuclear weapons. These ideas may be grouped into four distinct streams of thought. It is at this point necessary to emphasize that streams of thought are not equivalent to schools of thought. This study will adopt the definition of Steven Kull, who emphasizes that different streams are in no easy way identifiable with different groups or individuals. On the contrary, individuals are often drawn into varying streams of thinking at the same time. The fact that tensions between different streams of thought materialize not only between different groups of people, but also within individuals, makes it difficult to situate specific analysts—or for that matter government officials—in specific schools. A given writing nevertheless may stand for one particular stream, because authors usually attempt to concentrate on one message at a time.[9]

Observers following the first stream of thought have pointed out that nuclear weapons serve no military purpose whatsoever. Adherents to this thinking find nuclear weapons to be useless except to deter one's opponent from using them.[10] Because nuclear forces simply cancel each other out, quantitative nuclear superiority is of negligible political importance. This perspective leads to the argument that relative quantities of nuclear weapons play no role in the decision-making process in crisis situations. Proponents of this view stress instead the importance of the local conventional balance.[11] On the other hand, a second stream of thought takes the position that nuclear superiority is important. It is neither the balance of conventional forces nor the balance of resolve, but rather the balance of nuclear forces that keeps open the possibility of a military victory through the use of nuclear weapons, thereby enabling nations to pursue political ends with nuclear means.[12]

Scholars pursuing the third and fourth streams contend—like those following the first stream—that the strategic balance plays a secondary role, but these scholars emphasize—like scholars following the second stream—that nuclear weapons still influence policymaking in different ways. It is not nuclear superiority that affects political behavior, but rather the risk of nuclear war. Scholars in the third stream of thought stress that, given the inconceivable destructive consequences of nuclear use, nuclear threats need be neither subtle nor explicit to be credible. It is the nuclear danger inherent in the mere existence of nuclear forces that influences political behavior. The fear of escalation is a constant component in political calculations, forcing nuclear states to restrain themselves and to act cautiously.[13]

In the fourth stream of thought, on the other hand, scholars suggest that states will attempt to exploit the risk and insecurity of crisis situations. By deliberately manipulating the level of risk, the argument runs, states can advance their political aims. By threatening to unleash a process that they themselves cannot control, states can influence bargaining situations.[14]

While our thinking about the political role of nuclear weapons has been refined over time, a number of complications still preclude easy measurement of the impact of nuclear weapons on policy. First, decision makers tend to think simultaneously in terms of more than one of the four identified streams of thought and to justify their actions with explanations from different streams. Also, the four views outlined above are not by their own terms mutually exclusive. They can be combined in many different ways. For example, the first two views focus on direct links between military capabilities and political behavior. By contrast, the third and fourth streams of thought focus on the indirect connection between military power and political results, finding a substantial role for symbols and signals.

As to whether nuclear weapons have a generally stabilizing or destabilizing impact on global security, there is no consensus either. While the first and third streams of thought point to the stabilizing impact of nuclear weapons, the second and fourth streams of thought point to instability. Theory suggests no definite explanation of how nuclear weapons play their allegedly stabilizing role. These analytical complexities reflect real policy dilemmas.

This book is an effort to examine the question of the political role of nuclear weapons from a historical perspective. It approaches its subject not as a theoretical matter by way of testing one of the four streams of thought mentioned above, but instead asks how tensions between different views unfolded over a given time period. It traces the complex process by which different arguments interacted, conflicted, and overlapped in the laboratory of history.[15]

It is one of the most perplexing observations, from a historical perspective, that during the first decade of the Cold War people did *not* expect the conflict between East and West to develop into a "long peace." And certainly not many would have predicted that nuclear weapons would play a fundamentally stabilizing role in this process. On the contrary, people anticipated that a world in which the two superpowers threatened one another with utter destruction would be fraught with instability and danger. Perceptions of the role of nuclear weapons in international politics obviously changed over time.

The critical time period in which to observe these changes is the period from 1953 to 1963. As long as the United States possessed an atomic monopoly, worrying about the fundamental impact of the new weapons on the nature of conflict was primarily a theoretical issue. The situation changed once the Soviet Union broke the American atomic monopoly with its first atomic test in 1949. However, it was not until Dwight D. Eisenhower entered the White House that the American government had to face the fact that the U.S. homeland was becoming vulnerable to Soviet nuclear attack. Gone was the era of absolute security; the United States had to address the consequences of an irreversible situation of mutual vulnerability.

During Eisenhower's first term, it was generally anticipated that a future of mutual atomic plenty would be highly unstable. As atomic stockpiles grew, the two superpowers would become increasingly trigger-happy, as each felt that it was living with a gun to its head. In a world in which two mortally armed scorpions were facing one another, the advantage of attacking first was perceived as decisive. By 1963, however, the Cold War international system had achieved a certain stability, as mutual vulnerability gained general acceptance. After the Berlin crisis and the Cuban missile crisis, both the United States and the Soviet Union accepted the status quo of a divided Europe and a divided Germany. Furthermore, it had become clear that Germany would not control nuclear weapons of its own. Instead, U.S. troops would remain in Europe on a permanent basis. In short, by the time John F. Kennedy's presidency came to an abrupt end, the unexpected had happened: mutual vulnerability had arrived, but instead of fear and insecurity, mutual vulnerability brought relative calm and stability.

The central goal of this book is to explain the impact of American thinking about the political role of nuclear weapons on this somewhat unexpected process. How did two American administrations—Eisenhower's and Kennedy's—learn to live with the reality of a Soviet force capable of destroying the United States? What were their expectations regarding the military and political impact of the changing strategic nuclear balance? Did they perceive nuclear weapons as stabilizing respectively destabilizing factors in international politics? How would the fact that the American homeland was becoming vulnerable to Soviet nuclear attack affect the credibility of the U.S. security commitment to Europe? How did U.S. and Soviet possession of nuclear weapons influence the U.S. government's debate over national security policy, and what impact did this have on U.S. decision making in crisis situations?

The Eisenhower and Kennedy administrations, I will argue, reacted to the challenges of the changing nuclear equation by adjusting U.S. policy and thinking in ways that contributed to the avoidance of war. Building on new evidence and recent research, I would like to show how American officials came to see nuclear weapons themselves as the chief threat to their security—not nuclear weapons as instruments of Soviet strategy. Resulting from experiences such as the *Sputnik* shock, the Berlin crises, and the Cuban missile crisis, the political leadership of the United States learned that in a world of mutual nuclear plenty both the strategic balance and nuclear threats had lost in their political importance. In critical situations, with a high risk of war in particular, the nuclear danger would exert more influence on policy than any calculation of relative military power.

At the same time, however, I will emphasize that the American government did learn these central lessons of the nuclear age neither easily nor quickly. On the contrary, the story of American nuclear learning is a complex one, filled with puzzles and contradictions. This is so not least due to the transatlantic dynamic of the security debate. The extension of nuclear deterrence over U.S. allies heavily influenced the American debate over nuclear weapons policy. Driven by the need for continuous reaffirmation of U.S. security guarantees for Europe, excessive procurement of nuclear forces was kept alive—with all the dangerous implications for crisis stability. In a world in which impressions mattered as much as actual capabilities, claims of nuclear superiority and the prospect of an arms race became important psychological and political tools for the reassurance of allies.

In short, then, the nuclear peace, in its early days, might have been less stable than is generally assumed. Nuclear weapons had both a stabilizing *and* a destabilizing impact on American policy and on how the Cold War evolved. The Eisenhower and Kennedy administrations deserve credit for adapting U.S. policy to this new world of peril in ways that enhanced the stability of the international system.

There are great matters that I have omitted: By choosing to focus mainly on the thinking of the political leadership at the national policy level, I have taken into consideration interactions between the national policy level of the nuclear debate and other important policy levels such as programming, strategic planning, operational planning, or technological developments. My focus here is political. Both President Eisenhower and President Kennedy recognized the nuclear challenge to American security as essentially a political question.

A word is in order about organization: This book looks at three consecutive time periods during which American thinking on the political role of nuclear weapons evolved. The three periods are characterized by overwhelming U.S. nuclear superiority, evolving mutual nuclear vulnerability, and perceived mutual nuclear vulnerability. They correspond approximately to Eisenhower's first and second term and Kennedy's presidency. The following chapters are arranged thematically and address distinct lines of argument. With this structural organization, I could follow specific debates without losing sight of the larger historical process.

Part I addresses the American perception of the role of nuclear weapons in a time of overwhelming U.S. nuclear superiority. Chapter 1 provides an overview of Eisenhower's reappraisal of national security policy, which led to the integration of nuclear weapons into American defense strategy. Chapters 2 and 3 focus on the impact of the strategic balance and the thermonuclear revolution on U.S. policy during the first two years of Eisenhower's presidency. Chapter 4 discusses how tensions between the stabilizing and destabilizing effects of nuclear weapons were resolved in the nuclearization of NATO and the post–World War II settlement between the western powers and West Germany at the end of 1954.

Part II deals with the American perception of the role of nuclear weapons in a time of evolving mutual vulnerability. It focuses on the period after the launching of the first Soviet satellite, *Sputnik*, on 4 October 1957.[16] Chapters 5 and 6 trace subsequent policy dilemmas that emerged as Soviet nuclear capability to strike the American homeland grew. Chapter 7 charts Eisenhower's views on national security in a time of mutual nuclear plenty, the military meaning of the strategic balance, and the psychopolitical importance of nuclear superiority toward the end of his presidency.

Part III examines the American perception of the role of nuclear weapons in the Kennedy years, when mutual vulnerability was increasingly perceived as inevitable. Chapter 8 outlines President Kennedy's national security policy, discussing the continuing reevaluation of that policy during his first year in office. Chapter 9 focuses on the impact of nuclear weapons on the development of the Berlin crisis from 1958 through 1962. Chapter 10 deals with the trend toward using nuclear decision making to achieve symbolic (as opposed to substantive) ends or to signal intentions. Chapter 11, on the other hand, shows how in the Cuban missile crisis nuclear danger eclipsed these more subtle (psychological) goals of nuclear decision making. Finally, chapter 12 assesses how the Berlin crisis and the Cuban missile crisis changed the relationship between nuclear weapons and the further development of the Cold War.

In addition to the theoretical literature mentioned above, I have relied on the writings of three scholars. John Lewis Gaddis has outlined most clearly the scope of the question of how nuclear weapons relate to the development of the Cold War into a "long peace." He has explained how historical analysis can contribute to our understanding of the relationship between the development of nuclear weapons and the shaping of U.S. foreign policy.[17] McGeorge Bundy has made an enormous contribution to our understanding of the political impact of nuclear weapons by examining specific events in world politics since 1945. The main theme of Bundy's *Danger and Survival* is the impact of the nuclear danger on international politics. Bundy traces the roots of the major lessons of the nuclear revolutions, like the evolution of the tradition of nonuse, the absence of war between the superpowers, and the mutual acceptance of coexistence. Bundy also discusses the many failures of atomic diplomacy. Having served as an adviser to both Robert J. Oppenheimer and President John F. Kennedy, he is uniquely qualified to narrate the story of how these lessons took shape, first in the scientific arena and then in the political arenas.[18] On the impact of the shifting nuclear balance during the 1950s, the relationship between the nuclearization of NATO and U.S.–West European relations, and the influence of nuclear weapons on the Berlin crisis from 1958 through 1962, Marc Trachtenberg has presented an insightful analysis based on extensive archival research. Writing with an excellent sense of historical process, Trachtenberg explains how the basic themes of the nuclear revolution evolved in the 1950s.[19]

The myth of Eisenhower as a politically indecisive and passive president was challenged long ago. Among the first of the so-called Eisenhower revisionists, Fred I. Greenstein drew a portrait of Eisenhower as a skilled and articulate politician who consciously "hid his hand" to accomplish his political aims.[20] In his essay "Confessions of an Eisenhower Revisionist," Richard H. Immerman has outlined most comprehensively Eisenhower's core beliefs on war, peace, and security in the nuclear age. He points out that Eisenhower was among the first of his generation to acknowledge "the inversion of the relationship between force and statecraft because of the vulnerability of both sides to intolerable destruction."[21] Although Eisenhower generally acted very cautiously in planning for the eventual employment of nuclear weapons, as David Alan Rosenberg underscored in his authoritative study on the development of nuclear strategy and war plans, at the operational level President Eisenhower was unable to forgo the "institutionalization of overkill."[22]

The literature on the early 1960s is more scarce than the literature on the Eisenhower years. On Kennedy's foreign and defense policy, early biographies by Arthur M. Schlesinger and Theodore C. Sorensen are the most informative, however idealized they might be.[23] Standing out among the recent writings on President Kennedy is Michael R. Beschloss's well-documented account of the Kennedy-Khrushchev relationship. *The Crisis Years* brings both the individuals and the drama of their time to life. Beschloss focuses on how statements and actions of each affected the other. He finds that each leader paid insufficient attention to his counterpart's domestic political situation, leading to a spiral of misperceptions of dangerous proportions.[24] A detailed and well-documented analytical study of Kennedy's reappraisal of national security policy has yet to be done. Desmond Ball's *Politics and Force Levels* remains the most helpful account of the defense budget decisions of 1961. Ball explains the Kennedy administration's massive buildup of the nation's strategic missile forces—at a time, notably, when the United States already possessed vastly superior forces and the missile gap had been publicly exposed as a fiction—as a product of domestic political and bureaucratic pressures.[25] While I do not mean to belittle the influence of internal politics on nuclear decision making, I will argue that the decisions to build up the U.S. nuclear arsenal were also influenced by the international environment, particularly tension over Berlin.

This study emphasizes the link between Soviet nuclear strength and the security of the North Atlantic alliance, which itself rested on nuclear weapons. Three books on this issue deserve special mention. Jane E. Stromseth has provided a well-structured outline of the development of NATO strategy with particular emphasis on the debate within NATO in the 1960s.[26] John D. Steinbruner has elucidated the related issue of nuclear sharing between the United States and its allies. He has emphasized that the political aim of reassuring the allies of the U.S. commitment to their defense conflicted with the military goal of centralizing control over nuclear weapons.[27] Finally, Catherine McArdle Kelleher has completed the story of nuclear sharing in *Germany and the Politics of Nuclear Weapons*.[28] The nuclear status of Germany was a question of crucial importance to the debates on European stability in the late 1950s and early 1960s.

In addition to the literature mentioned above, this book draws on official and private papers recently released in the United States.[29] An advantage of studying nuclear politics of the 1950s and 1960s is that extensive archival sources are available today.[30] For the Eisenhower years, the published sources of the *Foreign Relations of the United States* contain massive documentation for most of the foreign policy decisions and diplomatic activities of the U.S. government discussed here. Furthermore, the *John Foster Dulles Papers* are available in the Seeley G. Mudd Library at Princeton University. The latter collection was completed with various documents from the relevant files in the Dwight D. Eisenhower Library. As to the development of nuclear strategy and war planning toward the end of the 1950s, the *Nathan F. Twining Papers* and the *Thomas D. White Papers*, both located in the Library of Congress, contain helpful material.

Availability of source materials presents a different challenge with respect to the Kennedy years. The *Foreign Relations of the United States* collection includes only two volumes (on the Berlin crisis, 1961–1963) related to this topic. For this reason, use of the *National Security Files*, the *President's Office Files*, the *White House Staff Files*, and the *White House Central Files* of the John F. Kennedy Library is absolutely essential. In addition, the *Maxwell D. Taylor Papers* and the *Lyman L. Lemnitzer Papers* in the National War College Archives contain valuable documentation. The *Papers of the Joint Chiefs of Staff* and the *Records of the National Security Council*, both located in the National Archives in Washington, D.C., offer further insight into Kennedy's national security policy. Finally, the document collections of the *National Security Archive* in Washington will be the starting point for the work of many future researchers on related topics. The archive's microfiche collections on the Berlin crisis, the Cuban missile crisis, and U.S. nuclear nonproliferation policy are among the richest source collections on national security policy in the 1950s and 1960s.

Part I

Eisenhower and Overwhelming Nuclear Superiority

1

The Integration of Nuclear Weapons into American National Security Policy

President Dwight D. Eisenhower's "new look" at U.S. defense strategy led to the integration of nuclear weapons into American national security policy. The conclusion of a year-long overhaul of basic national security policy, NSC 162/2 stated plainly that "in the event of hostilities, the United States will consider nuclear weapons to be as available for use as other munitions."[1] Nuclear weapons became the foundation of western security. The addition of the "absolute weapon" to other means of enforcing national security policy had lasting political and military implications for international politics.

Eisenhower's predecessor, President Harry S. Truman, had not worked out a strategy for securing political benefits from nuclear weapons. However, after the Soviet Union broke the American atomic monopoly with its first test of an atomic device in August 1949, Truman directed the Joint Chiefs of Staff (JCS) to devise a plan for the use of nuclear weapons. But the National Security Council (NSC) did little to articulate where, when, how, and against what targets to use nuclear weapons.[2] The Truman administration reacted to loss of the atomic monopoly not only by stepping up war planning efforts, but also by accelerating the production of atomic bombs. The outbreak of the Korean War in June 1951 gave a further boost to atomic weapons production. The atomic stockpile grew from fifty bombs in 1948 to about three hundred bombs in 1950 and to over one thousand bombs by the end of 1953.[3]

The efforts to produce and to plan for nuclear use were not matched by a similar effort to derive political leverage from nuclear weapons. Thinking about this political question during the Truman years ended with the statement that the decision to employ atomic weapons was to

13

remain with the president.[4] Although President Truman authorized the construction of the hydrogen bomb, he held fast to his belief that nuclear weapons had to be placed in a category apart from conventional forces.[5] In accordance with this view, the Truman administration, in its famous basic national security policy paper NSC 68, called for a buildup of both conventional and nuclear forces.[6] The goal of this administration was to avoid explicit reliance on nuclear weapons.

It was not until President Eisenhower's New Look that the links between the military and political implications of nuclear weapons became one of the determining factors in the evolution of the Cold War. Therefore, I begin by analyzing how Eisenhower came to rely on nuclear weapons as an integral part of U.S. national security strategy.

The State of Security upon Eisenhower's Election

Dwight D. Eisenhower was a reluctant politician. His decision to run for president in 1952 was rooted in a deep concern over the scope of the domestic debate about how best to respond to the Communist challenge.[7] In 1952, the American political leadership was confronted with a military stalemate in Korea. Increasingly, the American people were calling for the withdrawal of U.S. troops.[8] The Truman administration reacted to the danger of Soviet expansionism by calling for more defense spending and by warning that U.S. military forces were stretched dangerously thin. A leading Republican, Senator Robert Taft, on the other hand, publicly rejected the concept of collective security as too expensive. Taft used strong isolationist rhetoric, coupled with greater willingness for unilateral action, particularly in the Far East. Eisenhower's alarm at both Taft's isolationist philosophy and the free-spending Democratic agenda triggered his decision to enter the presidential race.

Eisenhower entered politics with a clearly defined strategy for securing the nation's fundamental interests.[9] Over his long military career as supreme commander, Europe, during World War II, army chief of staff, and NATO's first supreme allied commander Europe (SACEUR), he had developed certain strongly held core beliefs regarding national security strategy. Eisenhower believed that security and solvency were two sides of the same coin. He underlined their mutual dependency in a campaign speech: "We must achieve both security and solvency. In fact the foundation of military strength is economic strength. . . . The big spending is the $60 billion we pay for national security. Here is where the largest savings can be made. And these savings must be made without reduction of defensive power. That is exactly what I am now proposing."[10] According to Eisenhower, excessive military spending to counter the external threat posed by the Soviet Union would endanger the nation's internal cohesion, its institutions and values—in short, the American way of life. Eisenhower, unlike Truman, was convinced that defense had to be based on what the country could afford on the "long pull."[11] The United States had to design its military security to meet its permanent interests rather than to counter a temporary threat. Defense planning in the Eisenhower administration was analogized to a "floating D-day."[12]

However, it was the future secretary of state John Foster Dulles, who completed Eisenhower's security framework with concrete ideas regarding the nature of national security strategy. Dulles criticized Truman's foreign policy for being strategically reactive; the United States had lost the initiative in the struggle between East and West. The indecisive Korean War was proof of this lapse.[13] In an article in *Life* magazine, Dulles presented his answer to the problem: "The free world must develop the will and organize the means to retaliate instantly against open aggression by Red armies, so that, if it occurred anywhere, we could and would strike back where it hurts, by means of our own choosing."[14] Dulles coupled his preference for strategic asymmetry with a policy of boldness. Mere containment of the Soviet bloc should not be the only goal of American foreign policy. In a more proactive effort, the United States should strive to liberate the Soviet satellites, eventually rolling back the Kremlin's sphere of influence.

Eisenhower had reservations about both the doctrine of retaliation and the push for liberation.[15] However, he did not articulate his concerns publicly during the election. Eisenhower's call for a militarily and economically strong United States, supported by Dulles's proactive ideas, turned out to be successful. After twenty years of a Democrat-controlled White House, the Republicans returned with a landslide victory.

The Framework of National Security: The Dual Threat Approach

The driving force behind President Eisenhower's New Look was the mutual dependency of security and solvency. The country was faced with a dual threat: the external threat of Communism and the internal threat of a weakened economy. From this premise, the Eisenhower administration started on its year-long reappraisal of national security strategy. Primary concern remained with the external threat. The internal threat, however, was no longer ignored (as the new president feared it had been in the previous administration).

The newly elected president began his review of basic national security policy in February 1953, starting from the premise that an overhaul of policies must be considered in terms of financial costs. From the beginning, the president made it clear that the internal threat had to be taken into account along with the external threat posed by the Communist bloc. In one of the first meetings of the NSC, the president explained the rationale behind this core belief. Eisenhower feared that unrestricted spending would alter the very nature of American society. The United States could not afford to live "in a permanent state of mobilization" without destroying its "whole democratic way of life" in the process. National security could be secured only by balancing the danger of "national bankruptcy" and the danger of "national destruction." Secretary of the Treasury George M. Humphrey was even more fearful than the president was of an unbalanced budget. He described a process that would make the adoption of "totalitarian methods" unavoidable. The government was facing a huge debt as a result of the Truman budgets for fiscal years 1954 and 1955. This debt, according to Humphrey, would lead the country into "an inflationary cycle which could only end with a resort to controls and a planned economy along New Deal lines." Budget Director Joseph M. Dodge shared Humphrey's fear of budget deficits and demanded a balanced budget by fiscal year 1955. For the incoming Eisenhower administration, the immediate problem was, therefore, how to reduce the Truman budget.[16]

The Truman Legacy

It was clear from the beginning that Eisenhower would seek to reduce defense spending. It was just as clear that the outgoing president had favored an expansion of the defense budget. The new administration was confronted with a series of national security policy papers (NSC 20/4, 68/2, 135/3, and 141) that called for the development of U.S. military power in response to perceived Soviet foreign-policy gains.

NSC 20/4 (approved in November 1948) had been the NSC's first statement of overall U.S. objectives, policies, and programs for national security addressing the Soviet threat.[17] The outlined policy was based on the premise that peaceful coexistence would be possible once Russia had returned to its traditional borders. The first Soviet atomic explosion in September 1949 and the "fall" of China to communism only one month later led to an initial reexamination of basic national security policies. Against the background of increasing tensions, President Truman agreed to the suggestion of Paul H. Nitze, director of the Policy Planning Staff, that the concept of national security policy be evaluated in light of the possible development of a hydrogen bomb.[18] Nitze's advice led to NSC 68, which found existing programs to be dangerously inadequate and called for a rapid and sustained buildup of the political, economic, and military strength of the free world.[19] The Cold War, the paper argued, was in fact a real war in which the survival of the free world was at stake. Next to such a threat, questions of budget and expenditure paled. President Truman agreed with the theme of NSC 68 that difficult times for East-West relations lay ahead. Nevertheless, he did not approve the paper immediately. He first wanted to receive a clearer indication of the expected costs of the envisaged programs. However, in June 1950 the Korean War broke out, and in September of the same year, Truman approved NSC 68. Samuel F. Wells described the link between these two events aptly: "The real significance of NSC 68 was its timing—the tocsin sounded just before the fire."[20]

The next reappraisal of national security policies and programs grew out of an NSC meeting in October 1951. It ended with NSC 141, which was approved by President Truman on 19 January 1953, one day before the inauguration of President Eisenhower. It was the explosion of another atomic device in the Soviet Union that stimulated a renewal of the security debate. The fundamental question raised was whether U.S. national security strategy remained valid in light of the apparently rapid growth of Soviet atomic capacity. Or, did the change in the strategic balance mean that the United States had to overthrow the Soviet regime before the adversary attained the ability to hurt the United States?[21]

Nitze pondered thoroughly the consequences of the growing Soviet nuclear capabilities. Central in his mind was what he called the "atomic equation." The growing Soviet power to hurt the United States with a nuclear attack led Nitze to question whether the U.S. government would be willing "to use the atomic threat or to follow through on it in the event of any Soviet move short of direct atomic attack on the United States." Nitze was further concerned that the vulnerability of Europe and Japan to Soviet atomic attack would render the allies incapable of withstanding a Soviet threat. For Nitze, these unfavorable trends meant that the United States had to overcome its "dependence on the strategic use of atomic weapons in the event of general war." Building sufficient conventional forces would be a large task, but it could be done. Nitze also observed that the size of the American atomic stockpile enabled the United States "to use these weapons locally where their use would be militarily effective and did not involve more than offsetting political disadvantages." Nuclear weapons might in this way complement the limited capabilities of U.S. conventional forces. Great superiority in numbers of nuclear weapons could be to the advantage of the West with respect to the tactical use of nuclear weapons. However, Nitze qualified this last idea. He noted that it was difficult to see "how a precise dividing line can be drawn, or lived up to, separating tactical from strategic uses."[22] To avoid a situation in which cumulative Cold War "losses" could lead to defeat and in which the allies would become more and more neutralized, the United States had to expand its conventional forces. Nitze thought that the probability of war was high enough to justify striving for superior military power.[23]

The review made by the Democratic administration resulted in NSC 141. Eisenhower regarded the paper as Truman's national security policy legacy.[24] The document called for a general increase in U.S. security programs. A higher level of expenditures would have to be maintained over a long period before U.S. objectives would be attained. U.S. programs, the paper noted, should be expanded in two areas. First, military and civil defense of the continental United States should be enlarged substantially in order to reduce U.S. vulnerability to Soviet atomic capabilities. Second, military and economic aid to the Middle and Far East should be expanded in order to strengthen the free world's capacity to deter or counter local Communist aggression without sole reliance on the threat of general war. The expenditures for the increase in continental U.S. military and civil defense programs should originate, moreover, from new resources. A diversion from the buildup of land, sea, and air offensive readiness was to be avoided by all means.[25] In short, NSC 141, like its predecessor NSC 68, called for an accelerated buildup of the political, economic, and military strength of the free world. The document called for strengthening both conventional and nuclear forces. With respect to means, NSC 141 was very much a wish list.[26] It became the first task of the incoming administration to reconcile Truman's defense budget legacy with Eisenhower's goal of a sound economy.

The NSC Civilian Consultants

The Eisenhower administration set out to formulate defense policy guidance by establishing an ad hoc committee of civilian consultants to the NSC.[27] The NSC and the civilian consultants held their first important meeting on 31 March 1953. Budget Director Dodge and Secretary Humphrey opened the meeting by reminding the council of the projected future deficits absent cuts in the Mutual Security and Defense Department programs. Dillon Anderson then took the floor and presented the findings of the civilian consultants. It was their unanimous view that the United States had to strive for an adequate defense posture with a balanced budget. Neither continued deficit spending nor increased taxation was the right way to solve the problem. On the contrary, the United States had to accept, Anderson noted, that "we have bitten off more than we can chew." Accordingly, reductions in certain areas had to be made. A hasty rearmament program had resulted in much duplication that could be eliminated from the defense budget. Regarding the Mutual Security program, Anderson warned "that the United States should not undertake to shore up the whole non-Soviet world." One further aspect of the problem, Anderson noted, was that the "American public was quite unaware of the terrible fiscal mess" facing the country. The American people seemed to expect greater tax cuts than would be safe given the Soviet threat. The problem was not only fiscal, it was political as well—implicating the public image of the administration. Anderson recommended that the administration set forth with much greater candor the nature of the threat and the grave fiscal situation. In sum, it was the view of the consultants that a satisfactory national security posture could be reached while achieving a balanced budget for fiscal year 1954 and thereafter.[28]

The first suggestion of the civilian consultants, to eliminate redundancy in the programs of the Defense Department, was not heavily disputed. The buildup initiated by NSC 68 had fed the ambitions of the three armed services. Secretary of Defense Charles E. Wilson stated that substantial cuts could be made by eliminating duplication. Moreover, the military program was now designed to meet a "floating," rather than a "specific," D-day. This allowed review of missions, forces, and readiness levels on a continuing basis, resulting in a more efficient use of manpower. Therefore, some savings in overhead were possible. With these reorganizations, Department of Defense expenditures could be reduced by $2.3 billion for fiscal year 1954 and by $4 billion for fiscal year 1955.[29]

It was the second recommendation of the civilian consultants—that the Mutual Security program be cut—that led to the administration's first fierce internal argument. Budget Director Dodge and Secretary Humphrey took the side of the civilian consultants and insisted upon much larger savings than Governor Harold E. Stassen, director of the Mutual Security Agency (MSA), was prepared to allow. Secretary Humphrey bluntly described the MSA funds as "giveaway" money.[30] However, it was the president who took the lead in defense of the Mutual Security funds. Had it not been for the money the United States had spent on its European allies, beginning with the Marshall Plan, he noted, "many of the European nations would certainly have gone Communist."[31] MSA funds were a cheap way of buying U.S. security. The United States would not have to use its own troops. Furthermore, given the "fantastically higher" cost of maintaining an American soldier in the field than of maintaining a foreign soldier, it was cheaper to provide assistance to foreign military forces than to develop additional U.S. divisions.[32]

Questioned about the real deterrent value of the five American divisions in Europe, President Eisenhower who, after all, had served as NATO's first commander, jumped to the defense of these forces. He stressed that they were "a real physical deterrent to the Soviets and not merely a psychological one."[33] It was absolutely impossible to pull a single division out of Europe at the time. Given the task of German rearmament, Eisenhower was astonished that the MSA figure was not larger.[34] Secretary Dulles supported the president's position as sound foreign policy. He warned that the Europeans would interpret big cuts as signaling an American return to isolationism. The importance of the allies' perceptions could not be overemphasized.[35] The administration finally settled on moderate savings in MSA funds for both fiscal year 1954 and fiscal year 1955.[36]

Having agreed to the elimination of redundancy in Department of Defense programs, but not to big cuts in MSA funds, the Eisenhower administration had difficulties grappling with the third and final recommendation of the civilian consultants—that a balanced budget be reached beginning with fiscal year 1954. President Eisenhower stated that "he could not disagree with the dangers to our economy which the consultants had perceived."[37] But the problem was *when* to achieve the balanced budget. The United States had commitments and responsibilities to meet in the interest of national security. The nation could approach the goal of a balanced budget only gradually. The only thing that could be done initially was to show determination to move in the direction of a balanced budget.

The consensus from these discussions was documented in NSC 149/2. The paper set forth the goal of maintaining (over a sustained period) armed forces to provide for U.S. security and to strengthen the free world, while balancing the federal budget. The maintenance of a sound and strong U.S. economy was vital to the long-term survival of the free world. However, as NSC 149/2 concluded, it would be impossible to make substantial savings in the short term. The nation had to live up to its commitments and responsibilities around the world. As long as there was a war in Korea, the level of federal taxation could not be diminished.[38]

There was no immediate way to balance security and solvency. Moreover, the consensus behind this first statement on national security policies, given the cost of those policies, was quite fragile. When President Eisenhower tried to secure congressional support for what would be only a modest reduction in President Truman's fiscal year 1954 budget in a meeting with Republican leaders on 30 April, his comments drew severe criticism. Senator Taft was especially harsh in expressing his disappointment with the announced program: "The one primary thing we promised the American people was reduction of expenditures. Now you're taking us right down the same road Truman traveled. It's a repudiation of everything we promised in the campaign."[39] Adding to Eisenhower's problems, the outgoing director of the Policy Planning Staff, Paul H. Nitze, reminded the new administration of the problem of continental defense. It was true that NSC 149/2 wisely provided for increased emphasis on continental defenses. The problem, however, was how to do this within the budgetary constraints laid down in the same paper.[40]

Nitze identified the important question of how to translate the findings of NSC 149/2 into the basic national security policies set forth under the previous administration. The Eisenhower administration concluded its first restatement of basic national security policy in June 1953. NSC 153/1 opened with the acknowledgment that two principal threats endangered the survival of the fundamental values and institutions of the United States: One was the external threat by "the formidable power and aggressive policy of the communist world led by the USSR." The other was the internal threat of a "serious weakening of the economy of the United States." The basic problem for the future was to strike a balanced response to the risks arising from these two threats. This new emphasis on a *dual* threat did not imply that the Soviet threat to the free world was diminishing. The United States had to continue to give primary consideration to the threat of Soviet power, as NSC 68 had recommended. What was new was the realization "that increased emphasis on sound fiscal policy may involve assuming increased risks in relation to the Soviet threat."[41]

NSC 153/1 was essentially a summary of existing NSC policy, qualified by Eisenhower's core belief that national security could be achieved only by addressing both the external threat and the internal threat. In the first round of reexamination of existing national security policies, the Eisenhower administration had not found a way out of the dilemma between military security and economic security. The New Look had not been born yet. Key members of the government came to believe that only a complete reevaluation of security policy could result in a workable solution.

The Nature of National Security Policies: Project Solarium

While the broad framework of national security had been well defined as the balancing of a dual threat, little thought had been given to the detailed nature of national security policy. How could the objectives of American national security policy best be pursued within this general framework? To answer this question in a way that would not just restate existing national security policy, a thorough review of the foundations of this policy was needed. Project Solarium provided that review.[42]

The origins of Project Solarium are unclear and still disputed. Robert Cutler, special assistant to the president for National Security Affairs, recalled that Secretary of State Dulles conceived of the exercise. Cutler noted that on 2 May 1953, Dulles had the following four guests at his home: Robert Cutler, Undersecretary of State Walter Bedell Smith, Special Assistant to the President C. D. Jackson, and Dulles's brother, Director of the CIA Allen W. Dulles. In the course of the discussion, John Foster Dulles, according to Cutler, stated his conviction that only a complete evaluation of national security policy could lead to the formulation of a new, coherent security strategy. Three different scenarios, each one representing a possible conception of the future national security policy, should be analyzed for strengths and weaknesses. The result should be issued as one final statement, representing the consensus behind a new conception of national security policy. According to Cutler, the group was intrigued by the idea. In addition, Cutler stated, Smith suggested that the alternative scenarios should be developed by three small task forces.[43]

The informal discussion at Dulles's home was continued in a meeting of the same persons with the president on 8 May 1953. The small group met in the sun room of the White House, called the Solarium—hence the name of the project. The memorandum of the discussion suggests that President Eisenhower was involved in defining the methodology of the exercise and its scope to a far greater extent than is generally assumed. The meeting began with a series of points made by the secretary of state that show just how seriously Dulles took the Communist threat. The danger of Communist penetration loomed in Africa, the Middle East, India, Southeast Asia, the Far East, and South America. Dulles noted that it was "difficult to conclude that time is working in our favor." To the contrary, he thought that in "the world chess game, the Reds today have the better position."[44] Moreover, the western reaction to the Communist threat had been exclusively defensive. Dulles believed that such a policy would break the United States financially and result in the loss of the free world bit by bit. The secretary then proceeded to outline three alternative courses and suggested that they be explored further. Each of his alternatives focused on how to regain the strategic initiative in the Cold War. Dulles concluded by emphasizing that the administration should appraise alternative policies even if in the end "we conclude that perhaps the French and British are right and there is no other possible course than to wait and see."

President Eisenhower agreed with Dulles's point that existing national security policy was "leading to disaster, sapping our strength." However, the president emphasized factors other than taking the strategic initiative and adopting a more offense-oriented posture. First, Eisenhower stressed the importance of allies; they had to be convinced "about the rightness of any course we adopt." Second, he discarded at the outset a policy of "drawing the line." Third, he added a fourth alternative to the original Dulles three: "We should depend less on material strength and think more of improving the standards of living in the other countries as the way to gain true indigenous strength. We want people to see freedom and communism in their true lights." Emphasizing the need for allies and for worldwide acceptability of U.S. policy, Eisenhower limited the extent to which he was prepared to change existing policy. He made it clear that he did not support more aggressive, unilateral policies that would endanger existing alliances. However, Eisenhower was very sympathetic to further exploration of alternatives and even suggested how this should be done:

> The President said he would like to see set-up some teams of bright young fellows, each team to take an alternative, each team to tackle its alternative with a real belief in it just the way a good advocate tackles a law case—and then when the teams are prepared, each team should put on in some White House room, with maps, charts, all basic supporting figures and estimates, just what each alternative would mean in terms of goal, risk, cost in money and men and world relations. Against such a background, the NSC would be qualified to come to a decision. But don't talk about decisive action until all the facts are laid out cold and hard.[45]

On the day after the crucial Solarium meeting, the president approved, after a lengthy discussion with Robert Cutler, detailed guidelines on how to organize the undertaking. A working committee of the NSC, consisting of Walter Bedell Smith, Robert Cutler, and Allen Dulles, was set up to arrange the project organization: First, a panel had to be formed to draft precise and detailed terms of reference for each alternative. Second, the names of qualified persons for the three task forces had to be proposed. Finally, the project had to be prepared and executed at the National War College, which would provide a quiet atmosphere and limit public attention.[46]

After six more days, General James H. Doolittle was named chairman of the panel.[47] Together with four colleagues, he began to work on guidelines for the three task forces.[48] The panel started with a brief description of the three alternative courses as they had derived from the Solarium meeting.[49] On 1 June 1953, the panel offered more sophisticated guidance. The panel recognized that one could conceive of more than the three recommended courses of action, but it excluded three additional courses "as being in conflict with the realities of the world situation." The three rejected scenarios can be summarized as: isolationism, fundamental change of alliances and international institutions (NATO, UN), and preventive war.[50]

For the three remaining scenarios, the panel put together a long list of questions to guide the work of the task forces. The list included questions such as: What general results over what time period are expected to be accomplished by proposed policy? What specific actions should be undertaken to implement proposed policy? What lines of action should be abandoned in order to act economically? What are the costs of proposed actions? To what extent would proposed actions be supported by U.S. public opinion and the Congress? What would be the impact on allies and on world opinion? How would Soviet leaders be expected to interpret and react to proposed actions? To what degree would proposed actions affect the risk of general war? What would be the impact on the cohesion of the Communist bloc?[51] In short, Project Solarium was a very ambitious undertaking, especially in light of its six-week deadline.

Task force "A" analyzed a continuation of Truman's "strategy of containment," as elaborated in President Eisenhower's NSC 153/1. Although Secretary Dulles had dismissed him from the State Department the previous March, George F. Kennan, the "father" of containment, was asked to chair this group.[52] Task force "B" analyzed a "strategy of deterrence" that involved drawing a continuous line around the Soviet bloc beyond which the United States would not permit Soviet or satellite military forces to advance without general war. The chairman of this group was Major General James McCormack. Finally, task force "C" analyzed a "strategy of liberation," aimed at rolling back existing areas of Soviet influence. This group was headed by Admiral R. C. Conolly.[53]

On 16 July 1953, the three task forces presented their findings in a day-long meeting with the NSC. George Kennan opened the meeting. For task force "A" it was not possible to sponsor a course of action that would alter drastically President Truman's strategy of containment. Containment was characterized by the will of the United States to maintain armed forces to provide for its security over a sustained period and to assist in the defense of vital areas of the free world, to continue to build up the economic and military strength and cohesion of the free world, and—without materially increasing the risk of general war—to continue to exploit the vulnerabilities of the Soviet bloc.

The fundamental premise for the analysis by task force "A" was the conviction that "time can be used to the advantage of the free world."[54] If the free world built up and maintained its strength over a period of years, Soviet power would finally deteriorate from its internal weaknesses to the point where it no longer would constitute a threat to U.S. security. Task force "A" perceived "signs of a high state of instability and unclarity in the workings of Soviet power" since Stalin's death on 5 March 1953.[55] Against this background, the risk of a general war was judged to be not very high. The Soviets could and would be deterred further.

Moreover, the United States was in a "position to assume the strategic offensive in its conflict with Soviet Communism."[56] But Kennan's group qualified its call for a "strategic offensive" to bring about the eventual disintegration of the Soviet threat in four important ways: First, although the threat of war should not inhibit U.S. policy, Soviet expansion had to be stopped "without undue risk of war." If the United States had to use military force to reach its aims, it should follow through on its threat even "at the grave risk of general war." But an attempt should be made "to localize such military operations as far as possible." Second, the policy would require the assistance of the allies. Task force "A" perceived strengthening the free world to be of particularly great significance. The policy it called for involved "much less of the element of unilateral U.S. action" than the policies recommended by the two other task forces. Third, any conceivable progress toward a more peaceful world would at some point require some sort of formal agreement with the Soviet Union. It was, therefore, extremely important that the United States develop an "effective *stance* with relation to the problem of negotiation." After all, the United States should not be seen as responding to Soviet openness toward disarmament by insisting on continuation of the Cold War. Fourth, a precondition of continued containment was that there be no reduction in the defense establishment. It was important, therefore, "to generate increased public understanding on the vital importance today of military power as an instrument of policy for peace, its deterrent value and its confidence building aspects."

On the cost side, task force "A" expected its proposal to generate higher expenditures than the administration presently planned. The task force members believed, however, that the American economy had the capacity to provide a high level of preparedness. Any likely threat from a growing national debt did not seem comparable to the Soviet threat. Neither would it be wise to reduce the level of taxation. But then, the tax problem was primarily a political and psychological problem. In short, the United States had "the tax structure, debt situation, and general fiscal capability to *sustain* the security load" under the program proposed by task force "A."[57]

After George F. Kennan had finished his presentation, Major General J. McCormack presented the report of task force "B." McCormack's group regarded its proposed course of action more "as a support, rather than a substitute for existing policies"—the continuation of which Kennan had just recommended. Like task force "A," task force "B" rejected preventive war as a solution to the problem of the imminent U.S. loss of its lead in atomic weapons. The group believed time was on the side of the free world. Eventually, time would change the Soviet bloc from within. Moreover, U.S. policy had never promised liberation by military force of the captive people of the Soviet bloc.

The central problem for the future, task force "B" argued, was to adjust the not entirely successful policy "of reacting to Soviet pressures and aggressions as they have appeared at one point or another on the periphery." Group "B" proposed changing existing policies only as necessary to accommodate one new priority: "The warning of general war as the primary sanction against further Soviet Bloc aggression."[58] Any advance of Soviet bloc military forces beyond a certain line would be considered by the United States as initiating a general war, in which the full power (including nuclear weapons) of the United States would be used to bring about the defeat of the Soviet bloc forces. Moreover, the United States would make known in an unmistakable way that it had established and was determined to carry out such a policy. The uncrossable line would be the present borders of the Soviet bloc countries. The United States could not disregard the lesson of the Korean War that the Kremlin might regard any formulation of a "minimum" line other than present borders as an invitation to aggression. Task force "B" concluded that its proposed policy would have to be carried out unilaterally—that is, without relying on the allies.

Group "B" believed the primary benefit of its proposed course to be that it maximized the deterrent component of American national security policy. The policy made the most effective use of U.S. power. The threat of general war would reduce the likelihood that such a war would occur. And should such a war occur, the United States would be best prepared to conduct it. Such a policy would also assist in the settlement of ongoing wars in Korea and Indochina. McCormack and his team admitted that the weak point in their proposed policy was the risk that the adversary would call the American bluff. How would the executive convince the U.S. Congress to declare war? There was no answer to this question other than making the commitment to immediate retaliation as sober and irrevocable as possible.[59]

Although task force "B" did not foresee a reduction in defense expenditures, it emphasized that by ruling out the possibility of fighting wars at the periphery its proposal's "military costs will in the long term be less than the cost of any alternative that accepts such wars." Moreover, task force "B" agreed with task force "A" that the internal economic threat could not be compared with the Soviet threat: "Whatever the evils of inflation, whatever the economic problems involved in efforts to control it, these cannot be weighed in the same scales with the great danger to our national survival."[60]

Finally, Admiral Conolly took the floor. Task force "C" rejected the recommendations of both task force "A" and task force "B": "Mere containment is sterile as a continuing policy. Threat of retaliation by invoking general war will not suffice to restrain our enemy from continued erosive action against our world position. It is necessary that we create a climate of victory."[61] The fundamental point of departure for this call for a climate of victory was the assumption that "time has been working against us," and that this trend was irreversible. This assumption had its roots in the steadily growing Soviet nuclear capability, which in the not-too-distant future would allow the Soviets to strike a destructive blow against the U.S. homeland.

Task force "C" claimed that the United States had to add its war objectives to its peace objectives. Ending Soviet domination outside recognized borders, destroying the Communist apparatus in the free world, curtailing Soviet aggressive power, tearing down the Iron Curtain, and cutting down the strength of any Bolshevik elements left in Soviet Russia must be the *true* U.S. objectives. Whereas the authors of NSC 153/1 provided for the attainment of these objectives only by recourse to general war, task force "C" proposed to achieve the same objectives by perpetuating the Cold War. But Admiral Conolly had to admit that pursuit of such a course would generate "a greater risk of general war." The United States should not initiate general war, but it had to accept a greater risk of general war.

To achieve the aims defined by task force "C," the United States would have to "prosecute relentlessly a forward and aggressive political strategy in all fields and by all means: military, economic, diplomatic, covert and propaganda." Compared with existing policy, the emphasis on covert and propaganda means was new. Strong armed forces should be exploited to the fullest to achieve political, propaganda, and prestige objectives. Complete nuclear weapons would have to be placed in the hands of tactical units in order to ensure that they could be launched without delay.

The basic problem facing task force "C" was how to time specific actions in order to address the growing nuclear threat posed by the Soviet Union. The short-term phase of its timetable was five years, from 1953 to 1958. In many regards, the short term was the most important phase: By 1958, according to the timetable of task force "C," the strength of the free world would be greatly increased, Chinese prestige would be severely damaged through "the administration of a sound military defeat and the destruction of some of her industrial centers," and the strains between Communist China and the Soviet Union would reach a point at which the prospects of driving a final wedge between them would be good. To reach such a position, task force "C" counted on the continuation of hostilities in Korea. Prosecuting that war would destroy Soviet-supplied forces and equipment through means including nuclear weapons.[62]

Task force "C" admitted that the allies would undoubtedly oppose such an aggressive policy. But the United States should not tailor its policies to accommodate the internal politics of the allies. Admiral Conolly stated that it was his group's prediction that allied support "would snowball as the Soviets retreated."[63] Finally, the costs of implementing the recommendation of task force "C" were expected to approach $60 billion in the first two years and to rise even higher with resumed fighting in Korea. But task force "C" stated its view—concurring in this sole respect with task forces "A" and "B"—that the United States had the economic capacity to meet these costs.

After the three task forces had presented their respective findings, a lively discussion ensued, underscoring the essential differences between task forces "A" and "C." Their disagreement was basically a function of their differing perceptions of how the threat would evolve over time. Was time on the side of the United States or the Soviet Union? Was there any chance of change from within the Communist system? Task force "C" had adopted the premise that the United States could not live with the Soviet threat. So long as the Soviet Union continued to exist unchallenged by the United States "it will not fall apart." Therefore, so the argument ran, the Soviet Union must and could be shaken apart. This process would involve the use of force, and the United States had to be willing to risk general war. Task force "A" questioned such an aggressive course, asking, "If we won a war, what would we put in the place of the Soviet Government?" There did not exist among the Russian people elements from which a democratic government could be formed. But there were signs of evolution, particularly after the death of Stalin. The better course, according to task force "A," would be "to wait for an evolution in Soviet life and patterns of behavior."[64]

There were minor differences between task forces "A" and "B" as well. Whereas task force "B" thought in terms of the Communist bloc as a whole and believed it to be a tougher aggressive menace than did task force "A," Kennan's group ("A") thought mainly in terms of aggression by Russian forces. Moreover, task force "A" judged the existing deterrent to be basically adequate. Task force "B," however, wanted to create a further deterrent to general war and Soviet aggression.[65]

At the end of the day-long meeting, President Eisenhower made a personal statement about the whole range of problems discussed.[66] George F. Kennan recalled Eisenhower's remarks favorably thirty-five years later: "He [The President] spoke, I must say, with a mastery of the subject matter and a thoughtfulness and penetration that were quite remarkable. I came away from it with the conviction . . . that President Eisenhower was a much more intelligent man than he was given credit for being."[67]

President Eisenhower's summary remarks basically amounted to a rejection of a strategy of liberation. Although liberation and roll back were part of the Republican campaign program, they were most closely associated with the speeches of John Foster Dulles. Even during the campaign, Eisenhower had had reservations about these policies. At the conclusion of the Solarium meeting, the president opened his remarks by stating that "the only thing worse than losing a global war was winning one." Eisenhower stressed that there would be no individual freedom after the next global war. Moreover, the American people had demonstrated their reluctance to occupy conquered territory. The United States could act militarily only with the help of its allies, because U.S. forward bases were in the territories of its allies.[68] With these remarks, the president seemed to come down on the side of task force "A's" recommendation for future policy.[69] However, he might have intended simply to articulate his skepticism about rolling back the Soviet sphere of influence by use of force.[70]

Finally, President Eisenhower restated his basic belief that the internal threat of a weakened economy should not be overlooked: "If you demand of a free people over a long period of time more than they want to give, you can obtain what you want only by using more and more controls; and the more you do this, the more you lose the individual liberty which you are trying to save and become a garrison state."[71] With this remark, the president drew the attention of the NSC to the remarkable contradictions between Project Solarium and the emphasis of the first months of his presidency on fiscal as well as military security. During its first four months, the Eisenhower administration had shaped the framework of national security policy by equating the external threat and the internal threat. The three task forces of Project Solarium managed to agree on only one point: they each rejected the earlier framework for national security. The experts perceived the external threat to be qualitatively different from the internal threat. Moreover, the U.S. economy had the capacity to support higher defense expenditures than were previously planned.

President Eisenhower then underlined the many similarities among the three reports and asked the task forces to take the best features of each and combine them into a unified policy. But after the president left the meeting, the three groups were unable to overcome their fundamental differences and, finally, refused to synthesize their positions.[72] When Robert Cutler informed the president of the failure of the task forces to integrate their views, "he [Eisenhower] seemed very put out and left it to me [Cutler] to work out what I thought best."[73]

The special assistant to the president for national security affairs eventually presented a paper to the NSC enumerating points for consideration in drafting a new policy. After some further discussion of the issues at hand, the council directed the NSC Planning Board to draft a new basic national security policy paper. Cutler's two-page summary memorandum estimated the risk of general war resulting from aggressive action against the Soviet bloc as "less grave" than task force "A" had concluded. Cutler advocated accepting "moderately increased risks of general war by taking *some* of the aggressive actions" proposed by task force "C." Cutler proposed creating a "climate of victory." Within this framework, he suggested the following points for consideration: First, the United States should build and maintain at the lowest costs possible a strong retaliatory capability, a base for mobilization, and a continental defense. Second, the United States should create strong, independent groups of allied nations centered around Western Europe and the Far East. Third, the United States should provide more, but selective, foreign assistance. Fourth, the United States should designate areas in which any clearly recognizable Soviet military advance would be considered as initiating general war. Fifth, the United States should take selected aggressive actions of limited scope, moderately increasing the risk of general war, in order to reduce Soviet power at the periphery.[74]

This summary paper underscored the lack of consensus among the task forces. When it was discussed in the NSC, the key players in the administration confirmed their already stated personal preferences. Secretary Dulles succeeded in securing acceptance of the paper only by reminding the council that it was guidance, not policy. It was very loose guidance indeed for the drafting of the NSC 162 series. Secretary of Defense Wilson accepted the paper "if it didn't settle anything," but reminded the council that the JCS should have an opportunity to comment.[75]

The New Look of the New Joint Chiefs of Staff

On 12 May 1953, President Eisenhower had appointed an entirely new group of generals and admirals to fill the positions of the JCS.[76] The JCS consisted of General Matthew B. Ridgway (army chief of staff), Admiral Robert B. Carney (chief of naval operations), General Nathan F. Twining (air force chief of staff), and as chairman, Admiral Arthur W. Radford.

On 14 July 1953, one month before the appointment of the new group became effective, President Eisenhower met with the JCS-designates.[77] During the half-hour meeting, the president told the chiefs that he wanted them to make "a completely new, fresh survey of our military capabilities in light of our global commitments." The survey was to examine everything from weapons systems to strategic doctrine to service roles and missions.[78] Eisenhower was very clear in his instructions: the examination should be made with due regard to the dual threat approach as articulated in NSC 149/2 and 153/1: "While I do not fix any arbitrary budgetary or personnel limitations as a basis for this study, it should take into consideration our major national security programs for fiscal years 1954 and 1955, as outlined in NSC 149/2."[79] Moreover, Eisenhower did not want a long staff study. Starting from their great collective experience, the new chiefs should honestly and forthrightly state their individual views.

The JCS followed the instructions of the president to the letter: The main work was done on a two-day cruise on the *Sequoia* in early August without any prior staff discussions or close study of existing plans and programs. The effort resulted in a memorandum to the secretary of defense, dated 8 August 1953, the contents of which the JCS presented to the NSC on 27 August.

Two events that occurred at the same time as the presentation of the JCS study carried major significance for the future of military policy: the explosion of the first Soviet hydrogen bomb on 12 August, and the signing of the Korean armistice on 27 July. The Soviet test of a thermonuclear device underlined the growing vulnerability of the American homeland. The JCS, therefore, judged continental defense and the buildup of a retaliatory capacity to be the two most important problems for future defense policy.[80] The Korean War, on the other hand, had led to a serious overextension of U.S. armed forces. The war in the Far East had almost exhausted the available trained military reserves. The signing of the armistice now presented an opportunity to review U.S. commitments around the world and to redeploy overseas forces. The JCS suggested a course of redeployment and reorientation: "It would place in first priority the essential military protection of our Continental U.S. vitals and the capability for delivering swift and powerful retaliatory blows. Military commitments overseas—that is to say, peripheral military commitments—would cease to have first claim on our resources."[81]

Under such a policy, the United States would further deploy only naval and air forces abroad. There could be no retaliatory capacity without an extended overseas military base system. Moreover, air and sea power would have to back up local allied defenses. Finally, the United States would build up its reserves at home; this would enhance the mobility and flexibility of U.S. forces.[82]

Presenting the findings of the JCS report to the NSC, Admiral Radford emphasized that a policy of concentrating on both retaliatory forces and continental defense, and redeploying armed forces required one precondition: The integration of tactical and strategic nuclear weapons in American national security policy. Also, although the United States had spent vast sums on nuclear weapons, it was deferring their use because of concern for public opinion: "It was high time," the chairman of the JCS pointed out, "that we clarified our position on the use of such weapons if indeed we proposed to use them."[83] Radford thought that an evaluation by the NSC of the general concept advanced by the JCS report was needed. This evaluation could be relayed, in turn, to the president, who was absent from this crucial meeting.

The NSC reacted very favorably to the presentation by Admiral Radford. Secretary Humphrey took the lead in very warmly praising the work of the JCS. His enthusiasm was prompted by Radford's answer to the question of whether the military program set forth would cost more than the current program. Admiral Radford replied that, "on the contrary, it would ultimately cost less." After commitments were changed and redeployments made, there would be substantial savings.[84]

This was the New Look that would achieve security within the framework of the "great equation" between military and fiscal security. While the task force reports of Project Solarium had predicted heavy defense expenditures, Radford's presentation raised hopes that a balanced budget was attainable. Moreover, with the hydrogen bomb in the hands of the Soviets, Humphrey emphasized, the American people would demand a genuine reappraisal of U.S. national security policy: "The stage was now all set. If we did not walk out onto the stage, the results would be terrible."[85] The relief and enthusiasm of Secretary Humphrey was remarkable. He went as far as to recommend suspension of the Solarium study in light of the JCS report.

This surprisingly favorable reception of their report by the NSC caused two members of the JCS to elaborate on their views. Admiral Carney reminded the council that the report was largely constrained by the budgetary limitations set forth in President Eisenhower's guidelines.[86] General Ridgway wanted to make it crystal clear that he subscribed neither to the withdrawal of U.S. forces stationed overseas nor to any theory that war could be prevented through the deterrent effect of any single branch of the military. He emphasized "that the present report did not constitute the corporate view of the Joint Chiefs of Staff, but rather the view of the individual chiefs prior to their taking office."[87] One wonders to what extent the report reflected the views of Ridgway at all. The paper was obviously much more in line with Admiral Radford's and General Twining's thinking. Signs of a severe split within the JCS were written all over the presentation of their report.

John Foster Dulles had severe doubts about the desirability of the proposed strategy. While the secretary of state appreciated the report's approach, he was concerned about its likely impact on foreign policy. The free world greatly feared a revival of the Fortress America concept, Dulles noted, and the allies would "dismiss our proposed new policy as simply camouflaged isolation."[88] The proposed redeployments would force foreign governments and peoples to conclude that the United States thought that the menace of the Soviet Union and global war had vanished. This would frighten some European allies, who had been lowering defense expenditures. But not even the United States, Dulles stressed, could match the strength of a powerful totalitarian state on its own. The only solution was the "pooling of resources." The United States could not afford to take measures that could lead to a breach with its allies. Secretary Dulles believed that domestic opinion, of course, would be delighted with the new concept. But the new policy would be seen as a disaster in public opinion abroad. It was the "art of the thing," Dulles summarized his view, to reshape U.S. policy without damaging the vital cohesion of the free world. Redeployments had to be sold as an attempt to concentrate U.S. troops in a central reserve that could be deployed quickly to any potential danger zone.[89]

The JCS had recognized that their proposed course of action would have important and probably disruptive foreign policy consequences.[90] But while General Ridgway stated that the NATO powers would interpret the redeployment as abandonment, Admiral Carney was convinced that the concept could be sold without such consequences. After all, the United States had always planned to withdraw its forces after the European states had achieved the capacity to defend themselves. Admiral Radford emphatically agreed with the latter view. Moreover, the United States would state clearly that it was concentrating its great strength and not abandoning the allies. Finally, the council accepted the following suggestion made by John Foster Dulles: The NSC should recommend to the president that the secretary of state be authorized to explore the JCS concept from a foreign policy point of view.

When Cutler briefed the president about the council meeting, Eisenhower, too, reacted favorably to the JCS report: "This concept is a crystallized and clarified statement of this Administration's understanding of our national security objectives since World War II." But he realized immediately its disruptive potential with regard to foreign policy. His concern about how the allies would interpret the new policy caused him to go to great lengths in emphasizing that the concept was not new and should never be presented as new. The stationing of American troops abroad, Eisenhower stressed, had been a stop-gap operation "to produce among our friends morale, confidence, economic and military strength, in order that they would be able to hold vital areas with indigenous troops until American help could arrive." The U.S. military had always placed a premium on the safety of the United States from surprise attack, on the existence of highly mobile forces, and on comprehensive mobilization plans. The president thought that this return to original thinking should be included in the Solarium Policy Paper. But the way to do it, the president decided, was not to suspend the Solarium study (as Secretary Humphrey had suggested), but rather to include the JCS proposal quietly and without attribution.

President Eisenhower was concerned about the possible negative foreign policy implications of the JCS's proposed program. He was very concerned that the recent Soviet explosion of a hydrogen bomb would weaken the credibility of an aggressive foreign policy. Even before the explosion he had had doubts "about how much we should poke at the animal through the bars of the cage." It was with these considerations in mind that the president showed great interest in the "dramatic idea" about which John Foster Dulles had been thinking at that time.[91]

An Important Element of the New Look:
The Eisenhower-Dulles Partnership

In the days after the presentation of the JCS report, Dulles worked on a "dramatic idea" intended to solve the problem of reshaping U.S. national security policy without destroying the cohesion of the free world. On 1 September, he discussed his thoughts with Director of the Policy Planning Staff Robert R. Bowie and Robert Cutler. When Cutler briefed the president about the NSC meeting of 27 August, he also outlined the substance of the secretary's idea. President Eisenhower was extremely interested and suggested that Dulles should come and see him in Denver at his "Summer White House."[92] The secretary of state met the president on 6 September 1953. He had put his idea down on paper. That memorandum is a convincing argument for the "unexpected John Foster Dulles" who was a much more complex and multidimensional personality than his reputation for advocating "a policy of boldness" suggested at the time.[93]

Dulles first stated that there was a need for increased continental defense, increased emphasis on an effort to lead in nonconventional weapons, increased strategic reserves in lieu of commitments abroad (which were never intended to be permanent), budgetary balance and monetary stability, and adaptation to a manpower shortage. This was more or less a restatement of the priorities of the new JCS. But Secretary Dulles, unlike Secretary Humphrey, was sympathetic to such a policy approach for reasons other than its fiscal soundness. It was not only a question of "whether you've got the men to put there and the money to keep them there."[94] The policy had attractive features from a foreign policy point of view as well. As Soviet nuclear power grew, allied countries hosting the bases of the Strategic Air Command (SAC) would begin to look upon those bases "as lightning rods rather than umbrellas." Moreover, the semipermanent presence of U.S. land forces with their dependents abroad was an irritant with a potential to grow. These arguments led Dulles to the conclusion that "from the standpoint of European Allies the NATO concept is losing its grip." First, up to now, NATO had relied on U.S. atomic supremacy to deter the Soviet Union from an attack on Europe. Confidence in the credibility of the deterrent was now shaken in light of the recent evidence of a Soviet hydrogen bomb capacity. Second, the development of Soviet nuclear missiles frightened the close neighbors of the Soviet Union, because there was no defense against quick attack. Moreover, the United States was becoming vulnerable itself. This inspired fears that the Americans "might stay out if Europe were attacked first." Third and finally, the budget problems of the allies were even more acute than the budget problem of the United States. Against this background, Dulles warned, the Soviet "peace offensive" following the death of Stalin invited wishful thinking on the part of the allies. They might judge that "the danger is past and that neutralism and military economy is permissible."

All this made it probable that the JCS's proposed course would be interpreted abroad "as final proof of an isolationist trend and the adoption of the 'Fortress America' concept." The United States would drift into an isolated position where its defense expenditures would be doomed to rapid growth absent the pooled resources of the free world. The alternative Dulles proposed was "to make a spectacular effort to relax world tensions on a global basis." This could be done by withdrawal of Red Army forces from the satellite countries and U.S. forces from Western Europe. The plan would include limitation and control of weapons of mass destruction. This would allow the United States to reshape its policy in favor of continental defense, strategic mobility, and central reserves. Furthermore, the NATO allies could stabilize their forces at a level compatible with budgetary limits. It was Secretary Dulles's judgment that "within the framework of such a settlement the results desired could be achieved with an increase rather than a decline of U.S. influence and without risk of our being isolated." Finally, it was a propitious time for such a move "because we will be speaking from strength rather than weakness." The armistice in Korea had been achieved "in an atmosphere of our willingness to enlarge the war unless the armistice was accepted." U.S. deterrence obviously had worked in a compelling way. Moreover, the full impact of Soviet nuclear power had not yet been felt in Europe and Japan.[95]

From what we know, President Eisenhower was in general agreement with Dulles's line of argument, but he voiced one important reservation. While he acknowledged that the semipermanent presence of U.S. forces in foreign lands was an irritant, he warned that "any withdrawal that seemed to imply a change in *basic* intent would cause real turmoil abroad."[96] The president, who had not participated in the crucial NSC meeting of 27 August seemed to be as aware as his secretary of state of the possible adverse foreign policy implications of the course outlined by the JCS. Nevertheless, he thought that mutual withdrawal of Red Army forces and U.S. forces could be proposed as a step toward relaxing world tensions.

The president's position must be viewed in the context of what came to be known as Project Candor. After the explosion of the Soviet thermonuclear device, the Eisenhower administration began exploring with renewed vigor ways to prove U.S. interest in a peaceful settlement of the Cold War. Project Candor led to President Eisenhower's "Atoms for Peace" speech, analyzed in greater detail below.[97] Dulles's idea of mutual withdrawal was in one of the drafts of that speech. This draft prompted the planning board of the NSC to take a closer look at Dulles's proposed plan, and they criticized it harshly.[98] The representatives of the Defense Department on the NSC Planning Board stated that the mutual withdrawal idea would lead to political disaster, and Robert Bowie of the Department of State warned of military disaster.[99] Bowie reminded the planning board that the withdrawal of U.S. troops was linked to the control of nuclear weapons, "because we cannot withdraw our forces at the same time the Russians do without abandoning our bases. Obviously we cannot abandon forward bases until nuclear weapons are controlled."[100] President Eisenhower had used the same argument during the presentation of the Solarium reports to illustrate that the United States could not carry out its Cold War policies without its allies.

Two days after the president and the secretary of state had met in Denver, Eisenhower drafted a memorandum for Dulles that summarized his thoughts on their discussion. From this document it seems that their talk covered a much wider field than Dulles's idea of mutual withdrawal. Eisenhower was focused on the question of how increased defense expenditures could be explained to the American public and U.S. allies around the world. The very heart of the matter was that the American people expected tax relief after the end of the Korean War. But they were not well informed, the president wrote, "as to what drastic tax reduction would mean to the security of the country." If the administration was going to follow policies that might involve vastly increased expenditures over an extended time, it should begin to educate the

American people about the fundamental facts of these problems. The government should start to describe the capabilities now and in the near future of A-bombs and H-bombs. It should point out that as long as the Soviets refused to make an honest effort toward international control of nuclear weapons, the United States would assume that the leaders in the Kremlin were contemplating the offensive use of those weapons. President Eisenhower then set out to show that with the advent of the nuclear age the potential for industrial mobilization had lost a lot of its deterrent power: U.S. preparations for war "could no longer be geared to a policy that attempts only to avert disaster during the early 'surprise' stages of a war, and so gain time for full mobilization." The president found himself compelled by the doctrine of retaliation: "Rather, we would have to be constantly ready, on an instantaneous basis, to inflict greater loss upon the enemy than he could reasonably hope to inflict upon us. This would be a deterrent."[101]

Although Eisenhower said all of this in his memorandum to Dulles, in fact he was not wholly convinced of the merit of such a policy. If the contest to maintain relative advantage had to continue indefinitely, the country would be driven either to war or to some form of dictatorial government.

Eisenhower ended his analysis by contemplating the option of preventive war. Whereas Dulles envisioned a spectacular effort to lessen tensions, Eisenhower speculated: "In such circumstances, we would be forced to consider whether or not our duty to future generations did not require us to *initiate* war at the most propitious moment we could designate."[102]

The fact that the president and the secretary of state ended their respective analyses at opposite ends of the spectrum of options could lead one to conclude that they were in fundamental disagreement about the future of national security policy. But, to the contrary, their private meeting seems to have laid the foundation for a productive partnership that would shape American foreign policy during the 1950s.[103] Eisenhower feared the consequences of exorbitant defense expenditures over the long run, which he perceived as particularly dangerous in light of public expectations. Dulles, in addition, emphasized the delicacy of the foreign policy side of the problem and underlined the necessity of enhancing the credibility of U.S. deterrence.

This Eisenhower-Dulles dialogue happened at a very crucial moment. The meeting took place right before the final decisions regarding the formulation of a new basic national security paper (NSC 162 series) *and* the defense budget for fiscal year 1955 had to be made. Furthermore, the Europeans were increasingly eager to get a clear statement of the future of American security policy. And with the first round of consultations with the allies approaching, Project Candor was reaching its decisive phase as well. Political considerations had played a role in Eisenhower's choice of Dulles as secretary of state. But toward the end of 1953, the president and his secretary of state began to work as a team. This partnership was most responsible for the final shape of the New Look.

The New Look Takes Shape

The New Look took final shape during October 1953. It was the twin tasks of formulating a new basic national security policy paper and preparing the defense budget for fiscal year 1955 that triggered the final decisions of the year-long reexamination of national security policy. These two tasks influenced each other in many ways. The New Look, therefore, was a product of neither pure economic nor pure military strategic consideration.

Starting with the results of Project Solarium and integrating the views of the JCS, the planning board of the NSC, under the direction of Robert Bowie, drafted a first version of a basic national security policy paper.[104] NSC 162 did not much more than summarize in a comprehensive way the differences in opinion that had materialized so far. It pointed out the varying departmental positions and split views that had not yet been settled. Most of the differences were over three fundamental issues.

The first split concerned the nature of the threat the United States was facing. It went back to the first months of the administration, when the Treasury Department and the Budget Office had announced that the country was facing a dual threat.[105] The rest of the administration had given clear priority to the external threat posed by the Communist bloc. This division had furthermore become apparent during the discussion of Project Solarium. The majority view within the administration had then been that the United States could afford current levels of expenditure without damaging the economy. Moreover, the American public would support higher taxation if it fully understood the security needs of the country.[106] Like the discussion of the spring of 1953 with the civilian consultants, the October 1953 consultations revealed opposite views about the value of mutual security programs.[107]

A second difference of opinion concerned the redeployment of U.S. forces from Europe and the Far East. The planning board stated that under present conditions any major withdrawal of U.S. forces would seriously undermine the cohesion of the free world. In contrast, Admiral Radford emphasized that the United States was overextended to a degree that would deprive it of mobility and initiative in future military action in the defense of the free world.[108] U.S. diplomats, therefore, had to explain to the allies that the best defense of the free world rested "upon the mobility of U.S. forces, centrally based," upon the U.S. political commitment "to strike back hard directly against any aggressor who attacks such allies," and upon the allies' own forces.

The third disagreement concerned the problem of how to reduce the Soviet threat. It was basically a split between the State Department and the Defense Department, although in many respects it resembled the differences between task forces "A" and "C" of Project Solarium. While the State Department emphasized that the Soviet threat could be reduced only through a settlement in the interest of both East and West, the Defense Department stressed that reduction of the Soviet threat—short of initiating general war—could be achieved only by actions designed to result in Soviet accommodation to the security of the United States. The Defense Department pointed out that neither the detachment of any major European satellite from the Soviet Union nor a breakup between the Soviet Union and Communist China could be achieved in the short term without war or Soviet acquiescence. The State Department, on the other hand, interpreted the various Soviet peace gestures after the death of Stalin and the recent uprisings in East Germany as support for the proposition that in the long term the Communist system would change from within. Moreover, given the U.S. retaliatory capability, it was improbable that the Soviet Union would deliberately launch a general war against the United States. Deterrence could be expected to work.[109]

When the draft paper was discussed in the NSC, the president opened by defending the dual threat approach advocated by Secretary Humphrey and Budget Director Dodge. Placing too much importance on the military threat, the president believed, "would lead to both general mobilization and out-and-out regimentation." Encouraged by the president's statement, Secretary Humphrey and Director Dodge restated their well-known positions with renewed vigor. At this point, Secretary Dulles commented that the dual threat approach seemed to require that a balanced budget be reached at whatever cost to national security. Such an argument seemed doctrinaire. At the heart of the matter was the time factor: The dual threat group agreed in principle that the administration could get what it wanted from the American people in the short term, but that in the long term it was essential to balance the budget and to stabilize (or even lower) taxation.

Finally, President Eisenhower forced a consensus, basically supporting Dulles's line. In order to mollify Secretary Humphrey, the first statement in the policy paper should recognize that the United States was "engaged in defending a way of life as well as a territory."[110] In return, Secretary Humphrey and Director Dodge would have to accommodate a weaker stance on the fiscal threat.[111] President Eisenhower's reexamination of national security policy still took the internal threat of a weakened economy into account to a far greater extent than Truman's NSC 68 and NSC 141. Eisenhower's NSC 162/2 identified the Soviet Union as the primary threat to the security of the United States, but at the same time it underlined the significance of economic stability and democratic institutions.

The discussion then shifted to the problem of redeployment. The president and the secretary of state had made up their minds during their talk in Denver: The course suggested by the JCS was militarily sound, but politically unfeasible at the time. Secretary Dulles warned that "redeployment could bring about the complete collapse of our coalition in Europe." The president then pointed out that in order to redeploy, the United States would have to spend much more money on defense. In short, said the president, "that Western Europe not fall to the Communists was a *sine qua non*."[112]

From the very first, through the discussions of Project Solarium and the JCS report, both President Eisenhower and Secretary Dulles emphasized the absolute necessity for U.S. security of maintaining allies. There was never a danger that the United States would revert to isolationist policies. Isolation was rather perceived to be one of the greatest dangers to national security in the Cold War. The importance of allies was written into NSC 162/2: The United States could not "meet its defense needs, even at exorbitant cost, without the support of allies." The United States required overseas bases for the effective use of its air power, at least for some years to come. It also needed the military forces and economic resources of the major industrialized countries in order to retain the capacity to win a general war without undermining its democratic institutions.

NATO was clearly the product of common interest among the allied countries. According to NSC 162/2, however, at least four factors tended to weaken its cohesion. First, the economic and military recovery of the major allies had given them a greater sense of independence from the United States. Second, a major weakness was the instability of the governments of certain allies (i.e., France and Italy). Third, many Europeans feared that the United States would follow risky policies, ranging from preventive war and wars of liberation to withdrawal into isolation. Fourth, fear of general nuclear war had led the allies to press for renewed efforts to negotiate with the Soviet Union, and they were encouraged by recent overtures of the new Soviet leadership.[113] Against this background, the United States had to retain the cooperation of the allies by convincing them that it was following a strategy of collective security. Redeployment for the sake of regaining strategic mobility and initiative would be sound from a military point of view. After all, as the president often said, these forces had been brought overseas only as an emergency measure.[114] But until the allies resigned themselves to that reality, any redeployment had to be put on hold.

As to reduction of the Soviet threat, Dulles led the NSC to a carefully worded position advocating negotiated settlement without relaxation of the defense effort of the free world. It was again the president who inspired consensus. NSC 162/2 stated that the United States must seek to improve its own position of power and that of the free world relative to the Soviet Union. But the United States also had to keep open the possibility of general negotiations with the Soviet Union and Communist China on topics such as the control of armaments. NSC 162/2 concluded that the willingness of the Soviet leadership to negotiate acceptable settlements might increase over time "if the United States and its allies develop and increase their own strength, determination and cohesion, maintain retaliatory power sufficient to insure unacceptable damage to the Soviet system should the USSR resort to general war, and prove that the free world can prosper despite Soviet pressures, or if for any reason Soviet stability and influence are reduced."[115]

After the NSC members had discussed their differences over these three fundamental issues, they turned to the question of U.S. policy regarding the use of nuclear weapons. President Eisenhower immediately proposed a revision of the suggested language in favor of a clear statement that securing the "approval and understanding of our allies should precede the use of these special weapons."[116] Secretary Wilson and Admiral Radford then asked whether the Department of Defense could plan for the use of these weapons. Eisenhower replied that the president would make the ultimate decision as to the use of nuclear weapons. If U.S. security interests required their use, then he certainly would use them. The JCS "should count on making use of special weapons in the event of general war. They should not, however, plan to make use of these weapons in minor affairs."[117]

The issue was far from resolved and came up again six days later, during the discussion of the budget for fiscal year 1955. Secretary of Defense Wilson proposed a defense budget that would actually have *increased* the force levels of the armed services. He offered three reasons for this proposal: there had been no significant change in basic national security policy, no change in U.S. commitments, and no change with respect to U.S. policy on the use of atomic weapons. As long as the council did not clarify its views on the use of atomic weapons and the Department of State was worried about going forward with redeployment of U.S. overseas forces, it would be difficult to make any real progress toward reducing defense costs.

Secretary Humphrey and Director Dodge were aghast at the prospect of a defense budget of over $43 billion. The secretary of the treasury thought it absolutely essential to settle the issue of the use of atomic weapons once and for all. And Secretary Dulles asked whether these recommendations reflected the basic review of U.S. military strategy that the new JCS had so forcefully presented on 27 August 1953. In response, Admiral Radford stated that the current statement in NSC 162 on the use of nuclear weapons was regarded by the JCS as insufficient guidance: "He commented that unless we could use these weapons in a blanket way, no possibility existed of significantly changing the present composition of our armed forces."

Secretary Wilson and Admiral Radford believed that a decisive statement on when and how nuclear weapons might be used was a necessary precondition to the reduction of the defense budget. But when Robert Cutler suggested that the chairman of the JCS draft clearer guidance on nuclear use, the president stated that "we could not hope to do better than the presently agreed language."[118]

The final wording of NSC 162/2 on nuclear use was close to the proposal of the Defense Department. It read in part: "In the event of hostilities, the United States will consider nuclear weapons to be as available for use as other munitions." The sentence permitted the military to prepare plans on the assumption that nuclear weapons might be used. It was followed by two qualifications: First, the United States "should also seek, as and when feasible, the understanding and approval of this policy by free nations."[119] This formulation left ambiguous whether the approval of the allies would have to precede the actual use of these weapons.[120] Second, this policy "should not be made public without further consideration by the National Security Council."[121] This last qualification was intended to give the Department of State time to ascertain allied views.

The wording in NSC 162/2 was fuzzy enough to spark other differences of opinion on the new nuclear use doctrine. The Department of State believed that the language permitted the military "to make plans on the basis of the availability of nuclear weapons." It further agreed with the Department of Defense that "as a corollary, custody of atomic weapons should in large part be transferred from the AEC to the Department of Defense." However, State disagreed with the position that under the new policy "atomic weapons will, in fact, be used in the event of *any* hostilities." This decision should be made by the president "from case to case in the light of the actual circumstances."[122] Contradictory opinions regarding the use of nuclear weapons persisted within the administration after NSC 162/2 had become approved policy.[123]

But having a nuclear use policy in place allowed President Eisenhower to reduce the manpower of the U.S. armed forces. On 11 November 1953, he met with Secretary Dulles, Secretary Humphrey, and Secretary Wilson to discuss possible reductions in the proposed fiscal year 1955 defense budget. It was agreed that "the dependence that we are placing on new weapons would justify completely some reduction in conventional forces—that is, both ground troops and certain parts of the Navy."[124] Secretary Dulles suggested starting with the withdrawal of ground troops from Korea in order to demonstrate the administration's confidence in U.S. air and naval strength and to limit ground deployments in Asia. Also, service and support units in Europe could be scaled back, allowing further savings in manpower.[125]

The nuclear issue came up once more during discussion of the revised version of NSC 162 (NSC 162/1). Admiral Radford was not satisfied with the guidelines for the use of nuclear weapons. Officials in the army and the navy believed the emphasis on retaliatory power to be too strong. Admiral Carney pointed out that it was unwise "to put all our eggs in one basket of striking power," and eventually he withdrew his support (which had always been limited) for the JCS position articulated in the report to the NSC of 27 August 1953.[126] Eisenhower, however, liked the planning board version, because it provided some sense of priority for military planning. And, after all, "deterring war was even more important than winning a war. No deterrent to war could compare in importance with this retaliatory striking power." Finally, Secretary Dulles pointed out that the redeployment of American forces was a very delicate operation, if indeed it could be accomplished. Dulles estimated that the shift in priority toward retaliatory capability would require two or three years.[127]

NSC 162/2 integrated nuclear weapons into American security policy. It stressed the need for secure, massive retaliatory forces. The authors of the document acknowledged that the Soviet nuclear capability was increasing as well and that there would have to be a continual reexamination of national security policy.[128]

The year-long reappraisal of national security policy by the Eisenhower administration had started from the premise that security could only be achieved by giving equal weight to the external threat of the Soviet aggressive intent and immense power and the internal threat of a weakened economy and the accompanying pressures on democratic institutions. Project Solarium was largely the result of the pressure on President Eisenhower, which had been mounting since the campaign of 1952, to provide both fiscal and military leadership. The intensive policy exercise exposed the new administration to a range of possible future courses. The new NSC listened to different expert arguments, and then moved to build a consensus on national security policy. The result was really modification of President Truman's strategy of containment, rather than a fundamental shift in policy.

As instructed by the president, the JCS planned for the redeployment of U.S. overseas forces and the complete integration of nuclear weapons into American defense policy in a manner designed to implement the great equation between security and solvency. The JCS report bore the clear imprint of Admiral Radford, who shared the president's concern for this balance. Other members of the JCS were not persuaded by the final allocation of priorities. The president and Secretary Dulles both thought redeployment and increased integration of nuclear weapons to be militarily sound. At the same time they appreciated the diplomatic risk of the proposed policy. The New Look took shape from this understanding. The New Look provided for enough integration of nuclear weapons into American national security policy to permit manpower reductions, and thus considerable savings in the defense budget.[129] On the other hand, the New Look called for delayed redeployment of U.S. overseas forces so as to soften the blow to the allies.

The integration of nuclear weapons into American national security policy permitted the United States to adopt a financially bearable defense without abandoning Europe. Nuclear weapons made the cost of the Cold War tolerable. The savings made it easier to continue supporting collective security. The integration of nuclear weapons also responded to a perceived need for a more aggressive U.S. policy toward the Soviet Union. This is not to say that the New Look was primarily a product of fiscal considerations. As we will see in greater detail in the next chapter, the policy was also a product of military considerations.

The year-long reexamination of national security strategy had finally come to an end. President Eisenhower's answers to the complex challenges of American security were embodied in a new national security policy paper. NSC 162/2 tried to define aims, means, costs, and threats to American national security in a sensible way. Unfortunately, the public presentation of the New Look took the form of John Foster Dulles's speech before the Council on Foreign Relations on 12 January 1954. In one of the most famous moments of Cold War rhetoric, the secretary of state—arguably unintentionally—reduced the New Look to the concept of massive retaliation: "The way to deter aggression is for a free community to be willing and able to respond vigorously and at places and with means of its own choosing. The basic decision was made to depend primarily on a great capacity to retaliate, instantly, by means of our own choosing."[130]

Why had Dulles presented the New Look as the incarnation of the position first advanced in his 1952 article in *Life* magazine? Dulles was interested in maximizing deterrent power through the new policy. He also sought to explain the advantages of such a policy to the allies. Dulles believed the way to maximize U.S. deterrence was by linking the *certainty* of retaliation with the *uncertainty* of timing, place, and means of retaliation.[131] The secretary of state focused on the problem of deterrence as opposed to the problem of defense. After all, in the realm of daily politics the deterrence component of planning was more immediate than the defense component. The speech firmly established the public's image of Dulles as a proponent of massive retaliation at every opportunity, whatever the risks. A myth was born that overstated his confidence in nuclear weapons and understated his commitment to more flexible responses. Paradoxically, the secretary of state said what he said publicly not because of unshakable confidence in U.S. power, but rather because he believed in the necessity of strengthening American deterrence.[132]

Dulles emphasized the advantages of reliance on nuclear retaliation in the first instance in a way that would make the allies understand the common benefits of the new policy: "We keep locks on our doors, but we do not have an armed guard in every home. We rely principally on a community security system so well equipped to punish any who break in and steal that, in fact, would-be aggressors are generally deterred. That is the modern way of getting maximum protection at bearable costs."[133] The speech educated the allies in the nuclear business. Dulles's ultimate goal was to win allied acceptance of redeployments, which the secretary of state had called for several times during the year.[134]

Unfortunately, Dulles's remarks did not clarify allied understanding of U.S. policy, but only obscured it further. His rhetoric very quickly became the focus of Democratic criticism of the Republican defense policy: Did such a policy not invite piecemeal aggression by the Soviet Union, because it simply lacked credibility in the face of growing Soviet nuclear potential? Would the United States be forced to choose between humiliation and holocaust? In the words of Richard H. Immerman, the massive retaliation speech resulted in "a battle of words, a battle fought over nuance, emphasis, and context."[135] John Foster Dulles's article in the April 1954 issue of *Foreign Affairs* demonstrated the secretary's awareness of the complexities and the danger of oversimplified analyses.[136] But the popular interpretation of massive retaliation persisted.

2

The Impact of the Strategic Nuclear Balance on Policy

The relatively low financial cost of nuclear weapons permitted Eisenhower to pursue a modified strategy of containment, avoiding both isolationism and overspending. And the New Look was not only fiscally attractive. Its emphases on nuclear retaliatory forces, continental defense, and redeployment of overseas forces were sound strategic choices in light of the technological and military realities of the time. Nuclear capabilities were still relatively modest in contrast to what was to come. Nuclear war was not yet completely unthinkable and would not necessarily be tantamount to national suicide. The United States was still clearly the dominant nuclear power. From an American perspective, general war could have been fought and won.

The fact that nuclearization made military sense in the early 1950s had a direct impact on U.S. foreign and defense policies—and on the political choices of allies and adversaries. This chapter explores the impact of the strategic nuclear balance on policy at a time when the balance was lopsided. First, I will show how the United States coped with the anticipation of losing its nuclear advantage. Anxiety about the increasing nuclear capabilities of the Soviet Union generated serious consideration of preventive war even in the highest ranks of the American government. The preventive war debate came to a halt with rejection of the option toward the end of 1954. Second, I will analyze how the strategic balance influenced the Eisenhower administration's termination of the Korean War. In terms of chronology, this means a digression to 1953. However, insight into the learning process of the incoming Eisenhower administration regarding the military and political limitations of nuclear weapons will better explain why preventive war was rejected.

49

The New Look: Gigantic Bluff or
Coherent National Security Policy?

It was a widely held belief in the United States that the strategy of massive retaliation was primarily a cheap solution to balance Soviet conventional superiority. The strategy was perceived as nothing more than a gigantic bluff. From an essentially military point of view, according to popular perception, the strategy was misguided from the start. The following discussion is an attempt to show that in view of the military realities at the time, the New Look was not only economically sound but also militarily credible.

From the very beginning, the New Look was heavily criticized by Democrats and a majority segment of the strategic community. They disapproved of massive retaliation—the part of the New Look most visible to the public. Criticism increased over the years and reached its peak toward the end of the 1950s, inspired by the successful launch of the Soviet satellite *Sputnik* in 1957. Some critics concentrated on the credibility of the strategy in limited wars. Other critics concentrated on the changing nature of conflict in the thermonuclear age.

The most vocal critics were Bernard Brodie of Yale University, William W. Kaufmann of Princeton University, and Henry A. Kissinger of Harvard University.[1] All three agreed that the threat of massive retaliation lacked credibility as a response to limited aggression. After all, the punishment had to fit the crime. Bernard Brodie recalled Carl von Clausewitz's fundamental insight that the means of strategy must be proportional to its aims.[2] The credibility of massive retaliation as a deterrent to limited aggression was eroding in the face of growing Soviet nuclear capabilities. As the Soviets themselves became increasingly capable of retaliation, a massive nuclear strike would be "an act of desperation to be invoked only if national survival is unambiguously threatened."[3] In the eyes of its critics, the strategy of massive retaliation merely invited the adversary to execute limited aggression. In short, deterrence could fail. In that event, the nation would have to choose between humiliation and holocaust: "If the Communists should challenge our sincerity, and they would have good reasons for daring to do so, we would either have to put up or shut up. If we put up, we would plunge into all the immeasurable horrors of an atomic war. If we shut up, we would suffer a serious loss of prestige and damage our capacity to establish deterrents against further Communist expansion."[4] The critics' principal recommendation to avoid such a situation was to build up conventional forces as a deterrent to limited aggression.

Below the surface, objections to the New Look rested upon a more fundamental insight into the changing nature of conflict in the thermonuclear age. Atomic and hydrogen bombs had rendered total war aimed at unconditional victory unthinkable. In the thermonuclear age one could expect greater use of limited means to attain limited goals. Both sides would have to adopt a controlled and limited concept of warfare. Kaufmann noted that war would become "a function between the abstractness of a show of force and the terrible concreteness of annihilative conflict."[5]

Criticism of massive retaliation was not merely academic; it was taken up and confirmed by former members of the Truman administration, like Paul H. Nitze.[6] In addition, the split within the JCS over the heavy emphasis on retaliatory forces gained public attention. The army and navy were considering how to fight a general war with only limited employment of nuclear weapons.[7] The bottom line of all this criticism was that from an essentially military point of view, the New Look was an unsound strategy. According to the critics, Eisenhower was endangering the nation's security for the sake of fiscal conservatism.

Was there anything to this critique? The driving factor behind the JCS's New Look was the growing capacity of the Soviet Union to attack the American homeland with nuclear weapons. Ever since the Soviet Union had tested its first atomic bomb in 1949, the growing vulnerability of the U.S. homeland had led policy makers to address the problem of continental defense. Emphasis on continental defense had been Nitze's legacy as outgoing director of the Policy Planning Staff. The JCS had emphasized the matter in their report to the NSC on 27 August 1953. Continental defense had been assigned a high priority in NSC 162/2.[8] The explosion of the first Soviet thermonuclear device on 12 August 1953 underscored the necessity of concentrating on continental defense. And continental defense, in turn, was linked to acquiring a credible retaliatory capability. Making this capability credible by securing the weapons from a surprise nuclear attack was given highest priority in the final draft of the New Look. President Eisenhower approved the concentration on retaliatory forces, continental defense, and nuclear weapons not only because these priorities were fiscally attractive, but also because they were militarily logical adjustments to U.S. defense strategy in the face of growing Soviet nuclear and thermonuclear capabilities.

The problems with the new military policy lay in the potentially devastating foreign policy implications that redeployments would have. Eisenhower emphasized that redeployment should not be startling from a military point of view. According to the president, people who had seriously studied military problems had considered the stationing of U.S. troops abroad as a temporary expedient only. They had always placed a premium on "(1) safety of the US from surprise and destructive attack, (2) existence of highly mobile forces, (3) comprehensive mobilization plans quickly to marshal our entire strength in support of our national security."[9]

One reason why the sound military assumptions behind the New Look were often overlooked had to do with Eisenhower's background as a military man. As one of the country's leading soldiers, Eisenhower believed that the military theory behind the New Look was so evident as to require no explanation. David Alan Rosenberg has noted that "Eisenhower entered the presidency in January 1953 with a more thorough knowledge of nuclear weapons than any president before or since."[10] As NATO's first commander, General Eisenhower had relied on a strategy for the defense of Europe that would paralyze the enemy at the outset of war by delivering a massive air strike, including nuclear weapons. Eisenhower knew from firsthand experience that only with such a strategy could Europe be defended with numerically inferior forces.[11]

American war plans, too, were consistent with reliance on nuclear weapons. The JCS had interpreted the statement in NSC 162/2 on the use of nuclear weapons as an assurance that they could plan for their use in both limited war and general war.[12] The military strategy implementing NSC 162/2 (which was approved in December 1953) called for "tactical support for US or allied military forces in general war or in local aggression whenever the employment of atomic weapons would be militarily advantageous."[13] The assumption that tactical use of nuclear weapons could compensate for numerical inferiority in conventional forces predated the Eisenhower administration. As early as February of 1952, a scientific study called Project VISTA had concluded that "the tactical employment of our atomic weapons resources holds outstanding promise" for defending Western Europe.[14] And even army leaders believed that if nuclear weapons were used against concentrated forces, stockpiled supplies, and long lines of communications, NATO might be able to hold the line against a Soviet attack, even with numerically inferior forces.[15] The army was not generally opposed to the use of nuclear weapons. The army chief of staff General Matthew B. Ridgway was primarily concerned about the high priority assigned to procurement of strategic retaliatory forces.

At the beginning of the 1950s, procurement favored the SAC. The air force controlled the long-range bombers, and SAC controlled targeting, which was critical to general war planning. The plan for general war called for a combined offensive against military targets and urban-indus-trial targets. The goal was to blunt the adversary's threat by striking first. Massive retaliation, on the operational level, meant massive preemp-tion.[16] President Eisenhower was very clear about how to react to an impending strike. In January 1954, he lectured a group of congressmen about the tempo of a future war: "It is to hit the guy fast with all you've got if he jumps on you. War will be a very quick thing as fast as Congress can meet—24 hours."[17]

The emphasis on preemption has to be understood in terms of the warning time that the United States would have in the event of a nuclear attack and the time the Soviets would need to deliver their nuclear weap-ons. At the time, planners could count on days or even weeks. Key offi-cials were relatively confident that they would have enough warning time to destroy the bulk of the enemy's strategic forces before they could be launched. David Alan Rosenberg explains that "in this era before ballistic missiles, preemption appeared to be both militarily and consti-tutionally feasible."[18]

In addition to the time required to prepare a nuclear launch, the two most important factors limiting the effectiveness of a Soviet first strike would be the small numbers of atomic weapons in the Soviet arsenal and technical constraints on delivery. An NSC study estimated the Soviet Union's atomic stockpile to include 120 bombs containing about 80 kilotons of energy in 1953. The bombs could be delivered by about one thousand medium bombers of the TU-4 type, which could reach any target in the United States, but which would have enough fuel only for one-way missions.[19]

These operational handicaps on the Soviet side made a lasting impres-sion on the president. After the presentation of the NSC report he asked the NSC's Special Evaluation Subcommittee whether it had given any thought to what the Soviets thought the United States could do to them. President Eisenhower was convinced that "they must be scared as hell." The subcommittee's chairman stated that "any attack on the United States by the Soviets during this period would be an act of desperation and not an exercise of military judgment."[20] The report on the vulnera-bility of the United States paradoxically reassured the president that de-terrence would work, and that, should it fail, the United States would prevail in a general war.

All this is not to say that President Eisenhower overlooked or underes-timated the consequences of general war for the United States. He often expressed the view that if a third world war started with a Soviet surprise attack, the American public "would itself be required to accept a totalitarian regime."[21] A defeated Soviet Union, too, would only be governable by a totalitarian system for a considerable interval after the war. But this observation did not lead the president to conclude that in case of general war, the United States would have to restrain its use of force— especially nuclear force. Eisenhower believed that war had the inherent tendency to become total. A major war would become a nuclear war in which it would be self-defeating to restrain one's own use of force. In a war fought with nuclear and thermonuclear weapons, the president believed everything "would have to be subordinated to winning that war." In such a war, the United States "would be applying a force so terrible that one simply could not be meticulous as to the methods by which the force was brought to bear." The decision of how to fight the war would be determined by "where and how it would hurt most."[22]

General war was still thought to imply a long war, measured in years rather than months. After initial nuclear exchanges had paralyzed both sides, final victory, in the eyes of the president, might be achieved only with "a 12-year mobilization program."[23] In such a war, the mobilization potential of U.S. industry would still be decisive. NSC 162/2 concluded that national security required not only a strong military posture with both retaliatory and quick local reaction capabilities but also a protected mobilization base.[24] Nevertheless, as the potential size of the initial strike grew, it became increasingly important to be able to paralyze the enemy right at the beginning in order to bring the power of the U.S. mobilization base to bear.[25] These observations brought Eisenhower back to the central importance of retaliatory forces, which would have to be used at the outset of war, if possible in a preemptive strike—the potential success of which was still judged to be quite good. If the Soviets failed to gain strategic surprise, the above-mentioned Special Evaluation Subcommittee of the NSC had concluded that the damage to the United States would be greatly reduced and the success of the entire Soviet operation jeopardized "by alerting the defensive system and counteroffensive forces of the entire Western World."[26]

In light of the military realities at the time, the New Look was a credible and coherent national security policy. Nuclear weapons were still limited in numbers, and the destructive power of the majority of the bombs was relatively modest compared to the yield of hydrogen bombs. Nuclear war, it was perceived, need not lead automatically to mutual destruction. But as the New Look evolved, its proponents realized that what was a militarily sound policy for the present would require modification in the future. The need to adapt the policy led to serious consideration of preventive war.

The Shifting Strategic Balance and
Considerations of Preventive War

When the New Look was announced, the United States dominated the nuclear balance. However, assumptions about when and how the balance would shift influenced the political debate. The impact of the strategic nuclear balance on foreign policy became more apparent as the United States came to terms with the loss of its atomic monopoly. Anxiety about the expanding Soviet nuclear capabilities led policy makers even at the highest levels of the American government to consider preventive war.

From the very beginning of the nuclear age, it was clear that the U.S. atomic monopoly would not last. This basic insight prompted policy makers to ask what the United States should do when the Soviet Union developed atomic bombs. The urgency of this question increased with the test of the first Soviet atomic device in 1949. Wasn't preventive war the only solution to the threat of a Soviet Union in possession of a massive nuclear arsenal, given the fundamental hostility and aggressiveness of that superpower toward the West? Preventive war thinking had already been taken seriously within the administration and the strategic community before President Eisenhower came into office. The loss of the atomic monopoly and the outbreak of the Korean War resulted in several articles in the public press dealing with preventive war in the late summer of 1950.[27] But within the Truman administration, thinking about preventive war was overshadowed by concerns about American weakness at that time. The conventional wisdom was that it was in the interest of the West to have a period of stability in which to build up its forces. Further, important groups within the Truman administration believed that even after the Soviets achieved an extensive nuclear capacity, they would remain deterred. First, the adversary could not count on being able to destroy U.S. retaliatory capability in a first strike. Second, the Soviets preferred risk-averse courses of action. They would not deliberately embark on a course with serious risk to their own regime.[28]

The Korean War then led to an extraordinary military buildup from 1950 through 1953. The buildup included a great expansion in the production of fissionable material, which was used in an increasing number of tactical nuclear weapons.[29] With the growth of U.S. forces, the balance of power shifted in favor of the United States. Concerns about military weakness transformed into a window of opportunity. By the time Eisenhower entered office in January 1953, the military limitations counseling a policy of restraint had vanished. With the balance of power clearly in

favor of the United States, and the clouds of a huge Soviet thermonuclear capability gathering at the horizon, the time was ripe to give serious consideration to preventive war. Although such a policy was finally
rejected toward the end of 1954, it had a broad appeal and was seriously
discussed at the highest levels of the American government. The heart
of the support for preventive war was located in the military, and its
champions were found within the air force and the SAC.[30]

During the reappraisal of national security policy in 1953, preventive
war was not explicitly considered. However, strong coalitions within the
government were in favor of a more aggressive foreign policy approach
to the growing Soviet threat. Campaign calls for liberation and rollback
implied that the United States had to accept a greater risk of general
war. The issue was raised explicitly in Project Solarium. The directing
panel had excluded preventive war against the Soviet Union as being in
conflict with the realities of the world situation.[31] Nevertheless, even task
force "A" acknowledged the favorable strategic balance. It judged the
United States to be in a "position to assume the strategic offensive in its
conflict with Soviet Communism."[32] Also, task force "C" favored a much
more aggressive and positive policy. It assumed that time was against the
United States in view of the growing Soviet nuclear capability. Task force
"C" expected that a war with China would grow out of the war in Korea
by 1958. The approach taken by task force "C" was received coolly in
the NSC. The president touched on the two main problems with recommendations of task force "C": What would be done with the Soviet
Union after a general war? And what impact would a preventive war
policy have on U.S. allies?[33]

Although Eisenhower was skeptical about a more aggressive policy in
the early months of his administration, the issue would return as the
Soviet nuclear threat grew. At the beginning of September 1953, Eisenhower himself reopened the preventive war question in an exchange of
memoranda with Secretary John Foster Dulles. Against the background
of a Soviet explosion of a hydrogen device, the president struggled to
come to grips with the doctrine of massive retaliation. While he admitted its deterrent power, he was concerned about its consequences in
case the contest to maintain a relative advantage continued indefinitely.
This would drive the United States either to war or to some form of
dictatorial government. For fear of this untenable pair of options, Eisenhower contemplated preventive war. "In such circumstances," he concluded, "we would be forced to consider whether or not our duty to
future generations did not require us to *initiate* war at the most propitious moment we could designate."[34]

The Impact of the Indochina Crisis

The world situation changed for the worse from the   of
the American government in 1954. This was due, first, to
Soviet capacity to strike directly at the American homel
Soviet test of a thermonuclear device on 12 August 1953 ha
found effect on public opinion, particularly in Europe. Fea
war was aggravated by an American thermonuclear test in th
early 1954. The contamination of a Japanese fishing crew u
the suffering that would accompany nuclear war. Second, g
prehension of the nuclear danger exposed relations between th
States and its allies to unprecedented tensions. Allied gove
showed increasing reluctance to support an uncompromising U.
icy. The erosion of western unity became evident during the Indoch.
crisis in early 1954, and then in the failure of the European Defense
Community (EDC). These developments brought the question of preventive war back to the table during the summer of 1954.

On 13 March 1954, the Communists opened a major attack on an
encircled French outpost at Dien Bien Phu. The attack alarmed both
Paris and Washington. The loss of Indochina would endanger the western position in all of Southeast Asia. Japan was of course weakened at
the end of World War II. Then in 1949 the Nationalist Government of
the Republic of China was driven from the mainland to Taiwan by Mao
Tse-tung's Communist armies. Every new loss for democracy in this region, so the argument ran, would lead rapidly to additional setbacks,
which would eventually lead to the loss of the rest of Southeast Asia.[35] If
the French would lose their control over Indochina, it was very probable
that the Laniel government in France also would not survive. This turn
of events would threaten the cornerstone of the Eisenhower administration's plan for European security, the support of the European Defense
Community.[36]

With French forces faltering in Dien Bien Phu, the prospect of an
American rescue became more likely. It was Admiral Arthur W. Radford
who suggested American air intervention. He had already hinted to the
French and the British that U.S. intervention was likely.[37] Although the
president was attracted briefly to an air strike option, he decided that
there could be no intervention without congressional approval.[38] Also,
Secretary Dulles was opposed to unilateral military intervention and instead proposed a plan for "United Action," calling for multilateral military intervention.[39] Eisenhower and Dulles pushed the "United Action"
plan in early April. However, the idea quickly drew opposition from im-

portant quarters. Congressional leaders decided to back a resolution
calling for intervention only after the administration had received commitments from the allies (in particular Great Britain) to act collectively.
In addition, France had to be prepared to internationalize the war and
grant the Vietnamese independence.

When Secretary Dulles traveled to Europe to secure French and British support for "United Action," he encountered immediate opposition. Although the French foreign minister Georges Bidault on two
occasions directly appealed for an American air strike to save the encircled French garrison, the two nations never came close to agreeing on
their respective roles in the proposed coalition or on their war goals.[40]
The British flatly rejected "United Action," because they feared getting
bogged down in a war that could not be won. Outside intervention, in
their view, raised the danger of escalation and might precipitate general
war. This was all the more probable, the British secretary of state for
foreign affairs Sir Anthony Eden suspected, because the Americans
would use intervention to launch what he called "Radford's war against
China."[41] In the face of strong allied opposition to "United Action," the
Eisenhower administration decided not to attempt immediate intervention. This sealed the fate of the French troops in Dien Bien Phu. On 7
May, the garrison surrendered after fifty-five days of resistance.

The fall of Dien Bien Phu did not preclude future U.S. intervention.
On 9 May, Eisenhower discussed with a few key advisers U.S. options in
the event of the loss of Indochina to the Communists. The debate indicates just how far apart Dulles and Radford were regarding a more aggressive policy. Radford argued that the only military solution to the
Communist threat in Southeast Asia was to destroy China. Admiral Radford's primary objective in Indochina was to bring about war with China;
he did not believe that the United States would "at any point in the
future be confronted with as clear-cut a basis for taking measures directly against China as was the case now in Indochina." "[T]hree or four
years from now," he warned, "the balance of military power between the
Soviets and the US will have shifted in the former's favor because they
will then have a sufficient stockpile of nuclear weapons which, although
numerically less than the US stockpile, will give them the necessary capability to initiate and carry on general war on favorable terms."[42]

Secretary Dulles replied that Chinese Communist influence in the region was more likely to spread in "the form of subversive and indirect
aggression rather than open direct aggression." Accordingly, Dulles favored a policy of collective defense, some buildup of local forces, and
considerable economic aid. Even if Communist China were to exert its

influence militarily, Dulles did not believe that the United States should base its strategy exclusively on the prospect of an unlimited war. While he certainly did not favor a static defense as in Korea, he thought it "adequate to limit our offensive to areas and facilities which are related to China's offensive."[43] He emphasized that from a political viewpoint, it would be impossible to achieve a working coalition unless an effort were made to limit potential damage. The course suggested by Admiral Radford would isolate the United States from its allies. When the secretary of state discussed these options with the president, Eisenhower reacted favorably. He was "strongly opposed to any assumption that it was necessary to have a war with China."[44]

Meanwhile, the adversaries in Indochina had met at the conference table in Geneva in order to negotiate a peaceful settlement. The talks quickly deadlocked. Secretary Dulles did not want to have anything to do with the Chinese delegation and refused to shake hands with the Chinese minister of foreign affairs Chou En-lai. Richard H. Immerman has pointed out that the administration's posture at the conference suggested "that Geneva was a defeat, not a victory, thereby reinforcing the position of those in and out of the government who had little faith in negotiations to begin with."[45] The crisis formally ended with an agreement on 21 July to partition Vietnam. The settlement was better than what the military balance on the ground had led the West to expect. To preserve an anti-Communist foothold in Southeast Asia after the partition of Indochina, the Eisenhower administration negotiated a collective security treaty. The Southeast Asia Treaty Organization (SEATO) was signed by the United States, Great Britain, France, Australia, New Zealand, Pakistan, Thailand, and the Philippines on 8 September 1954. The members of the collective security pact pledged that an attack on one of them would be considered an attack on all of them.

The Aftermath of the Indochina Crisis: Guidelines under NSC 162/2

While the Geneva talks were still deadlocked, the NSC began to discuss guidelines for the implementation of NSC 162/2 in the fiscal year 1956 budget. However, the discussion shifted from details of implementation to the more fundamental question of whether the approved national security policy was still well suited to the likely threat. Repeating one of Dulles's famous phrases, Secretary of Defense Charles E. Wilson argued that it was time for an "agonizing reappraisal."[46] Although the military posture of the United States was good in theory, its policy had not been successful in practice—as Indochina had proved. Arms alone would not solve the problem posed by the Soviet threat. The majority of the NSC agreed with Wilson's description of events in Indochina as a failure of U.S. policy.

When Robert Cutler called on the unusually quiet secretary of state for comment, Dulles agreed that U.S. foreign policy needed reappraisal. The United States, the secretary said, was confronting two basic problems: "creeping Communist penetration and wide distrust of U.S. strategy among our allies." The first problem was due to the fact that the United States had no defense against Communist expansion by means short of war. Secretary Wilson was correct in his observation that "we will never get an adequate answer in purely military terms." The second major problem, Dulles added, "derived from the growing danger of nuclear war. In the light of this, our 'tough policy' was becoming increasingly unpopular throughout the world; whereas the British 'soft policy' was gaining prestige and acceptance both in Europe and Asia." The Geneva conference was ample proof that the tide was "clearly running against us in the channel of this tough policy." The result, he warned, would be loss of allies. The United States had to recognize the fact that it could no longer "run the free world," and accordingly the NSC should review basic security policy.

The president was not very happy with the almost defeatist mood of the NSC and expressed "some bewilderment over the term 'tough policy.'" The United States had only lost an argument over taking more positive action in Indochina. Secretary Dulles, then, illustrated what was meant by "tough policy" by referring to a JCS paper that concluded "that the United States should press the Russians hard during the few years in which it would retain atomic superiority." The problem with such a policy, the secretary of state pointed out, was that none of the allies would go along with it. The president replied "that if this were indeed the situation, we should perhaps come back to the very grave question: Should the United States now get ready to fight the Soviet Union? The president pointed out that he had brought up this question more than once at prior council meetings, and that he had never done so facetiously."[47]

Although seldom expressed, consideration of preventive war was implicit in all of the major national security policy deliberations during the summer of 1954. The discussion of guidelines for the implementation of NSC 162/2 was the vehicle for consideration of preventive war. Soviet nuclear potential was now serious enough to put the survival of the United States at risk. In March 1954, the NSC approved a new statement of U.S. objectives in the event of general war. The chief objective would be "to achieve a victory which will insure the survival of the United States."[48] The perceived failure of U.S. policy in Indochina and the fact that the nuclear capability of the Soviet Union was steadily growing brought the arguments into sharper focus. The opposing sides in the emerging fundamental policy dispute were represented by the State Department and the Defense Department, and their differences reached even minor issues.

While there was broad agreement regarding the changing nature of the Soviet threat, the State Department and the Defense Department disagreed fundamentally over the meaning of the change and the appropriate response. The basic problem with respect to U.S. security was the shifting strategic nuclear balance. It was already foreseeable that the end of the decade would witness a growth in both Soviet nuclear capabilities and the power of nuclear weapons, which would make total war a threat to the survival of both western civilization and Soviet civilization. Both sides, in effect, would attain nuclear plenty.[49] The Defense Department foresaw a scenario in which the United States and its allies would either have to acquiesce to the Soviet Union or react to Soviet aggression with military force. The department emphasized that there was an ultimate deadline by "which conditions must be created by the United States and the Free World coalition such as to permit the Soviet-Communist threat to be met with resolution."[50]

The State Department drew very different conclusions: The United States had to review its disarmament position and develop its military posture with a view to maximizing the support of the free world for U.S. policies. Moreover, the United States had to respond to Communist aggression on a scale and in a manner suited to the attainment of its political objectives. Finally, State Department officials contended that the United States should begin to consider what measures would be necessary for waging general war effectively in defense of vital U.S. interests "if the strategic use of nuclear weapons should become infeasible for military or other reasons."[51]

The JCS attacked the State Department position with a lengthy memorandum on the subject of negotiations with the Soviet Union. The JCS flatly rejected any negotiations on the "subjects of disarmament, atomic energy or any other of the world issues" until the United States "by means of positive action" had brought about a basic change of Soviet policy. While the West had regarded disarmament negotiations since 1946 as a means of reducing defense burdens alleviating the threat of war, the Soviet Union had used negotiations as a proxy for armed struggle, as a way to probe enemy weaknesses, and as a propaganda device.

In the face of Soviet atomic capability, U.S. allies had become more disposed toward agreement at any cost. The JCS concluded, "unless the Soviet attitude is altered by outside influences, the aggressive and irresponsible tactics pursued with success by the Soviets thus far will be only a prelude to the proportions which such tactics will attain once the present atomic superiority of the United States has been neutralized." For the JCS, the necessary course of action was to impose a lasting settlement by taking more proactive steps while "the United States still holds atomic superiority."[52]

When the issue of disarmament came up for discussion in the NSC, the president was not initially opposed to reexamining U.S. policy, notwithstanding Soviet exploitation of the process for military ends.[53] Robert Cutler then pointed out that the real question was "whether the U.S. should be willing to agree to effective nuclear disarmament in the absence of conventional disarmament." The president replied that it was certainly in the interest of the United States to agree to nuclear disarmament alone if it was enforceable. He asserted that "he would gladly go back to the kind of warfare which was waged in 1941." Eisenhower believed that the United States should explore whether a safe and enforceable system for assuring effective nuclear disarmament could be devised. However, until the United States could be sure of achieving enforceability—an improbable goal for the foreseeable future—it had to "maintain its present position of refusing to agree to atomic disarmament except as part of a general disarmament."[54]

The main theme in the more aggressive course that the Defense Department was advancing was freedom of action. The Department of State, on the other hand, emphasized the importance of preserving U.S. alliances. Because the president was not prepared to resolve this difference, the final language of the NSC statement struck a middle position.[55] The United States should attempt to gain maximum support from the free world through pressure or compromise. The United States should maintain the cohesion of the alliances and halt further Soviet expansion, particularly in Asia, by collective action. Furthermore, the United States should not overlook the possibility that unilateral action might bring about subsequent allied support. Finally, allied reluctance should not inhibit the United States from taking action "including the use of nuclear weapons, to prevent Communist territorial gains."[56]

Looking ahead to the advent of mutual deterrence, the NSC discussion focused on the issue of greater conventional war fighting capability. On this point, there was a split within the Department of Defense, between the army and the air force. The differences were over the role of conventional forces in general war and the need for more conventional weapons to fight local wars (although, it often was discussed without clear reference to one or the other).[57] Perspectives also differed according to whether one focused on the problem of deterrence or the problem of war fighting. When the conventional forces issue was raised in the NSC, the discussion reflected this analytical fuzziness. Perhaps the unclear analytical framework enlarged the impact of fiscal factors on the debate.

The army stressed the importance of conventional forces in general war. General Ridgway doubted whether the United States would be able to rely on the strategic use of nuclear weapons as a means of waging general war once the nuclear balance had shifted.[58] Ridgway foresaw major problems in organizing society after the end of a nuclear war. The army was capitalizing on an argument that the president himself had used a year before in rejecting the recommendation of task force "C" of Project Solarium. However, the president did not agree with General Ridgway's conclusion that the improbability of meaningful victory in a nuclear war required a buildup of conventional forces. He opposed greater conventional procurement due to the financial cost and dubious military value. The need to preserve a sound economy and democratic institutions, he had noted earlier in the year, made it "simply impossible to try to play safe in all possible kinds of warfare."[59] Also, Eisenhower did not believe that American restraint in nuclear use would encourage Soviet restraint. Eisenhower remained firm in his conviction that war tended to become absolute. Victory in a third world war against the Soviet Union would be achieved only by paralyzing "the enemy at the outset of the war."[60] The revised version of NSC 5422, accordingly, stated clearly that "if general war should occur, the United States should wage it with all available weapons and should continue to make clear its determination to do so."[61]

The conventional forces issue was analyzed differently in the State Department, which was reconsidering U.S. options should the strategic use of nuclear weapons become unfeasible. Robert Bowie pointed out that the United States should seek to convince the Soviets that it was prepared to counter aggression with strategic atomic attacks. This was the best policy from a deterrence point of view.[62] However, Bowie went on, "I am not sure that when nuclear balance is reached, the U.S. will indefinitely be able to base its strategy for fighting a general war on initiating the strategic use of nuclear weapons."[63] Secretary Dulles took up Bowie's point in the next NSC meeting. He proposed that the text of the NSC policy on nuclear use be changed to say that "our planning should be based on the assumption that if general war occurs we will use all available weapons." After all, he did not think it desirable "to have the paragraph contain a mandate to boast of our nuclear capabilities."[64] Secretary Dulles's proposal was approved.[65] Dulles's remarks also addressed the question of preparing public opinion in the United States and in Western Europe for the use of nuclear weapons. This topic had been discussed extensively during the drafting of President Eisenhower's "Atoms for Peace" speech.[66] Eisenhower doubted "the wisdom of preparing world opinion for some of the things we may have to do in case of war." And Dulles was even more frank: "Talk of atomic attack tended to create 'peace-at-any-price people' and might lead to an increase of appeasement sentiment in various countries."[67]

In conjunction with the discussion of procuring more conventional forces with which to fight a general war, Cutler raised the "hoary issue" of the increased probability of limited aggression. Some members of the NSC Planning Board were concerned that "a state of mutual deterrence, resulting from atomic plenty on both sides, might enable the Soviet Union to avoid atomic war and nibble the free world to death piece by piece." The president regarded this point as "completely erroneous." "The more atomic weapons each side obtains," the president said, "the more anxious it will be to use these weapons."[68] It is not completely clear where the president's statement was leading. Did he think that local war would automatically become general war? Or did he believe that limited war could be fought with tactical nuclear weapons? But Eisenhower made it clear that he was not inclined to discuss conventional weapons procurement and the risk of limited war further at the time. He stated that "speculation as to whether the Soviets will or will not become bolder was largely an academic exercise."[69]

To deter local Communist aggression, the NSC finally decided, the United States would rely on the deterrent power of its retaliatory forces. Should deterrence fail, the United States must be prepared to defeat local aggression "without necessarily initiating general war." The United States should give logistical support and assist with U.S. mobile forces, but the primary response would have to come from indigenous and UN forces. However, the adversary had to be convinced that the United States—unilaterally, if necessary—would take "whatever additional action its security requires."[70]

The debate over acquiring increased conventional capabilities was regarded by the supporters of a more aggressive course as academic at best. In their view, it was qualitative and numerical superiority in nuclear weapons that mattered. They did not necessarily disagree with the contention that mutual vulnerability would encourage limited aggression. But this threat of cumulative free world losses only reinforced the case for preventive war, as far as they were concerned.[71]

The Issue Comes to a Head: The Exclusion of Preventive War

The Indochina crisis renewed consideration of preventive war. The issue of a more aggressive policy shaped the discussion of guidelines for the implementation of NSC 162/2 during the summer of 1954 and came to a head toward the end of the year, when the departments had to file their proposals for change in basic national security policy. The discussion of their respective views led to the exclusion of preventive war as an acceptable policy. NSC 5501 stated: "The United States and its allies must reject the concept of preventive war or acts intended to provoke war."[72] While the crisis in Indochina had precipitated consideration of a more aggressive policy, the Quemoy/Matsu crisis led to the decision to rule out preventive war.

The departmental contributions to the annual review of basic national security policy made clear that the fundamental split was between the State Department and the JCS.[73] The Department of State regarded the "Soviet shift to a 'soft' line since the death of Stalin" as a major source of encouragement, reinforced by the end of hostilities in Korea and Indochina. Together with the growing fear of nuclear war, these developments tended to foster "neutralism" within the free world. On the other hand, the Soviet intent to relax tensions appeared genuine. And the Soviets might even exercise a restraining influence on Communist China, which remained bitterly hostile to the United States.[74] The Department of State believed existing national security policy to be an appropriate statement of how the United States should respond to the prevailing strategic environment. However, the policy required clarification in three respects. First, the United States should take measures to strengthen the political and economic stability and cohesion of the free world. Second, U.S. policy should take "full account of the fact that total war would be an incalculable disaster." The primary aim had to be to deter any Communist armed aggression. Should deterrence fail, aggression should be met in a manner and on a scale that would not inevitably broaden hostilities into total nuclear war. Moreover, the United States should forgo provocative actions. Third, without relaxing its defense posture, the United States should be ready to negotiate with the Communist powers.[75]

The members of the JCS believed that the Department of State was too encouraged by Soviet "soft" tactics and had underrated the likelihood of Communist armed aggression, particularly after the advent of atomic plenty. The solution to the problem of U.S. security, according to the JCS, lay not in an attempt to bring about a reorientation of the Soviet regime through diplomatic persuasion. Such a change had to be induced by convincing the Communist leaders that their expansionist policies "will be met by countermeasures which inherently will threaten the continued existence of their regimes."[76] The JCS opened their memorandum with a warning that the world conflict was now in "a critical era" and would probably soon reach a "decisive state." A major force in the evolving situation was the growing Soviet nuclear and thermonuclear potential that tended to drive the allies toward neutralism. The state of the conflict demanded action; the time, according to the JCS, was ripe for a more militarily proactive policy.

> The non-Communist world, if it takes positive and timely *dynamic* countermeasures, presently has ample resources to meet this situation, and with high chance of maintaining world peace without sacrifice of either vital security interests or fundamental moral principles, or in the event of war being forced upon it, of winning that war beyond any reasonable doubt. On the other hand, failure on the part of the free world and particularly of the United States to take such timely and dynamic action could, within a relatively short span of years, result in the United States finding itself isolated from the rest of the free world and thus placed in such jeopardy as to reduce its freedom of action to two alternatives—that of accommodation to Soviet designs or contesting such designs under conditions not favorable to our success.

The JCS complained that implementation of NSC 162/2 had thus far emphasized "reactive-type security measures" and, consequently, had not "resulted in a reduction of the Soviet-Communist threat." In their view, NSC 162/2 contained sufficient flexibility to permit the United States to counter Soviet aggression, but the United States had not applied its general policy to particular regions. Referring to the Indochina crisis, the JCS warned "that the timely achievement of the broad objective of U.S. security policy cannot be brought about if the United States is required to defer to the counsel of the most cautious among our Allies or if it is unwilling to undertake certain risks inherent in the adoption of dynamic and positive security measures."[77]

When the different approaches were discussed in the NSC, it was again Dulles who took the lead in arguing against the course recommended by the JCS. The secretary noted that basic security policy on the whole was pretty good. He admitted that he had called for a more proactive policy during the 1952 campaign. But while he had some sympathy with the JCS's viewpoint, he rejected their proposal because it did not make strategic sense, nor would the allies approve. He assumed that the supporters of a more aggressive policy were calling, in effect, for an effort to overthrow the Communist regimes in China and the European satellites. Dulles thought that it was probable that such a course of action would involve the United States in general war with the whole Communist bloc. And even if the United States succeeded in detaching Communist China and the satellites from the Soviet Union, the heart of the problem would still remain: Soviet atomic plenty. "Certainly no actions on the periphery of the Soviet Union," the secretary emphasized, "would stop the growth of the atomic capabilities of the Soviet Union."[78] Finally, such a policy "would almost certainly cause the disintegration of the free world bloc," because U.S. allies would never go along with it.[79]

The reaction of the president was characteristic. He underlined the similarities of the positions and declared that everyone seemed to be in fundamental agreement with basic policy. Differences in approach could only be resolved case by case. Robert Cutler asked the chairman of the JCS whether he would be able to recommend specific actions to implement his proposed modification of general doctrine. But Admiral Radford could give only one example of an instance in which the United States should have acted but did not: Indochina. There, the United States had had its chance. However, Radford added, the administration had "in effect given Britain and France a veto on U.S. actions."[80]

Although Admiral Radford did not mention it, there was at the time another obvious opportunity for more aggressive policy. Since September, tensions had grown between Communist China and Taiwan over the two islands of Quemoy and Matsu. The crisis had become a test to determine how far the United States was prepared to go to assist Taiwan's defense. Was the United States ready to risk general war over these islands, which were of no intrinsic value to U.S. security? By the time the NSC began discussing the proposed changes in basic national security policy, it had become clear that the administration would not go to war over these small islands.[81] Both Secretary George M. Humphrey and Secretary Wilson referred explicitly to Quemoy and Matsu as a crisis that clearly would not justify a more aggressive policy.[82] The crisis forced policy makers to think in concrete terms about stakes in national security policy, and this concrete cost-benefit analysis accelerated the decision to rule out preventive war.

The secretary of state summarized the main points of agreement on basic national security policy, and emphasized that he felt the policy was generally adequate.[83] Dulles underlined the value of collective security: "Our alliance system has staked out the vital areas of the world which we propose to hold even at the risk of general war. These vital areas include currently all the areas of immediate strategic value to us or which possess significant war potential." He was thinking particularly of SEATO and NATO; the latter remained the "greatest single U.S. asset."[84] Of course, Dulles admitted, there was justified concern at the prospect of a stronger Soviet bloc. But he confirmed the continued relevance of the general approach of President Truman's strategy of containment. The United States should also count on forces within the Communist bloc.[85] The secretary of state had discovered some evidence of internal erosion already. He added that time might bring about the disintegration "of the monolithic power structure of the Soviet orbit" by forces of nationalism that would drive China and the satellites toward greater independence. The majority of the NSC agreed with the secretary of state. Secretary Humphrey noted that the United States must "now learn to live the way many of the other nations of the world have lived for many centuries—that is, by co-existence based on the maintenance of the balance of power."[86]

Dulles rejected a more aggressive policy toward China for both foreign policy and strategic reasons. But what about a preventive strike aimed at the heart of Soviet power? Although Eisenhower did contemplate the idea of preventive war, he never came close to considering actual implementation of such a policy. He ruled it out not least because of the unsolvable problems that victory in a general war would pose. As early as the Project Solarium discussions, the question of what to do with Russia after winning a nuclear war had occupied the president's mind. Almost a year later, the president thought that "the colossal job of occupying the territories of the defeated enemy would be far beyond the resources of the United States at the end of such a war."[87] A defeated Soviet Union would be governable only by a totalitarian regime for a long time to come. Fearing the devastation a nuclear war would cause in civil society, the president urged the war planners of the SAC to concentrate on military as opposed to urban-industrial targets. "If we batter Soviet cities to pieces by bombing," he asked the JCS in June 1954, "what solution do we have to take control of the situation and handle it so as to achieve the objectives for which we went to war?"[88]

At the end of 1954, the Eisenhower administration rejected implementation of a more aggressive foreign policy course and formally ruled out preventive war as an option for U.S. national security policy. Particularly within the military bureaucracies the idea died only slowly. Moreover, as Marc Trachtenberg has shown, it occasionally flared up even in the mind of the president as an occasional expression of frustration.[89] But it had lost its impact as a major factor in American national security policy debates.

In the early 1950s, the strategic balance had been so lopsided that a policy of greater reliance on nuclear weapons made military sense for the United States. Corollarily, shifts in the balance of power carried a great deal of political weight. The lopsided balance affected the Soviets as well.[90] The Soviet "peace offensive" or "soft policy" after Stalin's death had been in part an accommodation to the shift in the strategic balance in favor of the United States that became apparent during the Korean War. At the beginning of the Berlin crisis of 1958, Nikita S. Khrushchev referred explicitly to the early 1950s as a time when the West had had the upper hand: "It is high time to realize that the times when the imperialists could act from 'positions of strength' with impunity have gone never to return, and try as they may, the imperialists will not be able to change the balance of forces in their favor."[91]

The Strategic Nuclear Balance and the End of the Korean War

The shifting nuclear balance influenced not only the long-term formulation of national security policy, but also the decision-making process during particular crises. We shift our attention momentarily back to 1953 to examine the impact of the strategic nuclear balance at the end of the Korean War. This short digression will offer some insight into the learning experience of the new Republican administration with respect to living with nuclear weapons.

The Eisenhower Approach to the Korean War Problem

Nuclear weapons had already influenced the development of the Korean War during the Truman presidency. Notable was President Truman's careless comment to the press after Chinese troops had crossed the Yalu River and stopped the UN forces' conquest of North Korea in late November 1950. President Truman triggered a major diplomatic crisis when he said that nuclear weapons had always been under consideration and that the military commander would be in charge of their use. Another dangerous turn in the fighting in April 1951 prompted additional ambiguous nuclear threats, including the dispatch of B-29s, armed with nuclear weapons, across the Pacific. However, while the Democratic government recognized the persuasive power of nuclear weapons, it was very reluctant to actually employ them.[92]

President Eisenhower entered office with a pledge to bring the Korean War to an early end. In December 1952 he visited Korea for two weeks. The trip convinced him that the stalemate could only be broken by broadening the war. And the following statement made upon his return to the United States caused speculation that he was considering the use of nuclear weapons: "We face an enemy, whom we cannot hope to impress by words, however eloquent, but only by deeds—executed under circumstances of our own choosing."[93]

In early February, the newly constituted NSC discussed the situation in Korea for the first time. The United Nations commander, General Mark W. Clark, had asked for permission to attack into the so-called Kaesong sanctuary in the event he received information that a Communist attack was imminent.[94] Eventually, no authority was delegated. Eisenhower, however, expressed the view "that we should consider the use of tactical atomic weapons on the Kaesong area, which provided a good target for this type of weapon." Surprisingly, neither he nor the secretary of state rejected such a course due to potentially negative consequences for U.S. relations with its allies. It was General Radford's predecessor as chairman of the JCS, General Omar N. Bradley, who thought it unwise to bring up the topic of the use of nuclear weapons with the allies. The president responded that if the allies objected to the use of nuclear weapons, the U.S. "might well ask them to supply three or more divisions needed to drive the Communists back, in lieu of use of atomic weapons." And Dulles used the opportunity to press his then favorite topic of breaking down the false distinction between nuclear and conventional weapons. He discussed "the moral problem and the inhibitions on the use of the A-bomb, and Soviet success to date in setting atomic weapons apart from all other weapons as being in a special category."[95]

The incoming Eisenhower administration was convinced from the beginning that the war could not be ended by conventional attack on the ground. The emerging strategy for winning the war comprised several new elements. One idea was to expand the war beyond Korea. Secretary Dulles emphasized "the necessity of creating a threat of pressures in the center (mainland China) to the end that it would make it less likely that the Chinese Communists would send . . . additional forces into Korea."[96] A second idea was to consider the use of nuclear weapons. Third and finally, the new strategy should be aimed at establishing a Republic of Korea including the territory up to the waist, the most narrow point of the country. Holding the line of the Yalu River would mean a one-third-longer defense line without gaining much in terms of industrialized areas.[97] The death of Stalin on 5 March represented the perfect opportunity to implement such a change in policy. Nitze declared at a meeting between Department of State officials and the JCS: "In the month after the funeral I think they [the Communists] might be reluctant to take dangerous actions."[98]

The president preferred an end to the war without expanding it by bombing the enemy's airfields in Manchuria. On the other hand, he understood that such a course would mean either a big buildup of conventional forces or the employment of tactical nuclear weapons. Eisenhower indicated that the military should plan for the use of nuclear weapons in a campaign to reach the waist line, depending "on military judgment as to the advantage of their use on military targets."[99] As it turned out, the JCS were very pessimistic about the use of tactical nuclear weapons in Korea because there were no concentrations of targets worth that degree of destruction.[100] The leading voice on the issue was the army chief of staff General Joseph Lawton Collins who pointed out that the Communist forces, "scattered over one hundred fifty miles of front, and well dug in," would not present a profitable target.[101] Moreover, he stressed that the harbors of Pusan and Inchon, which were central to the supply of the UN forces, presented ideal targets for the use of atomic weapons by the Communists. Air force chief of staff General Hoyt S. Vandenberg, agreed. He noted that from a military point of view the right way to employ nuclear weapons was to use them in Manchuria against the enemy's air bases.

While military officials emphasized the military disadvantages of nuclear use, Nitze, speaking for the State Department, in principle saw no unshakable policy barrier to use of atomic weapons. The real question, however, was "whether the advantages would outweigh the disadvantages." From a foreign policy point of view, according to Nitze, at least three disadvantages should be kept in mind: First, the United States would have to be concerned about the possibility that its remaining stockpile of nuclear weapons would appear less menacing if the use of nuclear weapons somehow did not produce the desired effect. Second, the political difficulties with the allies had to be taken into account. Tensions within the western alliances would grow if nuclear weapons were not effective at ending the war. Third, what if the Soviet Union retaliated in kind?[102]

The Planning Board of the NSC integrated the analyses of the JCS and the State Department. The resulting document, NSC 147, outlined a set of six military courses of action. The first three restricted military operations to Korea. The second three permitted the use of force against Manchuria and Communist China. NSC 147 summarized the military and political advantages and disadvantages of the use of nuclear weapons in a way that must have increased its reader's interest in a solution of the crisis without the risk associated with the employment of nuclear weapons.[103]

As always, President Eisenhower was concerned about fiscal cost. He raised the topic during the meeting between the NSC and the civilian consultants on 27 March.[104] If the West would increase its forces in Korea, the president argued, the Communists would similarly increase their deployment of soldiers on the North Korean side. Eisenhower concluded that the United States "would be forced ultimately into a situation very close to general mobilization in order to get such a victory in Korea." It was very much the cost of the conventional option that was driving Eisenhower to consider the use of tactical nuclear weapons in the Korean War. He admitted the absence of good targets, but nevertheless felt "it would be worth the cost if, through use of atomic weapons we could (1) achieve a substantial victory over the Communist forces and (2) get to a line at the waist of Korea." The president seemed to be prepared to pay the political price of differences with the allies as long as quick victory would heal the wounds. This is not to say that Eisenhower was unaware of allied reluctance to use nuclear weapons. Nevertheless—and here he agreed with the secretary of state—"the tabu which surrounds the use of atomic weapons would have to be destroyed."[105]

During the first months in office, both the president and the secretary of state were considering the use of nuclear weapons to end the Korean War, for economic and political-strategic reasons, respectively. And both underwent a painful, but important learning experience regarding the military and political limitations of nuclear weapons. It is especially noteworthy that this learning process was advanced by the outgoing members of the JCS.

Nuclear Threats and the Korean Armistice

While President Eisenhower and Secretary Dulles were learning about the military and political complexities inherent in considering the use of nuclear weapons, a statement made by Chinese premier Chou En-lai changed perceptions of the strategic landscape again. On 30 March, Chou En-lai proposed that negotiations should begin immediately on the exchange of sick and wounded military personnel, and he seemed to accept the principle of voluntary repatriation of prisoners of war.[106] The West interpreted these remarks as major concessions, because the question of voluntary repatriation had been the key obstacle during the armistice negotiations. The United Nations commander, General Clark, for example, sensed that the Communists probably wanted an armistice.[107] Officials in the Eisenhower administration were heartened by the correlation between the timing of Chou En-lai's speech and the difficulties within the Soviet Union after the death of Stalin. It looked like the Communists had settled on a peace offensive.[108] From an American perspective, the Communist interest in accommodation was further confirmed when the Communists issued an eight-point proposal on 7 May.[109] Officials in the Eisenhower administration concluded that the new Communist proposal "appears to represent a significant shift in their position and appears to offer a basis for negotiation of an acceptable agreement."[110]

When the NSC came together to discuss NSC 147, Cutler emphasized that it would be premature to make a choice among the six proposed options "in view of the new possibility that the Communists were really prepared to enter into an armistice in Korea." Secretary Dulles was thinking about increasing the stakes "in view of our much greater power and the Soviet Union's much greater weakness currently." Instead of an armistice at the 38th parallel, he thought that it now was possible to compel the Communists to accept a settlement along the line of the waist by threatening to call off the armistice negotiations.[111] In a later meeting of the NSC, Secretary Humphrey proposed building up the forces in Korea as rapidly as possible. The point was to maintain pressure on the Communists until negotiations were brought to a successful end. The president agreed with Secretary Humphrey, but added that it might be enough to provide the *appearance* of an increase of the forces in Korea. The United States should send out "only skeletonized units or headquarters units in place of the real thing." Such a strategy could be accompanied by deliberate leaks regarding troop movements to make sure that the other side got the message.[112]

The JCS were very skeptical about Eisenhower's proposal of a fake buildup aimed at reaching a final settlement. It was their view that without a prior decision to step up the pace of U.S. operations in the event of a collapse of the armistice negotiations, no additional units should be sent to Korea. The JCS initiated a reconsideration of the six alternative

courses of action that had been outlined in NSC 147. Chairman of the
JCS Bradley emphasized that the chiefs had deliberately avoided choosing among the alternatives because they did not want to interfere with
the political decisions of the government. In the course of the debate it
became clear that President Eisenhower was still interested in finding
targets for the use of tactical nuclear weapons. The JCS, on the other
hand, maintained their doubts about the usefulness of any targets within
Korea for this category of weapons. Finally, the president called on the
JCS to present, at the next NSC meeting, the military implications of the
six possible courses of action.[113]

When the JCS reported back to the NSC one week later, disagreement
between the president and his military advisers regarding the use of tactical nuclear weapons in Korea persisted. The JCS expressed "doubt as
to whether use of such weapons could really be justified in terms of the
large-scale destruction of enemy personnel and materiel." The president, nevertheless, insisted that "it might be cheaper, dollarwise, to use
atomic weapons in Korea than to continue to use conventional weapons
against the dugouts which honeycombed the hills along which the
enemy forces were presently deployed."[114] It was the president's primary
fear that the three courses restricting military operations to Korea would
only prolong the stalemate and ultimately cost the United States more
money.

The State Department stressed the dangers of the three alternatives
for extending the scope of operations to Manchuria and China. Under
each option there was a greater likelihood of Soviet intervention leading
to general war. In addition, U.S. allies might refuse to go along with
such actions and NATO might "fall to pieces temporarily." The alliance
system could be rebuilt if global war could be avoided and a bold course
of action would culminate in quick success. The president perceived at
the heart of the foreign policy problem the simple truth "that many
people in the European countries believe that global war is much worse
to contemplate than surrender to Communist imperialism."[115] At the
end of the meeting, Vice President Richard M. Nixon stated that a decision with respect to Korea "should be taken only in the context of the
longer-term problem which would confront us when the Soviet Union
had amassed a sufficient stockpile of atomic weapons to deal us a critical
blow and to rob us of the initiative in the area of foreign policy." The
president "agreed with the views of the Vice President, and explained
that Project Solarium was being initiated with this precise problem in
mind."[116]

Meanwhile, the NSC had pushed the reluctant JCS to select one of the proposed options. Picking up on the theme that Nixon had articulated, the JCS stated at the very beginning of their report that "the course of military action recommended will depend on the broader political objectives involving Korea." The JCS then proceeded to enumerate the risks involved in a decision to enlarge the Korean War. They warned of the danger of provoking a long-term war with China, of possible regional involvement of the Soviet Union, and of risking the outbreak of a global war. They noted further the risks of losing allies, suffering many casualties during offensive operations, and expanding the military budget. Only after setting out these qualifications, the JCS concluded that a combination of the three courses permitting the use of force in Manchuria and China "would be the most effective and the most economical in the long run for the United States to pursue in Korea." They emphasized that "the necessary air, naval, and ground operations, including extensive strategic and tactical use of atomic bombs, be undertaken so as to obtain maximum surprise and maximum impact on the enemy, both militarily and psychologically."[117]

When the JCS presented these findings to the NSC on 20 May, the president summarized their views thus: "If we went over to more positive action against the enemy in Korea, it would be necessary to expand the war outside of Korea and . . . it would be necessary to use the atomic bomb." The president believed that the United States "ought at once to begin to infiltrate these ideas into the minds of our allies" in a quiet and informal way. He added that he did not fear the Chinese as long as the blow fell swiftly. But his one great anxiety with respect to the course proposed by the JCS was the possibility of Soviet intervention, particularly an air attack on "the almost defenseless population centers of Japan." However, he decided that the record should show "that if circumstances arose which would force the United States to an expanded effort in Korea, the plan selected by the Joint Chiefs of Staff was most likely to achieve the objective we sought."[118]

Judging by the ongoing process of contingency planning, the threat of the use of nuclear weapons was in the air. The Eisenhower administration undertook to communicate the threat as part of a broader final attempt to search for an acceptable settlement. General Clark recommended stepping up conventional bombing of such critical targets as the North Korean capital of Pyongyang and the numerous irrigation dams in order to overcome the present hiatus in negotiations.[119] This proposal was carried out, and in May and June of 1953 the destruction caused by the air raids placed an increasing burden on North Korea.[120] On 25 May, the final settlement offer was made to the Communists.

After explaining that this position was final, a one-week recess in the talks was taken to allow the Chinese and North Koreans to consider a response.[121] Finally, Ambassador Charles E. Bohlen simultaneously made a confidential approach to the Soviet foreign minister Vyacheslav Mikhailovich Molotov in order to underline the seriousness of this last proposal.[122] The Americans hoped that the Soviets would have a restraining influence on China.

The threat of expanding the war outside Korea, including the threat of using nuclear weapons, was communicated in the form of a complex set of diplomatic and military actions. What, at the level of contingency planning, seemed to be a clear decision to use nuclear weapons, reached the other side in a much more ambiguous form. On 21 May, John Foster Dulles met Indian prime minister Jawaharlal Nehru during a trip to the Indian subcontinent. Assuming that his message would be relayed to Beijing, he told Nehru that "if the armistice negotiations collapsed, the United States would probably make a stronger rather than a lesser military exertion, and that this might well extend the area of conflict."[123] This is as close as the Eisenhower administration came to a direct threat. Moreover, it is not even certain that the message reached the Chinese.[124] Charles Bohlen in his talk with Molotov on 28 May was even more careful in his wording. Only after he had gone point by point through the concessions that the West would be making under these "extremely liberal proposals" did he tell the Soviet foreign minister that "a failure of the present armistice talks would lead to the creation of a situation which the US Government was most sincerely and earnestly attempting to avoid."[125]

Despite their ambiguity, the threats seem to have had an effect. The Communist delegation submitted a counterproposal that accepted most of the provisions of the western settlement offer.[126] The Communist reply was noted as very favorable in the West. Dulles informed the president that the counterproposal for the release of nonrepatriates to civilian status "far exceeds our most optimistic expectation." And General Clark expected early consummation of an agreement.[127] Nevertheless, over six weeks passed before the armistice was signed on 27 July. This postponement was mostly due to the fact that South Korean president Syngman Rhee was absolutely opposed to the UN proposal. Although the United States tried to appease the Korean president by offering a mutual defense treaty, Rhee, in the words of President Eisenhower, exploded a bombshell.[128] On 18 June, thanks to secretly and carefully planned actions by the Rhee government, approximately twenty-five thousand nonrepatriate North Korean prisoners of war escaped from

United Nations command camps.[129] For President Eisenhower the whole affair was extremely embarrassing. Secretary Dulles, however, remained optimistic due to problems elsewhere in the Soviet bloc. Dulles believed that the Soviets "were so anxious for an armistice that they would over-look what had happened."[130] The president admitted "that we can *do* all sorts of things to suggest to Rhee that we might very well be prepared to leave Korea, but the truth of the matter was, of course, that we couldn't actually leave."[131]

Although Washington never came close to actually using nuclear weapons in the Korean War, nuclear threats were part of the Eisenhower administration's not-very-coherent strategy for ending the conflict.[132] The important question for the present discussion is what impact nuclear threats had on the policy process leading up to the signing of the armistice on 27 July. To be sure, nuclear threats were not as central to ending the Korean War as conventional wisdom—deliberately cultivated by the president and Secretary Dulles—for a long time thought them to be.[133] After all, the specific messages conveyed from 21 May to 28 May came *after* the major Communist concessions articulated in Chou En-lai's speech of 30 March. Furthermore, in the period of transition and uncertainty after Stalin's death, peaceful coexistence was high on the agenda of Stalin's successors. Nuclear threats were never made in a clear and unambiguous manner. On the one hand, they were accompanied by increased conventional bombing and growing diplomatic pressures. On the other hand, the West was also making concessions to the Communists. Finally, the threats might not have gotten through to the Chinese and North Koreans, and even if they did, the Chinese might have discounted them for a variety of reasons related to Chinese military and strategic thinking.[134]

This is not to say that nuclear threats played no role whatsoever. The Communists certainly believed that a rejection of the UN proposal of 25 May would noticeably enhance the risk of an enlarged war that might include the use of nuclear weapons. However, the fact that they made their most important concessions before specific threats were made suggests that nuclear weapons influenced political behavior more by the overall strategic balance than by any particular threat to use them. The Communists realized the change of the tenor of U.S. policy under the Eisenhower administration. They must have paid attention to Eisenhower's statement at the end of his trip to Korea in December 1952, that only enlargement of the war would end it. And it is probable that the image of toughness portrayed by the American secretary of state had an impact. Clearly, the threat of an expanded war, including the possible employment of nuclear weapons, was in the air *before* the first major Communist concessions were made.

In short, what counted most was not a single isolated threat, but the general image of strength that was matched with clear willingness to apply superior power. In this context, the strategic nuclear balance came to bear as an underlying factor in the political process leading up to the end of the Korean War. On the U.S. side, this happened in the form of a general sense that the favorable nuclear balance *ought* to be useful in one way or another. On the Communist side, the threat had to be taken into account, because neither the absolute level of available destructive power nor the relative balance allowed the Communists to take the threat lightly.

The New Look and the Korean War

Whereas the Korean War problem in the first couple of months enhanced the sensitivity of the new administration to the political and military limitations of nuclear weapons, the signing of the armistice seemed to prove that nuclear threats on a fundamental level nevertheless worked. If judged by the result, the ending of the Korean War became the first demonstration of the New Look before the new national security strategy was actually approved. Hence, U.S. policy regarding Korea and the formulation of the New Look were mutually reinforcing.

The connection between the two aspects of policy making became obvious when Dulles grappled with the negative consequences of the new military policy, as proposed by the JCS, on U.S. allies. His solution was proposing mutual withdrawal of U.S. and Soviet military forces from Europe. He thought the moment particularly well suited for negotiations because the United States would be operating from a position of strength. And this situation was due in part to the fact that the Korean armistice had been achieved "in an atmosphere of our willingness to enlarge the war."[135] Dulles understood that perceptions shape reality. Therefore, he attempted to influence perceptions. On 11 November, he surprised even the president with his proposal that the United States start withdrawing ground troops from Korea. Not that Eisenhower did not like the message; he was eager for an opportunity to reduce the size of the army. More puzzling was Dulles's line of argument. The troops should be withdrawn "for the reason that we should show confidence in our air and naval strength."[136] The president agreed: It was of utmost importance that the Communists understand clearly "that any attack on the UN forces would mean general war."[137]

The perceptions of allies were as important as the perceptions of adversaries.[138] The president raised the topic when the NSC was discussing U.S. options in Korea in the absence of an acceptable political settlement.[139] Stating that it would be U.S. policy to react with nuclear weapons if the Communists resumed the fighting, the president asked if the "allies fully understood our position." Secretary Dulles replied that "he was quite certain our major allies did understand our view, even though there had not been formal discussions with them."[140] The opportunity for formal discussions arrived with the Bermuda conference from 4 December to 8 December 1953. The event brought together the heads of government and the foreign ministers of the United States, France, and the United Kingdom. The day after he had urged that NATO should integrate nuclear weapons into its strategic concept, John Foster Dulles explained the conclusion of the Korean War in a memorable passage: "The principal reason we were able to obtain the armistice was because we were prepared for a much more intensive scale of warfare. It should not be improper to say at such a restricted gathering that we had already sent the means to the theater for delivering atomic weapons. This became known to the Chinese Communists through their good intelligence sources and in fact we were not unwilling that they should find out."[141]

The message was clear: Nuclear threats had brought the Korean conflict to an end. The same threat, Secretary Dulles emphasized, "could be the greatest preventive to a resumption of hostilities."[142] But the message did not have the desired effect: British prime minister Winston S. Churchill stubbornly resisted "any idea of the automatic use of atomic weapons, even in the case of a Communist renewal of hostilities in Korea." The main reason for the British opposition was, as Secretary Dulles later pointed out to the NSC, "the very great anxiety of the British people lest, on account of their exposed position, they would suffer if the Soviets retaliated against our use of atomic weapons by attacking the population centers of the British Isles."[143] In an attempt to reassure the allies, the president noted that the United States would use nuclear weapons "only against a clear-cut breach of the armistice." The American government had "never proposed attacking cities such as Chungking, Peking, or Shanghai, but merely military installations such as air fields being used to support directly the conflict in Korea."[144]

As the New Look took final shape in October and November of 1953, the notion that nuclear threats brought an end to the Korean War helped to reassure the critics. The belief that nuclear threats had proved decisive was, as Rosemary J. Foot notes, "presumably of some comfort to

Eisenhower and Dulles" in making final decisions regarding the year-
long overhaul of national security policy.[145] In this sense, the last stages
of the Korean War became the foundation of the New Look. John Foster
Dulles perpetuated the image of a successful attempt at nuclear coercion with his famous brinkmanship interview in 1956.[146]

The Korean War example influenced the future U.S. policy with respect to Korea as well as the formulation of the New Look. The NSC
discussion of U.S. options in Korea in the absence of an acceptable political settlement triggered a reevaluation by the JCS. The new JCS, chaired
by Admiral Radford, translated its new strategic concept (as presented
in the report to the NSC on 27 August[147]) into military contingency planning in case of a resumption of hostilities in Korea. There could hardly
be a bigger difference in approach between the outgoing JCS, acting
very cautiously and emphasizing the ultimate responsibility of the political leadership, and the new JCS, recommending the destruction of the
Communist strength in the Far East once and for all if they resumed the
fighting. The new JCS pointed out that the old course had required a
buildup of nine to twelve months. This was compatible with the goal of
deterrence, which had been the goal of the former strategy. The course
of action previously recommended "was designed in part, to increase
the possibility of enemy acceptance of an armistice on U.S.-U.N. terms."
The new situation now required the United States to adopt much more
aggressive military objectives, including the destruction of "effective
Communist military power applied to the Korean effort" and rendering
"the enemy incapable of further aggression in Korea and the Far
East."[148] Upon the outbreak of hostilities, these military objectives were
to be achieved by launching "immediately a large-scale air offensive employing atomic weapons to destroy Chinese Communist forces and selected targets in China, Manchuria, and Korea." Finally, the JCS
thought it important to the success of such a course that they obtain in
peacetime the necessary presidential authority "to enable the immediate employment of nuclear weapons in sufficient quantity to insure success of the proposed course of action."[149]

The Department of State was very uneasy with the wording of the
JCS memorandum. Robert Bowie warned Secretary Dulles that it was
necessary to clarify the geographical location and general nature of the
targets that the JCS intended to attack. Did "selected targets" include
Chinese cities? Moreover, "the enemy" was defined only as Communists,
and to render all Communists incapable of further aggression in Korea
and the Far East would require the destruction of all Chinese *and* Soviet
military capabilities in the Far East.[150]

Presenting the policy to the NSC, Admiral Radford summarized that, while ground forces "would largely be limited to the actual theatre of war in Korea," the initial massive atomic air strike would make the Chinese Communists "incapable of aggression there or elsewhere in the Far East for a very considerable time." He saw no other way of responding to a Communist attack. However, such a policy would be justified, because the Communists "were unlikely to resume hostilities in Korea unless they were of the opinion that global war was a very strong possibility." The president replied that "this fitted exactly into his thinking, and he could see no other way of treating a renewed Communist attack." Resumption of hostilities would mean all-out war against China and the president expressed with "great emphasis the opinion that if the Chinese Communists attacked us again we should certainly respond by hitting them hard and wherever it would hurt most, including Peiping itself."[151]

As would happen so many times later in 1954, Dulles had to stand up against Admiral Radford's position. It was plain to the secretary of state that "Admiral Radford's course of action contemplated general war with China and probably also with the Soviet Union because of the Sino-Soviet alliance." In such a war, there would be virtually no UN participants other than the United States, and the "West European countries would immediately run to cover by seeking a neutrality pact with the USSR." Although any resumption by the Communists of hostilities in Korea might eventually end in general war, such a result should not be treated as inevitable. Secretary Dulles envisaged a strategy for victory *in* Korea as opposed to the prosecution of a war to achieve a total victory over China. This sharp reply by Dulles led Eisenhower to "admit the necessity of distinguishing between airfields adjacent to the Yalu River as opposed to targets in the South of China."[152]

At the Bermuda conference, British opposition to the use of nuclear weapons further swayed the president toward the position advocated by Dulles. On 8 January, Admiral Radford sought advance authorization for the U.S. commander to use atomic weapons to protect the security of his force in case of renewed hostilities. Again Secretary Dulles led the opposition, but this time he was joined by the president. Blaming the allies, "who had not as yet fully grasped the import of atomic warfare," the president stated that the "decision on use of this weapon would have to be referred to Washington."[153]

This tough position regarding contingency planning for resumption of hostilities in Korea appears to be in stark contrast to the president's careful consideration of possible negative consequences on allies of questions such as redeployment of overseas troops.[154] Part of the explanation for this contrast may be that the president's military background allowed him to distinguish clearly between contingency planning and what would actually happen during a crisis. But it is hard to avoid the conclusion that on a fundamental level Eisenhower was more impressed by the favorable strategic balance than Secretary Dulles, who sensed its limitation in foreign policy terms. With respect to the Korean War, their differences materialized in two important ways. First, there was no doubt in the president's mind that the United States, at the time, could win a general war against China. Second, he did not believe that the risk of Soviet involvement was very high—and this assumption was at the heart of the difference in opinion between the president and Secretary Dulles. The president realized that he seemed to be in disagreement with many members of the NSC on the following point. He did not believe "that the USSR was going to let itself get involved in full-scale warfare in the Far East. The risks were just too great and the distances for supply too extended."[155]

In the early 1950s, the strategic balance was characterized by limited destructive power (in contrast with what was to come) and a lopsidedness that had a direct impact on international politics. The strategic balance affected Eisenhower's approach to termination of the stalemated Korean War. Although nuclear threats were made in an ambiguous manner and only after the Communists had made major concessions, they nevertheless had considerable impact on the development of the Korean armistice. It was not a single, isolated threat that counted most, but rather the general impression that the United States militarily was strong, and the political leaders were clearly willing to apply their superior power. U.S. nuclear superiority influenced Eisenhower's decision to adopt a firm posture in Korea and the Communist decision to offer major concessions. During the final stages of its formulation, the Korean episode served to reassure the New Look's critics. However, Eisenhower never came close to actually using nuclear weapons. Both the president and Secretary Dulles underwent a learning process with respect to the political and military limitations of nuclear weapons.

Anxiety that the strategic balance would shift to the disadvantage of the United States, due to growing Soviet nuclear power, led the U.S. leadership to consider preventive war. The debate over a shift toward a more aggressive foreign policy posture reached its peak in the wake of the Indochina crisis. However, the Eisenhower administration never came close to implementing such a course. At the end of 1954, preventive war was formally rejected, due to perceived political and strategic disadvantages.

In the early 1950s, the one-sided strategic nuclear balance clearly affected international politics in manifold ways, some of them with quite destabilizing implications for the security of the free world. One might ask (with good reason) what was so destabilizing about American nuclear superiority when preventive war never came even close to implementation and when a very lesson of the Korean War was the military and political limitations of nuclear weapons. The destabilizing effects of the existence of a militarily useful nuclear advantage materialized indirectly through alliance politics. America's allies were scared by what they perceived to be the danger of a more aggressive U.S. foreign policy. The potential for disunity in the West reached such proportions as to lead Dulles to conclude that NATO was losing its grip. Tensions within western alliances became themselves a threat to American security. It was a dilemma for U.S. policy makers to choose between adopting a more positive policy, hoping that the allies would follow for lack of alternatives and once success was secured, or adopting a less independent and more cautious approach to foreign policy.

The reason why the allies opposed a more aggressive stand against perceived Communist expansionism had a lot to do with the thermonuclear revolution (discussed in the next chapter). From a European perspective, the window of opportunity for solving the problem of the Communist threat with a policy involving higher risks of war with the Soviet Union had already closed. A Soviet Union possessing thermonuclear weapons, however limited their number, exposed their countries to unacceptable risks.

3

The Impact of the Thermonuclear Revolution on Policy

People like Bernard Brodie had doubted that a nuclear war could be won (in any meaningful sense) since Hiroshima and Nagasaki. With the advent of the hydrogen bomb, however, these apprehensions spread to the mainstream of national security policy. The hydrogen bomb was revolutionary because its explosive power was a thousand times greater than either of the bombs dropped on Japan in 1945. This was the "absolute weapon" that Bernard Brodie had described in 1946.[1] The technological breakthrough paved the way for a growing acceptance of the inevitability of a nuclear stalemate. Once both superpowers had developed survivable second-strike forces, nuclear war would become an absurdity. The fundamental goal of strategy would shift from securing unconditional victory to limiting the scope and scale of war.

Because of their exposed position, U.S. allies in Europe and the Far East were particularly worried about the prospect of thermonuclear war. British Prime Minister Winston Churchill summarized his nation's fear in a talk with Henry Cabot Lodge, Jr., U.S. representative at the UN, in June 1954. Churchill noted that "when it came to trying to foresee the course of a future war, he thought that he could pretty well estimate how a future war could go, if it were fought with atomic bombs, but . . . when you come to figure it with hydrogen bombs it becomes absolutely impossible. Nobody can figure it. A nation that had one-tenth as many hydrogen bombs as another, can nevertheless win the war by being the first to attack and thereby completely destroying the 10 to 1 advantage which the other nation has got."[2] Statements of this sort led John Foster Dulles to fear that NATO was about to disintegrate. The allies possessed no defense against a hydrogen bomb attack. Increasingly, they feared that the United States might stay out of Europe, because the American homeland itself was becoming vulnerable to Soviet thermonuclear attack. The credibility of the U.S. commitment to the defense of its allies was shaken by the first Soviet test of a thermonuclear device.

In America the thermonuclear revolution fostered fears of neutralization of U.S. allies. We have seen earlier that the Eisenhower administration was extremely sensitive to these developments. President Eisenhower realized that the security of the United States depended on U.S. allies in two ways: First, the United States required overseas bases for the effective use of its strategic bomber forces. Second, the United States needed the military forces and economic resources of its allies in order to retain a capability to win a general war without sacrificing a healthy economy and democratic institutions. Concern about western unity affected Eisenhower's reappraisal of national security policy throughout 1953. Concern about allied reaction was the main reason why the president and Secretary Dulles had postponed major redeployments of U.S. ground forces in the fall of 1953. Fear about allied neutralization also had led Dulles to consider a spectacular effort to lessen world tension through mutual withdrawal of U.S. and Soviet troops from Europe in September 1953.[3]

The realization that the thermonuclear revolution had changed the nature of conflict prompted claims that only disarmament could secure world peace in the long term. This insight was articulated first by the physicists who had participated in building the bomb. They realized that the amount of destructive power available per pound of fissionable material was multiplying at an extraordinary rate toward the point where the use of this power would mean the end of civilization. This awareness, weighing heavily in its secrecy, led to interest in the control of nuclear armaments.

When the first details about the destructive power of the new weapon became public knowledge, the Europeans began to wonder where this development would lead. Once the Soviets possessed these weapons, European cities would be threatened with instant destruction. In the United States, the existence of a thermonuclear monopoly, and, once it was broken, the knowledge of overwhelming superiority, delayed such fears. For the Europeans, the security of invulnerability had long ago faded. But for the American continent, geography provided additional protection, and therefore an increased sense of security, despite impending vulnerability. Nevertheless, concern about allied fears increased the interest of the Eisenhower administration in the field of disarmament. President Eisenhower's famous "Atoms for Peace" speech evolved as a reaction to concern that the western coalition would lose its cohesion. A careful analysis of the background of the presidential address shows that it included a heavy propaganda element. However, during 1954, more and more officials in the American government, particularly in the State Department, became genuinely interested in nuclear arms limitation.

Nuclear Arms Limitation: The Origins of Project Candor

At an NSC meeting on 18 February 1953, a panel of consultants that had finished its report "Armaments and American Policy" in the middle of January proposed a policy of greater public openness about the politics of thermonuclear weapons. The panel had been set up by former secretary of state Dean G. Acheson in April 1952. It consisted of Robert J. Oppenheimer, Vannevar Bush, John S. Dickey, Allen W. Dulles, and Joseph E. Johnson. Its task was to review the UN plan for atomic energy, originally proposed by Bernard M. Baruch (U.S. representative at the United Nations) at the first meeting of the UN Atomic Energy Commission on 14 June 1946. Baruch's proposal had been refined over time and introduced in the form of a new offer in the newly established Disarmament Commission of the UN during 1951.[4]

During the period in which the panel was preparing its report, the United States had conducted two series of nuclear weapons tests. The second series culminated in the first H-bomb detonation at the Eniwetok Atoll in late fall of 1952.[5] The panel, therefore, was one of the first (and one of the most qualified) groups to grapple with the consequences of the thermonuclear revolution. The resulting study remains an impressive analysis of the changing character of conflict in the thermonuclear era, particularly because the authors related their knowledge about the technological power of the bomb to the sphere of politics.

The report began with a short summary of the unsuccessful history of arms regulation negotiations at the UN. The panel noted that these experiences indicated plainly that "it is hard to make progress in the limitation of armaments when there is a high level of tension in the international political situation." Unfortunately, recent developments in the field of nuclear technology had made it impossible to base future arms policy on the simple object of getting ahead of the Soviet Union. With the development and production of hydrogen weapons, a time of virtual nuclear plenty had to be foreseen in which both sides would have a stockpile of tens of thousands of nuclear weapons. The Soviet Union, although slower, would eventually attain the same level of destructive power as the United States. In such a situation, both sides would probably have placed themselves in a position in which their "basic destructive power cannot be destroyed by any single surprise attack by any enemy." The mechanics of a mass surprise attack were "singularly complex." Large stockpiles could be "widely dispersed." This analysis brought the panel to the heart of its concern:

> If the atomic arms race continues, therefore, we seem likely to have within a relatively few years a situation in which the two great powers will each have a clear-cut capacity to do very great damage to the other, while each will be unable to exert that capacity except at the gravest risk of receiving similar terrible blows in return. And this situation is likely to be largely unaffected by the fact that one side may always have many more weapons than the other. There is likely to be a point in our time when the Soviet Union will have "enough" bombs—no matter how many more we ourselves may have.

How would nations behave in such a situation? The panel thought it conceivable "that a world of this kind may enjoy a strange stability arising from general understanding that it would be suicidal to 'throw the switch.'" On the other hand, such a world might not be very calm, particularly since its coming would be gradual. There was always the "possibility that one nation or another may be tempted to launch a preventive war 'before it is too late,' only to find out that the time for such a blow has already passed." The panel regarded these developments with even greater concern, because American policy depended heavily on nuclear weapons. Since the initial decision to develop these weapons "the United States has decided to use it, to keep its control wholly unshared, to make as many as possible, to plan for their use, and to base that plan centrally on the concept of an immediate and devastating strategic blow at the center of hostile power."[6]

McGeorge Bundy, the panel's much-praised secretary, was to observe later that this analysis was "both startling and chilling."[7] The early 1950s were marked by overwhelming U.S. nuclear superiority and the Soviet Union had not yet developed a thermonuclear weapon.

The panel's conclusion was that the United States faced the twin task of dealing with the Soviet Union *and* the arms race. It was important that future proposals for arms limitation be judged against the existing dangerous situation and not against "some arbitrary vision of a world of total peace and harmony." The arms race was not black or white—

"either totally unlimited or firmly regulated by international treaties." It was crucial that the American government increase its freedom of action in the field of arms regulation.

From these general conclusions, the panel formulated five specific recommendations: First, it called for an act of candor to the American public. The government should tell the story of the atomic danger and direct public attention "specifically and repeatedly to the fact that the atomic bomb works both ways." The panel hoped that public understanding of the nuclear danger would lead to more serious attempts to deal with it.[8] Second, the report emphasized the danger of a failure to reach an understanding on atomic policy with the allies. The nation's major allies should be given a sense of shared responsibility in order to fight "a widespread feeling that the United States is clutching the atom to its bosom and may at any moment get angry and hurl it in the general direction of the Kremlin." Third, although it would hardly be possible to achieve 100 percent safety, the United States had every reason "to proceed with greatly intensified efforts of continental defense." Fourth, the United States should disengage from disarmament discussions in the UN, because they resembled an undertaking in psychological warfare. Fifth and finally, "a real effort should be made to find ways of communicating with the rulers of the Soviet Union on the range of questions posed by the arms race."[9]

When the report was discussed in the NSC, the president expressed his high opinion of the panel's analysis but stated that the paper was weak on possible means of carrying out its recommendations. He was particularly skeptical about the wisdom of disengaging from disarmament talks at the UN. Moreover, he was opposed to the idea of informing the American people "about the size of our stockpile of weapons, and Secretary Wilson joined him by stating that it seemed foolish to scare our people to death if we don't need to and can't really do anything about the problem."[10] Later in the same meeting, Eisenhower inquired "whether, when we finally achieved a sufficient stockpile of weapons, it would be possible to turn the atomic energy program toward peaceful uses."[11]

At the end of 1952, the Truman administration had instructed the U.S. representative at the UN Disarmament Commission "to begin tapering off negotiations and to avoid any further entanglement in fresh proposals."[12] After the change in leadership, in February 1953, Secretary Dulles stated that "the U.S. position was essentially a delaying tactic" at the forthcoming UN General Assembly. Vice President Nixon then had inquired "whether it might not be possible to make some kind of sensational offer on the disarmament side, which the Soviets would of course not accept, and which would therefore put them on the spot."[13] It was precisely this sort of proposal that led the panel to recommend that arms negotiations not be used as a tool for propaganda advantages in the UN. However, the whole issue was not perceived as pressing and, therefore, was referred to the NSC staff and Vannevar Bush for further study.

Interest in the panel's recommendation grew following the death of Stalin on 5 March 1953. Ever since George F. Kennan had outlined the strategy of containment in his famous "long telegram" in 1946, America's foremost experts on the Soviet Union had emphasized the great uncertainty involved in the transfer of power from one Soviet leader to another.[14] The Oppenheimer-Bush panel suggested that Stalin's death might afford an opportunity for more communication with the Soviet Union.[15] However, the president found his administration completely unprepared for the event: "Ever since 1946, I know that all the so-called experts have been yapping about what would happen when Stalin dies and what we, as a nation, should do about it. Well, he's dead. And you can turn the files of our government inside out—in vain—looking for any plans laid. We have no plan. We are not even sure what difference his death makes."[16] An ad hoc committee was set up in order to focus on the panel's recommendation of greater candor with the American public. Interest in Project Candor increased due to the gap in planning for the aftermath of Stalin's death.

The acceleration of events after Stalin's death, including the shift to a "peace offensive" by the new Soviet leadership, called for quick action. When the first news of Stalin's illness reached Washington, and the president realized that there was no planned response for a change in the Soviet leadership, Eisenhower considered a proposal made by C. D. Jackson, the special assistant to the president for Cold War operations. Jackson recommended that the United States exploit the situation after Stalin's death for political purposes. He suggested that the president make a public statement—taking advantage of this "first really big propaganda opportunity"—in order to prove the nation's devotion to peace.[17] Secretary Dulles, on the other hand, initially was very skeptical about the desirability of a presidential statement. The secretary of state opposed an early American response because he believed that Stalin's death would lead to a closing of ranks among the new Soviet leaders in the short run.[18] Only in the longer run would the forces of nationalism lead to serious strains within the monolithic structure of the Soviet bloc in the absence of the unifying force of the "demi-god" Stalin.

When Jackson's plan for political exploitation of Stalin's death was discussed in the NSC, Dulles expressed his desire to proceed carefully. He warned his colleagues that the United States had its own coalition to manage. The administration should be careful that an attempt to destroy the unity of the Soviet orbit "not jeopardize the unity of our own coalition." With even greater vehemence, Dulles opposed the proposal of a foreign ministers meeting to discuss German unity. He stressed that such a move would "ruin every prospect of ratification of the European Defense Community" and invite "the fall of the French, German and Italian governments," all of which had staked their future on the ratification of the EDC treaties.[19] However, Dulles's opposition to a presidential statement diminished as the Soviet peace-oriented rhetoric increased. Most influential in this regard was a speech by the new source of real power in the Soviet Union, Georgiy Maksimilianovich Malenkov. Malenkov underlined the readiness of the Soviet Union to settle peacefully all unresolved questions with other nations, including the United States.[20] The Soviets were submitting a more flexible resolution on disarmament in the UN General Assembly, and Chou En-lai's speech of 30 March broke the impasse in the armistice negotiations in Korea.[21]

Because of these hopeful signs, Dulles now agreed in principle to a speech by the president. However, he suggested that it focus on "a call for the end of hostilities in Asia generally, and in Korea and Indo-China specifically."[22] The president then introduced another new idea by stating that the United States should show its determination to raise the general standard of living throughout the world instead of supporting worldwide spending on armaments.[23] The process leading up to Eisenhower's highly praised "Chance for Peace" address was marked by improvisation and haste. As we will see, so was the follow-up once the speech was delivered.

The "Chance for Peace" Speech

President Eisenhower delivered his "Chance for Peace" address to the American Society of Newspaper Editors. The speech was broadcast nationwide over radio and television networks. Eisenhower began by describing the history of the Cold War since the end of World War II. Eight years of fear and force had brought the world to the point where the worst fate to be feared was "atomic war" and the best to be expected was "a life of perpetual fear and tension." The world was spending "the sweat of its laborers, the genius of its scientists, [and] the hopes of its children" on arms. With the death of Stalin, he noted hopefully, an era had ended.

The new Soviet leadership now had "a precious opportunity to awaken, with the rest of the world, to the point of peril reached and to help turn the tide of history." But the tide would turn only by deeds and not by mere rhetoric. The first step had to be peace in Asia, beginning with an honorable armistice in Korea and an end of indirect attacks on Indochina and Malaya. The next step would be a treaty with Austria and consideration of a united Germany. As progress in all these areas strengthened world trust, it would become possible to proceed with the reduction of armaments, including the limitation of military forces, the international control of atomic energy, the limitation or prohibition of other categories of weapons of great destructiveness, and the enforcement of these limitations "by adequate safeguards, including a practical system of inspection under the United Nations."

Finally, President Eisenhower called upon a new war against the brute forces of poverty and need. He proposed that a substantial percentage of the savings achieved by disarmament be deposited into a fund for world aid and reconstruction. He ended his address asking rhetorically how far the new leaders of the Soviet Union were prepared to go: "The test of truth," President Eisenhower emphasized, "is simple. There can be no persuasion but by deeds."[24]

Although the speech was praised extensively throughout the world, not much came of it in the short term. Eisenhower received much international acclaim for discussing the costs of the arms race and for the vague declaration of his government's interest in arms-limitation agreements.[25] The new Soviet leaders reprinted the speech without deletions in *Pravda*. Yet in Washington not everybody was happy with the response to the presidential address. Some of Eisenhower's national security advisers feared that the speech had projected an image of weakness. Only two days after President Eisenhower's address, Secretary Dulles gave a speech that reflected much less optimism.[26] Dulles's unyielding language provoked considerable anger on the Soviet side.

The new Soviet leaders had added to *Pravda*'s reprint of Eisenhower's address a long background analysis of their own. Ambassador Charles E. Bohlen sent a summary of the article to the State Department. He noted that the Soviets perceived the speech as an American reply to their own recent statements regarding the possibility of a peaceful solution to controversial international questions. While the language of the article was generally cautious, it was sharp in the rebuttal of Secretary Dulles's speech. Ambassador Bohlen underscored that the Soviets did not welcome the U.S. preconditions for disarmament negotiations. Summing up his impression of the article, he judged the "mildness of the rebuttal (with the exception of the attacks on the Secretary) plus the publication in full of the President's accurate and trenchant criticism of Soviet policies" as striking. He pointed out that the article appeared designed "to avoid the appearance of throwing cold water" on the U.S. proposals, and "to shift the onus . . . back on the US and its allies."[27]

A "Special Estimate" issued by all U.S. intelligence organizations, however, played down the publication of the full address as an "unusual but not unprecedented act." It was the overall sense that the *Pravda* article was "a skillful effort to promote dissension within the US Government, between the US Government and the American people, and above all, between the US and the rest of the non-Communist world." The authors of the "Special Estimate" saw the statement as a sign "that the rulers of the USSR envisage a prolonged political warfare campaign exploiting the 'peace' theme."[28]

When British prime minister Churchill informed President Eisenhower that he was thinking about making a personal visit to Moscow and convening a summit meeting, Eisenhower very clearly opposed these ideas. The president believed that "the *Pravda* editorial repeats all previous Soviet positions" and that the Communists had not taken any actions to demonstrate the seriousness of their intentions.[29]

The "Chance for Peace" effort remained propaganda. In this atmosphere, Project Candor was not making much progress either. On 27 May, Robert Oppenheimer and Vannevar Bush addressed the NSC. But the president did not want to terrify the American people. He was looking for a message of hope. The only decision made at the meeting, however, was not exactly in the interest of greater candor. The president directed the officials to suppress reference to the term "thermonuclear" in future official statements. Such weapons should be included in the definition of "atomic" weapons. Eisenhower directed Jackson to prepare a draft of a presidential address.[30] Meanwhile, disarmament negotiations in the UN remained a "holding operation." Secretary Dulles informed Henry Cabot Lodge that—while the president had placed major emphasis on disarmament in his speech of 16 April—he had made it clear that an agreement on disarmament matters "would come only as progress towards settlement of certain other political issues strengthens world trust."[31]

Eisenhower's "Atoms for Peace" Speech

The first explosion of a Soviet thermonuclear device on 12 August 1953 revitalized Project Candor. The end of the U.S. thermonuclear monopoly reminded officials of the earlier warning of Oppenheimer and Bush that the thermonuclear revolution would change the nature of conflict in the very near future. New interest in serious disarmament developed in the State Department. However, the story of the "Chance for Peace" address repeated itself; the "Atoms for Peace" speech ended with a serious setback for the United States' disarmament position.

Following the Soviet thermonuclear test, Robert Bowie stressed to the NSC the urgent need to reexamine the nation's disarmament position. The United States, Bowie pointed out, did not possess a plan that took account of the developments in the field of thermonuclear weapons. He warned that the administration "should not put forward any position on this important subject which we were not fully prepared to follow up on." Finally, Bowie repeated the view first articulated by Oppenheimer's panel that the UN was not the right forum for serious disarmament negotiations.[32]

In talks with the president in Denver on 6 September, Secretary Dulles proposed offering the Soviets a plan for mutual withdrawal from Europe.[33] Dulles's idea found its way into a new draft of Project Candor, which was put together in the State Department.[34] The NSC Planning Board, however, thought the plan to be doomed from a political as well as a military point of view. And eventually, Dulles was persuaded that the time was not yet ripe for such far-reaching proposals. In a memorandum to the president, the secretary concluded "that we ought not seriously to seek discussions with the Soviets until decisions have been taken on EDC." A firm foundation in Western Europe, in Dulles's view, was a sine qua non for a settlement with the Soviets. The secretary further asserted that the "specific and simple terms desirable for a speech are not a good basis for beginning negotiations. Either they seem to give away too much of our case," he noted, "or else they seem to be primarily propaganda, which would be likely to provoke only propaganda response." He thought that "the approaches [to the Soviets] should be primarily private."[35]

The Soviet explosion of a thermonuclear device was very much on the president's mind as well. While vacationing in Denver, he wondered about the capability of the Soviets to produce hydrogen weapons in the next several years.[36] The explosion also brought him back to his earlier consideration of peaceful uses of atomic energy. According to Eisenhow-

er's memoirs, he discussed his thoughts with Robert Cutler, who immediately wrote the following short letter to the chairman of the Atomic
Energy Commission, Admiral Lewis L. Strauss: "The President suggested that you might consider the following proposal. . . . Suppose the
United States and the Soviets were each to turn over to the United Nations, for peaceful use, X kilograms of fissionable material." What Eisenhower omitted in his memoirs was the second sentence of the short
letter from Cutler, which read: "The amount X could be fixed at a figure
which we could handle from our stockpile, but which it would be difficult for the Soviets to match."[37]

At first, Strauss was not very impressed with Eisenhower's proposal.
While he judged it novel and of some propaganda value, he informed
the president that "it has doubtful value as a practical move."[38] When
the president returned from Denver, he found a memorandum from
Cutler that summarized the adverse reaction to Dulles's mutual withdrawal proposal. Dulles's proposal had been far too complicated for a
presidential speech anyway. In a clear shift of emphasis away from a
search for a serious arms control offer, Cutler now turned his attention
to generating favorable propaganda. He found Project Candor to be a
valuable way of stimulating worldwide acceptability of the New Look:
"The virtue of making the proposals lies not so much in the likelihood
of their acceptability by the other side," he wrote to the president, "but
in the opportunity provided to the U.S.—once the proposals have been
made and not accepted—to put into effect a new and better (for the
long run) basic policy than that we now have."[39]

Such was the background when the president met with C. D. Jackson
and Admiral Strauss to discuss implementing the next stage of Project
Candor. The drafting of the speech increasingly became a "Strauss-Jack-
son" act, while the State Department lost close contact with the proposal.[40] The association that Cutler had drawn between Project Candor
and the New Look was becoming more important. In its final phase,
drafting of the "Atoms for Peace" speech was becoming heavily inter-
twined with the events leading up to the Bermuda conference of the
heads of governments and foreign ministers of the United States,
France, and the United Kingdom, from 4 December to 8 December,
1953. This suggests that the address was part of a broader attempt by the
Eisenhower administration to sell the New Look to the European allies.

The Bermuda conference had originated with Winston Churchill,
who had given up on his idea of a high-level meeting with the Soviets
due to American pressure. In place of a meeting with the Soviets,
Churchill proposed an informal meeting with the president and the

French premier.[41] British plans were shrouded in ambiguity, and the Americans were uncertain about what the British prime minister was really up to.[42]

In Bermuda, President Eisenhower took the initiative only minutes into the first substantive meeting. He introduced the idea of peaceful uses of the atom in order to underline U.S. interest in a peaceful end of the Cold War. The president noted that this new proposal would show the world that the West was struggling for peace.[43] French premier minister Joseph Laniel approved of the proposal in its entirety, but Winston Churchill expressed initial reservations.[44] Eisenhower's presentation of the proposal at the outset of the four-day conference put the U.S. delegation in a good position to press its two primary aims of the meeting. First, the Eisenhower administration hoped to encourage establishment of the EDC.[45] Second, the Americans hoped to convince the Europeans to accept the integration of nuclear weapons into NATO strategy.[46]

The fundamentally positive reaction of the British and the French convinced President Eisenhower to deliver the speech to the UN on the day he returned from Bermuda. Major revisions, taking account of the conference's results, were made during the flight to New York. In his memoirs, Eisenhower recalled that "only minutes before the delivery of the speech, the work was done."[47]

On 8 December 1953, before the UN General Assembly, President Eisenhower presented his plan for the International Atomic Energy Agency. The United States, the United Kingdom, and the Soviet Union, he suggested, should make contributions from their stockpiles of fissionable material, which then would be allocated to serve the peaceful pursuits of mankind.[48] As in the case of the "Chance for Peace" speech, delivery of the "Atoms for Peace" address took place against a backdrop of diplomatic contacts. Dulles instructed Ambassador Bohlen to contact Soviet foreign minister Vyacheslav Mikhailovich Molotov before delivery of the speech.[49] Bohlen met Molotov on 7 December and told the Soviet foreign minister that President Eisenhower would address the UN in a speech "devoted to [the] dangers of [the] atomic age." He added that the speech was not intended to make propaganda; its purpose was "to state US willingness to talk privately on [the] whole atomic armaments problem with Soviet Government." The ambassador ended by asking for the Soviet government's official response.[50]

President Eisenhower, initially, was pleased with the response to his speech at home and abroad. The reactions in the western democracies had been good. Eisenhower stressed the "tremendous amount of time" he personally had spent on the drafting of the speech in a letter to a personal friend.[51] But not everybody was happy with the reactions to the address, particularly once the reaction of the Soviets became known. The Soviet government accepted the U.S. proposal for talks, but rejected the substance of the "Atoms for Peace" idea. The Soviets objected to the idea that only small portions of fissionable material stockpiles would be turned over. Also, the Soviets feared that Eisenhower's plan would not limit the use of atomic weapons and therefore would not halt the atomic arms race. Ambassador Bohlen, to whom Molotov handed the Soviet reply, admitted that such a reaction "was to be anticipated in that in Soviet eyes it [the U.S. proposal] was probably regarded as means of maintaining superiority of US military stockpile."[52] But the Soviets went further and called for a mutual commitment not to use atomic weapons and other weapons of mass destruction. They regarded a proposal to outlaw nuclear weapons as a first important step toward abolition of atomic weapons. The Soviet answer was widely publicized over Moscow radio and in the Soviet press.[53]

Ambassador Bohlen regarded the answer as "not unskillful from [the] point of view of public opinion," but others judged it to be "diabolically clever" and "dangerously smart."[54] Jackson informed the president on 29 December that he was beginning to worry about the impression made by the Soviet reply on both sides of the Atlantic. In his view, it was a matter of urgency to put the ball back in the Soviet court. The Soviet reply, he added, had led to a deep and bitter quarrel between the State Department and the Defense Department. Robert Bowie believed that the language of the address, "plus Foster Dulles' personal impression in the two speech meetings prior to Bermuda, indicate that the U.S. is prepared to sit down with the Soviets to work out atomic disarmament without reference to total disarmament, including conventional weapons." But the Defense Department representative, Assistant Secretary of Defense for International Affairs Frank C. Nash, believed that this position amounted to "defense suicide, since the net result of exclusively atomic disarmament would reduce the U.S. defense position to a definite inferiority ration in conventional weapons and manpower." It would contradict the whole New Look philosophy.[55] The differences in departmental interpretations of the proposal were not surprising, since the speech was written by the president and a few close advisers.[56] Jackson informed Eisenhower that the president would have to clarify his intentions.

President Eisenhower's personal position was not clear. While in his reply to Jackson he stated that he was "not arguing either side of the question," Dulles came away from a meeting with Eisenhower convinced that the president's position was substantively in accordance with the position of the Department of Defense.[57] The result was ambiguity. For the president, the "question of total, as opposed to atomic, disarmament" was largely academic, because neither goal could be accomplished without the most rigid and complete system of inspection, and this, Eisenhower wrote to Jackson, "we feel perfectly certain the Soviets would never allow."[58] He was prepared "to listen to talks going beyond the pool proposal and dealing with atomic weapons generally although he was skeptical as to the possibility of any grandiose proposal being acceptable because of mutual suspicions."[59]

In a White House meeting with a few key advisers aimed at clearing up the remaining questions of interpretation of the presidential address, Eisenhower later went as far as to state his willingness to cancel out atomic and hydrogen weapons from the armaments of both the United States and the USSR:

> He would do this to protect the US economy and the US industrial base. He pointed out that in the final analysis it was the US industrial capacity which was the decisive factor in all major wars, from the Civil War on. Once the atomic and hydrogen threat to the US economy and industrial plant were removed, he believed the US could readily handle any other form of military attack on our country. However, he agreed that in the present state of world affairs, it is impossible that any effective agreement toward this end could be worked out which would provide the necessary safeguards.[60]

Acknowledging the many political problems that "Atoms for Peace" entailed, the president increasingly lost his interest in the proposal.[61] This became obvious when Secretary Dulles came back from the Berlin conference where he had talked to Molotov about the president's proposal.[62] While Dulles pointed out that the world was anxious to hear the follow-up to "Atoms for Peace," the president was in no hurry and wondered whether the vast problem "could not go forward in a series of phases."[63]

While "Atoms for Peace" was originally inspired by the serious interest in disarmament that followed the first Soviet thermonuclear test, it ended as the "Chance for Peace" initiative had, in a fight over propaganda advantages.[64] And even the propaganda was not as effective as anticipated. A member of the Policy Planning Staff summarized: "The Russians say in substance that we talked big in public before the U.N., emphasized the perils of the atomic age and suggested that we desired to meet them and were prepared to come forward with a new approach to them, but, when it came to private talks, we revealed our real position which is quite different. Our real position is that we want to continue the atomic armaments race."[65]

The Quandary of Nuclear Arms Limitation

Concern about the impact of hydrogen weapons increased in the wake of an American H-bomb test in the Marshall Islands on 26 March 1953. Allied pressure for a test moratorium grew, and the summer of 1954 witnessed a lively debate within the Eisenhower administration about the practicability of such a proposal. Although, in the end, the United States rejected a test moratorium, the decision makers developed an appreciation for the dangers of the thermonuclear age over the course of the debate.

Whereas the problem of disarmament was increasingly regarded as unsolvable, the realization of the changing nature of conflict materialized in the definite rejection of preventive war. In the summer of 1954, the tension between a more aggressive policy and a move in the direction of a general détente with arms control agreements reached its highest point. The impact of the shifting strategic nuclear balance and the onset of the thermonuclear revolution met one another at a decisive moment. And hanging in the balance were the United States' relations with its allies.

The U.S. hydrogen bomb test of 26 March created a worldwide uproar, because of the contamination of a Japanese fishing vessel and its crew. Rumors about contaminated fish alarmed Dulles. The event threatened U.S. foreign policy interests. In a phone conversation with Admiral Strauss, the secretary noted that he was afraid that the wave of hysteria would drive the allies into Soviet arms. The allies, he explained to Strauss, "think we are getting ready for a war of this kind. We could survive . . . but some of them would be obliterated in a few minutes. It could lead to a policy of neutrality or appeasement."[66] Out of fear, the western allies might stand behind the Soviet proposal to outlaw the use of nuclear weapons.

Experience bore out Dulles's concern. In the United Kingdom, the U.S. test led to parliamentary inquiries into why discussions on disarmament had not been held.[67] On 5 April, the House of Commons adopted a resolution "recognizing the threat to civilization posed by the hydrogen bomb and urging that the heads of government of the United States, the United Kingdom, and the Soviet Union meet to reconsider the question of regulation of armaments."[68] At the UN, Indian prime minister Jawaharlal Nehru introduced a proposal in the Disarmament Commission to suspend testing.[69] In a letter to the State Department, Henry Cabot Lodge, the U.S. representative to the UN, urged the U.S. government to reconsider the question of a test moratorium and emphasized the political benefits of such a posture.[70] The British were of the opinion that a moratorium on further hydrogen experiments could be monitored with available technology.[71]

The NSC was split on the issue of a moratorium. Admiral Strauss, Secretary Wilson, and Admiral Radford stressed the tremendous progress made with the recent tests on increasing the number of weapons in terms of available raw materials. They doubted the capacity to verify Soviet compliance with a moratorium. Both the president and the secretary of state, on the other hand, emphasized the political advantages of accepting such a proposal. President Eisenhower expressed the view that everybody "seems to think that we're skunks, saber-rattlers and warmongers." By accepting the moratorium, the United States could improve its public image. Secretary Dulles observed that the British were obsessed "over the H-bomb and its potential effect on the British Isles." He insisted that the U.S. government "could not sit here in Washington and develop bigger bombs without any regard for the impact of these developments on world opinion. In the long run, it isn't only bombs that win wars, but having public opinion on your side."[72] The insistence of the president and the secretary of state on the political desirability of a test moratorium led to further studies. The JCS feared that there was "no reason to expect that the Soviet Union would adhere in good faith to an agreement to suspend future tests." Therefore, the United States should not risk its present "advantage over the USSR with respect to the technical status of thermonuclear weapons development." The JCS believed any political advantage to be transitory in nature, "whereas the military disadvantages probably would be far-reaching and permanent."[73]

While the position of the JCS amounted to a clear "no," the view of the AEC was more complicated. Chairman Strauss emphasized the technological limitations to enforcing the proposal and stressed the importance of future tests for the development of small nuclear weapons for defensive purposes.[74] Strauss acknowledged, on the other hand, that just as the United States had gained an advantage from its recent test series, the Soviets, too, were planning their next tests for the near future. The AEC concluded that a temporary moratorium for weapons in the *megaton* range would not damage the U.S. weapon program. The likelihood of detection grew with increasing yields. Moreover, it was in the smaller-than-megaton range that the United States had to defend its present lead.[75]

In the State Department, however, the experience of the "Atoms for Peace" failure was fresh enough to foster skepticism about the AEC proposal. Dulles explained to the NSC why his department was opposed to the AEC proposal. If the United States suggested a moratorium to last no later than January 1956 and insisted that explosions under 100 kilotons be exempt, "the Soviets would quickly grasp the fact that the United States was advocating a position which had been tailored to its own advantage."[76] In response, the Soviets could easily suggest a limit of 50 kilotons, thereby stealing the propaganda advantage—again, one might say.[77]

At this point in the discussion, Secretary Dulles concluded that the United States must reject the test moratorium proposal. However, he believed that the United States should continue "to oppose total abolition of atomic weapons save as a part of an effective general disarmament program."[78] Although President Eisenhower too rejected the moratorium, he believed that the United States should not oppose abolition of nuclear weapons if an abolition could be enforced.

It seems that the concerns of the allies about the destructiveness of thermonuclear weapons led President Eisenhower to wonder when both sides would have "enough" nuclear weapons. One-and-a-half years earlier, Robert Oppenheimer and Vannevar Bush had asked how nations would behave in such a situation. The president did not expect a world of nuclear sufficiency to be quiet. Whereas the matter of "the morality of the use of these weapons was of no significance" to Eisenhower, the important thing was "that the advantage of surprise almost seemed the decisive factor in an atomic war."[79] He thought it important that his government should do everything to remove the threat of surprise. "Thanks to the element of surprise in the enemy's hands," the president stated, "the United States, for the first time in its history, was frightened at the prospect of an atomic war." Secretary Dulles immediately replied that these comments "were profoundly important and had a great bearing on our national strategy."[80] Dulles added that he did not entirely rule out the possibility of achieving effective abolition of nuclear weapons. Although the specific proposal for a test moratorium was finally rejected, the case for disarmament had received a serious boost.

The test moratorium issue came up again in the context of the reconsideration of basic national security policy in late 1954, which resulted in the exclusion of preventive war. As mentioned earlier, these discussions were marked by a fundamental split between the State Department and the Defense Department over how to protect the nation as the nuclear balance shifted. The departmental differences were irreconcilable with regard to arms limitation and disarmament.[81]

It was the view of the Defense Department that in the absence of demonstrated good faith by the Soviet Union, disarmament proposals were generally to the disadvantage of U.S. security interests. The State Department, on the other hand, perceived disarmament as the only way of escaping the peril of mutual nuclear plenty. Robert Bowie reiterated Eisenhower's fear: "Each side will get more jumpy as it increasingly comes to feel it is living with a gun at its head."[82] It was the prospect of mutual annihilation at the end of the arms race that inspired people like Robert Bowie to pursue disarmament. Nevertheless, suspicion of Soviet intentions outweighed fear of how an arms race might end.

At the very end of the year, Dulles summarized the fundamental problem of control of armaments as follows: The key question, he said, was "whether it was possible to have elimination of nuclear weapons without a corresponding reduction in the conventional armaments field." Whereas he thought it possible to work out effective controls in the nuclear field, this would never be feasible in the conventional field. If the administration agreed to eliminate nuclear weapons alone, "we would be depriving ourselves of those weapons in which the U.S. was ahead and would not be taking action in the area of Soviet superiority." While this was an obvious danger, Dulles noted, it could, on the other hand, be argued "that atomic weapons are the only ones by which the U.S. can be virtually destroyed through a sudden attack." If the danger of destruction could be removed, the U.S. industrial power would still act "both as a deterrent against total war and as a principal means of winning a war." These irreconcilable arguments drove Secretary Dulles to the discouraging conclusion "that this was the kind of a problem which fundamentally could not be solved by controls or by limiting weapons. Once weapons of great power had been discovered," he added, "it seemed most doubtful that they could be eliminated. In fact, there would seem to be more chance of success if one could eliminate war."[83]

The advent of the hydrogen bomb generated great concerns about a future of mutual atomic plenty. Within a few years, both the United States and the Soviet Union would develop "enough" nuclear capability to threaten one another with complete destruction. The fact that such a world would only come gradually led people to perceive the period ahead to be very dangerous and laden with instability. Although Oppenheimer and Bush could imagine that a situation of mutual vulnerability, once it had developed, might bring with it a strange stability, western leaders focused on the potential dangers that would precede the arrival of a stable peace. For both Churchill and Eisenhower, the advantage of striking first increasingly seemed decisive, and that lay at the heart of their concerns.

In summary, the Eisenhower administration's interest in the control of nuclear weapons grew from fears of the instabilities of a nuclear stalemate. The vulnerability of the allies played a major role in this process. Both the "Chance for Peace" and the "Atoms for Peace" proposals were designed primarily to reassure the allies. Neither of the proposals was seriously aimed at leading to nuclear arms limitation agreements with the Soviet Union. With the help of the Soviets, the proposals quickly degenerated into propaganda. It was not until the choice between a more aggressive foreign policy and a move in the direction of détente became more pressing, during the summer of 1954, that concern regarding a time of mutual atomic plenty grew within the Eisenhower administration, particularly in the State Department. Growing realization of what thermonuclear war would mean combined with fears of allied neutralization materialized in the definite rejection of preventive war at the end of 1954.

However, a policy of disarmament and arms limitation as a way of securing peace in the thermonuclear age collided with the American commitment to the defense of its allies. Nuclear weapons played a crucial role in providing for the security of the American allies. President Eisenhower's argument that U.S. industrial power would still be the decisive element once nuclear weapons were eliminated made sense for the security of the American homeland. However, it was doubtful that knowledge of the U.S. industrial capacity would keep the Soviets out of Western Europe. Although seldom mentioned, it was these concerns that tied conventional disarmament to nuclear disarmament. From a western perspective, nuclear disarmament without conventional disarmament would leave Europe unprotected against Soviet conventional superiority. This meant, as John Foster Dulles suggested at the time, "that there might well not be disarmament."[84]

4

The Nuclearization of NATO: A Delicate Balance

We have seen that nuclear weapons affected international politics and in particular American national security policy in manifold ways during the early 1950s. The relative inexpensiveness of nuclear weapons made it easier for Eisenhower to support the concept of collective security without weakening the nation's economy. At the time of its formulation, the New Look was not only a fiscally attractive strategy but also a sound military strategy. U.S. nuclear superiority could still be decisive in a general war. The expectation that the strategic balance was shifting had generally destabilizing implications. In particular, it exposed the western alliance system to unprecedented tensions. The thermonuclear revolution, on the other hand, strengthened the view that nuclear war between the United States and the Soviet Union would mean mutual destruction once both sides had developed "enough" nuclear weapons. In chapter 3, I proposed that fears of what the future would bring had generally stabilizing implications for the security debate. The development of serious interest in nuclear arms limitation agreements was a case in point.

However, it has to be emphasized that the strategic balance and the thermonuclear revolution were at once stabilizing and destabilizing phenomena. Besides its earlier described destabilizing effects, American nuclear superiority had also stabilizing effects, providing the U.S. and NATO with a credible deterrent. On the other hand, the thermonuclear revolution also influenced the strategic debate in destabilizing ways. The SAC, for example, perceived hydrogen bombs as means that would greatly enhance the possibility of delivering a single war-winning blow.[1] Politically more influential, however, were anticipations about the development of the two elements, that is, how the *shift* in the strategic balance and the worldwide *growth* in thermonuclear capabilities would affect policy.

In the early 1950s, nuclear weapons affected national security policy in both stabilizing and destabilizing ways. Both effects were felt most strongly in alliance politics. In this chapter I argue that a delicate balance was achieved in late 1954 with the nuclearization of NATO and the post–World War II settlement between the western powers and West Germany.

The story of how NATO went nuclear simultaneously with West Germany's accession is a complicated one. The nuclearization of the alliance was partly due to the same strategic, technological, political, and economic factors that had influenced the formulation of the New Look. In addition, the NATO framework was marked by the question of how to integrate the European defense efforts in order to contain historical animosities.

The Atlantic alliance was formed in 1949, principally as a means of preventing further expansion of Soviet influence in Europe. As the growing Soviet nuclear threat fundamentally changed this task, various national interests, threat perceptions, and capabilities had to be considered. The story of the transatlantic debate over these issues is a story of many diplomatic ruptures, quarrels, and clashes of opinion. However, the fact that NATO survived was proof of the strength of the underlying common security interest of its fourteen members.

Finally, and maybe most important, the nuclearization of NATO had consequences that proved to be essential for the development of American national security policy for the remainder of the Cold War. The stabilizing and destabilizing influences of nuclear weapons were in delicate balance at the end of 1954, because NATO went nuclear just when the U.S. nuclear deterrent was losing credibility. The growth of Soviet nuclear forces threatened the credibility of the nuclear foundation of alliance security.

The Eisenhower Administration and the Europeans

European expectations about future American-European relations were high when Eisenhower entered the presidency in January 1953. This was due to his service as commander of allied forces in Europe during World War II. He had gone on to become NATO's first commander at the end of 1950. Eisenhower, therefore, was well known in Europe and profited from his image as a war hero on both sides of the Atlantic.[2] Once in office, the new president immediately confirmed his "Atlanticist" image. In both his inauguration speech and his first State of the Union message, he stressed the importance of the political and economic unity of Western Europe and promised that his administration would further these goals whenever possible.[3]

Later in the year, when the drafts of the NSC 162 series were discussed in the NSC, he summarized his position on Europe by observing that "if the Communists succeeded in gaining control of Europe the world balance of power would be hopelessly upset." He added that it "would be necessary to spend many more billions than we are now spending to redress this balance of power. In short, said the President, that Western Europe not fall to the Communists was a *sine qua non*."[4] Aside from the fact that the United States needed the military forces and economic resources of the Western European nations in order to balance Soviet power, the Americans needed allied soil as a base for the effective use of their air power. Both Eisenhower and Dulles were strong believers in the concept of collective security and regarded it as a central element of U.S. national security policy.[5]

The State of NATO

Although there were important common transatlantic interests, NATO's future was uncertain in early 1953. The distress of European economies jeopardized the fulfillment of the Lisbon force goals, which NATO had adopted in February 1952. The Soviet Union's emergence as a nuclear power in August 1949, and the outbreak of the Korean War in June 1950, were the reasons for a NATO meeting in the Portuguese capital. The seriousness of the international situation and the growing Soviet threat led the alliance's members to adopt force goals calling for ninety-six NATO divisions by 1954.[6]

The Truman administration, initiating an increase in both the nation's conventional and nuclear forces, pressed the Europeans to fulfill their obligation under the Lisbon force goals. However, the British economy in particular was in deep trouble. Prime Minister Churchill must have realized that his nation would be unable to comply with the force goals. During the summer of 1952, the chief of the British Air Staff Sir John Slessor recommended to General Eisenhower's successor as commander of NATO, General Matthew Ridgway, that he project NATO force goals for 1956 under the assumption of reliance on nuclear weapons.[7] General Ridgway finished his study on NATO force goals in early summer of 1953, shortly before he was succeeded by General Alfred M.

Gruenther. Somewhat surprisingly to many, Ridgway's final report called for even more conventional forces than did the Lisbon force goals.[8] The British were not pleased with the results of the report and hoped for better judgment by General Gruenther and the incoming Eisenhower administration.

However, the first meeting between officials of the new Republican administration and their European counterparts at the eleventh session of the North Atlantic Council, only increased European concerns. In the days before the meeting, the Europeans emphasized their defense financing problems. The Americans, however, suspected that the Soviet peace initiative following Stalin's death was beginning to have an effect on the European public. The U.S. government believed that the Europeans were increasingly prepared to relax their defense efforts.[9]

In his opening statement at the NAC meeting, Secretary Dulles stressed that the U.S. government believed the Soviet initiative to be a tactical ploy rather than a basic change in Soviet policy.[10] He then mentioned two other themes that were central in the American debate over national security policy at that time. First, the secretary emphasized that the alliance should build up its forces over a sustained period rather than in a sudden burst, which would leave it exhausted in several years. Second, Dulles asserted that the western defense effort had to "reflect a proper balance between military and economic factors."[11] These were the two major themes of NSC 149/2, which the NSC approved two days after the secretary of state returned from Paris. As discussed above, the paper clearly reflected Eisenhower's dual threat approach to national security policy.[12]

John Foster Dulles summarized his government's views thus: "The new US administration believes by better planning we can have greater strength at lesser cost. Some may consider this naive," he added, "but we believe it and will try it. We wish not only to sustain present force goals, but see them enlarged in coming years."[13] From a European perspective, force expansion at lower cost sounded somewhat contradictory. The allied officials were also surprised that the secretary of state mentioned nuclear weapons only in a single and somewhat cryptic sentence, noting that the new weapons would inevitably change the character of NATO force requirements.

The American position on the question of economic aid (which was presented to the French and the British in bilateral meetings) had an even greater negative impact on the Europeans. The announcement that the United States would eliminate economic aid and substitute it with trade and off-shore procurement came as a shock to the Europeans.[14] While President Eisenhower and Secretary Dulles were fighting Congress to minimize cuts in the MSA funds, the first message they conveyed to the Europeans suggested willingness to cut foreign aid.[15]

The European reaction was one of utter despair. A member of the French delegation was quoted as saying: "This is the end of NATO." And the British warned the Americans that the NAC meeting had created a very delicate European situation. In a talk with Secretary Dulles, British minister of state John Selwyn Brooke Lloyd emphasized that some Europeans would view the American position "as return to isolationism, feeling that withdrawal first of general economic aid and then of special defense aid will be followed by withdrawal of troops." Moreover, from what the British knew about emerging U.S. trade policy, they doubted that trade would be an adequate substitute for aid. In addition, Selwyn Lloyd added, the American statement came at an "awkward moment because of Soviet 'peace' gestures."[16] Although Dulles seemed to be pleased by the results of his first NATO meeting, the Europeans were not happy with what the secretary of state had labeled a different American approach to the whole NATO concept: "We now propose to look on NATO as the defense of Europe by Europe with United States assistance."[17]

During the summer of 1953, the Europeans increasingly lost confidence in U.S. leadership. On the one hand, the reduction of the U.S. defense budget seemed to signal that even the Americans believed the risk of war to be diminishing. On the other hand, the U.S. government seemed to doubt that the European continent could be defended with available forces.[18] Last and most important, it was obvious that the gap between the existing NATO forces and the Lisbon requirements could not be closed, due to economic difficulties.[19] Against this background, the British concluded that the West would have to rely on the deterrent power of U.S. atomic superiority to close the gap between existing forces, and the projected requirements if NATO was going to implement a forward defense strategy.[20]

The State Department agreed that U.S. atomic superiority provided an effective deterrent at the present time. However, the department played down the deterrent power for two reasons: First, European confidence in U.S. atomic superiority would make it difficult to persuade the Europeans that further buildup of conventional forces was needed. Second, it was important that the Europeans close the conventional gap while U.S. atomic superiority prevailed, because at a certain point an atomic stalemate would develop. The State Department concluded that with NATO forces then available, only critical areas of Europe could be held in the event of an attack by the Warsaw Pact. From an American perspective, German rearmament was the key factor in the conventional forces debate. If the allies wanted to carry out a forward defense, Germany would have to be rearmed. In turn, a German contribution meant that the Europeans had to swallow "the bitter pill of EDC."[21]

The Question of EDC

The European Defense Community (EDC) had been designed in order to allow Germany to rebuild its defense structure in a context that would enable its neighbors to guard against the resurgence of militarism. In May 1952, France, West Germany, Italy, Belgium, the Netherlands, and Luxembourg had agreed to establish the EDC. The EDC would have its own army under an integrated high command. These forces were to be placed at the disposal of NATO.[22] However, by the end of 1952 none of the signatory nations had ratified the treaty.

From the very beginning of his presidency, Eisenhower had regarded the EDC as an integral part of collective security.[23] With the formulation of the New Look, the importance of the EDC for U.S. defense plans grew. The fact that the United States wanted to redeploy its overseas forces made a German contribution to the defense of Europe essential.[24] We have seen above that the new JCS concluded that withdrawing overseas forces would be a strategically sensible move, given the growing vulnerability of the American homeland. Unfortunately, the JCS view made its way into numerous press stories, raising European fears about the credibility of the American commitment for Europe.[25] Finally, the president decided against redeployments. Until the EDC was ratified, Eisenhower directed his administration, "let us all keep quiet on redeployment."[26] Eisenhower believed that if the Europeans knew that the United States wanted to pull out, they would not agree to German rearmament and the EDC, which were preconditions to pulling out.

At the Bermuda conference in December 1953, the Eisenhower administration got its chance to urge the ratification of the EDC.[27] In a talk with French prime minister Joseph Laniel, President Eisenhower stressed that the only practical way to ensure the defense of the free world "lay in the development of a greater unity on continental Europe by the association of France and Germany. He felt that the EDC was the only way a German contribution could be made available and France be given the guarantees to which she was entitled against a resurrection of Pan-Germanism."[28] Secretary Dulles went further and threatened that if the EDC were rebuffed, the U.S. Congress would not pass further appropriations for NATO, and the United States would have "to reevaluate their whole position" regarding Europe.[29] In the plenary meeting of the three heads of government, Winston Churchill urged the French to go forward with the ratification of the EDC. Churchill pointed out that as long as the United States did not like the idea of German rearmament within NATO, a failure of the EDC would lead to "something in the nature of peripheral defense"—the nightmare of the continental Europeans. In any case, he added, if U.S. troops were withdrawn from France, "British troops could not stay any longer."[30]

France was the weak link on ratification of the EDC. The Laniel government faced vigorous domestic opposition from the Socialists on one side, and from General Charles DeGaulle on the other side. DeGaulle was unshakably opposed to the idea of Franco-German rapprochement (which lay at the heart of the EDC). On a more fundamental level, the French were afraid that implementation of the EDC would lead to the withdrawal of U.S. and British troops from the continent. French foreign minister Bidault made it clear that the French were seeking additional commitments from the United States and the United Kingdom to stay on the continent once the EDC was ratified.[31]

In addition to discussing the EDC, the foreign ministers discussed the issue of NATO strategy with Lord Hastings Lionel Ismay, the secretary general of NATO. All three nations agreed on the necessity of maintaining the principle of forward defense.[32] British foreign minister Sir Anthony Eden, supported by French foreign minister Bidault, then asserted that because of economic limitations, NATO would have to rely increasingly on atomic weapons to deter a Soviet attack.

Secretary Dulles replied that the United States recognized the deterrent power of strategic air power. However, he added, the West had to think about the consequences of the growing Soviet atomic stockpile. Therefore, Dulles explained, the United States proposed that in the new NATO strategic concept, nuclear weapons should be "meshed in" with conventional armaments.[33] At the North Atlantic Council ministerial meeting in Paris, which began on 14 December, only six days after the end of the Bermuda conference, Secretary Dulles explained what the United States meant. The U.S. government was convinced that by arming NATO forces with tactical nuclear weapons, the alliance could provide an adequate defense.[34] And in a restricted session of the meeting, he confirmed that the United States had developed nuclear weapons "in number and variety such that they are assuming almost conventional roles."[35]

Dulles had thus outlined the consequences of the New Look for

NATO strategy. However, the Eisenhower administration had not had enough time to completely overhaul its approach to NATO, because it had focused primarily on the formulation of a *national* security policy.[36] When Secretary Dulles reported back to the NSC, he pointed out that "whereas last April's meeting had been 'pretty jittery,' " this time the NATO allies "felt much greater serenity and confidence." This was mainly due to the fact that the Europeans increasingly regarded the deterrent power of U.S. nuclear superiority as the base of NATO strategy. Dulles said that he had tried to bring the Europeans "to thinking in something like our terms of atomic weapons and of the atomic age." However, this had not been wholly successful, he added, "and the other Ministers were still very frightened at the atomic prospect."[37] Although the Europeans were ready to put their trust in the U.S. strategic deterrent, for lack of resources to pursue any alternatives, contemplating reliance on tactical nuclear weapons was something quite different. They were alarmed by the prospect of their countries becoming atomic battlefields, and were not yet prepared to accept the full consequences of the New Look.

NATO Goes Nuclear

In early 1954, allied fears of excessive reliance on nuclear weapons spread. Secretary Dulles perpetuated the myth that he favored massive retaliation as the response to threats of every magnitude in his famous speech before the Council on Foreign Relations on 12 January.[38] From a European perspective, extending nuclear deterrence to Europe was one thing; threatening massive retaliation to relatively minor conflicts in Asia was quite another. The Indochina crisis increased European anxieties that certain groups within the U.S. government might be actively seeking to provoke general war before the growing Soviet nuclear capability could alter the strategic balance.[39] From a European point of view, however, the Soviet Union possessed enough nuclear weapons already to leave Europe destroyed in a general war. The thermonuclear revolution had a heavy impact on the European outlook. Widespread fear of what would happen if hydrogen bombs were used in Europe increased with the American H-bomb test in the Marshall Islands on 26 March, which resulted in the contamination of a Japanese fishing crew.[40]

In light of these developments, the Europeans wrestled with the idea that the fate of their society rested in the hands of the American president. In response to a parliamentary query, Prime Minister Churchill publicly reconfirmed U.S. air-base rights in the United Kingdom for re-taliatory purposes, but only "subject to prior consultation between offi-cials of the two governments." The French immediately followed and suggested private discussions between the foreign ministers of the United States, the United Kingdom, and France on "the conditions for the utilization of atomic weapons in the general European area and specifically from bases in French North Africa and Metropolitan France."[41]

The Eisenhower administration reacted to European concerns over increased reliance on nuclear weapons with a concerted effort to push forward with the implementation of the New Look's consequences for NATO strategy. In a press conference on 16 March, Secretary Dulles stated that the president possessed the right to order instantaneous re-taliation "against any attack on the United States or upon its allies in Europe and the Western Hemisphere, without prior consultation with Congress."[42] And on 12 April, when the secretary of state was in London to discuss the situation in Indochina and Southeast Asia, he told British secretary of state Eden that the NSC had decided to incorporate tactical nuclear weapons into U.S. military planning. He then expressed the con-cern of the American government "that certain of our Allies apparently continued to draw a sharp line of distinction between the use of conven-tional weapons and atomic weapons." Dulles reminded his British col-league of Soviet superiority in manpower and conventional weapons and stressed the consequences of a refusal to integrate tactical nuclear weap-ons into NATO defense. "Were we to tie our own hands behind our back in this atomic area, where we have superiority," he emphasized, "we would all be at the mercy of blackmail." Finally, Dulles warned of the financial consequences of a decision "to maintain two separate mili-tary establishments, one along conventional lines and the other based on the integration of atomic weapons with conventional forces."[43]

The most important event in Secretary Dulles's campaign for the im-plementation of a NATO New Look was the North Atlantic Council min-isterial session in Paris on 23 April. In a long speech, the American secretary of state attempted to clarify the U.S. position regarding atomic and hydrogen weapons. The statement had been prepared in the State Department, and Secretary Dulles had cleared it with Secretary Wilson, Admiral Radford, and General Gruenther.[44]

Dulles opened his speech by stating that the primary strategic objec-tive of the United States and the rest of the free world was "to deter aggression and prevent the outbreak of war." The principal danger to western security was Soviet military power, including its growing stockpile of nuclear weapons. Such power, the secretary went on, would only be restrained by fear of retaliation, and it was therefore "indispensable that the free world possess and maintain a capacity for instant and formidable retaliation." It was difficult for the free world to match the non-atomic military strength of the Soviet bloc person for person. "Current NATO force programs," Dulles underscored, "fall short of providing the conventional forces estimated to be required to defend the NATO area against a full-scale Soviet Bloc attack." The United States had accepted the current force programs of the alliance only under the assumption that atomic weapons would be available for the support of presently programmed forces. Therefore, it was essential that NATO agree to a policy, in case of either general or local war, "to use atomic weapons as conventional weapons against the military assets of the enemy whenever and wherever it would be of advantage to do so, taking account of all relevant factors."

Due to European sensibilities on the issue, he added that this meant neither "that every local war must automatically be turned into a general war" nor "that because atomic weapons are used locally they would be used indiscriminately for the bombing of civilian populations." However, Secretary Dulles emphasized that NATO could not adopt a policy "that atomic weapons would be used only in retaliation for their use by the enemy." If such a policy became known, the deterrent power of these weapons would be gone. "The possession of a will, if need arises, to use strength," he stressed, "is as important as possession of strength."

Finally, Secretary Dulles touched on the delicate matter of consultation in the event of an enemy attack. He stressed that the United States intended to consult and cooperate fully with its allies. However, he added, under certain contingencies "time would not permit consultation without itself endangering the very security we seek to protect. So far as feasible, we must seek understanding in advance on the measures to be taken under various circumstances."[45]

Allied reaction to Secretary Dulles's statement was generally positive.[46] Anthony Eden emphasized in a letter to Dulles that "many considerations besides purely military ones must be taken into account in deciding in any given case whether or not there was a balance of advantage" in using nuclear weapons. And he underlined the strongly held views of his government "on the need for consultation before any decision is taken."[47] The Europeans were not yet convinced about the desirability of complete (that is, strategic and tactical) integration of nuclear weapons into NATO strategy. But now the related issue of the fate of the EDC was developing its own momentum.

The Failure of EDC and the NATO Solution

The Eisenhower administration had been urging ratification of the EDC ever since the Bermuda conference. Although the Netherlands, Belgium, and West Germany had ratified the treaty, progress was slow in early 1954. The central problem was still France. Dulles hoped that a deadlock on the German question on the occasion of the Four-Power conference in Berlin (23 January through 18 February) would create momentum for French ratification.[48] Although West and East found no solution for European security in Berlin, the French still made no progress toward ratification. French consideration of the EDC was further delayed by rapid deterioration of the French position in Indochina. Dien Bien Phu fell on 7 May, and the Laniel government fell shortly thereafter. Prime Minister Laniel's successor, Pierre Mendès-France, had never been an outspoken supporter of the EDC. His proposals for modification of the EDC treaty turned out to be completely unacceptable to the five nations that had signed on already (Germany, Belgium, the Netherlands, Luxembourg, and Italy). Not unexpectedly, the French National Assembly rejected the EDC in a vote on 30 August 1954.[49]

While the U.S. government lamented the death of the EDC, the focus of activity now shifted to the British government.[50] Winston Churchill had preferred NATO to the EDC since the Bermuda conference. When the Brussels conference ended without French adherence to the EDC, the British prime minister sought out Mendès-France to discuss future options. The day after their meeting, Churchill informed Secretary Dulles of the talk. He was surprised to learn that Mendès-France too favored NATO over the EDC. Churchill supposed that this was due to the very deep French feeling "that in E.D.C. they will be bound up in civil and military affairs with the much more active and powerful Western Germany, whereas in the N.A.T.O. system the United Kingdom and the United States of America counter-balance Germany to her proper proportions."[51]

The British pushed for German rearmament within NATO as rapidly as possible. However, there were several reasons for U.S. skepticism about the inclusion of a rearmed Germany in NATO. As long as the EDC remained an option, the United States did not want to discuss other alternatives. Once EDC failed, the United States could not easily shift positions. Secretary Dulles had threatened an agonizing reappraisal of U.S. NATO commitments should the Europeans reject the EDC.[52] Further, the United States did not completely trust Germany, and therefore preferred an all-European solution.[53] And one suspects that the United

States preferred the continental buildup to take place outside of NATO, because in this scheme there were higher chances for early redeployment of American troops. However, in the end the Americans agreed with the British that the security of Europe needed both the French *and* the German contributions. This common conviction became the moving force behind the developments leading to the final settlement between the western powers and Germany.

In the event, the foreign ministers from Belgium, Canada, France, Germany, Italy, Luxembourg, the Netherlands, the United Kingdom, and the United States met in a Nine-Power conference in London from 28 September through 3 October 1954. The meeting turned out to be very successful: the nine nations agreed to revive the Brussels treaty and invite both Germany and Italy to join. The executive body was named Western European Union (WEU) and its forces were wholly dedicated to NATO. This mechanism would allow the European allies to restrict the German buildup of naval and air forces as well as its manufacture of nuclear and chemical weapons. Germany, on the other hand, was granted sovereignty and membership in the Atlantic alliance.[54] On 5 May 1955, the occupation of Germany ended, and the western powers formally recognized the Federal Republic of Germany (FRG); four days later the FRG became a member of NATO.

NATO's New Approach

Meanwhile, SACEUR General Gruenther made plans for the integration of nuclear weapons into NATO strategy. In the wake of Dulles's clarification of the U.S. position regarding nuclear and hydrogen weapons in his speech before the NAC on 23 April, General Gruenther initiated the "New Approach" studies.[55] In November 1954, the Eisenhower administration was preparing its position regarding a draft of MC-48, which was scheduled for discussion at the forthcoming NAC meeting in December. The report entitled "The Most Effective Pattern of NATO Military Strength for the Next Few Years" stated that Soviet aggression could be deterred only if "NATO forces have the capability both to withstand a Soviet nuclear attack and to deliver an immediate effective nuclear counter-attack."[56]

It is interesting to note that when the report was discussed among the president, Secretary Dulles, Secretary Wilson, Admiral Radford, and General J. Lawton Collins (the U.S. representative to the NATO Military Committee), the expected economic costs of the new program were not yet clear. However, preliminary studies indicated that there was little hope that the new program would cost less than the one presently planned for and it might well cost more.[57] Nevertheless, the issue was not discussed further, and one suspects that the Americans believed that less talk about the costs of the new policy would make it easier to get European acceptance.

In any case, the Eisenhower administration realized the political problems inherent in a nuclear concept for NATO. The secretary of state, together with the secretary of defense, proposed to the president that the United States should be prepared to inform its allies at the NAC meeting that "we will not wage preventive war" and that "we will be prepared to explore reasonable bona fide disarmament proposals."[58] If these were the carrots to be offered at the forthcoming discussions, the sticks were warnings that if the NAC did not accept the report due to European opposition, the future of NATO would be in jeopardy.[59] Finally, the United States should make it abundantly clear that signs of disunity "on the intention to develop a capability to repel Soviet attack with everything that we have available would seriously jeopardize our political as well as our military posture as a deterrent to Soviet aggression."[60]

The debate in the NAC over MC-48 revealed that American concerns were not unfounded. Neither the French representatives nor the British representatives were happy with the draft paper.[61] The Europeans were concerned about the impact of the revised NATO strategy on their own sovereignty.[62] A solution was finally worked out in two meetings led by Secretary Dulles on 16 December in Paris, the first with the British and the Canadian foreign ministers and the second with French representatives.[63] Dulles proposed that MC-48 be approved "as a basis for planning and preparation of the forces." He then noted that "the approval did not involve any delegation of responsibility of the governments for putting plans into action in the event of hostilities."

In fact, neither the Europeans *nor* the Americans were prepared to delegate authority to declare war. Moreover, setting up a procedure requiring the approval of all NATO members in order to respond to a Soviet attack, Dulles pointed out, "would seriously hamper both the deterrent effect and defense." These problems involved very complicated constitutional and political issues that were virtually impossible to solve in the abstract, the secretary added, but that might be solved without difficulties by the events themselves.[64] Dulles pointed out that if the Soviets planned a nonatomic attack on NATO, such an attack would almost certainly be detected in advance due to the necessary mobilization and other preparations. This would give NATO time for consultations on the use of nuclear weapons.[65]

Dulles also threatened a fundamental reappraisal of U.S. policy in Europe in order to force the Europeans to accept MC-48. If the Europeans, who had always favored a forward strategy, rejected the report, the secretary warned, this would "raise serious questions for the U.S. in keeping its troops in Europe."[66] The threat of a peripheral strategy, paralleled on the political side by isolationism, loomed large in the background in Paris. Apparently, this mixture of carrots and sticks was successful: On 17 December, the secretary of state could report back to the president that the NATO Ministerial Council had unanimously approved MC-48.[67]

In the decisive NAC meeting, the secretary general of NATO, Lord Ismay, had introduced MC-48 offering the Dulles line of interpretation.[68] Lord Ismay first presented a resolution that read: "The council approves the report MC-48 as a basis for planning and preparations by the NATO military authorities, noting that this approval does not involve the delegation of responsibility of governments for putting the plans into action in the event of hostilities." The secretary general added that MC-48 allowed NATO "a defense so adequate that it would, in fact, operate as a deterrent to war." The new strategy would permit "an effective forward strategy and would constitute an actual defense so that there would not be the necessity of future liberation."[69] After this comprehensive outline of the positive military and political features of the new strategy, the council approved MC-48 without dissent—NATO had gone nuclear.[70]

How should the nuclearization of NATO and the parallel settlement between the western powers and Germany be understood? First of all, the integration of nuclear weapons into NATO strategy—like the New Look—made sense from a military point of view in 1954, because the nuclear balance was still very much in favor of the West. This meant that Soviet nuclear forces were quite vulnerable to quick attack, and the alliance could plan for the tactical use of nuclear weapons to make up for its conventional deficiencies. Marc Trachtenberg has noted that even the army, the service responsible for the ground defense of Europe, was early on attracted to a strategic concept in which nuclear weapons played a central role.[71]

On the European side of the Atlantic, these arguments had less impact, because they were countered earlier and in a much stronger way by the fear of thermonuclear war. The Europeans were more sensitive to arguments against the tactical use of nuclear weapons in Europe because of their exposed position. At the same time, however, serious economic problems led the Europeans to argue for greater reliance on the strategic deterrent. The economic case for the integration of nuclear weapons into western defense policy played a role on both sides of the Atlantic (although it might have had bigger impact on the European side). The relative inexpensiveness of nuclear weapons influenced the Americans in the formulation of the New Look and the Europeans in the acceptance of MC-48.

Since 1953, it had become clear to Europeans and Americans alike that the Lisbon force goals of 1952 could not be achieved. One wonders what would have happened at the end of 1954 if the allies had decided to implement the forward strategy without nuclear weapons. The economic case for nuclear weapons might well have been the strongest argument for them in the early 1950s. But economic and military factors do not adequately explain why the Europeans finally accepted a strategy that might endanger the survival of their societies and place their fate into the hands of the American president in certain contingencies.

If one attempts to explain why NATO went nuclear, certain political considerations deserve to be mentioned as well. After the failure of the EDC, the Europeans feared that the United States might follow through on its threats and adopt a peripheral strategy. That the settlement between the western powers and Germany was achieved within the institutional framework of NATO made it easier for the European nations to accommodate to the nuclear-oriented strategy outlined in MC-48. The coincidence of the European settlement and NATO nuclearization transformed the American commitment to the security of Europe into a more permanent feature of international politics. And the U.S. presence would help to contain historical animosities among the continental powers.

Why was the United States, on the other hand, prepared to reject a more aggressive foreign policy, accept limitations with regard to unilateral actions, and agree to a more permanent commitment for Europe (that is, no early redeployments)? The events of late 1954 satisfied two of the primary foreign policy goals of the Eisenhower administration. First, a rearmed Germany was integrated into the defense effort of the West without political disunity. Importantly, this augmented the pool of economic and military resources of the West. Second, increased reliance on nuclear weapons made a forward strategy an attainable goal in view of the military realities of 1954. For the first time since NATO's formation in 1949, a forward strategy seemed feasible.

However, with the failure of the EDC and the strengthening of NATO, early redeployment of U.S. ground troops in Europe was unlikely. Moreover, as the history of U.S. disarmament policy has shown, the United States increasingly felt the negative impact of an aggressive policy and was drawn toward a defensive strategy. Notably, preventive war was ruled out at the same time as these developments evolved. And the evidence shows that the decisions not to wage preventive war and to explore bona fide disarmament proposals were discussed within the Eisenhower administration in connection with its attempt to attain European acceptance of MC-48.

At the end of 1954, both the stabilizing and the destabilizing impacts of nuclear weapons found a delicate balance in the nuclearization of NATO and the integration of a rearmed Germany into the alliance. Why do I claim that the balance was delicate? NATO went nuclear precisely when the credibility of the nuclear deterrent was increasingly in doubt because of the growth of Soviet nuclear capabilities. The fundamental dilemma behind NATO's nuclearization was that evolving mutual vulnerability called into question the credibility of the nuclear foundation for the alliance's security. Did the fact that Western European security was based on the American nuclear guarantee not require nuclear weapons to do more than simply neutralize each other? Did it not demand that nuclear weapons influence political behavior in one way or another? This was the fundamental dilemma that became the driving force for the remainder of the 1950s. It exposed NATO and each of its members to serious tensions and fundamental choices.

Part II

Eisenhower and Evolving Mutual Vulnerability

5

Eisenhower's Approach: Buying Time with Tactical Nuclear Weapons

Since the conceptualization of the massive retaliation strategy, a growing group of critics had warned that in the face of increasing Soviet nuclear capabilities the concept would lose its credibility. In addition, with the onset of mutual deterrence, the strategy would invite limited attacks to test the will of the United States. The obvious conclusion, so the critics' argument ran, was to enlarge western conventional forces. Officials in the Eisenhower administration had been discussing the issue since 1953. However, the president had consistently refused to enlarge conventional forces.

In these early discussions regarding national security policy, the idea of compensating for Soviet conventional superiority with tactical nuclear weapons had played almost no role at all.[1] We have seen in chapter 4 that this argument developed some influence in connection with the nuclearization of NATO. In 1955, the Taiwan Strait crisis prompted even greater emphasis on tactical nuclear weapons in order to enhance the deterrent against Communist China. However, when it came to consideration of actually fighting a limited war, considerable skepticism about tactical employment of nuclear weapons prevailed through the middle of the decade. The allies in particular did not like the prospect of being defended by such weapons.

This reluctance to plan for the tactical employment of nuclear weapons changed in 1957, when the defense budget estimates grew because of additional costs for the missile development programs. During the early months of 1957, President Eisenhower decided to plan for the use of tactical nuclear weapons in any small war, even though the mostly younger members of the NSC Planning Board rejected this assumption.

Did Eisenhower stress reliance on tactical nuclear weapons simply to bypass a conventional buildup? Or was his decision also influenced by the belief that in a time of evolving mutual vulnerability, stability would arise from the realization that every war between the United States and the Soviet Union would involve the risk of mutual destruction, and, therefore, the conventional balance would not matter much beyond the sense of reassurance that it gave the allies?

Early Skepticism about Tactical Nuclear Warfare: NSC 5602/1

We have seen above, that there was division within the Eisenhower administration over whether procurement of conventional forces should be focused on preparation for general war or only for limited wars. In addition, it was often unclear whether either side in the debate was thinking in terms of deterrence or in terms of actually fighting a war. The same analytical ambiguity marked the debate over conventional capabilities through the middle of the decade.

In preparation for general war, the army still lobbied for additional conventional forces. At the beginning of 1955, Army chief of staff General Ridgway testified before the House Armed Services Committee that the proposed cuts in army personnel jeopardized U.S. security to a degree. Remarks of this sort fueled Democratic criticism that the administration was endangering U.S. security for fiscal reasons. The president was angered by Ridgway's statement. In a meeting with leading Republican congressmen, he exclaimed—while pounding the table—that he "was trying to talk sound sense," but General Ridgway was "talking theory." In a general war, nobody would think about shipping army divisions out of the country after it was hit by initial nuclear strikes. The reserve forces would be needed at home to restore order and get production going again. "What do you people think," the president asked with considerable heat, "would happen if this city were hit today by an H-bomb? Do you think you would vote or ask me to send the troops at Fort Meade overseas—or would you be knocking on my door to get me to bring them in to try to pick up the pieces here in Washington?"[2]

A year later, Ridgway's successor, General Maxwell D. Taylor, reminded the NSC of the fact that "approximately 40% of our ground forces would be fighting for their lives abroad while the air atomic war was going on."[3] However, increasingly the majority of the NSC perceived such statements as attempts by the army to get more money. The majority view, as espoused by Eisenhower himself, was that a general war would be a nuclear war.

The Impact of the Taiwan Strait Crisis

It was the Taiwan Strait crisis that triggered interest in the issue of how to deter and how to fight limited wars at the turn of the year from 1954 to 1955. Tensions between Communist China and the Nationalist Chinese in Taiwan had turned hot when the Communists started to shell the Nationalist-held islands in the Taiwan Strait at the beginning of September 1954. When Secretary Dulles met with the president in order to discuss the situation, Dulles raised the issue of "little wars." The secretary wondered whether the JCS were planning to deal with such wars "which might call for punishment related to the degree and the locality of the offense but which would not justify a massive retaliation against the Soviet Union itself."[4]

In a series of meetings in March 1955, the president and Secretary Dulles decided that the best policy would be to threaten the Chinese Communists with the tactical employment of nuclear weapons. Eisenhower and Dulles were firmly convinced that neither the Soviet Union nor China wanted a general war. Furthermore, the president made sure that the military understood that the United States did not want to actually use nuclear weapons—the essence of the undertaking would be to raise the pressure on the enemy. As part of an exercise in crisis bargaining, President Eisenhower and Secretary Dulles emphasized "the distinction between atomic missiles for tactical purposes and the big bomb with huge radio-active fallouts." The president proposed that Dulles include in his speech about his trip to Southeast Asia a paragraph "indicating that we would use atomic weapons as interchangeable with the conventional weapons."[5]

In a radio and television address on 8 March, the secretary told the American people and the world that the United States had "sea and air forces equipped with new and powerful weapons of precision which can utterly destroy military targets without endangering unrelated civilian centers."[6] A few days later, he elaborated on the issue in a press conference by expounding a policy of "less-than-massive retaliation" that was based on the use of small nuclear weapons against military targets rather than full-scale, city-destroying hydrogen bombs.[7] In short, the Taiwan Strait crisis exposed the weakness of massive retaliation for the deterrence of limited aggressions, prompting reliance on tactical nuclear weapons as a deterrent to limited aggression.[8]

Debating Basic National Security Policy

The fight over conventional force procurement during 1955 shaped the annual review of basic national security policy. Differences in opinion produced a national security policy paper that left all options open.

Secretary Dulles and the State Department, on the one hand, still emphasized deterrence. In a speech on 8 December, Dulles pointed out that the "essential thing is that a potential aggressor should know in advance that he can and will be made to suffer for his aggression more than he can possibly gain by it." To deter all forms of aggression, the capacity of massive retaliation was central. However, he now added to the message the doctrine of "less-than-massive retaliation" and noted that "the free world must have the means for responding effectively on a selective basis when it chooses. It must not put itself in the position where the only response open to it is general war."⁹ Since his speech before the Council on Foreign Relations in January 1954, Dulles had learned that in a time of thermonuclear weapons, the threat of massive retaliation alone would not deter. The threat had to fit the crime in order to be credible and supported by the allies.

The position of Dulles and the State Department rested on the premise that the main problems of the Cold War had started "to shift from safeguards against imminent aggression to preparations for long-term competition."¹⁰ Since early 1955, the Soviet leaders had made a series of conciliatory gestures: They had signed an Austrian peace treaty, accepted some important aspects of the western disarmament position, reduced the hostility of their propaganda, and substantially increased contacts with the West. The Soviet Union obviously felt overextended and had come to realize the horror of an atomic war.¹¹ The State Department anticipated prolonged negotiations with the Soviet Union. In the future, it would be primarily *political* leadership rather than military and strategic leadership that counted. And in this regard, the trend with respect to the strategic balance would not help the United States.

Dulles wrote to the president that as Soviet nuclear power grew, the U.S. retaliatory capability would lose its deterrent influence. "Repugnance to the use of nuclear weapons," he added, "could grow to a point which would depreciate our value as an ally, undermine confidence in our 'collective defense' concept, and make questionable the reliability of our allies and the availability to the SAC of our foreign bases." Moreover, Dulles went on, U.S. moral leadership would be challenged as well. The "Atoms for Peace" proposal had lost a lot of its popular influence. In this "vacuum," the secretary pointed out, the Soviets had moved with their proposals to "ban the bomb." The result was that "the great masses feel that at least the Russians *want* to end the thermonuclear danger while we are represented as stalling and trying to think up good reasons for perpetuating the danger and making it even greater."[12]

Against this background, Dulles and Robert Bowie fought with increased vehemence for greater procurement of conventional forces and against a policy of automatic employment of nuclear weapons in response to any hostilities.[13] These new emphases brought Dulles and Bowie into repeated conflict with the president. One of the first of these exchanges came when a small group of top officials was briefed on the new report of the Net Evaluation Subcommittee.[14] The president summarized the report's conclusion in his diary: A nuclear war between Russia and the United States on the hypothetical date of 1 July 1956 would lead practically to a total collapse of U.S. economy. Moreover, "on the order of 65% of the population would require some kind of medical care" most of them with no opportunity whatsoever to get it. Damage inflicted against the Soviets would be roughly three times greater. Eisenhower concluded that it "would literally be a business of digging ourselves out of ashes, starting again."[15]

During the meeting, Eisenhower expressed the view that "both sides would increasingly tend to avoid provoking such a situation as that played out in the war games." The Soviets would conduct similar exercises and they simply had to be given "credit for having some sense." None of the other participants doubted that the available capabilities provided a deterrent against all-out thermonuclear warfare, but some feared the increasing probability of peripheral wars. However, the president "was all the more convinced that we could not prepare for little wars at great distances from the United States, and commit several divisions here and several divisions there to resistance against local aggression. Rather, we should trust, he felt, to the kind of major deterrent that the prospect of strategic thermonuclear war would bring." Dulles replied that this approach "might be OK for us but that the people in these little countries who are friends of ours will continue to want to know what will happen if they are attacked." The president responded that these little countries would have to defend themselves on the ground, and the United States would only send in air, naval, and other mobile support.[16]

The same point came up again during the discussion of basic national security policy in the NSC meeting of 27 February 1956. President Eisenhower stated that the United States "must now plan to fight peripheral wars on the same basis as we would fight a general war." He asked rhetorically: "Had we not made up our minds that if the Communists renewed their aggression against Korea we would go 'all out' to meet it?" Again the secretary of state replied. He inquired what the United States would do if the Vietminh undertook to attack South Vietnam. "Would we proceed," he asked, "to drop atomic bombs on Peking?" The president answered that the United States might not drop bombs on Peking, but it would certainly "bomb the bases in China which were supporting the aggression."[17] In short, the president stubbornly resisted enlarging conventional forces for either general or limited wars.

The Department of Defense and the JCS, on the other hand, were not impressed by the conciliatory policy of the Soviet Union. On the contrary, the JCS felt strongly "that there has been a marked deterioration of the Free World position in the past year, due mainly to a new and more flexible approach on the part of the Communist Bloc."[18] They perceived a feeling throughout the world that the United States lacked the essential determination to carry through on its threats in time of crisis. With this, they noted, the danger of war—even general war—by miscalculation on the part of the Soviets increased considerably.[19] Against the background of this unfavorable analysis, the JCS called for a definite decision to use nuclear weapons in any hostilities "when the effectiveness of the operation of the U.S. forces employed will be enhanced thereby."[20] They were supported by Secretary Humphrey, who warned that absent a clear decision on this point the individual services would be able to protect their appropriations.[21] However, the president stressed that the United States could not ignore the political factors involved. He rejected the analysis of the JCS as too negative and called for a new report.[22]

The president was prepared neither to build up conventional forces nor to relinquish the power to launch nuclear weapons. The resulting basic national security policy paper, NSC 5602/1, reflected these wishes. Apart from this, the proposed language of the JCS prevailed on the question of preparation for a general war. The paragraph regarding limited wars, on the other hand, was very close to the proposal of the State Department.[23] NSC 5602/1 (which was approved on 15 March 1956) stated that it was the policy of the United States to integrate nuclear weapons with conventional weapons: "Nuclear weapons will be used in general war and in military operations short of general war as authorized by the President." The decision as to the employment of nuclear weapons clearly remained in the hands of the president.

With respect to limited war, the policy paper attempted to specify for the first time since the formulation of the New Look minimal requirements for conventional forces. NSC 5602/1 stated that within "the total U.S. military forces there must be included ready forces which, with such help as may realistically be expected from allied forces, are adequate a) to present a deterrent to any resort to local aggression, and b) to defeat or hold, in conjunction with indigenous forces, any such local aggression, pending the application of such additional U.S. and allied power as may be required to suppress quickly the local aggression in a manner and on a scale best calculated to avoid the hostilities broadening into general war." These ready forces should be "sufficiently versatile to use both conventional and nuclear weapons." Moreover, although these forces would need to have a flexible and selective nuclear capability, they should not become "so dependent on tactical nuclear capabilities that any decision to intervene against local aggression would probably be tantamount to a decision to use nuclear weapons." If the U.S. deterrent forces could adapt to both conventional and nuclear use, the "apprehensions of U.S. allies as to using nuclear weapons to counter local aggression can be lessened . . . thus avoiding the question of their use unless and until the deterrent fails."[24]

NSC 5602/1 shows that considerable skepticism about tactical nuclear warfare prevailed during the middle of the decade. Before summarizing the arguments against tactical nuclear weapons, I will outline the arguments for them. First, tactical nuclear weapons were cheap compared with conventional forces. Although this factor could not be overlooked by anybody, it made a particularly strong impression on those who valued a sound economy. Second, the United States possessed clear superiority in this category of weapon. Given the reluctance to build up and commit further conventional forces, tactical nuclear weapons offered the only response to limited Soviet aggressions. This line of thinking was prevalent in the Defense Department. Admiral Radford once said that "the idea of some dividing line between use and non-use of these weapons was getting us further and further from the realm of the possible and the actual."[25] And third, although the State Department was skeptical about actually using tactical nuclear weapons, Secretary Dulles had publicly threatened to use them in order to enlarge deterrence during the Taiwan Strait crisis.

On the other hand, the following three factors worked against tactical nuclear weapons. First, the people who were to be defended by their use did not like a strategy that would turn their countries into battlefields of tactical nuclear warfare. Allied opposition to the use of such weapons could lead to neutralism, thereby seriously weakening the cohesion of

the western alliances. Second, people feared that tactical nuclear warfare would get out of control and lead to general war. The danger of
escalation, like allied opposition, heavily influenced the thinking in the
State Department. Third, the president was not prepared to predelegate
authority to use any nuclear weapons. On balance, the factors against
tactical nuclear weapons outweighed the arguments for them.

High Tide for Tactical Nuclear Weapons: NSC 5707/8

The problem with the ambiguous language of NSC 5602/1 became obvious when the NSC discussed the defense budgets for fiscal year 1956
and fiscal year 1957. Secretary Wilson had the unfortunate job of informing the council that defense expenditures for the coming two years
could not be kept down to the levels estimated earlier. Furthermore, the
prospect for 1958, 1959, and 1960 was one of increasing defense budgets. In the missile age *both* bombers and missiles had to be developed.
On the other hand, neither U.S. commitments nor U.S. troop deployments abroad had diminished. This made it hard, Secretary Wilson emphasized, "to criticize the military requirements for carrying out these
commitments."[26]

The president was shocked at the prospect of such defense expenditures and noted that he had "nearly fainted when General Taylor, able
as he was, had suggested to him that the size of the Army should now be
increased to 28 divisions in view of the worldwide commitments." It was
the president's view that the security of the United States was "essentially
based on the aircraft and on the capability to deliver the bomb." Secretary Humphrey agreed with the president's concern for a healthy economy. Picking up the argument of Secretary Wilson, Humphrey
expressed great dissatisfaction with the present deployment of U.S.
forces overseas: "He pointed out that we had actually failed to live up to
the new-look strategy which the Administration had agreed upon shortly
after the new Administration had taken office." Redeployment was one
obvious possible response to the prospect of dangerously growing defense expenditures. However, the president remained opposed to following through on redeployment at the time and restated his earlier
view "that if we took our forces out of Europe today we would lose that
continent."

Admiral Radford then pointed out that the fiscal dilemma could be
eased by defining with certainty how nuclear weapons would be used in
any future war: "If the situation as to the use of such weapons remains

fuzzy," he warned, "the expense of maintaining the production of conventional weapons will continue to be saddled upon us."[27] He raised the issue again in a meeting between the JCS and the president on 30 March. President Eisenhower was very careful in his reply and stated only that the United States would use nuclear weapons in a direct war with the Soviets.[28] In a private talk between Radford and Eisenhower six weeks later, the chairman of the JCS came back to the issue. He warned the president that if the planners assumed that nuclear weapons would not be used in *small* wars, the way would then be "left open for a building up of service requirements." The president replied that "he was inclined to feel that we would not get involved in a 'small war' extending beyond a few Marine battalions or Army units. If it grew to anything like Korea proportions, the action would become one for use of atomic weapons." Participation in small wars would be primarily a matter of navy and air.[29]

Redeployments and Tactical Nuclear Weapons

During the congressional hearings on the defense budget for fiscal year 1957, interservice tensions and rivalries were becoming public—very much to the annoyance of the president.[30] Although such bureaucratic battles were partly inherent in an era of a quickly changing strategic environment and changing service roles due to technological developments, the ambiguous language of NSC 5602/1 added fuel to these quarrels. The mounting tension called for a clear decision on whether to secure a sound economy through redeployment or increased emphasis on tactical nuclear weapons.

On the one hand, redeployment of U.S. overseas forces was desirable from a military point of view, due to developments in nuclear weapons and delivery systems technology. The Soviets seemed to take account of these developments when they announced a reduction of their ground forces by 1.2 million men.[31] In addition, the Soviets now seemed sufficiently committed to policies of nonviolence as to allow for some reductions in U.S. overseas forces.[32] On the other hand, redeploying overseas forces was politically impossible because of the negative effect it would have on the cohesion of U.S. alliances. The solution of the Eisenhower administration was "streamlining." On 12 August, in a White House meeting with the Dulles brothers, Admiral Radford, General Alfred M. Gruenther, and some other advisers, President Eisenhower discussed American force levels in Europe. He decided that the units should be reduced in size by phasing out overhead and support elements. The new divisions should remain equal in strength due to increased firepower as a result of the integration of tactical nuclear weapons.[33]

During the summer of 1956, the army began to adapt the divisional organization to the atomic battlefield. Eisenhower was convinced that the adoption of these new divisions would make overall personnel reductions possible. He decided that there should be no publicity about these changes; specifically, no emphasis should be given to the placing of atomic weapons in the new divisions.[34] In short, "streamlining" U.S. overseas forces allowed the Eisenhower administration to make some savings without paying the political price of having to reduce NATO military force levels.

The questions of redeployment and the use of tactical nuclear weapons in limited wars were obviously connected. Because sizable redeployments were not feasible, emphasis shifted to the quick integration of tactical nuclear weapons. The army did not like the decision, and generals argued that emphasis on tactical nuclear weapons for all kinds of war actually contradicted the principle of flexibility set forth in NSC 5602/1. General Taylor presented the army's case to the president. The meeting deserves close attention because the army chief of staff made a strong argument, which elicited a sharp reply from the president.

General Taylor began by noting that during the discussion of the Joint Strategic Objectives Plan (JSOP) for 1960, the air force, the navy, and Admiral Radford had taken the view that all planning must be based upon the use of nuclear weapons.[35] The army and the Marine Corps, on the other hand, thought this premise to be contrary to NSC 5602/1, according to which a general war was envisioned as growing step by step from smaller action. Toward the end of the 1950s, General Taylor pointed out, a situation had to be envisaged where both sides would be deterred from deliberately starting a big war. It seemed to him that in such a situation, any war that occurred would be a small war. And the very nonnuclear forces that would be needed to fight such wars would be missing, because "programs for fighting a big war would absorb all available funds."

To this strong summary of the arguments, the president firmly replied that, regarding general war, he did not see any basis for believing that the opponent would refrain from using nuclear weapons at once and without restraint. Even if more divisions were available, it was unlikely that they could be moved during the early months of an atomic war. As to local wars, President Eisenhower emphasized that "over the past several years tactical atomic weapons have come to be practically accepted as integral parts of modern armed forces." He added that the tactical use of atomic weapons against military targets would not be more likely to lead to a big war than the use of some of the advanced conventional weapons. The president made clear that "planning should go ahead on the basis of the use of tactical atomic weapons against military targets in any small war in which the United States might be involved."

However, when Admiral Radford tried to take advantage of the situation and proposed telling the allies about modifications in support forces, President Eisenhower grew noncommittal. These changes could be implemented gradually.[36] Eisenhower refused to inform the allies, because he knew very well that allied countries "do not wish to be defended by nuclear weapons. They all regard these weapons as essentially offensive in character, and our allies are absolutely scared to death that we will use such weapons."[37] President Eisenhower was interested in the integration of tactical nuclear weapons not so much because of military and strategic considerations, but because it would justify some overall reductions of U.S. conventional forces in order to control defense expenditures.

Developments within NATO

In order to fully understand why President Eisenhower remained reluctant to implement the New Look, redeploying U.S. overseas forces and putting tactical nuclear weapons in their place, it is important to take a closer look at the events that were bringing NATO to the point of cracking during the summer of 1956. Shortly after Nikita Khrushchev held his de-Stalinization speech at the Twentieth Party Congress in February, Khrushchev and his minister of defense, Nikolay Aleksandrovich Bulganin, visited the United Kingdom. British ambassador Sir Roger M. Makins reported to Secretary Dulles that the Soviets were considering a unilateral troop reduction on the order of one million men. He noted that his government had the general impression that the likelihood of war was much reduced.[38]

The upcoming ministerial meeting of the NAC on 4 and 5 May in Paris provided the opportunity to discuss the consequences of the Soviet initiative. Most of the members of the NAC agreed with the analysis of British secretary of state John Selwyn Brooke Lloyd that the objective of Communist world domination remained the same, but that the new leadership had changed its tactics. The Soviets, Lloyd stressed, did not want war and would not risk war anymore. Their new tactic, he pointed out, was massive penetration, particularly of underdeveloped countries, by economic, technical, and cultural means. Secretary Dulles added that the new tactics were designed not only to dominate the newly independent nations, but also to disrupt the unity of the West.[39] Consequently, the threat to NATO was shifting from the military field to the political field. NATO had to retain its military strength, but it also had to strengthen its economic and political ties. The NAC agreed to set up a committee of "Three Wise Men," consisting of the Canadian, Norwegian, and Italian foreign ministers, to study what could be done in these fields to enhance unity within the Atlantic community.[40]

Reporting to the NSC about the meeting, Secretary Dulles was not very optimistic about the chances for greater unity within the alliance. How would its members react if the Soviets in fact went ahead with their troop reductions? During the meeting, the British had indicated that they might have to respond by reducing their forces. And, in fact, in the middle of June, the British proposed an early NAC meeting to issue a new directive to the NATO military authorities to review NATO strategy.[41]

In a letter to President Eisenhower, British prime minister Anthony Eden pointed out that since the development of thermonuclear weapons a condition of mutual deterrence was evolving. In this new strategic situation, he added, it would become increasingly difficult to justify the sacrifices required for the maintenance of large conventional forces. The British government, therefore, was of the opinion that the conventional forces stationed in Germany should be reduced. NATO would need shield forces, but it would not need the capability to fight a major land battle. Their primary military function, the British prime minister wrote, "seems now to be to deal with any local infiltration, to prevent external intimidation and to enable aggression to be identified as such."[42] The British were quick to add to this analysis of the situation that news stories indicated that the U.S. government, too, was seeking a major cut in its troop levels.[43]

President Eisenhower's initial reaction to Soviet troop reductions was that the Soviets would simply be imitating the New Look. However, Secretary Dulles warned that the Soviet announcement would weaken the cohesion of the alliance. Dulles warned that the Soviet move "would be focused on the German situation with the objective of upsetting Chancellor Adenauer's rearmament program." Moreover, he informed the NSC "of the widespread inclination among our NATO allies to downgrade in importance the role of the NATO ground forces because of their conviction that, at least in the initial phases of a future general war, the role of air atomic power would be crucial and ground forces would not have a very important part."[44] The fact that the NATO allies did not have nuclear armaments of their own contributed to the general feeling of discouragement. Hence, the Eisenhower administration was very reluctant to agree to an early NAC meeting.[45]

But at this point, events in the Middle East took center stage, and a definite answer from the United States would have to wait. While the "Three Wise Men" were formulating recommendations for coordinating NATO policies, the Suez crisis was creating a major rift through the alliance. On 26 July, the Egyptian government nationalized the Suez Canal Company. The fact that the British referred the dispute to the UN and fought with France against Egypt without informing the United States exposed NATO to considerable strain.[46]

Only in October did the anger and mistrust begin to calm. Meanwhile, the Eisenhower administration was in the middle of streamlining its own conventional forces. But it had reassured Germany that it had no intention of withdrawing U.S. forces from German soil.[47] Against this background, the Eisenhower administration had to formulate its answer to the British proposal for a new NATO political directive. The president had to make his decision despite a severe split between the Departments of Defense and State. The Defense Department recommended a sizable reduction not only of U.S. support forces but also of U.S. combat divisions in Germany. In a meeting with the president, Admiral Radford stated flatly that the British "were simply adopting the new look, which we had already adopted." Secretary Dulles replied "that it was one thing for us to rely on the new look, not being subject to insurrectionary or conventional attack as the Europeans are, and it is something else to propose it for the Europeans."[48] Finally, President Eisenhower decided that the United States could not take any divisions out of Europe for the time being. The effect on the German chancellor Konrad Adenauer and the German rearmament program would be too damaging.

The memorandum that was handed to the British on 12 October noted that the United States had no present plan to withdraw divisions from Europe and was only streamlining its force without weakening the defensive strength of NATO. Moreover, the memorandum explained the American opposition to a NATO strategy of total reliance on nuclear retaliation. It stated that the maintenance of effective shield forces, including conventional ground forces, was important to preserve flexibility. Finally, the memorandum set out the U.S. view on the future of NATO defense by introducing the "fair share" concept. Because of the increasing costs of maintaining the nuclear deterrent, the financial burden on the United States was growing asymmetrically compared with the burden on the Europeans. Eisenhower thought it fair that the Europeans assume greater responsibility for the conventional shield forces of NATO.[49]

The British, however, did not alter their draft proposal for a new NATO political directive and presented it to the NAC on 19 October.[50] The ministerial meeting of the NAC, which was held in Paris, promised to be very important.[51] In Paris, the Americans found themselves in the somewhat unexpected position of arguing in favor of conventional shield forces. The Europeans, on the other hand, had modified their earlier skepticism toward tactical nuclear weapons and were arguing for their integration down to the divisional level.[52] The principal question in this new setting was whether the United States was prepared to help the Europeans out with tactical nuclear weapons. This became clear in bilateral talks between the United Kingdom and the United States, which were held during the meeting. In order to solve their financial problems, the British were prepared to accept integration of tactical nuclear weapons. However, they would need atomic weapons from the United States to make their reduced forces the equivalent of their existing forces.[53]

This overview of the development of NATO politics during the summer of 1956 helps us better understand why President Eisenhower remained reluctant to redeploy U.S. overseas forces. Financial difficulties and the changing nature of the Soviet threat convinced the Europeans that they had to accept the integration of tactical nuclear weapons in NATO strategy and force posture. However, they still feared becoming wholly dependent on nuclear weapons. This was the very dilemma that had faced the U.S. government for the previous several years.

Debating Basic National Security Policy

In 1956, President Eisenhower managed to keep the growth of the defense budget within limits. The increasing costs of the missile development programs were countered by savings due mainly to the reorganization of the army into smaller divisional units. But below the surface, tensions within the defense community were growing. They had not yet reached the breaking point when the NSC began discussing the military program for fiscal year 1958. The differences in opinion, which in most cases went back to the initial positions taken in 1953, were evident during the debate of the threat that the nation was facing.

Admiral Radford said that though he valued a sound economy very highly, he felt compelled to point out the risks involved in increasing tensions within Soviet satellite states and in situations such as the Suez crisis. President Eisenhower, on the other hand, held firmly to the view that in his opinion the likelihood of war was not increasing. On the contrary, he added, in reference to the Hungarian uprising of 1956, "the USSR had taken a worse beating lately than at any time since 1945." While the secretary of state agreed with the president's view that the position of the Soviet Union had deteriorated dramatically, he was not sure whether or not this would reduce the risk of war. As he had warned the NATO allies only a few days earlier, he now pointed out to the NSC that the unfortunate course of events might result in a terrific effort by the Kremlin to achieve some kind of offsetting success: "To achieve this," he added, "the Soviets might therefore be willing to take risks which could be very dangerous to the free world, since they would be risks born of desperation."[54] Clearly, Dulles was implying that under this new condition the risk of limited aggression might increase.[55] The problem of how to deter and fight local wars had not yet been solved.

The different views within the Eisenhower administration regarding the future of the nation's national security posture clashed with the review of basic national security policy (as stated in NSC 5602/1) beginning in February 1957. This time, the split in opinion occurred essentially along generational lines, rather than departmental lines. Different views were represented by, on the one hand, the younger men of the NSC Planning Board and, on the other hand, the older men of the NSC, represented by the president, Secretary Dulles, and Secretary Humphrey.

On the occasion of an NSC meeting on 28 February 1957, Robert Cutler presented the first draft of a reviewed policy paper (NSC 5707), consisting of seven major problems identified by the planning board. The first issue proved to be the most controversial. Cutler summarized the planning board's view that increasing nuclear capabilities of the United States and the Soviet Union tended, on the one hand, "to create a deterrent to general war. On the other hand, the increasing capabilities enhanced the risk of local conflict and of general war through miscalculation." It was the view of the planning board that this problem would seriously endanger U.S. alliances, because allies would become increasingly susceptible to Soviet threats. The question was whether the United States possessed the means to defend against local aggression.

Simply asking this question was heresy to the ears of the older men of the NSC. Dulles was quick to point out that the statement "ran contrary to the entire basic strategy of the United States." He felt (and so did the president) that "our policy should be that our friends and allies supply the means for local defense on the ground and that the United States should come into the act with air and naval forces alone." The deterrence of local aggression depended, for example, on an effective German army in Western Europe and similar effective forces of U.S. allies elsewhere in the world. Both the president and the secretary of state commented that one notable fallacy underlying the statement of the planning board was the assumption that any war in which nuclear weapons were used would necessarily develop into a general nuclear war. President Eisenhower played down the danger of escalation by indicating that the United States now possessed tactical nuclear weapons that "would create only one-twentieth of the damage wrought on Tokyo by the fire bomb raids of 1945." Secretary Humphrey added that the planning board's statement was purely theoretical. Three times this administration had faced the possibility of local war: in Korea, Indochina, and Taiwan. "In each case," Humphrey explained, "when the chips were finally down, the military people came in and said that we could not undertake to fight such a war without the use of nuclear weapons." These examples, in his view, clearly demonstrated that the United States had crossed a bridge in the matter of the use of nuclear weapons.

Robert Cutler then turned to the second question—the continued decline in the power of Western Europe. The decline had been emphasized by the Franco-British failure in the Suez crisis. Western Europe's decline could result in a greater need for U.S. support. In the eyes of Secretary Dulles, however, "there was now for the first time a real prospect that the position of Western Europe was definitely improving," given the move toward European unification. For Secretary Dulles, the Anglo-French debacle in the Suez crisis exposed not military weakness, but rather moral weakness. The president again agreed with Dulles's analysis. In answer to a more skeptical assessment of the speed of European integration by Governor Harold E. Stassen, he predicted that if the European integration did not happen "the Western European nations would perish in spite of anything the United States could do to help them."[56]

Through March and April, the planning board revised its draft and produced a paper that called essentially for the continuation of existing national security strategy.[57] With respect to the question of local wars, this meant that the NSC again had to deal with the ambiguous language of NSC 5602/1. On 11 April 1957, the council addressed the matter again. Admiral Radford explained that the JCS were in fact already engaged "in carrying out a policy that, in any action in which U.S. forces were involved, we would make use of nuclear weapons if it proved necessary." Accordingly, he now called for a clearly written directive, taking account of that fact, which would avoid the confusion of earlier basic national security papers.

While Robert Cutler tried to defend the language proposed by the planning board, President Eisenhower firmly supported Admiral Radford. The current revision, Eisenhower noted, offered a chance "to see to it that from now on our basic policy gets into line with the planning which had been going on in the Department of Defense for over two years." The president decided that "he would very much like to see a draft of a revised statement of the military elements of our national strategy as written in the Defense Department." In the absence of the secretary of state, Cutler noted that the Department of State had a certain interest in this policy area as well and "that Secretary Dulles felt that the U.S. still needed a considerable degree of flexibility in the weaponry of our armed forces." But the president had made up his mind. He stated "very clearly his opinion that we had now reached a point in time when our main reliance, though not our sole reliance, should be on nuclear weapons."[58]

What the president was advocating during this meeting is quite remarkable: The formulation of basic policy was to follow actual planning in the Defense Department. President Eisenhower simply suppressed further discussion of the issue of how to deter and fight local wars.[59] Secretary Dulles was caught in the middle of the turmoil that the president's decision must have caused in the State Department. When the NSC discussed the proposed language of the Defense Department in its meeting on 27 May 1957, Robert Cutler began by pointing out the view of the State Department on the issue. State was of the opinion that in order to fulfill the nation's political purposes, U.S. military strategy for dealing with limited hostilities had to provide the president with options "to choose the appropriate means (including choice as to nuclear or nonnuclear weapons) for responding to limited hostilities in the light of the actual political and military circumstances." Military strategy for limited wars had to limit the risk of escalation into general war and take account of allied sensibilities.[60]

Robert Cutler then called on Secretary Dulles to speak on the issue. Dulles said "that he believed he accepted as fully as anyone present, and certainly more fully than any of his State Department colleagues, the inevitability of the general use of nuclear power as conventional."[61] However, he added, this was not the time to go as far as the language suggested by the Defense Department.[62] On the one hand, he went on, "our so-called 'little bang weapons' are actually of the type which produced such sensational results at Hiroshima." On the other hand, the concept of selectivity simply could not be disregarded. Whereas NSC 5602/1 had emphasized that the United States should be prepared to make use of *force* selectively, the revised language would say that the United States will use *atomic weapons* selectively. Secretary Dulles doubted "that we were yet ready and prepared to exercise a selective nuclear capability."

Admiral Lewis L. Strauss, the chairman of the AEC, interrupted to reply that the United States was now developing nuclear weapons "which were approximately 10%, or even 5%, of the size of the weapon used at Nagasaki." Secretary Dulles answered that if this was so, it would be extremely important that the NSC be kept informed. Changing the focus of his argument, he added that U.S. allies did not realize that the United States possessed such a capability. And until they were convinced of this, a revision of basic policy along the lines of the proposed language would be very dangerous.[63] Admiral Radford and Secretary Wilson replied that NSC 5707/7 was a secret policy paper, which was supposed to be forward looking. They both stressed that the existing language of NSC 5602/1 was just too ambiguous to be useful for planning purposes and would leave the Department of Defense to develop two very costly strategies.

Eisenhower ultimately settled the issue. It was the opinion of the president that use of force should be selective and flexible only with respect "to conflicts occurring in less developed areas of the world." He justified his recommendation by pointing out "that military action in Berlin could not be kept local in character; nor, probably could military action in the Near East. Limited wars could really only be limited in underdeveloped areas."[64]

NSC 5707/8, which was approved by the president on 3 June 1957, followed the president's recommendation. The paper emphasized greater reliance on nuclear weapons as follows: "It is the policy of the United States to place main, but not sole, reliance on nuclear weapons; to integrate nuclear weapons with other weapons in the arsenal of the United States; to consider them as conventional weapons from a military point of view; and to use them when required to achieve national objectives." The paper dealt with local aggression as a distinct issue only with regard to conflicts occurring in less developed areas of the world, where limited U.S. forces would participate, because U.S. interests were involved. In such cases, "military planning for U.S. forces to oppose local aggression will be based on the development of a flexible and selective capability, including nuclear capability for use as authorized by the President. When the use of U.S. forces is required to oppose local aggression, force will be applied in a manner and on a scale best calculated to avoid hostilities from broadening into general war."[65]

Although it seems that considerable doubts about the availability of small nuclear warheads persisted, Dulles and the State Department did not oppose the new basic national security policy.[66] When the secretary of state addressed the annual Department of Defense Secretaries' Conference in June, he acknowledged that massive retaliation, "which has served us so well and which will continue to serve us well, has certain weaknesses which have become increasingly apparent during the last two or three years as the Soviet Union as well as we have developed the increasingly massive destructive capability of nuclear weapons." Citing the adage that "the punishment should fit the crime," Secretary Dulles noted that as destructive capability increased, the credibility of the threat to retaliate massively in response to any aggression anywhere had diminished. Fortunately, Dulles continued, the United States was gradually developing small-yield nuclear weapons to counter the threat of "nibbling operations" by the Soviet Union. He hoped that these new possibilities would provide adequate deterrence and adequate defense without destroying "the economic foundation which is one of the indispensable requisites of a vigorous and free society."[67]

The adoption of NSC 5707/8, with its emphasis on nuclear weapons, renewed the question of redeployment.[68] Would the integration of tactical nuclear weapons allow the United States to use smaller conventional forces in limited wars? Following the guidance of the basic national security policy paper, the Defense Department proposed a military program for fiscal year 1958 and fiscal year 1959, based on a budget ceiling of $39 billion. A first draft presented by Secretary Wilson to the president in a memorandum of 10 July, made clear that a balanced military program could be maintained only through massive reductions in the personnel strengths of the military services.[69] What was called for was the application of the New Look to the U.S. defense effort overseas.[70]

However, the precarious state of the peace in Korea, and upcoming elections in Germany would make U.S. force reductions politically untenable.[71] And the services themselves believed that the force levels outlined in Secretary Wilson's memorandum would be militarily untenable. When the military program for fiscal year 1958 and fiscal year 1959 was discussed in the NSC, Admiral Radford again explained that the plan "was an extension of the New Look of 1953 brought up to date."[72] While the president pointed out that reductions had to be made somewhere in order to free up funds for missile development, Secretary Dulles gave notice of the State Department's reservations regarding redeployment. The dilemma was familiar to everyone, and so was the solution with respect to the reductions for fiscal year 1958. The State Department, finally, agreed to the proposed troop reductions, because they could be accomplished without redeployment of combat units from Europe.[73] Once more, the tough decision of whether to redeploy was pushed into the future; but it had become clear that reductions for fiscal year 1959 would bring this process to an end. Then, the launch of the Soviet satellite *Sputnik* on 4 October 1957 thoroughly reshaped the strategic environment for the remainder of the 1950s and forced the Eisenhower administration to shift course dramatically. The consequences of the *Sputnik* launch will be discussed in chapter 6.

In 1957, the earlier skepticism about tactical nuclear warfare had eroded to a considerable degree. Why did Eisenhower decide to place greater reliance on nuclear weapons against the advice of the younger men on the planning board? The explanation is a complex mix of political, economic, technological, and strategic considerations. First, in 1957 there was no acute crisis, like the Taiwan Strait conflict in 1954–55, to focus attention on the problems and risks involved in a decision to use tactical nuclear weapons in local wars. Second, allied reluctance to support further integration of nuclear weapons into NATO strategy had eased, due to fiscal problems in the allied countries. Third, the economic problems of the United States had become more pressing due to the additional costs for the development of missiles. The principal question was how to offset the costs of these new weapons systems. Fourth, the growing availability of small nuclear warheads allowed the president and Secretary Dulles to downplay the danger of escalation inherent in a decision to use tactical nuclear weapons, although doubts regarding the danger of escalation persisted, particularly within the Department of State. Finally, the case for greater integration of tactical nuclear weapons was aided by the perception that the Soviet threat was on the decline.

Whereas fiscal considerations played their role in the process leading to greater emphasis on tactical nuclear weapons, Eisenhower pulled into such a direction not simply because he was not prepared to pay for an increase in conventional forces. On a more fundamental level, the president doubted that the Soviets would take a risky course of action. Because Eisenhower thought that every conflict between the United States and the Soviet Union would escalate quickly to the level of nuclear war, he did not think that local aggression would become more probable. It was on this point that Dulles and others disagreed with the president. Dulles believed that the weakening of the Soviet Union increased the probability of taking the risk of initiating local aggression. Eisenhower recognized the merit in the latter position. Therefore, he decided not to redeploy overseas forces so as to avoid sending the wrong signals to allies and enemies.[74]

Eisenhower's confidence that limited aggression and the risk of miscalculation had not become more likely was based on an understanding that the nature of conflict was changing in an environment of mutual vulnerability. We have seen that in the first half of the decade, U.S. leaders expected mutual vulnerability to be highly destabilizing. In June 1954, the president himself feared that once both sides had "enough" nuclear weapons the advantage of surprise would become decisive.[75] However, his view on this point had changed over the years. When the NSC discussed U.S. arms control policy in connection with its review of basic national security policy in April 1957, the president took issue with the assumption that there would be no security for either the United States or the Soviet Union if both nations kept building up their nuclear capabilities. President Eisenhower believed that the United States would be secure "for the good and sufficient reason that each side would realize the folly of resorting to a course of action in the shape of nuclear general war in which each country would be completely destroyed." This, he explained, was "the security of the stalemate."[76]

The president was strengthened in his view by the results of the annual report of the Net Evaluation Subcommittee. In 1957, the NESC reached the conclusion that "in 1959 the USSR will have the net capability of delivering a nuclear attack which could kill approximately 40% of the U.S. population, seriously injure another 13%, and disrupt the political, social, and economic structure of the United States." In 1959, a nuclear war initiated by the Soviet Union would result in mutual devastation, and "neither side could expect to destroy the nuclear capability of the other or to be able to defend itself adequately against nuclear attack."[77] The president concluded from these calculations that the United States should concentrate on producing a strategic nuclear force that was so big and so well distributed that the Soviets would not attack the United States or any U.S. allies.[78]

In early 1953, Robert Oppenheimer and Vannevar Bush had wondered whether a situation of mutual atomic plenty might give rise to stability, due to the general understanding that it would be suicidal to "throw the switch," or whether the world would end in nuclear disaster, because one side might be tempted by the advantage of attacking first.[79] By 1957, Eisenhower believed that mutual vulnerability had become a formula for stability. Both sides now seemed to have all the deterrence power they needed. Would mutual vulnerability lead to mutual security and bring the costly arms race to an end? The answer, to be discussed in chapter 6, was negative.

6

Into the Missile Age: Does Relative Strength Matter?

We have seen in the previous chapter that Eisenhower's unwillingness to enlarge the nation's conventional forces and the related decision of placing greater emphasis on tactical nuclear weapons were not prompted by fiscal considerations alone. The president had become convinced that mutual nuclear plenty would generate stability, stemming from the mutual realization that any war between the United States and the Soviet Union would eventually escalate to the nuclear level. So why commit so much of the nation's resources to defense and, in Eisenhower's view, undermine its institutions? Despite mutual vulnerability, did relative strength still matter? If not, how much nuclear power was enough? Would the arms race come to an end?

The president's views on the changing nature of conflict were not widely shared. Several groups of consultants pondered the consequences of growing Soviet nuclear strength. Both the Killian Panel (1955) and the Gaither Panel (1957) addressed the danger in the changing *relative* military strengths of the United States and the Soviet Union. Both reports recommended maintaining American military and, in particular, nuclear superiority, because they perceived mutual vulnerability to be fraught with instability and danger. Both panels called on the Eisenhower administration to take advantage of the nuclear superiority of the West and translate it into political gain before it was too late.

Based on the prediction that western nuclear superiority would be temporary, Eisenhower made sure that the U.S. strategic forces would never become vulnerable to an immobilizing attack. However, Eisenhower and Dulles found it difficult to translate nuclear superiority into political leverage. Feeling that mutual vulnerability might already be close, they recognized that the meaning of war as an instrument of policy was changing.

But if nuclear superiority had only limited military significance, then why did the arms race continue? Eisenhower and Dulles came to learn that as long as allies believed in the value of military superiority, that measure of status would remain important psychologically and politically. Military superiority was necessary in order to reassure allies and those domestic groups which perceived superiority as essential. To provide this reassurance, Eisenhower agreed to accelerate the nation's missile development programs though he did not perceive missiles as militarily very valuable weapons. Political pressure also explains the president's proposal of a bigger defense budget than he thought was justified from a military point of view.

Finally, the question remained whether NATO could survive the growth of Soviet nuclear strength. Or was an independent European nuclear force the better answer? The end of the decade witnessed an intense European-American debate on the issue of nuclear sharing. Numerous proposals were discussed, but none were made into policy. The prospect of nuclear sharing mitigated European fears of abandonment by the United States as a consequence of the American homeland becoming vulnerable to retaliation. On a more fundamental level, however, Eisenhower seems to have been increasingly prepared to share nuclear information with the Europeans and, at least in theory, accepted the idea of a European nuclear force.

Meeting the Threat of Surprise Attack

Since the first Soviet test of an atomic device in 1949, the consequences of the new threat to American security had been discussed in the NSC. In the first years, American nuclear superiority seemed to be more than an adequate match to the Soviet threat. Things began to get complicated in April 1954, when four strategic experts of the RAND Corporation finished their soon-to-be-famous report R-266. Albert J. Wohlstetter, F. S. Hoffman, R. J. Lutz, and Henry S. Rowen revealed that SAC's eighty-two overseas air bases would be highly vulnerable to an attack by Soviet bomber forces. SAC had planned to use these bases as staging areas for several days before an actual strike. R-266 now showed that SAC could reduce its vulnerability by limiting its use of overseas bases to refueling.[1] Air Force chief of staff General Thomas D. White ultimately approved the recommendation of the RAND report.[2]

The question of the vulnerability of the SAC was taken up again during the NSC discussions of the continental defense program in June 1955. The view of the council's consultant on continental defense, Robert C. Sprague, turned out to be most controversial. Robert Bowie summarized Sprague's report thus: "At the present rate of development of our continental defense system the Soviets by mid-1957 will be able to destroy our nuclear retaliatory power by surprise attack."[3] During the NSC meeting, both the director of the CIA and the air force chief of staff emphasized that this conclusion was based on an improbable worst-case scenario. Allen Dulles pointed out that the findings reflected highly uncertain and disputable intelligence estimates with respect to the Soviet bomber force. He was personally inclined to a more conservative estimate, and so was the president.[4] General Nathan F. Twining, likewise, stressed the technical difficulties of a large surprise attack. He doubted that "the Soviets would sacrifice their heavy, long-range aircraft on a one-way mission with complete strategic surprise, as suggested by Mr. Sprague."[5] The president added that "he would think it odd if we received no warning at all." He pointed to the example of the U.S. Air Force during World War II, which was never able to effect attacks with complete surprise. He did not believe that the Soviets would decide to launch a "bolt out of the blue" without taking into account the negative effects on public opinion.

Accordingly, Eisenhower believed that production of the B-52 bomber should not exceed approved levels.[6] However, the president also recognized the central importance of safe SAC bases for U.S. security. Therefore, he approved measures for improvement of SAC's situation. Highest priority was given to measures for the dispersal of the strategic bomber force, the improvement of the early warning system, the enhancement of the SAC's control and communications capabilities, the study of an alert force concept, and the initiation of research on protective shelters.[7] A guiding principle behind these improvements was that the best protection of long-range bombers was ensuring that they would be in the air, on their way to their targets, as soon as the enemy struck.

The Killian Report

In March 1954, the president requested the Technological Capabilities Panel of the Science Advisory Committee of the Office of Defense Management (ODM) to make a study of U.S. technological capability to reduce the threat of surprise attack. A panel of forty-two members, directed by James R. Killian, Jr., president of the Massachusetts Institute of Technology, was established to accomplish this task. The panel analyzed how science and technology could be used to reduce the nation's vulnerability based on a comparison of military strength of the United States with that of the Soviet Union. The resulting timetable defined four phases, which characterized the pattern of change in relative nuclear strength.

The panel explained that the prevailing balance was characterized by an offensive advantage of U.S. air-atomic power, limited only with respect to large multimegaton weapons. But because the United States had no reliable early warning system and only inadequate defenses, the SAC was vulnerable to surprise attack. This balance would change in 1956–57, because by then the United States would acquire a substantial number of multimegaton weapons and increase its defense capabilities. Period II, starting in 1956–57 and ending in 1958–60, therefore would be marked by a very great U.S. offensive advantage and a strengthening of the SAC's ability to defend against surprise attack. The United States would be able to mount a decisive air strike, while the Soviet Union would not. The Killian Panel predicted that these years would be "a very favorable period for political moves and diplomatic negotiations" from the standpoint of relative military strength.

Period III would be a time of transition, characterized by a growth of Soviet multimegaton capability and substantially increased U.S. defenses. These developments would lead into period IV, possibly beginning within a decade and lasting indefinitely. In this time period, an attack by either side would result in mutual destruction. Each side would possess enough multimegaton weapons and adequate delivery means to break through the defenses of the adversary and destroy its country, even if the adversary managed to initiate hostilities with a surprise attack. The Killian Panel expected this period to be "so fraught with danger to the U.S. that we should push all promising technological development" in order to stay in periods II and III as long as possible.[8]

Because the panel perceived the advent of mutual vulnerability to be fraught with instability and danger, it made recommendations to prolong U.S. security as long as possible. Although difficult times seemed to lie ahead for the United States, the report included at least one positive message: The panel members foresaw opportunities to turn military superiority into political gains before the strategic balance would change. The panel also produced a long list of recommendations for strengthening the U.S. offensive striking power and the continental defense system, and for improving intelligence gathering, communications, and maintenance of equipment.[9] The panel assigned the highest priority to development of ballistic missiles. If the United States achieved an intercontinental ballistic missile (ICBM) capability first, the nation would be able to maintain a position of advantage into the next decade.[10]

On 17 March 1955, the panel briefed the NSC on its findings and recommendations. The NSC then referred the recommendations to the appropriate departments and agencies of the executive branch for study and comment.[11] The NSC discussed the report again in August, focusing on controversial issues. First, the council emphasized the importance of the timetable as a basis for all the panel's recommendations. Secretary Dulles made sure that nobody was left with the erroneous impression "that our international policy was determined and enforced by obliteration and warfare such as was envisaged in the Timetable and the panel's recommendation." Governor Harold Stassen replied that this was not what the panel had in mind; it did not mean "that we should use our relative military advantage for military purposes." The president assumed that the panel meant the same thing as "when we talked about negotiating from strength."[12] The secretary's remarks were a first hint that from a foreign policy point of view relative military advantage may not be easily translated into political gains.

Second, the discussion made transparent that it was not yet clear how a quick missile capability should be reached. Should efforts be concentrated on the development of ICBMs, while intermediate range ballistic missiles (IRBMs) would only be achieved as a by-product? Or should the development of IRBMs be advanced with the same priority as the ICBMs because IRBMs could cancel out Soviet ICBMs due to the advantage of U.S. overseas bases close to the Soviet Union? Should the different development projects remain in the hands of various departments and agencies, or should the whole undertaking be centrally managed?

The president was convinced that it was useless to produce missiles in quantity, "because we can't fight that kind of a war." He added that "if this is the only means of waging war, he would never wage it." He agreed that the United States needed some missiles as a threat and deterrent, but it did not need a thousand or more. The president proposed that social scientists be brought into U.S. security planning "to study how long civilization can take these weapons developments." It seemed to him that the "nature of conflict has gotten beyond man." Eisenhower expressed the hope "that the future character of war will repel men from the use of force."[13] The president firmly believed that at some point, both sides would have all the deterrent power they needed. He began to wonder whether, at that point, both sides would be in danger or in peaceful stability.

The Development of Missiles

In early September, the NSC examined the question of why the development of ballistic missiles was so important for the nation's security. Secretary George M. Humphrey asked how ballistic missiles would fit in with the bomber forces. And Governor Stassen inquired whether the terrific speed of Soviet ICBMs would not endanger U.S. bomber forces on the ground. The advent of intercontinental missiles seemed all the more threatening, because there would be no defense against missiles in the near future. The secretary of the air force, Donald A. Quarles, replied to these queries. He pointed out that in the period up to 1960, the Soviets were not likely to achieve a sufficient number of ICBMs with the requisite degree of accuracy to endanger the bomber force of the SAC. In the short term, the ICBM would be a backup weapon. Precisely because missiles would be relatively inaccurate in the near future, the president was concerned about a war fought with missiles. Because of their low accuracy, they would be easier to use against cities than against bomber bases. The president once noted that "the world would be a shamble before an atomic war was over. War up to now has been a contest, but with nuclear missiles, it is no longer a contest, it is complete destruction."[14]

In the course of the NSC meeting, Undersecretary of State Herbert Hoover, Jr., addressed missile development in the context of U.S. foreign relations. He stressed that if the Soviets were the first to demonstrate to the world an ICBM capability, "the result would have the most devastating effect on foreign relations of the United States of anything that could possibly happen." The security of NATO rested on nuclear weapons. If the allies doubted the ability of the United States to deter attacks against them, Hoover pointed out, "neutralism would advance tremendously throughout the free world."[15] It was not, as further analyses within the State Department showed, that Soviet development of an ICBM would increase Soviet willingness to initiate general war. Rather a Soviet ICBM would encourage groups within allied countries that had advocated a policy of greater independence from the United States. The allies would wonder "whether the U.S. willingness to act in their behalf would be reduced by the apparently greater U.S. vulnerability to nuclear attack." In such a climate, the allies would increase their resistance to U.S. policies perceived to be risky or dangerous.[16]

For fear of allied "neutralism," the State Department believed that the United States should make the most complete use of all its resources to achieve development of an ICBM. Herbert Hoover recommended that the ICBM be placed at the very top of the priorities within the Defense Department, set apart from the other 180 defense projects in the category of "highest priority."[17] In the view of the Department of State, the ICBM project should be "very much in the same category as the Manhattan Project during World War II."[18] With this, the question was put on the table as to whether the project should remain the responsibility of the air force and the Department of Defense, or whether, instead, a separate organizational structure should be set up, comparable to the Manhattan project.

President Eisenhower agreed with the foreign policy analysis of the Department of State, but he disagreed with the proposal for a new missile development bureaucracy. The president approved the recommendation of the NSC that the ICBM program be a research and development program "of the highest priority above all others."[19] But the president thought it unwise to establish a Manhattan-type project. In his view, this would postpone the date of operational capability rather than accelerate it, because the project would lose some of its momentum. He believed that the people who knew most about missile development were already in the armed services.[20]

The question had been asked, from the first discussion of the Killian Panel's recommendations, whether the achievement of an early IRBM capability was not as important as the development of an ICBM. An IRBM might be achieved more easily and more quickly. An IRBM capability, so the argument ran, could offset to a considerable degree the military advantage that would be gained by the Soviets in case they achieved an ICBM capability first. The reason for this was that U.S. IRBMs could be stationed overseas, close to the Soviet Union. Besides being able to reach targets within the Soviet Union, they would strengthen allied confidence in U.S. retaliatory power.

The State Department studied the issue and concluded that U.S. achievement of an IRBM would diminish the impact of Soviet acquisition of an ICBM on the cohesiveness of U.S. alliances.[21] The Department of Defense came to the conclusion that it "had the technical capability to undertake the development of an IRBM concurrently with the present ICBM effort, with a reasonable assurance of bettering the time schedule set for the ICBM." The department proposed a twofold program: While the air force was developing a land-based IRBM, a joint army-navy program would have the dual objective of developing a ship-launched capability and also providing a land-based alternative to the air force program. The secretary of defense recommended that the president approve the whole program as of "equal priority to the ICBM program, but with no interference to the valid requirements of the ICBM program."[22]

President Eisenhower agreed that development of an IRBM was of critical importance to the security of the United States. But he was skeptical as to whether it should be given the same priority as the ICBM program. He was reluctant to have all three services working on the problem of missile development. He feared difficulties in achieving adequate coordination among the services. He suspected that such interservice rivalries had delayed the decisions within the Defense Department. But the secretary of defense assured the president that both programs could be carried on simultaneously, without mutual interference. Eisenhower, finally, directed "that the IRBM and ICBM programs should both be research and development programs of the highest priority above all others." Whereas mutual interference between these programs should be avoided as far as practicable, conflicts of interests endangering the security of the United States should be referred to the president. In addition, the president directed the secretary of defense to report each month on the development of the programs.[23]

Already in late 1955, when the Department of State had proposed a Manhattan-type program for the ICBM, Secretary Charles E. Wilson had reminded the NSC of the financial costs. He had pointed out that, according to the estimates of the armed services, "it would cost approximately $45 billion a year for some years if the Defense Department were to carry out the recommendations of the Killian Panel together with the regular military and military assistance programs."[24] However, at the time more urgent than cost was the question of how to set up a program and an organizational structure best suited to achieve a quick success. Once these organizational questions were settled at the end of the year, the financial issue became prominent again. Secretary Humphrey, in particular, warned that "some of the ideas in the Killian report would ruin us." Commenting further on the extensive ballistic missile research programs, he added, "that the scientists these days showed a tendency to run wild."[25] However, as we have seen in the preceding chapter, the increasing costs of the missile development programs were counterbalanced by savings due to the reorganization of the army based on a smaller divisional structure.

Financial pressures with respect to the missile development programs grew during the summer of 1957. The administration would have to find massive savings if it wanted to keep the defense budget within a budget ceiling of $39 billion. As a first step, the administration dealt with the question of whether the development of missiles would justify reductions in the production and technological development of bombers. The Weapons Systems Evaluation Group of the Defense Department reached the conclusion that from a military point of view a mixture of missiles and bombers would be needed by 1967.[26]

After it had become clear that more missiles would not justify fewer bombers, the Eisenhower administration, in a second step, began the difficult task of reorganizing the missile development programs. The summarized costs of all development programs for fiscal year 1956 and fiscal year 1957 (approximately $11.8 billion) made the NSC realize that the resources of the United States would be insufficient to support all the programs in the future. In addition, the president pointed out that "so many of the missile systems . . . seemed to him to resemble one another quite markedly in their capabilities."[27] In short, the administration had to face the difficult decision of which specific programs to eliminate—a task loaded with political and bureaucratic hurdles.

In August 1957, the reviewed program slowly began to emerge. The NSC and the president approved the recommendation of the secretary of defense with respect to the two ICBM programs. While the Atlas program was to be continued at the highest priority, the Titan program was given lower priority "in an effort to make substantial economies in this alternative development."[28] This was a relatively easy decision, because both ICBM programs were managed by the air force. More difficult was the question of what to do about the IRBMs. Because of excessive costs, a simultaneous development of more than one IRBM program seemed no longer justified. The Department of Defense, the air force, and the army were directed to recommend a program to be placed under the management of the air force alone.[29] Meanwhile, the IRBM program would be reduced to a test program. The navy, finally, had taken up the development of the Polaris submarine-based missile. Because such a weapon had the potential to be a nearly invulnerable deterrent, the project was carried on with a high defense priority.[30]

As for the IRBM, the army and the air force were unable to come up with a clear choice in favor of either Thor or Jupiter.[31] Meanwhile, numerous press stories were referring to deep interservice rivalries and questioned whether such a situation did not delay the missile programs. The slow progress, finally, led the president to reconsider the idea of a Manhattan-type organization.[32] But before the issue could be decided, *Sputnik* reshaped the strategic environment, with consequences that will be discussed in the following section.

How did the Eisenhower administration react to the recommendations of the Killian Panel? First, it reduced the vulnerability of the nation's strategic strike complex, to ensure that the country could never be disarmed by a Soviet surprise attack. Second, although it regarded missiles as only supplementary weapons, it recognized quick development to be of overriding political and psychological importance. The race to develop missiles would have an important impact on international politics and particularly on the confidence of the allies. Secretary Dulles once explained the matter to the NSC by pointing out that "while these terrible missiles . . . might never be used, they are nevertheless essential to national security. We simply cannot afford to be inferior to the USSR."[33] The message was clear: As long as the United States possessed military superiority and the Soviets (and the world) knew it, the Soviet Union could not and would not "checkmate" the United States.

How did the administration deal with the Killian Panel's recommendations to make the most of the nation's existing military superiority? The truth is that the Eisenhower administration found it difficult to translate nuclear strength into political leverage; it never even set up a comprehensive program to analyze the possibilities. On the contrary, the prospect of a missile war reassured Eisenhower in his growing conviction that war as an instrument of policy had to be reappraised.[34] Each side now possessed all the deterrent power necessary to deter the other. A time of mutual deterrence might produce stability.

Sputnik and the Missile Gap

On 4 October 1957, the Soviet Union launched the first orbiting earth satellite. *Sputnik*, as the satellite was called, immediately became the symbol of Soviet technological achievement. It signaled that the Soviet Union had overtaken the United States in the field of long-range missile technology. Although the Eisenhower administration had been collecting intelligence data indicating that the Soviets had been making rapid progress in the development of long-range ballistic missiles since July, the shock of *Sputnik* was profound: The United States had been challenged in the one field—science and technology—in which almost everybody had taken American preeminence for granted.[35] *Sputnik* led to a wave of near-hysteria in the United States (which was paralleled by deep allied concerns) about the perceived inadequacy of the nation's defense. People speculated that Eisenhower's economic policy and the country's poor educational system had caused this crisis.[36]

Since 1955, the Eisenhower administration had anticipated the psychological and political impact that the first demonstration of a long-range missile capability had caused. Now *Sputnik* had confirmed the administration's worst fears. And before the first wave of anxiety had time to abate, the next shock was already agitating the nation. At the end of November, numerous press stories spread the word that a far from optimistic top-secret report to the president had been made in the NSC.[37] The articles referred to the so-called Gaither report, which was presented to the president on 4 November 1957. The report ended with a call for immediate action: "If we fail to act at once, the risk, in our opinion, will be unacceptable."[38]

The Gaither Report

The Gaither report originated in a recommendation of the ODM of the previous April, which had endorsed a major bomb shelter program for civil defense. In the course of the NSC's discussion of that recommendation, Secretary of State Dulles questioned the value of passive defense measures and instead proposed to concentrate the nation's resources on the buildup of active deterrent forces. Although the president leaned toward Dulles's view, he pointed out that if both sides possessed hydrogen bombs, but only one was ready to dig in and ride out a nuclear war, the "side which had the shelters to take refuge in was likely to win the war after the initial exchange of nuclear blows." However, he immediately added that this would no longer be "war in any traditional sense, but rather a contest between death and survival." The Science Advisory Panel of the ODM was then directed to study "the relative value of various active and passive measures to protect the civil population in case of nuclear attack and its aftermath."[39]

A panel was set up to analyze the matter under the direction of H. Rowan Gaither, chairman of the board at both the Ford Foundation and the RAND Corporation. Because of Gaither's ill health, he was succeeded as director by Robert C. Sprague in September 1957, a Massachusetts industrialist and expert on continental defense.[40] Before long, the panel expanded the scope of the study to include an assessment of the deterrent value of U.S. retaliatory forces and the economic and political consequences of any significant shift in the direction of the nation's defense programs.[41] A key influence in the drafting of the report was a visit that Sprague made to NORAD in September 1957. Sprague witnessed a spontaneous alarm, during which only a relatively small number of SAC planes was able to take off within the tactical warning time available.[42]

The Gaither Panel adopted the approach of the Killian Panel and based its recommendations on a comparison of the relative military strengths of the United States and the Soviet Union over the next few years. At the heart of the Gaither Panel's concern lay the vulnerability of SAC. Existing active defense systems (air defense systems against bombers and missiles) and passive defense systems (blast and fallout shelters) provided little protection for the civilian population. It was primarily the deterrence provided by the SAC, which was responsible for the security of the civilian population. However, the panel found that in a hypothetical "bolt from the blue"—a surprise strike without SAC's being on alert—SAC itself could be knocked out while its planes were still on the ground. And the panel expected that the Soviets would soon achieve an early ICBM capability (probably by 1959).

Based on this analysis, the panel recommended securing the strategic deterrent as the nation's highest priority, and it proposed a whole package of measures. First, SAC's alert system, tactical warning system, and base defense should be improved to reduce the vulnerability to a Soviet surprise *bomber* attack. Second, an early warning system should be developed, SAC bombers should be dispersed to the widest extent practical, and a large number of bombers should be protected by blast shelters to reduce vulnerability to an *ICBM* attack. Third, the nation should accelerate the IRBM, ICBM, and Polaris missile programs to enhance SAC's offensive capability. Finally, the United States and its allies should strengthen their ability to fight limited military operations in order to enhance deterrence of small wars.

The Gaither Panel was split on the advisability of active and passive defense measures to protect people and big cities. Although recognizing the impossibility of absolute protection (even at a very high price), the report proposed (as a relatively low priority) a mixed program of active and passive defenses, including a fallout shelter program to protect the civilian population. A shelter program, in the panel's opinion, would strengthen the nation's deterrence, because the enemy would not be tempted to strike targets that it had a low likelihood of destroying. Civil defense would also increase the credibility of U.S. willingness, if necessary, to employ the SAC arsenal, because the risk of retaliation would be somewhat reduced by the inability of a retaliatory strike to destroy certain targets. The Gaither Panel valued a shelter program as a symbol of the nation's will to survive in the nuclear age.[43]

A glance at the projected costs of these recommendations indicates that the panel was considering more than a minor correction of the nation's defense programs. The estimated cost of strengthening offensive capabilities over the next five years (1959–1963) was $19 billion.

Improving the active and passive defenses would cost an additional $25 billion over the same time period. The report determined that these expenditures were "well within our economic capabilities."

While the president believed that nuclear stalemate might not necessarily be fraught with danger, the report described the situation as "a period of extremely unstable equilibrium" where a "temporary technical advance . . . could give either nation the ability to come near to annihilating the other." The panel set its sites on SAC's acquisition of an effective alert status and the ability to strike back decisively, even if taken by surprise. The panel found further that, once attained, such a capability should be exploited for its political advantage: "This could be the best time to negotiate from strength, since the U.S. military position vis-à-vis Russia might never be as strong again."[44] A similar position had already been taken by the Killian Panel. However, the experience of the Eisenhower administration had demonstrated an inability to translate nuclear superiority into political leverage.

The Reaction of the Eisenhower Administration

How did the Eisenhower administration respond to the message of the Gaither report? On the occasion of the presentation of the panel's findings to the NSC, the president pointed out that it was essential that his government become neither panicked nor complacent.[45] It was the view of both the president and the secretary of state that the panel had not taken a well-rounded view of the prevailing state of national security.[46] The struggle against the Soviet Union had an economic side and a public relations side, as well as a military. The twin shocks of *Sputnik* and the press accounts of the Gaither report had complicated the task for the future in ways that the panel had not taken into account.

Part of the difficulty the administration had with the report was that key members of the administration understood the problem of strategic deterrence differently than members of the panel did. When Gaither presented the report to the president on 4 November 1957, Eisenhower's first remark indicated his skeptical view of the study's approach. The president agreed that U.S. military strength was relative to that of the adversary. However, he felt "that we are getting close to absolutes when the ability exists to inflict 50% casualties on an enemy."[47] In other words, while the report was premised on the possibility of prolonging absolute military superiority, the president believed that mutual vulnerability might be rapidly approaching.

At a later meeting of the whole NSC, Secretary Dulles explained that the panel had only dealt with the military aspects of containing the Soviet Union. "It should be remembered," he observed, "that the Soviet Union had made its greatest gains in terms of taking over other people and other areas during the years from 1945 to 1950 when the United States was more powerful than it had ever been before in peacetime and the USSR had not made any appreciable gains even though they now had great nuclear capabilities and general military capacity."[48] Up to now, he pointed out, the struggle with the Soviet Union had primarily been a cold war. "Accordingly," he added, "there was a great danger that we should so focus our eyes on the military aspects of the struggle that we lose the cold war which is actually being waged, forgetting that an actual military conflict may never be waged."[49] Both the president and the secretary of state concluded their general criticism of the panel's approach by stating that there was no real defense to a nuclear strike and that the most that could be done would be to retaliate. Therefore, the United States should concentrate on maintaining its deterrent capabilities. And the country should use additional resources to conduct its foreign policy in a manner that would assure victory in the political cold war.

Although doubtful of the value of superior forces from a military point of view, and accepting the inevitability of mutual vulnerability, both the president and the secretary of state were becoming confident that the Soviets would be deterred. First, given the gruesome consequences, they regarded the possibility of a massive Soviet surprise attack as very remote. They recognized that the Gaither Panel's gloomy assessment of SAC's vulnerability was based on worst-case assumptions: The report considered what would happen in a time of relative tranquillity and reduced international tensions if the Soviets were to mount a massive surprise attack against the United States and simultaneously against all important U.S. overseas bases. Realistically, not even Soviet rulers would contemplate such an assault, as Secretary Dulles explained in a telephone conversation with the president on the very day the Gaither report was discussed in the NSC. He pointed out to the president that such an attack without provocation would involve casualties of perhaps one hundred million and would create terrible conditions for all who survived in any part of the world.[50]

In addition to the enormous toll in human lives that would result from a massive surprise attack, several other factors led American leaders to conclude that this worst-case scenario was extremely improbable, if not impossible. In the course of discussions leading to the rejection of preventive war in late 1954, members of the Eisenhower administration had gained an understanding of the military complexities behind such a massive strike. Even if technical and organizational problems could be overcome, there remained the unanswered question of what to do with the remnant of the adversary's society once the war was won. And if the problems posed by winning a general nuclear war looked insurmountable to the U.S. government in the early 1950s, how would they look to the Soviet government at the end of the decade, by which time nuclear capabilities would have multiplied? Finally, a Soviet decision to start a general nuclear war *without* strategic surprise, that is while U.S. forces were on full alert, was even more remote, because the prospect of the United States striking first would deter Soviet escalation.[51]

President Eisenhower rejected the defense program outlined in the Gaither report. During discussions of the defense budget for fiscal year 1959, the president made clear how far and in what direction he was prepared to go. Only four days after the Gaither report was presented in the NSC, the president met with the secretary of defense, Neil H. McElroy, to discuss budget adjustments that would be necessary in light of the Gaither Panel's recommendations. Eisenhower recognized the importance of making the strategic striking forces invulnerable. The president indicated that he would agree to additional money for dispersing SAC's bombers and improving the alertness of its forces. Moreover, he would accept moderate acceleration of the missile development programs, particularly of the nearly invulnerable Polaris submarine-based missile.[52]

On the other hand, Eisenhower clearly rejected the panel's recommendation for initiating a fallout shelter program. The president and Secretary Dulles urged three main arguments to justify this decision. First, Eisenhower argued that even with a shelter program the nation would not be able to survive "as an organized society."[53] Second, the limited value of shelters had to be measured against their enormous cost. "Was the Panel," the president asked the NSC, "proposing to impose controls on the U.S. economy now?" In short, the president repeated his fundamental belief that security was the product of economic *and* military strength. Third, both the president and Secretary Dulles were concerned about how the allies would receive a huge shelter program for the United States. The secretary of state pointed out that "to say that the American people must be saved from the effects of radiation and not the British and the French and the others was tantamount to losing our Allies."[54]

The president's response to the Gaither report did not evolve in a political vacuum. Eisenhower operated in an environment open to domestic and external pressures. The discussion of further acceleration of the IRBM missile programs best reveals the impact of domestic pressures. The debate over additional funds for conventional forces best reveals external pressures. The president agreed to accelerate the two ICBM programs (Atlas and Titan), but he was reluctant to spend more money on the development of IRBMs. He reminded his advisers that the administration's position was to rely primarily on the bomber force as the principal weapon system of U.S. deterrence for the next few years.[55] Secretary Dulles believed the president's position to be sound on foreign policy grounds. In Dulles's view, a crash program for IRBMs was not needed, because neither the British nor other NATO allies would be ready to receive IRBMs in the next two years. The Europeans would need more time to build the bases for these missiles and train their troops in the use of the missiles. Dulles saw no point in being able "to send an imperfect IRBM to NATO before our European Allies were ready to use it."[56]

Vice President Richard Nixon, on the other hand, outlined the argument *for* acceleration by warning of congressional pressure in case the administration failed to propose additional funds in this area. Referring to the forthcoming congressional hearings on the defense budget, Nixon advised more rapid production of operational missiles even if the administration was not completely satisfied with their quality.[57] The issue was discussed further at a meeting attended by the vice president, the secretary of defense, the secretary of state, and others, on 27 November. Secretary Dulles, who was again speaking against further spending on the IRBM, summarized the consensus as being in favor of moderately accelerating both the Jupiter and Thor programs, largely for psychological reasons. "It seemed to be felt," he noted in his memorandum of the conversation, that "there was an irresistible pressure to accelerate the program and demonstrate our capacity as rapidly as possible."[58] The argument based on the perception of the domestic public eventually won the day, and the defense budget for fiscal year 1959 included supplementary funds for both IRBM programs.[59]

Eisenhower's justification for the extension of the funds for conventional forces reveals comparable concern for the perception of the allies. Within a month of the launching of *Sputnik*, it had become clear that further redeployments of U.S. overseas forces were out of the question for the near future. President Eisenhower had assured Paul-Henri Spaak, the secretary-general of NATO, that "while the number of men in divisions might be reduced, there will be no reduction in actual strength for a long time."[60] The force reduction planned for the fiscal year 1959 military program could not be carried out. On the contrary, the NSC and the president had to recommend that Congress appropriate additional funds to keep two divisions in Korea and five divisions in Europe.[61]

The Eisenhower administration was very reluctant to implement the recommendations of the Gaither report. Nevertheless, defense expenditures for fiscal year 1959 exceeded the planned budget ceiling of $38 billion by $1.44 billion.[62] The increase in defense spending was due partly to concern about the vulnerability of the strategic striking complex, but mostly to concern about domestic (public and bureaucratic) and external pressures. Eisenhower noted to Secretary McElroy that "he thought that about two-thirds of the supplementary funds are more to stabilize public opinion than to meet the real need for acceleration." The secretary of defense agreed. From Eisenhower's perspective, the important question after the twin shock of *Sputnik* and the Gaither report was, "what is the [defense budget] figure that will create confidence?" He thought that "a feeling of greater confidence in the security sphere might go over into economic confidence as well."[63] Looking back on the period following *Sputnik*, the president, in his own account of his second term, concluded that additional defense expenditures do not automatically increase security: "Because security is based upon moral and economic, as well as purely military strength, a point can be reached at which additional funds for arms, far from bolstering security, weaken it."[64]

In Eisenhower's security equation, the first factor, moral strength, was the least clearly defined. Richard Immerman has argued that Eisenhower entered office with a strong sense of the Communist threat as challenging the American way of life, the nation's values, institutions, and social cohesion, by making excessive demands on the country's economic strength.[65] But in the atmosphere of near-hysteria after *Sputnik*, moral strength hit an all-time low. The president was least concerned about the military factor in his security equation. Security increasingly depended on public relations, aimed at bridging the gap between the president's confidence and public fears. This was not an easy task, because the administration had to persuade both domestic and allied groups of U.S. strength. Was there a single formula to address both constituencies? Or did the domestic message undermine the allied message (and vice versa)?

The Domestic Versus the Foreign Policy Context

A key question is why the president never attempted to explain the remarkable differences between his view and the domestic and foreign public's perception of *Sputnik*, the Gaither report, and the alleged missile gap. A brief answer is that Eisenhower never found a way to mitigate domestic fears without endangering the nation's relations with its allies.

The missile gap hysteria initiated a major defense controversy that shaped defense policy discussion into the Kennedy administration. President Eisenhower seems to initially have underestimated the depth of the *Sputnik* shock, if only because inside the administration the prospect of quick Soviet progress in the field of missile technology and the fact that American nuclear superiority was eroding had been commonly accepted since the middle of the decade. But it quickly became clear that the president's critics were absolutely dissatisfied with what, in their view, was a minor acceleration of the defense program in the wake of *Sputnik*. These critics continued to base their views on a numerical comparison of relative American and Soviet strengths. This approach lay at the heart of intelligence assessments, the results of which were leaked to the press regularly and which nourished domestic criticism for the remainder of the decade. Others have analyzed thoroughly how this critique grew in a complex political and bureaucratic environment.[66]

First, officers from all three armed services, including General Maxwell D. Taylor, General Thomas S. Power, and Admiral Arleigh A. Burke, initiated the doctrinal controversy, the gist of which became public during congressional hearings. In connection with the organization of the missile development programs, we have seen that service rivalries had become increasingly fierce and public, and that President Eisenhower appealed in vain to the services' loyalty. The press played on the various dissenters' views. Joseph and Stewart Alsop in particular warned of the consequences of a Soviet missile advantage. Newspaper articles titled "After Ike, the Deluge," and "Our Gamble with Destiny" voiced their conclusions.[67] Scholars cautioned that a Soviet advantage with respect to strategic nuclear weapons would have important political consequences. Albert Wohlstetter captured this view in describing the strategic balance as "precarious."[68] And Henry Kissinger warned that the missile gap would precipitate Soviet nuclear blackmail.[69] The democratic opposition, finally, capitalized on the widespread criticism of President Eisenhower's defense policy.

Senator John F. Kennedy made foreign policy a central issue of the presidential election campaign of 1960.[70] He criticized massive retaliation as leaving the American president no choice but nuclear devastation or submission, a situation that necessarily would leave the initiative with the enemy.[71] He pointed to deficiencies in the development of ballistic missiles as being critical in the near future and called for a buildup of the country's strategic forces.[72] Finally, he warned of a Soviet attempt to exploit their new strength on a substrategic level of violence: "Their missile power will be the shield from behind which they will slowly, but surely, advance—through Sputnik diplomacy, limited brush-fire wars, indirect non-overt aggression, intimidation and subversion, internal revolution, increased prestige or influence, and the vicious blackmail of our allies."[73] These threats could be credibly deterred only with conventional forces.[74] Kennedy articulated the concerns of people who thought the United States should amass more conventional forces as well as the concerns of those who were calling for expanding the U.S. strategic nuclear arsenal.

The advocates of a larger defense effort were dissatisfied with the fiscal year 1959 defense budget. The intelligence estimates, the summary assessments of which were regularly passed on to the press, reinforced their concerns.[75] The national intelligence estimate (NIE) of 1958 projected a Soviet ICBM force of one hundred by the middle of 1960 and a force of more than five hundred ICBMs by 1961.[76] Estimates made by the air force and by the SAC were much higher.[77] All these estimates were based not on any reconnaissance results of Soviet ICBMs, but rather on different assumptions about what the Soviets would decide to do with the resources they were known to have and the weapon levels they could achieve if they launched a crash program. Because there turned out to be fewer Soviet bombers than had been predicted in the middle of the 1950s, intelligence experts predicted that the Soviets were concentrating on maximizing their missile forces.[78]

President Eisenhower never spelled out why he rejected such gloomy predictions. He could have pointed to the photographic evidence from the U-2 flights—as he later did in his memoirs.[79] These photographs refuted claims that Soviet ICBM deployment was multiplying rapidly.[80] But at the time, although Eisenhower was aware that the Soviets knew of the U-2 flights, he decided to keep the program from the public in order to avoid potentially negative repercussions in international politics. The president's silence led his critics to believe that he did not take the danger seriously. If there was any gap at all, it was a communication gap that placed the president in an essentially defensive position in the domestic security policy debate after the *Sputnik* shock.

Matters became even worse in 1960. The NIE of 1960 predicted that there would be 35 Soviet ICBMs on launchers by mid-1960, 140 to 200 by mid-1961, and 250 to 350 by mid-1962.[81] The most serious blunder came with Secretary of Defense Thomas S. Gates's statement before the House Appropriations Committee. Gates seemed to explain the reduced estimates, compared with the 1958 estimate, as the result of a shift from predicting Soviet capabilities to predicting Soviet intentions and plans.[82] This explanation immediately aroused suspicion that the government was using political trickery to fend off congressional criticism.[83] The fact that Secretary Gates's denial of a deterrence gap was reported in the press alongside General Thomas S. Power's controversial claim that the Soviets "could virtually wipe out our entire nuclear strike capability within a span of 30 minutes" added fuel to the controversy.[84]

The characteristic Eisenhower response to the Gaither report, as well as to public fears of a missile gap, was to "play down the whole thing."[85] Eisenhower had his way on the defense budget. While reducing the vulnerability of the strategic striking forces, his administration resisted large missile deployment programs, the acceleration of new bomber development programs, and new conventional forces. But Eisenhower's critics feared that he did not fully appreciate the extent of the Soviet threat. In this regard, others have criticized Eisenhower's inadequate public relations work.[86] Without denying these critiques, we will see that Eisenhower realized that there was a communications gap. But he perceived foreign policy limitations on what and how much he could explain to the American public without unduly frightening U.S. allies.

During his last three years in office, Eisenhower regularly presented to the public a detailed overview of the different kinds of U.S. forces and their assigned missions. He emphasized the availability of the almost invulnerable submarine-based nuclear missiles, underlined the strength of the U.S. bomber force, which was widely dispersed on bases all over the world, and described the capabilities of the nation's early warning system. He ended his public assessments of U.S. military strength with general assurances of U.S. strategic superiority. The United States was ahead in the nuclear field and intended to stay ahead.[87] What Eisenhower did not do was give a detailed account of how he saw the strategic nuclear balance. Nor did he ever give a reason for his reluctance to accept his own administration's intelligence estimates of Soviet ICBM deployment.

While his failure to discuss intelligence estimates may be explained as a conscious decision not to make public the secret U-2 flights, Eisenhower's failure to assess the nuclear balance cannot be dismissed that easily. McGeorge Bundy pointed out that Eisenhower never offered his personal views on the strategic nuclear balance. Nor did Eisenhower spell out his opinion regarding other fundamental issues in the struggle with the Communists, such as the value of nuclear superiority or the stability of a nuclear stalemate. Bundy notes that the president could have made the compelling argument that even if a missile gap really did open up, this would not increase the risk of surprise attack, because the Soviets would still be unable to prevent a devastating reply, and, therefore, would be deterred. Bundy concludes that it was "a large missed opportunity for leadership that the man with the rank, the record, and the personal understanding to make this argument fully and persuasively appears to have made it, as far as the record now shows, only to himself."[88]

We have seen that Eisenhower was increasingly prepared to accept a nuclear stalemate toward the end of the 1950s. He clearly realized the limited value of a mere numerical advantage in nuclear weapons from a military point of view. Moreover, his government had experienced difficulty in translating military superiority into political gains in a time of mutual nuclear plenty. On the other hand, the president was sensitive to the fact that superiority was necessary to reassure the allies. It was this psychological and political reassurance that had made the achievement of the first demonstrated missile capability so important. To be sure, the reassuring effect of superiority helped in the domestic context as well, as long as there were individuals and groups who perceived superiority as important. And the nation's reaction to *Sputnik* was the best evidence that such thinking was still very widespread, indeed. Even the president, who believed that nuclear superiority was of limited value, might still have felt a vague sense of greater security at the prospect of numerical superiority.[89] But what mattered most was allied sensibilities. To the allies, security depended on the American nuclear guarantee, the credibility of which was still perceived as resting on nuclear superiority. In short, Eisenhower had to explain the actual unimportance of a missile gap (in case one should develop) without undermining the country's credibility as the allies' security-guarantor. Eisenhower seems to have been well aware of the dilemma. When the NSC discussed how to react to the shift in Soviet emphasis from military to economic competition—signaled by Khrushchev's claim that the Soviet Union would soon surpass the United States in the field of peaceful production—Eisenhower commented that "in terms of our setting forth our military capabilities before the world, we were damned if we did and damned if we didn't." The problem was, he added, "how to inform our own people in a logical way of our military capabilities, without at the same time scaring our allies to death."[90]

It is obvious that the president had to modulate his reaction to *Sputnik* and missile gap fears according to the divergent demands of domestic policy and foreign policy. From Eisenhower's perspective, the reaction

of the American public and the reaction of America's allies had to be
dealt with together. This becomes evident in Eisenhower's memoirs, in
which he deals with the two issues in two consecutive, thematically interrelated sections.[91] The contention that foreign policy precluded a clear
statement of nuclear realities and frank discussion of the value (or lack
of value) of superior forces at that time can be seen from the NATO
allies' reaction to the launching of the Soviet satellite *Sputnik*. How was
this evidence of a Soviet lead in missile technology perceived within the
alliance? And what proposals were made, and what conclusions were
drawn from this event on both sides of the Atlantic?

NATO and the Question of Nuclear Sharing

From a European perspective, *Sputnik* challenged the credibility of
the U.S. nuclear guarantee. Deterrence depended not only on capabilities, but also on the will to carry out the threat.[92] Was the American
promise to defend Europe with nuclear weapons credible once the U.S.
homeland became vulnerable? The significance of *Sputnik* was that it
drove home to the general public and the European allies the message
that the United States was now vulnerable to nuclear attack. Germany's
chancellor Konrad Adenauer put the matter very clearly in a talk with
John J. McCloy, former high commissioner for Germany and at the time
chairman of the Board of Chase Manhattan Bank, who recorded the
chancellor's serious doubt in American "participation and interest in
NATO as a result of the military-scientific advances of the USSR."[93]

These fears resulted in European pressure for control over nuclear
forces. The Germans repeatedly stated their dissatisfaction with the U.S.
policy of consulting on possible nuclear use and pointed out that the
United States had brought NATO close to war on several occasions without consultation. Within six days of the launching of the Soviet satellite,
the British began urging the American government to cooperate more
closely in the field of nuclear weapons and ballistic missiles.[94]

Against this background, it becomes clear why the Eisenhower administration perceived the need to assure the allies of U.S. superiority in the
nuclear field. But simply confirming western strategic superiority was no
longer enough. To mitigate fears of U.S. isolationism, the United States
adopted a policy of nuclear sharing. John D. Steinbruner has noted that
for the United States, the issue of nuclear sharing brought two fundamental values into conflict. On the one hand was the political aim of
reassuring the Europeans of the U.S. commitment. On the other hand
was the problem of the military defense of Europe in the nuclear era,

which demanded that nuclear weapons be centrally controlled.[95] Regarding the latter point, Dulles pointed out in several exchanges with German foreign minister Heinrich von Brentano that it would be impossible for the United States to generally agree *not* to act before consultations were possible.[96] In a letter to Chancellor Adenauer, the secretary explained that central control of strategic nuclear forces was necessary, because the appearance of indecision "could have serious consequences, and increase the likelihood of a major conflict."[97]

However, in the days after *Sputnik*'s launch, the British pressed the issue of closer cooperation in nuclear weapon and missile development and called for a U.S.-U.K. meeting.[98] Secretary of State Dulles interpreted these diplomatic moves as signals that the British were becoming dissatisfied with the alliance.[99] While the British were becoming increasingly dependent on nuclear weapons, the secretary explained to the president, they felt "remote from the decisions regarding these weapons."[100] On the occasion of several bilateral meetings between President Eisenhower and Prime Minister Harold Macmillan between 22 October and 25 October 1957, Eisenhower proposed that the coming NATO meeting might be a meeting of heads of government.[101] The secretary-general of NATO, Paul-Henri Spaak, who happened to be in Washington at the time, was asked to invite the heads of government to the meeting.[102]

The day before, Secretary Dulles and Secretary-General Spaak had discussed privately the issue of NATO defense strategy. The secretary-general of NATO stated that NATO was unable to reach the minimum figures required by General Lauris Norstad's recent "SHAPE Minimum-Force Study, 1958–1963."[103] Secretary Dulles replied by noting that the United States had lived up to its commitments. Moreover, the burden in the atomic field had grown, and perhaps "the Soviets got ahead because the U.S. was spending too much on its ground forces in Europe." It was the view of the Eisenhower administration that the U.S. contribution should be primarily nuclear, and the European contribution should be primarily conventional. While the secretary-general agreed that the Germans and the French, in particular, were lagging, he warned Dulles of the negative impact that the American "fair share" concept would have. It was important, Spaak emphasized, that the idea not persist in Europe "that the U.S. would contribute all of the modern weapons while Europe would contribute only manpower." This would lead the larger European countries further down the road to independent nuclear forces, and the shield forces would get thinner and thinner.[104]

Conceding the logic of the secretary-general's argument, the administration agreed to accept the plan for a NATO atomic stockpile, which originally had been put forward by the French in May 1956. Second, the administration planned to inform the allies about its accelerated missile programs and tell them that American IRBMs would be deployed in the NATO area whenever NATO nations were ready to receive them. Third, the administration decided to announce that it would recommend to Congress that the Atomic Energy Act be amended in order to permit a more liberal exchange of atomic energy information.[105]

General Lauris Norstad, the NATO commander in Paris, had advocated both the nuclear weapons stockpile and the development of a NATO ballistic missile force. The stockpile would make tactical nuclear weapons available to the forces of more countries—while the warheads remained in U.S. custody. The NATO ballistic missile force would match the emerging Soviet missile force, which was capable of hitting Western Europe. While implementation of the stockpile scheme was well under way by 1960, General Norstad's missile force under direct NATO control never saw the day.[106] Instead, the Eisenhower administration pushed for the deployment of IRBMs in the NATO theater under bilateral control arrangements. This policy had been initiated before the *Sputnik* launch. At the beginning of 1957, the main problem within NATO was still Britain's insistence on a sharp reduction of its own NATO forces, which would bring their level substantially below the commitment contained in the Brussels treaty. Moreover, Britain indicated that it wished to acquire nuclear weapons from the United States in order to make its reduced force the equivalent of the existing one. Only days before President Eisenhower met the British prime minister in Bermuda, Macmillan signed a Defense White Paper laying out a plan to stretch British force reductions over two years.[107] Supreme Allied Commander, Europe, Lauris Norstad, and the members of the WEU agreed reluctantly to the British reductions.

Such was the state of affairs when President Eisenhower and his party arrived in Bermuda on 20 March 1957. Eisenhower had two important goals for the conference. First, he sought to restore confidence in the Anglo-American relationship by overcoming the mutual mistrust resulting from the Suez crisis. While the *Sputnik* shock provided the decisive spark for nuclear sharing proposals, it was the earlier Suez crisis that had prompted British, and particularly French, interest in developing independent national nuclear forces.[108] Second, Eisenhower sought to obtain a reaffirmation of British support for U.S. policies, particularly regarding Europe.[109] As an incentive, Eisenhower suggested that the United States might make IRBMs available to the British.

In the course of the three-day meeting, Prime Minister Macmillan described the British overall defense plan and philosophy. Over the next four years, he said, the British would attempt to adjust their military forces and strategy to the nuclear age. They intended to expand their atomic and hydrogen capabilities. They also planned to reduce their military forces from a total of about 750,000 troops in 1957 to about 400,000 troops in 1962. President Eisenhower reacted to Macmillan's presentation by noting that the plan "in fact reminded him a bit of the US 'new look' idea." However, in what amounted to a summary of the U.S. experience with its New Look strategy, Eisenhower warned Macmillan that the New Look "had been considerably affected since its formulation a few years ago by political considerations around the world."[110] By the end of the conference, Eisenhower agreed in principle to work out arrangements for making IRBMs available to the British. As required by U.S. law, the nuclear warheads for the IRBMs would remain in U.S. custody.[111] Because the missile was still under development, detailed arrangements and the precise schedule of deployment would have to be worked out later.[112]

The plan to place IRBMs in NATO countries under some variation of a "dual key" arrangement was taken up in December 1957 at the first top-level meeting of the NAC since the alliance had been created eight years earlier. While the NATO members in principle agreed to accept U.S. IRBMs, location and control over their use remained to be decided "in conformity with NATO defense plans and in agreement with states directly concerned."[113] Eventually, General Norstad secured placements in Italy and Turkey (in these two cases the weapons were controlled directly by SACEUR) as well as in Britain (the British insisted on dual control). But as early as the NAC meeting it had become clear that France would not agree to such a formula. The French attributed "special importance to equality in weapons distribution and opposed any discrimination."[114] France's leaders pointed out that French control over warheads and IRBMs was a political necessity. The distribution issue brought France into conflict with SACEUR, while the control issue brought France into conflict with the American Congress. Out of the felt need of national control, France also refused to have tactical nuclear weapons stockpiled on French soil. After General Charles DeGaulle's return to power in 1958, he proposed a triangular relationship with the United States and Great Britain, in the framework of which strategic plans and actions regarding the use of nuclear weapons should be decided.[115] Once that proposal was rejected by Washington, France began a policy of distancing itself from its NATO partners.

Pressure from the French led officials in the Eisenhower administration to realize that proposals under which the United States retained control over nuclear warheads would never be enough to overcome European reluctance to accept complete nuclear dependence on the United States. In 1960, President Eisenhower was prepared to move toward some more liberal arrangement. Since the Europeans insisted on winning some control over nuclear weapons, it was preferable, from an American perspective, to develop an integrated European nuclear force worked into the NATO defense programs and presumably subordinated to a European NATO commander.[116] This policy happened to correspond well with Eisenhower's view that the American presence in Europe would be only temporary. At some point in the future, Europe had to become an independent and unified power base that could withstand the Soviets on its own. And for this, Europe would need some control over nuclear forces. However, there were signs of opposition to such changes. Members of the Congressional Joint Committee on Atomic Energy were enraged over the control arrangements for tactical nuclear weapons. During their inspection tour in Europe, they found fighter aircraft loaded with nuclear bombs and manned by German pilots.[117]

In 1960, U.S. policy regarding nuclear sharing was very much in flux. The Eisenhower administration's initiatives ended on an ambivalent note. In the NAC meeting of December 1960, Secretary of State Christian A. Herter, John Foster Dulles's successor, outlined what would later become known as the multilateral force (MLF). The United States was to assign five Polaris submarines to NATO, which in a second stage could be manned with European crews if desired. The proposal originated in a report by Robert Bowie, the former director of the State Department's Policy Planning Staff, who then became a professor at Harvard. His proposal for a collective nuclear force controlled by Europeans can be read as a first step in the direction of a more radical change in the nuclear status quo.[118] In the short term, the collective force proposal gave the State Department a constructive position to counter proposals for proliferation of national nuclear weapons programs, particularly a German program.[119]

The nuclear sharing policy of the Eisenhower administration prevented neither the British nor the French from developing independent national nuclear forces. But then, preventing independent forces was not a high priority aim of the Eisenhower administration. The British had successfully tested a nuclear device in 1952 and had developed their first thermonuclear weapon by 1957. The first French test of a fission weapon came on 13 February 1960. The nuclear sharing policy provided for a nuclear-armed *Bundeswehr* and brought the Germans very close to effective control over nuclear weapons. On the other hand, the United States retained formal control over the nuclear warheads. From a purely legal perspective, the German finger was kept off the nuclear trigger. Nuclear sharing mitigated European fears of U.S. neutralism in time of mutual American-Soviet vulnerability to nuclear attack. Together with general assurances of western strategic superiority, U.S. nuclear sharing initiatives were thought to reassure U.S. allies when Nikita Khrushchev seemed loaded with self-confidence due to the new Soviet nuclear strength. However, would this be enough to secure the alliance in the long term? Or was some kind of independent and unified European nuclear force the better solution? Eisenhower seems to have preferred the second alternative toward the end of the 1950s.

7

Eisenhower, Nuclear Weapons, and Policy at the End of the 1950s

By the end of his second term, Dwight D. Eisenhower had gained an appreciation for the magnitude of the nuclear revolution.[1] The nature of conflict was changing and a nuclear stalemate was becoming reality. But Eisenhower had come to realize that these circumstances need not make the world a more dangerous place. On the contrary, these developments could be stabilizing, because both sides would be deterred by the prospect of mutual annihilation. Eisenhower repeatedly pointed out that both sides possessed all the deterrent power needed to threaten the complete destruction of one another. This understanding led Eisenhower to his strong conviction that the Soviets did not want war and would be deterred. Finally, Eisenhower recognized that the links between the military capabilities and the political behavior of states were growing ever weaker in a time of mutual vulnerability. Nuclear superiority had only limited military meaning, and it did not easily determine political behavior.

We have seen that in public, President Eisenhower never expressed his views in such explicit terms. Nevertheless, his government's policy and actions during his last years in office generally reflect this outlook on the Cold War. President Eisenhower pressed for banning nuclear tests in the years after *Sputnik* and supported his new advisers, particularly James R. Killian, Jr., and George B. Kistiakowsky, the first two special assistants to the president for science and technology, who truly believed in the ban.[2] In August 1958, Eisenhower announced that negotiations for a test ban treaty would begin at the end of October. He also proposed a one-year moratorium on all nuclear tests during the period of the negotiations. The moratorium went into effect in November 1958 and lasted until September 1961. However, Eisenhower's hopes to conclude a test ban treaty faded in the aftermath of the downing of a U-2 reconnaissance plane over the Soviet Union, which led to the breakup of the Paris summit conference in 1960. Eisenhower's efforts in the field of arms control were paralleled by a cautious but confident effort to reach agreement with Khrushchev on the status of Berlin.[3]

Eisenhower defined security as the product of moral, economic, and military strength. Of these three factors, he was clearly least concerned about the third. There was no real military defense except the ability to retaliate, as he frequently pointed out with supreme confidence. The United States should therefore concentrate on maintaining its deterrent by investing its resources in strategic striking forces and securing them from attack. Because any military confrontation with the Soviet Union was bound to escalate to general nuclear war, Eisenhower saw no point in building up conventional forces. While the United States was prepared to help its allies with logistic, mobile air, and sea support, local defense would be the primary responsibility of the allies themselves. Although there is some evidence that Eisenhower increasingly developed concern about the danger of rapid escalation of limited war once tactical nuclear weapons were employed, he never wavered in his position regarding limited war.[4] He was helped in reaching this conviction by his fiscal conservatism—which brings us to the second element in his security equation.

Concern for a sound economy was an important element in Eisenhower's security equation. Excessive demands on the nation's economic strength, the president kept reminding his government and the American public, would lead to a "garrison state," and would endanger the nation's values, institutions, and social cohesion. The fact that Eisenhower passed over much bigger defense programs owes much to the relative inexpensiveness of nuclear weapons. Nuclear weapons minimized the costs of deterrence.[5] In 1953, the integration of nuclear weapons into national security policy had allowed the Eisenhower administration to build a financially bearable defense framework after the Korean War expansion without withdrawing from global engagement. In 1954, the cost effectiveness of acquiring nuclear weapons had made it easier for the Europeans to accept the nuclearization of NATO. And in 1957, both the Europeans and the Americans were willing to put more emphasis on tactical nuclear weapons rather than conventional weapons in order to ease financial burdens. They expected that savings from reduced conventional armaments would make up for the costs of missile development. The economy of nuclear armaments facilitated the goal of keeping NATO together, a task that became increasingly difficult as the Soviet Union developed the capacity to strike the U.S. homeland.

Moral strength was the least clearly defined of the three factors in Eisenhower's security equation. Moral strength comprised the will of the public in the nation and the western alliance system as a whole. It depended, to a large extent, on public (domestic and allied) perceptions of the general military and economic strength of the United States. It was in this area that Eisenhower sensed the biggest problems during his last years in office. Allied fears of U.S. isolationism, which were increasing as the Soviet capability to damage the U.S. homeland was growing, pushed the president to recommend procuring vastly superior strategic forces. But it was not only the fears of America's allies that inspired rhetoric of the importance of superiority. Domestic reaction to *Sputnik* and hysteria about the missile gap proved that many in the United States itself believed in the value of superiority. Apart from the negative foreign policy consequences, an honest discussion by Eisenhower of his true beliefs concerning national security would have aroused powerful domestic opposition. It was the need to communicate resolve to the American and European public that led Eisenhower to accelerate the nation's missile development programs and to recommend an enlargement of the fiscal year 1959 defense budget, for which he saw only very limited military justification.

The dilemma in reconciling Eisenhower's personal understanding of strategic deterrence with what he felt necessary for the reassurance of allies and the American public had real costs in his last years in office. First, if nuclear superiority had lost most of its meaning from a military point of view, it was, nevertheless, perceived to be important as a device for signaling U.S. resolve. This quandary was reflected in the fact that the differences between those attempting to build a full first-strike capability and those looking for just the right sized nuclear force to reassure allies was never very clear. There was no single accepted assessment of the consequences of the nuclear revolution, and the president kept his own view on this matter to himself. This situation created a huge gray area where bureaucratic and political pressures for bigger nuclear forces could play themselves out. As a consequence, a broad range of strategic weapons systems was developed and maintained, and no one really knew how much was enough. Toward the end of 1960, the United States had at its disposal a strategic bomber force of 538 B-52s, 1,291 B-47s, and 19 B-58s. This force was complemented by 12 Atlas ICBMs (deployed in the United States), 60 Thor IRBMs (deployed in Great Britain), and 30 Jupiter IRBMs (deployed in Italy). Moreover, Eisenhower had approved the

construction of 780 additional Atlas, Titan, and Minuteman ICBMs and
19 submarines, each of which would carry 16 Polaris missiles.[6] Acceleration of the production of nuclear warheads was even more impressive:
Between 1958 and 1960, the number of nuclear warheads trebled from
six thousand to eighteen thousand.[7]

Second, Eisenhower believed that the Soviets would be deterred, and
that prudence would assure that they would act as rational actors. But
allied doubts as to how the Soviets would act once they achieved nuclear
parity made it necessary to strengthen the credibility of deterrence as
much as possible. One way to do this was to emphasize rapid and massive
retaliation in case of attack; only preparations for war would sustain the
credibility of the nuclear threat. Therefore, the president subscribed to
the position that if the SAC were used, it should be used at once and in
full force. For Eisenhower the purpose of the capability to retaliate was
deterrence. But once this was translated into operational planning, such
a goal was no longer distinguishable from SAC's commitment to preemption in order to achieve a single war-winning blow. The question of
nuclear targeting and warplanning came to a head in 1960 as a response
to the development of the Polaris missile, the first strategic nuclear
weapons system not controlled by the air force. In a crucial meeting of
11 August 1960, Eisenhower assigned the task of developing a national
strategic target list (NSTL) and a single integrated operational plan
(SIOP) to the commander of the SAC. Eisenhower assigned this job to
the air force for practical and organizational reasons. Only SAC had
the computer resources necessary to undertake the task. Also, the battle
between the navy and the air force over control of the nation's nuclear
forces was another reminder of the unhealthy impact of interservice rivalries, which had had such a disastrous effect on the effort to develop
missiles. The result of the decision to make SAC responsible for targeting was the SIOP-62, the first single integrated operational plan, which
institutionalized plans for a massive, simultaneous nuclear offensive
against the full set of military and urban-industrial targets in the Soviet
Union, China, and Eastern Europe.[8]

Third, emphasis on nuclear superiority and massive retaliation to satisfy public perception worked against serious consideration of alternative concepts of deterrence. For example, the navy, led by Admiral
Arleigh Burke, had formulated a strategy of finite deterrence, built
upon the relatively invulnerable Polaris missiles. Burke repeatedly
pointed out that with the advent of Soviet ICBMs all-out war had become
obsolete as an instrument of national policy. He emphasized that acquisition of strategic forces be guided by "an objective of generous ade-

quacy for deterrence alone (i.e., for an ability to destroy major urban areas), not by the false goal of adequacy of 'winning.' "[9] The air force, by contrast, perceived finite deterrence as a threat to its central position in the nuclear field. It criticized the navy's suggestion as potentially harmful to American credibility in the eyes of NATO allies. The Air Force defended the value of a counterforce target system. Air force officials, in collaboration with strategists of the RAND Corporation, then developed a strategic alternative that centered on the exclusion of city targeting. Once attacked, the United States, so the argument ran, should limit its retaliatory strike to destruction of the adversary's own strategic striking forces, preserving the cities as hostages. This would in effect extend the process of deterrence into war itself and establish an opportunity to terminate a war without completely destroying both sides' civil societies. There were doubts about the technical and operational feasibility of this strategy, even among its proponents. But more important was that the SAC was not prepared to accept the plans' emphasis on damage limitation. The no-cities strategy therefore never became official air force thinking.[10]

Both finite deterrence and the no-cities strategy would have directed U.S. nuclear war plans away from pure capabilities planning. All this was discussed at a time when the writings of people in academia indicated that differences in employment strategy might matter. A relatively small circle of civilian strategists developed a body of thought that centered around the exploitation of uncertainty in crisis situations. In what was essentially a bargaining situation, governments must attempt to manipulate risk in order to achieve their political goals. In such a situation, the most important thing was not that a particular employment strategy make military sense, but rather that it function as a signal of how far the government was prepared to increase the level of risk.[11] Alternative deterrence strategies were unfolding in theory, but during Eisenhower's tenure they did not have a major impact on the way in which the nation's strategic forces were developed.

Dwight D. Eisenhower recognized the costs of the direction in which U.S. national security strategy was moving due to political and psychological pressures and the direction in which strategy might have moved if influenced exclusively by real risks and realistic assumptions. He was aware of the unnecessary size of the nation's strategic forces. He realized that the difference between strictly military needs and foreign and domestic policy needs opened a wide field for bureaucratic pressures. Eisenhower's frustration in this matter showed in his much-cited warning of the "military-industrial complex" in his farewell address to the nation on 17 January 1961.[12] The president reacted with horror to the SIOP-62. He was concerned that the "integrated targeting plan could be used to generate military requirements for tremendous additional forces, especially when the new administration takes over and the new people will not know the background, i.e., how these requirements were generated."[13] Kistiakowsky's presentation frightened Eisenhower and caused him to wrestle with the question of how to limit nuclear demand during his last days in office.[14] Eisenhower left the White House "with a definite sense of disappointment" regarding accomplishments in the field of disarmament, which had become a serious issue during his second term.[15] Although Dwight D. Eisenhower had developed a comprehensive body of thought on war, peace, and security for an era of mutual thermonuclear plenty, he ended his presidency knowing that he had been unable to assert his acquired wisdom against the force of political pressure.

Eisenhower's legacy for the future of national security policy was an atmosphere of remarkable discord within the nation's defense establishment. Discord had been growing since *Sputnik*. The president had tried to play down the danger the nation was facing. This, however, only aroused his critics, who feared that the country's top leaders underestimated the extent of the Soviet threat. Eisenhower's very narrowly elected successor was on record with his own views with respect to the defense debate. The new administration would have to formulate its security strategy in response to the strategic discussion of the late 1950s.

Part III

Kennedy and Perceived Mutual Vulnerability

8

Kennedy's Approach: A Strategy of Multiple Options

A good way to begin analyzing John F. Kennedy's national security policy is to understand it as a response to the strategic discussion of the late 1950s. The new administration absorbed the body of strategic thinking by relying heavily on the fairly small circle of civilian strategists that had developed new themes in opposition to the official policy of the New Look. However, an influential circumstance limiting the freedom of action of the administration was President Kennedy's narrow victory (the closest result since 1824), which gave him only a limited margin of flexibility in maneuvering among domestic and bureaucratic pressures.

The group of people President Kennedy brought into government shared his criticism of his predecessor's defense policy and believed that the American military posture needed to be strengthened and made more flexible. These officials and advisers included former Truman administration officials, such as Dean Acheson and Paul Nitze, many analysts from the RAND Corporation, such as Charles Hitch, Henry Rowen, William Kaufmann, and Alain Enthoven, and one of the leading military opponents of massive retaliation, General Maxwell Taylor.[1]

Change was announced not only with respect to the military element of the nation's security, but also with respect to the economic element. The new administration was committed to Keynesian economics. It emphasized employment and economic growth with little regard to budget deficits and inflation. A transition task force report by Paul Samuelson noted that "any stepping up of these programs [defense programs] that is deemed desirable for its own sake can only help rather than hinder the health of our economy in the period immediately ahead."[2] This was quite a dramatic departure from Eisenhower's fiscal conservatism.

Kennedy's secretary of defense had the freedom to make his appraisal of the entire defense strategy without direct regard to fiscal limits.[3]

Secretary of Defense Robert S. McNamara, former president of the Ford Motor Company, promised to tackle this task with vigorous leadership.[4] McNamara encouraged centralization of defense planning and enlargement of the secretary of defense's authority.[5] In fact, Eisenhower had been moving in this direction. Under the Department of Defense Reorganization Act of 1958, the secretary of defense was provided with the authority to centrally direct the Defense Department in all matters, including determination of the nation's force structure. Command channels were established from the president and the secretary of defense directly to the unified commands.[6] Greater concentration of authority in the secretary of defense and his staff worked to the disadvantage of the military leadership. The Joint Chiefs of Staff quickly realized that their influence on the appraisal of defense policy was restricted under the new civilian leadership.[7]

Although the new president defined security differently than Eisenhower had, the two administrations perceived the Soviet threat similarly. The main danger was the growing Soviet power to attack the American homeland and the consequences of that power for the ability of the United States to guarantee the security of its allies. The Soviets seemed to count on the range of their recently developed missiles to intimidate the United States, and thus to widen the scope of action they could take without substantial risk of war. President Kennedy expressed this apprehension during his campaign, and again in countless memoranda during his presidency.[8] Would the Soviets take advantage of their conventional superiority and nibble the free world to death piece by piece? Walt W. Rostow, at that time an aide to the new assistant to the president for national security affairs, McGeorge Bundy, characterized the anticipated direction of Soviet foreign policy: "Essentially, Khrushchev's strategy comes to this: he exerts pressure at some point on our side of the line; by such pressure he creates a situation in which we can only reply at the risk of starting a nuclear war or escalating in that direction; faced with this prospect, we look for compromise; he backs down a little; and a compromise is struck which, on balance, moves his line forward, and shifts us back."[9]

It was precisely such thinking, so the argument ran, that led the Soviets to instigate the Berlin crisis in 1958. And now, in early 1961, Khrushchev seemed to step back from earlier, vague signals expressing interest in arms control.[10] On 6 January 1961, the Soviet leader announced support for wars of national liberation. President Kennedy considered this speech to be the most important of the year.[11] His administration perceived the "Wars of Liberation" speech as proof of Soviet expansion by limited action—overlooking the possibility that the speech was primarily an effort by Khrushchev to counter Chinese criticism of his policies.[12] From an American perspective, Soviet intentions seemed clear. Then, Khrushchev reiterated his threat of a separate peace treaty with East Germany.

Rejected Elements of the Eisenhower Approach

The differences between the Eisenhower and Kennedy administrations lay in their solutions to the strategic dilemma. I have already mentioned that the incoming Democratic administration did not believe that growing defense expenditures would have a negative impact on the nation's economy and, ultimately, the American way of life. The Kennedy administration also rejected three other elements of Eisenhower's national security policy, all of which had shaped Republican defense policy until 1961: adherence to massive retaliation, emphasis on tactical nuclear weapons, and nuclear sharing.

To the Kennedy administration, massive retaliation was not a credible strategic answer to the underlying nuclear dilemmas; more than that, it was dangerous. During the campaign, Kennedy had warned that massive retaliation limited in a dangerous way the president's options in case of an acute crisis: "We have been driving ourselves into a corner where the only choice is all or nothing at all, world devastation or submission—a choice that necessarily causes us to hesitate on the brink and leaves the initiative in the hands of our enemies."[13] Emphasis on tactical warning and immediate response raised the danger of accidental or unintended nuclear war. During his first days in office, the president was warned by McGeorge Bundy that pursuing a policy of massive retaliation meant that "a subordinate commander faced with a substantial Russian military action could start the thermonuclear holocaust on his own initiative if he could not reach you."[14] Only a few days later, the acting chairman of the AEC, John S. Graham, informed the president that "the civilian control of atomic weapons contemplated in the atomic energy act had been eroded away."[15]

The briefing of Secretary of Defense McNamara and President Kennedy on the SIOP-62 only confirmed the alarming inflexibility of the nation's nuclear war plan. When McNamara visited General Thomas S. Power at the SAC headquarters in February 1961, he was shocked to learn of SIOP-62's extremely high damage goals, which would lead to fantastic overkill if the plan ever had to be carried out.[16] And when, in September 1961, at the height of the Berlin crisis, the president was briefed on the war plan, he saw nothing that would make the nuclear option attractive as a policy.[17]

Members of the Kennedy administration also feared that local use of tactical nuclear weapons would rapidly escalate into general nuclear war. The president had expressed this fear even before he entered the presidency: "If it [nuclear force] is applied locally, it can't necessarily be confined locally. The Russians would think it a prelude to strategic bombing of their industrial centers. They would retaliate—and a local use would become a world war."[18] Walt Rostow pointed out that the case for tactical nuclear weapons had weakened over the last few years because of the "danger of escalation, the lack of terrain and targets which would avoid the mass destruction of civilian populations, and the difficulty of distinguishing tactical from strategic targets."[19] The Bowie report had concluded that NATO's tactical nuclear "shield" concept had been rendered obsolete by Soviet acquisition of similar capabilities.[20] This view was reinforced by the Acheson report, which became the backbone of the new administration's NATO policy.[21]

Despite staking out a skeptical position, the Kennedy administration's policy on tactical nuclear weapons was not very consistent during 1961. On the one hand, the administration diminished their role in overall planning and pressed for the installation of permissive action links (PALs: electromechanical locks that would prevent a nuclear detonation unless the user inserted the proper code). By the summer of 1962, all short-range nuclear weapons in Europe were equipped with PALs.[22] On the other hand, the delivery of tactical nuclear weapons to Europe increased from 2,500 in 1961 to 4,000 in 1963 and over 7,000 in 1968.[23] Delivery continued in order to appease the allies. In his Athens address on the occasion of the NATO ministerial meeting in May 1962, Secretary McNamara attempted to reconcile general skepticism regarding the use of tactical nuclear weapons with political respect for his European audience. These weapons were needed, the secretary of defense pointed out, to deter their first use by the Soviet Union. But on the other hand, NATO could not expect to avoid retaliation if it used them first. McNamara also stressed the grave damage that would be caused in Europe by a local nuclear exchange. Tactical nuclear use was unlikely to give NATO any military advantage. And, finally, he warned of the danger of rapid escalation:

> To be sure, a very limited use of nuclear weapons, primarily for purposes of demonstrating our will and intent to employ such weapons, might bring

Soviet aggression to a halt without substantial retaliation, and without escalation. This is a next-to-last option we cannot dismiss. But prospects for
success are not high, and I hesitate to predict what the political consequences would be of taking such action. It is also conceivable that the limited tactical use of nuclear weapons on the battlefield would not broaden
a conventional engagement or radically transform it. But we do not rate
these prospects very highly.[24]

The prevailing view in the Kennedy administration was that tactical nuclear weapons could not credibly make up for manpower deficiencies.[25]
Nuclear sharing brought two fundamental values of U.S. foreign policy into conflict: the political goal of reassuring allies of American commitment to their defense and the military goal of centralizing control
over nuclear weapons. Concerned about the possibility of accidental war
and the danger of escalation, the Kennedy administration sought to
achieve central control. Indeed, the new administration did *not* want to
encourage national nuclear forces. Secretary of State Dean Rusk thus
justified this policy: "Our policy of trying to slow down acquisition [of]
nuclear weapons capabilities is based on [the] view that such acquisition
will increase [the] risk of war by accident or miscalculation, diminish
[the] possibility [of] controlled nuclear response in event of hostilities,
raise new obstacles [for] arms control, and pose [a] very grave threat to
allied political cohesion."[26] While aware of political constraints and the
legacy of past agreements, the Kennedy administration explicitly
adopted the recommendation of the Acheson report: "Over the long
run, it would be desirable if the British decided to phase out of the
nuclear deterrent business. . . . The U.S. should not assist the French to
attain a nuclear weapons capability, but should seek to respond to the
French interest in matters nuclear in . . . other ways."[27] McNamara informed the allies of this policy in his Athens address:

> In particular, relatively weak national nuclear forces with enemy cities as
> their targets are not likely to be sufficient to perform even the function of
> deterrence. . . . Indeed, if a major antagonist came to believe there was a
> substantial likelihood of its being used independently, this force would be
> inviting a preemptive first strike against it. In the event of war, the use of
> such a force against the cities of a major nuclear power would be tanta-
> mount to suicide, whereas its employment against significant military tar-
> gets would have a negligible effect on the outcome of the conflict.
> Meanwhile the creation of a single additional national nuclear force en-
> courages the proliferation of nuclear power with all of its attendant dan-
> gers. In short, then, limited nuclear capabilities, operating independently,

are dangerous, expensive, prone to obsolescence, and lacking in credibility as a deterrent.[28]

Kennedy's call for central nuclear control (together with his call for more conventional forces) led to immense tensions within the Atlantic alliance.[29] However, after the Berlin crisis President Kennedy realized the importance of compromising with the allies, and eventually he committed five Polaris submarines to NATO (depending on the success of the European conventional buildup).[30] In addition, the secretary of defense proposed more nuclear information sharing in his Athens address. And under the so-called Athens guidelines, the government committed itself to consultations before the employment of nuclear weapons, time and circumstances permitting.[31]

Rejected Alternative Strategies

In addition to rejecting the above mentioned aspects of its predecessor's policy, the Kennedy administration rejected the notion of striving to attain a first-strike capability (or win capability) for delivering a decisive blow to the enemy.[32] The transition task force headed by Paul H. Nitze articulated the importance of the decision between "a politically meaningful 'win' capability in general nuclear war versus the creation of a secure retaliatory capability."[33] The task force's report rejected the win strategy for several reasons: it was not feasible with the foreseeably available technology; it would be immensely expensive both economically and politically; it would require the United States to be ready to launch a first or a preemptive strike; and, therefore, it would be destabilizing.[34]

The new administration quickly decided to develop strategic forces that were geared for a second-strike role, as McNamara informed the Congress: "We sought to place greater emphasis on . . . the kind of forces which could ride out a massive nuclear attack and which could be applied with deliberation and always under complete control of the constituted authority."[35] With this decision, the new administration sought to reduce the dependence of the nation's military policy on tactical warning and immediate response to attack.[36] With a second-strike capability as the goal, vulnerability and survivability became the dominant factors of concern.[37] Survivability was the theme that guided Kennedy's defense budget amendments, which he presented in a special message to the Congress on 28 March 1961. While proposing acceleration of the second generation missile programs, particularly the Polaris and the Minuteman programs, and extending the ground alert program for the bomber force, the new administration proposed limiting the development of the B-70 bomber to a few prototypes, cutting the Titan II ICBM program, and accelerating the phase-out of the B-47 bombers.[38] Under the new defense program, the United States would have 1,298 missiles at its disposal in 1965—202 more than projected under the Eisenhower program.[39]

Deterrence was the primary goal of the new administration, as it had been with the Eisenhower administration. But the Kennedy administration rejected not only the goal of a full first-strike capability, it also seemed to accept a general no-first-use posture. President Kennedy stated in his budget message of March 1961 that "our arms will never be used to strike the first blow in any attack." Later in the same speech, he added that as "a power which will never strike first, our hopes for anything close to an absolute deterrent must rest on weapons which come from hidden, moving, or invulnerable bases which will not be wiped out by surprise attack."[40] McNamara's guidelines for the task force report on strategic weapons systems requirements were even more specific. Strategic nuclear forces should be developed on the assumption "that we will not strike first with such weapons."[41]

The administration grew more cautious during its first year in its statements regarding the first use of nuclear weapons. Kennedy's budget message had a negative impact on European allies and their faith in the American nuclear guarantee. The United States was explicitly committed to initiating the use of nuclear weapons rather than accept major defeat on the ground in the defense of Western Europe. A basic national security policy paper draft of March 1962 summarized the no-first-use dilemma: "In short, we should not preclude the possibility of launching the first nuclear blow as to deny ourselves the deterrent advantage of Soviet uncertainty on this point; nor should we so commit ourselves to this concept as to maximize its destabilizing effect in periods of tension, or to create an unbalanced resource allocation which would render U.S. and allied forces vulnerable to non-nuclear attack and require a nuclear *riposte* contrary to our and allied interests, if such attack were to be countered."[42]

The obvious lesson was to avoid talking about no-first-use whenever possible. But in its rejection of a full first-strike capability, the administration remained firm. First, the strategy was unfeasible, because even a devastating first strike inevitably would miss Soviet submarines at sea. Second, the buildup necessary to reach a first-strike capability would provoke an arms race. And third, it would be very costly.[43]

However, the Kennedy administration was not prepared to adopt a finite deterrence posture either.[44] There were supporters of finite deterrence in the White House, who relied on the results of the WSEG-50 report of the Weapons Systems Evaluation Group, finished in December 1960, which projected strategic offensive weapons systems for 1964 through 1967. The report proposed a finite deterrence strategy, because even a counterforce first strike would not prevent unacceptable levels of damage to the United States. Some forces, such as Soviet submarine-based missiles, would be nontargetable, while other forces would survive because of unknown location.[45] Moreover, an effort to gain a first-strike capability could not succeed, even with an accelerated buildup, because the adversary could strengthen its offensive capability at far less cost. More than one missile would be needed to destroy a single enemy missile. WSEG-50 therefore called for sufficient strategic forces to ensure high levels of damage, regardless of how a war started, and emphasized the development of conventional forces to meet local aggression locally.[46] An expert on the WSEG panel told George Rathjens, a member of Eisenhower's Science Advisory Committee, that "a counter-force capability is unrealistic and that retaliation requirements are really rather modest." One-eighth of the B-52 force carrying Hound Dog missiles on air alert, three hundred mobile Minuteman missiles, and about twenty Polaris submarines might be sufficient "to destroy the bulk of Soviet industrial capability and a very large fraction of the population."[47]

Secretary McNamara was briefed on the report's findings in January 1961. WSEG-50 seems to have made a favorable impression on the new secretary of defense, and its results were widely circulated in the Defense Department and the White House.[48] At the time of Kennedy's budget message, support for a strategy of finite deterrence was centered in the White House staff.[49] However, over the course of the summer, particularly against the background of the Berlin crisis, arguments against that strategy prevailed. McNamara ultimately rejected finite deterrence in his memorandum to the president in September 1961 for the following two reasons: First, deterrence may fail, or war may break out for accidental or unintended reasons. In that case, the strategy would allow neither damage limitation nor early war termination. Second, finite deterrence weakened the U.S. ability to deter Soviet attacks against American allies.[50] The Berlin crisis proved the political and public relations importance of superior nuclear forces in order to keep the alliance together and credibly threaten nuclear response in defense of Europe.[51] Finite deterrence would weaken the credibility of the American nuclear guarantee for Europe. Incidentally, finite deterrence would have been difficult to explain to the American public, in view of President Kennedy's harsh criticism of the Eisenhower defense policy.

Kennedy's New National Security Strategy:
The Multiple Options Approach

The reasons why the Kennedy administration rejected both a full first-strike posture and a finite deterrence strategy referred directly to the fundamental strategic dilemma that evolved during the late 1950s. As both superpowers were now equally vulnerable to nuclear attack, initiating a nuclear war had become tantamount to national suicide. The nature of conflict had changed. Nuclear superiority now had only limited military meaning. However, reliance on nuclear threats remained at the basis of European security. These threats had to be credible. Therefore, nuclear weapons had to be useful beyond mere deterrence of the other side's first use of its nuclear capabilities. Strategic superiority remained important as a measure of credibility. What was Kennedy's solution to this strategic dilemma?

In answer to the realization that nuclear war was becoming tantamount to national suicide, the Kennedy administration proposed building up conventional capabilities. Failure to do so had been the principal weakness of Eisenhower's national security policy. During his campaign, John F. Kennedy had called for increased conventional forces in order to credibly deter limited aggression in NATO Europe.[52] Paul Nitze's transition task force report summarized President Eisenhower's policy with respect to limited war: "The last Administration has never clearly faced up to the issue of the degree to which we should rely on nuclear weapons in limited wars. In essence they have said we will do what we can with conventional weapons; what can't be handled by conventional weapons must be handled by nuclear weapons."[53] With respect to NATO, the Bowie report of 1960 and the Acheson report in 1961 had recommended strengthening conventional forces. The aim of the conventional buildup was to enhance the credibility of the nuclear deterrent: "Such an attainable increase in non-nuclear capabilities in Europe would not enable NATO to defeat every conceivable Soviet aggression in Europe without using nuclear weapons. . . . However, it would give NATO flexibility to meet a wide range of Soviet aggressions without recklessness, since it would provide a non-nuclear capability to impose a pause in the event of quite large attacks by the Soviet non-nuclear ready forces, i.e., by the bulk of the Soviet forces in the satellites reinforced by such forces as the Soviets could quickly deploy to the central front."[54]

The principal aim of the "pause" was to give the adversary time to consider the grave consequences of an escalation to the nuclear level.[55] However, the military, both the JCS and SACEUR Norstad, had severe reservations about the pause concept from a military point of view.[56]

Because of these concerns, the Kennedy administration decided against an overall change on NATO's political directive. Changes with regard to the nuclear threshold should be implemented within the existing guidelines.

It was Secretary of Defense McNamara, in particular, who made an effort to implement a conventional option for NATO.[57] The Berlin crisis proved, in his opinion, the necessity for a conventional option. Also, new studies in the System Analysis Office of the Department of Defense indicated toward the end of the year that the conventional superiority of the Warsaw Pact in Europe might be far smaller than previously had been assumed, thus making a conventional defense of Western Europe more credible.[58] In his Athens address, McNamara underscored the importance of a conventional option in order to enhance the credibility of the nuclear deterrent and called for fulfillment of the thirty-division force goals for NATO's central region, as outlined in MC 26/4.[59]

While the responsibility of the European partners was to build up the alliance's divisional strength, the responsibility that the United States assigned to itself was to build up airlift and sealift capabilities. McNamara noted in his guidelines for the task force on limited war requirements that the present U.S. limited war capabilities provided for only one limited war situation at a time, without drawing on the forces deployed in Europe, Korea, Hawaii, and Okinawa. The task force was directed to study how much and what kind of additional forces the United States would need to redeploy its reserve forces in combination with its overseas forces in order to deal with more than one limited war situation at a time.[60] In his budget message, the president asked for $212 million to spend on acquiring limited war capabilities, especially airlift and sealift capabilities.[61]

European criticism of the new emphasis on a conventional option for NATO spread quickly. DeGaulle's France was confirmed in its doubts that the Americans would risk one of their cities in order to save Paris, and Adenauer's Germany was reluctant to support a strategy that would enlarge the risk of Germany's becoming a conventional battlefield.[62] Both nations preferred a strategy whereby any Warsaw Pact aggression would be treated as tripping the wire that would cause the United States to launch its nuclear weapons. They were skeptical of any strategy that entailed a pause to allow the aggressor to consider the consequences of its actions.

European criticism reached a new level of intensity in the aftermath of McNamara's Ann Arbor speech (which was basically a declassified version of his Athens address). From a European perspective, the American emphasis on central nuclear control combined with the rejection of independent national nuclear forces meant that Europe had to supply manpower while leaving the decision on nuclear options to the Americans.[63] And the principal European critique of the proposed buildup of NATO's conventional forces remained that such a buildup would only undermine the credibility of the American nuclear guarantee. This, finally, brings us to the second part of the fundamental strategic dilemma of the time, which was how to strengthen the credibility of a security guarantee resting on nuclear threats. And this part of the dilemma proved to be much harder to answer.

To reassure the allies, the Kennedy administration stressed that in case of Warsaw Pact aggression in Europe, the level of violence would have to be controlled, in order to make the nuclear deterrent credible. Consistent with that policy, Secretary McNamara articulated a no-cities counterforce strategy, as it had been developed by the air force, with the help of RAND Corporation analysts at the end of the 1950s.[64] In February 1961, McNamara was briefed on the strategy by William W. Kaufmann who had taken part in the effort to develop the new concept.[65] Seven months later, the secretary of defense used the strategy as a yardstick for the adequacy of the nation's strategic forces in his draft memorandum to the president:

> The forces I am recommending have been chosen to provide the United States with the capability, in the event of a Soviet nuclear attack, first, to strike back against Soviet bomber bases, missile sites, and other installations associated with long-range nuclear forces, in order to reduce Soviet power and limit the damage that can be done to us by vulnerable Soviet follow-on forces, while, second, holding in protected reserve forces capable of destroying the Soviet urban society, if necessary, in a controlled and deliberate way.[66]

McNamara reiterated the no-cities counterforce strategy in the secret session of NATO in Athens on 5 May 1962: "The U.S. has come to the conclusion that to the extent feasible, basic military strategy in general nuclear war should be approached in much the same way that more conventional military operations have been regarded in the past. That is to say, our principal military objectives, in the event of a nuclear war stemming from a major attack on the Alliance, should be the destruction of the enemy's military forces while attempting to preserve the fabric as well as the integrity of allied society."[67] In his Ann Arbor speech, McNamara emphasized that the "very strength and nature of the Alliance forces make it possible for us to retain, even in the face of a massive surprise attack, sufficient reserve striking power to destroy an enemy society if driven to it. In other words, we are giving a possible opponent the strongest imaginable incentive to refrain from striking our own cities."[68]

McNamara's use of the no-cities counterforce concept must be understood in terms of the European audience to which it was addressed. Only then does it become clear that the Kennedy administration emphasized a no-cities counterforce strategy not so much because the administration believed in its feasibility, but rather because the strategy was well suited for the presentation of U.S. policy goals regarding its European partners.

The no-cities strategy conveyed three important messages: First, superiority had important significance; hence the credibility of the U.S. nuclear deterrent was very good, indeed.[69] The fact that the United States could seriously think about the strategy signaled the value and extent of U.S. nuclear superiority, which bolstered the credibility of the U.S. nuclear guarantee for Europe.[70] Communication of the strategy to the public came only after the administration had driven home the extent of both quantitatively and qualitatively superior U.S. nuclear force in a series of speeches in connection with the Berlin crisis. During the last three months of 1961, Deputy Secretary of Defense Roswell L. Gilpatric, Assistant Secretary of Defense for International Security Affairs Paul Nitze, and Secretary McNamara echoed the message of American nuclear strength.[71] On 19 December, Nitze commented to the NSC on McNamara's statement of U.S. nuclear superiority at the NATO ministerial meeting of December 1961 and stressed that the "NATO members were impressed by this statement and particularly by Robert McNamara's and Dean Rusk's assurances in this context of the depth of the U.S. commitment to NATO."[72] Second, since the strategy's main goal was to spare cities, a no-cities counterforce strategy allayed European fears that the United States would not risk New York for Paris. Third, the strategy underlined the aim of a central nuclear command and control system and exposed independently operating forces as expensive, prone to obsolescence, and lacking credibility as a deterrent.[73]

There were other reasons, as well, that led the Kennedy administration to adopt a no-cities counterforce strategy in 1961. Quantitative, as well as qualitative, U.S. nuclear superiority made the goal of limiting damage to the United States in case of a nuclear war seem possible in 1961. Comprehensive mapping of Soviet strategic forces provided by air force and CIA reconnaissance satellites confirmed that, in reality, if there was any missile gap at all it was in favor of the United States.[74] With respect to the U.S. homeland, the strategy was an expression of hope that the damage of a nuclear war could be limited and the war terminated before civil society was destroyed. Also, further buildup of the nation's strategic forces could be justified only with a strategy that included counterforce targets. In 1961, McNamara used the no-cities counterforce strategy as a yardstick for determining strategic forces requirements (a decision from which he would later retreat because such a yardstick turned out to be so indeterminate).[75]

However, McNamara did not believe that the no-cities counterforce strategy really would be implemented in case of nuclear war. The strategy was not even extensively discussed in the top echelons of the government. During congressional hearings on the fiscal year 1963 defense budget in January 1962, the defense secretary noted that he was not implying that the strategy "is our tactic or . . . is one that should be considered as an operational tactic."[76] A few days later, he elaborated on this point and stressed that the administration endorsed the no-cities counterforce approach because of the high standards it set with respect to the survivability of strategic weapons and the nation's command and control systems. The strategy, he continued, "is not considered as an indication of our operational plans but rather as the basis for a higher requirement of survivability for both the weapons systems and the communication links between them and the military and political authorities having command over them."[77]

The reasons why members of the Kennedy administration doubted the operational feasibility of a no-cities counterforce strategy can be summarized in four points. First, there was reason to doubt that a nuclear war would proceed as envisioned by the strategy. Why should the Soviets restrain themselves in a first strike and attack only military targets? From a Soviet perspective, the first American strike, whether retaliatory or preemptive, threatened to be disarming because of the limited number and poor quality of Soviet strategic forces.[78] With this consideration in mind, the Soviet war planners had to think in terms of a preemptive strike on military as well as urban-industrial targets.[79] Secretary of Defense McNamara commented in a press conference: "I think it at least as likely that our cities would be attacked as that our military targets would be attacked. I don't share the views of some that only the military installations would be targeted."[80] Moreover, was it not more probable that the alliance would have to make the decision to go nuclear? Deputy Assistant Secretary for System Analysis Alain Enthoven later confirmed that "as a practical matter it was impossible to communicate a clear distinction between McNamara's view of deliberation, control, and 'no-cities' as a last desperate hope to make the best of a catastrophe, and

General [Curtis] LeMay's view that we could fight and win a nuclear war. . . . The Ann Arbor theme was too subtle an idea to be effective in the political arena."[81]

A second flaw in a no-cities counterforce strategy was that the strategy demanded a degree of flexibility and restraint not available with the existing nuclear weapons. In April 1961, the chairman of the JCS Lyman L. Lemnitzer pointed out that "we do not have adequate defenses, nor are our nuclear retaliatory forces sufficiently invulnerable, to permit us to risk withholding a substantial part of our effort, once a major thermonuclear attack has been initiated."[82] Nevertheless, the no-cities counterforce strategy became part of the guidelines for the SIOP-63.[83] Although the new war plan allowed more flexibility and included more options than the SIOP-62—it distinguished military targets from cities and command and control systems—its options were all still massive, each envisioning the launch of thousands of weapons.[84] The central problem remained that the amount of radioactive fallout could not be limited to desired levels because of the big circular errors of probability of the carrier systems and the huge explosive power of the available warheads.[85] Finally, scientific knowledge of the electromagnetic effects of nuclear explosions on nuclear command and control systems was very limited at the time.[86] The vulnerability of the nation's command, control, and communication systems was generally regarded as a critical factor in 1961.[87] Although McNamara could inform the Senate Appropriations Committee about the components of a new Post-Attack Command and Control System (PACCS) in February 1962, the system could not be implemented for several years.[88]

A third weakness of the no-cities counterforce concept came to light in the course of the Berlin crisis of 1961, when Kennedy administration officials realized that damage to Europe in a nuclear war could not be limited.[89] The Soviets had emphasized the development of regional-range ballistic missiles at the end of the 1950s, due to technical problems in their ICBM program and the political priority of regional security.[90] This meant that while they had only a very limited number of ICBMs at their disposal in 1961, the Soviets had enough IRBMs and sea-based ballistic missiles to assure destruction of Europe even after a massive preemptive strike by the United States.

A fourth weakness of counterforce was that given the growing invulnerability of the Soviet nuclear force, the possibility of limiting damage to the United States by destroying Soviet weapons was eroding quickly. On 13 September 1961, the chairman of the JCS briefed the president on the SIOP-62. On this occasion, General Lemnitzer warned President

Kennedy that even if the United States preempted a Soviet attack, he could not guarantee that the entire Soviet nuclear arsenal would be destroyed: "Under any circumstances—even a preemptive attack by the US," he pointed out, "it would be expected that some portion of the Soviet long-range nuclear force would strike the United States."[91] McNamara summarized the last two points in a speech to the Fellows of the American Bar Foundation on 17 February 1962: "It [the USSR] does have the power today to damage severely the nations of Western Europe, and we must anticipate that over the years the Soviets can, and undoubtedly will, produce weapons with sufficient range and destructive power to inflict similar damage on the United States, even while we ourselves retain a substantial margin of strategic power."[92]

While doubting its operational feasibility, the Kennedy administration made political use of the no-cities counterforce strategy. Ironically, the strategy was endorsed at a time when damage limitation had become increasingly doubtful due to the growing invulnerability of the Soviet nuclear force. And the strategy was endorsed for the benefit of a European audience for which the goal had become impracticable as early as 1961.

Notwithstanding the rhetoric, Secretary of Defense McNamara had never been prepared to make any advance commitment with respect to nuclear doctrine and targets. He made this clear in an address to the Fellows of the American Bar Foundation in February 1962. His address represents U.S. nuclear strategy at the end of 1961 more accurately than the Athens speech: "Our new policy gives us the flexibility to choose among several operational plans, but does not require that we make any advance commitment with respect to doctrine and targets."[93] In this regard, he was in complete agreement with the president, who decided never to sign a basic national security policy paper as a binding guidance for defense planning.[94] The key element for planning had to be flexibility. The most important factor was to assure that nuclear forces could be used in a controlled and deliberate way, under a wide range of contingencies: "We may have to retaliate with a single massive attack. Or, we may be able to use our retaliatory forces to limit damage to ourselves, by knocking out the enemy's bases before he has had time to launch his second salvos. We may wish to terminate a war on favorable terms by using our forces as a bargaining weapon—by threatening further attack."[95] The two most important preconditions for flexibility were invulnerable nuclear weapons systems and a secure command and control system. On these two elements, the Kennedy administration focused its efforts. Beyond that, preplanning of detailed nuclear options would be a hopelessly difficult task. In an actual crisis situation, a response would have to be improvised.

The unwillingness of the Kennedy administration to make any commitment to one, detailed nuclear strategy reflected the basic insight of the civilian strategists that it was uncertainty that made nuclear threats work in circumstances of mutual vulnerability. The Kennedy administration's multiple options approach to military strategy reflected the same basic insight. The Kennedy administration broadened the options available, made no advance commitments with respect to nuclear doctrine and targets, and built up conventional strength so that the question of when and how to use nuclear weapons would never have to be faced.

9

The Berlin Crisis:
Example of Self-Deterrence or
Successful Manipulation of Risk?

For the United States, the Berlin crisis was a test of will. The Soviet leaders seemed to anticipate that the effectiveness of the U.S. deterrent would decrease as Soviet nuclear capabilities increased. The crucial question was whether the U.S. government remained prepared to defend West Berlin by whatever means, notwithstanding the vulnerability of the United States itself. At stake in West Berlin was the credibility of the superpowers' security guarantees to their respective allies.

Tension over the future of West Berlin grew in 1958 and did not completely abate until 1963. Sometimes acute, sometimes simmering, but never far from the minds of defense policymakers, the crisis was a touchstone of American perceptions of the Soviet threat during this period. Khrushchev seemed to be probing for western concessions, exploiting the growing Soviet IRBM threat to Europe and western fears of an ICBM gap in the wake of *Sputnik*. The greatest danger to the West was that Soviet threats would split NATO. The Europeans increasingly doubted the will of the United States to guarantee their security by all means. Such doubts could translate into major changes in Western European foreign policy. The United States had to allay European fears and ensure the close association of the Federal Republic of Germany to the West. West Berlin became the test of U.S. commitment.[1]

We have seen that sharing nuclear weapons with the allies was one way that President Eisenhower sought to reinforce the NATO alliance. But what was intended to reassure the allies, at the same time threatened the Soviets. Khrushchev's decision to rearrange the politics of Berlin was strongly influenced by fear of a nuclear-armed Germany.[2] Eisenhower had presented to NATO the plan for a U.S.-controlled nuclear stockpile system in late 1957. In March 1958, Konrad Adenauer had obtained a majority vote in the Parliament authorizing him to arm the *Bundeswehr* with atomic weapons. And in late 1958, when Khrushchev provoked the Berlin crisis, Germany had just completed the training of a nuclear-capable fighter-bomber unit and the construction of a nuclear weapons storage facility.[3]

The coincidence of the German move toward nuclear weapons and Soviet pressure in Berlin did not escape the notice of Ambassador Llewellyn E. Thompson in Moscow.[4] But to officials in Washington, a nuclear-armed *Bundeswehr* did not appear to pose a fundamental threat to the Soviet Union. The Eisenhower administration valued the delivery of nuclear warheads to Europe as an important signal of U.S. resolve. The reassuring effect of nuclear deployments would countervail Soviet attempts to lull Germany into a state of neutrality.[5]

There might have been other reasons, in addition to his fear of a nuclear-armed Germany, that explain Khrushchev's instigation of the Berlin crisis. These reasons may include a desire of Khrushchev to strengthen the leaders of East Germany or to contain his Chinese critics.[6] The most striking feature of all of this is that the spiral of misperception and flawed communication, which would become a characteristic element of Soviet-American relations in the early sixties, was there from the very beginning of the Berlin crisis in 1958.

The Reaction of the Eisenhower Administration

Border tension over West Berlin was becoming more frequent during the summer of 1958.[7] The Berlin crisis was incited by Khrushchev's speech at a Soviet-Polish meeting in Moscow on 10 November. Subsequently, the Soviet Union sent notes on Berlin to the United States, the United Kingdom, France, and the Federal Republic of Germany. Khrushchev demanded that there be a peace treaty between the former wartime allies and Germany. He announced that the Soviet Union regarded the four-power agreements over the control of Berlin and Germany as "null and void." These agreements had been violated by the West, according to Khrushchev, particularly with the rearmament of West Germany. Khrushchev then proceeded to propose a demilitarized free-city status for West Berlin. He warned the West that if a peace treaty was not accepted within six months, the Soviet Union would make separate arrangements with East Germany on the basis of which that country would "fully deal with questions concerning its space, i.e., exercise its sovereignty on land, water, and in the air."[8] The Soviet threat was clear: The West had to prepare for the moment when Khrushchev would relinquish control over access to West Berlin to the East Germans, thereby forcing the West to deal with a state it refused to recognize.

The Eisenhower administration assumed that the Soviets did not want general war but that they would keep probing. Both Eisenhower and Dulles were convinced that the Soviet threat was a bluff. The president pointed out in a talk with congressional leaders that "Khrushchev does not desire war more than we."[9] Nevertheless, the danger of the situation, in the words of Secretary Dulles, was that the western position would be "nibbled away."[10] Secretary Dulles concluded that if the West was perfectly firm in its position "there is not one chance in 1000 the Soviets will push it to the point of war."[11] The president insisted that because the Soviet threat was essentially a long-term problem, in which this particular case was only one of many probes to come, the best way to protect western interests was by being prepared to defend them with nuclear weapons.[12] Secretary Dulles once commented that "the basic philosophy of our current program is that if we show that we are prepared to use whatever force may be required to assure our rights in respect to Berlin, and if the Soviets are in no doubt of this, then we will not in the event have to use that force."[13] In other words, if the risk of nuclear war was accepted, the Soviets would withdraw from their present position. Both the president and the secretary of state recognized that a crucial factor in this strategy was that the West remain united in its response to Soviet pressure.[14]

Officials in the Eisenhower administration believed that the threat of general war would be a sufficient deterrent. Extensive military preparations were unnecessary and would lead to a dangerous accumulation of costs in the long run. More important was that the West demonstrate its resolve in order to assure the Soviets that the West would defend West Berlin with nuclear weapons. What counted was not so much the military value of military preparations, but rather the psychological impact of preparation on Soviet beliefs. Eisenhower and Dulles favored quiet precautionary military measures that would attract no public attention, but that would be detectable by Soviet intelligence, in order to manipulate Soviet perceptions of nuclear risks. The scope of the program is only partly identifiable; it included measures such as increased military traffic and communications between West Berlin and the FRG, the expansion of U.S. forces in Europe, and the acceleration of the nuclear stockpile program in the FRG.[15]

Contingency Planning

The Eisenhower administration's approach to the Berlin crisis entailed some risk of escalation due to unexpected developments, miscalculation, or muddling. Eisenhower admitted that the nation could become embroiled in a general war as a result of miscalculations on either side.[16] He ordered a review of contingency planning in case deterrence of a Communist attempt to close western access to Berlin should break down.[17] The initial approach of the Eisenhower administration to contingency planning sought to meet a challenge to surface access to Berlin on the ground. It was understood that retaliation on the ground could quickly escalate to general war. This risk had to be accepted.[18]

However, the British were wary of such risk taking, because they perceived their survival as a functioning society to be at stake. They recommended responding to restrictions on surface access with an airlift. The British also urged a bigger role for diplomatic action before deploying military force in response to interruption of access to West Berlin.[19] The French, agreeing with the British on this particular matter, opposed any commitment to plans that would lead "semi-automatically" to all-out war. However, the French were even more prepared than the Americans to oppose quickly, with military force, any interference with access to Berlin.[20] Under the evolving compromise, the allies would launch a small probe to determine whether the Soviets were prepared to use force to prevent allied passage. If the initial probe or probes were rebuffed, the allies would increase pressure on the Soviet Union and East Germany by stepping up propaganda campaigns, diplomatic pressures, readily observable military measures, and possibly economic measures. If all of these measures proved futile, the allies would then decide how to restore the free passage by use of force.[21]

Allied opposition to an early nuclear response led to further discussion of military contingency plans within the administration. The debate shows that Eisenhower was not prepared to contemplate conventional war in Europe. At the beginning of March, the Department of State examined two alternative ways to follow up once an initial probe was obstructed. One option was to use substantial conventional force to reopen passage to Berlin. The other option was a counterblockade of the Soviet Union in the Pacific.[22] President Eisenhower liked neither option.[23] Christian Herter, soon to be secretary of state, informed the hospitalized John Foster Dulles that the president had convinced his advisers "that we cannot fight a ground battle around Berlin." He then conveyed the president's view that if the Soviets took Berlin by force, "we have to then face up to the big decision but in the meanwhile we would do everything feasible to negotiate."[24]

American planners seem to have finally settled on the use of a reinforced battalion to reopen access to delay facing the decision of whether to escalate to general war.[25] General Nathan F. Twining summarized the purpose of such a move as being "to require the Soviets to respond in sufficient force so that they would realize that they were initiating general war."[26] However, Eisenhower qualified his support for a strategy of risk manipulation in two respects: First, the studies outlining the U.S. view of how to follow up in the event the initial probe failed should not be shown to the allies. Second, "advance planning regarding the alternative uses of force would necessarily be subject to review and decision in the light of circumstances as they develop."[27]

Western Unity

The central problem for the Eisenhower administration in responding to Khrushchev's threat became maintenance of western unity. The British, on the one hand, were convinced that the only appropriate way to solve the differences over Berlin in the nuclear age was through negotiations.[28] They called for a summit meeting. Prime Minister Harold Macmillan of Great Britain described the fears of the British people in a talk with President Eisenhower. He said that "eight thermonuclear weapons, which . . . the Soviets could now deliver against England, would destroy their country and kill 20 million people."[29] British ambassador Sir Harold Caccia cut to the heart of the matter in a remark to Under Secretary of State C. Douglas Dillon to the effect that "the British people will never be atomized for the sake of Berlin."[30] Some time later, the president replied to Caccia "that speaking for himself he would rather be atomized than communized."[31]

The Germans, on the other hand, were fearful that the British would show weakness. After a visit from Adenauer on 27 May, President Eisenhower noted that the chancellor seemed "to have developed almost a psychopathic fear of what he considers to be 'British weakness.' "[32] The Soviets attempted to capitalize on European fears of nuclear war. Khrushchev's discourses on Soviet rocket and atomic prowess are well known. One of his most famous pronouncements was made in a conversation with W. Averell Harriman on 25 June: "One bomb is sufficient to destroy Bonn and the Ruhr, and that is all of Germany. Paris is all of France; London is all of England. You have surrounded us with bases but our rockets can destroy them. If you start a war, we may die but the rockets will fly automatically."[33]

Members of the Eisenhower administration had discussed how to best reassure the Europeans even before Khrushchev's threats of November 1958. The spring debate on basic national security policy, which centered, as in the preceding years, on the question of more conventional forces for limited wars, outlined the scope of the dilemma of maintaining western security despite mutual nuclear plenty. Deputy Secretary of Defense Donald Quarles noted that "the danger of speaking about limited war involving the United States and the USSR is precisely that it would encourage this kind of erroneous thinking. It would be extremely dangerous, for example, to allow a concept to get out that if we were attacked in Berlin we would not apply all the necessary force required to repel the attack." Chairman of the JCS Twining expanded on this point, observing that "a deterrent would cease to be a deterrent if the enemy came to believe that we had lost our will to use it." Twining advised against increased limited forces to cope with limited aggressions, "because of the serious adverse psychological reactions at home, in the minds of our allies, and in the minds of the Soviets." Dulles then presented the counterargument that "unless we could satisfy our allies that they possess some kind of local military capability to defend themselves by other means than our resort to massive nuclear retaliation, we would lose our allies." While recognizing that local wars in Europe might very well spread rapidly into general nuclear war, the secretary of state noted that "we do not want to lose our allies before the war even starts."[34]

However, President Eisenhower affirmed his often-stated position that local wars would quickly escalate into general nuclear war in Europe. Moreover, the additional expense of deploying conventional forces would require a controlled economy and, finally, would render the United States a garrison state. For these reasons, the president concluded as he had in August 1960, that "we must be ready to throw the book at the Russians should they jump us."[35] In the nuclear age, the unity of the alliance depended not primarily on military preparation, but rather on how military measures were perceived by allies, adversary, and the American public. President Eisenhower, as a believer in the value of exploiting uncertainty, decided to speak as little as possible about military courses of action for hypothetical situations.[36] However, the president was not unaffected by European fears of nuclear war. While leaving the decision of whether to use all available means to reopen passage to Berlin for the future, he was increasingly prepared to search for a negotiated settlement of the Berlin problem.[37]

Tensions between what Adenauer perceived to be British weakness and what Macmillan perceived to be German inflexibility led Eisenhower to consider bilateral talks with the Soviets more favorably.[38] After the Geneva foreign ministers' conference had failed to lead to a solution, a bilateral meeting was scheduled for September 1959. One advantage of a direct encounter with Khrushchev was that Eisenhower could expose nuclear threats as a bluff. On 13 July Eisenhower told a few key advisers that if "Khrushchev were to threaten war or use of force, he would immediately call his bluff and ask him to agree on a day to start."[39] The celebrated meeting between Eisenhower and Khrushchev at Camp David resulted in abandonment of the Soviet deadline for a peace treaty. The friendly "spirit of Camp David" was due to mutual understanding that the conflict over Berlin and Germany should not be solved by a war that would lead to mutual suicide.[40]

Against this background, Eisenhower was looking for possible arrangements with the Soviets. On 19 June, he suggested that the United States might use the offer to abandon plans to station IRBMs in Greece as a bargaining chip for Berlin. His comments about the desirability of a trade-off are of interest, in light of the events leading up to the Cuban missile crisis:

> The President said one thing is bothering him a great deal in the present situation, and that is the plan to put IRBMs in Greece. If Mexico or Cuba had been penetrated by the Communists, and then began getting arms and missiles from them, we would be bound to look on such developments with the gravest concern and in fact he thought it would be imperative for us to take positive action, even offensive military action. He could see the reason for Redstone, Corporal or Honest John missiles, which are short-range, but not IRBMs. He wondered if we were not simply being provocative, since Eastern Europe is an area of dispute in a political sense.[41]

On 1 October, Eisenhower noted that "the time was coming and perhaps soon when we would simply have to get our forces out" of West Berlin. He was willing to consider developing Berlin into "some kind of a free city," which might "require that the U.N. would become a party guaranteeing the freedom, safety, and security of the city."[42] However, Eisenhower's proposal was rejected by both the Department of State and the Department of Defense as backing down in the face of the Soviet threat. And it was clearly anathema to Chancellor Adenauer. On 15 March 1960, Eisenhower noted in frustration that "the West, except for Adenauer, thinks we should explore alternatives on Berlin." Secretary of State Herter agreed and underscored that the problem was "that the Germans are unwilling to explore any alternatives to the present status on Berlin."[43] In the end, Adenauer's veto was binding on President Eisenhower. Although Eisenhower was moving toward the idea of accommodation with the Soviets, as Marc Trachtenberg has noted, there "was in fact very little that the Americans were willing to negotiate about."[44]

The Camp David meeting had led to an agreement on an East-West summit, scheduled for May 1960 in Paris. But as early as the spring of 1960, the "spirit of Camp David" had given way to increased tensions. Then came the shooting down of the American U-2 photographic reconnaissance airplane deep inside the Soviet Union. The incident resulted in the cancellation of the Paris summit.[45] Khrushchev then postponed discussion of the crisis until the new American administration took office.

The Crisis Builds Up under Kennedy

Kennedy's national security policy team shared the Eisenhower administration's perception of the threat that the nation was facing over Berlin. Both the Republican administration and the Democratic administration agreed on the crucial importance of maintaining the western position in West Berlin. Both believed that any Soviet interference with basic western interests should be firmly resisted. Finally, both Eisenhower and Kennedy attempted to manipulate risk, that is, exploit the uncertainty inherent in the crisis, in order to remind the Soviets of the unacceptable risk of nuclear war.

However, the two administrations differed over the means by which to achieve the intended result. While President Eisenhower was supremely confident that minor, "quiet," precautionary measures would be enough to convince Khrushchev that the West would stand firm, President Kennedy was of the opinion that only a clear display of force would make the danger clear.[46] As discussed below, Kennedy concluded that only a publicly announced buildup of conventional forces in Central Europe would be a credible deterrent. In addition, the Kennedy administration turned out to be even more flexible with respect to the German question and negotiations over the status of Berlin than the Eisenhower administration. This greater flexibility regarding Berlin and Germany was probably closely related to Kennedy's doubts about the credibility of the U.S. deterrent.[47]

Khrushchev had clearly hoped that Kennedy would defeat Richard

Nixon in the 1960 election. During the election campaign, the Soviet premier had criticized both Kennedy and Nixon, following the advice of Averell Harriman, who had warned him that to express one-sided support for Kennedy was the surest way to hinder his election. After Kennedy's narrow victory on 9 November 1960, Khrushchev quickly moved to signal that he wanted "to make a fresh start," using W. Averell Harriman and Adlai E. Stevenson, III, as intermediaries.[48] The Soviets were worried that Germany and China would obtain nuclear weapons and urged the Americans to prevent the spread of nuclear weapons.[49] When Kennedy met with Harriman, Thompson, Charles E. Bohlen, and George F. Kennan on 11 February to discuss the thinking of the Soviet leadership, the nation's leading specialists on Soviet affairs agreed that the Soviets sounded conciliatory. They stated that "Khrushchev would very much like some specific diplomatic successes in 1961" in order to secure rapid Soviet economic progress. They believed that Khrushchev was not likely to bring the Berlin situation "to a boil unless there is a break-down of negotiations on disarmament, or perhaps an increase in tension in such a place as Laos."[50]

In fact, the situation in Laos was deteriorating very rapidly in early 1961. The Soviet-supported forces of the Pathet Lao had threatened to expel the American-supported forces of General Phoumi Nosavan from every key city of the country.[51] This threat proved to the incoming administration that Khrushchev was serious about supporting wars of national liberation, as he had announced in a speech on 6 January 1961. We have seen previously that the "Wars of Liberation" speech became somewhat of an obsession with President Kennedy and received wide attention.[52] On the other hand, President Kennedy's alarming rhetoric in his State of the Union message of 30 January cannot have pleased Khrushchev either. Kennedy declared that each "day, the crises multiply. Each day, their solution grows more difficult. Each day, we draw nearer the hour of maximum danger."[53] Although Kennedy made a point of not mentioning the Berlin problem (causing considerable West German uneasiness), the alarmist language could hardly have been interpreted by the Soviets as signaling U.S. willingness to solve differences by negotiations.[54]

Tensions between East and West developed quickly during 1961. And with increasing tensions, the spiral of misperceptions and flawed communications preempted the agenda of negotiation. Both Khrushchev's "Wars of Liberation" speech and Kennedy's State of the Union Address were directed toward domestic audiences. Kennedy spoke to an audience that had elected him on campaign promises that he would do more about the Soviet danger than Eisenhower had done. Khrushchev spoke to an audience before which he felt a need to prove that he was a tougher Communist than Soviet hard-liners and his Chinese critics believed him to be. But amidst growing tensions, people on the other side forgot that this was rhetoric designed for domestic consumption. Threats were taken seriously for fear of the consequences if they were ignored.[55]

The Bay of Pigs and the Kennedy-Khrushchev Meeting in Vienna

Then came the dramatic failure of the Bay of Pigs invasion. On 17 April 1961, a CIA-trained, -armed, and -transported force of some 1,500 anti-Castro Cuban exiles landed at the Cuban Bay of Pigs. The force was crushed in less than three days by the military forces of Fidel Castro. Although most of the planning and preparations had been done during Eisenhower's presidency, President Kennedy made the decision to go ahead with the invasion. With the Bay of Pigs failure, the Kennedy presidency reached its all-time low.[56] Columnist Stewart Alsop captured the general mood in Washington's foreign policy circle at that time: "He [the President] knew that he was in for trouble, but I am quite sure he had no idea that he would take such a left and right to the jaw as Cuba and Laos, which have been taken together by far the worst foreign policy failures suffered by an American President in our times. Add the signs of weakness all around the Soviet periphery, the disarray of NATO, the threat to Berlin, and all the rest of it. Given this grim picture, can Kennedy come back?"[57]

The Bay of Pigs failure exposed the young president as indecisive and immature. These were signs of weakness that Khrushchev could not fail to notice. The Soviet premier decided to exploit this opportunity in the forthcoming Vienna meeting of the two heads of state. In the aftermath of his somber direct encounter with Khrushchev, Kennedy admitted in a talk with Prime Minister Macmillan of Britain that the West might have become weaker in the view of the Soviets as a result of recent developments in Laos and Cuba.[58]

In the late 1950s, Khrushchev had committed himself to the position that a peace treaty was essential to contain a potential West German nuclear threat to the Soviet Union.[59] On 17 February 1961, the Soviets reiterated that they were not prepared to simply drop their Berlin demands. In a memorandum to the FRG, Khrushchev did not rule out an interim settlement on Berlin pending the conclusion of a peace treaty within a specified time limit.[60] On 9 March, Ambassador Llewellyn

Thompson told Khrushchev that Kennedy was reviewing American policy on Germany and inquired into the possibility of a meeting between President Kennedy and Premier Khrushchev. The Americans abandoned active pursuit of a meeting in the wake of the Bay of Pigs crisis. After this embarrassment for Kennedy, however, it was the Soviet side that revived the idea with a formal proposal for a summit meeting on 4 May.[61] Against the background of their earlier proposal, the Americans had little choice but to accept the invitation.

The Vienna meeting of 3–4 June 1961 brought the Soviet threat to block access to Berlin to a new climax: Khrushchev flatly threatened war over Berlin. During his conversation with President Kennedy, the Soviet premier reiterated his threat of a separate peace treaty, imposing a new six-month deadline for the resolution of the problem.[62] The Vienna talks were a sobering experience for President Kennedy. From the transcripts of their conversation, it appears that the Soviet premier was always on the offensive.[63] Needling Kennedy by noting that the former senator had been late on the occasion of a meeting between Khrushchev and congressional leaders in September 1959, the Soviet premier drew Kennedy into a debate over ideology—very much to the annoyance of Kennedy's advisers. President Kennedy acknowledged Khrushchev's belief in the inevitability of the spread of Communism. He then went on to point out that "our basic objective should be preservation of peace and if we fail in that effort both our countries will lose. Our two countries, possess modern weapons. . . . However, if our two countries should miscalculate they would lose for a long time to come." Khrushchev was annoyed at the word "miscalculation": "It looked to him as if the United States wanted the USSR to sit like a school boy with his hands on his desk." The West had been using the term far too often, but the Soviet Union, though not wanting war, would not be intimidated either.

During the afternoon meeting, Kennedy attempted to explain what he meant by "miscalculation": "In Washington," he noted, "[the President] has to attempt to make judgments of events, judgments which may be accurate or not; he made a misjudgment with regard to the Cuban situation." This admission of an American mistake led only to a further outburst by the Soviet leader: "The President had said that the US had attacked Cuba because it was a threat to American security. Can six million people really be a threat to the mighty US? The United States has stated that it is free to act, but what about Turkey and Iran? . . . they have US bases and rockets. If the US believes that it is free to act, then what should the USSR do?"

Aside from the "miscalculation" issue, one other remark by Kennedy

was bound to leave a lasting impression on Khrushchev. In an attempt
to explain that U.S. policy was fundamentally aimed at securing the
status quo, Kennedy stated that "we regard the present balance of power
between Sino-Soviet forces and the force of the United States and Western Europe as being more or less in balance."[64] While not everybody in
Washington liked this remark, Khrushchev surely did.

But the toughest exchanges came on the second day of the meeting,
when the two leaders met at the Soviet Embassy to discuss the Berlin
issue. During the afternoon session, President Kennedy, referring to his
forthcoming meeting with Macmillan, inquired as to whether he should
inform the British premier "that he had gained the impression that the
USSR was presenting him with the alternative of accepting the Soviet act
on Berlin or having a face to face confrontation." This inquiry led to
the final exchange, which set the stage for the coming summer:

> Mr. Khrushchev continued by saying that he wanted peace and that if the
> US wanted war, that was its problem. It is not the USSR that threatens with
> war, it is the US. The President stressed that it was the Chairman, not he,
> who wanted to force a change. Mr. Khrushchev replied that a peace treaty
> would not involve any change in boundaries. In any event, the USSR will
> have no choice other than to accept the challenge; it must respond and it
> will respond. The calamities of a war will be shared equally. War will take
> place only if the US imposes it on the USSR. It is up to the US to decide
> whether there will be war or peace. This, he said, can be told Macmillan,
> DeGaulle and Adenauer. The decision to sign a peace treaty is firm and
> irrevocable and the Soviet Union will sign it in December if the US refuses
> an interim agreement. The president concluded the conversation by ob-
> serving that it would be a cold winter. [65]

President Kennedy returned from Vienna shocked at Khrushchev's
belligerence and feeling that the Soviet leader perceived him to be inex-
perienced and indecisive.[66] On 6 June 1961, Kennedy reported to the
nation in a televised address on "the very somber 2 days" in Vienna.
The president pointed out how valuable it had been that both sides had
had the opportunity to make clear what they considered as vital, "for
the facts of the matter are that the Soviets and ourselves give wholly
different meanings to the same words—'war', 'peace', 'democracy', and
'popular will'." Noting that the "most somber talks were on the subject
of Germany and Berlin," Kennedy reiterated the American commitment to defend western access rights to West Berlin at any cost.[67] The
crucial question for the future, therefore, was whether Khrushchev
would carry out his threat to sign a separate peace treaty with Eastern

Germany before the end of the year. In the wake of Vienna, his threat looked more credible than ever before.

The Reaction of the Kennedy Administration: A Strategy of Risk Manipulation

The Kennedy administration began to formulate its strategy for dealing with the Berlin problem against a background of increasing Cold War tensions. Kennedy overhauled Eisenhower's Berlin plans as part of the new administration's general reappraisal of national security policy. We have seen that Kennedy's advisers agreed that the threat of massive retaliation lacked credibility and, therefore, aimed at developing multiple options for the use of nuclear weapons. The Kennedy administration advocated a non-nuclear buildup in order to make the nuclear deterrent more credible, thereby enhancing the West's bargaining position. The Europeans regarded the new emphasis on conventional alternatives as a dangerous shift in American strategic thinking. They argued that a substantial increase in conventional forces would serve to degrade rather than strengthen the nuclear deterrent.[68] The Berlin crisis provided the Kennedy administration with the opportunity to advance its strategic ideas within NATO. The reappraisal of NATO strategy and the overhaul of contingency planning for Berlin reinforced each other and evolved along parallel tracks during 1961.

The close weave between the redirection of national security policy and the overhaul of the Berlin policy is particularly evident in the role that Dean Acheson, the secretary of state under President Truman, played in this process. Acheson had publicly criticized Eisenhower's approach to the Berlin crisis in 1959 as relying too much on nuclear threats and neglecting the conventional effort.[69] Now, in early 1961, he had the chance to reshape the nation's NATO policy.[70] When he presented his NATO report to the president, Kennedy asked him to review the Berlin planning as well.[71] Acheson laid out the essential premises of his approach in a memorandum of 3 April 1961, before leaving for a tour of Europe and just in time for the visit of British prime minister Harold Macmillan to Washington.[72] The Kennedy administration's Berlin policy was based upon two fundamental assumptions: First, Berlin was no place for compromise, and the West had to stand firm. Second, the credibility of the western deterrent needed to be enhanced by a conventional buildup.[73]

McGeorge Bundy transmitted what he called Acheson's "first-rate interim memorandum on Berlin" to President Kennedy, summarizing its argument in view of the forthcoming Macmillan visit: "Attempts to ne-gotiate this problem out of existence have failed in the past, and there is none which gives promise of success now. . . . Berlin is no place for compromise."[74] Acheson's memorandum outlined his premises for analysis of the Berlin problem: First, it seemed "more likely than not that the USSR will move toward a crisis this year." Second, there was "no 'solution' for the Berlin problem short of the unification of Ger-many. All sources of action are dangerous and unpromising. Inaction is even worse. We are faced with a 'Hobson's choice'. If a crisis is provoked a bold and dangerous course may be safest." Acheson declared that the importance of Berlin was very great and that the West had to be pre-pared for military response in order to save the power status quo in Europe:

> If USSR is not to dominate Europe, and, by doing so, dominate Asia and Africa also, a willingness to fight for Berlin is essential. Economic and politi-cal pressures will not be effective; they would degrade the credibility of the United States commitment to NATO. Nor would threatening to initiate general nuclear war be a solution. The threat would not carry conviction; it would invite a preemptive strike; and it would alienate allies and neutrals alike. The fight for Berlin must begin, at any rate, as a local conflict. The problem is how and where will it end. This uncertainty must be accepted.[75]

It was the fundamental logic of Acheson's approach that western willing-ness to use substantial conventional forces in defense of West Berlin would signal to the Soviets that further escalation would mean the use of nuclear weapons. Once the West had committed itself to such a degree, according to Acheson, nuclear threats would become more credible.[76]

Following the formulation of Acheson's preliminary conclusions, President Kennedy requested a first review of available military planning for a possible Berlin crisis.[77] The JCS were directed to undertake three studies on the basis of the recommendations put forward by Acheson.[78] As early as 5 May, McNamara informed the president that the military planning for Berlin was based on policy guidance of February 1958 (NSC 5803), which did "not reflect new developments in U.S. strategic thinking." Therefore, he thought that an early restatement of American national policy with regard to Berlin contingency planning was desir-able.[79] The Kennedy administration had already reviewed Berlin contin-gency planning as part of its general reappraisal of national security policy before Kennedy's encounter with Khrushchev in Vienna. All of the studies so far underscored the importance of a conventional buildup in order to strengthen the western deterrent. Finally, allied governments were briefed about the shift in U.S. strategic thinking in personal talks between President Kennedy and Harold Macmillan, Konrad Adenauer, and Charles DeGaulle.[80] Khrushchev's Vienna threats generated a sense of pressure and an atmosphere of anxiety that allowed the new administration to push for the implementation of its new approach to national security strategy.

In his address to the American people on the eve of his return from Vienna, Kennedy kept silent on Khrushchev's December ultimatum, noting that there were "no threats or ultimatums by either side."[81] If the point of this evasion was to give the Soviets a chance to retreat without undue loss of prestige, Khrushchev's reaction was disappointing. On 4 June, he made public the text of the Aide-Mémoire that he had handed to the American delegation in Vienna. Moreover, the Soviet premier publicly committed himself in two speeches to the signing of a peace treaty with the GDR "at the end of this year."[82] Khrushchev raised the ante further on 8 July 1961, announcing the temporary suspension of the reduction of Soviet armed forces planned for 1961 and an increase in defense spending for the year by the equivalent of $3.4 billion.[83] The Kennedy administration now was forced to formulate its response to Khrushchev's challenge in a tense atmosphere. At the heart of the American response lay the Acheson report of 28 June.[84]

Acheson's Berlin Report

Acheson's Berlin report started from the premise that the significance of Berlin was that it "has become an issue of resolution between the U.S.A. and the U.S.S.R., the outcome of which will go far to determine the confidence of Europe—indeed, of the world—in the United States."[85] Until this conflict of wills was resolved, it would be dangerous to attempt to solve the Berlin issue by negotiations. Negotiations could only resolve the issue once the United States had demonstrated that Khrushchev would not get what he wanted. Khrushchev's determination in Berlin indicated that he did not believe that the United States would be willing to use nuclear weapons to defend the city.[86] Apparently, the Soviet leader's fears that interference with western rights would lead to nuclear war had diminished over the last years.[87] This expectation had to be reversed.

In order to bring about a reversal of Khrushchev's appraisal of American unwillingness to go to nuclear war over Berlin, the United States, first of all, had to decide that it could accept nuclear war rather than submit to the Soviet demands. Otherwise U.S. policy would be a bluff, and a bluff would be exposed quickly. The report pointed out that there was a substantial chance that nuclear war might result either through miscalculation or through Moscow's refusal to be deterred; however, this risk had to be accepted. Second, to convince the Soviets that the United States was earnest about defending Berlin, it had to ready the military, economic, and political power needed for the defense of the city. There were two purposes to these preparatory measures: one was to convince the Soviets of U.S. willingness to use nuclear weapons rather than submit to Soviet demands; the other was to assure the Soviets that the U.S. would have, at the appropriate time, the power necessary to achieve its purpose.[88] These preparations had to be wholly authentic; they should be neither dramatized nor concealed. They had to be portrayed as related to world tensions generally rather than to Berlin alone. Khrushchev should not be challenged directly on Berlin. Military preparations had to include the rapid buildup of the nation's capabilities for conventional and nuclear war, including the expansion of nonnuclear ground, air, and naval forces as well as the enhancement of SAC's readiness and the buildup of the country's civil defense system. However, political preparations might be even more credible. Planning a major long-term increase in U.S. force levels might have a substantial deterrent effect.

The report then came to the crucial question of the use of force in case a sizable probe would establish that access to Berlin was physically blocked. The paper noted that the purpose of the operation which would then be initiated would not be military defeat; this would not be feasible. The operation would rather serve "the political purpose of moving the Soviets to negotiate a resumption of access by giving the most convincing demonstration of which the West was capable that the Western Allies were not prepared to submit to Soviet demands and would use whatever force was necessary, up to and including general war, in resisting them." The difficult question was how large the force had to be so "that the Soviets would appreciate the great risk that conflict involving this force would, if not terminated by early negotiations, get out of control and escalate into nuclear war."[89] The report proposed that the force be strong enough to overcome the GDR's own forces and able to fulfill its defensive task without the use of tactical nuclear weapons. The JCS believed that seven divisions and four air wings would achieve this end.

Apart from the risk of escalation to nuclear war, the report listed one other pitfall should the recommended strategy fail: allied discord. The report noted that European governments might come to a different appraisal of the dangers and advantages involved and might dissociate themselves from the U.S. position.[90] Acheson expected the allies to proceed more cautiously, because "none of them has the prestige or world position which we do; and, therefore, none of them can have that position and prestige at stake."[91] The Acheson report portrayed the Berlin issue as a test of wills between the United States and the Soviet Union over the credibility of the American commitment. The report proposed a strategy of risk manipulation in order to signal resolve and increase the deterrent to the greatest extent possible.

Dean Acheson's report was discussed in the NSC meeting of 29 June. As a result, the president directed the departments concerned to evaluate its various proposals, and he called for a long series of studies.[92] The report accentuated the possibility of nuclear war, as Carl Kaysen, one of Bundy's aides, explained: "Our own plans emphasize that we must face the risk of war."[93] The Kennedy administration began to seriously focus on war plans. That Berlin contingency planning assumed rapid escalation to nuclear war was confirmed as early as 13 June, when McNamara informed the NSC that supplies for U.S. forces in Berlin consisted of ammunition and combat rations for only eighteen days.[94] With respect to general war, Kaysen informed Bundy that "it is clear that the 'general war' which the JCS discussed is exactly the one-shot response with all out nuclear forces" outlined in SIOP-62.[95] After Bundy had discussed the issue with Carl Kaysen, Henry D. Owen, and Henry A. Kissinger, he informed the president that "the strategic war plan is dangerously rigid and . . . may leave you very little choice as to how you face the moment of thermonuclear truth . . . In essence, the current plan calls for shooting off everything we have in one shot, and it is so constructed as to make any more flexible course very difficult."[96] It is clear from the record that Kennedy was not satisfied with the available war options. He sought more flexible options. The integration of such options into Berlin contingency planning will be discussed below.

When the NSC came together on 13 July to discuss the recommendations of the different departments, a vigorous debate ensued. Secretary of State Dean Rusk pointed out that the essential point of the Acheson report was that currently the United States was not in a good position to negotiate.[97] In the preceding days, however, Arthur Schlesinger and others had criticized the report for failing to relate proposed military measures to political objectives. Accordingly, President Kennedy asked Acheson to provide a political program for Berlin.[98] The NSC meeting did not yield an answer to the question of when and about what the United States should be prepared to negotiate. Even more disputed was

Acheson's call for prompt declaration of a national emergency, which was supported only by Vice President Lyndon Johnson. Both Secretary Rusk and Secretary Robert McNamara voted against such a step, as it would generate a dangerous mobilization psychology.[99] Clear decisions on both questions were postponed until the next meeting of the NSC on 19 July.[100]

During the next six days, the consensus within the administration shifted against Acheson's position on both issues. With respect to a silent diplomatic posture, Henry Kissinger noted in a thoughtful memorandum that he felt "uneasy to have refusal to negotiate become a test of firmness." On the contrary, he pointed out, "firmness should be related to the substance of our negotiation position." According to Kissinger, the United States should not leave the diplomatic and propaganda initiative to Khrushchev, but instead should seek the initiative itself. If the West stated its own program and Khrushchev rejected it, the free world would be in a much stronger tactical position.[101] Kissinger's argument was picked up by others, and by 22 July, Bundy summarized the majority view, noting that the president "should indicate not only our willingness to negotiate, but our intent to take the lead" in his upcoming speech.[102]

Regarding declaration of national emergency, the general consensus was that it was not necessary at the time.[103] Arguably, the decisive exchange with regard to this issue came in the NSC meeting of 19 July, when Secretary McNamara convinced Acheson that postponement of a declaration of emergency would nevertheless "permit a sufficiently rapid deployment in the event of deepening crisis."[104] President Kennedy made his final decisions on 19 July.[105] The next day, he informed Prime Minister Macmillan, President DeGaulle, and Chancellor Adenauer about the course of action the United States recommended.[106] And on 25 July, the president addressed the American people in a dramatic presentation of the situation that the nation was facing over Berlin.

Kennedy's Berlin Speech

Substantively, President Kennedy's address followed the strategic approach outlined in the Acheson report. Differences materialized only on minor issues. Kennedy's strategy of risk manipulation centered on a highly visible buildup of conventional forces in order to improve the credibility of the nuclear deterrent. Kennedy's call for $3.24 billion additional appropriations for the armed forces, devoted primarily to giving the U.S. the capability to deploy six additional divisions and supporting air units to Europe at any time after 1 January 1962, signaled U.S. resolve over West Berlin. However, the president immediately made it clear that the United States would honor its commitments by nuclear as well as conventional means: "The NATO shield was long ago extended to cover West Berlin, and we have given our word that an attack in that city will be regarded as an attack upon us all. . . . We need the capability of placing in any critical area at the appropriate time a force which, combined with those of our allies, is large enough to make clear our determination and our ability to defend our rights at all costs and to meet all levels of aggressor pressure with whatever levels of force are required."[107]

The rhetoric of the speech was gloomy and underscored the American willingness to go to war, nuclear war if necessary.[108] Kennedy requested new funds for the nation's civil defense program even though not much could be done to reduce casualties should a war break out by the end of the year. The president took great pains to relate the requested emergency funds to the long-term military buildup, which had been under way since January. He referred to the improved readiness of the reserve forces and the expansion of air- and sealift capabilities, and he emphasized the accelerated development of invulnerable missile power and the nation's ability to hold 50 percent of its bomber forces on a fifteen-minute alert. Though neglecting to mention the possibility of a future declaration of national emergency, Kennedy strongly hinted that additional force would be called up if such steps became necessary. Finally, President Kennedy did not rule out settlement of the crisis by negotiation. On the contrary, following the advice of his White House aides, he perceived it as his duty to mankind to seek actively a peaceful solution of the crisis. "Our peacetime military posture," he noted, "is traditionally defensive; but our diplomatic posture need not be."[109] The response of the United States to the Berlin crisis would not be merely military; it would be more than just standing firm.

The Kennedy administration counted on the deterrent impact of announced military preparations. The buildup of troop levels was highly visible and thus served the public-image goal well.[110] As the Acheson report had emphasized, military preparations had to be authentic in order to convey the intended message. Contingency planning may have had a comparable function. Marc Trachtenberg has pointed to evidence that the Kennedy administration believed that the Soviets would get a fairly good understanding of western contingency plans through spy penetration of certain NATO governments.[111] Acquisition of such information via espionage would enhance its credibility in the eyes of Soviet analysts.

Contingency Planning

While one can only speculate as to whether the Kennedy administration deliberately used western contingency plans as a way to enhance the
western deterrent, it seems safe to say that consultation within NATO
regarding Berlin contingency planning served the Kennedy administration as a vehicle for advancing its new strategic thinking.[112]

Before Kennedy's 25 July speech, the reappraisal of Berlin contingency planning seems to have been sketchy. There is some evidence
that some thought was given within the Kennedy administration to the
selective and threatening use of nuclear weapons. A paper by Thomas
Schelling observed that the Berlin crisis was a competition in risk taking.
Schelling proposed that the government develop plans to use nuclear
weapons selectively as part of a bargaining strategy in order to convey to
the Soviets the message that a war may get out of hand.[113] McGeorge
Bundy forwarded the paper to the president, inviting him to act on its
proposal: "If you find this paper at all persuasive," Bundy wrote, "you
will wish to start to work on these problems in the Defense Department
where there is still a hideous jump between conventional warfare and a
single massive all-out blast."[114] The fact that Schelling's reasoning was
taken up in later contingency plans suggests that his paper had a major
impact. The administration also started to work on alternative general
war planning. It concentrated its efforts on working out an attack on
Soviet strategic forces alone, excluding Soviet cities from the target
list.[115] It is difficult to say what impact these efforts had on further contingency planning.

After Kennedy's 25 July speech, and in particular after the Berlin wall
went up on 13 August, the Kennedy administration accelerated its Berlin
contingency planning efforts.[116] The evolving wisdom held that an allied
response to obstruction of access to Berlin should be gradual, aimed at
making the Soviets progressively more aware of the danger of general
nuclear war. Contingency plans should include a wider range of nonnuclear options and preparations for the selective use of nuclear weapons.
Increased flexibility would improve the credibility of the nuclear threat.
It would also raise the nuclear threshold. The Soviet Union should be
given as many opportunities as possible to pause and reassess its
policy.[117]

However, at first, neither the British nor the French liked the new
American guidelines for Berlin contingency planning.[118] NATO's supreme commander, General Norstad, shared the skepticism of the Europeans. He questioned whether NATO could sustain a conventional

defense against massive conventional attack over an extended period and whether NATO would be able to enforce a gradual, controlled escalation of the fighting, particularly in a situation where it was unlikely that the West would have the initiative. Consequently, he thought that the West had to be prepared for explosive escalation.[119] Finally, he doubted that the Europeans believed that the new emphasis on nonnuclear options would increase the credibility of the nuclear deterrent; on the contrary, they seemed to interpret it as a shift away from reliance on nuclear weapons.[120]

Meanwhile, Assistant Secretary of Defense Paul Nitze worked on further integrating American views on Berlin contingency planning.[121] President Kennedy officially approved the results of these efforts when he signed National Security Action Memorandum No. 109 in October 1961. The memorandum is available as an enclosure to a letter from President Kennedy to General Norstad.[122] The president approved a flexible response strategy for restoring western access to Berlin and directed General Norstad to adjust his military plans and his discussions with U.S. allies according to the provided guidelines. The President opened the substantive part of the letter by making clear that he wanted "a sequence of graduated responses to Soviet/GDR actions in denial of our rights of access."[123] The proposed sequence of actions started with diplomatic and economic initiatives, including economic embargo, maritime harassment, and UN action and proceeded up to military measures, including everything from small probes of Soviet intentions to nonnuclear air action, nonnuclear ground operations in GDR territories in division and greater strength and supplementary naval blockade, selective nuclear attacks for the primary purpose of demonstrating the will to use nuclear weapons, limited tactical employment of nuclear weapons, and finally to general nuclear war.[124]

The president emphasized that nonnuclear air and ground operations were politically oriented military operations "aiming to display to the Soviets the approaching danger of possibly irreversible escalation." The strategy was aimed at creating firebreaks to permit negotiations before all-out war began. Additional firebreaks were planned above the nuclear threshold to demonstrate selective employment of nuclear weapons. With respect to nuclear options, the president called on General Norstad to "spell out for me with particularity your operational concepts for the command and control procedures within your command."[125] Finally, the president reaffirmed the general approach of his strategy of risk manipulation, the logic of which was originally outlined in the Acheson report:

At this juncture I place as much importance on developing our capacity and readiness to fight with significant non-nuclear forces as on measures designed primarily to make our nuclear deterrent more credible. In saying this I am not in any sense depreciating the need for realization by the U.S.S.R. of the tremendous power of our nuclear forces and our will to use them, if necessary, in support of our objectives. Indeed, I think the two aspects are interrelated. It seems evident to me that our nuclear deterrent will not be credible to the Soviets unless they are convinced of NATO's readiness to become engaged on a lesser level of violence and are thereby made to realize the great risks of escalation to nuclear war.[126]

Even after this presidential clarification of U.S. policy, SACEUR Norstad resisted the implementation of NSAM 109. In a meeting with Kennedy on 7 November, he proposed drafting a memorandum that would be consistent with the president's wishes and at the same time alleviate concern in NATO.[127] However, both Rusk and McNamara rejected Norstad's version as being inconsistent with U.S. policy on military actions in a Berlin conflict as outlined in the president's letter of 20 October. They then drafted a letter asking General Norstad to accommodate the outlined course of action.[128] Their letter reached Norstad with a cover letter from the president, ending SACEUR's unsuccessful resistance to the implementation of NSAM 109.[129] Though it is not clear to what extent the Kennedy administration succeeded in securing European support for the outlined contingency plans, John C. Ausland informed the president in August 1962 that there was "considerable agreement on them" among the United States, Great Britain, France, and Germany.[130]

The Berlin Wall As a Symbol of Mutual Acceptance of the Status Quo

The western strategy of risk manipulation worked better than American policy makers realized at the time.[131] Soviet Premier Khrushchev was frightened by the war hysteria generated by President Kennedy's speech of 25 July. The construction of the Berlin wall in order to stop the mass exodus of refugees, which had increased dramatically during July, signaled Soviet acceptance of the status quo of a divided Europe. Though the Kennedy administration had to mitigate the psychological crisis in West Berlin, on a fundamental level the administration saw the erection of the wall as facilitating a Berlin settlement based upon the status quo.[132]

The West received a firsthand account of Khrushchev's reaction to

Kennedy's speech from the president's adviser on disarmament, John J. McCloy, who had been visiting Khrushchev's summer residence on the Black Sea. McCloy cabled Washington that Khrushchev reacted to the speech using "rough war-like language returning to cordiality after the storm had passed."[133] A combination of threats and appeals to reasonableness characterized Khrushchev's reaction. On the one hand, the Soviet premier termed the president's address a declaration of war, and pointed to the force that would be unleashed by Soviet missiles should war occur. On the other hand, he appealed to the president's common sense, emphasized that the Soviets did not want war, and invited the West to advance its own proposals.[134]

Khrushchev expanded on the same themes in two emotionally charged speeches on 7 and 11 August. He repeatedly warned of the danger of military preparations and the specter of nuclear war: "War hysteria shall lead to nothing good," he noted on 11 August. "If the feelings are let loose and they predominate over reason, then the flywheel of war preparations can start revolving at a high speed. Even when reason prompts that a brake should be put on, the flywheel of war preparations may have acquired such speed and momentum that even those who had set it revolving will be unable to stop it." This process may end in "the abyss of thermonuclear war," because a war over Berlin would be a nuclear war. Khrushchev then appealed "to those who have not lost the faculty of thinking calmly and soberly. . . . Come to your senses, gentlemen." Imploring the United States to behave in a reasonable fashion, he called for a conference: "Let us not try to intimidate each other," he said and proposed "to sit down at the conference table and discuss calmly, without inflaming passions and in a businesslike way, what is to be done to prevent the seeds of new conflicts from taking root in the soil left from the last war."[135] While the Soviet Union wanted a German peace treaty, Khrushchev added, any "barring of access to West Berlin, any blockade of West Berlin" was entirely out of the question.[136] Finally, a third message in Khrushchev's reaction to Kennedy's speech was directed more at the Europeans than at the Americans: The Soviet Union possessed the means to destroy all of Europe! The Soviet leader warned Italian president Amintore Fanfani that "the first two countries to be destroyed would be Italy and Great Britain, since they contain many missile bases."[137] And he threatened the Germans that after a war over Berlin "there probably will be nothing and nobody left in Germany to unite."[138] Whether these threats were primarily intended to split the western alliance or instead to provoke Europe's leaders to persuade the United States to adopt a less aggressive course of action is unclear.

Meanwhile, mass exodus from the GDR of many of its most skilled citizens was becoming a major problem for the Eastern bloc. The tide of refugees had grown in the wake of the Vienna meeting and had reached a daily average of more than one thousand in July. Following Khrushchev's August speeches, the rate reached over two thousand refugees per day.[139] In the early morning hours of 13 August, the East Germans began to seal off the border between the Soviet sector and the western sectors of Berlin. And by 18 August, the construction of the wall had begun. The border closing effectively stopped the refugee flow. Between 13 and 18 August only 492 persons crossed the sector borders.[140] As Marc Trachtenberg has stated, "If one were looking for something that would express Soviet acceptance of the status quo in Europe—of a divided Berlin and a divided Germany—what better symbol could there be than the Berlin Wall?"[141]

Initially, members of the Kennedy administration perceived the sector border closing as a possible solution to the Berlin problem. Secretary Rusk noted in a meeting with the Berlin Steering Group on 15 August that, though a serious matter, the border closing, in realistic terms, might make a Berlin settlement easier.[142] Lawrence J. Legere, an aide to Maxwell Taylor, told the general that nobody "wants to go to war . . . over this recent business, but everyone hopes somebody else will come up with an impressive and effective countermeasure." It was important, he added, not to "lose sight of the object of our impending exercise in brinkmanship: the preservation of the security and freedom of *West Berlin*."[143] Indeed, State Department officials had anticipated that the East Germans might take measures to control the refugee flow. A few analysts even had foreseen the closing of the sector borders.[144] Fearing that an unrestricted mass exodus might lead to an East German uprising, they agreed that there was little that Washington could do in such a case. Others have pointed out that Kennedy's emphasis on the defense of *West* Berlin (as opposed to all of Berlin) as a vital aim of western policy might have invited the events of 13 August.[145]

American policy makers may have been genuinely relieved by the dividing of Berlin. This goes a long way to explain the slow and cautious reaction of the Kennedy administration. On 13 August, Secretary Rusk noted publicly that "limitation on travel within Berlin" was a violation of "the four-power status of Berlin" and would be vigorously protested through the appropriate channels.[146] However, for the next five days not much more happened. This state of affairs produced a major crisis of confidence in West Berlin itself. President Kennedy had promised firmness in his 25 July speech, and now it seemed that the United States had let the people of West Berlin down.[147]

The Kennedy administration had seriously underestimated the psychological impact of the wall on German stability. Measures to prevent a serious rift in U.S.-German relations and to restore the confidence of West Berlin citizens became a top priority in Washington. As part of an exercise in damage control, the president announced on 18 August that the U.S. garrison in West Berlin would be reinforced by a battle group of 1,500 men.[148] He also decided to send Vice President Johnson to West Berlin in order to reassure its people and its mayor, Willy Brandt.[149] And on 30 August, the president appointed retired general Lucius D. Clay, the hero of the 1948 Berlin airlift, as his personal representative on a temporary assignment to Berlin.[150] The administration argued that the building of the wall should be treated not as an isolated act, but rather as part of the broader context of the conflict with the Soviet Union. In this connection, the administration contemplated stepping up the pace of its military preparations as outlined in Kennedy's 25 July speech.[151]

The erection of the Berlin wall, symbolizing mutual acceptance of the status quo of a divided Europe, marks the watershed for the settlement of the Berlin crisis. To be sure, the crisis did not abate immediately; indeed, it did not disappear until the Cuban missile crisis took its place. But after 13 August, the quest for a negotiated settlement took top priority on the agenda, replacing the strategy of brinkmanship.

Nuclear Danger and Its Influence on Politics

Although the U.S. deterrent strategy seemed to work well, it is surprising to learn how far the Kennedy administration was prepared to go to accommodate the Soviet Union (and thus avoid war). While the favorable nuclear balance helped stiffen the political resolve of the United States, it meant little militarily. Perhaps American nuclear superiority raised U.S. policymakers' confidence that Khrushchev would act cautiously. However, at no point did the Kennedy administration assume that a war in which nuclear weapons were used would end in anything less than disaster for all.[152] President Kennedy made the point with particular clarity when he was asked by the press days after the wall went up whether he saw a possibility for the settlement of the crisis by force: "Well, I do not see that there could be any solution, which would serve the world, on Berlin by force. Therefore, I am hopeful that all people involved will realize that in these days of massive forces available on every side, that for the future of the countries involved and for the human race, that we should attempt to work out a peaceful solution, and neither side should attempt to impose its will by brute force because in that case it would be unsuccessful and disaster would be the common result."[153]

The Acheson report had emphasized that the United States must face the risk of war. Against this background, policy makers began to focus on war plans and damage estimates for nuclear exchanges. They did not like what they saw. Columnist Stewart Alsop found President Kennedy preoccupied with a study that "predicted 'on the order of 70 mega-deaths' in case of nuclear war with the Soviet Union" during a dinner in July 1961. Alsop noted in a private letter that one "has the feeling that he [Kennedy]—and perhaps later all the rest of us—is coming up against a reality which he always knew cerebrally existed, but never really believed in."[154] As to a civil defense system, Carl Kaysen reminded McGeorge Bundy that the question was not one of zero rather than five million casualties, but thirty-five rather than forty million. The available estimates showed that only three to four nuclear weapons allocated to cities would cause approximately ten million fatalities.[155]

However, it became clear that it did not make much sense to quibble over numbers and what was an acceptable threshold of fatality for the United States when it could be taken for granted that Europe was doomed for destruction in a nuclear scenario. In 1961, Soviet concentration on developing regional-range ballistic missiles rendered Europe more vulnerable than the United States. The Kennedy administration knew that Khrushchev's threatened destruction of Europe had to be taken seriously.

How the Kennedy administration would have made the ultimate decision is uncertain. We know that Acheson advised Kennedy to arrive at his own private conclusion in advance and, then, not reveal it to anybody.[156] The president appears to have followed this advice. There is some evidence that even hard-liners, like Dean Acheson and Paul Nitze, would have sacrificed West Berlin rather than start a nuclear war.[157] Recently, McNamara stated that he "recommended, without qualification" to President Kennedy never to initiate "under any circumstances, the use of nuclear weapons."[158] However, his advice might well have come once the Berlin crisis was already fading from memory. Nobody can say with certainty what President Kennedy would have decided. It was a political imperative to maintain unity by stating that the United States would defend Western access to West Berlin by whatever means. French foreign minister Maurice Couve de Murville summarized the issue in a tripartite ministerial meeting on 5 August, noting that "Khrushchev says this is an issue on which the West will not fight and that we will finally accept his position. Perhaps in the last analysis, he is right but it would certainly be wrong to give him the immediate impression that he is right."[159]

Kennedy's Initial Approach to Negotiation

American nuclear superiority did not make it easier for the Kennedy administration to accept the risk of nuclear war. The nuclear danger deterred the United States despite U.S. superiority. While the U.S. government attempted to exploit the risk of nuclear war in order to bring the fear of escalation to bear on the other side, it too shared that fear. Nuclear danger imposed *mutual* restraint. The settlement of the Berlin conflict by peaceful means was in the interest of both sides.

The self-deterring impact of a strategy of risk manipulation can best be seen in the way that the supporters of negotiations justified the diplomatic approach. The danger of mutually unintended escalation to nuclear war, they argued, was inherent in this test of will. Public opinion demanded that everything possible be done to avoid becoming involved in a nuclear war over West Berlin. Ambassador Thompson made this point in May 1961. "Both sides," he wrote to the secretary of state, "consider [the] other would not risk war over Berlin." The danger in such a situation, he added, was that if both Khrushchev and Kennedy were to carry out their declared intentions, the situation was likely to "get out of control and military as well as political prestige would become involved making retreat for either side even more difficult."[160] Thompson concluded that world opinion demanded a flexible position.

Secretary Rusk used the same argument in December 1961 in order to bring the French to the negotiation table. "One of the quickest ways to have a nuclear war," he noted in a quadripartite foreign ministerial meeting, "is to have the two sides persuaded that neither will fight. Precisely because a *casus belli* is involved in this situation it would be irresponsible for governments that have nuclear weapons under their control not to be in contact with each other even up to the last few seconds before the holocaust." Moreover, he pointed out that the "American people . . . would only go to war with good consciences. They would wish to believe that they were fighting for a just and honorable purpose."[161] The shortest possible exposition of the same thought was given by Adenauer during a talk with Acheson in November. Pointing to Soviet conventional strength in Europe, Adenauer noted that "nothing could be done against them with conventional power. Nuclear power must not be used. Therefore, we must negotiate."[162]

The Kennedy administration never completely ruled out negotiations with the Soviet Union over Berlin. Kennedy was even more flexible than Eisenhower had been regarding the substance of negotiations. In April 1961, British prime minister Harold Macmillan emerged from a meeting with President Kennedy with the view that Kennedy was moving toward the eventual acceptance of de facto relations with the GDR.[163] President Kennedy was more inclined than Eisenhower to resist allied opposition to schemes that moved toward the acceptance of the status quo in central Europe. Ultimately, however, Kennedy's hands were tied by the political commitment to West Berlin and the FRG—exactly as Eisenhower's had been.

In the spring of 1961, there was no political program for settling the Berlin crisis. Dean Acheson soon filled the conceptual vacuum.[164] His report excluded any attempt to settle the conflict by negotiation until the test of will was resolved in favor of the United States. Only once it became clear that Khrushchev would not get what he wanted could negotiations play a role as a face-saving device. However, we have seen that McGeorge Bundy's White House staff convinced Kennedy that it would be unwise to leave the diplomatic initiative to the Soviets. This group proposed that the president take the lead in negotiations. Bundy referred to "such items as the Oder-Neisse line and a de facto acceptance of a divided Germany" as needing further discussions.[165] The president himself doubted that the idea of German unification had much appeal around the world.[166] However, in the early summer of 1961, the substance of a negotiating position was regarded as having only secondary priority, next to the more important issue of enhancing the deterrent by adopting appropriate military measures.

It seems that this framework allowed Acheson to carry the day.[167] At the end of July 1961, Acheson presented a political program for Berlin that would supplement the military measures, which he had outlined in his report of 28 June. Acheson advised against calling a peace conference. However, he agreed that the West had to call a foreign ministers' conference before the German elections in the fall of 1961. In the period between these elections and the Soviet signing of a peace treaty, the West should present a counterproposal to Khrushchev's proposed conference on treaties with either one or both of the Germanies. The proposal would "amount to a dressed-up form of the status quo," Acheson noted in a meeting of the Inter-Departmental Coordination Group on Berlin on 26 July. The status quo, he added, "might eventually include a four-nation agreement that they are not going to fight over Berlin, perhaps endorsed by NATO and by the members of the Warsaw Pact." At a later stage of the negotiations, issues on the table might include immigration, trade, assurances on the Oder-Neisse boundary, a central European security zone, and German nuclear weapons.[168]

Western Disagreement with Respect to Negotiations

This was the state of affairs when Secretary of State Rusk presented the American position to the foreign ministers of Great Britain, France, and Germany in Paris in August. Immediately, it became apparent that there was substantial disagreement in the alliance as to when the West should initiate negotiations with the Soviet Union. Secretary Rusk outlined the position of the U.S. government. First, he stated, "some Ambassadorial contact in Moscow was in any event inevitable."[169] Second, he proposed calling a foreign ministers' meeting, hoping that the Soviets would accept the invitation. As to the substance of the western negotiating position, Rusk followed the Acheson line: "The West might start with proposals on which we would not necessarily expect to end but which would improve the status quo. From these," he added, "we might expect to move to some de facto regulation of the situation in conformity with our interests and consistent with the maintenance of something like the status quo." Secretary Rusk justified the U.S. approach with reference to the danger of nuclear war and the influence of public opinion:

> If we can not convince most UN countries that our position is reasonable and that we are not just being stubborn, the pressure will be towards some position which will be difficult for us. In democratic societies people do not think much of war as an instrument of policy unless they believe war is unavoidable. We believe nuclear war to be possible in the Berlin crisis although we do not say this is inevitable. If we ask our peoples to take a risk of this magnitude, we must make clear that every feasible effort is being made to achieve our objective by other means. Democracies must be led to conflict with clear consciences.[170]

The French refused to be committed in advance to a foreign ministers' conference.[171] French foreign minister Maurice Couve de Murville noted that before deciding to negotiate, the West should agree on the substance of policy. Couve de Murville defended the French rejection of an early diplomatic initiative in Achesonian terms: "Khrushchev says, this is an issue on which the West will not fight and that we will finally accept his position." He added that if "we now went to Khrushchev and said that we wanted to negotiate, he would immediately conclude that we were not serious." The French foreign minister agreed "that it was not impossible that the crisis would lead to nuclear war but we must accept this risk. If what we accept instead weakens our position and our unity it will be possible to avoid a nuclear war in 1961. But this would merely lead to nuclear war in 1962 or 1963."[172] This was not a policy. The allied powers had learned that in the past and had to evaluate the present situation in that light. For the remainder of the year, it would be the French alone who would stick to an uncompromising position regarding negotiations—a position remarkably similar to Acheson's original concept.

The Germans covered the middle ground between the U.S. position and the French position. German foreign minister Heinrich von Brentano acknowledged "that public opinion exercised pressures for direct negotiations." Therefore, he agreed that the West must not give the impression that it was seeking a purely military solution to the conflict. However, von Brentano echoed French concerns, saying "that an expression of willingness to negotiate under current conditions would be interpreted as a sign of weakness."[173]

Secretary of State Rusk attempted to alleviate friction within the alliance in two direct talks with President DeGaulle and Chancellor Adenauer. However, DeGaulle confirmed his conviction that it was Khrushchev's goal to compel the West to negotiate. DeGaulle noted that if negotiations were started, it would be "because Mr. Khrushchev has whistled." The West should therefore tell the Soviets: "No, we will not change the status of Berlin. We will not have our rights interfered with. We are there legitimately. We have been there for sixteen years. If you change the status of Berlin by force, we will reply by force."[174] One day later, Secretary Rusk had a conversation with Chancellor Adenauer that brought Rusk's frustration with the French position to the fore. Pointing to President Kennedy's grave responsibility for the use of nuclear weapons, Rusk noted that "General DeGaulle believes we are in Berlin and that if the Soviets disturb us we will shoot." However, he added, this "is not an adequate position in the sixties when we are considering a nuclear war."[175]

The French were confirmed in their rejection of negotiations by the wall episode and the Soviet resumption of nuclear tests at the end of August 1961. Henceforth, they refused to be part of any diplomatic initiative until the atmosphere of deadline and ultimatum had changed to détente. The Americans urged the French to change their strict no-negotiations position, pointing out that France was virtually isolated in NATO with respect to this matter. Secretary Rusk emphasized in a conversation with the French ambassador that the "disunity of the alliance is what will impress Khrushchev most."[176] Around the same time, President Kennedy reminded Adenauer, who was still trying to bridge the gap between France and the United States, that "both public opinion in democratic countries and the sheer logic of thermonuclear war" demanded every effort to find a peaceful solution.[177]

Finally, the French agreed to a new American proposal that an announcement be made saying in effect that "with French and United Kingdom approval . . . the United States would undertake explorations with the Soviet government with a view to possibilities of negotiations" and that it "was anticipated that these exploratory conversations might take place between the Secretary and Mr. Gromyko at the opening of the United Nations General Assembly in New York in September as well as through normal diplomatic channels."[178] President Kennedy announced western readiness for serious "talks about Germany and other problems" in a White House statement issued on 13 September.[179]

The Development of Kennedy's Negotiating Posture

Meanwhile, the Kennedy administration was moving toward a dramatic shift in the substance of negotiations. While the Berlin wall episode entrenched French opposition to a diplomatic initiative, it had the opposite effect on the Kennedy administration, enhancing its interest in a more flexible western negotiating position. On 28 August, McGeorge Bundy informed the president that it was "the main line of thought among those who are now at work on the substance of our negotiating position . . . that we can and should shift substantially toward acceptance of the GDR, the Oder-Neisse line, a non-aggression pact, and even the idea of two peace treaties." Instead of talking about occupation rights, the West should focus on "the three fundamentals of freedom for Berlin, free access, and a western presence, in that order."[180] The government's assessment of the probability of a crisis and the risks involved in an escalation of the crisis to nuclear war had prompted this shift.

Kennedy's White House staff took the lead in drafting a more flexible negotiating position. Informed by Khrushchev's reaction to Kennedy's 25 July speech, which was marked by fluctuation between threats and appeals to reasonableness, and the rapidly growing exodus of refugees from East Germany, McGeorge Bundy called his White House aides together in order to discuss the possibility of "major departures from the Acheson line."[181] The group discussed advantages and disadvantages of various negotiating positions. It attempted to relate these positions to the broader policy question of what the United States wished Europe to be like in a few years.[182] On 11 August, Bundy informed the president that he would soon have to decide on the substance of a negotiating position. Bundy noted that he was "greatly attracted by the notion of shifting our basic stand in West Berlin from occupation rights to self-determination and a free choice of protectors by the West Berliners themselves."[183] The formulation of a negotiating posture, Bundy pointed out, was the most important foreign policy problem of the time. He proposed that the president meet with a small group in order to discuss the matter. The group should include Kissinger, Charles Bohlen, Taylor, Theodore Sorensen, and Owen in addition to Secretary Rusk and Foy D. Kohler.

Two days later, the Berlin wall went up. The event strengthened the opinion of the White House staff that a diplomatic initiative was urgent. On 14 August, Bundy told the president that "we should take a clear initiative for negotiation within the next week or ten days." He indicated that the State Department was dragging its feet, arguing that the substance of the negotiating position could be discussed only once negotiations had begun. Bundy argued that, on the contrary, it was about time to move forward and concentrate on the fundamental western interests in Berlin.[184]

Two staff papers, one by Kissinger the other by Kaysen, indicate the tenor of thinking in the White House staff at this time. The group concluded that instability was inherent in the prevailing situation in Europe. This group asked *why* Khrushchev was forcing the issue at that particular time. Both Kissinger and Kaysen acknowledged that the Soviets were driven by legitimate security concerns aimed at containing the revival of German military power, particularly if a revitalized German military meant a nuclear military. Kaysen noted that "the outcry that the Soviet Union has raised about nuclear weapons in West Germany in my own judgment reflects a genuine concern, one which is widely shared among satellites, and which goes deeper than the level of Communist propaganda."[185]

Both analysts agreed that the Soviet Union wanted stabilization of the situation in Eastern Europe through western recognition of the Oder-Neisse boundary and the legitimacy of the GDR. They then proceeded to ask what aims the United States had with respect to West Berlin. Besides the fact that it was an area of western freedom that the United States was specifically committed to defend, Berlin was an important item in U.S.-German relations, tying West Germany to the United States. The U.S.-German relationship operated as a two-way street: Just as the United States sought the FRG's commitment to western security, so the

FRG sought American commitment to German unification. This was where Soviet and western goals clashed: Unification of the two Germanies was inconsistent with the recognition of the East German regime and acceptance of the Oder-Neisse boundary.

One or the other side would have to modify its aims; otherwise, the world would drift toward war. Carl Kaysen concluded that the United States could not achieve Soviet acceptance of the status quo without risking war.[186] Therefore, the United States would have to modify its own aims. Kaysen proposed that the United States concentrate on the freedom of West Berlin, including the freedom of access. However, Henry Kissinger warned that if "the West understands its interests correctly it *must* stand for the unity of Germany despite the experience of two world wars and despite the understandable fear of a revival of German truculence." The call for unification was an imperative of German domestic policy. Kissinger believed that the "division of Germany is almost certainly unavoidable."[187] However, the "future cohesion of the North Atlantic Community," he added, "depends on our ability to demonstrate what makes it so." The West might have to acquiesce in the division of Germany but could never condone it. He concluded that if "the West settles for the *status quo* it should make clear that it does so not by preference but because it prefers the *status quo* to nuclear war."[188]

President Kennedy's White House staff stated western interests as freedom for the people of West Berlin, the clear maintenance of allied right to be there, and the right of access. The group discussed what the West should be prepared to offer in exchange for Soviet guarantees of these fundamental western aims. The debate moved toward possible recognition of the GDR and the Oder-Neisse line, the idea of two peace treaties, a nonaggression pact, mutual security guarantees for both Germanies by the Warsaw Pact and NATO, and the creation of a nuclear-free zone in Germany.

A memorandum from Kennedy to the secretary of state of 21 August shows that the president was eager to move forward on negotiations: "I want to take a stronger lead on Berlin negotiations. Both the calendar of negotiation and the substance of the Western position remain unsettled, and I no longer believe that satisfactory progress can be made by Four-Power discussion alone. I think we should promptly work toward a strong U.S. position in both areas and should make it clear that we cannot accept a veto from any other power. We should of course be as persuasive and diplomatic as possible, but it is time to act."

The president noted that he wanted to issue an invitation for negotiations before 1 September. Secretary Rusk should make "it plain to our three Allies that this is what we mean to do and that they must come along or stay behind." As to the substance of U.S. policy, he regarded the Acheson paper as a good start, but emphasized that it was "*not* a finishing point." Picking up on an earlier proposal by McGeorge Bundy, he directed the secretary of state to set up a small and relatively invisible group, separated from the day-to-day operational work, to prepare a policy paper for decision. The group, he added, should include people such as Bohlen, Owen, and Martin J. Hillenbrand from the State Department and Bundy and Sorensen from the White House. Kennedy ended the memorandum with guidelines regarding substantive matters. The U.S. negotiating position, he said, should protect "our support for the *idea* of self-determination, the *idea* of all-Germany, and the *fact* of viable, protected freedom in West Berlin."[189]

It is clear that Kennedy was looking for a way to "square the circle" with respect to German reunification. On the occasion of a quadripartite foreign ministers meeting later in the year, Secretary of State Rusk translated Kennedy's instructions, saying that "what we needed was some theory that would in a theoretical way prevent the permanent division of Germany."[190] In addition, the president noted that he thought the United States should "*not* insist on maintenance of occupation rights if other strong guarantees can be designed." And he invited consideration of "the option of proposing parallel peace treaties."[191]

On 12 September, one day before Kennedy publicly announced western readiness for serious talks with the Soviet Union, the president met with Secretary Rusk in order to agree on a negotiating position. The details of this discussion are not yet known. However, the president sent a memorandum to Dean Rusk recording the agreement that they had reached. Kennedy wrote that the "approach of calling a Peace Conference and working toward Parallel Peace Treaties is agreed between us, and you will proceed to have it developed in detail." The peace treaty would have been a first step toward the recognition of the East German state. Kennedy and Rusk agreed that Ambassador Thompson "should open negotiations on this basis with the Soviet Union."[192] All of this shows that the Kennedy administration was prepared to accommodate the Soviet Union through serious bilateral talks and was moving toward a negotiated settlement, as Khrushchev's deadline for a separate peace treaty approached.

Communication with the Soviets

The Soviets announced their readiness to enter into an exchange of opinions between Secretary Rusk and Soviet foreign minister Andrei I.

Gromyko at the United Nations General Assembly, one day after Kennedy had publicly stated western interest in negotiations.[193] Eventually, Rusk and Gromyko would meet three times in New York. Secretary Rusk opened their first meeting by saying that each side must clearly know what the vital interests of the other side were, so that there could be no mistake. The United States and the Soviet Union, he added, shared a common interest in preventing war. Rusk proceeded to point out that the problem was not the conclusion of a peace treaty. "As we see it," he said, "the crisis occurs because the Soviet Government states that this act will terminate allied rights and that access to West Berlin will then be subject to the agreement and consent of the East German regime." It was this particular Soviet claim that clashed with "what President Kennedy has described as three vital interests of the United States. Not only are these vital interests," he added, "but they represent fundamental commitments of the United States and its NATO allies." Rusk underlined that prestige was involved: "For political purposes . . . West Berlin is not 110 miles inside East Germany, but right on the demarcation line between West and East Germany."

Gromyko replied that the "reason why the Soviet Government believed it to be necessary to have a peace treaty signed is that it is convinced that such a treaty would place obstacles in the way of the development of revanchism and militarism in West Germany." He added that the West German leaders kept raising the question of a revision of borders in Europe, and "West Germany does not conceal its intention to swallow the GDR."[194] Secretary Rusk noted in reply that the United States "could understand why the peoples of Eastern Europe after their terrible experiences of the last war would be concerned about the rearmament of a Germany with aggressive designs." However, West German rearmament was not aggressive and was thoroughly integrated within the broader North Atlantic community.[195]

The Kennedy administration endeavored to communicate three important messages to the Soviet side: First, there was a real danger of unintended nuclear war involved in the crisis. Second, the vital interest of the United States was the freedom of *West* Berlin and access thereto. Third, the United States acknowledged the fact that Soviet security interests were involved.[196] The same three issues were addressed by President Kennedy in his speech to the United Nations General Assembly on 25 September.[197] He opened his address with one of the most memorable passages on the meaning of the nuclear revolution: "War appeals no longer as a rational alternative. Unconditional war can no longer lead to unconditional victory. It can no longer serve to settle disputes. It can no longer concern the great Powers alone. For a nuclear disaster, spread by winds and waters and fear, could well engulf the great and the small, the rich and the poor, the committed and the uncommitted alike. Mankind must put an end to war—or war will put an end to mankind."

He pointed to the danger that nuclear war might come despite everyone's best intentions at a time when every "man, woman and child lives under a nuclear sword of Damocles, hanging by the slenderest of threads, capable of being cut at any moment by accident or miscalculation or by madness." And he ended his speech on the same grave note: "The events and decisions of the next ten months may well decide the fate of man for the next ten thousand years. . . . And we in this hall shall be remembered either as part of the generation that turned this planet into a flaming funeral pyre or as the generation that met its vow to 'save succeeding generations from the scourge of war.' "

Regarding Berlin, President Kennedy emphasized that there was a dangerous crisis "because of threats against the vital interests and the deep commitments of the Western Powers, and the freedom of West Berlin." Kennedy went on to confirm western interests and commitments: "The Western Powers have calmly resolved to defend, by whatever means are forced upon them, their obligations and their access to the free citizens of West Berlin and the self-determination of those citizens." After shifting attention to what the United States regarded as vital interests, the president underscored his readiness to negotiate, noting that "we shall never negotiate out of fears and we shall never fear to negotiate." Finally, he noted that his government believed that "a peaceful agreement is possible which protects the freedom of West Berlin and allied presence and access, while recognizing the historic and legitimate interests of others in assuring European security." Besides this appeal to Soviet interests in greater stability for Central Europe, Kennedy's address included as part of a disarmament proposal the prohibition of "transfer of control over nuclear weapons to states that do not own them"—signaling that the Kennedy administration had no interest in a nuclear Germany.[198]

On 3 October, Secretary Rusk briefed representatives of Great Britain, France, and Germany on his talks with Gromyko. He emphasized that the Soviets seemed to want to solve the Berlin problem through discussions rather than let the crisis develop. Most important, the Soviets had in effect removed the year-end deadline for the signing of the peace treaty.[199] The secretary of state further conveyed his impression that the "Soviets are seriously aware" of the three vital western interests. The Soviets wanted to consolidate their position in Central Europe: "They will resist any plan for the reunification of Germany." The Soviets seemed interested in the broader, long-range problems of European security; however, Rusk noted, they did not expect arrangements in this field to be related to arrangements on Germany or Berlin.[200]

Not everybody agreed with Rusk's optimistic assessment. McGeorge Bundy informed President Kennedy that the Soviets had signaled their willingness to renew their guarantees of western access to West Berlin in return for recognition of the German borders, respect for the sovereignty of the GDR, prevention of the spread of nuclear weapons in Europe, and agreement to West Berlin's free-city status. If this was the trade-off, Bundy warned, "we are on a dangerous slope of appeasement, and I am certain that this will be the view of the Germans, the Frenchmen and the Republicans."[201]

This was the situation when the American president met personally with Foreign Minister Gromyko on 6 October. Kennedy warned Gromyko that the Soviet government had asked for too many western concessions. A settlement along the lines discussed between Rusk and Gromyko "was not a compromise, but rather meant trading an apple for an orchard." In his reply, Gromyko again indicated that his government placed particular stress on nuclear-free Germanies, as well as on prohibition of the manufacture of nuclear weapons in the two states. The Soviet foreign minister emphasized that it was "in the interest of both the U.S. and the U.S.S.R. . . . to prevent the two Germanies from acquiring nuclear and rocket weapons."[202]

German and French Opposition to a Broad Approach

However promising the elimination of the deadline seemed to be, now the problem of German opposition to everything implying recognition of the GDR and abandonment of the goal of unification came to bear. The White House had anticipated that German resistance would be the biggest obstacle to the shift in the American negotiating position.[203]

These expectations were quickly confirmed when Secretary Rusk introduced the new emphases in American policy in a quadripartite foreign ministers' meeting. Foreign Minister von Brentano stated that the German government would not agree to any general security arrangement in Central Europe unless Germany was unified. Germany must not be inferior to any other ally, as she would be in a neutral zone, and any NATO-Warsaw Pact arrangements were unacceptable as long as Germany remained divided.[204] In the aftermath of the Rusk-Gromyko talks,

German ambassador Wilhelm C. Grewe informed representatives of the United States, Great Britain, and France that his government believed "the discussions with Gromyko had now reached a stage where we should pause and reflect." A number of previously unconsidered questions had been discussed on which the German government needed clarification such as, "What did the discussion on acquisition and possession of nuclear weapons mean? How was this related to the nuclear power of NATO and the nuclear armament of the NATO allies? . . . What about the proposals for a NATO-Warsaw Pact relationship? In the past," he added, "this had been ruled out because of the implications of GDR recognition."[205]

In a further bilateral U.S.-FRG talk, Ambassador Grewe again emphasized that Bonn "had been concerned over the fact that European security had been broached at all." Pointing out that the whole western press was talking of recognition of the GDR, and noting that the secretary himself had said "that there was no real difference between *de facto* recognition and *de jure* recognition," Grewe emphasized that any East-West talks on Germany must incorporate reunification in all future negotiations. He admitted that "the *status quo* cannot, of course, be changed, but it is important to keep the *status quo* as a nonrecognized *status quo*."[206]

On the day of this exchange, Chancellor Adenauer communicated the same fears in a letter to President Kennedy. The president replied with a lengthy letter. Kennedy wrote that the United States had no intention of withdrawing from Berlin, nor did it intend to give western rights away. However, "the logic of history and the needs of the Alliance demand that every effort, consistent with our vital interest, be made to solve this problem by peaceful and diplomatic methods before the ultimate confrontation." Regarding German concerns about European security, he wrote that "we think it would be worthwhile to see how the confrontation in Central Europe might be reduced." He then proceeded to state two specific proposals, although the Germans had strongly opposed them in earlier meetings. "It would certainly be to the great advantage of the West," Kennedy stated, "if the concentration of Soviet forces in the satellites could be lowered."[207] "Steps should be also studied that would assure both sides that no surprise attack is being prepared, or is about to be launched." The president closed his letter with a reminder of his government's policy regarding nuclear weapons: "As far as the nuclear weapons component of European security is concerned, I need not remind you that it has been the long-established policy of the US Government not to relinquish control of nuclear warheads to any nation not owning them and not to transmit to any such nation information or material necessary for their manufacture."[208]

With the new German government in office, Ambassador Grewe informed Secretary Rusk that there was a broad consensus in Germany for "no abandonment of reunification, no recognition of the GDR, and settlement of the boundary question only in a peace treaty."[209] The U.S. government could only go as far as the German government agreed to go.[210] General Secretary Khrushchev emphasized the weak point of the U.S. negotiating position when he wrote to Kennedy in early November that it "is not an exaggeration to say that the FRG hinders also the US Government in the free conduct of the policy which the latter believes to be reasonable."[211] Indeed, the fundamental American commitment to West Berlin and West Germany reduced the chances of a negotiated settlement on the basis of the broader approach envisaged by Kennedy's White House staff during the fall of 1961.

As the Acheson report had foreseen, maintaining the unity of the NATO alliance would become the central U.S. foreign policy problem, as it had been under Eisenhower.[212] The president would have to convince the Germans that negotiations were the right approach to solving the crisis peacefully.[213] In a series of meetings between 20 November and 22 November, Kennedy impressed on Adenauer that the nuclear balance was in favor of the West, and that the West by no means would negotiate from a position of military inferiority. On the contrary, the United States and NATO were stronger from the nuclear standpoint now than they would be in another two or three years. Therefore, Kennedy pointed out, "we might do as well or better in negotiating now than later."[214] Kennedy's insistence was successful. Adenauer finally agreed that the American-Soviet talks should continue in Moscow.[215]

President Kennedy did not miss the opportunity to tell Adenauer that the United States thought it important for European security that Germany remain a nonnuclear state. He inquired whether Germany was continuing to adhere to its declaration of 1954 that it would not manufacture nuclear, biological, or chemical weapons.[216] Adenauer replied that Germany would stick to the policy stated in 1954 but did not want to make new statements in the context of Berlin.[217]

Germany was not the only obstacle to negotiations, France, too, opposed a broadening of talks on Berlin to include security in Central Europe generally. In a foreign ministers' meeting on 11 December, French foreign minister Maurice Couve de Murville affirmed his government's opposition to negotiations. Two things had happened in the seven months since Vienna: "the splitting of Berlin and the lifting of the time limit for a peace treaty." The Western powers should not let themselves be pushed into discussing the broader issues of European security. "They should say that they would not discuss Berlin under Soviet blackmail and threat. The Soviets were not going to risk war over Berlin any more than we were, and the situation could therefore continue for a long time."[218]

The United States, on the other hand, was not prepared to give up further exploration of the Soviet position, and Rusk went so far as to threaten that "the U.S. would have to review the whole situation to see if it and its allies were in fact agreed on substance."[219] Finally, a compromise was struck in a phone conversation between DeGaulle and Kennedy. The agreement allowed Secretary Rusk and Ambassador Thompson to conduct further meetings with Soviet representatives from January through August under the rubric of exploratory discussions.[220] However, after so many meetings with the Germans and the French, there was not much substance left for these talks.[221] Prime Minister Macmillan noted sarcastically that what the West was doing "was rather like inviting someone to dinner without telling him just what there would be to eat. We would be saying that there would be soup, probably fish and perhaps a little meat, although the latter was not certain."[222]

Not surprisingly, then, the Thompson-Gromyko talks did not make any progress at the beginning of 1962. On 15 January, President Kennedy informed Secretary Rusk that he was not satisfied with the Berlin negotiations and was wondering whether everything had to be cleared with the allies first and whether Thompson was the right channel. He summarized the disadvantages of the present situation by noting that "we are unable to talk frankly to the Russians, and yet we cannot really pull our Allies into a position of responsible participation."[223]

A few days later, President Kennedy opened a different channel of communication in order to inform the Soviet leader that he was concerned about the increasingly formal nature of the exchange in the Thompson-Gromyko meetings. The initial contact in the new channel probably was made by Robert F. Kennedy, who had frequent secret meetings with Georgi N. Bolshakov, a Soviet military intelligence agent.[224] The new arrangement was developed further in a conversation between Bolshakov, Alexei I. Adzhubei (Khrushchev's son-in-law and editor in chief of Isvestiia) and President Kennedy on 31 January. The president introduced a new approach to Berlin negotiations, which he later confirmed in a personal letter to Khrushchev. Because there was little chance, the president explained, of finding a perfect solution to the Berlin situation, the United States and the Soviet Union should instead make every effort to reach some mutually acceptable accommodation that would minimize the hazards of the present situation. While the Berlin crisis might work itself out by force of evolution, it was important to reach some accommodation now. The United States recognized that the Soviet Union was concerned about a "future excess of German nationalism and the proliferation of nuclear weapons." In these areas, however, accommodation might be found. Moreover, he warned Khrushchev, "further pressures on the West in Berlin only increase the pressure within France and the Federal Republic of Germany to build a greater military force, to secure an independent nuclear capacity and to adopt a more rigid attitude on any accommodation."[225]

It is unclear how much of these personal exchanges entered into the formal talks between Gromyko and Thompson. According to the account of Paul H. Nitze, Secretary Rusk presented a proposal to Soviet foreign minister Andrei Gromyko in March 1962 that "held out the prospect of an agreement that would prevent the spread of nuclear weapons, secure a nonaggression pact between NATO and the Warsaw Pact, establish several committees to be composed of equal numbers of East and West Germans to handle 'technical' contacts between the two Germanies, establish an international access authority (with a seat for East Germany) to supervise travel between West Berlin and West Germany, and organize a permanent conference of deputies of the foreign ministers of the four powers (United States, Great Britain, France, and the Soviet Union) to meet regularly on the Berlin situation."[226] Somebody in Bonn, apparently with Adenauer's support, leaked word to the press on the substance of the U.S. proposal. Adenauer expressed concern about the course of the talks in a letter to President Kennedy. Finally, the Soviet-American talks bogged down, apparently because the Soviets insisted on the withdrawal of the U.S. garrison from West Berlin. This, Kennedy was not prepared to do, because "Europe would lose its confidence in U.S. leadership."[227]

The Berlin Crisis and Nuclear Weapons:
Risk Manipulation and Self-Deterrence

During the summer of 1962, high-level talks on the Berlin issue proceeded between Soviet and American officials. Although no significant progress was made on substantive questions, neither side precipitated a crisis.[228] However, anxieties remained and the confrontation over Berlin simmered right into the Cuban missile crisis. It was only after October of 1962 that tensions over Berlin abated.[229] The resolution of the Cuban crisis resulted in Soviet acquiescence to the status quo in Berlin, which was finally codified in the Quadripartite Berlin Agreement of 1971.[230]

By the time the Cuban missile crisis overtook the Berlin crisis, American perspectives on policy making had evolved. Marc Trachtenberg observes that the world at the end of 1962 was very different from the world of November 1958. In the interim, the issue of the structure of power in post–World War II Europe had come to a head. A key issue was how the German question would be resolved. Independent national nuclear forces also had become a concern. Was Germany becoming a nuclear power, following the example of Great Britain and France?[231]

With the advent of the Berlin wall, symbolizing both sides' acceptance of the status quo of a divided Europe, the European security system had attained a certain stability. With respect to the political goal of German unification, the Kennedy administration tempered its support, acknowledging the *idea* of one Germany. In reality, American policymakers increasingly accepted the fact of a permanently divided Europe. On the military side, the Kennedy administration made it clear that it was not willing to support a nuclearized *Bundeswehr*—a position that had been less clear under Eisenhower. Moreover, Kennedy conveyed to his Soviet counterpart his willingness to discuss broader issues of European security, paying deference to genuine Soviet security interests, and acknowledging the common interest in stopping further nuclear proliferation.

With respect to the unity of NATO, the United States had proved its willingness to defend West Berlin at whatever costs. Moreover, the Kennedy administration's call for a conventional option signaled an American intention to stay in Europe. In this respect again, Kennedy broke with Eisenhower. Eisenhower consistently had emphasized that the U.S. troops were in Europe only as a limited stopgap operation. Finally, both Great Britain and France were building independent national nuclear forces, making them less dependent on the American nuclear guarantee.[232] Germany, however, had to rely exclusively on the U.S. deterrent. Yet Germany could still hope that a multilateral nuclear force would facilitate integration of Europe's nuclear shield.[233]

While common fear of nuclear war favored superpower acceptance of the status quo, the American attempt to manipulate risks in order to deter the Soviets and reassure the allies had its costs. Khrushchev's withdrawal of the deadline for a treaty as a visible sign of Soviet failure opposed to the relative secrecy of the Kennedy administration's willingness to compromise perpetuated the conflict. Khrushchev had committed his personal prestige to the signing of a peace treaty that would leave regulation of access to Berlin to the East German government. Twice, Khrushchev was forced to back down. Each month without a treaty rendered Khrushchev more vulnerable to criticism from domestic and Chinese hard-liners.[234] Furthermore, the fact that the Americans attributed postponement of Khrushchev's deadline to U.S. nuclear superiority can only have increased Soviet interests in quick achievement of nuclear parity.[235]

And finally, the Kennedy administration had perceived the Berlin crisis as a test of its will to defend Berlin by nuclear means. The crisis focused attention on the nuclear arm of NATO's defenses. The Berlin crisis had proved the political relevance of superior nuclear forces to European security. This extended the realm of nuclear signals and symbols; a fact that will be further analyzed in chapter 10.

10

Nuclear Politics—Symbols and Signals: How Political Considerations Affected Military Strategy, Planning, and Budgets

We have seen that as early as the late 1950s the link between the super-powers' military capabilities and their political behavior had become weaker as their vulnerability increased. Nuclear plenty limited the impact of purely military considerations regarding the role of nuclear weapons. In addition, the fact that NATO's security rested on nuclear threats shifted emphasis on political considerations. Strictly military analysis gave way to political and diplomatic analysis. The Berlin crisis, for instance, was perceived as a test of will, not a test of capabilities. The crucial problem was to influence others' beliefs about one's resolve. The very nature of this goal opened a wide field for psychological factors, symbols, and signals. Nuclear threats had to be converted into favorable political outcomes by psychological processes guided by highly subjective factors. Increasingly, defense decisions were made with an eye to their potential impact on international perception.[1]

While nuclear superiority may have made little difference militarily, it became the symbol for the credibility of U.S. policy with respect to Europe. A signal of resolve in connection with the Berlin crisis was a speech given by Deputy Secretary of Defense Roswell Gilpatric in October 1961. The speech made powerful claims about the enormous superiority of American nuclear capabilities. Gilpatric focused not so much on the question of what this meant for military strategy. His speech, rather, illustrated the resolve of the U.S. government. First of all, the speech was intended to reassure the Europeans of the credibility of the American commitment to the defense of West Berlin and Europe. It is less clear

241

whether the speech was part of a calculated decision by the Kennedy administration to make political use of a strategic threat. In any event, members of the Kennedy administration came to believe that U.S. nuclear superiority had had an impact on the Soviet decision to relax its insistence on a peace treaty.

It was possible to use nuclear rhetoric as a credible political tool, because the United States did, in fact, have superior forces. We have seen that the intelligence community had lowered its estimates of Soviet ICBM deployments substantially in the National Intelligence Estimate (NIE) of 1960. However, this reduction did not convince those who believed in a missile gap favoring the Soviets, because of the unfortunate way in which the new estimates were presented to Congress. President Eisenhower left office noting in his last State of the Union message on 12 January 1961 that the "bomber gap of several years ago was always a fiction and the 'missile gap' shows every sign of being the same."[2] After only two weeks in office, Secretary of Defense McNamara hinted in a press conference that he had reached the same conclusion. Several news articles reported that Kennedy's advisers had determined that there was no missile gap. Rapidly, the issue became the first major scandal of the new government. President Kennedy quickly intervened in an exercise of damage control, stating that a sound judgment of the issue had to await further studies.[3]

For political reasons, members of the Kennedy administration were reluctant to admit that there was no missile gap so soon after the election campaign. In reality, however, officials like Roswell Gilpatric, Charles Hitch, Paul Nitze, Jerome Wiesner, McGeorge Bundy, Herbert York, and David E. Bell later admitted that they were convinced by the time of the fiscal year 1962 defense budget decisions (March 1961) that the United States was not behind the Soviet Union in missile production.[4]

Within the intelligence community, the missile gap remained an issue in dispute through the summer of 1961. Not until the NIE of September 1961 were the estimates of Soviet capabilities materially reduced. The September 1961 NIE corrected the number of Soviet ICBMs on launchers for the middle of 1961 from ten to twenty-five, and estimated the Soviet ICBM force for the middle of 1962 to be in the range of thirty-three to fifty operational missiles.[5] The intelligence community explained that new data stemming from the CIA's secret reconnaissance satellite program (Discoverer) permitted more accurate estimates of Soviet capabilities.[6] Furthermore, there was evidence that the Soviets were concentrating their resources on the development of their second-generation missiles, as a CIA representative pointed out to General Maxwell Taylor: "Our estimate was based on the belief that for several years the Soviets had engaged in a relatively steady though deliberately paced program to deploy first generation ICBM's. . . . We now believe that the Soviet leaders recognized the serious disadvantages of their extremely cumbersome first-generation system and proceeded to the vigorous development of a more suitable second-generation system."[7] Once campaign myths were dispelled, it became apparent that the United States enjoyed both quantitative and qualitative nuclear superiority. At the end of 1961, the United States had a strategic triad of more than 1,650 long-range bombers, 30 Atlas D ICBMs, 32 Atlas E ICBMs, 1 Titan ICBM, and 80 Polaris missiles at its disposal, and these capabilities were rapidly growing.[8]

Nuclear Superiority As a Signal of Resolve and Reassurance

Although the Kennedy administration discovered within weeks that the missile gap was a myth, the problem in the fall of 1961 was convincing the allies of this. The Europeans still seemed to believe in a Soviet missile advantage. These fears were reinforced by Khrushchev's threats that his missiles could destroy European societies in a matter of minutes. The Soviets had resumed nuclear testing at the beginning of September with nuclear devices of yet unmatched yields. This made the Europeans wonder whether the new Soviet nuclear strength had inspired the sudden American interest in Berlin negotiations.

We have seen that allied unity was an important item on the political agenda in October 1961. The Kennedy administration confronted the problem of soliciting German and French support for the new U.S. negotiating posture. As outlined in Kennedy's UN address and in the Gromyko-Rusk talks, the American negotiating position centered on three vital western interests: allied presence in West Berlin, freedom of the city, and access thereto. Especially the German leaders were disappointed with the American leaning toward recognition of the GDR and the Oder-Neisse line. They feared that the United States would become involved in discussions of the broader subject of European security, making the goal of German unification a secondary priority. In addition, the Kennedy administration tightened American control over nuclear warheads in Europe and made clear that it would not support the further proliferation of nuclear weapons. This in effect meant that if the *Bundeswehr* were to gain nuclear capability, it would be under some dual key arrangement. The Germans would have to rely on the American nuclear guarantee.

The above mentioned speech by Roswell Gilpatric was intended primarily to reassure the Europeans, particularly the Germans, about the strength of the American commitment. On 21 October, the deputy secretary of defense explained that "our forces are so deployed and protected that a sneak attack could not effectively disarm us. The destructive power which the U.S. could bring to bear, even after a Soviet surprise attack upon our forces, would be as great as—perhaps greater than—the total undamaged force which the enemy can threaten to launch against the U.S. in a first strike—in short, we have a second strike capability which is at least as extensive as what the Soviets can deliver by striking first."[9]

The message was clear. There was a deterrence gap disproportionately favorable to the United States.[10] On 11 November, Secretary Robert McNamara echoed the theme of American nuclear strength in a speech in Atlanta, noting that "Khrushchev's boasts about his 100-megaton terror weapon are transparent attempts to conceal his nuclear inferiority. With a limited number of ICBM's and submarine launched missiles, and his two or three hundred bombers capable of reaching the North American continent, the strategic nuclear power that he could bring to bear on the United States, even on a surprise attack, is less than a third as much as we could launch against the Sino Soviet Bloc, even after we had sustained the most successful assault that he could mount against us." And the implication of all of this, Secretary McNamara concluded, was that "[w]e have less reason to fear all-out nuclear war than do the Soviets."[11] "Nuclear superiority," as McNamara later emphasized in his Athens address, "has important meanings."[12]

We have seen that President Kennedy emphasized American nuclear strength in order to convince Chancellor Adenauer that negotiations were necessary on the occasion of several meetings from 20 November through 22 November. While pointing out that the U.S. government felt that Germany should not acquire its own nuclear weapons, President Kennedy emphasized that the nuclear balance favored the West. Kennedy believed that the West should negotiate while it held a position of military strength.[13] Emphasizing the American commitment to the defense of Germany, President Kennedy hoped to win Adenauer's agreement to further negotiations.

The Kennedy administration offered reassurance to key officials in Europe over the course of several speeches. Assistant Secretary of Defense for International Security Affairs Paul Nitze, attempted to clarify U.S. defense policy in an address to the International Institute for Strategic Studies in London in December. Nitze underlined that an increase in nonnuclear capabilities was intended to enhance the nuclear deterrent and had nothing to do with the potential vulnerability of the U.S. strategic deterrent. On the contrary, the United States believed that the West had a definite nuclear superiority. Nitze added that the Kennedy administration believed "this superiority, particularly when viewed from the Soviet side, to be strategically important in the equation of deterrence and strategy."[14] Secretary McNamara and Secretary Dean Rusk echoed Nitze's point in their presentations at the NAC ministerial meeting of December 1961. And the American effort to provide reassurance worked: The Europeans *did* derive political comfort from the debunking of Soviet nuclear capability. Nitze reported to the NSC that the NATO members were impressed by McNamara's and Rusk's assessment of U.S. nuclear superiority and particularly by their "assurances in this context of the depth of U.S. commitment to NATO."[15]

Similarly, Henry Kissinger persuaded the German chancellor to relax his concerns about the vulnerability of U.S. retaliatory forces. In the course of the discussion, Kissinger underscored that even after a Soviet first strike, the United States would "have more weapons and delivery vehicles remaining than [the] Soviet Union." He indicated the invulnerable nature of the Polaris force, described the kind of forces that would survive a Soviet attack, and discussed the damage that these forces could inflict on the Soviet Union. One day later, Secretary of State Rusk was informed that the "Chancellor grew progressively more interested and cordial as [the] exposition progressed." Adenauer was quoted as saying that "he had never understood the degree of thought that went into U.S. planning." Moreover, the chancellor had "stressed repeatedly how enormously reassuring this exposition was."[16] Two days later, President Kennedy complained to the German ambassador in Washington that the United States had been making the points stressed by Kissinger since June 1961. "Yet," he added, "there was this constant need to reassure the Germans."[17]

McGeorge Bundy has noted that "to the degree that German officials believed in the value of superiority, Gilpatric's assurance was bound to be important."[18] Capitalizing on that perception, the Kennedy administration had launched a lecture tour to advertise U.S. nuclear superiority, in effect reinforcing the very same beliefs. In late 1961, American nuclear superiority became a symbol for the resolve of the American commitment to the defense of Berlin and Western Europe. It reassured the Europeans that the United States was not going to negotiate from weakness and, more generally, enhanced European confidence in NATO and in the western position in Berlin. To the extent nuclear superiority conveyed resolve, it was politically important.

Reassurance and Deterrence

What was reassuring to the allies was threatening to the Soviets. Khrushchev cannot possibly have liked Gilpatric's persistent debunking of the myth of Soviet nuclear superiority. The American rhetoric only exacerbated tension between Khrushchev and his domestic critics at the twenty-second Communist party congress. Several scholars have suggested that Gilpatric's speech was consciously directed at both the allied audience and the Soviet audience. Secretary of State Rusk emphasized the importance of letting Khrushchev know that the United States was strong in a television interview on the day after Gilpatric's speech.[19] Roger Hilsman, Jr., has observed that Kennedy believed that if Khrushchev "were allowed to continue to assume that we still believed in the missile gap, he would probably bring the world close to war."[20] By the same token, apprising Khrushchev of American nuclear superiority would strengthen the American negotiating position. And since regarding the negotiations over Berlin winning allied support was the central problem at the time, I would argue that Gilpatric's speech was primarily directed at the allied audience.

However, there is some evidence that the Kennedy administration made political use of a strategic threat. According to a declassified Defense Department history, President Kennedy invoked U.S. strategic strength in his 25 July speech describing the nation's rapidly growing, invulnerable strategic weapons programs. Announcing the necessity of constructing fallout shelters, Kennedy warned that the Berlin crisis had the potential of developing into general nuclear war. Kennedy later learned that Khrushchev had been greatly distressed by this speech.[21] When Khrushchev sent a personal letter to Kennedy on 29 September 1961, urging a settlement of the crisis through a secret channel, Kennedy did not answer until 16 October, the day before the opening of the twenty-second party congress.[22] His reply, warning that the alternatives to a settlement were "dire," may have impelled the Soviet leader to back down from the deadline on 17 October.[23]

There is some evidence that members of the Kennedy administration concluded that the attempt to advertise the strategic balance as a means of political coercion was a success. On 20 October, Ambassador Llewellyn Thompson wrote a letter to George F. Kennan, at that time U.S. ambassador in Belgrade, including the following passage: "I attach importance, as does Chip [Bohlen], to his [Khrushchev's] public statement to the Congress putting off the deadline. This is probably related not only to the evidence of our willingness to negotiate but also to the 'correlation of forces.' I don't think they have an answer to the Polaris and, moreover, you will doubtless have seen in the public press . . . that there has been a reappraisal here of Soviet ICBM capabilities very much downward!"[24]

Apart from his domestic political situation, there were other reasons for Khrushchev to be extraordinarily sensitive to American boasts of nuclear superiority. The Soviet leader acknowledged that the Americans had successfully used their strategic superiority as political leverage in earlier times, implying that this had now changed. In his speech on 11 August, in reply to Kennedy's 25 July address, Khrushchev underscored that there "was a time when American Secretary of State Dulles brandished thermonuclear bombs and followed a position of strength policy with regard to the socialist countries. . . . That was barefaced atomic blackmail, but it had to be reckoned with at the time because we did not possess sufficient means of retaliation, and if we did, they were not as many and not of the same power as those of our opponents."[25] This line of argument left Khrushchev, at least in his own mind, vulnerable to the American program of exposure of Soviet nuclear inferiority in the fall of 1961.[26]

In June 1962, Secretary McNamara considered how relative strength had related to Soviet hesitancy in pushing the Berlin issue. Looking back on 1961, McNamara concluded that the acceleration of the U.S. military programs, particularly a major increase in operational missiles, had impressed the Soviets "as a manifestation of United States determination and has also forced them to confront the economic implications of a new round of arms competition." McNamara believed that the rhetoric of superiority had conveyed a message of resolve. McNamara noted that the U.S. buildup had caused the Soviets "to realize that the shift in the political-military relation of forces in the world has been less significant than they anticipated two or three years ago [and] that the West cannot be persuaded to accept their inflated strategic claims." McNamara ended on an optimistic note: The Berlin crisis might have enhanced Soviet awareness of realities under conditions of nuclear plenty, particularly regarding the limits of political leverage that could be extracted by claims of superiority. He emphasized that the Soviets "have become aware that their real accomplishments in strategic weapons cannot be so readily translated into concessions by the West as they had earlier imagined."[27] From an American perspective, this might have been a sensible assessment of the limited political impact of nuclear superiority. Less clear is whether this assessment accurately reflected Soviet experiences of 1961.

The Arms Race As a Functional Substitute for War

In December 1961, the Kennedy administration decided to propose to Congress a huge buildup of strategic forces, even though the United States already possessed vastly superior forces. President Kennedy proposed a buildup even though he realized the danger of a nuclear arms race. Scholars like Desmond Ball have emphasized the political and bureaucratic pressures behind these decisions. However, if one puts the fiscal year 1963 defense budget decisions in the context of the administration's struggle to enhance the credibility of the American commitment to Europe and the military buildup initiated during the Berlin crisis, these decisions present themselves in a new light. The minimum that can be said is that the positive side effect of the buildup in terms of signaling resolve was a good reason for not paying the political price of cutting service propositions further down. It was the *act* rather than the *result* of the defense buildup, the readiness for hard and expensive tasks, that carried political weight. Arms competition increasingly became the functional substitute for actual war.

In October 1961, Secretary McNamara presented the Defense Department's proposal for the fiscal year 1963 defense budget and the fiscal year 1963 to fiscal year 1967 defense program to the president. It was the first defense program and budget to be prepared wholly by the Kennedy administration under the new planning, programming, and budgeting procedure.[28] With respect to strategic forces, McNamara recommended no further funds for the nation's heavy bomber forces and no further development of first-generation ICBMs (Titan and Atlas programs). However, he proposed a rapid expansion of the country's Minuteman and Polaris missile programs as follows:[29]

	FY 63	FY 64	FY 65	FY 66	FY 67
Minuteman ICBMs	150	600	700	800	900
Polaris missiles	144	288	480	560	656

The position of the Defense Department was opposed by Kennedy's White House staff, Budget Director David Bell, and the army. General Maxwell Taylor, McGeorge Bundy, and Carl Kaysen thought McNamara's proposal to be too generous on the strategic side and too conservative on the conventional side. McNamara's recommendations in effect represented a manpower reduction below the Berlin buildup of active duty forces, because the National Guard divisions would return to reserve status. Rusk and Bundy feared the proposed reduction from a foreign policy point of view.[30] General Taylor believed that the United States needed at least two additional divisions.[31]

As to strategic forces, opposition to McNamara's position was articulated in a series of memoranda by Carl Kaysen of McGeorge Bundy's White House staff.[32] Kaysen argued that McNamara's recommendations were based on old estimates of the probable development of Soviet missile strength. McNamara's numbers did not fully take into account the intelligence breakthrough of September 1961, which had shown that the missile gap actually favored the United States.[33] Kaysen proceeded to warn that such an "error on the side of generosity has the undesirable consequence of stepping up the arms race. In a world of missiles and thermonuclear warheads, more arms do not in any simple way add more security."[34] The most sensible interpretation of the Soviet missile deployment so far, Kaysen noted, was that it rested "on the concept of finite deterrence." U.S. long-range missile strength was now in the neighborhood of 120, and, based on McNamara's proposal, would grow to over 500 by July 1963. By July 1964, it would double again to over 1,100. The important question, often overlooked, was whether such a sharp increase would not "present the appearance of our seeking a first strike posture, and thus have a high probability of provoking a response in kind by the Soviets."[35]

On the basis of these considerations, Kaysen proposed a program that would take account of updated intelligence estimates, minimize the risk of generating an arms race, and accomplish military objectives:[36]

	FY 63	FY 64	FY 65	FY 66	FY 67
Minuteman ICBMs	150	300	400	500	600
Polaris missiles	144	288	464	464	464

A slower development and procurement schedule would enable scientists to eliminate technical shortcomings of both missiles before deployment.[37] Arthur Schlesinger has noted that President Kennedy showed "a certain sympathy" with the views of his staff.[38] However, in the proposal that was delivered to Congress, Secretary of Defense McNamara's original recommendations were changed only marginally.[39]

The Impact of the Domestic Policy and Bureaucratic Policy Environment

Desmond Ball has explained the political and bureaucratic pressures behind Kennedy's fiscal year 1963 defense budget decisions. Kennedy's campaign promises generated expectations within Congress, industry, and the military for an enlargement of the defense budget. Even in his fiscal year 1962 budget amendment proposals of March 1961, Kennedy had found it politically necessary to commit the nation to more missiles.[40] This happened before his administration had developed a strategic policy of its own and even though some key officials had already recognized the missile gap to be fiction. Once the estimates of Soviet capabilities were reduced in the fall of 1961, the U.S. missile programs had already developed a momentum of their own. To have slowed them down at that time would have been politically even more costly than in the spring.[41] David Bell warned the president in November that even McNamara's proposal might "require a major effort on the part of the Administration to change what appears to be a fairly widespread national attitude that national security requires ever-increasing strategic missile forces and airpower."[42]

Ball has argued that the magnitude of the buildup was a product of bargaining within the defense bureaucracy. In the face of far larger demands from the armed services, it was not possible for McNamara to compromise on smaller levels of forces.[43] On 6 October, the secretary of defense informed the president that the proposals of the individual services exceeded the financial sum he was recommending for the period 1963 through 1967 by $74 billion.[44] If McNamara's original program, for example, recommended 100 nonmobile Minuteman ICBMs for procurement in fiscal year 1963, the air force demanded 600. And the navy desired 160 Polaris missiles, as opposed to McNamara's recommendation of 96.[45] The air force called for 2,300 Minuteman ICBMs by the end of fiscal year 1967, and the navy wanted 720 Polaris missiles.[46] The force proposals made by the secretary of defense were not an expression of a theory of requirements—what his DPM-61 made believe—but rather the result of a bureaucratic compromise. However, pressures from within the military-industrial complex do not tell the whole story.

The Fiscal Year 1963 Defense Budget and the Berlin Crisis

We have seen that risk manipulation over Berlin rested on rhetoric surrounding military preparations. Acheson had written in his report that the deterrent effect on the Soviets of foreshadowing a major long-term increase in U.S. force levels "would probably be substantial." Dean Acheson thought that the Soviets "even now bitterly regret the lasting jump in US defense expenditures brought on by the Korean war. It would be useful to convince them that a similar increase might result from a Berlin crisis."[47] At the heart of Acheson's line of thinking was the conviction that the most important result of the military buildup would be felt *before* it came to a ground probe in Berlin. The principal goal of the announcement of a long-term military buildup was to make steps short of military force, like economic countermeasures, an airlift, or a blockade, more effective. Military preparations should be made so evident that the eventual use of force would be believed by the adversary to be virtually automatic.

In announcing a proposal to appropriate an additional $3.24 billion to the armed forces, Kennedy emphasized that these emergency funds would be used for the long-term buildup of the nation's conventional *and* nuclear forces. In addition, the president foreshadowed the call-up of additional forces should such a step become necessary. Khrushchev was extremely sensitive to the "flywheel of war preparations" announced by Kennedy.[48] The Soviets did not want the Berlin crisis to be a cause of western rearmament.[49] To threaten with the prospect of an arms race seemed to work.

When the wall went up, President Kennedy inquired about the possibility of an increased buildup. Additional increases in military capabilities, Kennedy wrote to the secretary of defense, "would, of course, have a direct relation to the development of our longer term posture to be reflected in the FY '63 budget."[50] However, for the rest of August the matter was overshadowed by the need to restore confidence in West Berlin and Germany. The military buildup question was back on the table when the Kennedy administration had to decide how to react to the Soviet announcement (30 August) that troops scheduled to be discharged would remain, and the Soviet announcement (31 August) that nuclear testing would resume.[51] There was a widespread feeling, to use General Taylor's words, "that the moment has come to shift into a higher gear" regarding the general defense effort.[52] On 31 August, President Kennedy asked the secretary of defense for recommendations on expanding the nation's military forces. On 7 September, the president met with the secretary of state, the secretary of defense, and some other key officials in order to discuss McNamara's recommendations.[53] However, differences of opinion precluded any decision.

The next day, President Kennedy sent a series of questions, based on the previous day's discussion, to Rusk and McNamara. Two of the inquiries are of special interest in this context. First, the president reopened discussion of a fundamental assumption of his government's Berlin strategy. "Will an increase of our conventional force in Europe," he asked, "convince Khrushchev of our readiness to fight to a finish for West Berlin or will it have the opposite effect?" Second, he inquired about the interaction of Soviet and Western military postures: "If we add 6 divisions to NATO, may not Khrushchev add 6 or more divisions to the conventional forces facing NATO?"[54]

Secretary of Defense McNamara replied to the presidential inquiries on 18 September.[55] McNamara concluded that "further mobilization and deployment actions should be taken at this time in order to convey to the USSR and to our Allies a firm determination and resolve to defend our interests in Berlin." He proceeded to propose the early deployment of at least one additional U.S. division to Europe and the call up of four National Guard divisions to active duty in order to assure an adequate strategic reserve. Such action, he added, would enhance deterrence, strengthen the western negotiating position, and, if deterrence should fail, increase the capability of the alliance for waging war without resort to nuclear weapons. Apart from these general conclusions, the secretary of defense replied to Kennedy's first question that while a conventional buildup alone would be unlikely to convince Khrushchev of U.S. willingness to fight to a finish over Berlin, the absence of a buildup would probably increase his doubts about U.S. determination. He added that to "continue efforts focused mostly on nuclear forces and nuclear threats would carry less conviction than building up *both* non-nuclear and nuclear forces."[56]

McNamara's proposals must be viewed against the background of criticism from General Lauris Norstad. We have seen above that NATO's supreme commander was skeptical about NATO's ability, in case of war, to enforce a graduated, controlled development of the fighting and about notions that NATO could successfully sustain a conventional defense over an extended period of time. Norstad warned (in an appendix to McNamara's memorandum to the president) that "the credibility of the deterrent can be destroyed by emphasizing a policy that could be construed by the Soviets as permitting them to become involved, and then, if they decide the risks are too great, to disengage."[57] Therefore,

Norstad advised against deploying additional troops to Europe at that time. Henry Kissinger supported Norstad on this particular point noting that "the Acheson approach pays insufficient attention to the psychological situation in Europe." The European obsession with nuclear weapons, Kissinger emphasized, could "not be overcome by subterfuge, but only by a strategic concept in which both nuclear and conventional weapons have their place."[58] Norstad finally had to acquiesce in the implementation of National Security Action Memorandum (NSAM) 109 and its sequence of graduated, flexible options. But, at least, he had succeeded in reminding Kennedy of the importance of allied trust in U.S. nuclear forces.

With regard to President Kennedy's second query, whether an increase of U.S. divisions in Europe would trigger a similar or larger reinforcement of Soviet forces in East Germany, McNamara answered affirmatively. However, the net total, the secretary of defense noted, might still shift in favor of NATO. The Soviets faced a number of difficulties, like "logistical problems, dispersal required by the threat of nuclear operations, potentially hostile populations, vulnerability of the [lines of communication] (particularly the rail net) to sabotage and air interdiction, and the restrictive geography of the European peninsula."[59]

The final decision on an additional military buildup was made in a small meeting on 18 September. McGeorge Bundy argued against any call-up at this time "because of the adverse impact on the negotiating attitude of the USSR." Only a few days earlier, the Soviet Union and the United States had agreed on an exchange between Rusk and Andrei Gromyko on the occasion of the United Nations General Assembly meeting. However, Bundy lost the argument, and McNamara's view carried the day. Secretary Rusk, via Foy Kohler, indicated no concern over the impact of a military buildup on current negotiations. Finally, President Kennedy decided to call up two National Guard divisions with supporting forces and directed McNamara to inform the press.[60]

Deterrence and the Arms Race

It seems likely that President Kennedy saw the buildup as a deterrent and a tool that would strengthen the American negotiating posture in the forthcoming talks between Gromyko and Rusk. The decision was shaped so as to minimize European concerns about a one-sided increase in conventional forces. No additional divisions were transferred to Europe.[61] The buildup was kept small enough that Khrushchev would not conclude that the United States was moving away from its emphasis on nuclear weapons as the main deterrent.

In fact, Secretary Rusk repeatedly used the threat of an arms race in his conversation with Soviet foreign minister Gromyko on September 21. Only minutes into their talk, Rusk warned Gromyko that Soviet insistence on a peace treaty that would leave access to West Berlin subject to East German control could be dangerous. "He was not threatening, but he would say that we consider ourselves to be under a threat. We do not want an arms race, but we will not draw away from it in these circumstances." Secretary Rusk closed the conversation on the same note, with an even more obvious hint that an arms race would slow Soviet economic plans and endanger Khrushchev's major political commitment to increased production of agricultural machinery. Rusk "agreed that it was important not to let the situation get out of hand and develop into a direct clash. There was no reason why this should be as between the Soviet Union and the United States, both of us had big things to do at home; moreover, the arms race should be stopped and the arms burden reduced."[62] Secretary Rusk used the prospect of war only to underline the common interest of the Soviet Union and the United States in preventing it. When it came to put on some pressure on the Soviets, he was falling back on the issue of arms competition.[63]

And again, the threat of an arms race seemed to work. On 17 October, Khrushchev relaxed his commitment to a deadline for the signing of a peace treaty. Later, Secretary of Defense McNamara confirmed that "the United States acceleration of military programs beginning in 1961 has clearly impressed them [the Soviets] as a manifestation of United States determination, and has also forced them to confront the economic implications of a new round of arms competition."[64] As discussed above, preserving a unified negotiating posture became first priority after disappearance of the Soviet deadline.[65] U.S. rhetoric now emphasized nuclear superiority as discussed in Roswell Gilpatric's speech.

Against this background, the Kennedy administration made its final fiscal year 1963 defense budget proposal during November and December 1961. During the preceding months, the government had come to realize that a credible deterrent needed *both* a conventional buildup and a nuclear buildup. The threat of an arms race had been applied successfully, and the usefulness of the rhetoric of nuclear superiority as a means of reassuring the allies had been proven. Recent experiences with the rhetoric of military superiority provided a powerful case for further expansion of the nation's general defense forces. Indeed, Secretary Rusk and McGeorge Bundy questioned what in their opinion were insufficient increases in conventional forces from a foreign policy point of view.[66] And Kaysen noted that a return of the National Guard divisions to reserve status "may diminish significantly the message conveyed by our other military preparations to the Soviets, who are impressed by ground force strength."[67]

In contrast to the case for a conventional buildup, it is more difficult to prove a correlation between the 1963 strategic missile buildup and the Berlin crisis rhetoric of superiority. This may be due to the lack of declassified records on the final decisions regarding the Minuteman and Polaris programs in late December.[68] In addition, Secretary McNamara told the Senate Armed Services Committee that "in contrast to other military requirements, the requirement for strategic retaliatory forces lends itself rather well to reasonably precise calculation."[69] McNamara rationalized the buildup of the nation's strategic forces as the product of a precise theory of requirements. In effect, this argument served to conceal the domestic and foreign policy influences on the defense budget decisions.[70]

However, the timing of the final budget proposals suggests that they were affected by the developments in the Berlin crisis. On 11 and 12 December, the Kennedy administration pressed the French into acceptance of Soviet-American talks under the guise of exploratory discussions. At the same time, Paul Nitze was trying to convey to the Europeans that nuclear superiority had important meanings. A similar message by Rusk and McNamara on the occasion of the NATO ministerial meeting seemed to convince the Europeans of the depth of the American commitment.[71] From a foreign policy viewpoint, there were strong incentives to expand the nation's nuclear forces. Those incentives complement the domestic political and bureaucratic explanations of why the Kennedy administration accelerated its strategic missile programs after the myth of the missile gap had been exposed.[72] The positive side effect of the buildup in terms of signaling resolve was a good reason for not paying the political price of cutting further down service propositions for larger strategic forces.

Political Considerations and Military Planning: The Case of Nuclear Testing

Mutual vulnerability meant, paradoxically, that the nuclear force that was needed for deterrence could never be used. However, the superpowers and their allies continued to act as if nuclear weapons actually could be used. This initiated a process in which the link between the physical capabilities and the political behavior of states waned and became distinctly one-sided. As long as military force could physically secure political goals, the important question was how military factors (like the correlation of forces) affected political decisions. Once military power could only be transformed into favorable political outcomes by indirect psychological processes, the essential question became how military decisions could and would support the highly subjective assessment of the situation by adversary, allies, and the nation itself. Since in an era of mutual nuclear plenty a threat with nuclear weapons was not very credible, it was crucial for nations to establish their resolve. We have seen above that because the Berlin crisis was perceived as a test of will, both sides thought it central to influence others' beliefs. Nuclear superiority and arms competition became important signaling tools for influencing allies and the Soviet Union alike.

The need to signal resolve led members of the Kennedy administration to emphasize U.S. nuclear superiority in the fall of 1961. The dominance of political considerations can be seen in the debate over whether the United States should resume nuclear testing. On 30 August, the Soviets announced the resumption of nuclear weapons testing. The Soviets announced that because the West was threatening war as its response to a separate peace treaty, and because any war would quickly escalate into nuclear-rocket war, the Soviet Union had to be prepared.[73] The timing of the decision suggests that Moscow thought resumption of testing would serve its political aims in Berlin. With their first test of a weapon yielding approximately 150 kilotons on 1 September, the Soviets broke the three-year informal test moratorium, which had gone into effect after the beginning of the Geneva Conference on the Discontinuance of Nuclear Weapons Tests in November 1958. However promising the chances for an agreement seemed to be in the spring of 1960, the Geneva conference came to a standstill in the aftermath of the downing of the American U-2 reconnaissance aircraft over Sverdlovsk. Soon after Kennedy's sober encounter with Khrushchev in Vienna, the new administration, pushed by criticism from Congress, found itself drifting toward resumption of testing.[74]

The Panofsky Panel Report

The president was still in doubt about whether to resume testing. On 24 June, he appointed a special panel from the President's Science Advisory Committee to study the pros and cons of testing. The panel was chaired by Stanford University professor Wolfgang Panofsky.[75] The group submitted its final report on 21 July. The Panofsky panel's conclusion indicated no immediate need for the resumption of testing. The panel's report noted that weapons tests might result in improvements in the yield-to-weight ratios of strategic warheads. This would add flexibility to the design of U.S. strategic systems "in particular with regard to reduced vulnerability and increased mobility." However, the significance of these developments depended in part on other technical factors, like the accuracy, reliability, and vulnerability of delivery systems, the level of intelligence data on enemy targets, and enemy defense capabilities.

In addition, a crucial decision would be whether to emphasize deterrent or counterforce strategies. For deterrent strategies, improvements in yield-to-weight ratios of strategic warheads were of little significance, because "warheads of present yields delivered with the CEP's [accuracy] of existing systems would so completely over-kill the population and over-destroy the floor space of urban area targets by blast and fire, that further increases in yields would produce little additional damage." Yield-to-weight ratios were of greater importance in connection with counterforce strategies. The critical factor for success of counterforce strategies was that a sufficient force would survive an initial enemy attack. This depended more on the number of delivery vehicles than the available warhead yields. Moreover, the ability to obtain precise knowledge of the location of a very large proportion of Soviet strategic delivery systems was central to a counterforce strategy. However, the report noted, "we do not now have this information on Soviet missiles; and, even if it is obtained on fixed missile installations . . . the problem of maintaining continuously accurate knowledge of the locations of mobile systems such as Polaris will be extremely difficult."[76]

On the basis of this analysis, the Panofsky report concluded that "none of the specific weapons tests now discussed appear to be of such urgency from the technical and military point of view that a reasonable delay in reaching a formal decision on resumption of nuclear testing would be critical." Finally, the panel advised Kennedy to focus on the political impact of nuclear testing: "Any decision in the near future concerning resumption of nuclear testing can be governed primarily by non-technical considerations."[77]

Members of the Kennedy administration discussed the Panofsky report during the first week of August. The JCS rejected the panel's conclusions and recommended the resumption of testing as a matter of urgency. In their comments on the report, they noted that there "are many points in the report which are considered to be inaccurate or which express opinions and military judgments with which the Joint Chiefs of Staff [JCS] do not agree." The military leaders went on to question the report's conclusion that from a military point of view there was little urgency to testing and that the decision therefore could be guided primarily by nontechnical considerations.[78] However, the JCS position was opposed strongly in the White House. President Kennedy asked General Taylor who had written the comments of the JCS. The president was surprised at the position of the military, because the AEC seemed to be "in general agreement in the findings and conclusions of the report."[79]

Subsequently, General Taylor himself set out to present the military arguments in favor of resuming testing. In his opinion, established military strategy required testing. With regard to strategic warfare, Taylor noted that "if we are to absorb the first strike, we need a secure retaliatory force, which is mobile and uses lightweight warheads." Progress in developing light strategic warheads was "worth more to us than to the USSR" due to U.S. strategy for global nuclear warfare. The same was true for development of tactical nuclear weapons.[80]

However, McGeorge Bundy did not buy into Taylor's arguments when he briefed the president before the next NSC meeting. While the military benefits of resuming testing seemed to be minimal in the short term, Bundy underscored "the political reasons for playing out the test ban negotiations both at Geneva and at the UN."[81] When the Panofsky report was discussed in the NSC meeting on 8 August, John McCloy, who was in charge of disarmament negotiations, warned that the UN General Assembly was about to meet. Any indication that the United States intended to resume testing would lead to vigorous protests by the nonaligned states.[82] The evolving sense of the meeting was that from a military point of view there was no urgent need for resuming testing, and such a decision would have serious disadvantages from a foreign policy perspective.

The Soviet Test Series and Its Impact on the Berlin Crisis

The political environment changed dramatically with the sudden and unexpected announcement of 30 August that the Soviet Union would resume nuclear testing. Bundy has written that of all Soviet provocations during 1961 and 1962, "it was the resumption of testing that disappointed [Kennedy] most."[83] On 31 August, the president met with his advisers to formulate a response. Chairman of the Atomic Energy Commission Glenn T. Seaborg's notes of these discussions make clear that the administration regarded the Soviet announcement as a *political* challenge in connection with the Berlin crisis. Some advisers thought that the decision for the United States to resume testing should be postponed in order to fully capitalize on the propaganda advantage that the Soviet announcement presented. Others favored an immediate commitment to testing, so that nobody would perceive the president as being indecisive.[84]

As it turned out, the president chose a third approach between these two options. On 2 September, the United States and Great Britain proposed an immediate atmospheric test ban and gave the Soviets until 9 September to reply. Khrushchev rejected the offer on 9 September.[85] On 1 September, the Soviets exploded their first device and by 5 September they had conducted their third test. It was this third test that convinced the president that he had to act. Later the same day, President Kennedy announced that in view of the Soviet test series the United States would resume underground testing, which produced no fallout. Kennedy's decision was a product of purely political considerations. This also suggests Arthur Schlesinger's account of how the president answered Adlai Stevenson's comment that he would not have resumed testing:

> Kennedy quickly said, "What choice did we have? They had spit in our eye three times. We couldn't possibly sit back and do nothing at all. We had to do this." Stevenson remarked, "But we were ahead in the propaganda battle." Kennedy said, "What does that mean? I don't hear of any windows broken because of the Soviet decision. The neutrals have been terrible. The Russians made two tests *after* our note calling for a ban on atmospheric testing. Maybe they couldn't have stopped the first, but they could have stopped the second. . . . All this makes Khrushchev look pretty tough. He has had a succession of apparent victories—space, Cuba, the thirteenth of August [the Berlin wall], though I don't myself regard this as a Soviet victory. He wants to give out the feeling that he has us on the run. The third test was a contemptuous response to our note. . . . Anyway, the decision has been made. I'm not saying that it was the right decision. Who the hell knows? But it is the decision which has been taken."[86]

According to Seaborg, political considerations continued to affect the American test program once underground testing was begun. On 5 September, the chairman of the AEC indicated in a meeting with the president that a first test of approximately twenty tons could be prepared by 15 September. Seaborg's remark, according to his personal journal, triggered the following exchange with the president: "The President felt that the disparity between a 20-*ton* yield and the first Soviet test of about

150 *kilotons* would invite much averse comment. He wanted a much larger test, 20 or more kilotons, if possible, but he did not want to accept any delay. I [Seaborg] told him that, while we could ready a device in the desired size range, such a large test conducted so soon would jeopardize the availability of the rest of the tunnel complex where it might be carried out." However, because of political concerns, the temptation was big to match kilotons for kilotons. Eventually, a device of approximately six kilotons was tested. The test led to the contamination of one of the two available test tunnels. When the president requested acceleration of the testing schedule in late September, the chairman of the AEC replied: "It is the conclusion of the Commission that we cannot accomplish any significant speedup in the presently planned program without resorting to atmospheric testing, although it is not the purpose of this letter to make a recommendation for atmospheric testing at this time."[87] The administration found itself drifting toward the resumption of atmospheric testing. The development of the two test series did nothing to mitigate fears of an adverse impression on world opinion regarding U.S. nuclear strength.

On 17 October, the first day of the twenty-second party congress and the day on which the Soviets withdrew the deadline for the signing of the separate peace treaty, Khrushchev announced that an explosion of a 50-megaton device would take place on 31 October.[88] The Associated Press quoted Khrushchev telling the Communist Party congress that "we have a 100 million ton bomb, but we do not intend to explode it. If we happen to explode it in the wrong place, we might break our own windows. May God grant that we never have to explode such a bomb."[89] The actual explosion came one day earlier than announced.

The Kennedy administration felt that it had to react. On 2 November, the president announced that the United States would start the preparations for nuclear tests in the atmosphere so as to be ready in case it would become necessary to conduct them.[90] President Kennedy wanted to avoid the perception that the United States might be falling behind the Soviet Union in nuclear strength. The president showed more respect for the Soviet tests than previously. While continuing to denounce them as part of a Soviet campaign of fear, he did not dismiss them as mere bluff and acknowledged that "these tests are, no doubt, of importance to Soviet leaders and scientists in developing and improving nuclear weapons." Nevertheless, he quickly emphasized, "in terms of total military strength, the United States would not trade places with any nation on earth." Pointing to his nation's superiority in nuclear power, he added that "it will be the policy of the United States to proceed in developing nuclear weapons to maintain this superior capability for the defense of the Free World against any aggressor." Kennedy's statement was clearly intended to reassure the allies. The United States was willing to maintain superior nuclear force relative to the Soviet Union, because this was what many Europeans (and Americans) thought to be essential for the defense of the Free World.[91]

Kennedy's decision to reassure allies with Gilpatric's speech of 21 October was clearly a reaction to the Soviet test series and, in particular, to Khrushchev's announcement of the unprecedented explosion of a device of 50 kilotons.[92] The apparent success and power of Soviet testing made it even more urgent from an American point of view to signal resolve by emphasizing its nuclear superiority. The intensity of the Soviet test series, and the impression that the tests made on world opinion, heavily influenced the atmosphere in which the Kennedy administration decided to publicize American nuclear superiority and in which it made the fiscal year 1963 defense budget decisions. The test race was part of the psychological balance which became so important to the Berlin issue in the fall of 1961.

The psychological balance tipped in favor of the Soviet Union when the results of the evaluation of the Soviet test series became known. A scientific panel headed by Hans Bethe concluded that the tests would help the Soviet Union to achieve important advances in nuclear technology. Moreover, in some respect Soviet nuclear capability seemed to have surpassed U.S. capabilities. In a memorandum to the JCS, Paul Nitze summarized a preliminary technical evaluation of the Soviet test series as indicating "a highly successful Soviet effort to achieve greater thermonuclear efficiencies, to improve yield-to-weight ratios, and to reduce fissionable materials requirements. In some cases, the Soviet results appear to go beyond present US technology."[93] The sobering meeting at which the Bethe Panel's results were discussed indicated that it was no longer only a matter of decreasing confidence among U.S. allies; a chink had appeared in American self-confidence. Secretary Rusk indicated that the United States had to consider whether it was still in its interest to sign the comprehensive test ban treaty, which it had tabled in Geneva in the spring of 1961.[94]

During the winter of 1961–62, the United States was moving toward the resumption of atmospheric testing. However, the president seemed to vacillate about the final decision to test. This was due to his doubts about whether resuming atmospheric tests would bury the chances for a test ban agreement. In addition, the British opposed the resumption of atmospheric tests. They also had some political leverage with regard to the American decision, because the United States wanted to use

Christmas Island, a British possession, for the tests.[95] And finally, the military reasons for atmospheric tests were still being debated.[96]

It was now the secretary of defense who outlined the immediate military need for testing.[97] Secretary McNamara based his case for testing on different arguments than the JCS and General Taylor had made in the summer. McNamara did not imply that atmospheric testing would lead to major changes in the military balance.[98] Nor did he justify further testing on the grounds of U.S. military strategy. He did *not* argue that tests would enable the United States to pursue a no-cities counterforce strategy. Leaving the question of civil versus military targets aside, he justified further testing on grounds of the general goal of insuring the nation's ability to inflict unacceptable damage to any enemy. The test results were needed, McNamara wrote to the president, first, to "minimize the vulnerability of our delivery systems and provide measures to penetrate their defenses." Second, tests were important to increase the capabilities of the U.S. antimissile weapons. Third, there was an urgent requirement for increased knowledge about the effects of nuclear explosions on bases, missiles, radar, and communications. "The high altitude tests," he pointed out to the president, "will provide critical data necessary to evaluate 'blackout' and associated electromagnetic effects."[99]

The JCS still did not follow McNamara's line of thinking. Their call for an acceleration of nuclear tests in various environments, including the atmosphere, was based on an assessment of the *political* effects of a failure to resume unrestrained testing. Their analysis started from the fundamental assumption that U.S. national security policy was based on technological superiority. Chairman of the JCS Lyman L. Lemnitzer wrote to the president that the "security of the United States depends to a large extent upon our ability to assure superiority in nuclear weapons and our ability to employ them effectively."[100] If the United States lost its technological edge, the implications for the nation's security would be extremely dangerous. On 22 December 1961, the JCS wrote to the secretary of defense that "continued US inaction to resume atmospheric testing in the face of Soviet nuclear advances will certainly bring into question US nuclear superiority and will tend to undermine the future confidence of our Allies and our own people."[101] The JCS justified testing by referring to the political importance of allied trust in U.S. nuclear superiority. Given the background of the Berlin crisis and European concerns about the new U.S. emphasis on a conventional option, this was a powerful attempt to remind the president of the nation's strategic Achilles' heel.

As to the question of whether a comprehensive test ban would still be in the interests of the United States, the secretary of defense believed that a ban, if observed, was likely to be to the advantage of the United States. Even if the Soviets were to cheat, the second-strike capability of the nation seemed to be in no doubt.[102] McNamara added that a comprehensive test ban would have some effect on slowing the diffusion of nuclear power. Finally, he said, "the cooperation that may develop between the US and the USSR, as a result, has a potential importance."[103] Secretary Rusk agreed with McNamara's analysis that the gains from a test ban would outweigh the risks. The JCS alone opposed any further call for a comprehensive test ban, because its members believed that any such treaty would endanger the nation's military superiority.[104]

Kennedy's Decision to Resume Testing

President Kennedy finally decided to resume atmospheric testing in a meeting with his top national security advisers on 27 February. Glenn Seaborg's account of the meeting confirms that the decision to resume testing was primarily due to the perception of an overriding political need to demonstrate technological and nuclear superiority to the allies. According to Seaborg, Secretary Rusk noted that the "reputation of the United States must not be endangered by suggestions we might be falling behind."[105] Word was getting around at the UN that the United States was behind and may have to bargain from weakness.[106] Finally, Kennedy concluded that resumption of testing might even be the quicker route toward a test ban agreement. When President Kennedy announced his decision to resume atmospheric testing on 2 March, he emphasized that failure to respond to the Soviet tests would cause many to "lose faith in our will and our wisdom, as well as our weaponry." He once again combined his decision to go ahead with testing with an offer for a comprehensive test ban treaty: "If the Soviet Union should now be willing to accept such a treaty, to sign it before the latter part of April and apply it immediately—if all testing thus be actually halted—then the nuclear arms race would be slowed down at last—the security of the United States and its ability to meet its commitments would be safeguarded—and there would be no need for our tests to begin."[107]

With the conference of the eighteen-nation Disarmament Committee resuming in Geneva in March 1962, it quickly became clear that there was little hope for progress toward a test ban treaty. On 25 April, the United States began its atmospheric test series with an air drop off Christmas Island.[108] Eventually, the series comprised forty tests, yielding a total of approximately 20 megatons. The scientific evaluation of the test data was not encouraging for those who sought missile defense. Seaborg noted that the results "should have a sobering effect on any who believe that the earth's outer environment could emerge from a full nuclear exchange without severe damage."[109]

The decision-making process of the Kennedy administration regarding the question of underground and atmospheric nuclear test resumption was dominated by political considerations. Washington evaluated the necessity of nuclear tests first of all regarding their impact on the balance of resolve. The influence of the test race on others' assessment of the balance of resolve developed importance against the background of the test of will over Berlin. This was the case because in an era of nuclear plenty, military power had to be transformed into political gains by psychological processes depending on highly subjective assessments of national power. The Kennedy administration did not assume that nuclear tests would change the military balance in a fundamental way; what the tests would change, though, was the perception of this balance among allies, adversary, and the American public. This political concern influenced not only the decision to resume testing, but also the way in which the test series developed. The perception of urgent political need for quick and powerful tests adversely affected the planning, the conduct, and the efficiency of the American test series; the United States did not gain the maximum possible scientific and technical information per kiloton of exploded nuclear power.

Due to the growing symbolic and signaling substance of defense policy decisions the dividing line between the political and military dimensions of nuclear weapons was becoming blurry. The JCS, for example, were defining the *military* requirements for testing almost exclusively by referring to the *political* impact of a failure to strive for military and technological superiority. On the other hand, people tended to rationalize political goals with military requirements. Why, for instance, did McNamara underscore the military requirements for testing even though he perceived no danger to the nation's second-strike capability? He might have been thinking in terms of a no-cities counterforce strategy, which called for technologically superior forces. As will be shown in the next section, however, his interest in that strategy seems itself to have been motivated by strong political considerations. This process goes a long way toward explaining why in the final meeting on the decision to resume atmospheric testing on 27 February 1962 diametrically opposed assessments of the matter could persist: While Adlai Stevenson felt "that a good technical case had not been made for the resumption of testing,"

Vice President Lyndon Johnson thought "that there was military necessity [for test resumption] not counterbalanced by political considerations."[110]

Nuclear Strategy: The Growing Gap
between Theory and Practice

Not only were the links between military capabilities and the behavior of states becoming weaker, but also the role of strategic concepts was changing. The nuclear strategy that was publicly declared was no longer determined primarily by a military assessment of what was feasible on the operational level with available technology.[111] Of greater importance was what political impact a particular employment strategy would have. It has been argued above that the Kennedy administration endorsed the no-cities counterforce strategy not because it believed in its feasibility, but rather because it believed that this strategy would send the right political signals. Sending the right political signals had become particularly important in mediating differences between the United States and its European allies.

We have seen that the Kennedy administration made a big effort to enlarge NATO's conventional forces in order to deter limited aggression credibly. More conventional power would enable NATO to enforce a pause in the event of a Soviet attack with conventional forces. It was the purpose of this firebreak to make the adversary appreciate the risk of escalation to the nuclear level. Hopefully, this would further early war termination.[112] Consultation over Berlin contingency planning served the Kennedy administration in promulgating its new strategic thinking within the alliance.[113] However, the Europeans were anything but happy about Washington's efforts to change NATO strategy. They interpreted the new emphasis on a conventional option by the Kennedy administration as a shift away from a reliable nuclear deterrent. They feared that, as a consequence, the risk of Europe again becoming the theater of a large conventional war would increase.

European opposition to the new American strategic thinking was bolstered by General Norstad's own resistance to the implementation of a strategy of graduation for NATO. The effect of this was to awaken the Kennedy administration to the fact that a conventional buildup alone would not be enough to strengthen deterrence as long as Europe did not believe in it. European political realities called for *both* a conventional and a nuclear buildup. The European obsession with nuclear weapons, Henry Kissinger emphasized, could only be overcome with a strategy in which both nuclear and conventional weapons had their place. This was exactly what the Kennedy administration proposed in its fiscal year 1963 defense budget. Washington began to stress its nuclear superiority as a signal of U.S. resolve with regard to the defense of West Berlin and Europe. The message was clear: A conventional buildup was appropriate, but the United States would not abandon its nuclear superiority.

In one interview, after explaining the state of American nuclear capability, Secretary McNamara added: "I think it's a fact that nuclear power has not been a universal deterrent. Our superior nuclear power did not deter the invasion of South Korea, it did not deter the construction of the wall in East Berlin on the 13th of August, it has not deterred the communist invasion and infiltration of Southeast Asia over a period of years." McNamara came to the heart of his argument: "I think it's quite clear that the addition of non-nuclear forces broadens and expands the deterrent power of the nuclear force. The non-nuclear forces must rest on the firm foundation of superior nuclear power." These were the premises on which the proposed fiscal year 1963 defense budget rested and that provided the foundation to U.S. foreign policy.[114]

The problem the Kennedy administration was facing with respect to NATO in early 1962 was how to sell the conventional option to the Europeans without destroying their already shaky trust in the American nuclear guarantee. With regard to long-term European stability, it was also important to the United States to stop the trend toward national nuclear forces. With an eye on a potential German interest in nationally controlled nuclear forces, the United States had to make a stand, in particular, against the French *force de frappe*. McNamara's solution to these political dilemmas was to propose a no-cities counterforce strategy. We have seen above that the secretary of defense saw reason to doubt the feasibility of the strategy. First, it was doubtful that the Soviets would "cooperate" with the logic of the strategy and restrain themselves from attacking U.S. population centers. Second, the desired level of restraint was unattainable with present technology, and third, the strategy could not save Europe from destruction.[115] However, the strategy sent the right political messages. The no-cities counterforce concept was an expression of American strategic superiority, signaling American confidence in the ability of this force to destroy Soviet forces. The strategy's main goal was to terminate a nuclear war *before* the cities were destroyed. It thus allayed European fears that the United States would never risk New York for Paris. Moreover, the strategy justified keeping nuclear forces centrally controlled. It allowed McNamara to criticize independent nuclear forces as unnecessary, at best.

McNamara's Athens Address

It was McNamara's aim to convince the allies of these goals in his famous speech in Athens before NATO's assembled foreign and defense ministers in May 1962. The address is often quoted as an explanation of U.S. nuclear strategy, overlooking the political context in which it was presented. It is worth examining closely what McNamara actually said. The secretary of defense opened his address by reminding his audience that in the NATO meeting of December 1961 he had emphasized U.S. nuclear superiority but demanded a buildup of NATO's nonnuclear forces. Today, he continued, he "would like to discuss in greater depth our views on the problem of general nuclear war and its deterrence, the role and level of non-nuclear forces, and the linkage between these two types of forces in relation to deterrence." As to general nuclear war, McNamara defined American strategy using the no-cities counterforce concept: "The U.S. has come to the conclusion that to the extent feasible basic military strategy in general nuclear war should be approached in much the same way that more conventional military operations have been regarded in the past. That is to say, our principal military objectives, in the event of a nuclear war stemming from a major attack on the Alliance, should be the destruction of the enemy's military forces while attempting to preserve the fabric as well as the integrity of allied society."

The secretary of defense indicated that this strategy had many advantages over a strategy that targeted only cities or a mixture of civil and military targets for the purpose of both deterrence and the conduct of general war. In particular with regard to casualties suffered by the participants, the results would vary over wide ranges.[116] The most important implication of such wide variations in outcomes of nuclear war, McNamara went on, was "that nuclear superiority has important meanings." Because the nuclear defense of NATO was undertaken on a global basis, that is, the United States targeted Soviet nuclear forces threatening Europe with the same priority as those forces being able to reach North America, he was confident "that the Soviet Union will not initiate the use of nuclear weapons in the face of our nuclear superiority." For the same reason, a Soviet first use of nuclear weapons following a limited engagement in Europe appeared equally unlikely.

McNamara proceeded to question the value of relatively weak national nuclear forces. He underscored that the theater in a major nuclear war would be worldwide. In such a war, the target system would be indivisible. The efficient use of NATO resources required that such a war be conducted as a centrally controlled campaign. It was essential that the decision to use nuclear weapons be centralized to the greatest extent possible. McNamara warned of the risks in case the alliance failed to achieve central control of nuclear forces: "We would all find it equally intolerable to have one segment of the Alliance force attacking urban-industrial areas while, with the bulk of our forces, we were succeeding in destroying most of the enemies' nuclear capabilities. Such a failure in coordination might lead to the destruction of our hostages—the Soviet cities—just at a time at which our strategy of coercing the Soviets into stopping their aggression was on the verge of success."[117] These considerations led the American secretary of defense to a critique of national nuclear forces. He emphasized that "weak nuclear capabilities, operating independently, are expensive, prone to obsolescence, and lacking in credibility as a deterrent."

While the West could defend its interests with considerable confidence that the Soviets would not wish to escalate a conflict, McNamara continued, it was the more likely contingency that NATO, not the Soviets, "would have to make the momentous decision to use nuclear weapons, and we would do so in the knowledge that the consequences might be catastrophic for all of us." McNamara now proceeded to stress that "despite our nuclear superiority and our ability to destroy the Soviet target system, all of us will suffer deeply in the event of major nuclear war." With an eye on Berlin contingency planning, McNamara then discussed the prospect of the tactical and demonstrative use of nuclear weapons as a way of dealing with a less than all-out direct assault. Whereas these were next-to-last options that could not be dismissed, the United States did not rate these prospects very highly. "As we understand the dynamics of nuclear warfare," the secretary of defense noted, "we believe that a local nuclear engagement would do grave damage to Europe, be militarily ineffective, and would probably expand very rapidly into general nuclear war."[118] The only credible deterrent of lesser Soviet actions was the buildup of NATO's conventional capabilities to the level of a thirty-division-equivalent force. Additional nonnuclear strength would enhance the overall deterrent by bolstering credibility.[119]

McNamara's Ann Arbor Speech and the Reaction of the Europeans

European reaction to American strategic thinking became evident after McNamara had distilled the substance of his Athens address into the public commencement address at the University of Michigan at Ann Arbor in the middle of June.[120] Initially, the president had expressed general concern about a first draft of the address on grounds that "it might seem to be a continuation of our debate with the French and might offer the Soviet Union a hand-hold for charges of missile rattling."[121] The president approved a revised draft, though McGeorge Bundy still doubted the wisdom of a passage on weak national nuclear forces in the face of the "messy dialogue with the French."[122] As was to be expected, McNamara's Ann Arbor speech provoked negative reactions in Paris.[123] The French leaders perceived the speech as a direct attack on their national nuclear weapons program. The Americans, however, were especially surprised by the uproar that the address produced in Great Britain. McNamara's assessment of the lack of value of national nuclear forces poured oil onto the flames of the Labour Party's critique of Macmillan's conservative government.[124] In order to reconcile the difficulties that his address had produced for the British government, McNamara announced on 23 June that in his critique of independently operating nuclear forces he had not been referring to the thoroughly coordinated British bomber command.[125]

From a European perspective, McNamara's argument in favor of central control of NATO nuclear forces was touching on delicate matters, like sovereignty and prestige. If translated from the field of strategic logic into the political domain, the speech meant that while Europe had to provide foot soldiers, it had to leave the nuclear capability and the decision to use it to the United States. The differences in outlook between Europe and the United States cannot be better demonstrated than with a reference to a meeting between Alain Enthoven and Raymond Aron in April 1962. The French sociologist pointed out to the American strategist "that U.S. military policy regarding Europe is based on technical considerations rather than an understanding of European political realities."[126] Although Secretary Rusk tried to allay European concerns in a tour of allied capitals beginning in Paris on 19 June, the United States could not stop France from building a separate nuclear force.[127]

It is clear that in his Athens and Ann Arbor addresses the secretary of defense had attempted to make a primarily political statement through a discussion of military strategy. While McNamara doubted the practicability of a counterforce strategy, he found the counterforce rhetoric useful in conveying policy goals to the European partners. It is true that the Athens address did not trumpet nuclear counterforce strategy as a panacea:

> We in the United States are prepared to accept our share of this responsibility [for the decision to use nuclear weapons]. And we believe that the

combination of our nuclear superiority and a strategy of controlled response gives us some hope of minimizing damage in the event that we have
to fulfill our pledge. But I would be less than candid if I pretended to you
that the United States regards this as a desirable prospect or believes that
the Alliance should depend solely on our nuclear power to deter the Soviet
Union from actions not involving a massive commitment of Soviet force.
Surely an Alliance with the wealth, talent, and experience that we possess
can find a better way than this to meet our common threat.[128]

However, as this quote indicates, he made this clarification most clearly
while explaining the need for additional nonnuclear forces. It is impossible to say exactly how optimistic the secretary of defense really was
about the chances that a counterforce strategy would limit damage to
the American homeland in May 1962. We have seen that this aim was
not completely out of the question at the end of 1961. Quantitative and
qualitative nuclear superiority inspired some hope that a counterforce
strategy could work in practice. Since nuclear war could come by accident or miscalculation, no-cities counterforce was a next-to-last option
that prudence forbid the United States to dismiss. Finally, McNamara
also might have been driven by the idea of a strategy that held open the
possibility of war termination before American cities were destroyed,
because that strategy might have made it easier to live in the complex
world of nuclear dilemmas.[129]

While one can only speculate as to motivation, the point is that the
Athens address was delivered for its political impact. It was the irony of
the Athens speech that McNamara endorsed a no-cities counterforce
strategy to an audience for which the goal of damage control had become meaningless in 1961. Three months before the NATO meeting in
Athens, the secretary of defense had noted that the Soviet Union "does
have the power today to damage severely the nations of Western Europe,
and we must anticipate that over the years the Soviets can, and undoubtedly will, produce weapons with sufficient range and destructive power
to inflict similar damage on the United States, even while we ourselves
retain a substantial margin of strategic power."[130] McNamara used the
strategy in order to underscore the meaning of superiority as a symbol
of U.S. resolve and to justify the need for central control of NATO's
nuclear forces. This, however, he did without setting forth in clear language his own doubts—recorded in other places—as to whether the
Kremlin would "cooperate" in a counterforce strategy and *before* admitting that all would suffer deeply in case of nuclear war.

What this suggests, then, is that there was a widening gap between declaratory strategy and realistic operational planning. Politics dictated rhetoric, despite a weakened grounding in what really could be accomplished. The military and technical feasibility of a strategy might never be tested, but political demands were real and immediate. The growing symbolic character of public rhetoric regarding national security strategy, which became evident during the Berlin crisis, accelerated the growth of the gap between theory and practice.

With the advent of mutual vulnerability, deterrence had less to do with what could be accomplished in a nuclear war than with the ability to manipulate perceptions of what could be accomplished in a nuclear war. Nuclear threats became less credible as both superpowers became vulnerable. This is not to say that nuclear weapons lost all their political utility, simply canceling each other out. Henceforth, nuclear threats had to be converted into favorable political outcomes by psychological processes open to highly subjective factors and assessments. A heavy dose of rhetoric was noticeably employed first at the end of the 1950s in connection with the need to reassure the Europeans regarding the American nuclear guarantee in the face of highly public Soviet missile successes.[131]

The American commitment to the defense of Europe remained the single most important reason for these developments. The Berlin crisis, which from an American perspective developed over the question whether the United States was still prepared to go to nuclear war over Berlin, enhanced the importance of manipulating the symbolic value of defense decisions. The Berlin crisis was a test of will, not of capabilities. It was about influencing the beliefs of the adversary, the allies, and the domestic public about U.S. resolve. It was about how to best manipulate risks. During the crisis, the Kennedy administration learned that claims of nuclear superiority and the prospect of an arms race could be used for psychological and political effects. The rhetoric of nuclear superiority was used as a signal of resolve, aimed at bolstering the credibility of the American security commitment to its European allies. However, when it came to enhancing the pressure on the Soviets directly, the Kennedy administration used the threat of an arms race. It was the *act* of a defense buildup, in particular of conventional forces, that seemed to impress the Soviets as a signal of American determination.

Finally, I have shown that increasingly, rhetoric more than military-technical considerations drove strategic policy. Signals and symbols came to play an important role in nuclear politics, reflecting the foreign policy need to demonstrate resolve in a time of evolving mutual vulnerability.

11

The Cuban Missile Crisis: The Impact of the Nuclear Danger on Policy

While the Berlin wall marked a watershed, tensions over Berlin did not completely abate until after the Cuban missile crisis. The Cuban missile crisis originated in a Cold War environment that was shaped by the superpower conflict over the future of West Berlin and, more generally, the European security structure. We have seen in earlier chapters that the Berlin crisis proved the political value of nuclear weapons in two important ways. First, fear of nuclear war affected American behavior during the crisis, despite superior nuclear capabilities. Nuclear danger led restraint in the Kennedy administration's policy goals for Berlin and Europe. The possibility of escalation of the conflict to the nuclear level was an important influence on those working in favor of a negotiated settlement. Second, the unfavorable strategic balance might well have inspired Khrushchev to lift the year-end deadline for a separate peace treaty.

In June 1962, Secretary of Defense Robert McNamara summarized the lessons of the Berlin crisis. He emphasized that nuclear superiority was only of limited political importance.[1] While this was an appropriate summary of the American experience, it clearly cannot have been the lesson the Soviets learned. Having himself acknowledged and exploited the political utility of atomic diplomacy, Khrushchev had to lift the deadline in the face of superior western military power. The Kennedy administration perceived Khrushchev's decision to have been the result not only of U.S. willingness to negotiate but also of the correlation of forces. The American government capitalized on the view that the Soviet withdrawal was due to U.S. nuclear superiority in order to reassure its European allies about the depth of the American commitment to their defense. Finally, the Europeans *did* believe in the value of nuclear supe-riority. To the extent the strategic balance reassured the Europeans—and for that matter the U.S. public—it *was* politically important. This atmosphere can only have driven the Soviet desire to achieve parity in numbers of strategic nuclear weapons as quickly as possible. We will see soon that Khrushchev's decision to install medium-range and intermedi-ate-range ballistic missiles in Cuba was driven partly by this very motive.

The Cuban missile crisis came somewhat as an aftershock to the Berlin crisis. In contrast to the Berlin crisis, the strategic balance played less of a role during the Cuban missile crisis. Emphasis shifted to the mutually self-deterring impact of nuclear weapons. The Cuban missile crisis, by highlighting the nuclear danger, carried home the message that the United States and the Soviet Union each had a more important goal than worldwide competition: the prevention of nuclear war.[2] Recogni-tion of this fact led to mutual restraint. Nuclear weapons had become a stabilizing factor in international politics.

The factor of time distinguishes the Cuban missile crisis from the Ber-lin crisis. The experiences and arguments of the year-long Berlin crisis were compressed into less than two weeks. It was the tempo of the Cuban crisis of October 1962 that led to mutual recognition that events could spill out of control. The political leaders of both the United States and the Soviet Union learned that the manipulation of risk was a highly speculative art. At a certain point in a crisis, the "noise" in the situation in the form of misinformation, miscalculation, misjudgment, and mis-management could lead to inadvertent escalation. Given the devastating consequences of a failure in the manipulation of nuclear risk, it was important to focus attention on the avoidance of crises and their quick termination through mutual restraint and compromise.

This is not an argument that with the Cuban missile crisis nuclear weapons lost all their political utility. Neither is it an argument that nu-clear weapons simply cancel each other out. The shift from the percep-tion of nuclear weapons as bargaining tools toward the perception of nuclear weapons as cause for self-restraint was *gradual* in nature. The Cuban missile crisis showed both sides that nuclear superiority is only of limited political importance, particularly in crisis situations. For the nuclear learning process, which McNamara hoped had been strength-ened on both sides in the aftermath of the Berlin crisis, the experience of being on the brink of a nuclear conflict was important.

It is most striking that the key lessons of the Cuban missile crisis grew stronger as more became known about the details of the story. The first twenty-five years of the debate over the meaning of the Cuban missile crisis was dominated, first, by the memoirs of former Kennedy administration officials, in particular Robert Kennedy's *Thirteen Days: A Memoir of the Cuban Missile Crisis*.[3] Later scholarly works were built around Graham Allison's seminal book, *The Essence of Decision*.[4] These writings discussed the October 1962 episode as a successful model of crisis management. Arthur Schlesinger, Jr., for example, described John F. Kennedy's decision making as a "combination of toughness and restraint, of will, nerve, and wisdom, so brilliantly controlled, so matchlessly calibrated, that it dazzled the world," thereby perpetuating the view that the crisis ended as it did because of Kennedy's masterful management of U.S. policy.[5]

This mythology of the Cuban missile crisis was undermined by several retrospective conferences between 1987 and 1992 that brought together American, Soviet, and Cuban participants in the event to reevaluate what had happened. The conferences resulted in a new body of information that was presented in a series of books and articles by James G. Blight and others.[6] The new revelations about the missile crisis emphasize the extent to which decision making in Washington, Moscow, and Havana was characterized by flawed communication and miscalculation. The new information stresses how close the crisis came to spinning out of control and underscores how problematic it is to rely on the belief that governments can manage severe international crises.

The Cuban Missile Crisis

On Tuesday morning, 16 October 1962, McGeorge Bundy informed the president that photographic evidence had been obtained showing Soviet MRBMs in Cuba.[7] The president immediately called for a meeting of a group of advisers that became known as the ExComm (Executive Committee of the National Security Council). Two days earlier, two U-2 aircraft had flown over Cuba taking pictures. The photographs obtained from these flights were analyzed by the National Photographic Interpretation Center. Intelligence officers found the first hard evidence of Soviet MRBM sites in Cuba and confirmed twenty-four SAM (surface-to-air missile) sites on the island.

After five days of analysis and debate in the ExComm, President Kennedy decided on 20 October to implement a naval blockade on the further delivery of all offensive military equipment to Cuba and to insist on the withdrawal of Soviet missiles already delivered to Cuba. On the evening of Monday, 22 October, Kennedy announced his decision to the nation. At the same time, he warned the Soviet government that the United States will "regard any nuclear missile launched from Cuba against any nation in the Western Hemisphere as an attack by the Soviet Union on the United States, requiring a full retaliatory response against the Soviet Union."[8]

There followed the most dangerous week of the Cold War. The two superpowers were facing each other in a conflict that had broken out over nuclear missiles. It is generally agreed that at the time the risk of nuclear war—however high its probability might have been in reality—was believed to be greater than at any time before.[9] The U.S. naval quarantine of Cuba was accompanied by a series of military and diplomatic moves and countermoves. Some of these military and diplomatic initiatives were not authorized by the political leadership of the two main contestants.

The crisis reached its climax on Saturday, 27 October. At that time, the strategic nuclear forces of the United States were widely dispersed and for the first time in history placed on "DEFCON 2," the second highest alert posture. In addition, the United States was assembling the troops necessary for an invasion of Cuba. Meanwhile, some of the Soviet missile sites in Cuba were reported to be operational, and the Cuban military forces were fully mobilized. During the morning of 27 October, an American U-2 aircraft entered Soviet airspace as a result of a navigational error. Around noon of the same day, another U-2 reconnaissance plane was shot down over Cuba. Meanwhile, different proposals were being debated, including the idea of trading Soviet missiles in Cuba for American missiles in Turkey.

The acute phase of the crisis ended on Sunday, 28 October, when Nikita Khrushchev publicly announced his decision to remove the missiles from Cuba. However, the question of the withdrawal of the Soviet Ilyushin-28 bombers from Cuba, the verification of the withdrawal of the Soviet missiles and bombers, and the formalization of the U.S. noninvasion pledge were not resolved until November. In April 1963, the last Jupiter missile left Turkey, finalizing the private deal that had been communicated during a secret meeting between Robert Kennedy and Soviet ambassador Anatoly F. Dobrynin on 27 October 1962.[10]

The Roots of the Crisis

The Cuban missile crisis had its roots in a Cold War environment that was shaped by tensions over the Berlin issue. The military, ideological, and geopolitical struggle between the Soviet Union and the United States converged in the city of Berlin. The spiral of misperception and flawed communication, which went back to the buildup of the Berlin crisis during the first few months of 1961, finally culminated in October 1962. A discussion of why Khrushchev and Kennedy thought they had to act as they did shows the extent to which misperceptions lay at the heart of the issue. Before discussing what motivated the Soviet leader to implement his personal idea to deploy nuclear missiles in Cuba, we will consider why the American president believed he had to react with more than diplomatic means to what he perceived as a reckless Soviet initiative.

American Perceptions and Misperceptions

When McGeorge Bundy informed the president about the missile deployment, Kennedy's first reaction was that "there had been a concerted Soviet effort to mislead the United States government and its president on a matter of the highest importance, so that they could be presented with a fait accompli at some moment of Khrushchev's choice."[11] Kennedy felt particularly deceived because of the secrecy of the Soviet move.[12] Moreover, the news of Soviet missiles in Cuba broke in a charged domestic political environment. Senator Kenneth Keating of New York previously had raised an alarm about the possibility of offensive weapons reaching Cuba.[13] In answer to such concerns, President Kennedy had denied repeatedly that there was evidence of the installation of such weapons. Now, Senator Keating had turned out to be right. Furthermore, President Kennedy had received repeated Soviet assurances that no offensive weapons would be installed in Cuba. On 4 September, Attorney General Robert Kennedy met with Soviet ambassador Anatoly Dobrynin. According to Robert Kennedy, Dobrynin told him that he had been instructed by the Soviet chairman, Nikita Khrushchev, to assure President Kennedy that there would be no surface-to-surface missiles or offensive weapons placed in Cuba.[14] On 11 September 1962, TASS released an authorized statement condemning U.S. overseas bases and pointing out "that there is no need for the Soviet Union to set up in any other country—Cuba, for instance—the weapons it has for repelling aggression, for a retaliatory blow."[15]

With regard to Soviet assurances, President Kennedy was particularly angry about the conversation he had with Soviet foreign minister Andrei Gromyko on the occasion of their meeting on 18 October, two days after the president had learned about the missiles in Cuba. Gromyko stated that he was instructed to make clear that the Soviet military assistance to Cuba was "by no means offensive"—without further defining what the Soviet government meant by this.[16] Kennedy had decided not to discuss U.S. awareness of the missiles with Gromyko and, therefore, did not press the matter further. However, he interpreted Gromyko's statement as a lie and felt betrayed by the Soviet government.

Initially, President Kennedy thought that Khrushchev had made his decision to station missiles in Cuba despite American warnings. However, the Soviet decision was made before the United States issued its warnings. Kennedy's September warnings were meant more as an assurance to his countrymen than a direct warning to Khrushchev. His 4 September press conference has to be read in the context of the heated domestic debate over the meaning of the Soviet shipments to Cuba. President Kennedy stated that "there is no evidence of any organized combat force in Cuba from any Soviet bloc country; of military bases provided to Russia; of a violation of the 1934 treaty relating to Guantanamo; of the presence of offensive ground-to-ground missiles; as of other significant offensive capability either in Cuban hands or under Soviet direction and guidance. Were it to be otherwise the gravest issue would arise."[17]

On 13 September, Kennedy committed himself to act in case Cuba should acquire a capacity to carry out offensive actions against the United States. "If at any time," the president stated, "the Communist buildup in Cuba were to endanger or interfere with our security in any way . . . or if Cuba should . . . become an offensive military base of significant capacity for the Soviet Union, then this country will do whatever must be done to protect its own security and that of its allies."[18] These warnings reflected a strong national conviction that having Soviet missiles in Cuba was absolutely unacceptable.

In addition to the president's pledge, on 26 September, the United States Congress adopted a joint resolution stating that "the United States is determined . . . to prevent in Cuba the creation or use of an externally supported military capability endangering the security of the United States."[19] By the time the CIA discovered the missiles in Cuba, it was the declared position of the administration and the Congress that any deployment of this kind simply was intolerable. Against the background of these promises, more than mere diplomacy was called for.[20]

Kennedy's assessment of the nation's attitude toward missiles in Cuba is captured in his brother's remembrance of a private exchange that the two of them had on 24 October. "It looks really mean, doesn't it?" said the president referring to the possibility that the approaching Soviet ships would challenge the quarantine. "But then, really there was no other choice," the president went on. "If they get this mean on this one in our part of the world, what will they do on the next?" His brother replied: "I just don't think there was any choice, and not only that, if you hadn't acted, you would have been impeached." The president agreed.[21]

McGeorge Bundy reminded the ExComm during its first meeting on 16 October 1962, that Khrushchev must have made his decision to install missiles in Cuba prior to President Kennedy's September warnings.[22] The Soviets had not made their decision in spite of American warnings. Why did the Kennedy administration fail to issue a warning earlier? It seems probable that the Soviets would have decided against an adventurous course in May 1962—when Khrushchev is believed to have begun contemplating the decision—if the president and the Congress had articulated their warnings in the spring.

The failure of the Kennedy administration to give an earlier warning was rooted in a widespread assumption that it was too obvious to be emphasized that the United States would not tolerate such a development. The belief, particularly in the White House, that Khrushchev would never dare to deploy missiles in Cuba was very powerful. Around 22 August 1962, the leading members of the administration began to consider the theory of John A. McCone, director of the CIA, that the extensive SAM installations in Cuba indicated that the buildup would end with the deployment of MRBMs.[23] Arthur Schlesinger expressed what was a consensus view when he wrote to McGeorge Bundy that any "military construction will probably be defensive in function; a launching pad directed against the U.S. would be too blatant a provocation."[24] On 5 October, McCone again articulated his concern in a talk with McGeorge Bundy. McCone's summary memorandum of their conversation notes that Bundy "was satisfied that no offensive capability would be installed in Cuba because of its worldwide effects and therefore seemed relaxed over the fact that the intelligence community cannot produce hard information about this important subject."[25] These incidents indicate that from an American perspective the unacceptability of Soviet nuclear missiles in Cuba was so self-evident that no one saw a need to communicate that fact.

Soviet Perceptions and Misperceptions

The Soviet decision secretly to install nuclear missiles in Cuba was motivated by the Soviet outlook on the underlying problems of the Cold War in the aftermath of the acute phase of the Berlin crisis. It is now generally agreed that Khrushchev's decision to deploy MR/IRBMs to Cuba originated with three main concerns: first, the perceived need to prevent the loss of Cuba and deter a U.S. invasion; second, the perceived need to redress a highly unfavorable strategic balance; and, less important than the first two reasons, third, the desire to expose the United States to a direct threat comparable to the threat the Soviet Union faced, due to the U.S. deployment of nuclear weapons on the Soviet periphery.

A majority of western analysts have assumed that the second concern was the primary motivation for Khrushchev's decision.[26] They regarded Soviet emphasis on the first, as in Khrushchev's speech to the Supreme Soviet on 12 December 1962, as a post hoc justification for the outcome of the crisis.[27] The statements of the Soviet participants at the recent conferences on the missile crisis, however, have made it clear that fears of an American invasion were in fact as much on Khrushchev's mind as the desire to redirect the strategic balance.[28] Finally, when and how was the Soviet decision made? In his memoirs, Khrushchev has noted that he developed the idea to deploy nuclear missiles to Cuba during his visit to Bulgaria between 14 and 20 May 1962.[29] During the recent conferences on the Cuban missile crisis, other Soviet officials have described how Khrushchev explored the idea in the weeks before, during, and after his trip to Bulgaria. It is particularly striking that both Anastas I. Mikoyan and Andrei Gromyko, two of the foremost Soviet experts on American politics, reported that they had expressed concern about the feasibility of the plan. Whereas Mikoyan did not believe that it was possible to install the missiles secretly, Gromyko warned of the political consequences in the United States. Khrushchev's advisers, moreover, doubted that Fidel Castro would agree to such a proposal. However, the Cuban leader responded positively, whereupon Khrushchev decided to go ahead with the deployment in early June 1962.[30] In general, it seems that the whole idea was very much Khrushchev's personal game, marked by improvisation, and not thought out thoroughly.

With regard to the loss of Cuba, Khrushchev in his memoirs explained: "One thought kept hammering away at my brain: what will happen if we lose Cuba? I knew it would have been a terrible blow to Marxism-Leninism. It would gravely diminish our stature throughout the world, but especially in Latin America. . . . We had to establish a tangible and effective deterrent to American interference in the Caribbean. But what exactly? The logical answer was missiles."[31] Cuba had become the most important asset of Soviet foreign policy in the Western Hemisphere. From a Soviet perspective, there emerged a deliberate pattern of American activity to isolate Cuba diplomatically, militarily, and economically. First of all, the United States had already tried once to overthrow Fidel Castro's regime. They would try again, and this time make sure that they would do it right.[32]

In late 1961, President Kennedy had authorized a covert program, known as Operation Mongoose, which aimed at helping Cuba to overthrow the Communist regime. In February 1962, the chief of the operation, Major General Edward G. Lansdale, defined a plan of covert operations that was supposed to culminate in the overthrow of the Castro government in October—the very month in which the Cuban missile crisis erupted.[33] In March, the American planners recognized that the final success of the operation "will require decisive U.S. military intervention."[34] Parallel to this program of covert operations, U.S. forces carried out a series of highly visible military exercises, clearly simulating an invasion of Cuba.[35] Moreover, the Cubans and Soviets knew about the scope of Operation Mongoose, because Cuban intelligence had managed to penetrate the CIA.[36] The United States also pursued a wide range of political and economic pressures on the Castro regime. In January 1962, the Kennedy administration managed to gain enough Latin American votes to suspend Cuba from the Organization of American States (OAS). And in February, Kennedy declared an embargo on all trade with Cuba.[37] From a Soviet perspective, there was reason enough to be concerned over the possibility of a U.S. invasion of Cuba.

Khrushchev in his memoirs noted that his purpose in installing the missiles in Cuba was not limited to protecting Cuba. In addition, he writes, "our missiles would have equalized what the West likes to call 'the balance of power.'"[38] Against the background of the Berlin developments discussed above, it is obvious that the Soviets thought it important to redress the strategic balance. By early 1962, it was clear that the United States possessed a substantial nuclear superiority. Moreover, the Kennedy administration had shown no hesitation to exploit this advantage politically. U.S. officials had underscored the meaning of nuclear superiority in order to reassure the Europeans in a series of speeches. Nuclear superiority had proved politically useful, because Europe felt reassured. From a Soviet perspective, these American statements seemed to be a concerted effort to intimidate the Soviet Union.[39] If one takes all of this together with Khrushchev's own earlier attempts in nuclear diplomacy, it is clear that the Soviet leader also perceived the missile deployment as a means to minimize the political power that the Americans could derive from their superior nuclear capabilities.

Finally, there is little doubt that Khrushchev was influenced in his decision by a desire to counter the American deployments of nuclear missiles at the Soviet periphery. As early as the Vienna meeting in June 1961, Khrushchev had compared the Cuban situation with Turkey.[40] In his speeches during the Bulgarian visit in May 1962, he repeatedly referred to the presence of U.S. nuclear missiles in Turkey.[41] His memoirs confirm the impression that the missiles in Turkey made on him. "The Americans," Khrushchev wrote, "had surrounded our country with military bases and threatened us with nuclear weapons, and now they would learn just what it feels like to have enemy missiles pointing at you; we'd be doing nothing more than giving them a little of their own medicine. And it was high time America learned what it feels like to have her own land and her own people threatened."[42]

Why did the United States fail to see Khrushchev's motives for changing the situation over Cuba? The American belief that the Soviet leaders would never pursue such a course was supported by two misperceptions. First, the U.S. leadership did not consider the possibility that the Soviets would interpret their hostile words and their military, economic, and political pressure as indications of an impending invasion of Cuba. Pointing to the domestic political context, McGeorge Bundy, in hindsight, has underscored that the covert operations program "was not a prelude to stronger action but a substitute for it."[43] This assertion is confirmed by the fact that the ExComm did not refer to any previous intentions to invade Cuba when it discussed the available options to react on 16 October.[44]

Second, the political leaders of the United States had learned during the Berlin crisis that the political utility of superior nuclear forces was only limited. McGeorge Bundy is correct when he notes that most of the Kennedy administration "thought it self-evident that our country had already been exposed" to mutual nuclear danger.[45] However, officials in the Kennedy administration failed to take into account how the rhetoric of western nuclear superiority would affect the Soviet Union. They did not realize the extent to which their program for the reassurance of European allies combined with their declared emphasis on a no-cities counterforce strategy would push the Soviet leaders to take action to redress the strategic balance. Raymond Garthoff has noted that in one sense "the United States failed to anticipate the Soviet action in Cuba because it failed to recognize how desperate the Soviet plight seemed in Moscow!"[46] Moreover, there remained within the American government powerful groups that believed in the overriding political and military importance of military superiority. Director of the CIA John McCone, Secretary of the Treasury C. Douglas Dillon, and the members of the JCS were concerned about the effect of the Soviet missiles in Cuba on the strategic balance. Chairman of the JCS General Maxwell D. Taylor, for example, warned the president on 16 October that the missiles in Cuba—if followed by further deployments—"*can* become . . . a rather important adjunct and reinforcement . . . to the strike capability of the Soviet Union."[47] A CIA memorandum written by Raymond Garthoff on 27 October 1962, estimated that the approximately forty Soviet IR/MRBMs in Cuba "will increase the first-strike missile salvo which the USSR could place on targets in the continental United States by over 40 percent."[48] People who thought superiority to be indispensable tended to be concerned about the strategic consequences of the Soviet missiles in Cuba.

During the ExComm meetings on 16 October, President Kennedy repeatedly came back to the question of why Khrushchev had chosen to place missiles in Cuba. Secretary Rusk replied by referring to a statement by McCone who had noted "that one thing Khrushchev may have in mind is that . . . he knows that we have a substantial nuclear superiority, but he also knows that we don't really live under fear of his nuclear weapons to the extent that . . . he has to live under fear of ours."[49] However, as will be discussed in greater detail below, President Kennedy believed that the missiles had only a marginal impact on the overall strategic nuclear balance and that the problem was, first of all, a political and psychological one.

The Kennedy administration underestimated the desire of Khrushchev to adjust the strategic balance, because it underestimated how highly Khrushchev valued the political and psychological impact of the strategic balance. Because of uncertainties and misperceptions regarding Khrushchev's motives, the Kennedy administration began to speculate that the Soviets intended to use the Cuban missiles to enhance their bargaining position in Berlin. Failing to see the Soviet desire to preempt an invasion of the Caribbean island and to minimize the political power the United States could derive from nuclear superiority, the administration overemphasized what it believed to be the central motivation for the Cuban missile deployment—reprisal for Berlin.

From Crisis Bargaining to Not Losing Control

The development of U.S. policy during the Cuban missile crisis was marked by a shift from considerations of bargaining toward efforts at not losing control over the events. The discussions within the ExComm from the discovery of the missiles through the announcement of the naval quarantine by President Kennedy centered on the question of what initial response had to be contemplated and what military preparations initiated. The debate was clearly dominated by the element of bargaining. From the announcement of the quarantine to the settlement, however, considerations of bargaining were increasingly superseded by the endeavor of not losing control over the events. The American recognition that the crisis had a potential to spill out of control was paralleled by comparable recognition on the Soviet side.

Once the CIA discovered the Soviet missiles, an immediate consensus developed among the key U.S. decision makers that the missiles had to be removed. At the beginning of the first ExComm meeting on 16 October 1962, Secretary Rusk summarized: "Now . . . I do think we have to set in motion a chain of events that will eliminate this base. I don't think we [can?] sit still."[50] While the goal of U.S. policy was clear from the beginning, the question of how to best achieve it became the object of a fierce debate over the next few days. Initially, President Kennedy leaned toward eliminating the missiles by an air attack with conventional forces. At the end of the first ExComm meeting, Kennedy stated flatly that there certainly would be an air strike to take out the missiles, which might have to be extended to a general air strike against a wider set of targets.[51] Looking back, Kennedy emphasized how important the factor of time had been to developing a prudent policy: "If we had to act . . . in the first twenty-four hours, I don't think we would have chosen as prudently as we finally did."[52] Kennedy's first reaction was anger at the Soviet deception. Khrushchev had a similar reaction to the imposition of the quarantine. Kennedy's announcement of 22 October caught Khrushchev by surprise. The Soviet leader reacted by ordering accelerated construction of the missile sites and ordering Soviet ships to ignore the naval quarantine. (The order subsequently was changed.)[53]

Air Strike versus Naval Blockade

As early as the first ExComm meeting, some of the president's advisers voiced reservations about the air strike option. What were the political consequences of such an action? Was a surprise air attack compatible with American principles? At the second meeting of the ExComm, McNamara became the first to suggest a course between mere diplomacy and a preemptive strike. A third alternative would involve a blockade against offensive weapons entering Cuba in the future, twenty-four-hour surveillance, and a statement to the world by the president. The presidential statement would comprise an ultimatum to Khrushchev indicating "that we have located these offensive weapons; we're maintaining a constant surveillance over them; if there is ever any indication that they're to be launched against this country, we will respond not only against Cuba, but we will respond directly against the Soviet Union . . .

with a full nuclear strike."[54] Over the next four days, key officials started to group around the two alternatives of an air strike and a naval blockade. Robert McNamara, Robert Kennedy, Theodore Sorensen, and former secretary of defense Robert Lovett became the leading advocates of the blockade option.[55] The option of taking out the missiles by means of some military attack was supported by Dean Acheson and the Joint Chiefs of Staff.[56] Other individuals, for example McGeorge Bundy, were less consistent in their support for one particular option, speaking on behalf of different courses of action at different times.[57]

An air strike promised to take out the missiles instantly. General Taylor, for example, emphasized the point: The action would be decisive, it would maximize the element of surprise, and it would confront the world with a fait accompli.[58] However, three major objections to the air strike option evolved. First, as Robert Kennedy argued during the debate on the different courses of action, a "sneak attack" was not in the tradition of the United States. He noted on 19 October that President Kennedy would find it very difficult to opt for an air strike "with all the memory of Pearl Harbor."[59] Undersecretary of State George Ball agreed that a surprise attack on Cuba would destroy the moral position of the United States and alienate its friends. He warned that such action would endanger the whole alliance structure through which the United States had organized the strength of the West in the post–World War II era.[60] Second, and perhaps more significant, an air strike involved a higher risk of escalation than less dramatic courses. It would lead to the instant killing of several hundred Soviet soldiers manning SAM sites and working on the missile sites. This again would push the Soviet leaders toward taking retaliatory action, possibly against Berlin, as McNamara pointed out. President Kennedy agreed that "at some point Khrushchev would say that if we made a move against Cuba, he would take Berlin."[61] Third, a clear, swift strike was militarily impractical. The JCS insisted on a large-scale attack of several hundred sorties against SAM sites, fighter bases, and missile sites. McNamara repeatedly warned that such a widespread attack probably would lead to invasion with all its consequences.[62]

The blockade option, on the other hand, had the disadvantage that it would not eliminate the missiles already in Cuba. It would not prevent the installations from becoming operational if the Soviets had all the necessary material already in Cuba. And, finally, it might produce a counterblockade.[63] A blockade, nevertheless, had two essential advantages: First, it was, in the words of Theodore Sorensen, the "step least likely to precipitate general war."[64] It might entail the risk of a counterblockade; however, it would not lead immediately to sudden death. Second, it was a prudent first step. If the blockade failed to compel the removal of the missiles, further U.S. action could be taken. An air strike or an invasion at a later point would not have the Pearl Harbor association.[65]

Although on Thursday night it seemed that a majority of the ExComm supported the blockade, this consensus broke down when the committee presented its recommendations to the president.[66] The debate on Friday morning was marked by sharp disagreement. The ExComm then decided to split into two working groups in order to provide the president with clear options.[67] During the day, air strike supporters began to shift their support to the blockade option. The blockade became a naval quarantine and, as Bundy has noted, acquired "the additions of diplomatic planning, legal justification, political exposition, and connection . . . to further action if necessary."[68] Overnight, in a considerable tour de force, Theodore Sorensen produced a draft speech for the president on the blockade. On Saturday, 20 October, both options were presented to the president, who quickly decided on the naval quarantine, subject only to a final military briefing on an air strike. However, the presentation by the responsible military commander included nothing to persuade the president. General Joseph Sweeney informed the president on 21 October that in an air strike "even under optimum conditions, it was not likely that all of the known missiles would be destroyed." General Taylor added: "The best we can offer you is to destroy 90% of the known missiles."[69]

The Announcement

At 7:00 p.m. on Monday, 22 October, President Kennedy addressed the nation and the world. Only a few trusted allied governments had received advance notice of his speech.[70] "Within the past week, unmistakable evidence has established the fact that a series of offensive missile sites is now in preparation" on the island of Cuba, the president began. Describing the capabilities of the detected missiles, which could only have the purpose of providing "a nuclear strike capability against the Western Hemisphere," Kennedy announced what "*initial* steps" he had directed to be taken immediately. "To halt this offensive buildup," he stated, "a strict quarantine on all offensive military equipment under shipment to Cuba is being initiated." The military buildup in Cuba would further be subject to close surveillance, and should any missile be launched against any nation in the western hemisphere, the United States would regard it "as an attack by the Soviet Union on the United

States, requiring a full retaliatory response upon the Soviet Union." Finally, Kennedy called upon Chairman Khrushchev "to halt and eliminate this clandestine, reckless and provocative threat to world peace and to stable relations between our two nations."[71]

The Kennedy administration had made its decision on how to react to the Soviet challenge. Fear of rapid escalation with the potential of leading to nuclear war cautioned Kennedy to decide on a less violent course than an air attack. The decision to try out the naval quarantine was dominated by considerations of bargaining. It was, in the words of McGeorge Bundy, "only a first step, not a last."[72] If the quarantine did not lead to the removal of the missiles—and not many were convinced that it would—further steps could be taken. Because the decision was announced as an initial step only, it was important to impress the Soviets with readiness to move to the next level if necessary. At the time of the president's speech, troops were moving down to Georgia and nearly all U.S. military forces worldwide increased their alert status to DEFCON 3; an alert which had not been activated since the Korean War.[73] Polaris submarines were dispatched to sea, and ICBM missile crews were alerted. The SAC had one-eighth of its B-52 bomber force airborne and began to disperse 183 B-47 bombers to thirty-three civilian and military airfields.[74] On 24 October, the SAC took the unprecedented action of increasing its alert posture to still higher alert, DEFCON 2, only one step away from war.[75]

The events following the announcement of the quarantine promptly proved the strength of the chosen policy. On the diplomatic front, foreign support for the quarantine was stronger than the Kennedy administration had expected. The OAS voted nineteen to zero to endorse the quarantine. The NATO allies also expressed their full support for the American decision. Tensions, however, began to rise when the quarantine went into effect at 10:00 a.m. on 24 October. Would the Soviet ships challenge the quarantine line? In Washington, the members of the Ex-Comm waited; the ball was in the Soviet court.[76] And then, in the middle of the meeting, intelligence reports started to trickle in indicating that the Soviet ships were turning around.[77] It was at this point that Dean Rusk uttered his famous comment: "We are eyeball to eyeball, and the other fellow just blinked."[78] As we now know, Khrushchev's blink may have come just in time. The Soviet leader's first reaction to Kennedy's announcement of the quarantine apparently was to order his ships to proceed to Cuba. According to Soviet historian Roy Medvedev, it was Anastas Mikoyan who preempted Khrushchev's order from being sent, and instead directed the Soviet ships to stop short of the quarantine line.[79] On Thursday, the quarantine was challenged by a tanker, which the president decided to leave unboarded due to its cargo.[80] A stalemate began to set in. The Soviets seemed to have accepted the quarantine.

This, however, did not resolve the problem of inducing Khrushchev to remove the missiles already in Cuba. On the contrary, work on the missile sites in Cuba was continuing rapidly. On 26 October, the CIA notified the ExComm that, according to intelligence gathered by air reconnaissance on the day before, the two MRBM sites at San Cristobal were estimated to achieve "a full operational capability" during the day.[81] Meanwhile, the ExComm debated how to increase the pressure on the Soviet Union by military measures such as tightening the quarantine (to include gasoline), placing aggressive, day and night air reconnaissance of the missile sites, and imposing the first enforced inspection of a Soviet ship at sea. Secretary McNamara repeatedly spoke in favor of such measures. The supporters of the air strike/invasion option, however, argued that it was better to risk war with the Soviet Union over the missiles already in Cuba than over a confrontation with Soviet ships at sea. The president seemed to summarize the general consensus on Friday morning when he noted that "we will get the Soviet missiles out of Cuba only by invading Cuba or trading." He added that he "doubted that the quarantine alone would produce the withdrawal of the weapons."[82] Time was running short for the quarantine option.

The continuing work on the missile sites seemed to make it clear that the Soviets would not withdraw their offensive weapons without further U.S. action. While the ExComm pondered the matter, the first cause for hope emerged. Aleksandr Fomin, known to be the senior KGB official at the Soviet embassy in Washington, met John Scali, a respected correspondent for ABC news, for lunch. Fomin asked Scali, who had good connections with the State Department, to determine whether the United States would be interested in settling the crisis along the following lines: the Soviet bases would be removed under UN supervision if the United States would pledge not to invade Cuba.[83] Later in the day, the State Department received a letter from Khrushchev to Kennedy proposing a deal along the same lines.[84] From an American perspective, it looked as if Khrushchev's letter and Fomin's approach were part of a coherent Soviet negotiating position. New information, however, has since made clear that Fomin was acting on his own initiative. Moreover, his talk with Scali would have been too late to influence the content of the letter.[85]

Friday, 27 October: The American Side

On 27 October, the cautious optimism of Friday night gave way to the "blackest hour" of the crisis. As we will see, alarm and despair were felt in both Washington and Moscow. However, for the moment we will focus on the American side of the story. While the ExComm was meeting to consider a positive reply to Khrushchev's letter of 26 October, Radio Moscow broadcast a new message from the Soviet Chairman. Khrushchev now insisted that the United States remove its IRBM Jupiter missiles from Turkey in return for the removal of the Soviet missiles from Cuba.[86] Khrushchev's quick change of heart confused the members of the Ex-Comm. In contrast to Khrushchev's private letter of 26 October, the new message was formal in tone. Had Khrushchev been overruled by his hard-line colleagues?[87] When we read the transcripts of the ExComm meetings, the distress of its members becomes obvious. They felt a tremendous shortage of time. There was the disappointed hope of Friday night, the fact that five MRBMs were reported to be fully operational,[88] not knowing whether nuclear warheads had already reached Cuba,[89] reports that the Soviet personnel in New York were preparing to destroy sensitive material,[90] the need to keep the political and diplomatic initiative, and the problem of maintaining the nation's strategic forces and the forces assembled for the invasion or an air strike in a high state of readiness over an extended period of time.

During the course of the day, more news was to come that underscored the danger that the crisis was on the point of spinning out of control. Between 10:00 and 11:00 a.m., a U-2 aircraft on a routine air sampling mission off the cost of Alaska accidentally strayed into Soviet airspace. Although Soviet MiGs took off to intercept it, the American pilot managed to turn home without any shots being exchanged.[91] Would the Soviets interpret the incident as a last-minute intelligence reconnaissance in preparation for nuclear war?[92] Around noon, another U-2 reconnaissance plane was shot down over Cuba, leading to the only life lost by hostile action during the crisis. When word of the killing of Major Rudolf Anderson, Jr., reached the meeting, the ExComm assumed (incorrectly as we now know) that the attack had been ordered by Khrushchev, and perceived the incident as further escalation of the crisis. However, President Kennedy decided to wait a day before deciding whether to react with limited fire against the offending antiaircraft batteries or instead to destroy all the batteries. The delay was received with disbelief in the Pentagon, because the ExComm had approved the concept of immediate reprisal earlier in the week.[93]

Clearly, the dominant issue on this Saturday was the question of how to respond to Khrushchev's second proposal to trade American Jupiter missiles in Turkey for Soviet missiles in Cuba. More than once during the previous few days, administration officials had worried that the two issues might become entangled.[94] The possibility of a trade had been put forward publicly in a column by the prominent U.S. writer Walter Lippmann, as well as in a statement by Austrian foreign minister Bruno Kreisky. On this Saturday morning, the president was so upset about the fact that the Jupiter missiles seemed the only remaining obstacle to a peaceful solution to the crisis that he expressed himself as if he had given orders to remove them earlier.[95] In reality, as both McGeorge Bundy and Dean Rusk have since made clear, the decision never had been taken to remove the missiles from Turkey. Although everyone agreed that they were militarily obsolete, the decision had been postponed, because of political repercussions the decision would have within NATO.[96]

The transcripts of the ExComm meetings reveal that the president favored trading the missiles in Turkey for the missiles in Cuba.[97] In fact, he was by far the strongest advocate of a trade. Kennedy emphasized that the trade had "appeal" and that "to any man at the United Nations or any other rational man it will look like a very fair trade."[98] The president recognized that if the United States rejected the missile trade and went ahead with an air strike or an invasion, it would quickly find itself in an impossible position. Such a U.S. action very likely would lead to a Soviet reprisal, possibly against Berlin or Turkey, with all its dangerous consequences of rapid escalation to nuclear war. Everybody, and in particular the Europeans, would then see a missile trade as having been "a pretty good proposition."[99] He made the same point even more strongly at the end of the afternoon meeting of the ExComm: "We can't very well invade Cuba with all its toil, and long as it's going to be, when we could have gotten them out by making a deal on the same missiles in Turkey. If that's part of the record I don't see how we'll have a very good war."[100]

On the other hand, as almost all advisers warned the president, a public trade was diplomatically impossible. McGeorge Bundy summarized the view of others when he stressed that in the minds of the allies "it would be already clear that we were trying to sell out allies for our interests. That would be the view in NATO," he added. "It's irrational, and it's crazy, but it's a *terribly* powerful fact."[101] Moreover, neither General Norstad nor Thomas Finletter, permanent representative to the North Atlantic Council, believed that NATO would agree to such a deal.

Eventually, several advisers, including Sorensen, Bundy, Ball, Llewellyn Thompson, and Robert Kennedy, proposed the idea of replying to Khrushchev's first proposal, simply ignoring the second proposal. The president at first did not accept this proposal, because he was convinced that Khrushchev would not budge from his latest demand for a trade. The options seemed to have narrowed to two: trade or armed conflict.[102] In one of the central exchanges of the day, Llewellyn Thompson, the former ambassador to the Soviet Union, challenged this assumption. Thompson argued that there might still be a chance to resolve the crisis on the basis of Khrushchev's first proposal, because the "important thing for Khrushchev . . . is to be able to say, 'I saved Cuba, I stopped an invasion.' "[103] Bundy, Sorensen, and Robert Kennedy insisted that Thompson might be right, and the president finally agreed to the negotiation ploy and directed a letter to be sent to Khrushchev along these lines.[104]

After the ExComm afternoon meeting broke up, a smaller group, consisting of the president, Rusk, McNamara, Robert Kennedy, Ball, Roswell Gilpatric, Thompson, Sorensen, and Bundy, met in the Oval Office. The group agreed that the main point of Kennedy's letter (no Soviet missiles in Cuba, and no U.S. invasion) should be reinforced with an oral message passed through Ambassador Dobrynin. The Soviet Union should be informed that if it did not agree to a solution along these lines, the United States would have to take further action. Finally, Secretary Rusk proposed one additional component. While there could be no public deal over the Turkey missiles, the missiles in fact would be removed once the crisis was resolved. However, if the Soviets made public any reference to this assurance, the proposal would become void.[105]

At 7:45 p.m., Robert Kennedy met Dobrynin and delivered his message. When the ExComm came together for the last time on this long day at 9:00 p.m. to review possible courses of action for the following day, expectations for success of a diplomatic solution were not very high. McNamara in particular was skeptical of dealing with the crisis on the basis of Khrushchev's letter of 26 October. He had reread it and found to his astonishment that it was "twelve pages of—of fluff."[106] The meeting ended with McNamara worrying about what to do with the Cuban government after an invasion and about how to respond to Soviet action in Europe.[107]

In 1987, Dean Rusk informed his former colleagues that President Kennedy had been prepared for another diplomatic contingency with respect to a missile trade. Here is Rusk's recollection of what is now known as the "Cordier ploy":

It was clear to me that President Kennedy would not let the Jupiters in Turkey become an obstacle to the removal of the missile sites in Cuba because the Jupiters were coming out in any event. He instructed me to telephone the late Andrew Cordier, then at Columbia University, and dictate to him a statement which would be made by U Thant, the Secretary General of the United Nations, proposing the removal of both the Jupiters and the missiles in Cuba. Mr. Cordier was to put that statement in the hands of U Thant only after further signal from us.[108]

However, the "Cordier ploy" was never implemented. It was a contingency plan, and Bundy has noted correctly that it "does not tell us what the president would have done if Sunday produced a dusty answer from Moscow."[109] Nevertheless, as commentators Laurence Chang and Peter Kornbluh conclude, "the instruction to Rusk, together with Kennedy's remarks at the October 27 ExComm meeting and the messages to Dobrynin, indicate that President Kennedy was extremely reluctant to allow obsolete missiles in Turkey to stand in the way of a negotiated settlement to avert nuclear war."[110] Moreover, several other authors have pointed out that other alternatives remained, such as tightening the quarantine.[111]

Friday, 27 October: The Soviet Side

The tension, alarm, and despair experienced by the members of the ExComm on 27 October were paralleled by comparable feelings on the Soviet side. During the night from Saturday to Sunday, Khrushchev decided to end the confrontation. The way in which his letter of 28 October, accepting Kennedy's noninvasion pledge in return for withdrawal of the missiles in Cuba, was prepared is indicative of the sense of urgency that the Soviet chairman felt. According to Fyodor Burlatsky, the new message was drafted at Khrushchev's dacha and then rushed by a driver to Radio Moscow where it was broadcast at 9:00 a.m. on 28 October.[112] Why was there such a sense of urgency in Moscow? The vast American preparations for both an air attack and an invasion were highly visible. On 26 October, Soviet intelligence apparently reported that an American attack on Cuba was imminent. Khrushchev knew that an attack would end with local Communist defeat.[113]

On 27 October, Khrushchev received a letter from Castro written from the bomb shelter in the Soviet embassy in Havana the night before. Castro warned Khrushchev that "the aggression is almost imminent within the next 24 or 72 hours." The Cuban leader urged the Soviet chairman to react if the United States invaded Cuba: "If . . . the imperialists invade Cuba with the goal of occupying it, the danger that that aggressive policy poses for humanity is so great that following that event the Soviet Union must never allow the circumstances in which the imperialists could launch the first nuclear strike against it."[114] This reminder that the conflict could escalate to the nuclear level can only have encouraged Khrushchev, who knew what this would mean, to accept the deal with Kennedy.[115]

Other factors apparently also played a significant role. There was real danger that events were slipping out of control. First, the U-2 flight over Soviet territory undoubtedly contributed to the mounting tensions. Although Khrushchev seems to have been sensitive to the possibility that it was in fact an accident, the incident, coming in the middle of an acute crisis, was highly provocative.[116] In addition, the shooting down of the American U-2 over Cuba seems to have shaken the Soviet chairman seriously, because he had not ordered the attack. According to evidence presented by several Soviet participants at the Moscow conference, the shooting down was indeed an unauthorized act of Soviet air defense forces in Cuba, ordered by local Soviet commanders.[117] The event highlighted the extent to which Khrushchev's control over the events in Cuba had eroded at the height of the crisis.[118]

Verbal messages from the American side might have contributed to Khrushchev's sense of urgency. However, if earlier accounts have emphasized Robert Kennedy's meeting with Dobrynin on Saturday, 27 October, it is now generally agreed that John Scali's outburst of Saturday afternoon was of greater influence. At the request of Secretary Rusk, Scali had asked Fomin to meet again to inquire about the cause of the shift in the Soviet position. According to Scali's own account of the meeting, he did much more than ask for an explanation. Scali denounced Fomin for "a stinking double cross" and warned him that an invasion of Cuba was "only a matter of hours away." Fomin apparently relayed this information to Moscow. After the resolution of the crisis, Fomin communicated a message from Khrushchev to Scali that his outburst had been "very valuable" toward the Soviet decision to end the crisis.[119]

Finally, Khrushchev did not make a deal without consideration from the United States. A decision to end the confrontation would be compensated by an American noninvasion guarantee. Since fear of U.S. takeover of Cuba had been a major motive for the installation of the missiles, Khrushchev could argue that the crisis had ended successfully for the Soviet Union.[120] The noninvasion pledge was a means to save face, justify the withdrawal of the missiles, and assuage Fidel Castro.[121] Moreover, there was the private assurance that the Jupiter missiles in Turkey would be removed.[122] Anatoly Dobrynin revealed that he already had met with Robert Kennedy on the night of Friday, 26 October. In the course of the meeting, Dobrynin, on his own initiative, raised the point that there seemed to be a double standard with respect to Soviet missiles in Cuba and American missiles in Turkey. According to the Soviet ambassador, Robert Kennedy went as far as to call the president in order to confirm that the U.S. government intended to remove the missiles once the current crisis was settled. There is, therefore, a possibility that Khrushchev's second proposal, including the demand for a Turkey-Cuba missile trade, was a reaction to Robert Kennedy's remarks to Dobrynin.[123] Moreover, Dobrynin recently has contradicted Robert Kennedy's account of their meeting on Saturday, 27 October, in two important respects. First, he denied that the president's brother threatened further American military action against the missile sites if the Soviet government did not remove the missiles.[124] Second, the Soviet ambassador insisted that Robert Kennedy did not say that the Jupiters had been ordered to be removed earlier; on the contrary, he portrayed their removal as a concession by the United States as part of an explicit deal.[125]

Six of the principal participants in the resolution of the crisis—Rusk, McNamara, Bundy, Ball, Gilpatric, and Sorensen—wrote twenty years later that "the decisive military element in the resolution of the crisis was our clearly available and applicable superiority in conventional weapons within the area of the crisis. U.S. naval forces, quickly deployable for the blockade of offensive weapons . . . and the availability of U.S. ground and air forces sufficient to execute an invasion if necessary, made the difference."[126] American conventional superiority was definitely a major factor, both for the formulation of the quarantine as an initial response by the United States and for Khrushchev's decision to end the confrontation. With regard to the political process, one might add that the balance of resolve also favored the United States. After all, it was the Soviet side that secretly had taken the initiative in seeking to change the status quo. However, it was the increasing *mutual* realization that the events could slip out of control that advanced the political resolution of the crisis. The fact that both sides showed a steady determination to settle the conflict without war was directly related to the possibility of escalation to the nuclear level.

The question of how nuclear weapons influenced both sides' decision making will be examined more closely in the following section. McGeorge Bundy and others have argued that, in reality, chances for an unlimited escalation of the conflict might not have been very high. The reason for this is, Bundy has argued, that both sides were willing to trade the Turkish and the Cuban missiles. There would have been several limited diplomatic and military moves available to the United States if the Soviets had responded differently on Sunday.[127] However, McNamara has reminded us that even though chances for rapid escalation might have been overestimated at the time, they were real. He has pointed to the fact that we now know that there actually were both nuclear warheads for IRBMs and several tactical nuclear missiles (including launchers) in Cuba. The tactical missiles were to be used against a U.S. invasion force and the authority for their employment was delegated to the Soviet field commander in Cuba. Where would an invasion have ended?[128]

Nuclear Superiority Versus Nuclear Danger in the Settlement of the Crisis

The question of what role nuclear weapons played in the Cuban missile crisis has proved to be of enduring interest. Several generations of political scientists have looked at the history of the Cuban missile crisis for answers to the question of the impact of nuclear weapons on international politics. It is not surprising that people went back to the most dangerous crisis of the Cold War to search for answers. That these debates often have been somewhat speculative has been emphasized by the new information on the Cuban and Soviet side of the story, which recently has been made available through James G. Blight's oral history program.[129]

One frequently asked question is whether it was conventional or nuclear superiority that was responsible for the outcome of the crisis. With regard to the political process, however, the more important question is whether it was nuclear superiority or nuclear danger that was more important for the settlement. How did U.S. nuclear superiority and Soviet nuclear inferiority affect the decision making of the two governments? Did the United States feel comfortable because of its nuclear advantage? Were members of the Kennedy administration prepared to take greater risks because they were more willing to face a nuclear conflict than were leaders of the Soviet Union? Did the Soviet leaders, on the other hand, feel so inhibited by their nuclear "inferiority" as to be limited in their freedom of maneuver? Did they feel compelled to bring about a quick settlement of the crisis? Or were both sides motivated by fear of escalation?

Looking back on the Cuban missile crisis, a number of American participants of the ExComm have emphasized that U.S. nuclear superiority did not translate into usable military power to support political objectives. In 1982, Rusk, McNamara, Bundy, Ball, Gilpatric, and Sorensen wrote that the Cuban missile crisis "illustrates not the significance but the insignificance of nuclear superiority in the face of survivable thermonuclear retaliatory forces."[130] General Taylor implied that this was true for both sides when he wrote in 1974 that "the strategic force of the United States and the U.S.S.R. simply canceled each other out as effectual instruments for influencing the outcome of the confrontation."[131] Others, like Paul H. Nitze, have insisted that the outcome of the crisis had a good deal to do with the strategic balance. It is not so much its influence on American policy but rather its impact on Soviet policy that counts for Nitze. "I think," Nitze noted during a recent interview, "it mattered a great deal to the Soviets, and I thought it properly mattered a great deal to the Soviets."[132] Although the impact of the strategic balance on Soviet policy seems to be more disputed, I first will examine how American policy was affected by the nuclear factor.

The American Case

As in the Berlin crisis, the Kennedy administration at no point concluded that a war in which nuclear weapons were employed would end with anything less than common disaster. While the Americans had used the concept of no-cities counterforce strategy to underscore the significance of nuclear superiority, thereby reassuring Europe of the commitment to defend Berlin, the whole notion of controlled nuclear war gave the United States no comfort in October 1962. There was no counting of missiles, bombers, and warheads, and no one argued that the United States could limit damage to an acceptable degree in case of nuclear war. Such considerations were simply missing from the discussions of the ExComm. On the contrary, one has the impression that the atmosphere was marked by a visceral feeling of mutual vulnerability well captured in the following remark of the president on 16 October: "What difference does it make? They've got enough to blow us up now anyway."[133] In his first letter to Khrushchev, announcing his speech of 16 October, Kennedy warned of the nuclear danger: "I have not assumed that you or any other sane man would, in this nuclear age, deliberately plunge the world into war which it is crystal clear no country could win and which could only result in catastrophic consequences to the whole world, including the aggressor."[134]

Clearly, members of the Kennedy administration did not think that U.S. nuclear superiority would be decisive, and they did not even make use of a strategic threat. But how did they value the shift in the strategic balance as a consequence of the installation of the Soviet missiles in Cuba? Were the Americans concerned about the military significance of the Soviet missile deployment? McGeorge Bundy brought the topic up on 16 October: "What is the strategic impact on the position of the United States of MRBMs in *Cuba*? How gravely does this change the strategic balance?" And it was the direct reply of Secretary McNamara that preempted further debate within the ExComm of the matter almost completely: "Mac, I asked the Chiefs that this afternoon, in effect. And they said, substantially. My own personal view is, not at all." Chairman of the JCS Maxwell Taylor attempted to explain the reasoning of the JCS. Although these were only a few missiles, he noted, "they can become . . . a rather important adjunct and reinforcement . . . to the strike capability of the Soviet Union. We have no idea how far they will go." General Taylor then pointed to the nonmilitary influence of the missiles: "But more than that . . . to our nation . . . it means a great deal more. You all are aware of that, in Cuba and not over in the Soviet Union."

President Kennedy was trying to imagine a world with substantially enlarged Soviet nuclear forces in Cuba. He was momentarily concerned about the impact of such a situation on Berlin: "Then they start getting ready to squeeze us in Berlin." However, he immediately realized that with regard to the fundamental military balance not much would have changed: "You may say it doesn't make a difference if you get blown up by an ICBM flying from the Soviet Union or one that was ninety miles away. Geography doesn't matter that much." It was clearly not the military impact of the Soviet missiles that worried the ExComm, but rather their political and psychological impact. "It makes them look like they're coequal with us," said the president. Edwin W. Martin, the assistant secretary of state for inter-American affairs, expressed it best: "Well, it's a psychological factor that we have sat back and let 'em do it to us, that is more important than the direct threat." Moreover, there was a distinct domestic political factor involved. The president had publicly announced that he would act if offensive weapons were detected in Cuba. McNamara brought the issue to the point: "I don't think there *is* a military problem here. . . . This is a domestic, political problem."[135]

It was the assessment of the Kennedy administration that the political consequences, both domestic and international, of acquiescence in the missile deployment counted most. Once there was agreement on this point, no member of the ExComm pushed for a detailed assessment of the military significance of the Soviet missiles.[136] For most of the senior advisers, the decisive factor was a feeling that both sides had enough to blow each other up anyway. The president explained his thinking in a television and radio interview on 17 December: "The Cuban effort . . . was an effort to materially change the balance of power . . . not that they were intending to fire them [the Soviet missiles in Cuba], because if they were going to get into a nuclear struggle, they have their own missiles in the Soviet Union. But it would have politically changed the balance of power. It would have appeared to, and appearances contribute to reality."[137]

Most members of the ExComm did not disagree with McNamara's assessment that, in purely military terms, the Soviet missile deployments did not affect the strategic balance. Some individuals, like Paul H. Nitze, John McCone, Douglas Dillon, and the members of the JCS, did not completely agree with that assessment. However, they were not primarily concerned with the impact of the missile deployment on the local military situation in Cuba. They rather focused on possible repercussions on the situation in Europe. The U.S. position in Berlin rested on the notion that superior nuclear capabilities were meaningful in the face of Soviet conventional advantages.[138] The central problem, therefore, was how the Soviets would value the shift in the strategic balance. Would they conclude that they could now get away with aggression in Berlin? Because the Kennedy administration had misread Khrushchev's motives for installing missiles in Cuba, nobody in the ExComm had an answer to this question. The Kennedy administration did not think that it would *gain* any military or political advantage from its nuclear superiority in the short term. However, some members of the administration feared that the United States would *lose* political influence around the world in the longer term, particularly with respect to the Berlin question. However, this would depend more on Soviet (and allied) perceptions than on American strategic analyses. The fact of geographical proximity of Soviet missiles to the United States would be politically and psychologically important as long as others perceived it as important.

Finally, whatever urgency the Kennedy administration might have felt to act in order to save its nuclear superiority was outweighed by fear of escalation. As we have seen above, the Americans acted very cautiously during the whole crisis. The realization that the events could quickly lead to nuclear holocaust had a powerful effect on U.S. policy; it affected both the decision in favor of a quarantine and Kennedy's clear preference for a missile trade over a military solution on 27 October.

McNamara emphasized right from the beginning that an air strike would have to be executed *before* the Soviet missiles became operational. Otherwise, the secretary of defense noted, "I do not believe we can state we can knock them out before they can be launched; and if they're launched there is almost certain to be . . . chaos in part of the east coast."[139] Moreover, both General Taylor and Secretary McNamara underscored that in order to minimize the probability that surviving missiles could strike back, it was important that the initial air strike be extensive, covering the enemy missiles, plus the airfields, plus potential nuclear storage sites.[140] Furthermore, because such an air strike would lead to the killing of several hundred Soviet personnel, McNamara added, it seemed "almost certain that any one of these forms of direct military action will lead to a Soviet military response of some type some place in the world."[141] Finally, in order to preserve the advantage of surprise, there should be no announcement of the strike. But again, as Undersecretary of State Ball noted: "You go in there with a surprise attack. You put out all the missiles. This isn't the *end*. This is the *beginning*."[142]

However, there were powerful political advantages to limiting the attack to the missile sites only. Both Secretary Rusk and McGeorge Bundy questioned the assumption that the Soviets would retaliate immediately with all their surviving nuclear forces. Dean Rusk emphasized that he did not believe "that the critical question is whether you get a particular missile before *it* goes off because if they shoot *those* missiles we are in general nuclear war." This was not just some sort of automatic, limited retaliation. "The Soviet Union has got quite a different decision to make."[143] McGeorge Bundy joined the same line of thinking and stressed the political advantage of a situation where the adversary would be responsible for the escalation. "Their bombers take off against us," he said, "then *they* have made a general war against Cuba of it . . . it then becomes much more *their* decision."[144]

McNamara replied that he was not thinking so much about a deliberate Soviet decision to escalate the conflict. On the contrary, what worried him was whether the central Soviet authorities would stay in control in order to make a rational decision: "We don't know what kinds of communications the Soviets have with those sites. We don't know what kinds of control they have over the warheads."[145] It was primarily the risk of escalation posed by an air strike that led McNamara to propose the blockade option; he did initially regard it not as a perfect solution but rather as a less-dangerous one.[146] Such fears were shared to some degree by most of the ExComm members, particularly the strong quar-

antine supporters. Theodore Sorensen, for example, named as one of
the fundamental advantages of the blockade option that it "is the step
least likely to precipitate general war."[147] When the air strike was defini-
tively rejected on 21 October, Robert Kennedy observed: "It would lead
to unpredictable military responses by the Soviet Union which could be
so serious as to lead to general nuclear war."[148]

President Kennedy's strong advocacy of a missile trade on Saturday,
27 October, was caused primarily by fear of conflict escalation as a consequence of an air strike or an invasion. We have seen above that the
president increasingly felt that the options had narrowed to either trade
or war. Thus, he initially rejected the advice that he ignore Khrushchev's
second proposal for a Turkey-Cuba missile trade. The Soviets simply
would reply that they were not interested in such a deal, and the work
on the missile sites would go on. "Then I think," Kennedy said, "we're
going to have to do *something* . . . but the escalation is going to go on,
and we think this is very likely, that there would be some reprisal against
possibly Turkey and possibly against Berlin." Furthermore, the president did not believe that the NATO allies realized that war was imminent and that military action in Cuba could quickly lead to military
action in Europe. "They [the Europeans] don't . . . realize . . . what's
coming up," Kennedy noted in frustration. Once it was too late, everybody would wish they had opted for the trade—and the U.S. government would be held responsible for the decision. In short, President
Kennedy was extremely reluctant to allow obsolete missiles in Turkey to
stand in the way of a negotiated settlement, because he expected dire
consequences for failing to reach an agreement: "What we're going to
be faced with is—because we wouldn't take the missiles out of Turkey,
then maybe we'll have to invade or make a massive strike on Cuba which
may lose *Berlin*. That's what concerns me."[149]

The Soviet Case

During the Cuban missile crisis, fear of the nuclear danger clearly
outweighed whatever advantages were associated with U.S. nuclear superiority. I will now turn to the Soviet case. The Soviet side of the story is
somewhat speculative, because a well-documented account of the decision making of the Soviet government is still not yet possible to achieve.

A popular thesis is that the fact of strategic "inferiority" profoundly
affected Soviet policy. This conclusion is an inference based on the fact
that the Soviet leaders failed to enhance their bargaining position during the crisis in two important ways. They did not exploit their compara-

ble conventional advantage in Europe and answer the blockade of Cuba with any move in Berlin. Nor did they prepare their strategic nuclear forces for war as a signal of their resolve.

With regard to the Berlin analogy, Paul Nitze has argued that if it were not for American nuclear superiority, the Soviets would have reacted in Berlin.[150] Others have argued that the situation in the Caribbean was the mirror image of the situation around Berlin: one side possessed conventional superiority, which could be contained only by nuclear threat. If U.S. conventional superiority was decisive in the Caribbean, one would expect Soviet conventional superiority to be decisive in Berlin. And since this was not the case, so the argument runs, nuclear weapons must have had asymmetrical effects.[151]

However, I do not think that the Berlin analogy is convincing beyond a certain point; there are other explanations for the fact that the Soviets did not react in Berlin. Khrushchev did not set up the missile deployment with his mind singularly focused on Berlin. There is no evidence that the Soviet chairman was thinking in terms of a deliberate ploy aimed at enhancing Soviet bargaining power over Berlin. In fact, all the former members of the Soviet government who have orally presented the Soviet side of the story have insisted, without exception, that the Cuban move was not part of a larger scheme involving the status of Berlin.[152] To be sure, the Berlin experience did enhance Khrushchev's interest in equalizing the balance of power in a general way. Therefore, it is probable that a feeling that the missiles in Cuba would minimize the political power that the United States could achieve from their huge nuclear superiority was involved, to some degree, in Khrushchev's deployment decision. But this is quite different from the assumption that the Soviets would have moved in Berlin once the missiles were installed. In short, Washington, more than Moscow, perceived a connection between Cuba and Berlin. Moreover, once Kennedy had announced the detection of the missiles, there was nothing in the situation that could make expansion of the crisis attractive to the Soviets. The detection of the missiles took Khrushchev by surprise, and this was certainly not the time to enlarge the crisis and the risk of escalation by blockading Berlin. Finally, the balance of resolve favored the United States: Khrushchev secretly had taken the initiative to change the status quo but was caught in the middle of the action.

The observation of the missing Soviet countermove in Berlin is often closely associated with the observation that the Soviets did nothing to reduce the vulnerability of their strategic striking forces during the crisis. While the Americans were making serious preparations for general nuclear war, the Soviets neither placed their strategic nuclear forces on enhanced alert conditions nor dispersed them.[153] Marc Trachtenberg has argued that the reason why the Soviets did nothing to enhance their bargaining power had a good deal to do with their view of U.S. nuclear superiority and doctrine. "The danger of provoking an American preemptive strike tended to rule out countermeasures—or even the serious threat of countermeasures, around Berlin or elsewhere—that would significantly increase the risk of war."[154] The evidence that the Soviets really did think in these terms, however, is very thin. It consists of the famous remark of Soviet deputy foreign minister Vasily V. Kuznetsov to John McCloy after the crisis—"You Americans will never be able to do this to us again"—which is interpreted as indicating that the Soviets drew back because of their relative weakness in strategic nuclear forces.[155]

There are other credible explanations for the fact that the Soviets did not counterbalance U.S. general war preparation. Using military preparations in order to strengthen one's bargaining position was part of the American tradition of strategic thinking, originating in the writings of the civilian strategists in the late 1950s. The Soviets did not necessarily think the same way. The American thinking was a product of the extension of nuclear deterrence over its European allies, a geostrategical fact missing in the Soviet case. Also, Khrushchev consistently followed a somewhat cruder version of atomic diplomacy which rested on the pure threat value of nuclear weapons. The decisive elements in his calculation were his assumptions about the psychology and firmness of his opponents. There also might have been some technical considerations that prevented the Soviets from holding their strategic forces on an extended alert posture.[156] It is possible, too, that Khrushchev did not want to bring his generals too much into decision making. After all, the Soviet decisions during the whole affair were very much Khrushchev's personal ones.[157]

Although it remains somewhat inconclusive to what degree Soviet policy was affected by the strategic balance, there certainly is no reason to conclude that it had a profound impact on the Soviet side. On the other hand, there is strong evidence that fear of uncontrolled escalation and the nuclear danger played an important role in Khrushchev's decision to end the crisis. As we have seen above, the unauthorized shooting down of the American U-2 plane over Cuba, in particular, illustrated the danger that the events were on the verge of spilling out of control. But the single most important piece of evidence for the claim that the Soviet leader was heavily affected by fear of inadvertent escalation to nuclear war is his letter to President Kennedy on 26 October. Khrushchev's style of writing manifested anxiety, a feeling that the Soviet Chairman later described as "intense."[158]

Khrushchev's letter contained an eloquent argument about the calamitous nature of modern warfare. He warned the American president that "should war indeed break out, it would not be in our power to contain or stop it, for such is the logic of war. I have taken part in two wars," he reminded Kennedy, "and I know that war ends only when it has rolled through cities and villages, sowing death and destruction everywhere." Khrushchev then moved on to emphasize that the danger was mutual: "You may regard us with distrust, but you can at any rate rest assured that we are of sound mind and understand perfectly well that if we launch an offensive against you, you will respond in kind. But you too will get in response whatever you throw at us. And I think you understand that too." The letter repeatedly stressed that the weapons in Cuba were not intended to be offensive and their sole purpose was the defense of Cuba. Khrushchev, finally, proposed removing the missiles in return for American assurances not to take part in any attack upon Cuba. The letter concludes with the often-quoted appeal to solve the crisis by peaceful means before it was too late:

> If you have not lost command of yourself and realize clearly what this could lead to, then, Mr. President, you and I should not now pull on the ends of the rope in which you have tied a knot of war, because the harder you and I pull, the tighter this knot will become. And a time may come when this knot is tied so tight that the person who tied it is no longer capable of untying it, and then the knot will have to be cut. What that would mean I need not explain to you, because you yourself understand perfectly what dread forces our two countries possess. Therefore, if there is no intention of tightening this knot, thereby dooming the world to the catastrophe of thermonuclear war, let us not only relax the forces straining on the ends of the rope, let us take measures for untying this knot. We are agreeable to this.[159]

With regard to the Soviet decision to end the confrontation, fear of escalation and the plain danger of nuclear war were clearly more important than considerations about the military impact of the strategic balance.

I propose that with regard to the role of nuclear weapons in the Cuban missile crisis, it was not nuclear superiority but rather nuclear danger that was of the essence. The U.S. quantitative nuclear advantage gave the American leaders no comfort, and certainly did not enhance their willingness to take greater risks. And the fact of strategic "inferiority" was not decisive for Khrushchev's termination of the crisis. More important for the advancement of a peaceful settlement of the crisis was the *mutual* realization that the events could slip out of control and that nuclear war would know no winner. The possibility that developments were approaching a point where events could become unmanageable was a recurring theme in the exchange of letters between Kennedy and Khrushchev. Each leader took it for granted that the other did not want nuclear war.[160]

It is not the point here, however, to argue that the strategic balance had no effect whatsoever on the development of the crisis; the argument is one of relative importance. Considerations of relative power were involved in both the Soviet decision to deploy missiles in Cuba and the American decision to take great risks to undo the deployment. Both sides were to some extent caught in their experiences from the Berlin crisis. And the crisis over Berlin had advanced a feeling that the strategic balance was of a certain political importance. I cannot improve on Mc-George Bundy's compelling conclusion on the role of nuclear weapons: "Nuclear ambition caused the crisis; a sense of nuclear affront forced the response; an awareness of nuclear danger drove both governments toward rapidity of resolution; but it was conventional superiority on the scene [and I would add the balance of resolve] that determined the eventual outcome."[161]

12

The Détente of 1963: Lessons of the Cuban Missile Crisis

The end of the Cuban missile crisis brought two important changes: First, the end of the crisis saw diminished pressure against West Berlin. It sealed the mutual acceptance of the status quo that was, finally, codified in the Berlin Quadripartite Agreement of 1971. Second, following the crisis, the threat of an American invasion of Cuba abated. The Kennedy administration was not prepared to formalize a noninvasion commitment and it continued to undermine the Castro government; however, the call for open military aggression against Cuba was increasingly superseded by an understanding that Fidel Castro had to be accepted as a fact of life.

Within the Kennedy administration, there was a strong feeling that the West should take advantage of the crisis's outcome in order to bring about a major change in East-West relations. President Kennedy alluded to such an opportunity in his letter to Khrushchev of 28 October: "Perhaps now, as we step back from danger, we can together make real progress" in the field of disarmament. He listed the areas that seemed to be most promising: "I think we should give priority to questions relating to the proliferation of nuclear weapons, on earth and in outer space, and to the great effort for a nuclear test ban."[1] In general, initiatives in the field of disarmament were regarded as more promising than a revival of the Berlin negotiations.[2] However, the hawks within the administration opposed any move toward a détente with the Soviet Union. The leadership of the president, therefore, was of central importance. And in this regard, Kennedy's handling of the crisis improved his level of respect within the administration, and with Congress and the nation. The president had proved his ability to stand up to the Soviet Union. At the same

time, the Cuban missile crisis had focused attention on the danger of a
nuclear confrontation. The combination of these two factors allowed
Kennedy to set a new tone in East-West relations with his famous
"peace" speech on 10 June 1963. His address at American University
stemmed from a new awareness of the importance of improving relations with the Soviet Union in the thermonuclear age.[3]

As to the effects of the crisis on the Soviet Union, Khrushchev succeeded in containing domestic criticism about his handling of the affair,
at least in the short term.[4] On 12 December 1962, the Soviet premier
presented his views on the matter in a speech at a meeting of the Supreme Soviet. Khrushchev justified the missile deployment noting that
its "purpose was only the defense of Cuba." And this, the Soviet government had accomplished: the American president had declared "that the
United States would not attack Cuba." Therefore, the missiles had been
withdrawn. As to the question of who had won, Khrushchev stressed
"that reason won, that the cause of peace and of the security of nations
won." The outcome of the crisis was "a result of mutual concessions and
compromise." The Cuban missile crisis was "peaceful coexistence policy
in action"—and the only alternative would have been mutual thermonuclear disaster.[5] With regard to the future of East-West relations, Khrushchev, in his letter agreeing to withdraw the missiles, underlined the
importance of progress in the field of disarmament.[6] In another letter
to Kennedy on 19 December, Khrushchev suggested that the "time has
come now to put an end once and for all to nuclear tests."[7] However, a
misunderstanding regarding the number of inspections each side would
be allowed to make of the other's military sites bedeviled the negotiations for a test ban for several months to come.[8] Besides efforts in the
field of disarmament, the Soviets tried to bring up the Berlin issue on
several occasions.[9] However, they were not prepared to press the issue.
And the Americans decided against pursuing the matter at that time. So
tensions abated and arms control took over the agenda.

The experience of the missile crisis stimulated mutual interest in arms
control and a turn toward détente in U.S.-Soviet relations. A first sign
that agreement was possible came with the establishment of the so-called
hot line in June 1963. The Cuban missile crisis had shown the importance of swift and reliable communication between antagonists during
dangerous international crises. The "hot line" established a direct communication link between Washington and Moscow.[10] Meanwhile, the test
ban negotiations had reached an impasse over the question of the number of inspections and the number and location of unmanned seismo-
logical stations. In June 1963, President Kennedy decided to make a

"fresh start." He stressed the importance of a test ban in his "peace" speech: "The conclusion of such a treaty—so near and yet so far—would check the spiraling arms race in one of its most dangerous areas. It would place the nuclear powers in a position to deal more effectively with one of the greatest hazards which man faces in 1963, the further spread of nuclear arms."[11] Kennedy went on to announce that the United States would not conduct nuclear tests in the atmosphere so long as other states did not do so either. A few days later, Khrushchev shifted attention away from a comprehensive test ban to an agreement on the cessation of nuclear tests in the atmosphere, in outer space, and under water. After only two weeks of bargaining, Averell Harriman, Andrei Gromyko, and Viscount Quinton Hailsham (for Great Britain) initialed the Limited Test Ban Treaty (LTBT) on 25 July 1963.[12] The LTBT was the first successful step in the field of disarmament and arms control in the negotiations between the Soviet Union and the United States since the end of World War II.[13] The turn toward détente was further strengthened with the U.S.-Soviet agreement of September 1963 to jointly support a UN General Assembly resolution banning the placement of weapons of mass destruction in outer space.[14]

The development of the détente of 1963 had a lot to do with what the Soviet and the American leadership regarded as the single most important lesson of the Cuban missile crisis. The central problem of the previous few years had been how the situation of evolving mutual vulnerability would affect the balance of power between the United States and the Soviet Union. Whereas the Soviets had been seeking to test how much political influence they could exert through their new military strength, the Americans had been seeking to contain the perception created by such changes in relative political power, particularly because of the changes' disruptive consequences for the cohesion of western alliances. While the Berlin crisis proved that nuclear superiority still played a political role, this point was overshadowed by the central lesson of the Cuban missile crisis: The prevention of nuclear war was a more important goal for the security of both the United States and the Soviet Union than relative gains and losses in political power. The nuclear danger had been understood before; but never before had leaders felt that the danger of nuclear war, generated by the pace of a crisis itself, could lead to a situation where events slipped out of control. Mutual fear of escalation advanced both restraint and willingness to resolve the issue by peaceful means. And it was impetus enough for increased efforts toward a general reduction of tensions in East-West relations.

There is no better assessment of the age of mutual vulnerability than the one delivered by President Kennedy in his "peace" speech:

I speak of peace because of the new face of war. Total war makes no sense in an age when great powers can maintain large and relatively invulnerable nuclear forces and refuse to surrender without resort to those forces. It makes no sense in an age when a single nuclear weapon contains almost ten times the explosive force delivered by all of the allied air forces in the Second World War. It makes no sense in an age when the deadly poisons produced by a nuclear exchange would be carried by the wind and water and soil and seed to the far corners of the globe and to generations yet unborn. Today the expenditure of billions of dollars every year on weapons acquired for the purpose of making sure we never need to use them is essential to keeping the peace. But surely the acquisition of such idle stock-piles—which can only destroy and never create—is not the only, much less the most efficient, means of assuring peace.

The United States and the Soviet Union, Kennedy emphasized, had a "mutually deep interest in a just and genuine peace and in halting the arms race." And the mutual recognition that both sides could only lose in a nuclear war had become stronger. "Almost unique, among the major powers," Kennedy pointed out, "we have never been at war with each other."[15]

Apart from the lesson that it was imperative to avoid such crises in the future, the Cuban missile crisis demonstrated that nuclear superiority was of limited psychopolitical importance only. And unlike in the Berlin crisis, this time the lesson was mutual. Both sides realized that nuclear risks were too dangerous to be exploited given the possibility of uncontrolled escalation and its devastating consequences. In critical situations with a high risk of leading to war, the nuclear danger was by far more potent than any calculation of relative military power. In times of relative tranquillity, prestige effects of nuclear weapons and political gains stemming from nuclear advantages might still be of some use. In times of high international tensions, however, when such political leverage would be used most, prestige effects of nuclear weapons would become overshadowed by nuclear danger.[16]

The Cuban missile crisis emphasized the nuclear danger and enhanced the visibility of the limits of the political utility of nuclear superiority. At the same time, the crisis decreased the need to use relative nuclear advantage to reassure allies. I have argued above that with the Berlin wall as symbol of the acceptance of a divided Europe by both East and West, the European security system attained a certain stability. This perception was supported by the Kennedy administration's new emphasis on a conventional option for NATO (signaling U.S. willingness to stay in Europe on a permanent basis) and the development of national nuclear forces by those nations (France and Great Britain) that perceived the lack of such symbols of power as incompatible with their roles. Even more important, the Kennedy administration's emphasis on central nuclear control kept the German finger off the nuclear trigger. This mitigated both Soviet and European fears. However, while the Berlin wall symbolized the de facto physical division of Europe, it was only after the Soviet Union failed to move in Berlin during the Cuban missile crisis that the West developed trust in the durability of the division of Europe. These developments reduced the pressure on the American government to reassure its European allies through U.S. nuclear superiority.

The Cuban missile crisis had a lasting influence on how we perceive the role of nuclear weapons in international politics. The world had moved toward the nuclear brink, the political leaders of the two superpowers had realized that there was a real chance of slipping over it, and it was understood that the result would be disaster. After the Cuban missile crisis, nuclear weapons were perceived as a stabilizing factor in international politics. The continuing relevance of these lessons has been reinforced with the burst of new attention to the missile crisis in the wake of momentous changes within the Soviet Union that brought the Cold War to an end. While the Cuban missile crisis was a time of nuclear learning for all participants, the learning still goes on.

However, one should be careful not to overstate the message: These changes were gradual in nature. The stabilizing force of nuclear weapons did not go unchallenged in the aftermath of the Cuban missile crisis. Nuclear threats did not become completely useless in a political sense. The lesson of the Cuban missile crisis was not so simple as to leave everyone convinced that nuclear weapons simply cancel each other out. The best evidence for the fact that the strategic balance remained of some political importance is that the arms race continued. What factors kept the race going? First, the invocation of the idea of a nuclear stalemate in the early 1960s was more anticipation than perception of the actual situation. If Europe was doomed for destruction, the possibility of reducing damage to the American homeland to an acceptable level could be discussed. This is not to say that U.S. policymakers obtained much confidence from their nuclear superiority. The analysis of the decision-making process of the Kennedy administration during the Cuban missile crisis shows that this was not the case. However, the strategic balance was one-sided enough that people like General David Burchinal could explain the outcome of the crisis (which he perceived as a very one-sided victory for the United States) as a direct consequence of a military fact: U.S. nuclear superiority.[17] The motivation for the Soviets to close the gap in strategic capabilities was real.

Second, intermingled with this thinking was the argument that superior nuclear forces were valuable in order to limit damage to the United States in case of a deterrence failure. It was precisely the experience of the Cuban missile crisis that showed that accidental or inadvertent nuclear war was a real possibility. And if a war could come as a mutually unintended product, a strategy to limit damage in case of war was the prudent political choice. A pure deterrent strategy, like a minimum deterrence posture, would only leave open the worst of all choices: humiliation or holocaust. Secretary of Defense McNamara justified U.S. counterforce capabilities using such an argument in his memorandum to the president only one month after the missile crisis. Counterforce capabilities were the insurance "to make the best of a bad situation."[18] But McNamara realized that a force designed for damage limitation inevitably had in it a first-strike capability. The problem was to reach what he called a balanced damage-limiting force structure that would stop short of capabilities where the additional money spent was not worth the diminishing marginal returns in terms of damage limitation.[19] The problem was that the recommendations dictated by such reasoning could not be distinguished from the recommendations of individuals and groups arguing in favor of a full first-strike posture. As part of the bureaucratic battle over the size of the strategic forces, the services could exploit the admitted desirability of a balanced damage-limiting force structure. Bureaucratic pressure drove the balance of counterforce capabilities in the direction of a first-strike posture—with all the negative implications for the development of the arms race and for crisis stability.

Third, and possibly most important, nuclear superiority had proven to be politically useful for the reassurance of allies. Threats of an arms race had been used to exert pressure on an opponent and seemed to have worked to a certain degree. Claims of nuclear superiority and willingness to carry on with the expensive burden of the arms race became important signals of resolve. And because the deterrent effects stopped flowing directly from the relative balance of physical capabilities, it was the balance of resolve that mattered increasingly. In a process that later would be called the "greater-fool perceptual rationale," relative nuclear capabilities remained important.[20] There would always be audiences—for example allies, Third World countries, or the U.S. public—that would interpret the balance of power in a conventionalized perspective, counting the relative numbers of nuclear weapons. In a world that was to a large extent built in the minds of people, the nuclear balance remained of some importance.

My point is not that such arguments became irrelevant in the aftermath of the Cuban missile crisis. However, from the perspective of the American and Soviet political leadership, the advantage of relative gains or losses was increasingly perceived as having only marginal value, compared with the nuclear danger in particular times of high tension. Further evidence for this gradual change in the relative weight of policy goals (in the case of the United States) is the shift in emphasis from damage limitation to assured destruction. While in 1961 Secretary McNamara had defined U.S. nuclear strategy in the framework of the no-cities counterforce strategy, he came to place more stress on assured destruction capabilities from 1963 onward. In December 1963, the secretary of defense noted to the president that the central objective for the strategic nuclear forces was to assure U.S. ability to destroy, after a well-planned and well-executed Soviet surprise attack on U.S. strategic forces, "the Soviet government and military controls, plus a large percentage of their population and economy (e.g. 30% of their population, 50% of their industrial capacity, and 150 of their cities)."[21] The damage-limiting objective was not given up completely. However, toward the end of the decade damage limitation was mentioned mainly in connection with the nuclear threat from China. A Draft Presidential Memorandum of January 1969, after Robert McNamara had left the Pentagon, stated that "we believe it would not be feasible to limit damage by strategically significant amounts against the Soviets because they can and would react to maintain their Assured Destruction capability. Against China, however, effective Damage Limiting appears feasible, at least for the next decade."[22] The same paper concluded that it was doubtful that U.S. superiority in nuclear warheads "can be converted into meaningful political power, particularly now that the Soviet Union also has a large and well-protected strategic force."[23]

The new emphasis on assured destruction as opposed to damage limitation sent new signals into the world of international politics. First, assured destruction was an expression of the acceptance of mutual vulnerability. Second, assured destruction gave a better answer to the question of how much is enough. It served Secretary McNamara far better than the no-cities counterforce strategy in his bureaucratic battles over military programs and budgets. The new emphasis was thought to dampen incentives for prolonging the arms race. Finally, the new strategic concept underscored the gap between declared strategy and operational war planning, between theory and practice. On the operational level, emphasis remained on flexibility and control, and no substantive changes were made to the SIOP-63.[24] In his last memorandum for President Johnson in 1968, McNamara noted that the lack of war plans for the controlled and deliberate use of the nation's nuclear power "is one of the main weaknesses in our posture today."[25] In this regard, assured destruction emphasized that pure military considerations lost their influence on the formulation of nuclear strategy in an era of mutual vulnerability. Assured destruction was primarily a product of political considerations.

Strengthened by the shock of October 1962, nuclear weapons proved to have a predominantly stabilizing impact on international politics in the future. The underlying cause of this development was widespread recognition in the East and the West alike of what John F. Kennedy had already spelled out before the Cuban missile crisis (in words which are of striking relevance to today's security debate): "War appeals no longer as a rational alternative. Unconditional war can no longer lead to unconditional victory. It can no longer serve to settle disputes. It can no longer be of concern to great powers alone. For a nuclear disaster, spread by winds and waters and fear, could well engulf the great and the small, the rich and the poor, the committed and the uncommitted alike. Mankind must put an end to war—or war will put an end to mankind."[26]

Conclusions

The international system attained a certain stability in 1963, at the very moment when mutual vulnerability became evident. From today's perspective, it is precisely this coincidence that makes us so receptive to the proposition that, by and large, nuclear weapons have a stabilizing impact on international politics. However, this stability had not been expected during the 1950s, at the height of the Cold War. On the contrary, most observers anticipated that a time of mutual atomic plenty would be characterized by instability and the danger that the Cold War might turn hot. The role of nuclear weapons, or at least our perception of their role, changed over time.

This study has inquired into the American thinking about the political role of nuclear weapons. It has narrated the story of how the Eisenhower and Kennedy administrations reacted to the reality of a growing Soviet nuclear threat against the American homeland. The lesson to be drawn from this historical approach to understanding the political impact of the absolute weapon is a complex one, filled with puzzles and contradictions.

The lesson is hopeful insofar as its shows that both President Eisenhower and President Kennedy adapted United States policy to evolving mutual nuclear vulnerability in ways that contributed to the avoidance of war. Over the years, the political leadership of the United States learned to fear the nuclear danger, it learned to accept the political limitations of both nuclear superiority and nuclear threats, and it learned that coexistence with the Soviet Union was an essential prerequisite to the future survival of the two superpowers.

But still, the lesson is also one of many failures, of nuclear arms races, and of crisis decision making bringing the world dangerously close to the nuclear brink. The American example of nuclear learning, therefore, does not inspire much confidence in the proposition that "more

313

may be better" and that nuclear learning would necessarily produce stability in other circumstances and in relations between other countries.

Nuclear learning under Eisenhower and Kennedy evolved in three distinct phases, characterized by the changing strategic nuclear balance between the United States and the Soviet Union. The first phase was a time of overwhelming American nuclear superiority. President Eisenhower's New Look defense policy led to the integration of nuclear weapons into American national security policy. The relatively low financial cost of nuclear weapons permitted Eisenhower to pursue a strategy of modified containment instead of fundamentally reorienting American national security policy. Nuclear weapons allowed him to avoid isolationism, the attractiveness of which had loomed large following the Korean War. The low price tag on nuclear weapons made it possible to strike a balance between security and solvency, thereby preserving the nation's institutions and the American way of life.

However, the New Look was more than fiscally attractive, it was also strategically sound, in light of the technological and military realities of the time. The quantity of nuclear weapons in the world was still relatively small, and the imbalance was sufficient to matter militarily. The overwhelming nuclear superiority of the United States directly affected the policy choices of both East and West, facilitating the end of the Korean War. Expectations of a shift in the strategic balance due to growing Soviet nuclear capabilities carried political weight. These expectations resulted in even louder calls for a more aggressive U.S. foreign policy and serious consideration of preventive war even at the highest ranks of the American government.

At the same time, the advent of the hydrogen bomb generated great concerns about a future of mutual thermonuclear plenty. Within a few years, both the United States and the Soviet Union would develop "enough" nuclear capability to threaten one another with complete destruction. Because such a world would evolve only gradually, people expected the period ahead to be laden with instability and danger. In a world of mutual thermonuclear plenty, so the argument ran, the advantage of striking first would be increasingly decisive. The realization that the thermonuclear revolution had changed the nature of conflict led to claims that only disarmament and nuclear arms control could secure world peace in the long term.

The superpowers' possession of nuclear weapons had both stabilizing and destabilizing effects in the early 1950s. These effects were most clearly reflected in alliance politics. America's European allies were worried by the prospect of a more aggressive U.S. foreign policy, because they felt more exposed to the growing Soviet nuclear threat than did their American security guarantors. The seemingly contradictory effects of nuclear weapons reached a delicate balance in late 1954 with the nuclearization of NATO and the post–World War II settlement between the western powers and West Germany. The arrangements were embodied in the London and Paris Accords, adopted by the western powers at the end of the year.

The events of late 1954 and early 1955 meant that Europe would be defended by an integrated western defense effort, German power would be contained, and the United States would become permanently involved in Europe. Nuclear weapons had an impact on all three of these developments. First, the nuclearization of NATO eased American concerns about the military strength of the alliance. The integration of nuclear weapons made NATO's forward strategy a realistic military goal for the first time since NATO's birth in 1949. American nuclear superiority enabled the alliance to contemplate the tactical use of nuclear weapons in order to make up for conventional deficiencies. Second, while German rearmament was kept within limits, particularly on the nuclear side, German military and economic resources were added to the western defense effort. Third, the fact that the settlement between the western powers and Germany was finally achieved within the institutional framework of NATO made it easier for the Europeans to accept the nuclear-oriented strategy outlined in MC-48. The coincidence of the European settlement and NATO's nuclearization meant that the American commitment to the security of Europe had become a permanent feature of international politics, thereby containing historical animosities between the continental powers. Furthermore, it meant that the danger of America moving to a peripheral strategy for the defense of Europe had passed, and that the United States would not adopt a more aggressive foreign policy posture. The step back from an aggressive posture was reflected in the Eisenhower administration's elimination of preventive war as a policy option.

Finally, the relatively low price tag on nuclear weapons influenced the Europeans' acceptance of MC-48, as it had already affected Eisenhower's formulation of the New Look. Since 1953 it had become clear to Europeans and Americans alike that the Lisbon force goals for the conventional defense of Europe would not be achieved. It is easy to imagine history having taken a different, potentially more dangerous turn if the fiscal logic of nuclear weapons had not allowed the West to develop a powerful military alliance to contain Soviet expansionism.

In the second phase, Americans came to terms with the evolving state of mutual vulnerability. While stability prevailed in the settlement of late 1954, the equilibrium was delicate, because NATO went nuclear at the very moment when the credibility of the nuclear threat was increasingly in doubt, due to growing Soviet nuclear capabilities. It was the fundamental dilemma of NATO's nuclearization that evolving mutual vulnerability undermined the alliance's security, which rested on nuclear threats. Would the world go up in flames because one side wanted to launch a preemptive strike before it was too late, only to find that the window of time in which to deliver such a blow had passed already? Or would the Soviet Union undermine the position of the West bit by bit?

These questions produced growing pressure for a more flexible military posture in order to deal with the likely threats of the future. Eisenhower, however, was never prepared to enlarge the country's conventional forces. Instead, he emphasized the temporary American advantage in tactical nuclear weapons. He was motivated in part by rising fiscal demands due to the development of missiles in addition to bombers. But more important, the president believed that the nature of conflict was changing in an environment of mutual vulnerability. Eisenhower was increasingly convinced that mutual nuclear plenty would bring stability, because both sides would realize that any war between the United States and the Soviet Union would eventually become nuclear. So why overcommit the nation's resources (building up unnecessary conventional forces), while undermining its institutions?

Eisenhower's beliefs were not widely shared at the time. Both the Killian Committee (1955) and the Gaither Panel (1957) dealt differently with the changing balance of military strength between East and West. The reports of both bodies concluded that maintaining U.S. nuclear superiority was essential, because mutual vulnerability would bring instability and danger. Moreover, both groups of consultants urged the Eisenhower administration to take advantage of the present western lead in nuclear forces and to translate that lead into political gains before it was too late.

The Eisenhower administration, however, found it difficult to translate nuclear superiority into political leverage in its dealings with the Soviet Union. The prospect of a missile war with thermonuclear warheads led Eisenhower to realize that the meaning of war as an instrument of policy was changing. Nuclear superiority was losing its military significance. In Eisenhower's opinion, mutual vulnerability was becoming reality. As a consequence, Eisenhower followed a fundamentally defensive, status quo–oriented foreign policy. Both his readiness to engage in negotiations over Berlin and his increased interest in the process of arms control reflect his outlook on the fundamental dynamic of the Cold War in a time of mutual nuclear plenty.

President Eisenhower believed that in this new environment neither the military element nor the economic element of policy was critical for the security of the nation. Rather, it was the element of moral strength, comprising the psychology of the nation and of the West as a whole, that Eisenhower sensed to be the biggest problem during his last years in office. As long as others believed in the value of superiority, then superiority remained of political and psychological importance. And the most important reason why others perceived superiority to be essential was that the security of the Atlantic alliance rested on nuclear threats. Nuclear weapons simply had to influence policy in one way or another, or NATO would fall apart. Claims of superiority were necessary to reassure allies and domestic groups that perceived superiority to be essential. It was in the hope of harnessing this psychological function that Eisenhower agreed to accelerate the nation's missile development programs, though he did not perceive missiles to be very valuable militarily for some time to come. And it was in response to political pressure that he proposed a bigger defense budget in the aftermath of Sputnik, though he thought the new budget was unjustified from a military point of view.

Eisenhower realized that the credibility of the American commitment to the defense of Europe required nuclear superiority as a signaling device of U.S. resolve. He was aware that the necessary size of these forces depended on highly subjective factors. The question was, therefore, whether it was ultimately less costly to let the Europeans defend Europe with their own forces, including their own nuclear capabilities. Whether NATO would survive the growth of Soviet nuclear strength remained doubtful at the end of the 1950s. It seems that Eisenhower was increasingly prepared to solve the problem through independent (and preferably integrated) European nuclear forces.

Toward the end of the Eisenhower presidency, mutual vulnerability evolved without leading to disaster. If many had not expected this result in the first half of the decade, even fewer observers had anticipated that nuclear superiority would remain of considerable political importance. The balance between stabilizing and destabilizing effects of nuclear weapons remained delicate. President Eisenhower recognized the inevitability of mutual vulnerability and accordingly followed a cautious foreign policy. The constant imperative to reassure allies and domestic groups that believed in the value of nuclear superiority, on the other hand, drove Eisenhower to advocate heavy procurement of nuclear forces, with all the dangerous implications for crisis stability.

In phase three, Americans perceived mutual vulnerability as inevitable. During the Kennedy presidency, NATO's fundamental dilemma and the tensions between stabilizing and destabilizing effects of nuclear weapons came to a head. Before the international system developed a certain stability, the world had to live through the two most dangerous crises of the Cold War.

The fundamental strategic dilemma described above affected Kennedy's reappraisal of national security policy. Responding to the fact that the prospect of nuclear war was becoming tantamount to national suicide, the new Democratic government proposed building up the West's conventional forces so that the question of when and how to use nuclear weapons would never have to be faced. Given the growing vulnerability of the American homeland to nuclear attack, the allies, however, interpreted this shift in strategy as a sign that the Americans were no longer prepared to defend Europe by whatever means. In order to reassure the Europeans of the continuing credibility of the U.S. security guarantee, the Kennedy administration emphasized the concept of controlled, graduated response, while remaining doubtful as to its feasibility. Purely military considerations played a much smaller role in the 1961 reappraisal of national security policy compared with Eisenhower's evaluation of the New Look. This was reflected in the part that the JCS played in the process: While in 1953 their recommendations had formed the basis of the New Look, in 1961 their role was deliberately limited by the political leadership.

The conflict over the city of Berlin brought NATO's nuclear dilemma to a head, because West Berlin was locally indefensible. From an American perspective, the Berlin crisis starkly posed the question of whether the United States still had the will to defend the city by whatever means necessary in light of Soviet power to harm the American homeland. From a Soviet perspective, the nuclear factor was also at stake in the crisis but in a very different way. Khrushchev's decision to force the German question was heavily influenced by fear of a nuclear-armed Germany. Eisenhower's liberal views regarding nuclear sharing with the Europeans only intensified Soviet concerns.

The development of the crisis during the summer of 1961 confirmed to the Kennedy administration the lesson (which Eisenhower too had learned) that nuclear superiority had only limited psychopolitical meaning. The nuclear balance counted for very little with respect to military planning. At no point did Kennedy conclude that a war in which nuclear weapons were used would end in anything other than shared disaster.

The nuclear danger led the Kennedy administration to search for a negotiated settlement. The fear that the conflict would reach the nuclear level as a result of an uncontrolled escalation forced the United States to move toward acceptance of the status quo of a divided Europe (the construction of the Berlin wall symbolized Soviet acceptance of the same solution). Kennedy tempered his support for the political goal of German reunification. He came to accept the fact that Europe was divided permanently. The Kennedy administration acknowledged that genuine Soviet security interests were at stake. Both Kennedy's willingness to discuss the broader issue of European security and his interest in stopping further nuclear proliferation were communicated to the Soviets. In this connection, the shift from Eisenhower's liberal views on nuclear sharing toward tight central control over NATO's nuclear forces (in effect keeping the German finger off the nuclear trigger) was of utmost importance.

At the beginning of the crisis, however, it was not clear whether the Soviets would be deterred, nor whether the Atlantic alliance would stick together. The Kennedy administration counted on highly visible military preparations having a deterrent effect. The Americans emphasized that the buildup of conventional forces would enhance the nuclear deterrent. Increased conventional capabilities would signal U.S. readiness to stay in Europe permanently and become engaged at a lower level of violence, thereby giving the Soviets time to contemplate the great risk of escalation to nuclear war. The problem with this approach was that the Europeans interpreted it as a shift away from reliance on nuclear weapons in response to the vulnerability of the American homeland to Soviet nuclear attack. In order to reassure the allies of the credibility of the American nuclear guarantee, the Kennedy administration began to stress the extent of U.S. nuclear superiority, implying that it was of continuing significance.

The Berlin crisis magnified the inverse relationship between military force and statecraft that Eisenhower had already witnessed. Mutual vulnerability created the situation that the nuclear power that was needed for deterrence, if it served its purpose, would never be used. The correlation between the physical capabilities and the political behavior of states became ever weaker. As long as military forces could still secure political goals, the important question was how military factors (like the correlation of forces) affected political decisions. Once military power could be transformed into favorable political outcomes only indirectly by manipulation of perception, the essential question became how military decisions would affect the highly subjective assessment of the situation by adversaries, allies, and the nation itself. Since, in an era of mutual vulnerability, nuclear threats were not very credible, it was crucial for nations to establish their resolve.

Because the Berlin crisis was perceived as a test of wills (as opposed to a test of capabilities), it was crucial to influence others' beliefs. In a world in which impressions mattered as much as, if not more than, actual capabilities, claims of nuclear superiority and the prospect of an arms race became important psychological and political signaling tools for the reassurance of allies as well as the deterrence of adversaries. Arms competition became the functional substitute for war. This process caused the gap between theory and practice to widen. Declaratory strategy was cut loose from operational planning. While the military and technical feasibility of a strategy might never be tested, its political presentation might deter the very contingencies in which the strategy would be employed.

If the Kennedy administration learned from the Berlin crisis that nuclear weapons had only limited psychopolitical utility, the Soviets did not learn the same lesson. Twice in two years, Nikita Khrushchev had to ignore a deadline that he had imposed for a separate peace treaty with East Germany in the face of superior western power. Moreover, the American government capitalized on the idea that Soviet concessions were due to U.S. nuclear superiority. And to the extent that the Europeans felt reassured by claims of western nuclear superiority, this political packaging was important. From a Soviet perspective, there was a real incentive to redress the unfavorable strategic balance. Thus Khrushchev decided to deploy MR/IRBMs in Cuba.

It was the tempo of the Cuban missile crisis that led to the mutual recognition that events could eventually slip out of control. At a certain point in the crisis, the "noise" of misinformation, miscalculation, misjudgment, and mismanagement could lead to inadvertent escalation. The U.S. nuclear advantage gave the American leaders no comfort in October 1962 and certainly did not enhance their willingness to take greater risks. Nor did strategic "inferiority" inspire Khrushchev to end the crisis. It was rather the mutual realization that events could develop their own escalation dynamic that was important for a peaceful settlement of the crisis.

I have argued that the lesson of the Cuban crisis on both sides was that nuclear superiority was of limited psychopolitical importance. Both sides realized that nuclear risks were too great to be exploited and that they had a common goal that was far more important: the prevention of nuclear war. The shock of the Cuban experience led to increased efforts toward a general reduction of tensions in East-West relations. While there was no new pressure around Berlin, a stronger Kennedy and a more conciliatory Khrushchev moved the world toward détente. The most important achievement of the détente of 1963 was the signing of the Limited Test Ban Treaty as the first successful step in the fields of arms control and disarmament since World War II.

It was only after the Berlin crisis and the Cuban missile crisis that the stabilizing effects of nuclear weapons *gradually* began to prevail. Nevertheless, the arms race continued, and nuclear weapons did not become politically obsolete. But the destabilizing impact of nuclear weapons became more *visible*, because the Cuban missile crisis had shed light on the danger involved in a strategy of risk manipulation and underscored the limits of the political utility of nuclear weapons in an era of mutual vulnerability. The nuclear danger had been understood before; but never before had the political leaders in Washington and Moscow felt that the danger of nuclear war, generated by the pace of the crisis itself, could lead to a situation where events might slip out of control.

Also, U.S. leaders no longer needed to exploit the destabilizing effects of nuclear weapons, because the European security system had acquired a certain stability. The Soviets had proven themselves deterrable, and the allies no longer needed to be constantly reassured by boasts of western nuclear superiority. The Cuban missile crisis confirmed what the Berlin wall had symbolized, namely that both the United States and the Soviet Union accepted the status quo of a divided Europe. While France and the United Kingdom were developing independent national nuclear forces, Germany was bound to abstain from acquiring a nuclear capability of its own. The Germans had to rely on the American security guarantee. They were compensated by the permanent American presence in Europe.

Again, I emphasize that the notion of nuclear weapons as a stabilizing force did not go unchallenged in the aftermath of the Cuban missile crisis. Neither the strategic balance nor nuclear threats became completely obsolete in political terms. Several factors kept the old patterns in force in 1963: First, while the American political leadership perceived the balance of power in terms of mutual vulnerability, this perception had not yet attained total legitimacy. Kennedy's buildup of the nation's strategic forces had produced such a nuclear advantage that some observers could still argue that the United States would survive a nuclear war without unacceptable damage. Second, a larger group of people concluded from the Cuban missile crisis that miscalculation or accident could launch a nuclear war. It was therefore politically prudent to have superior nuclear forces in order to limit damage as much as possible in the event of war. Third, nuclear superiority had proven to be of some psychological and political importance. There would always be audiences—for example allies, Third World countries, or the U.S. public—who would interpret the balance of power in a "conventionalized perspective," counting the relative number of nuclear weapons.

However, I argue that the political leadership of the United States (and of the Soviet Union) regarded such advantages in relative political gains or losses as marginal. Both sides came to learn that in critical situations, with a high risk of war in particular, the nuclear danger would exert more influence on policy decisions than any calculation of relative military power.

By 1963, the international system had developed a certain stability and mutual vulnerability had gained general acceptance. A time of mutual nuclear plenty had become reality without having led to disaster. Not many observers had expected this peaceful transformation of the Cold War in the early 1950s, and even fewer had predicted that nuclear decision making would play an increasingly stabilizing role in this process. If one attempts to explain the peaceful transformation of the Cold War into a "long peace," one should pay tribute to the fact that President Eisenhower and President Kennedy proved capable of nuclear learning. Both Eisenhower's and Kennedy's nuclear choices contributed to the enhanced stability of the international system of the 1960s.

While the lesson to be drawn from the evolution of American policy on nuclear weapons is essentially a positive one—since its shows that nuclear learning is possible—it should not be overlooked that the nuclear peace of the 1950s and 1960s might have been less stable than is generally assumed. These observations are relevant for today's security debate, which is characterized by considerable nostalgia for the stability and simplicity of the strategic environment of the Cold War days. If the post–Cold War era is a time of transition and fluidity, so too the 1950s and the early 1960s witnessed fundamental changes in the security environment. It is important that our discussions of the future role of the "absolute weapon" in a changing international system are not guided by false historical premises. Enhanced recognition of the historical complexities, puzzles, and contradictions in our thinking about the military and political role of nuclear weapons will provide a more appropriate basis for debating the future.

Notes

Introduction

1. The term "long peace" was coined by John Lewis Gaddis, "The Long Peace: Elements of Stability in the Postwar International System," *International Security* 10, No. 4 (Spring 1986): 99–142; John Lewis Gaddis, *The Long Peace: Inquiries into the History of the Cold War* (New York: Oxford University Press, 1987). The general idea that nuclear weapons imposed peace has been advanced by many scholars, although with varying emphasis: McGeorge Bundy, *Danger and Survival: Choices about the Bomb in the First Fifty Years* (New York: Vintage Books, 1988); Robert Jervis, *The Meaning of the Nuclear Revolution: Statecraft and the Prospect of Armageddon* (Ithaca, N.Y.: Cornell University Press, 1989); Joseph S. Nye, "Nuclear Learning and U.S.-Soviet Security Regimes," *International Organization* 41 (Summer 1987): 371–402; Michael Mandelbaum, *The Nuclear Revolution: International Politics before and after Hiroshima* (New York: Cambridge University Press, 1981); Kenneth Waltz, "The Spread of Nuclear Weapons: More May Be Better," *Adelphi Papers* 171 (London: The International Institute for Strategic Studies, 1981); Robert Gilpin, *War and Change in World Politics* (New York: Cambridge University Press, 1981).

2. John Mueller, *Retreat from Doomsday: The Obsolescence of Major War* (New York: Basic Books, 1989); John Mueller, "The Essential Irrelevance of Nuclear Weapons: Stability in the Postwar World," *International Security* 13, No. 2 (Fall 1988): 55–79.

3. For an interesting critique of Mueller's argument: Carl Kaysen, "Is War Obsolete? A Review Essay," *International Security* 14, No. 4 (Spring 1990): 42–64; John Lewis Gaddis, "Nuclear Weapons, the End of the Cold War, and the Future of the International System," in *Nuclear Weapons in the Changing World*, ed. Patrick J. Garrity and Steven A. Maaranen (New York: Plenum Press, 1992), 15–31.

4. Bernard Brodie, *The Absolute Weapon: Atomic Power and World Order* (New York: Harcourt, Brace & Company, 1946); Bernard Brodie, *Strategy in the Missile Age* (Princeton: Princeton University Press, 1959).

5. William Liscum Borden, *There Will Be No Time* (New York: Macmillan, 1946). The enduring influence of these two streams of thought through the Cold War is documented by Steven Kull, *Minds at War: Nuclear Reality and the Inner Conflicts of Defense Policymakers* (New York: Basic Books, 1988), 3–16.

6. In the late fifties and the early sixties, when a situation of mutual deterrence was evolving, the ideas of three scholars heavily influenced strategic thought in the West. Albert Wohlstetter's distinction between first- and second-strike capabilities, Glenn Snyder's treatise of the stability-instability paradox, and Thomas Schelling's discussion of "threats that leave something to chance" and the "reciprocal fear of surprise attack" proved to be of lasting significance. Albert Wohlstetter, "The Delicate Balance of Terror," *Foreign Affairs* 37, No. 3 (January 1959): 211–34; Glenn Snyder, "The Balance of Power and the Balance of Terror," in *The Balance of Power*, ed. Paul Seabury (San Francisco: Chandler, 1965), 184–201; Thomas Schelling, *The Strategy of Conflict* (Cambridge: Harvard University Press, 1960); Thomas Schelling, *Arms and Influence* (New Haven: Yale University Press, 1966).

7. Graham T. Allison, *Essence of Decision: Explaining the Cuban Missile Crisis* (Boston: Little, Brown & Company, 1971); Morton H. Halperin, *Bureaucratic Politics and Foreign Policy* (Washington, D.C.: The Brookings Institution, 1974); John D. Steinbruner, *The Cybernetic Theory of Decision: New Dimensions of Political Analysis* (Princeton: Princeton University Press, 1974).

8. Regarding psychological factors: Robert Jervis, *The Logic of Images in International Relations* (Princeton: Princeton University Press, 1970); Robert Jervis, *Perceptions and Misperceptions in International Politics* (Princeton: Princeton University Press, 1976); Robert Jervis, *The Illogic of American Nuclear Strategy* (Ithaca, N.Y.: Cornell University Press, 1984); Robert Jervis, Richard Ned Lebow, and Janice Gross Stein, *Psychology and Deterrence* (Baltimore: Johns Hopkins University Press, 1985); James G. Blight, "The New Psychology of War and Peace," *International Security* 11, No. 3 (Winter 1986–87): 175–86; Ole Holsti and Alexander George, "The Effects of Stress on the Performance of Foreign Policy-makers," in *Political Science Annual* 6 (1975), ed. Cornelius Cotter (Indianapolis: Bobbs-Merrill, 1975); Robert Axelrod, *The Evolution of Cooperation* (New York: Basic Books, 1984). Alexander George and Richard Smoke were among the first to call for more empirical writing: Alexander George and Richard Smoke, *Deterrence in American Foreign Policy: Theory and Practice* (New York: Columbia University Press, 1974).

9. Kull, *Minds at War.*

10. This argument was most clearly spelled out by Robert S. McNamara, "The Military Role of Nuclear Weapons: Perceptions and Misperceptions," *Foreign Affairs* 62, No. 1 (Fall 1983): 59–81.

11. This line of argument is often identified with statements of former members of the Kennedy administration with respect to the Cuban missile crisis: Dean Rusk, Robert McNamara, George W. Ball, Roswell L. Gilpatric, Theodore Sorensen, and McGeorge Bundy, "The Lessons of the Cuban Missile Crisis,"

Time, 27 September 1982, 85–86; Maxwell D. Taylor, "The Legitimate Claims of National Security," *Foreign Affairs* 52, No. 3 (April 1974): 577–94.

12. For an argument in this vein: Colin S. Gray, "Nuclear Strategy: The Case for a Theory of Victory," *International Security* 4, No. 1 (Summer 1970): 54–87.

13. The concept of existential deterrence is best explained by Bundy, *Danger and Survival.*

14. This stream of thought goes back to the works of Schelling, *The Strategy of Conflict* and *Arms and Influence.*

15. While several generations of political scientists have considered the role of nuclear weapons in international politics, only recently have historians, most notably John Lewis Gaddis and Marc Trachtenberg, turned to this issue. However, it is still not very clear how the theoretical and historical fields relate to each other. For a good outline of how historical analyses could make a distinctive contribution to the field of strategic studies see: Marc Trachtenberg, *History and Strategy* (Princeton: Princeton University Press, 1991), 261–86. For another view regarding relations between the two fields: John Lewis Gaddis, "Expanding the Data Base: Historians, Political Scientists, and the Enrichment of Security Studies," *International Security* 12, No. 1 (Summer 1987): 3–21; for a more provocative development of the same topic: John Lewis Gaddis, "International Relations Theory and the End of the Cold War," *International Security* 17, No. 3 (Winter 1992–93): 5–58. See also: Lynn Eden, "The End of U.S. Cold War History? A Review Essay," *International Security* 18, No. 1 (Summer 1993): 174–207.

16. This emphasis means that the middle years of the decade are not covered to the same degree as Eisenhower's first and last years in office. It means in particular that this book does not analyze the two Taiwan Strait crises of 1954–55 and 1958, which would provide interesting case studies for the impact of nuclear weapons in crises of limited scope.

17. See his writings as cited in notes 1, 3, and 5. John Lewis Gaddis's earlier study, *Strategies of Containment: A Critical Appraisal of Postwar American National Security Policy* (New York: Oxford University Press, 1982), showed that Eisenhower's New Look comprised more than the military dimension of massive retaliation, pointing in particular to Eisenhower's emphasis on the mutual dependency of security and solvency.

18. Bundy, *Danger and Survival.* In contrast, this study elaborates the different directions, some of them rather destabilizing, in which mutual vulnerability led the debate over the political and military role of nuclear weapons in the fifties and the sixties. I will stress in particular that both the stabilizing and destabilizing effects of nuclear weapons were most apparent in the context of alliance politics. It was primarily the need to reassure the Europeans that prevented the central lessons of the nuclear revolution—as outlined by Bundy—from taking hold much earlier and at a lower level of nuclear armaments.

19. Trachtenberg, *History and Strategy.* See in particular chapter 3, "A 'Wasting Asset': American Strategy and the Shifting Nuclear Balance, 1949–1954," chapter 4, "The Nuclearization of NATO and U.S.-West European Relations," and chapter 5, "The Berlin Crisis."

20. Fred I. Greenstein, "Eisenhower As an Activist President: A New Look at the Evidence," *Political Science Quarterly* 94 (Winter 1979–1980): 575–99; Fred I. Greenstein, *The Hidden-Hand Presidency: Eisenhower As Leader* (New York: Basic Books, 1982). The reassessment of Eisenhower also has influenced historians' views of John Foster Dulles's role during the Eisenhower presidency. Although some observers have concluded that the rise of Eisenhower devalued the importance of Dulles's diplomacy, I prefer the judgment of Richard Immerman, who describes Eisenhower and Dulles as a team, emphasizing consultation and interchange between the president and his secretary of state. See Richard H. Immerman, ed., *John Foster Dulles and the Diplomacy of the Cold War* (Princeton: Princeton University Press, 1990).

21. Richard H. Immerman, "Confessions of an Eisenhower Revisionist: An Agonizing Reappraisal," *Diplomatic History* 14, No. 3 (Summer 1990): 319–42, 325.

22. David Alan Rosenberg, "The Origins of Overkill: Nuclear Weapons and American Strategy, 1945–1960," *International Security* 7, No. 4 (Spring 1983): 3–71. In successive articles, Rosenberg stressed that nuclear weapons policy is as much a result of a governmental process as an intellectual exercise. He noted that the gap between theory and practice, declaratory and operational policy is an inherent feature of the structure of U.S. nuclear strategy. See David Alan Rosenberg, "Reality and Responsibility: Power and Process in Making of United States Nuclear Strategy, 1945–1968," *The Journal of Strategic Studies* 9, No. 1 (March 1986): 35–52; David Alan Rosenberg, "U.S. Nuclear Strategy: Theory vs. Practice," *Bulletin of the Atomic Scientists* 43, No. 2 (March 1987): 20–26.

23. Arthur M. Schlesinger, Jr., *A Thousand Days: John F. Kennedy in the White House* (Cambridge: The Riverside Press, 1965); Theodore C. Sorensen, *Kennedy* (London: Pan Books Ltd., 1965).

24. Michael R. Beschloss, *The Crisis Years: Kennedy and Khrushchev, 1961–1963* (New York: HarperCollins Publishers, 1991). For an excellent review of Beschloss's book, setting it apart in quality compared to other recently published biographies of John F. Kennedy, see Fred I. Greenstein, "Coming to Terms with Kennedy," *Reviews in American History* 20 (1992): 96–104.

25. Desmond Ball, *Politics and Force Levels: The Strategic Missile Program of the Kennedy Administration* (Berkeley: University of California Press, 1980). Still valuable as well is Fred Kaplan, *The Wizards of Armageddon* (New York: Simon & Schuster, 1983).

26. Jane E. Stromseth, *The Origins of Flexible Response: NATO's Debate over Strategy in the 1960s* (New York: St. Martin's Press, 1988). The early debate within NATO, leading the alliance to "nuclear dependency" during the 1950s, has been researched and documented extensively by Robert Wampler. See Robert Allen Wampler, *Ambiguous Legacy: The United States, Great Britain and the Foundations of NATO Strategy, 1948–1957*, Ph.D. diss. (Ann Arbor, Mich.: University Microfilms, 1991).

27. John D. Steinbruner, *The Cybernetic Theory of Decision.*

28. Catherine McArdle Kelleher, *Germany and the Politics of Nuclear Weapons* (New York: Columbia University Press, 1975).

29. The archival sources and the published sources are listed in the bibliography (including their abbreviations).

30. Wampler provides an excellent overview of U.S. sources regarding nuclear weapons and NATO. See Robert A. Wampler, *Nuclear Weapons and the Atlantic Alliance: A Guide to U.S. Sources.* Produced for the Nuclear History Program (College Park, Md.: Center for International Studies, 1989). For another valuable overview of the sources for the Eisenhower years see Roger M. Anders, "Essay on Sources," in *Atoms for Peace and War, 1953–1961,* ed. Richard G. Hewlett and Jack M. Holl (Berkeley: University of California Press, 1989), 657–74.

Chapter 1

1. NSC 162/2, "Basic National Security Policy," 30 October 1953, FRUS, 1952–1954, 2: 577–97, 593.

2. David Alan Rosenberg's excellent account of the origins of nuclear war planning during the Truman and Eisenhower years is by far the best available, see Rosenberg, "The Origins of Overkill," 3–71.

3. David Alan Rosenberg, "U.S. Nuclear Stockpile, 1945–1960," *Bulletin of the Atomic Scientists* 38, No. 3 (May 1982): 25–30.

4. This decision was stated in NSC 30, "United States Policy on Atomic Warfare," FRUS, 1948, 1: 624–28.

5. For an excellent assessment of President Truman's position with regard to nuclear weapons, see Bundy, *Danger and Survival,* 197–235.

6. NSC 68 was drafted mainly by Paul H. Nitze, director of the Policy Planning Staff under Truman. The paper was a comprehensive analysis of American national security policy in light of the development of the hydrogen bomb. NSC 68 became the basis of the American strategy of containment of the Sino-Soviet bloc, and its basic assumptions remained valid for the next forty years. The document is printed in FRUS, 1950, 1: 234–92. For a good analysis see Samuel F. Wells, Jr., "Sounding the Tocsin: NSC-68 and the Soviet Threat," *International Security* 4, No. 2 (Fall 1979): 116–58; Steven L. Rearden, *The Evolution of American Strategic Doctrine: Paul H. Nitze and the Soviet Challenge* (Boulder: Westview Press, 1984); John Lewis Gaddis and Paul H. Nitze, "NSC-68 and the Soviet Threat Reconsidered," *International Security* 4, No. 1 (Spring 1980): 164–76.

7. For the reasons that Eisenhower allowed his name to be placed before the Republican national convention, see Dwight D. Eisenhower, *The White House Years: Mandate for Change, 1953–1956* (New York: Doubleday & Company, 1963), 13–22.

8. Ralph B. Levering, *The Public and American Foreign Policy, 1918–1978* (New York: Morrow, 1978), 102. Against this background, Eisenhower's promise to go to the battlefield proved to be one of the most valuable moves of his campaign.

Robert A. Divine, *Foreign Policy and U.S. Presidential Elections, 1952–1960* (New York: New Viewpoints, 1974), 84–85.

9. Several authors have emphasized that Eisenhower had strong beliefs with regard to questions of national security strategy before entering the presidential campaign. See Glenn H. Snyder, "The 'New Look' of 1953," in *Strategy, Politics, and Defense Budgets,* ed. Warner R. Schilling, Paul Y. Hammond, and Glenn H. Snyder (New York: Columbia University Press, 1966), 379–525, 516–22; Gaddis, *Strategies of Containment,* 127–45; Immerman, "Confessions of an Eisenhower Revisionist," 327.

10. Eisenhower in an election speech on 25 September 1952, *New York Times,* 26 September 1952.

11. Eisenhower, Annual Message to the Congress on the State of the Union, 2 February 1953, Eisenhower PPS, 1953, 12–34.

12. NSC 149/2, "Basic National Security Policies in Relation to Their Costs," 29 April 1953, FRUS, 1952–1954, 2 (part 1): 305–10. Eisenhower explained this concept to the press on 30 April 1953: "The essence of the change is this: We reject the idea that we must build up to a maximum attainable strength for some specific date theoretically fixed for a specified time in the future. Defense is not a matter of maximum strength for a single date. It is a matter of adequate protection to be projected as far into the future as the action and apparent purposes of others may compel us" (Eisenhower, The President's News Conference, 30 April 1953, Eisenhower PPS, 1953, 242).

13. Both Kaplan and Freedman have stressed the influence of the Korean War on the formulation of a new national security strategy. See Kaplan, *The Wizards of Armageddon,* 177–81; Lawrence Freedman, *The Evolution of Nuclear Strategy* (New York: St. Martin's Press, 1981), 90.

14. John Foster Dulles, "A Policy of Boldness," *Life* 32, 19 May 1952, 146–60.

15. Gaddis, *Strategies of Containment,* 128–29; Harold Stassen and Marshall Houts, *Eisenhower: Turning the World toward Peace* (St. Paul: Merrill/Magnus Publishing Corporation, 1990), 48.

16. All quotations from: Memorandum of NSC meeting, 25 March 1953, FRUS, 1952–1954, 2 (part 1): 260–62. See also Memorandum of NSC meeting, 11 February 1953, ibid., 236; Memorandum of NSC meeting, 31 March 1953, ibid., 265.

17. NSC 20/4, "U.S. Objectives with Respect to the USSR to Counter Soviet Threats to U.S. Security," 23 November 1948, FRUS, 1948, 1 (part 2): 662.

18. The development of the hydrogen bomb was a highly controversial issue within the United States. George F. Kennan, Robert Oppenheimer, and David E. Lilienthal (the last two of whom were members of the Atomic Energy Commission) described the thermonuclear bomb as a weapon of genocide. Such a weapon was, in their view, not consistent with traditional moral and ethical values of their country, especially if the United States did not follow a no-first-use policy. But these concerns failed to convince the Truman administration: First, the hydrogen bomb was technologically feasible. Second, the Soviets, so the ar-

gument ran, would not be restrained in their hydrogen bomb development program by ethical reservations. Third, with the increasing tensions in East-West relations, the hope for a solution to the problem through arms control was quickly fading. See Richard G. Hewlett and Francis Duncan, *Atomic Shield, 1947–1952*, vol. 2, A History of the U.S. Atomic Energy Commission (University Park: Pennsylvania State University Press, 1969), 378–94; David E. Lilienthal, *The Atomic Energy Years, 1945–1950*, vol. 2, The Journals of David E. Lilienthal (New York: Harper & Row, 1964); David Alan Rosenberg, "American Atomic Strategy and the Hydrogen Bomb Decision," *Journal of American History* 66 (June 1979): 62–78.

19. NSC 68, "United States Objectives and Programs for National Security," 14 April 1950, FRUS, 1950, 1: 234–92.

20. Wells, "Sounding the Tocsin," 139.

21. Memorandum, Executive Secretary of the Policy Planning Staff to the Counselor, 12 May 1952, FRUS, 1952–1954, 2 (part 1): 12–17. Schwartz, the executive secretary, presented the fundamental question very clearly. It was his personal judgment that the Soviet Union could and would be deterred even after achieving such a capacity. He pointed to the fact that the Soviets could not wage general war without serious risk to their own regime. Moreover, he perceived that the Russians preferred risk-averse courses of action.

22. All quotations from Memorandum, Paul H. Nitze to the Secretary of State, 12 January 1953, FRUS, 1952–1954, 2 (part 1): 202–5.

23. Memorandum, Nitze to the Deputy Undersecretary of State, 14 July 1952, FRUS, 1952–1954, 2 (part 1): 58–59.

24. Memorandum of NSC meeting, 11 February 1953, FRUS, 1952–1954, 2 (part 1): 236. NSC 141 dealt with the question of whether the allocation of resources under the existing programs was appropriate to the perceived threat and the outlined strategy. For a broader statement of the U.S. position in the world, the threat in the period ahead, and the basic strategy, see NSC 135/3, "Reappraisal of U.S. Objectives and Strategy for National Security," 25 September 1952, FRUS, 1952–1954, 2 (part 1): 142–56.

25. NSC 141, "Reexamination of United States Programs for National Security," 19 January 1953, FRUS, 1952–1954, 2 (part 1): 209–22. For the summary that was presented to the incoming Eisenhower administration: Memorandum to the NSC by the Executive Secretary, 9 February 1953, FRUS, 1952–1954, 2 (part 1): 228–30.

26. Douglas Kinnard, *President Eisenhower and Strategy Management: A Study in Defense Politics* (Lexington: University of Kentucky Press, 1977), 7.

27. The consultants included Dillon Anderson, James B. Black, John Cowles, Eugene Holman, Deane W. Mallott, David B. Robertson, and Charles A. Thomas. See editorial note, FRUS, 1952–1954, 2 (part 1): 244.

28. All quotations from: Memorandum of NSC meeting, 31 March 1953, FRUS, 1952–1954, 2 (part 1): 264–81.

29. NSC 149/2, "Basic National Security Policies in Relation to Their Costs," 29 April 1953, FRUS, 1952–1954, 2 (part 1): 305–16.

30. Memorandum of NSC meeting, 8 April 1953, FRUS, 1952–1954, 2 (part 1): 287–90. For Dodge's insistence see Memorandum of NSC meeting, 22 April 1953, FRUS, 1952–1954, 2 (part 1): 291–301.

31. Memorandum of NSC meeting, 31 March 1953, FRUS, 1952–1954, 2 (part 1): 273.

32. Memorandum of NSC meeting, 25 March 1953, FRUS, 1952–1954, 2 (part 1): 260.

33. Memorandum of NSC meeting, 31 March 1953, FRUS, 1952–1954, 2 (part 1): 273.

34. Memorandum of NSC meeting, 22 April 1953, FRUS, 1952–1954, 2 (part 1): 298.

35. Memorandum of NSC meeting, 31 March 1953, FRUS, 1952–1954, 2 (part 1): 278.

36. NSC 149/2, "Basic National Security Policies in Relation to Their Costs," 29 April 1953, FRUS, 1952–1954, 2 (part 1): 312–15.

37. Memorandum of NSC meeting, 31 March 1953, FRUS, 1952–1954, 2 (part 1): 269–71; see further: Draft Memorandum Prepared for the NSC, n.d., ibid., 282.

38. NSC 149/2, "Basic National Security Policies in Relation to Their Costs," 29 April 1953, FRUS, 1952–1954, 2 (part 1): 305–16. NSC 149/2 was approved by the NSC on 28 April 1953.

39. Quoted in Thomas Peter, *Abschrecken und Ueberleben im Nuklearzeitalter: Präsident Eisenhowers Sicherheitspolitik des "New Look,"* Ph.D. diss. (Grüsch: Verlag Rüegger, 1990), 79. See editorial note, FRUS, 1952–1954, 2 (part 1): 316–17.

40. Memorandum by Paul H. Nitze and Carlton Savage of the Policy Planning Staff, 6 May 1953, FRUS, 1952–1954, 2 (part 1): 318–23.

41. All quotations from NSC 153/2, "Restatement of Basic National Security Policy," 10 June 1953, FRUS, 1952–1954, 2 (part 1): 378–86.

42. For an excellent account of Project Solarium that analyzes the three final task force reports in considerable detail, see Peter, *Abschrecken und Ueberleben*, 84–111. For an earlier attempt that mainly draws on interviews for lack of access to the final reports (declassified between 1984 and 1987), see Snyder, "The 'New Look' of 1953," 379–525. See also, Robert J. Watson, *The Joint Chiefs of Staff and National Policy, 1953–1954*, vol. 5, History of the Joint Chiefs of Staff (Washington, D.C.: Historical Division, Joint Chiefs of Staff, 1986), 11–14; Gaddis, *Strategies of Containment*, 145–46.

43. Robert Cutler, *No Time for Rest* (Boston: Little, Brown & Company, 1966), 307–8.

44. Memorandum, "Solarium Project," 8 May 1953. I thank Jennifer L. Ottavinia for providing me with a copy of the memorandum.

45. All quotations from Memorandum, "Solarium Project," 8 May 1953. In his account of the meeting, Snyder has overlooked the fact that Dulles was present. See Snyder, "The 'New Look' of 1953," 407.

46. In an interview in 1988, George Kennan, the chairman of one of the

three task forces, recalled the high secrecy of the project. See John Foster Dulles Centennial Conference, " 'Project Solarium': A Collective Oral History," 27 February 1988, 3. For the project's organization: Memorandum for the Record by the Special Assistant to the President for National Security Affairs, 9 May 1953, FRUS, 1952–1954, 2 (part 1): 323–26.

47. General Doolittle was retired; at this time, he was vice president of Shell Corporation. See Peter, *Abschrecken und Ueberleben*, 86.

48. The four colleagues were Robert Amory, Jr., Lt. General L. L. Lemnitzer, Dean Rusk, and Admiral Leslie C. Stevens. See Memorandum for the Record by the Special Assistant to the President for National Security Affairs, 15 May 1953, FRUS, 1952–1954, 2 (part 1): 327–28. The panel formulated the guidelines in close cooperation with the task forces themselves, which had already been formed. The task forces were simultaneously briefed on intelligence and background materials. See Memorandum by the President to the Secretary of State, 20 May 1953, FRUS, 1952–1954, 2 (part 1): 353. It remains unclear from the documentation in the FRUS what role John Foster Dulles played in further preparation of the project. A letter from the president proves that he was at least participating in the organization of the project. See Memorandum by the President to the Secretary of State, 20 May 1953, FRUS, 1952–1954, 2 (part 1): 349–54. But General Andrew Goodpaster, a member of task force "C," suggests that Dulles played a much more active role. According to Goodpaster, Dulles discussed directly with the task forces "some of the questions that he had in mind such as the background of the study, the kind of assumptions that we shared, and the ultimate purpose of the safeguarding of our security. . . . On that premise, what would be the best route to try to pursue this?" (*"Project Solarium": A Collective Oral History*, 11–12).

49. Memorandum for the Record by the Special Assistant to the President for National Security Affairs, 9 May 1953, FRUS, 1952–1954, 2 (part 1): 325–26.

50. For the precise wording of the four rejected courses: Paper Prepared by the Directing Panel of Project Solarium, 1 June 1953, FRUS, 1952–1954, 2 (part 1): 361–62. See also, Snyder, "The 'New Look' of 1953," 409.

51. Paper Prepared by the Directing Panel of Project Solarium, 1 June 1953, FRUS, 1952–1954, 2 (part 1): 362–64.

52. For Kennan's outline of containment see [George F. Kennan], "The Sources of Soviet Conduct," *Foreign Affairs* 25, No. 4 (July 1947): 566–82. The assignment as chairman of task force "A" gave Kennan a certain satisfaction. He recalled that during the presentation of the final reports before the NSC, he "could talk, and he [Secretary Dulles] had to listen" (*"Project Solarium": A Collective Oral History*, 5–6).

53. Paper Presented by the Directing Panel of Project Solarium, 1 June 1953, FRUS, 1952–1954, 2 (part 1): 365–66.

54. Memorandum to the NSC by the Executive Secretary, 22 July 1953, FRUS, 1952–1954, 2 (part 1): 400.

55. Task force "A" was the only group emphasizing the death of Stalin as a

sign of Soviet weakness. See Report of Task Force "A," OSANSA, NSC, S, Folder "Project Solarium" Task Force A (3) to (7), Box 9, DDEL, 11.

56. Memorandum to the NSC by the Executive Secretary, 22 July 1953, FRUS, 1952–1954, 2 (part 1): 400. See Notes Taken at the First Plenary Session of Project Solarium, 26 June 1953, FRUS, 1952–1954, 2 (part 1): 388–89.

57. All quotations from Memorandum to the NSC by the Executive Secretary, 22 July 1953, FRUS, 1952–1954, 2 (part 1): 400–11. In this connection Kennan's group was against a fixed defense budget: "Task force 'A' considers that absolute dollar costs are neither comprehensible to the average American nor a proper yardstick for estimating the capabilities of our economy over the long-term. The costs of military power, like power itself, are relative matters, in this case relative to the threat it meets and to the gross national product, and should be viewed as such" (Report of Task Force "A," OSANSA, NSC, S, Folder "Project Solarium" Task Force A [3] to [7], Box 9, DDEL, 42).

58. All quotations from Memorandum to the NSC by the Executive Secretary, 22 July 1953, FRUS, 1952–1954, 2 (part 1): 413. For a discussion of the differences between task force "A" and task force "B," see Notes Taken at the First Plenary Session of Project Solarium, 26 June 1953, FRUS, 1952–1954, 2 (part 1): 391.

59. Notes Taken at the First Plenary Session of Project Solarium, 26 June 1953, FRUS, 1952–1954, 2 (part 1): 391.

60. Both quotations: Memorandum to the NSC by the Executive Secretary, 22 July 1953, FRUS, 1952–1954, 2 (part 1): 415.

61. Report of Task Force "C," OSANSA, NSC, S, 16 July 1953, Folder "Project Solarium Task Force C," Box 9, DDEL, 13.

62. All quotations from Memorandum to the NSC by the Executive Secretary, 22 July 1953, FRUS, 1952–1954, 2 (part 1): 417–30.

63. Notes Taken at the First Plenary Session of Project Solarium, 26 June 1953, FRUS, 1952–1954, 2 (part 1): 392. Task force "C" attempted to exploit the principle that "nothing succeeds like success" (Memorandum to the NSC by the Executive Secretary, 22 July 1953, FRUS, 1952–1954, 2 [part 1]: 418).

64. All three quotations from Memorandum to the NSC by the Executive Secretary, 22 July 1953, FRUS, 1952–1954, 2 (part 1): 434. For a CIA study as to whether time was on the side of the U.S.: Memorandum of NSC meeting, 30 July 1953, FRUS, 1952–1954, 2 (part 1): 436.

65. Memorandum to the NSC by the Executive Secretary, 22 July 1953, FRUS, 1952–1954, 2 (part 1): 434.

66. According to General Goodpaster it was characteristic for President Eisenhower to use the opportunity to bring the bureaucracies in line with his own thinking: "The President would come to a line of action, he wanted everybody to hear it, everybody to participate in it, and then he wanted everybody to be guided by it" (*"Project Solarium": A Collective Oral History*, 20). Building on such statements, Richard Immerman has asserted that "the Solarium exercise was fundamentally an extension of Eisenhower's beliefs as well as his leadership."

Admitting that there is so far little documentary evidence to substantiate such an argument, he declares that Eisenhower "stacked the deck so that Solarium would produce the results he desired" (Immerman, "Confessions of an Eisenhower Revisionist," 337).

67. *"Project Solarium": A Collective Oral History*, 7. General Goodpaster agreed with this assessment of the president's summation (Ibid., 12).

68. Memorandum by the Special Assistant to the President for National Security Affairs, 16 July 1953, FRUS, 1952–1954, 2 (part 1): 397.

69. The new director of the Policy Planning Staff, Robert Bowie, at least seems to have made such an interpretation. See *"Project Solarium": A Collective Oral History*, 22.

70. For this claim, see Andrew Goodpaster, "Presidential Transitions and Foreign Policy: Eisenhower and Kennedy," in *Papers on Presidential Transitions and Foreign Policy*, vol. 5, Reflections of Five Public Officials, ed. Kenneth W. Thompson (Lanham, Md.: University Press of America, 1987), 15–34, 26. Immerman notes that the president by insisting on Goodpaster's membership in task force "C" ensured "that its conclusions be within the bounds of prudence" (Immerman, "Confessions of an Eisenhower Revisionist," 339; also, *"Project Solarium": A Collective Oral History*, 13, 22).

71. Memorandum by the Special Assistant to the President for National Security Affairs, 16 July 1953, FRUS, 1952–1954, 2 (part 1): 397.

72. Moreover, all of the participants were tired, and some of them had other commitments. See Memorandum by the Special Assistant to the President for National Security Affairs, 16 July 1953, FRUS, 1952–1954, 2 (part 1): 398; see also, *"Project Solarium": A Collective Oral History*, 13–14.

73. Memorandum by the Special Assistant to the President for National Security Affairs, 16 July 1953, FRUS, 1952–1954, 2 (part 1): 398.

74. All quotations from Memorandum by the Special Assistant to the President for National Security Affairs, 31 July 1953, FRUS, 1952–1954, 2 (part 1): 440–41.

75. Memorandum of NSC meeting, 30 July 1953, FRUS, 1952–1954, 2 (part 1): 438.

76. Snyder indicates that Senator Taft played an important role in bringing about the appointment of the new chiefs. Radford shared a close relationship with Senator Taft. Both held the view that greater emphasis should be put on Asia (as opposed to Europe) and on the use of sea and air forces. See Snyder, "The 'New Look' of 1953," 410–12; Watson, *The Joint Chiefs of Staff and National Policy*, 14–15.

77. There was one exception: General Twining succeeded General Vandenberg on 30 June. See editorial note, FRUS, 1952–1954, 2 (part 1): 326–27.

78. Editorial note, FRUS, 1952–1954, 2 (part 1): 394. See also Matthew B. Ridgway, *Soldier: The Memoirs of Matthew B. Ridgway* (New York: Harper, 1956), 266–67.

79. Dwight D. Eisenhower, Memorandum for the Secretary of Defense, 1 July 1953, AWF, A, Folder "Joint Chiefs of Staff," Box 23, DDEL.

80. Memorandum by the JCS to the Secretary of Defense, 8 August 1953 (I thank Marc Trachtenberg for supplying me with a copy of this document). Admiral Radford underlined the increasing nuclear threat in his presentation before the NSC: "The atomic factor, however, now looms much larger, and the problem of continental defense is now much more important than it seemed in the summer of 1950" (Memorandum of NSC meeting, 27 August 1953, FRUS, 1952–1954, 2 [part 1]: 450).

81. Memorandum by the JCS to the Secretary of Defense, 8 August 1953.

82. The best analysis of the JCS's suggestions that I have seen is Watson, *The Joint Chiefs of Staff and National Policy*, 18–21. See also Snyder, "The 'New Look' of 1953," 414–15.

83. Memorandum of NSC meeting, 27 August 1953, FRUS, 1952–1954, 2 (part 1): 447.

84. Memorandum of NSC meeting, 27 August 1953, FRUS, 1952–1954, 2 (part 1): 443–45. The memorandum by the JCS did not make such a claim. See Memorandum by the JCS to the Secretary of Defense, 8 August 1953.

85. Deputy Secretary of Defense Kyes thought the report was "an historic event." All quotations from Memorandum of NSC meeting, 27 August 1953, FRUS, 1952–1954, 2 (part 1): 443–55.

86. General Twining, on the other hand, denied that he would have expressed different views absent the budget problem. See Memorandum of NSC meeting, 27 August 1953, FRUS, 1952–1954, 2 (part 1): 448.

87. Memorandum of NSC meeting, 27 August 1953, FRUS, 1952–1954, 2 (part 1): 447.

88. Memorandum of NSC meeting, 27 August 1953, FRUS, 1952–1954, 2 (part 1): 453. For recognition of European fear of U.S. isolationism, see Memorandum from Dulles to Eisenhower, 23 July 1953, WHMS, "White House Correspondence, 1953 [3]," DPEL.

89. All quotations from Memorandum of NSC meeting, 27 August 1953, FRUS, 1952–1954, 2 (part 1): 443–55.

90. Memorandum, JCS to the Secretary of Defense, 8 August 1953.

91. All quotations from Memorandum, Cutler to the Secretary of State, 3 September 1953, FRUS, 1952–1954, 2 (part 1): 455–57.

92. Memorandum, Cutler to the Secretary of State, 3 September 1953, FRUS, 1952–1954, 2 (part 1): 455–57.

93. John Lewis Gaddis, "The Unexpected John Foster Dulles: Nuclear Weapons, Communism, and the Russians," in *John Foster Dulles and the Diplomacy of the Cold War*, ed. Richard H. Immerman (Princeton: Princeton University Press, 1990), 47–77. For Dulles revisionism, see Immerman, *John Foster Dulles and the Diplomacy of the Cold War;* Ronald W. Pruessen, *John Foster Dulles: The Road to Power* (New York: Free Press, 1982).

94. Memorandum of NSC meeting, 27 August 1953, FRUS, 1952–1954, 2 (part 1): 446.

95. All quotations from Memorandum by Dulles, 6 September 1953, WHMS,

"White House Correspondence 1953 [2]," DPEL. For a broader analysis of the Korean War see chapter 2.

96. Memorandum from Eisenhower to Dulles, 8 September 1953, WHMS, "White House Correspondence, 1953 [2]," DPEL.

97. For a more detailed analysis of Project Candor and the "Atoms for Peace" speech, see chapter 3.

98. In the end, Secretary Dulles expressed reservations about his own idea. See Memorandum, Dulles to Eisenhower, 23 October 1953, FRUS, 1952–1954, 2 (part 2): 1234–35.

99. The representative of the Defense Department stated that "The long range effect of an offer of a settlement to withdraw would be to blow up NATO" (Memorandum of discussion at the Planning Board of the NSC, 19 October 1953, FRUS, 1952–1954, 2 [part 2]: 1229).

100. Memorandum of discussion at the Planning Board of the NSC, 19 October 1953, FRUS, 1952–1954, 2 (part 2): 1228.

101. All quotations from Memorandum, Eisenhower to Dulles, 8 September 1953, WHMS, "White House Correspondence, 1953 [2]," DPEL.

102. Memorandum, Eisenhower to Dulles, 8 September 1953, WHMS, "White House Correspondence, 1953 [2]," DPEL.

103. For the Eisenhower–Dulles partnership, see Immerman, *John Foster Dulles and the Diplomacy of the Cold War*, 3–20; Richard H. Immerman, "Eisenhower and Dulles: Who Made the Decisions?" *Political Psychology* 1 (Autumn 1979): 21–38; Ronald W. Pruessen, "John Foster Dulles and the Predicaments of Power," in *John Foster Dulles and the Diplomacy of the Cold War*, ed. Richard H. Immerman (Princeton: Princeton University Press, 1990), 21–46; Greenstein, *The Hidden-Hand Presidency*.

104. For the organizational details, see Editorial note, FRUS, 1952–1954, 2 (part 1): 463–64.

105. Robert Cutler summarized the opposing views in the following words: "Side "A" . . . sees the threat to the United States as the basic Soviet hostility to the United States and the Soviets' formidable military power. While acknowledging a sound U.S. economy is essential, Side "A" believes the United States *must* first meet necessary security costs. Side "B", on the other hand, sees the threat to the United States as a dual threat—the external threat of Soviet power; the internal threat of weakening our economy and changing our way of life. Side "B" believes the U.S. must strike a proper balance between the risks arising from these two threats" (Memorandum of NSC meeting, 7 October 1953, FRUS, 1952–1954, 2 [part 1]: 515).

106. NSC 162, "Review of Basic National Security Policy," 30 September 1953, FRUS, 1952–1954, 2 (part 1): 491, 503–5, 510–11.

107. Whereas the Treasury Department and the Budget Office called for progressive reductions of military aid for Europe, the rest of the administration thought that aid reduction should be tied to the ability of the European economies to assume this burden. See NSC 162, "Review of Basic National Security Policy," 30 September 1953, FRUS, 1952–1954, 2 (part 1): 507.

108. Robert Cutler had seen to it that the view of the JCS was integrated into the draft of the Planning Board. NSC 162, "Review of Basic National Security Policy," 30 September 1953, FRUS, 1952–1954, 2 (part 1): 508.

109. NSC 162, "Review of Basic National Security Policy," 30 September 1953, FRUS, 1952–1954, 2 (part 1): 491–93, 508–12.

110. Memorandum of NSC meeting, 7 October 1953, FRUS, 1952–1954, 2 (part 1): 515–21. According to the wording of NSC 162/2, it was the basic problem of national security "to meet the Soviet threat to U.S. security [and] . . . in doing so, to avoid seriously weakening the U.S. economy or undermining our fundamental values and institutions" (NSC 162/2, "Statement of Basic National Security Policy," 30 October 1953, FRUS, 1952–1954, 2 [part 1]: 578).

111. For the details of the discussion, see Memorandum of NSC meeting, 7 October 1953, FRUS, 1952–1954, 2 (part 1): 521–26. For the final version, see NSC 162/2, "Statement of Basic National Security Policy," 30 October 1953, FRUS, 1952–1954, 2 (part 1): 591, 593–94.

112. Both quotations from Memorandum of NSC meeting, 7 October 1953, FRUS, 1952–1954, 2 (part 1): 527–28.

113. All quotations from NSC 162/2, "Statement of Basic National Security Policy," 30 October 1953, FRUS, 1952–1954, 2 (part 1): 583–87.

114. Memorandum of NSC meeting, 7 October 1953, FRUS, 1952–1954, 2 (part 1): 527, 528–30. The NSC was sympathetic to redeployment of U.S. forces over the next few years. But it excluded such a statement from NSC 162/2 out of fear that its contents would be leaked to the allies and have unwarranted consequences.

115. NSC 162/2, "Statement of Basic National Security Policy," 30 October 1953, FRUS, 1952–1954, 2 (part 1): 594–95.

116. Memorandum of NSC meeting, 7 October 1953, FRUS, 1952–1954, 2 (part 1): 532. The president emphasized that "nothing would so upset the whole world as an announcement at this time by the United States of a decision to use these weapons."

117. Memorandum of NSC meeting, 7 October 1953, FRUS, 1952–1954, 2 (part 1): 533.

118. All quotations from Memorandum of NSC meeting, 13 October 1953, FRUS, 1952–1954, 2 (part 1): 542–47.

119. Both quotations from NSC 162/2, "Statement of Basic National Security Policy," 30 October 1953, FRUS, 1952–1954, 2 (part 1): 593.

120. See President Eisenhower's statement in the NSC meeting of 7 October, which had included such a connection.

121. NSC 162/2, "Statement of Basic National Security Policy," 30 October 1953, FRUS, 1952–1954, 2 (part 1): 593.

122. All quotations from Memorandum, Undersecretary of State to the President, 3 December 1953, FRUS, 1952–1954, 2 (part 1): 607–8.

123. On 11 March 1955, Eisenhower approved an interpretation of the original language of NSC 162/2 similar to the State Department interpretation. The

use of nuclear weapons would be automatic only in case of a Soviet nuclear attack on the United States or Western Europe. In cases of more limited aggression, the president would decide on a case-by-case basis. See Memorandum, James Lay to the Secretary of State and Others, "Policy Regarding Use of Nuclear Weapons," 14 March 1955, NPP 45–91, No. 00193, NSA.

124. Memorandum for the Record by the President, 11 November 1953, FRUS, 1952–1954, 2 (part 1): 597.

125. In the final defense budget, the army had to cut its manpower to 1,164,000 men on 30 June 1955 (despite its stated goal of growing to 1,500,000 men), the navy had to reduce its personnel from 740,600 to 688,900 men, whereas the air force increased in manpower from 955,000 to 970,000 during fiscal year 1955. All numbers from Snyder, "The 'New Look' of 1953," 448–60.

126. Memorandum of NSC meeting, 29 October 1953, FRUS, 1952–1954, 2 (part 1): 571, 572. He reminded the council that the original JCS report had had its roots in the financial guidelines set by the president. For an excellent account of differences within the JCS, see Watson, *The Joint Chiefs of Staff and National Policy*, 33–34.

127. All quotations from Memorandum of NSC meeting, 29 October 1953, FRUS, 1952–1954, 2 (part 1): 572–74.

128. NSC 162/2, "Statement of Basic National Security Policy," 30 October 1953, FRUS, 1952–1954, 2 (part 1): 595.

129. Savings were also facilitated by the more efficient use of defense resources and the end of the Korean War.

130. John Foster Dulles, "The Evolution of Foreign Policy," *Department of State Bulletin*, 25 January 1954, pp. 107–10.

131. For the origins and the evolution of John Foster Dulles's certainty/uncertainty principle, see Richard D. Challener, "John Foster Dulles: The Certainty/ Uncertainty Principle," *Zürcher Beiträge zur Sicherheitspolitik und Konfliktforschung* 10 (Zürich: Center for Security Studies, 1989).

132. At this point, one is very much reminded of the differences in approach between task forces "A" and "B" of Project Solarium. Whereas "A" started from the premise that the existing deterrent was enough, "B" wanted to create a further deterrent, because it perceived the Soviet Union as part of a wider Communist bloc and as a tougher aggressive menace than "A" did.

133. Dulles, "The Evolution of Foreign Policy," 108. The secretary of defense had used a comparable analogy during the NSC meeting of 27 August in order to show how to gain acceptance for the course suggested by the JCS among the people of the free world. Memorandum of NSC meeting, 27 August 1953, FRUS, 1952–1954, 2 (part 1): 453.

134. See for example, Memorandum of NSC meeting, 11 February 1953, FRUS, 1952–1954, 15 (part 1): 770.

135. Immerman, *John Foster Dulles and the Diplomacy of the Cold War*, 11.

136. John Foster Dulles, "Policy for Security and Peace," *Foreign Affairs* 32, No. 3 (April 1954): 353–64. For background, see Samuel F. Wells, "The Origins of

Massive Retaliation," *Political Science Quarterly* 96, No. 1 (Spring 1981): 31–52; Peter, *Abschrecken und Ueberleben*, 144–55.

Chapter 2

1. The rationale behind the strategy of massive retaliation was also criticized from outside the United States. See for example the writings of two British strategists, B. H. Liddell Hart, *The Revolution in Warfare* (New Haven: Yale University Press, 1946); B. H. Liddell Hart, *Deterrent or Defense: A Fresh Look at the West's Military Position* (New York: Praeger, 1960); P. M. S. Blackett, *Fear, War, and the Bomb: The Military and Political Consequences of Atomic Energy* (New York: Whittlesey House, McGraw–Hill Book Company, 1949).

2. Bernard Brodie, "Nuclear Weapons: Strategic or Tactical?" *Foreign Affairs* 32, No. 2 (January 1954): 217–28. See also, Carl von Clausewitz, *On War*, ed. and trans. by Michael Howard and Peter Paret (Princeton: Princeton University Press, 1976); Bernard Brodie, "Unlimited Weapons and Limited War," *The Reporter* 11, No. 9 (18 November 1954): 16–21.

3. Henry A. Kissinger, *Nuclear Weapons and Foreign Policy* (New York: Published for the Council on Foreign Relations by Harper & Brothers, 1957), 111.

4. William W. Kaufmann, "The Requirements of Deterrence," in *U.S. Nuclear Strategy: A Reader*, ed. Philip Bobbitt, Lawrence Freedman, and Gregory F. Treverton (London: Macmillan, 1989), 168–90.

5. William W. Kaufmann, "Limited Warfare," in *Military Policy and National Security*, ed. W. W. Kaufmann (Princeton: Princeton University Press, 1956), 118. See also: Robert E. Osgood, *Limited War: The Challenge to American Security* (Chicago: University of Chicago Press, 1957). Such a concept of warfare was particularly unfamiliar to Americans, who traditionally perceived a clear separation between peace and war. See Kurt R. Spillmann, *Aggressive USA? Amerikanische Sicherheitspolitik, 1945–1985* (Stuttgart: Klett–Cotta, 1985), 11–29.

6. Paul H. Nitze, "Atoms, Strategy and Policy," *Foreign Affairs* 34, No. 2 (January 1956): 187–98.

7. See for example, Memorandum of NSC meeting, 25 March 1954, FRUS, 1952–1954, 2 (part 1): 637–44.

8. NSC 162/2 called for the development and maintenance of a "mobilization base, and its protection against crippling damage, adequate to insure victory in the event of general war" (NSC 162/2, "Statement of Basic National Security Policy," 30 October 1953, FRUS, 1952–1954, 2 [part 1]: 582).

9. Memorandum, Cutler to the Secretary of State, 3 September 1953, FRUS, 1952–1954, 2 (part 1): 456.

10. Rosenberg, "The Origins of Overkill," 10.

11. For the origins of NATO defense strategy, see Trachtenberg, *History and Strategy*, 152–65. Trachtenberg describes General Eisenhower's view as a middle position between a peripheral strategy and a forward defense. Whereas the for-

mer wanted to withdraw from the Continent and rely primarily on air and naval power, the latter would defend Europe with forces in place as far to the east as possible.

12. "In the event of hostilities, the United States will consider nuclear weapons to be as available for use as other munitions" (NSC 162/2, "Statement of Basic National Security Policy," 30 October 1953, FRUS, 1952–1954, 2 [part 1]: 593).

13. JCS 2101/113, 10 December 1953, "CCS 381 U.S. (1-31-50) Sec. 31," JCS, NARS. For an excellent account and assessment of the developments within the Defense Department leading to JCS 2101/113, see Watson, *The Joint Chiefs of Staff and National Policy*, 26–32.

14. Quoted in Rosenberg, "The Origins of Overkill," 30.

15. For the army concept of warfare between 1949–1954, see Trachtenberg, *History and Strategy*, 156–59.

16. For the war plans of the SAC, see Rosenberg, "The Origins of Overkill," 28–38; Trachtenberg, *History and Strategy*, 134.

17. AWF, Legislative Meetings Series, 5 January 1954, "Legislative Meetings—1954 (1) (Jan.–Feb.)," DDEL.

18. Rosenberg, "The Origins of Overkill," 34.

19. Report of the Special Evaluation Subcommittee of the National Security Council, 15 May 1953, FRUS, 1952–1954, 2 (part 1): 334–39.

20. Memorandum of NSC meeting, 4 June 1953, FRUS, 1952–1954, 2 (part 1): 369.

21. Memorandum of NSC meeting, 4 March 1954, FRUS, 1952–1954, 2 (part 1): 636.

22. All quotations from Memorandum of NSC meeting, 25 March 1954, FRUS, 1952–1954, 2 (part 1): 637–44.

23. Memorandum of NSC meeting, 24 June 1954, FRUS, 1952–1954, 2 (part 1): 689. Secretary Dulles was also on record as indicating that he "was not at all sure that a future war, in which we were ranged against both the USSR and Communist China, would not last for even ten years" (Memorandum of NSC meeting, 19 November 1953, FRUS, 1952–1954, 2 [part 1]: 602).

24. NSC 162/2, "Statement of Basic National Security Policy," 30 October 1953, FRUS, 1952–1954, 2 (part 1): 582.

25. See President Eisenhower's remarks to congressional leaders in Notes by the Assistant Staff Secretary to the President on the Legislative Leadership Meeting, 14 December 1954, FRUS, 1952–1954, 2 (part 1): 824–27.

26. Report of the Special Evaluation Subcommittee of the National Security Council, 15 May 1953, FRUS, 1952–1954, 2 (part 1): 334.

27. Trachtenberg, *History and Strategy*, 100–15, 117. Trachtenberg gives an excellent account of preventive war thinking in the late forties and early fifties. Of special interest in this context is his conclusion that NSC 68 was not a defensive, status quo–oriented document. Concerns about the shifting balance, he argues, played a major role in shaping the policy outlined in the document.

28. See for example, Memorandum, Executive Secretary of the Policy Planning Staff (Schwartz) to the Counselor (Bohlen), 12 May 1952, FRUS, 1952–1954, 2 (part 1): 12–17.

29. American nuclear capabilities expanded from fifty bombs in 1948 to around three hundred bombs in 1950 and reached one thousand toward the end of 1953. See Rosenberg, "U.S. Nuclear Stockpile," 25–30. Moreover, nuclear weapons evolved not only in numbers but also in yield. For the qualitative improvement of U.S. nuclear weapons, see Rosenberg, "The Origins of Overkill," 23–25.

30. On that matter, see Curtis E. LeMay, *Mission with LeMay: My Story*, with the assistance of K. MacKinlay (New York: Doubleday, 1965), 481–82; Thomas S. Power, *Design for Survival* (New York: Coward-McCann, 1965), 79–84. For a more thorough evaluation of this point, see Trachtenberg, *History and Strategy*, 105–7.

31. Memorandum, Executive Secretary to the NSC, 22 July 1953, FRUS, 1952–1954, 2 (part 1): 400.

32. Paper Prepared by the Directing Panel of Project Solarium, 1 June 1953, FRUS, 1952–1954, 2 (part 1): 361–62. Snyder describes a fourth course in which the United States would undertake active negotiations with the Soviet Union for two years. The Soviets would know that if they did not agree to U.S. terms within this period, they would risk general war. See Snyder, "The 'New Look' of 1953," 409.

33. See chapter 1.

34. Memorandum from Eisenhower to Dulles, 8 September 1953, WHMS, "White House Correspondence, 1953 [2]," DPEL. See chapter 1.

35. Eisenhower explained the threat in terms of the "domino theory" in a news conference on 7 April 1954. See Eisenhower, The President's News Conference, 7 April 1954, Eisenhower PPS, 1954, 381–90.

36. For detailed accounts of the American role in the Dien Bien Phu crisis, see George C. Herring and Richard H. Immerman, "Eisenhower, Dulles, and Dienbienphu: 'The Day We Didn't Go to War' Revisited," *The Journal of American History* 71, No. 2 (September 1984): 343–63; George C. Herring, " 'A Good Stout Effort': John Foster Dulles and the Indochina Crisis, 1954–1955," in *John Foster Dulles and the Diplomacy of the Cold War*, ed. Richard H. Immerman (Princeton: Princeton University Press, 1990), 213–33; Bundy, *Danger and Survival*, 260–70; John Prados, *The Sky Would Fall: Operation Vulture: The U.S. Bombing Mission in Indochina, 1954* (New York: The Dial Press, 1983), which includes further bibliographical references.

37. See for example, Memorandum of conversation between Dulles and Eden, 30 April 1954, SS, "Mr. Merchant TOP SECRET, Indochina 1954 [9]," DPEL.

38. Eisenhower's personal position is somewhat elusive. On the one hand, some of Eisenhower's comments made Radford believe that an air strike had the president's approval. On the other hand, Eisenhower did not have a good

deal of faith in the chances for success of an air strike and insisted on satisfactory military and diplomatic arrangements with the French. See Herring and Immerman, "Eisenhower, Dulles, and Dienbienphu," 348–49; Bundy, *Danger and Survival*, 260–63.

39. Memorandum of conversation between Dulles, Eisenhower, et al., 2 April 1954, WHMS, "Meetings with the President, 1954 [4]," DPEL.

40. Herring and Immerman, "Eisenhower, Dulles, and Dienbienphu," 356–63. It is unclear whether Dulles offered the French the support of tactical nuclear weapons in one of his meetings with Bidault. For this episode, see Bundy, *Danger and Survival*, 260–79.

41. Memorandum, McCardle to the Secretary of State, 30 April 1954, FRUS, 1952–1954, 16: 629–30.

42. Both quotations from Memorandum of conversation between Dulles, Radford, et al., 9 May 1954, SS, "Mr. Merchant TOP SECRET, Indochina 1954, 1960 [1]," DPEL.

43. Memorandum from Dulles to the President, 28 May 1954, SS, "Mr. Merchant TOP SECRET, Indochina 1954, 1960 [1]," DPEL.

44. Memorandum of conversation between the President, Dulles, et al., 25 May 1954, SS, "Mr. Merchant TOP SECRET, Indochina 1954, 1960 [1]," DPEL.

45. Richard H. Immerman, "The United States and the Geneva Conference of 1954: A New Look," *Diplomatic History* 14, No. 1 (Winter 1990): 43–66.

46. Memorandum of NSC meeting, 24 June 1954, FRUS, 1952–1954, 2 (part 1): 690. Dulles had used these words on 14 December 1953, in a speech before the North Atlantic Council. He had warned the Europeans that a failure to build the European Defense Community would leave Germany and France apart and "would compel an agonising reappraisal of basic United States policy" (Statement by the Secretary of State to the North Atlantic Council, 14 December 1953, FRUS, 1952–1954, 5: 461–68).

47. All quotations from Memorandum of NSC meeting, 24 June 1954, FRUS, 1952–1954, 2 (part 1): 693–96.

48. NSC 5410/1, "U.S. Objectives in the Event of General War with the Soviet Bloc," 29 March 1954, FRUS, 1952–1954, 2 (part 1): 645–46.

49. NSC 5422/2, "Guidelines under NSC 162/2 for Fiscal Year 1956," 7 August 1954, FRUS, 1952–1954, 2 (part 1): 717. See also NSC 5422, "Tentative Guidelines under NSC 162/2 for Fiscal Year 1956," 14 June 1954, FRUS, 1952–1954, 2 (part 1): 649–55.

50. Annexes to NSC 5422, Study Prepared by the Department of Defense, 14 June 1954, FRUS, 1952–1954, 2 (part 1): 675.

51. Annexes to NSC 5422, Study Prepared by the Department of State, 14 June 1954, FRUS, 1952–1954, 2 (part 1): 669–71.

52. All quotations from Memorandum, JCS to the Secretary of Defense, 23 June 1954, FRUS, 1952–1954, 2 (part 1): 680–86. Watson has stressed that the JCS's views on negotiations with the Soviets were closely related to the Indochina crisis. See Watson, *The Joint Chiefs of Staff and National Policy*, 45–46.

53. For the precise wording of the respective positions, see NSC 5422, "Tentative Guidelines Under NSC 162/2 for Fiscal Year 1956," 14 June 1954, FRUS, 1952–1954, 2 (part 1): 656.

54. All quotations from Memorandum of NSC meeting, 24 June 1954, FRUS, 1952–1954, 2 (part 1): 687–88. For the final wording of the guidelines regarding disarmament, see NSC 5422/2, "Guidelines under NSC 162/2 for Fiscal Year 1956," 7 August 1954, FRUS, 1952–1954, 2 (part 1): 717–18.

55. President Eisenhower thought that the question had to be decided in relation to concrete cases. The formula "to decide on a case-by-case basis" became a euphemism for lack of consensus on specific issues or for the president's wish to avoid the consequences that a clear decision would entail.

56. NSC 5422/2, "Guidelines under NSC 162/2 for Fiscal Year 1956," 7 August 1954, FRUS, 1952–1954, 2 (part 1): 721.

57. A good case in point is the presentation of the issue in NSC 5422, the basis for the discussion in the NSC. The paper analyzed the problem of increasing probability of peripheral aggression in the paragraphs regarding general war. See NSC 5422, "Tentative Guidelines under NSC 162/2 for Fiscal Year 1956," 14 June 1954, FRUS, 1952–1954, 2 (part 1): 656–58.

58. For the wording of the split, see NSC 5422, "Tentative Guidelines under NSC 162/2 for Fiscal Year 1956," 14 June 1954, FRUS, 1952–1954, 2 (part 1): 656–57.

59. Memorandum of NSC meeting, 24 June 1954, FRUS, 1952–1954, 2 (part 1): 689.

60. Memorandum of NSC meeting, 3 December 1954, FRUS, 1952–1954, 2 (part 1): 804–5. General Ridgway had a special opportunity to present the minority position of the army before the NSC. While the president accepted that the general was sincere in his view and that he was not merely presenting a "parochial" army viewpoint, Secretary Wilson contended that the army chief of staff was trying to justify a larger army.

61. Memorandum of NSC meeting, 5 August 1954, FRUS, 1952–1954, 2 (part 1): 706, fn. 7.

62. In May 1954, Dulles summarized the experiences with the doctrine of retaliation after sixteen months of efforts: Although the policy was opposed by the allies, he noted, "there has been no open armed aggression and none seems likely, so long as we retain effective atomic supremacy and the will, if need be, to use it" (John Foster Dulles, United States Foreign Policy, 16 May 1954, WHMS, "General Foreign Policy Matters [2]," DPEL).

63. Memorandum, Bowie to Secretary of State, 4 August 1954, FRUS, 1952–1954, 2 (part 1): 699–700.

64. Both quotations from Memorandum of NSC meeting, 5 August 1954, FRUS, 1952–1954, 2 (part 1): 706.

65. For the final wording of the paragraph, see NSC 5422/2, "Guidelines under NSC 162/2 for Fiscal Year 1956," 7 August 1954, FRUS, 1952–1954, 2 (part 1): 718.

66. For a broader analysis of the speech, its origins and consequences, see chapter 3.

67. Both quotations from Memorandum of NSC meeting, 5 August 1954, FRUS, 1952–1954, 2 (part 1): 706–7.

68. All quotations from Memorandum of NSC discussion, 24 June 1954, FRUS, 1952–1954, 2 (part 1): 689.

69. Memorandum of NSC meeting, 5 August 1954, FRUS, 1952–1954, 2 (part 1): 702–3.

70. Both quotations from NSC 5422/2, "Guidelines under NSC 162/2 for Fiscal Year 1956," 7 August 1954, FRUS, 1952–1954, 2 (part 1): 718.

71. For this argument, see Annexes to NSC 5422, Study Prepared by the Department of Defense, 14 June 1954, FRUS, 1952–1954, 2 (part 1): 672–75.

72. NSC 5501, "Basic National Security Policy," 7 January 1955, FRUS, 1955–1957, 19: 24–38.

73. Other departments filed some interesting proposals for particular areas of national security policy, but the basic question of how to shape overall policy with respect to the changing threat was clearly fought out between State and JCS. For comments of other departments, see Paper Prepared by the Director of the Foreign Operations Administration, 9 November 1954; Paper Prepared by the Director of Central Intelligence, 18 November 1954; Memorandum by the Director of Defense Mobilization, 19 November; Memorandum by the Director of the United States Information Agency, 19 November; all in: FRUS, 1952–1954, 2 (part 1): 770–84.

74. The CIA confirmed the latter view when it estimated that the Soviet Union "will try to restrain its Far Eastern allies and satellites from deliberately initiating a hot war or overt military aggression within the next five years" (Paper Prepared by the Director of Central Intelligence, 18 November 1954, FRUS, 1952–1954, 2 [part 1]: 772–81).

75. All quotations from Paper Prepared by the Department of State, 15 November 1954, FRUS, 1952–1954, 2 (part 1): 772–76.

76. Memorandum, JCS to the Secretary of Defense, 17 December 1954, FRUS, 1952–1954, 2 (part 1): 828–32. See the wording of the split in NSC 5440, "Basic National Security Policy," 14 December 1954 (Ibid., 806–22).

77. All quotations from Memorandum, Secretary of Defense to the Executive Secretary of the National Security Council, 22 November 1954, FRUS, 1952–1954, 2 (part 1): 785–87.

78. Memorandum of NSC meeting, 24 November 1954, FRUS, 1952–1954, 2 (part 1): 789–90.

79. Memorandum of NSC meeting, 21 December 1954, FRUS, 1952–1954, 2 (part 1): 834.

80. Memorandum of NSC meeting, 24 November 1954, FRUS, 1952–1954, 2 (part 1): 796. Dulles replied to this by stating that Indochina was a setback, but that it "stemmed from decisions and policies taken long ago by the French" (Ibid., 795–97).

81. For the Taiwan Strait crisis, see Bundy, *Danger and Survival*, 273–87; George and Smoke, *Deterrence in American Foreign Policy*, 266–94.

82. Memorandum of NSC meeting, 21 December 1954, FRUS, 1952–1954, 2 (part 1): 837–41.

83. The President agreed and expressed his view "that our national security policies were now well-stated" (Memorandum of NSC meeting, 24 November 1954, FRUS, 1952–1954, 2 [part 1]: 799).

84. Both quotations from Memorandum of NSC meeting, 21 December 1954, FRUS, 1952–1954, 2 (part 1): 834–35.

85. Secretary Wilson supported this view: "While we ourselves can't do very much externally to destroy it [Communism], he was sure that ultimately it would destroy itself. . . . China had been a dictatorship for centuries; so had the Soviet Union. These countries had new kinds of dictators now, but these dictators still faced the problem of how to control their population" (Memorandum of NSC meeting, 21 December 1954, FRUS, 1952–1954, 2 [part 1]: 840).

86. Both quotations from Memorandum of NSC meeting, 21 December 1954, FRUS, 1952–1954, 2 (part 1): 834–37.

87. Memorandum of NSC meeting, 4 March 1954, FRUS, 1952–1954, 2 (part 1): 636.

88. Quoted in Rosenberg, "The Origins of Overkill," 35.

89. Trachtenberg, *History and Strategy*, 145–46.

90. Trachtenberg stresses that, whereas the 1948 Berlin crisis followed the creation of the West German state and the 1958 Berlin crisis occurred at a time when Germany was on its way to acquiring nuclear weapons, the Soviets did not respond to the rearmament of Germany, which was underway in the early 1950s. See Trachtenberg, *History and Strategy*, 150–51.

91. Address by Premier Khrushchev at a Soviet-Polish Meeting, 10 November 1958, DG, 339–43.

92. Dingman has presented an account of the atomic diplomacy during the Korean War that includes a detailed analysis of the Truman years. See Roger Dingman, "Atomic Diplomacy during the Korean War," *International Security* 13, No. 3 (Winter 1988–89): 50–91. For further accounts, see Rosemary J. Foot, *The Wrong War: American Policy and the Dimensions of the Korean Conflict, 1950–1953* (Ithaca: Cornell University Press, 1985); Rosemary J. Foot, "Nuclear Coercion and the Ending of the Korean Conflict," *International Security* 13, No. 3 (Winter 1988/89): 92–112; Edward C. Kiefer, "President Dwight D. Eisenhower and the End of the Korean War," *Diplomatic History* 10, No. 3 (Summer 1986): 267–89; Bundy, *Danger and Survival*, 238–45; Watson, *The Joint Chiefs of Staff and National Policy*, 223–46.

93. Eisenhower, *Mandate for Change*, 93–97.

94. Intelligence reports had confirmed that the area was used by the Communists as a staging and resupply area for the entire western front. General Clark demanded an end to the immunity of the "Kaesong sanctuary," which had been designed to facilitate armistice negotiations that were stalemated at the time. See Clark to the JCS, 7 February 1953, FRUS, 1952–1954, 15 (part 1): 742–45.

95. All quotations from Memorandum of NSC meeting, 11 February 1953, FRUS, 1952–1954, 15 (part 1): 769–72.

96. Memorandum, Dulles to Eisenhower, 6 March 1953, FRUS, 1952–1954, 15 (part 1): 805–6.

97. For a general outline of the strategy, see Memorandum, Dulles to Eisenhower, 6 March 1953, FRUS, 1952–1954, 15 (part 1): 805–6; Memorandum, Cutler to Secretary Wilson, 21 March 1953, FRUS, 1952–1954, 15 (part 1): 815. See also Eisenhower, *Mandate for Change*, 178–80.

98. Memorandum of the Substance of Discussion at a Department of State–JCS meeting, 6 March 1953, FRUS, 1952–1954, 15 (part 1): 806–12.

99. Memorandum, Cutler to Secretary Wilson, 21 March 1953, FRUS, 1952–1954, 15 (part 1): 815.

100. The influence of such an argumentation on U.S. policies in the Korea, Indochina, and Taiwan Strait crises has been analyzed in detail by John Lewis Gaddis, *The Long Peace*, 104–46.

101. As proof, he referred to tests that had shown that men could be close to an atomic explosion without being hurt if they were well dug in. See Memorandum of the Substance of Discussion at a Department of State–JCS meeting, 27 March 1953, FRUS, 1952–1954, 15 (part 1): 817–18.

102. Memorandum of the Substance of Discussion at a Department of State–JCS meeting, 27 March 1953, FRUS, 1952–1954, 15 (part 1): 817–18.

103. NSC 147 estimated that the Communists would recognize the employment of such weapons as indicative of western determination to carry the Korean War to a successful conclusion. The paper, however, was unable to estimate "whether this recognition would by itself lead the Communists to make the concessions necessary to reach an armistice" (NSC 147, "Analysis of Possible Courses of Action in Korea," 2 April 1953, FRUS, 1952–1954, 15 [part 1]: 838–57.

104. See chapter 1.

105. John Foster Dulles added that while "in the present state of world opinion we could not use an A-bomb, we should make every effort now to dissipate this feeling." All quotations from: Memorandum of NSC meeting, 31 March 1953, FRUS, 1952–1954, 15 (part 1): 825–27; for the context: FRUS, 1952–1954, 2 (part 1): 264–81.

106. For the text of his statement, see *Department of State Bulletin*, 13 April 1953, 526–27; Editorial note, FRUS, 1952–1954, 15 (part 1): 824.

107. Clark to the Joint Chiefs of Staff, 11 April 1953, FRUS, 1952–1954, 15 (part 1): 903.

108. See Dulles's remarks in the NSC and at a meeting with the Korean ambassador: Memorandum of NSC meeting, 8 April 1953, FRUS, 1952–1954, 15 (part 1): 892–95; Memorandum of Conversation between Secretary Dulles, Dr. You Chan Yang, et al., 8 April 1953, FRUS, 1952–1954, 15 (part 1): 897–900. Julian Harrington, the consul general in Hong Kong, wrote to the State Department that the decision for Chou En-lai's move was reached during his visit to Moscow

on the occasion of Stalin's funeral: "It may be an element in Soviet 'peace offensive' designed to reduce world tensions and lower guard of Western powers during critical period of consolidation Communist bloc following Stalin's death" (The Consul General in Hong Kong to the Department of State, 31 March 1953, FRUS, 1952–1954, 15 [part 1]: 828–29).

109. For the proposal, see Clark to the JCS, 7 May 1953, FRUS, 1952–1954, 15 (part 1): 979–81.

110. Collins to Clark, 7 May 1953, FRUS, 1952–1954, 15 (part 1): 981–83.

111. All quotations from Memorandum of NSC meeting, 8 April 1953, FRUS, 1952–1954, 15 (part 1): 893–95.

112. Memorandum of NSC meeting, 28 April 1953, FRUS, 1952–1954, 15 (part 1): 945–47.

113. Memorandum of NSC meeting, 6 May 1953, FRUS, 1952–1954, 15 (part 1): 975–79.

114. Memorandum of NSC meeting, 13 May 1953, FRUS, 1952–1954, 15 (part 1): 1012–17. With respect to interest in the use of tactical nuclear weapons, Dingman is for once mistaken when he notes that the president "steered the full NSC away from a firm decision on contingency plans for tactical use of nuclear weapons" (Dingman, "Atomic Diplomacy during the Korean War," 85). On the contrary, Eisenhower was the one insisting on planning for the use of tactical nuclear weapons. Moreover, the president did not reject, as Dingman further notes, "a suggestion to fake a manpower buildup" (Ibid., 84). This had been the president's own idea, which then triggered a rejection by the JCS.

115. Both quotations from Memorandum of NSC meeting, 13 May 1953, FRUS, 1952–1954, 15 (part 1): 1016. It seems that the State Department in fact was favoring alternative C, which was the one the president was most skeptical about—especially if nuclear weapons were not employed. For the position of the State Department, see Memorandum by the Deputy Assistant Secretary of State for Far Eastern Affairs to the Secretary of State, 6 April 1953, FRUS, 1952–1954, 15 (part 1): 880–82.

116. Both quotations from Memorandum of NSC meeting, 13 May 1953, FRUS, 1952–1954, 15 (part 1): 1016.

117. All quotations from Memorandum by the JCS to the Secretary of Defense, 19 May 1953, FRUS, 1952–1954, 15: 1059–64.

118. All quotations from Memorandum of NSC meeting, 20 May 1953, FRUS, 1952–1954, 15 (part 1): 1065–67.

119. Clark to the JCS, 14 May 1953, FRUS, 1952–1954, 15 (part 1): 1022–24.

120. For details on the bombing campaign, see David Rees, *Korea: The Limited War* (New York: St. Martin's Press, 1964), 381–82; Robert Jackson, *Air War over Korea* (London: Allan, 1973): 156–57.

121. Editorial note, FRUS, 1952–1954, 15 (part 1): 1096–97; Clark to the JCS, 23 May 1953, ibid., 1090–95.

122. Memorandum of the Substance of Discussion at a Department of State-JCS meeting, 18 May 1953, FRUS, 1952–1954, 15 (part 1): 1038–44; Memoran-

dum by the Acting Secretary of State to the President, 18 May 1953, ibid., 1046–48.

123. In the next sentence, however, the secretary of state noted that the United States was sincerely trying to get an armistice and "that only crazy people could think that the United States wanted to prolong the struggle" (Memorandum of conversation between Dulles and Nehru, 21 May 1953, FRUS, 1952–1954, 15 [part 1]: 1068–69). Moreover, when Nehru one day later brought up the issue of intensified hostilities, Dulles did not comment and simply dropped the topic. Memorandum of conversation between Dulles and Nehru, 22 May 1953, ibid., 1071.

124. Prime Minister Nehru at least repeatedly denied such an action. For the details of the argument, see Foot, "Nuclear Coercion," 104–5.

125. Ambassador Bohlen to the Department of State, 28 May 1953, FRUS, 1952–1954, 15 (part 1): 1109–11. For the exchanges between the State Department and Bohlen leading to the talk, see Ambassador Bohlen to the Department of State, 24 May 1953, in ibid., 1095–96; The Acting Secretary of State to the Embassy in the Soviet Union, 26 May 1953, ibid., 1103–4. Molotov replied five days later with a fundamentally positive answer, see Ambassador Bohlen to the Department of State, 3 June 1953, ibid., 1133–34.

126. The Communist delegation had requested and received a three-day postponement for administrative reasons. Therefore, the delegations did not reconvene negotiations at Panmunjom until 4 June. See editorial note, FRUS, 1952–1954, 15 (part 1): 1137.

127. Memorandum by Dulles to Eisenhower, 4 June 1953, FRUS, 1952–1954, 15 (part 1): 1138.

128. Eisenhower, *Mandate for Change*, 185.

129. Editorial note, FRUS, 1952–1954, 15 (part 2): 1196–97.

130. Memorandum of NSC meeting, 18 June 1953, FRUS, 1952–1954, 15 (part 2): 1200–1205; Memorandum of Telephone Conversation between Dulles and Eisenhower, ibid., 1264–65.

131. Memorandum of NSC meeting, 2 July 1953, FRUS, 1952–1954, 15 (part 2): 1300–1312.

132. Edward Kiefer has stressed that Eisenhower's approach to the ending of the Korean War was not very coherent, see Kiefer, "President Dwight D. Eisenhower and the End of the Korean War," 268.

133. For expressions by Eisenhower and Dulles of their common conviction that primarily nuclear threats brought about the Korean armistice, see Eisenhower, *Mandate for Change*, 179–80; Sherman Adams, *Firsthand Report: The Inside Story of the Eisenhower Administration* (New York: Harper & Brothers, 1961), 102; James Shepley, "How Dulles Averted War," *Life*, 16 January 1956, 70–72; Bermuda Conference meeting, 7 December 1953, FRUS, 1952–1954, 5: 1808–18.

134. Rosemary Foot's article is the best essay that I have seen on the impact of nuclear threats on the ending of the Korean War. See Foot, "Nuclear Coercion," 93–112, 104–7.

135. Memorandum by Dulles, 6 September 1953, WHMS, "White House Correspondence 1953 [2]," DPEL. For background see chapter 1.

136. Memorandum for the Record by the President, 11 November 1953, FRUS, 1952–1954, 2 (part 1): 597.

137. Memorandum of NSC meeting, 28 October 1953, FRUS, 1952–1954, 15 (part 2): 1572.

138. Memorandum of NSC meeting, 19 November 1953, FRUS, 1952–1954, 15 (part 2): 1617.

139. At that time the threat that the Communists would not agree to a political conference was less important than the threat that President Rhee would unilaterally resume hostilities. See NSC 167, "U.S. Courses of Action in Korea in the Absence of an Acceptable Political Settlement," 22 October 1953, FRUS, 1952–1954, 15 (part 2): 1546–50. In such a case, the JCS opposed further UN participation in military actions. The State Department went even further and proposed instigating the ouster of Rhee if he against all persuasion initiated the action. See Memorandum, JCS to the Secretary of Defense, 27 October 1953, ibid., 1563–67; Memorandum of NSC meeting, 29 October 1953, ibid., 1573.

140. Both quotations from Memorandum of NSC meeting, 29 October 1953, FRUS, 1952–1954, 15 (part 2): 1571.

141. Second Restricted Tripartite Meeting of the Heads of Government, 7 December 1953, FRUS, 1952–1954, 5: 1811. The secretary of state was very likely referring to a decision by the president on the eve of the truce to authorize the transfer of nuclear weapons to military custody for overseas deployment. See Dingman, "Atomic Diplomacy during the Korean War," 87.

142. Second Restricted Tripartite Meeting of the Heads of Government, 7 December 1953, FRUS, 1952–1954, 5: 1813.

143. Both quotations from Memorandum of NSC meeting, 10 December 1953, FRUS, 1952–1954, 15 (part 2): 1653–55.

144. Second Restricted Tripartite Meeting of the Heads of Government, 7 December 1953, FRUS, 1952–1954, 5: 1818. See Memorandum of Conversation between Eisenhower and Churchill, 4 December 1953, ibid., 1739–40. In fact, only four days earlier the president had suggested striking at Peking if the Chinese resumed the attack. See Memorandum of NSC meeting, 3 December 1953, FRUS, 1952–1954, 15 (part 2): 1638.

145. Foot, "Nuclear Coercion," 112.

146. Shepley, "How Dulles Averted War," 70–72.

147. See chapter 1.

148. All quotations from Memorandum, JCS to the Secretary of Defense, 27 November 1953, FRUS, 1952–1954, 15 (part 2): 1626–29. By contrast, the old report contained important limitations: "a. Destroy effective Communist military power in Korea. b. Reduce the enemy's capability for further aggression in Korea and the Far East" (Memorandum, JCS to the Secretary of Defense, 19 May 1953, FRUS, 1952–1954, 15 [part 1]: 1059–64).

149. All quotations from Memorandum by the JCS to the Secretary of Defense, 27 November 1953, FRUS, 1952–1954, 15 (part 2): 1626–29.

150. Memorandum, Bowie to Secretary of State, 3 December 1953, FRUS, 1952–1954, 15 (part 2): 1634–36.

151. All quotations from Memorandum of NSC meeting, 3 December 1953, FRUS, 1952–1954, 15 (part 2): 1636–45.

152. All quotations from Memorandum of NSC meeting, 3 December 1953, FRUS, 1952–1954, 15 (part 2): 1636–45. Eventually, the JCS changed their memorandum to read: "Employing atomic weapons, conduct offensive air operations against military targets in Korea, and against those military targets in Manchuria and China which are being used by the Communists in direct support of their operations in Korea, or which threaten the security of US/UN forces in the Korean area" (Memorandum, JCS to the Secretary of Defense, 18 December 1953, in FRUS, 1952–1954, 15 [part 2]: 1674–75).

153. All quotations from Memorandum of NSC meeting, 8 January 1954, FRUS, 1952–1954, 15 (part 2): 1704–10.

154. From the beginning, President Eisenhower emphasized the necessity of allies and usually weighed the impact of policy decision on allies carefully. See chapter 1.

155. Memorandum of NSC meeting, 8 January 1954, FRUS, 1952–1954, 15 (part 2): 1704–10. A special national intelligence estimate of March 1954 is of particular interest regarding this question. The SNIE estimated that the Chinese Communists would avoid courses of action that would involve serious risk of U.S. action against the Chinese mainland. Moreover, the majority view of the SNIE anticipated the reaction of the Kremlin to a situation in which the Chinese Communist regime was about to be destroyed and lost to the bloc in a way that forced the dissent of the Department of State. The special assistant, Intelligence, Department of State, and the assistant chief of staff, G-2, stated that the present language "minimizes the danger that the USSR would give all out assistance to Communist China rather than accept its loss to the bloc" (SNIE 100-2-54, "Probable Reactions of Communist China, the USSR, and the Free World to Certain US Courses of Action in Korea," 5 March 1954, ibid., 1758–62).

Chapter 3

1. Bernard Brodie wrote his seminal study on the "absolute weapon" in 1946. The book, however, was clearly written with an eye for the strategic problems of the future. See Brodie, *The Absolute Weapon.* In his marvelous piece about strategic thought in America, Marc Trachtenberg has emphasized that for the strategists it was the hydrogen bomb "that marked the decisive break with the past" (*History and Strategy,* 6).

2. Memorandum of Conversation between Winston Churchill and Henry Cabot Lodge, 26 June 1954, SS, "Churchill-Eden Visit June 25–29 1954 [1]," DPEL.

3. See chapter 1.

4. For a detailed history of international control of nuclear energy in the early years of the Cold War, see Bundy, *Danger and Survival,* 130–235; Barton J. Bernstein, "The Quest for Security: American Foreign Policy and International Control of the Atomic Bomb, 1942–1946," *The Journal of American History* 60, No. 4 (March 1974): 1003–44; Lilienthal, *The Atomic Energy Years,* 1–30; Dean Acheson, *Present at the Creation: My Years in the State Department* (New York: W.W. Norton & Company, 1969), 149–56, 314–21.

5. For information about the four U.S. test series between April 1952 and April 1954, see editorial note, FRUS, 1952–1954, 2 (part 2): 881–82.

6. All quotations from Report by the Panel of Consultants of the Department of State to the Secretary of State, January 1953, FRUS, 1952–1954, 2 (part 2): 1056–91.

7. Bundy, *Danger and Survival,* 289, gives an excellent account of the report. He has published an abbreviated version of the report in McGeorge Bundy, "Early Thoughts on Controlling the Nuclear Arms Race: A Report to the Secretary of State, January 1953," *International Security* 7 (Fall 1982): 3–27. For additional analysis, see Richard G. Hewlett and Jack M. Holl, *Atoms for Peace and War, 1953–1961: Eisenhower and the Atomic Energy Commission* (Berkeley: University of California Press, 1989), 41–44. The book includes an interesting bibliographical essay (pp. 657–74) regarding the history of the AEC in the Eisenhower years.

8. All quotations from Report by the Panel of Consultants of the Department of State to the Secretary of State, January 1953, FRUS, 1952–1954, 2 (part 2): 1056–91. Oppenheimer repeated his call for a public exposition of the facts in an article in July. See Robert Oppenheimer, "Atomic Weapons and American Policy," *Foreign Affairs* 31 (July 1953): 525–35.

9. All quotations from Report by the Panel of Consultants of the Department of State to the Secretary of State, January 1953, FRUS, 1952–1954, 2 (part 2): 1056–91.

10. Memorandum of NSC meeting, 25 February 1953, FRUS, 1952–1954, 2 (part 2): 1110–14. This had already been the reaction of former secretary of state Acheson. See Notes of a Meeting in the Office of the Secretary of State, 30 December 1952, ibid., 1051–53.

11. Memorandum of NSC meeting, 25 February 1953, FRUS, 1952–1954, 2 (part 2): 1110–14. See Memorandum of NSC meeting, 18 February 1953, ibid., 1106–09.

12. Notes of a Meeting in the Office of the Secretary of State, 30 December 1952, FRUS, 1952–1954, 2 (part 2): 1049–55.

13. Both quotations from Memorandum of NSC meeting, 18 February 1953, FRUS, 1952–1954, 2 (part 2): 1106–09.

14. George F. Kennan, "Long Telegram," FRUS, 1946, 6: 696–709. See also Kennan, "The Sources of Soviet Conduct," 570.

15. Report by the Panel of Consultants of the Department of State to the Secretary of State, January 1953, FRUS, 1952–1954, 2 (part 2): 1086.

16. Quoted in Emmet J. Hughes, *The Ordeal of Power: A Political Memoir of the*

Eisenhower Years (New York: Athenaeum, 1963), 101. The president made this comment at the Cabinet meeting on 6 March. See editorial note, FRUS, 1952–1954, 8: 1098.

17. Memorandum of NSC meeting, 4 March 1953, FRUS, 1952–1954, 8: 1091–95.

18. For such an argument, see Memorandum Prepared by the Counselor of the Department of State, 10 March 1953, FRUS, 1952–1954, 8: 1108–11.

19. All quotations from Memorandum of NSC meeting, 11 March 1953, FRUS, 1952–1954, 8: 1117–25. There is some evidence that Secretary Dulles's general opposition to Jackson's plan had its roots (besides the reasons mentioned) in bureaucratic and personal rivalry. The secretary of state was obviously much concerned about the role of the State Department in Jackson's conception of political warfare. See Paper Prepared by Walt Whitman Rostow, Massachusetts Institute of Technology, 11 May 1953, FRUS, 1952–1954, 8: 1173–83. See the exchange between Jackson and Dulles during the NSC meeting in Memorandum of NSC meeting, 11 March 1953, ibid., 1119–23.

20. Memorandum of Telephone Conversation between Dulles and the President, 16 March 1953, FRUS, 1952–1954, 8: 1130–31.

21. The Assistant Secretary of State for United Nations Affairs to the U.S. Representative at the UN, 2 April 1953, FRUS, 1952–1954, 2 (part 2): 1139–40. For a summary of Soviet peace gestures after Stalin's death, see Memorandum by Carlton Savage of the Policy Planning Staff to the Director of the Staff, 1 April 1953, FRUS, 1952–1954, 8: 1138–39.

22. Memorandum of NSC meeting, 11 March 1953, FRUS, 1952–1954, 8: 1117–25. It was Paul H. Nitze who had suggested to Secretary Dulles that the United States should make a settlement of the Korean War the principal target after Stalin's death. Such a settlement would improve western military strategic flexibility, remove a potential danger to the western alliance, and create a situation in which the possibilities of a rift between Mao and Malenkov would be enhanced. However, Nitze thought it important that "we make this effort in a serious, therefore covert, way rather than as part of a propaganda program" (Memorandum by the Director of the Policy Planning Staff to the Secretary of State, 10 March 1953, FRUS, 1952–1954, 8: 1107–8).

23. Memorandum of NSC meeting, 11 March 1953, FRUS, 1952–1954, 8: 1122.

24. Address by the President, "The Chance for Peace," 16 April 1953, FRUS, 1952–1954, 8: 1147–55.

25. Sherman Adams, for example, considered it the most effective speech of Eisenhower's public career. See Adams, *Firsthand Report*, 97.

26. John Foster Dulles, "Address before the American Society of Newspapers Editors, 18 April 1953," *Department of State Bulletin*, 27 April 1953, 603–8.

27. Bohlen to the Department of State, 25 April 1953, FRUS, 1952–1954, 8: 1165–66.

28. SE–44, "The Soviet Statement of 25 April 1953 in Reply to President Ei-

senhower's Speech on 16 April 1953," 30 April 1953, FRUS, 1952–1954, 8: 1168–69.

29. For the exchange of letters between Churchill and Eisenhower, see President Eisenhower to Prime Minister Churchill, 5 May 1953, FRUS, 1952–1954, 8: 1170–71; President Eisenhower to Prime Minister Churchill, 25 April 1953, ibid., 1166–67; Prime Minister Churchill to President Eisenhower, 4 May 1953, ibid., 1169.

30. Memorandum of NSC meeting, 27 May 1953, FRUS, 1952–1954, 2 (part 2): 1169–74.

31. The Secretary of State to the U.S. Representative at the UN, 4 June 1953, FRUS, 1952–1954, 2 (part 2): 1175–76. For policy guidance regarding U.S. activities in the UN Disarmament Commission from May through September 1953, see Memorandum by the Executive Committee on Regulation of Armaments to the Executive Secretary of the NSC, 26 May 1953, ibid., 1160–69.

32. Memorandum of NSC meeting, 9 September 1953, FRUS, 1952–1954, 2 (part 2): 1210–12. For Bowie's views on the "Chance for Peace" speech, see Memorandum of Discussion at the Planning Board of the NSC, 19 October 1953, ibid., 1227–32.

33. For the connection to the reexamination of basic national security policy, see chapter 1.

34. For the Department of State proposal, see Memorandum, Cutler to the Secretary of State, 19 October 1953, FRUS, 1952–1954, 2 (part 2): 1232–33.

35. All quotations from Memorandum for the President by the Secretary of State, 23 October 1953, FRUS, 1952–1954, 2 (part 2): 1234–35.

36. Memorandum, Cutler to Strauss, 10 September 1953, FRUS, 1952–1954, 2 (part 2): 1213–14.

37. Memorandum by Cutler, 10 September 1953, FRUS, 1952–1954, 2 (part 2): 1213. For Eisenhower's recollection, see Eisenhower, *Mandate for Change*, 251–53. Admiral Strauss joined Eisenhower in excluding the second sentence in his later account. See Lewis L. Strauss, *Men and Decision* (Garden City, N.Y.: Doubleday & Company, 1962), 357.

38. Memorandum, Strauss to Eisenhower, 17 September 1953, FRUS, 1952–1954, 2 (part 2): 1218–20.

39. Memorandum, Cutler to the President, 19 October 1953, FRUS, 1952–1954, 2 (part 2): 1233–43.

40. Memorandum for the Files, 30 September 1954, FRUS, 1952–1954, 2 (part 2): 1526–27. Secretary Dulles informed Robert Bowie only very late in the game that the Candor speech was likely to be made at the Bermuda conference. Memorandum of telephone conversation, 1 December 1953, ibid., 1250. Hewlett and Holl have shown that the debate of Project Candor was heavily affected by the "Oppenheimer case." Going back to the discussion of whether the United States should develop the hydrogen bomb, people like Strauss suspected Oppenheimer of being a Soviet agent. This was the time of McCarthy's hunt for Communists within the American government. Eisenhower suspended Oppen-

heimer's clearance for classified information shortly before leaving for Bermuda. At the very time when Project Candor was implemented, one of its initiators was heavily accused. By this time, the aim of the project had shifted from serious arms control negotiations to pure propaganda. See Hewlett and Holl, *Atoms for Peace and War,* 34–72. For further details on the "Oppenheimer case," see Bundy, *Danger and Survival,* 305–18.

41. Prime Minister Churchill to President Eisenhower, 5 November 1953, FRUS, 1952–1954, 5: 1711–12; Memorandum of NSC meeting, 12 November 1953, ibid., 1713–15.

42. See the diplomatic correspondence between the American ambassador in London and the Department of State, FRUS, 1952–1954, 5: 1715–25.

43. First Restricted Tripartite Meeting of the Heads of Government, 4 December 1953, FRUS, 1952–1954, 5: 1750–54.

44. It seems that Churchill was holding back his approval in order to get more leverage for closer U.S.-U.K. collaboration in the field of atomic energy intelligence, especially regarding the effects of thermonuclear weapons on various targets. See Eisenhower-Churchill Meeting, 5 December 1953, FRUS, 1952–1954, 5: 1767–69; NSC 151/2, "Statement of Policy by the NSC on Disclosure of Atomic Information to Allied Countries," 4 December 1953, FRUS, 1952–1954, 2 (part 2): 1256–84; Prime Minister Churchill to President Eisenhower, 7 December 1953, ibid., 1289; Prime Minister Churchill to President Eisenhower, 16 December 1953, ibid., 1301–2; First Restricted Tripartite Meeting of the Heads of Government, 4 December 1953, FRUS, 1952–1954, 5: 1753.

45. Eisenhower-Laniel Meeting, 5 December 1953, FRUS, 1952–1954, 5: 1769–74. The question of the EDC turned out to be the main topic of the Bermuda conference.

46. See Dulles's lecture on this topic during a special meeting of the foreign ministers on NATO strategy. See Telegraphic Summary by the U.S. Delegation, 6 December 1953, FRUS, 1952–1954, 5: 1788–91. Project Candor was not the only way of selling the New Look to the Europeans. It was also in Bermuda that Secretary Dulles revealed the view of the U.S. government that nuclear threats were responsible for the ending of the Korean conflict. See chapter 2.

47. Eisenhower, *Mandate for Change,* 253.

48. For the full text of the address, see Dwight D. Eisenhower, Address before the General Assembly of the United Nations on Peaceful Uses of Atomic Energy, 8 December 1953, Eisenhower PPS, 1953, 813–22.

49. For the secretary's instructions, see The Secretary of State to the Embassy in the Soviet Union, 6 December 1953, FRUS, 1952–1954, 2 (part 2): 1286–87.

50. Bohlen to the Department of State, 7 December 1953, FRUS, 1952–1954, 2 (part 2): 1287–88. It seems that the State Department through Secretary Dulles at least was successful in securing that the address was paralleled with a call for private talks.

51. The President to Captain E. E. Hazlett, 24 December 1953, FRUS, 1952–1945, 2 (part 2): 1309–10. On the domestic and international reaction to Eisenhower's address, see Hewlett and Holl, *Atoms for Peace and War,* 209–11.

52. Bohlen to the Department of State, 22 December 1953, FRUS, 1952–1954, 2 (part 2): 1303–5; see: Bohlen to the Department of State, 21 December 1953, ibid., 1302–3. David Lilienthal came to think that Eisenhower's speech was a pure propaganda ploy. See David E. Lilienthal, *The Venturesome Years, 1950–1955*, vol. 3, The Journals of David E. Lilienthal (New York: Harper & Row, 1966), 474.

53. Bohlen to the Department of State, 22 December 1953, FRUS, 1952–1954, 2 (part 2): 1303. Bohlen to the Department of State, 26 December 1953, FRUS, 1952–1954, 2 (part 2): 1310–12.

54. Bohlen to the Department of State, 22 December 1953, FRUS, 1952–1954, 2 (part 2): 1304. Also see Memorandum, Jackson to the President, 28 December 1953, FRUS, 1952–1954, 2 (part 2): 1316–18.

55. Memorandum, Jackson to the President, 29 December 1953, FRUS, 1952–1954, 2 (part 2): 1314–16.

56. Watson, *The Joint Chiefs of Staff and National Policy*, 189–90; Hewlett and Holl, *Atoms for Peace and War*, 209–17.

57. Memorandum, Eisenhower to Jackson, 31 December 1953, FRUS, 1952–1954, 2 (part 2): 1321–22. Memorandum of Conversation with the President, by the Secretary of State, 5 January 1954, FRUS, 1952–1954, 2 (part 2): 1322–23.

58. Memorandum, Jackson to the President, 31 December 1953, FRUS, 1952–1954, 2 (part 2): 1321–22.

59. Memorandum of Conversation with the President, by the Secretary of State, 5 January 1954, FRUS, 1952–1954, 2 (part 2): 1322–23. When Secretary Dulles informed other officials of his talk with the president, he stressed that the "President thought that we should be *prepared* to talk atomic disarmament, if the USSR raised the matter." The president had told him that he felt he made this clear in his 8 December speech. See Memorandum of Conversation of Members of the Department of State, the Atomic Energy Commission, and the Department of Defense, n.d., FRUS, 1952–1954, 2 (part 2): 1324–30.

60. Summary of Meeting in the White House, 16 January 1954, FRUS, 1952–1954, 2 (part 2): 1342–43.

61. Bundy has noted that Eisenhower had "a notable tendency to overrate the power of a major formal address and to underrate the need for follow-up" (Bundy, *Danger and Survival*, 293).

62. See editorial note, FRUS, 1952–1954, 2 (part 2): 1355.

63. Memorandum of NSC meeting, 26 February 1954, FRUS, 1952–1954, 2 (part 2): 1364–65.

64. The Soviets played their side of the propaganda game as well and insisted on the link between the "Atoms for Peace" proposal and their outlaw proposal. See The Secretary of State to the Department of State, 28 April 1954, FRUS, 1952–1954, 2 (part 2): 1398–99; Memorandum of Conversation by the Assistant Secretary of State for European Affairs, 1 May 1954, FRUS, 1952–1954, 2 (part 2): 1413–17. For a comparable judgment of the "Atoms for Peace" speech, see Bundy, *Danger and Survival*, 292–95. For accounts that assess the address in a

more positive way as an expression of Eisenhower's concern over the nuclear danger, see James R. Schlesinger, "Atoms for Peace Revisited," and Robert R. Bowie, "Eisenhower, Atomic Weapons and Atoms for Peace," both in *Atoms for Peace: An Analysis after Thirty Years*, ed. Joseph F. Pilat, Robert E. Pendley, and Charles K. Ebinger (Boulder: Westview Press, 1985), 5–24.

65. Memorandum by Alexander Bickel of the Policy Planning Staff to the Consultant to the Secretary of State on Atomic Energy Affairs, 29 April 1954, FRUS, 1952–1954, 2 (part 2): 1402–03. It is worthwhile to note that draft notes for a meeting of the president with congressional leaders on 17 November 1954, listed the "Atoms for Peace" issue under "Propaganda." Draft notes for a Bipartisan meeting with the president, 17 November 1954, WHMS, "Meetings with the President, 1954 [1]," DPEL. The Project Candor failure was still recalled several years later. When at the beginning of 1957 the NSC discussed the suggestion of the Panel on the Human Effects of Nuclear Weapons Development for a program of "involvement" of the broader public, Robert Cutler —who had been part of the small circle drafting the speech—warned that "we do not wish to get involved again in anything like our ill-fated 'Operation Candor.' " Memorandum of NSC meeting, 7 February 1957, FRUS, 1955–1957, 19: 414. For a summary of the report's recommendations, see Report to the President and the NSC by the Panel on the Human Effects of Nuclear Weapons Development, 21 November 1956, ibid., 374–75.

66. Memorandum of Telephone Conversation between Dulles and Strauss, 29 March 1954, FRUS, 1952–1954, 2 (part 2): 1379–80.

67. Memorandum, Deputy Undersecretary of State to Secretary of State, 1 April 1954, FRUS, 1952–1954, 2 (part 2): 1380–82.

68. Editorial note, FRUS, 1952–1954, 2 (part 2): 1382–83.

69. For a fuller summary of the international reaction to the hydrogen bomb test, see Memorandum, Bowie to the Secretary of State, 5 May 1954, FRUS, 1952–1954, 2 (part 2): 1419–20.

70. The U.S. representative to the UN Lodge to the Department of State, 12 April 1954, FRUS, 1952–1954, 2 (part 2): 1383; Lodge to the Department of State, 14 April 1954, ibid., 1385.

71. For the British side of the story, see The Secretary of State to the Department of State, 2 May 1954, FRUS, 1952–1954, 2 (part 2): 1418–19; Memorandum by the Assistant Secretary of State for UN Affairs to the Deputy Undersecretary of State, 5 May 1954, ibid., 1421–22.

72. All quotations from Memorandum of NSC meeting, 6 May 1954, FRUS, 1952–1954, 2 (part 2): 1423–29.

73. The Acting Secretary of Defense to the Secretary of State, 17 May 1954, FRUS, 1952–1954, 2 (part 2): 1437–40. See The Secretary of Defense to the Secretary of State, 4 June 1954, ibid., 1457–58.

74. Memorandum of NSC meeting, 23 June 1954, FRUS, 1952–1954, 2 (part 2): 1467–72.

75. Memorandum by the Secretary of State to the Executive Secretary of the

NSC, 23 June 1954, FRUS, 1952–1954, 2 (part 2): 1463–67; Memorandum of NSC meeting, 27 May 1954, ibid., 1452–56.

76. Memorandum of NSC meeting, 23 June 1954, FRUS, 1952–1954, 2 (part 2): 1469.

77. Memorandum of NSC meeting, 27 May 1954, FRUS, 1952–1954, 2 (part 2): 1454. For a broader outline of the State Department's position, see Memorandum by the Secretary of State to the Executive Secretary of the NSC, 23 June 1954, ibid., 1463–67.

78. Memorandum of NSC meeting, 23 June 1954, FRUS, 1952–1954, 2 (part 2): 1468.

79. Memorandum of NSC meeting, 23 June 1954, FRUS, 1952–1954, 2 (part 2): 1469. The president, moreover, stressed that soon even "little countries will have a stockpile of these bombs, and then we *will* be in a mess" (Memorandum of NSC meeting, 27 May 1954, ibid., 1455).

80. Both quotations from Memorandum of NSC meeting, 23 June 1954, FRUS, 1952–1954, 2 (part 2): 1467–72.

81. See for example, The Secretary of Defense to the Secretary of State, 11 December 1954, FRUS, 1952–1954, 2 (part 2): 1583–84. See also chapter 2.

82. Summary of Discussion in the NSC Planning Board Meeting, 18 October 1954, FRUS, 1952–1954, 2 (part 2): 1537–40. See Memorandum of Conversation, by Howard Meyers of the Office of UN Political and Security Affairs, 17 November 1954, ibid., 1563–66.

83. All quotations from Memorandum of Conversation, by Howard Meyers of the Office of UN Political and Security Affairs, 29 December 1954, FRUS, 1952–1954, 2 (part 2): 1585–89.

84. Memorandum of Conversation, by Howard Meyers of the Office of UN Political and Security Affairs, 29 December 1954, FRUS, 1952–1954, 2 (part 2): 1585.

Chapter 4

1. Rosenberg, "The Origins of Overkill," 36–37.

2. See for example John Foster Dulles's first statement to the North Atlantic Council on 24 April 1953. The new secretary of state stressed that President Eisenhower's past association with NATO had given him a great appreciation for the alliance's importance. The U.S. Delegation at the North Atlantic Council Meeting to the Department of State, 24 April 1953, FRUS, 1952–1954, 5 (part 1): 373–78.

3. Eisenhower, Inaugural Address, 20 January 1953, Eisenhower PPS, 1953, 1–8; Eisenhower, Annual Message to the Congress on the State of the Union, 2 February 1953, Eisenhower PPS, 1953, 12–34.

4. Memorandum of NSC meeting, 7 October 1953, FRUS, 1952–1954, 2 (part 1): 527–28. NSC 162/2 contained a statement that the United States could

not meet its defense needs, even at exorbitant costs, without the support of its allies. See NSC 162/2, "Statement of Basic National Security Policy," 30 October 1953, FRUS, 1952–1954, 2 (part 1): 583.

5. For an excellent overview of Eisenhower's policy with regard to Europe, see Thomas U. Schöttli, *USA und EVG: Truman, Eisenhower und die Europa-Armee.* Ph.D. diss. (Bern: Lang Verlag, 1994).

6. These forces were to be contributed by Belgium, Canada, Denmark, France, Iceland, Italy, Luxembourg, the Netherlands, Norway, Portugal, the United Kingdom, and the United States (Greece and Turkey joined NATO later in the year). The exact force goals can be found in Watson, *The Joint Chiefs of Staff and National Policy,* 282.

7. In July 1952, the British chief of staff anticipated Eisenhower's New Look in an outline entitled "Defense Policy and Global Strategy," which was discussed with the Americans, but was at that time rejected. Robert Wampler has presented a detailed analysis of the British-American debate over NATO strategy from 1948 through 1957. His study emphasizes the critical role of the United Kingdom in pushing NATO to adopt a more avowed strategy of nuclear deterrence. See Wampler, *Ambiguous Legacy.*

8. Whereas the study itself is still classified, British sources allow a fair judgment of its findings. This account is based on Wampler, *Ambiguous Legacy,* 452–506; Peter, *Abschrecken und Ueberleben,* 233–35; Robert C. Richardson III, "NATO Nuclear Strategy: A Look Back," *Strategic Review* 9, No. 2 (Spring 1981): 35–43.

9. The U.S. Permanent Representative on the North Atlantic Council to the Department of State, 4 April 1953, FRUS, 1952–1954, 5 (part 1): 364–66; The Ambassador in France to the Department of State, 23 April 1953, ibid., 369–71.

10. The U.S. Delegation at the North Atlantic Council Meeting to the Department of State, 24 April 1953, FRUS, 1952–1954, 5 (part 1): 373–78. Secretary Dulles was echoing "the-prove-by-deeds-only" topic, which President Eisenhower had emphasized in his "Chance for Peace" speech. See chapter 3.

11. The U.S. Delegation at the North Atlantic Council Meeting to the Department of State, 24 April 1953, FRUS, 1952–1954, 5 (part 1): 373–78.

12. For background see chapter 1.

13. The U.S. Delegation at the North Atlantic Council Meeting to the Department of State, 24 April 1953, FRUS, 1952–1954, 5 (part 1): 373–78.

14. For the bilateral meetings see The Ambassador in France to the Department of State, 23 April 1953, FRUS, 1952–1954, 5 (part 1): 369–71; The Ambassador in France to the Department of State, 23 April 1953, ibid., 371–73.

15. Secretary Humphrey's remarks in the meetings with the Europeans that from a fiscal point of view the United States and the United Kingdom had similar problems, and had to find ways to reduce government expenditures, must have had a very unfortunate impact in this situation. See The Ambassador in France to the Department of State, 23 April 1953, FRUS, 1952–1954, 5 (part 1): 372.

16. All quotations from The Ambassador in France to the Department of State, 26 April 1953, FRUS, 1952–1954, 5 (part 1): 385–88.

17. Memorandum of NSC meeting, 28 April 1953, FRUS, 1952–1954, 5 (part 1): 397–99.

18. See for example Draft of Memorandum by the Assistant Secretary of State for European Affairs to the Secretary of State, 7 July 1953, FRUS, 1952–1954, 5 (part 1): 427–32.

19. During the NAC meeting of April 1953, NATO had already slightly reduced the Lisbon force goals. For the exact amount of the reductions, see Watson, *The Joint Chiefs of Staff and National Policy*, 287.

20. For the British position, see Memorandum by the Deputy Assistant Secretary of State for European Affairs to the Secretary of State, 24 September 1953, FRUS, 1952–1954, 5 (part 1): 440–44; Telegraphic Summary, by the U.S. Delegation, 6 December 1953, FRUS, 1952–1954, 5 (part 2): 1788–91.

21. Both quotations from Memorandum by the Deputy Assistant Secretary of State for European Affairs to the Secretary of State, 24 September 1953, FRUS, 1952–1954, 5 (part 1): 442–43. On the point that the Eisenhower administration regarded a German cooperation with other European nations as indispensable for a strong and stable Europe, see Hans-Jürgen Grabbe, "Konrad Adenauer, John Foster Dulles, and West German-American Relations," in *John Foster Dulles and the Diplomacy of the Cold War*, ed. Richard H. Immerman (Princeton: Princeton University Press, 1990), 109–32.

22. Schöttli, *USA und EVG*.

23. Eisenhower, *Mandate for Change*, 139–43.

24. For detailed background on this point, see Watson, *The Joint Chiefs of Staff and National Policy*, 306–11.

25. Secretary Wilson's press conference of 19 October, at which he discussed the question of troop levels in Europe, had a major impact in this regard. In an effort of damage control, the American representative on the Atlantic Council, John C. Hughes, stressed to his European partners that the "US does not contemplate any withdrawal of US troops under NATO command" (The U.S. Permanent Representative on the North Atlantic Council to the Department of State, 28 October 1953, FRUS, 1952–1954, 5 [part 1]: 447–48).

26. Memorandum of NSC meeting, 10 September 1953, FRUS, 1952–1954, 5 (part 1): 449–54. It was decided that it would be the responsibility of the State Department to prepare the allies for the acceptance of the new strategic concept. Public statements regarding new weapons and redeployment would be left to the president.

27. For the origins of the conference see chapter 3.

28. Eisenhower-Laniel Meeting, Bermuda, 5 December 1953, FRUS, 1952–1954, 5 (part 2): 1769–74. See the conversation between Douglas MacArthur II and Laniel in MacArthur-Laniel Meeting, Bermuda, 4 December 1953, ibid., 1740–44.

29. Eisenhower-Laniel Meeting, Bermuda, 5 December 1953, FRUS, 1952–1954, 5 (part 2): 1773. See also Second Tripartite Foreign Ministers Meeting, 5 December 1953, ibid., 1763–67. In the same vein, Dulles threatened "an agoniz-

ing reappraisal of basic United States policy" at the North Atlantic Council meeting in December 1953. Statement by the Secretary of State to the North Atlantic Council, 14 December 1953, FRUS, 1952–1954, 5 (part 1): 463.

30. Both quotations from Third Plenary Tripartite Meeting of the Heads of Government, Bermuda, 6 December 1953, FRUS, 1952–1954, 5 (part 2): 1794–1806. See Memorandum by the Director of the Office of British Commonwealth and North European Affairs to the Counselor of the Department of State, 16 November 1953, ibid., 1715–18.

31. For the French views, see Third Plenary Tripartite Meeting of the Heads of Government, Bermuda, 6 December 1953, FRUS, 1952–1954, 5 (part 2): 1794–1806. Whereas the EDC treaty would run for fifty years, the North Atlantic Pact would expire after twenty years. Thus, by 1969 U.S. and British troops could conceivably depart from the continent, leaving Germany dominant.

32. Telegraphic Summary, by the U.S. Delegation, 6 December 1953, FRUS, 1952–1954, 5 (part 2): 1788–91; Third Plenary Tripartite Meeting of the Heads of Government, Bermuda, 6 December 1953, ibid., 1795.

33. Telegraphic Summary by the U.S. Delegation, 6 December 1953, FRUS, 1952–1954, 5 (part 2): 1790.

34. Statement by the Secretary of State to the North Atlantic Council, 14 December 1953, FRUS, 1952–1954, 5 (part 1): 461–68.

35. Note Prepared by the Assistant Secretary of State for European Affairs on the Restricted Session of the North Atlantic Council, 16 December 1953, FRUS, 1952–1954, 5 (part 1): 476–79.

36. The JCS, for example, could still not agree on the future of NATO strategy. Whereas the army and the navy thought that the forward strategy could be implemented if tactical nuclear weapons were provided to NATO, the air force doubted the feasibility of such a strategy. See Watson, *The Joint Chiefs of Staff and National Policy*, 297–301.

37. All quotations from Memorandum of NSC meeting, 23 December 1953, FRUS, 1952–1954, 5 (part 1): 479–81.

38. See chapter 1.

39. See chapter 2.

40. See chapter 3. In May 1954, Eugene Rabinowitch, the editor of the *Bulletin of the Atomic Scientists*, expressed his alarm "that statesmen (and ordinary citizens) discuss (and some of them advocate) 'massive retaliation' as an answer to local aggression, at the very moment when the Bikini test should have taught them that 'atomic retaliation' has become something no sane person should ever consider as a rational answer to *any* political or military situation (short of direct Soviet aggression against the United States or Western Europe—if then" (Eugene Rabinowitch, "The Hydrogen Bomb and the Great Unsolved Problems," *Bulletin of the Atomic Scientists* 10 [May 1954]: 146–47, 168).

41. Both quotations from Memorandum of Conversation, by the Special Assistant to the Counselor of the Department of State, 30 March 1954, FRUS, 1952–1954, 5 (part 1): 486–87.

42. Editorial note, FRUS, 1952–1954, 5 (part 1): 497–98.

43. All quotations from Memorandum of Conversation between Dulles and Eden, et al., 12 April 1954, FRUS, 1952–1954, 5 (part 1): 499–501.

44. For the origins of the statement, see editorial note, FRUS, 1952–1954, 5 (part 1): 497–98; Statement by the Secretary of State to the North Atlantic Council Closed Ministerial Session, 23 April 1954, ibid., 509–14. The latter source notes the differences between the delivered version and an earlier draft, which were in some parts substantial.

45. All quotations from John Foster Dulles, "Talking Paper" for NATO Meeting in Paris on 22–23 April 1954, SS, "Disarmament-Atomic Weapons and Proposal, 1953, 1954, 1955 [2]," DPEL.

46. The United States Permanent Representative to the North Atlantic Council to the Department of State, 24 April 1953, FRUS, 1952–1954, 5 (part 1): 515.

47. Letter from Eden to Dulles, 28 April 1954, SS, "Disarmament-Atomic Weapons and Proposal, 1953, 1954, 1955 [2]," DPEL.

48. In the aftermath of Stalin's death, and with the first signs of a Soviet "peace offensive," the western powers initiated diplomatic efforts to deal with the major European problems left over from World War II. The Eisenhower administration was reluctant to encourage these developments, doubting the sincerity of the Soviet desire for peace. The Berlin conference was the result of these efforts. France, the United Kingdom, the United States, and the Soviet Union met to discuss the status of Austria and Germany.

49. For background on the history of the EDC, see Schöttli, *USA und EVG*; Rolf Steininger, "John Foster Dulles, the European Defense Community and the German Question," in *John Foster Dulles and the Diplomacy of the Cold War*, ed. Richard H. Immerman (Princeton: Princeton University Press, 1990), 79–108. For an account of the depressing atmosphere in Brussels, see FRUS, 1952–1954, 5 (part 1): 1052–69.

50. For the reaction of the Department of State and in particular of John Foster Dulles, see FRUS, 1952–1954, 5 (part 2): 1114–28.

51. Prime Minister Churchill to the Secretary of State, 24 August 1954, FRUS, 1952–1954, 5 (part 1): 1077–78. See Foreign Secretary Eden to the Secretary of State, 24 August 1954, ibid., 1078–79.

52. The comment of the U.S. observer to the Interim Committee of the EDC, Bruce, on Secretary Dulles's reaction to the rejection of the EDC in the French National Assembly is a good case in point. See The U.S. Observer to the Interim Committee of the EDC to the Department of State, 31 August 1954, FRUS, 1952–1954, 5 (part 2): 1118–19.

53. On this point see Steininger, "John Foster Dulles," 93–94. Ronald Pruessen, for example, demonstrates that doubts about the trustworthiness of Germany were one of the key stimuli for John Foster Dulles's thoughts in the postwar period. See Pruessen, *John Foster Dulles*, 307–12, 330–42.

54. For source material on the London Conference, see FRUS, 1952–1954, 5 (part 2): 1294–1542. See also Lawrence S. Kaplan, *NATO and the United States: The Enduring Alliance* (Boston: Twayne Publishers, 1988), 16–21, 62–66.

55. For the origins and development of General Gruenther's work, see Wampler, *Ambiguous Legacy*, 517–653; Peter, *Abschrecken und Ueberleben*, 250–56; Robert E. Osgood, *NATO: The Entangling Alliance* (Chicago: University of Chicago Press, 1962), 105–26; David N. Schwartz, *NATO's Nuclear Dilemmas* (Washington: The Brookings Institution, 1983), 3–34.

56. Memorandum by the Secretary of State and the Secretary of Defense to the President, 2 November 1954, FRUS, 1952–1954, 5 (part 1): 529–32. MC-48 is still classified, but secondary sources give a reasonable overview of its main points.

57. Memorandum by the Assistant Secretary of State for European Affairs to the Secretary of State, 1 November 1954, FRUS, 1952–1954, 5 (part 1): 527–29; Memorandum by the Secretary of State and the Secretary of Defense to the President, 2 November 1954, ibid., 531.

58. Memorandum by the Secretary of State and the Secretary of Defense to the President, 2 November 1954, FRUS, 1952–1954, 5 (part 1): 531.

59. The Assistant Secretary of State for European Affairs to the U.S. Permanent Representative on the NAC, 24 November 1954, FRUS, 1952–1954, 5 (part 1): 538–39. This was essentially John Foster Dulles's "agonizing reappraisal" threat reconsidered.

60. The Assistant Secretary of State for European Affairs to the U.S. Permanent Representative on the NAC, 24 November 1954, FRUS, 1952–1954, 5 (part 1): 538.

61. The U.S. Permanent Representative on the NAC to the Department of State, 4 December 1954, FRUS, 1952–1954, 5 (part 1): 539–40.

62. The French at one point suggested the formation of a high-level political standing group in which to register the approval of all members before the employment of nuclear weapons in case of attack. See Memorandum of Conversation, by the Assistant Secretary of State for European Affairs, 20 November 1954, FRUS, 1952–1954, 5 (part 1): 535–36.

63. The Secretary of State to the Department of State, 17 December 1954, FRUS, 1952–1954, 5 (part 1): 548–49.

64. All quotations from Memorandum of Conversation, by the Director of the Policy Planning Staff, 16 December 1954, FRUS, 1952–1954, 5 (part 1): 548; Memorandum of Conversation, by the Assistant Secretary of State for European Affairs, 19 December 1954, ibid., 560.

65. Memorandum of NSC meeting, 21 December 1954, FRUS, 1952–1954, 5 (part 1): 560–62.

66. Memorandum of Conversation, by the Director of the Policy Planning Staff, 16 December 1954, FRUS, 1952–1954, 5 (part 1): 548.

67. The Secretary of State to the Department of State, 17 December 1954, FRUS, 1952–1954, 5 (part 1): 548–49.

68. The State Department realized the advantages of Lord Ismay taking the lead in presenting the report. However, it took great care to make sure that Ismay's statement was along U.S. lines. The Assistant Secretary of State for Euro-

pean Affairs to the U.S. Permanent Representative on the NAC, 24 November 1954, FRUS, 1952–1954, 5 (part 1): 538–39.

69. All quotations from the U.S. Delegation at the NAC Meeting to the Department of State, 18 December 1954, FRUS, 1952–1954, 5 (part 1): 557–59.

70. NATO decided with MC-48 that the future security of the alliance would depend on nuclear weapons and that military planning should take account of tactical nuclear weapons. With the endorsement of MC-14/2 in December 1956, NATO agreed on a new strategic concept stemming from these changes. See J. Michael Legge, "Theater Nuclear Weapons and the NATO Strategy of Flexible Response," *RAND Report R-2964-FF* (Santa Monica: The RAND Corporation, 1983), 2–7.

71. Trachtenberg, *History and Strategy*, 154–60.

Chapter 5

1. Of the civilian strategists, both Bernard Brodie and Henry Kissinger at one point called for bigger reliance on tactical nuclear weapons. See Brodie, "Nuclear Weapons: Strategic or Tactical?" 226–28; Kissinger, *Nuclear Weapons and Foreign Policy*, 145–68.

2. Both quotations from Diary Entry by the President's Press Secretary, 1 February 1955, FRUS, 1955–1957, 19: 39–40.

3. Memorandum of NSC meeting, 27 February 1956, FRUS, 1955–1957, 19: 210.

4. Memorandum of Conversation with the President, 22 December 1954, WHMS, "Meetings with the President, 1954 [1]," DPEL.

5. Both quotations from Memorandum of Conversation with the President, 7 March 1955, WHMS, "Meetings with the President, 1955 [7]," DPEL.

6. Quotation from editorial note, FRUS, 1955–1957, 19: 60–61. See *Department of State Bulletin*, 21 March 1955, 459–64.

7. Editorial note, FRUS, 1955–1957, 19: 61. In a news conference on 16 March, President Eisenhower said he could see no reason why, in a combat situation where they could be used on strictly military targets, tactical nuclear weapons should not be used "just exactly as you would use a bullet or anything else" (Ibid.).

8. The Taiwan Strait crisis and the impact of nuclear weapons on its development deserve a broader analysis. In our context, it is sufficient to show how the crisis affected the debate over more limited forces. For a detailed analysis of the crisis, see Bundy, *Danger and Survival*, 273–87; George and Smoke, *Deterrence in American Foreign Policy*, 266–94, 363–89; Herring, "A Good Stout Effort," 213–33; H. W. Brands, Jr., "Testing Massive Retaliation: Credibility and Crisis Management in the Taiwan Strait," *International Security* 12 (Spring 1988): 124–51.

9. Address by John Foster Dulles before the Illinois Manufacturers' Associa-

tion, 8 December 1955, Selected Correspondence and Related Materials: 1955, "Massive Retaliation Policy 1955," DPP. See editorial note, FRUS, 1955–1957, 19: 173.

10. Department of State General Comments on NSC 5501, 3 October 1955, FRUS, 1955–1957, 19: 123–25.

11. Outline for a speech by the Secretary of State, 19 May 1955, FRUS, 1955–1957, 19: 79–81; NIE 100-7-55, "World Situation and Trends," 1 November 1955, ibid., 131–45.

12. All quotations from John Foster Dulles, Draft #11, 28 January 1956, SS, "Paper on Nuclear Weapons—1/56 [1]," DPEL. See John Foster Dulles, Draft #10, 22 January 1956, SS, "Paper on Nuclear Weapons—1/56 [1]," DPEL. For Eisenhower's answer, see Eisenhower to Dulles, 23 January 1956, SS, "Disarmament—Papers on Nuclear Weapons, January 1956 [1]," DPEL.

13. For an excellent outline of Robert Bowie's approach to the problems of an era of mutual deterrence, see Memorandum from Bowie to Dulles, 4 January 1956, SS, "Paper on Nuclear Weapons—1/56 [5]," DPEL.

14. On 14 February 1955, the president had approved the recommendation of the NESC that the evaluation of the net capability of the USSR, in the event of general war, to inflict injury upon the United States should be carried out on a continuous basis. See editorial note, FRUS, 1955–1957, 19: 56–57. The annual report of 1955 had been discussed in the NSC on 27 October, but in the absence of the president. See Memorandum of NSC meeting, 27 October 1955, ibid., 126–30.

15. Diary Entry by the President, 23 January 1956, FRUS, 1955–1957, 19: 187–88.

16. All quotations from Memorandum for the Record by the President's Special Assistant for National Security Affairs, 23 January 1956, FRUS, 1955–1957, 19: 188–91.

17. All quotations from Memorandum of NSC meeting, 27 February 1956, FRUS, 1955–1957, 19: 201–18.

18. Memorandum, JCS to the Secretary of Defense, 24 February 1956, FRUS, 1955–1957, 19: 200; Memorandum, Secretary of Defense to the Executive Secretary of the NSC, 24 February 1956, ibid., 199.

19. Memorandum of NSC meeting, 27 February 1956, FRUS, 1955–1957, 19: 201–18; Memorandum, JCS to the Secretary of Defense, 22 March 1956, ibid., 234–38.

20. Memorandum of NSC meeting, 27 February 1956, FRUS, 1955–1957, 19: 203.

21. All quotations from Memorandum of NSC meeting, 27 February 1956, FRUS, 1955–1957, 19: 201–18.

22. The president himself proposed the structure for a new report. He urged the JCS to show what had been accomplished over the last three years and to recognize that a sound economy was a fundamental element of overall U.S. security. See Memorandum of a Conference with the President, 13 March 1956, FRUS, 1955–1957, 19: 238–41.

23. Memorandum of NSC meeting, 27 February 1956, FRUS, 1955–1957, 19: 204, 206.

24. All quotations from NSC 5602/1, "Basic National Security Policy," 15 March 1956, FRUS, 1955–1957, 19: 242–68.

25. Memorandum of NSC meeting, 27 February 1956, FRUS, 1955–1957, 19: 203.

26. Memorandum of NSC meeting, 22 March 1956, FRUS, 1955–1957, 19: 268–74.

27. All quotations from Memorandum of NSC meeting, 22 March 1956, FRUS, 1955–1957, 19: 268–74.

28. Memorandum of Conference with the President, 30 March 1956, FRUS, 1955–1957, 19: 280–83.

29. All quotations from Memorandum of a Conference with the President, 14 May 1956, FRUS, 1955–1957, 19: 301–3.

30. In this connection, Eisenhower came to think that the chief of staff system had failed. Although he discussed alternative organizational solutions, nothing concrete came of these ideas. Notes on a Meeting with the President, 29 March 1956, FRUS, 1955–1957, 19: 276–79; Memorandum of a Conference with the President, 5 April 1956, ibid., 285–90; Memorandum of a Conference with the President, 18 May ibid., 303–5.

31. Memorandum of a Conference with the President, 18 May 1956, FRUS, 1955–1957, 19: 303–5. See the president's remarks at a meeting of the NSC: Memorandum of NSC meeting, 17 May 1956, FRUS, 1955–1957, 19: 305–11.

32. See Secretary Dulles's comments in Memorandum of a Luncheon Conversation among the Secretary of State, the Secretary of the Treasury, and the Secretary of Defense, 19 April 1956, FRUS, 1955–1957, 19: 299.

33. Memorandum for the Record, 13 August 1956, FRUS, 1955–1957, 4: 94; Memorandum of Conversation, 13 August 1956, ibid., 93–95.

34. Memorandum of Conference with the President, 11 October 1956, FRUS, 1955–1957, 19: 369–70.

35. Through the JSOP the JCS gave guidance to the service staffs, which served as the basis for programs and funds.

36. All quotations from Memorandum of a Conference with the President, 24 May 1956, FRUS, 1955–1957, 19: 311–15.

37. Memorandum of NSC discussion, 17 May 1956, FRUS, 1955–1957, 19: 307.

38. Memorandum of a Conversation between Dulles and British Ambassador Makins, 19 April 1956, FRUS, 1955–1957, 27: 655–56. Around the same time, Eisenhower wrote to Churchill that he thought that mutual nuclear plenty tended "to reduce very materially the possibility of *any* war; but I think it would be unsafe to predict that if the West and East should ever become locked up in a life and death struggle, both sides would still have sense enough not to use this horrible instrument" (Letter, Eisenhower to Churchill, 27 April 1956, NNP 1945–91, No. 00255, NSA).

39. Telegram from the U.S. Delegation at the NAC Ministerial Meeting to the Department of State, 5 May 1956, FRUS, 1955–1957, 4: 57–62.

40. Telegram from the U.S. Delegation at the NAC Ministerial Meeting to the Department of State, 5 May 1956, FRUS, 1955–1957, 4: 66–70; Telegram from the U.S. Delegation at the NAC Ministerial Meeting to the Department of State, 5 May 1956, ibid., 70–71; Message, Secretary of State to the President, 5 May 1956, ibid., 75; Message, Secretary of State to the President, 6 May 1956, ibid., 76–77.

41. Memorandum of a Conversation between the Secretary of State and British Ambassador Makins, 29 June 1956, FRUS, 1955–1957, 4: 84–88; Memorandum of NSC meeting, 10 May 1956, ibid., 77–84.

42. Letter, Eden to Eisenhower, 18 July 1956, FRUS, 1955–1957, 4: 90–92.

43. Memorandum of a Conversation between the Secretary of State and British Ambassador Makins, 13 July 1956, FRUS, 1955–1957, 4: 89–90.

44. Both quotations from Memorandum of NSC meeting, 10 May 1956, FRUS, 1955–1957, 4: 77–84.

45. Memorandum Prepared in the Department of State, 29 June 1956, FRUS, 1955–1957, 4: 87–88.

46. For the influence of the Suez crisis on the special relationship between the United Kingdom and the United States, see Roger Wm. Louis, "Dulles, Suez, and the British," in *John Foster Dulles and the Diplomacy of the Cold War*, ed. Richard H. Immerman (Princeton: Princeton University Press, 1990), 133–58. For the Suez crisis, see Peter, *Abschrecken und Ueberleben*, 281–343; Dwight D. Eisenhower, *The White House Years: Waging Peace, 1956–1961* (New York: Doubleday & Company, 1963), 20–57.

47. On the occasion of visiting Chancellor Adenauer on 28 September, Senator George had given his host the complete assurance of the president that the United States had no intention of withdrawing. See Memorandum, Dulles to Eisenhower, 1 October 1956, FRUS, 1955–1957, 4: 96–99.

48. Both quotations from Memorandum of Conference with the President, 2 October 1956, FRUS, 1955–1957, 4: 99–102. For the position of the State Department, see Memorandum for the President, 1 October 1956, WHMS, "White House Correspondence—General, 1956 [1]," DPEL.

49. For the contents of the American answer (the memorandum itself is not available), see Memorandum, Dulles to Eisenhower, 1 October 1956, FRUS, 1955–1957, 4: 96–99; Memorandum of Conference with the President, 2 October 1956, ibid., 99–102.

50. Editorial note, FRUS, 1955–1957, 4: 102.

51. In his departure statement, John Foster Dulles noted that "this meeting would perhaps be the most important meeting NATO had held" (editorial note, FRUS, 1955–1957, 4: 103).

52. Telegram from the U.S. Delegation at the NAC Ministerial Meeting, 14 December 1956, FRUS, 1955–1957, 4: 149–56.

53. The solution of this question involved difficult political and constitutional

issues and was not developed much further before the Bermuda Conference between British prime minister Harold Macmillan and President Eisenhower, 21–23 March 1957, which will later be discussed. See chapter 6.

54. Both quotations are from Memorandum of NSC meeting, 21 December 1956, FRUS, 1955–1957, 19: 384–94.

55. See the remarks of the French representative at the NAC meeting: On 18 November 1956, Bulganin had written in a letter to the president of the French Council of Ministers, Mollet, that the balance of forces was now such as to allow the Soviets to attack without nuclear weapons. See Telegram from the U.S. Delegation at the NAC Ministerial Meeting to the Department of State, 14 December 1956, FRUS, 1955–1957, 4: 151.

56. All quotations from Memorandum of NSC meeting, 28 February 1957, FRUS, 1955–1957, 19: 425–41.

57. See the remarks of Robert Cutler while presenting the second draft (NSC 5707/1) to the NSC in Memorandum of NSC meeting, 28 March 1957, FRUS, 1955–1957, 19: 446–56.

58. All quotations from Memorandum of NSC meeting, 11 April 1957, FRUS, 1955–1957, 19: 465–80.

59. The decision-making process on how to deter and fight local wars shows a president who is in charge of national security policy matters. The fact that he suppressed further discussion of the topic within the NSC and forced the language of the basic national security policy paper into line with actual policy, sheds light on the political weight of both the council and the policy paper. The most important decisions regarding these matters were reached outside the NSC, in smaller meetings between the president and key members of the administration. A good case in point is Eisenhower's meeting with General Taylor. After listening to the arguments of the army chief of staff, he outlined his own ideas regarding the future of U.S. military strategy, expecting the army to fall in line. The council then gave its formal blessing to these decisions, making them visible for all its members. For a study of President Eisenhower's use of the NSC machinery, see Greenstein, *The Hidden-Hand Presidency*, 124–38.

60. The State Department did not actually suggest alternate language. It only informed the Council of its general views in the form of an annex to NSC 5707/ 7. See Memorandum of NSC meeting, 27 May 1957, FRUS, 1955–1957, 19: 497.

61. All quotations from Memorandum of NSC meeting, 27 May 1957, FRUS, 1955–1957, 19: 488–507. Secretary Dulles had played an important part in burying the earlier attempt of the Planning Board to revise the language of the policy paper with respect to local wars. He was, therefore, in the difficult position to argue against the position of the Defense Department without contradicting his earlier statement.

62. For the precise language used by the Defense Department, see Memorandum of NSC meeting, 27 May 1957, FRUS, 1955–1957, 19: 493–96.

63. All quotations from Memorandum of NSC meeting, 27 May 1957, FRUS, 1955–1957, 19: 488–507. The secretary of state warned that world opinion was not yet ready to accept the general use of nuclear weapons in local conflicts.

64. Memorandum of NSC meeting, 27 May 1957, FRUS, 1955–1957, 19: 502–3.

65. NSC 5707/8, "Basic National Security Policy," 3 June 1957, FRUS, 1955–1957, 19: 507–24.

66. Following a request of the president, Admiral Strauss presented a report about the stock numbers of nuclear weapons below the 10-megaton range in a meeting of most of the members of the NSC on 7 June. The brief presentation provoked considerable questioning and Secretary Dulles demanded that the topic should be taken up again in a formal NSC meeting. The details of further discussions remain classified. See Memorandum of NSC meeting, 13 June 1957, FRUS, 1955–1957, 19: 524–26.

67. Excerpts of the speech are quoted in editorial note, FRUS, 1955–1957, 19: 526–27.

68. The connection is most clearly spelled out in a memorandum by Admiral Radford. It was his opinion that the definition of local aggression provided in NSC 5707/8 indicated that "there will be no large-scale employment of U.S. forces, particularly ground forces, in armed conflict short of general war." The Chairman of the JCS therefore stressed the necessity for reduction of overseas deployments, particularly from Europe. See Memorandum, Radford to Wilson, 16 July 1957, FRUS, 1955–1957, 19: 549–53.

69. Of all the services, the army was hit hardest with a projected reduction from presently approved 1,000,000 men to 900,000 at the end of fiscal year 1958, and to 850,000 at the end of fiscal year 1959. For the numbers, see Memorandum, Secretary of Defense to the President, 10 July 1957, FRUS, 1955–1957, 19: 540–46.

70. Memorandum, Cutler to the President, 1 July 1957, FRUS, 1955–1957, 19: 533–35; Memorandum, Radford to Cutler, 3 July 1957, ibid., 538–39; Memorandum, Cutler to the President, 5 July 1957, ibid., 539–40.

71. Memorandum, Cutler to the President, 1 July 1957, FRUS, 1955–1957, 19: 533–35.

72. Memorandum of NSC meeting, 25 July 1957, FRUS, 1955–1957, 19: 556–65.

73. For the details of the decision, see Memorandum, Secretary of Defense to the President, 10 July 1957, FRUS, 1955–1957, 19: 540–46; Memorandum of a Conference with the President, 16 August 1957, ibid., 586–91; Memorandum, Secretary of Defense to the President, 12 September 1957, ibid., 595–97.

74. For a comparable argument, see Immerman, "Confessions of an Eisenhower Revisionist," 330–32.

75. See chapter 3.

76. Memorandum of NSC meeting, 17 April 1957, FRUS, 1955–1957, 19: 480–86.

77. Memorandum of NSC meeting, 20 December 1956, FRUS, 1955–1957, 19: 379–84.

78. The President used this argument several times during the debate in the

NSC leading to NSC 5707/8. See Memorandum of NSC meeting, 20 December 1956, FRUS, 1955–1957, 19: 380; Memorandum of NSC meeting, 7 February 1957, ibid., 413–19.

79. See chapter 3.

Chapter 6

1. A. J. Wohlstetter, F. S. Hoffman; R. J. Lutz, and H. S. Rowen, "Selection and Use of Strategic Air Bases," *RAND Report R-266* (Santa Monica: The RAND Corporation, 1962).

2. Decision on AFC 22/4a, "Vulnerability of the USAF Strategic Striking Complex," 10 March 1953, Air Force Council Decisions, Vol. I, Box 103, Twining Papers, LC; Decision on AFC 22/4b, "Vulnerability of the Strategic Striking Complex," 2 November 1953, ibid.

3. Memorandum of NSC meeting, 16 June 1955, FRUS, 1955–1957, 19: 87–94, particularly fn. 4, 88.

4. Memorandum of NSC meeting, 16 June 1955, FRUS, 1955–1957, 19: 89. For a systematic analysis of intelligence estimates regarding the Soviet threat, see Lawrence Freedman, *U.S. Intelligence and the Soviet Strategic Threat* (London: The Macmillan Press, 1986); with respect to the time period under consideration, see pp. 63–67.

5. Memorandum of NSC meeting, 16 June 1955, FRUS, 1955–1957, 19: 91. The bulk of the Soviet bomber force, consisting to a high percentage of TU-4, could reach targets within the continental United States only on a one-way mission. For the development of the Soviet strategic forces, see Robert P. Berman and John C. Baker, *Soviet Strategic Forces: Requirements and Responses* (Washington: The Brookings Institution, 1982).

6. Memorandum of NSC meeting, 16 June 1955, FRUS, 1955–1957, 19: 87–94.

7. On 9 August 1955, the Defense Department briefed the NSC on the measures taken and planned to reduce the vulnerability of the SAC, including cost estimates. See Memorandum of NSC meeting, 9 August 1956, FRUS, 1955–1957, 19: 338–41. See also Decision on FC 20/7, "Strategic Plan of Operations," 6 March 1956, Air Force Council Decisions, Vol. I, Box 103, Twining Papers, LC.

8. The Killian Committee finished its report on 14 February 1955. The report is partially reprinted in Report by the Technological Capabilities Panel of the Science Advisory Committee, "Meeting the Threat of Surprise Attack," 14 February 1955, FRUS, 1955–1957, 19: 41–56.

9. For the full list of all general and specific recommendations, see Report by the Technological Capabilities Panel of the Science Advisory Committee, "Meeting the Threat of Surprise Attack," 14 February 1955, FRUS, 1955–1957, 19: 46–60.

10. Report by the Technological Capabilities Panel of the Science Advisory

Committee, "Meeting the Threat of Surprise Attack," 14 February 1955, FRUS, 1955–1957, 19: 44, 46.

11. Memorandum of NSC meeting, 17 March 1955, FRUS, 1955–1957, 19: 63–68.

12. Memorandum of NSC meeting, 4 August 1955, FRUS, 1955–1957, 19: 95–96.

13. All quotations from Memorandum of NSC meeting, 4 August 1955, FRUS, 1955–1957, 19: 95–108.

14. Supplementary Notes on the Legislative Leadership Meeting, 14 February 1956, FRUS, 1955–1957, 19: 196–98.

15. Both quotations from Memorandum of NSC meeting, 8 September 1955, FRUS, 1955–1957, 19: 111–22.

16. Memorandum Prepared in the Department of State, n.d., FRUS, 1955–1957, 19: 154–61.

17. In a preparatory memorandum, Robert Bowie had briefed the acting secretary of state to this end. See Memorandum, Bowie to the Acting Secretary of State, 7 September 1955, FRUS, 1955–1957, 19: 110–11.

18. Memorandum of NSC meeting, 8 September 1955, FRUS, 1955–1957, 19: 111–22.

19. This language newly included the supplementary phrase "above all others." Memorandum of NSC meeting, 8 September 1955, FRUS, 1955–1957, 19: 111–22.

20. The president explained his opposition to a Manhattan-type project in a letter to Secretary Wilson and repeated it in the above-mentioned diary entry. See Memorandum of NSC meeting, 8 September 1955, FRUS, 1955–1957, 19: 118; Diary Entry by the President, 30 March 1956, FRUS, 1955–1957, 19: 275–76.

21. Memorandum Prepared in the Department of State, n.d., FRUS, 1955–1957, 19: 154–61.

22. Report Prepared in the Department of Defense, n.d., FRUS, 1955–1957, 19: 161–66.

23. For the exchange between the president and Secretary Wilson, see Memorandum of NSC meeting, 1 December 1955, FRUS, 1955–1957, 19: 166–70.

24. The director of the ODM, Arthur Flemming, immediately replied to Secretary Wilson's statement that he did not hope that "doubts as to national security programs would be resolved in favor of some fiscal advantage unless there were very sound reasons for such a resolution" (Memorandum of NSC meeting, 15 November 1955, FRUS, 1955–1957, 19: 145–50).

25. Memorandum of NSC meeting, 16/17 August 1956, FRUS, 1955–1957, 19: 345–57; Memorandum of NSC meeting, 11 January 1957, ibid., 401–9.

26. The president had called for such a report (Memorandum of NSC meeting, 28 March 1957, FRUS, 1955–1957, 19: 446–56). After listening to the results of the study, he noted that comparable studies in the future should always take into account the total cost of the weapon system in relation to its effectiveness. This remark showed the president's preference for bombers from a strictly mili-

tary point of view. He presumably expected better results for the manned aircraft because of the fact that bombers could be used more than once, whereas missiles, once launched, would never return. See Memorandum of NSC meeting, 20 June 1955, ibid., 528–30.

27. Memorandum of NSC meeting, 3 July 1957, FRUS, 1955–1957, 19: 535–38.

28. Memorandum of NSC meeting, 1 August 1957, FRUS, 1955–1957, 19: 565–72.

29. The president only reluctantly agreed to place the missile under the management of the air force because of the problem this would pose for the army. But finally the argumentation of Secretary Wilson, who stressed that the air force should be responsible in accordance with its roles and missions and moreover had the required funds in its fiscal year 1958 budget, seemed to have convinced the president. See Memorandum of NSC meeting, 1 August 1957, FRUS, 1955–1957, 19: 565–72.

30. Memorandum of NSC meeting, 3 July 1957, FRUS, 1955–1957, 19: 535–38; Letter, Secretary of Defense to the President, 9 August 1957, ibid., 580–83. For the development of the Polaris program, see Harvey M. Sapolsky, *The Polaris System Development: Bureaucratic and Programmatic Success in Government* (Cambridge: Harvard University Press, 1972).

31. Memorandum of NSC meeting, 10 October 1957, FRUS, 1955–1957, 19: 601–5. The problem seems to have been that it was impossible at the moment to cancel the Jupiter—which would have been more desirable from an organizational point of view—because the Jupiter missile at that time showed the better test results. See Memorandum of a Conference with the President, 16 August 1957, ibid., 587–91; Memorandum of a Conference with the President, 8 October 1957, ibid., 589–601.

32. Memorandum of a Conference with the President, 16 August 1957, FRUS, 1955–1957, 19: 586–88; Memorandum of a Conference with the President, 8 October 1957, ibid., 589–601.

33. Both quotations from Memorandum of NSC meeting, 11 January 1957, FRUS, 1955–1957, 19: 405–9.

34. See his remarks to members of the Science Advisory Committee in Memorandum of a Conference with the President, 29 March 1957, FRUS, 1955–1957, 19: 456–59.

35. Regarding the accumulating intelligence data, see editorial note, FRUS, 1955–1957, 19: 593–94. For the impact of *Sputnik* on the scientific community, see James R. Killian, Jr., *Sputnik, Scientists, and Eisenhower: A Memoir of the First Special Assistant to the President for Science and Technology* (Cambridge: MIT Press, 1977), 2–3.

36. Eisenhower gives a lively impression of the anxiety that *Sputnik* aroused in Eisenhower, *Waging Peace,* 220–26.

37. For the press coverage see *Washington Post,* 20 December 1957; *New York Times,* 23 November 1957; Joseph and Stewart Alsop, *The Reporter's Trade* (New York: Reynal & Company, 1958), 361–64.

38. The report was declassified in 1983, see NSC 5724, "Deterrence and Survival in the Nuclear Age: Report to the President by the Security Resources Panel of the Science Advisory Committee," 7 November 1957, OSANSA, NSC, Box 22, DDEL (hereafter cited as Gaither report). The report is in part reprinted in FRUS, 1955–1957, 19: 638–61.

39. All quotations from Memorandum of NSC meeting, 4 April 1957, FRUS, 1955–1957, 19: 459–64.

40. More than ninety persons (including advisors and staff) were working on the report, including William C. Foster, John J. McCloy, Robert A. Lovett, Dr. Frank Stanton, Admiral Carney, and Paul H. Nitze. For a list of the members of the Steering Committee, see editorial note, FRUS, 1955–1957, 19: 628–29.

41. Apparently, the president was not informed about the expansion of the study's scope. See Peter, *Abschrecken und Ueberleben*, 214–15; Fred Kaplan underlines the influence of Albert Wohlstetter's vulnerability studies with respect to this expansion. See Kaplan, *The Wizards of Armageddon*, 125–43; Thomas D. White, Memorandum for General LeMay, 15 August 1957, "1957—Top Secret File," Box 41, White Papers, LC.

42. Sprague's visit is described by Kaplan, *Wizards of Armageddon*, 132–34, 150–54. See Sprague's report to the president and a few of his key advisers: Memorandum of NSC meeting, 7 November 1957, FRUS, 1955–1957, 19: 635. The vulnerability of SAC was of great concern to its new commander, General Thomas S. Power, who had succeeded General LeMay on 1 July 1957. Power wrote to air force chief of staff General Thomas D. White, that under worst conditions "no warning can be guaranteed to any of my bases" (Letter, General Power to General White, 23 December 1957, "1957—Top Secret Folder," Box 41, White Papers, LC).

43. Gaither report, see appendixes B and F.

44. Gaither report. David Alan Rosenberg has noted that the president was privately informed that three of the Gaither Panel's members advocated reconsidering preventive war as a means of preempting future instability. See Rosenberg, "The Origins of Overkill," 46–49.

45. Memorandum of NSC meeting, 7 November 1957, FRUS, 1955–1957, 19: 632.

46. Eisenhower told Dulles in a phone call on 26 December 1957, that the Gaither exercise had definitely proved "the unwisdom of calling in outside groups" (Memorandum of a Conversation between the President and the Secretary of State, 26 December 1957, FRUS, 1955–1957, 19: 712).

47. Memorandum of a Conference with the President, 4 November 1957, FRUS, 1955–1957, 19: 621.

48. Memorandum of NSC meeting, 7 November 1957, FRUS, 1955–1957, 19: 633–34. Eisenhower made use of this passage to describe his government's reaction to the Gaither report in his memoirs. See Eisenhower, *Waging Peace*, 221–22.

49. Memorandum of NSC meeting, 7 November 1957, FRUS, 1955–1957, 19: 632.

50. For the phone conversation, see Memorandum of a Conversation between the President and the Secretary of State, 7 November 1957, FRUS, 1955–1957, 19: 638.

51. President Eisenhower reached this conclusion during the discussion of the report by the Net Evaluation Subcommittee on 12 November 1957. The report concluded that "in the event of a Soviet attack on the U.S. in 1960, both the U.S. and the USSR would be devastated" (Memorandum of NSC meeting, 12 November 1957, FRUS, 1955–1957, 19: 672–76).

52. Memorandum of a Conference with the President, 11 November 1957, FRUS, 1955–1957, 19: 662–64. Eisenhower was already moving in such a direction in his comments on the two presentations of the Gaither report, one in the NSC, and the other in a smaller meeting. See Memorandum of a Conference with the President, 4 November 1957, ibid., 620–24; Memorandum of NSC meeting, 7 November 1957, ibid., 630–35.

53. Memorandum of a Conference with the President, 4 November 1957, FRUS, 1955–1957, 19: 622.

54. Both quotations from Memorandum of NSC meeting, 7 November 1957, FRUS, 1955–1957, 19: 632–34.

55. Memorandum of a Conference with the President, 22 November 1957, FRUS, 1955–1957, 19: 687–88; Memorandum of NSC meeting, 22 November 1957, ibid., 694.

56. Memorandum of NSC meeting, 22 November 1957, FRUS, 1955–1957, 19: 693.

57. Memorandum of NSC meeting, 22 November 1957, FRUS, 1955–1957, 19: 693–94.

58. Memorandum of a Conversation, FRUS, 1955–1957, 19: 697.

59. When the administration presented the defense program in a bipartisan congressional meeting, the president indicated his personal skepticism with respect to the acceleration of the missile development programs. In reply to a query of Senator Anderson, who thought that the United States had too many different, redundant missile programs, Eisenhower referred the senator to the specialists. "He invited Sen. Anderson to go over to the Defense Department where they would brief him for two solid days—and leave him thoroughly confused" (Minutes of a Bipartisan Congressional Meeting, 3 December 1957, FRUS, 1955–1957, 19: 701–2).

60. Memorandum of a Conversation, 25 October 1957, FRUS, 1955–1957, 4: 182–83.

61. For the details of the discussion on this issue, see Memorandum of a Conference with the President, 11 November 1957, FRUS, 1955–1957, 19: 664; Memorandum of NSC meeting, 14 November 1957, ibid., 677–86; Memorandum of NSC meeting, 22 November 1957, ibid., 689–95.

62. Memorandum of a Conference with the President, 5 December 1957, FRUS, 1955–1957, 19: 704.

63. All quotations from Memorandum of a Conference with the President, 5 December 1957, FRUS, 1955–1957, 19: 702–4.

64. Eisenhower, *Waging Peace*, 217.

65. In a brilliant article, Immerman reflects on Eisenhower's conception of national security strategy, particularly as related to the nuclear age. Immerman succeeds in giving a comprehensive picture of Eisenhower's core beliefs regarding national security. See Immerman, "Confessions of an Eisenhower Revisionist," 319–42.

66. Both Richard Aliano and Desmond Ball concentrate in their writings on showing how factors of the domestic environment influenced the nation's reaction to *Sputnik* and the missile gap during the transition from Eisenhower to Kennedy. Both emphasize that foreign policy cannot be understood only as a reaction to external stimuli (like the Soviet threat), but must also be seen as a function of the domestic policy process. Internal factors, so their argument runs, provide a superior explanation for the changes in defense policy from Eisenhower to Kennedy. See Richard A. Aliano, *American Defense Policy from Eisenhower to Kennedy: The Politics of Changing Military Requirements, 1957–1961* (Athens: Ohio University Press, 1975); Ball, *Politics and Force Levels*, 1–88.

67. Joseph Alsop, "After Ike, the Deluge," *Washington Post*, 7 October 1959, A17; Stewart Alsop, "Our Gamble with Destiny," *Saturday Evening Post*, 16 May 1959, 23, 114–18.

68. Wohlstetter pointed out that a survivable second-strike capability as the basis of a strategy of deterrence did not come automatically: "Deterrence is a matter of comparative risks. The balance is not automatic. First, since thermonuclear weapons give an enormous advantage to the aggressor, it takes great ingenuity and realism at any given level of nuclear technology to devise a stable equilibrium. And second, this technology itself is changing with fantastic speed. Deterrence will require an urgent and continuing effort" (Wohlstetter, "The Delicate Balance of Terror," 211–34).

69. Henry A. Kissinger, *The Necessity for Choice: Prospects of American Foreign Policy* (New York: Harper & Brothers, 1961), 26, 39.

70. For the election campaign, see Theodore H. White, *The Making of the President 1960* (New York: Athenaeum, 1961); Sorensen, *Kennedy*, 191–253; Schlesinger, *A Thousand Days*, 62–76.

71. See for example the following collection of Kennedy's foreign policy speeches: John F. Kennedy, *The Strategy of Peace*, ed. by Allan Nevins (New York: Harper & Brothers, 1960), 184.

72. Speech by Senator Kennedy, *Congressional Record*, Senate, 29 February 1960, 3801.

73. Kennedy, *The Strategy of Peace*, 37–38.

74. As early as 1957, Kennedy had called for increased attention to the problem of limited war. See John F. Kennedy, "A Democrat Looks at Foreign Policy," *Foreign Affairs* 36, No. 1 (October 1957): 44–59. Moreover, he read and agreed with General Maxwell D. Taylor's *Uncertain Trumpet* (New York: Harper, 1960) and Liddell Hart's *Deterrent or Defense*. See John M. Taylor, *General Maxwell Taylor: The Sword and the Pen* (New York: Doubleday, 1989), 8; Robert Frank Futrell,

Ideas, Concepts, Doctrine: A History of Basic Thinking in the United States Air Force, 1907–1964 (Maxwell Air Force Base, Ala.: Air University, 1974), 317.

75. The best study of the reliability of intelligence estimates with respect to the missile gap remains the one by Edgar M. Bottome, *The Missile Gap: A Study of the Formulation of Military and Political Policy* (Rutherford, N.J.: Fairleigh Dickinson University Press, 1971). See also Colin S. Gray, " 'Gap' Prediction and America's Defense: Arms Race Behavior in the Eisenhower Years," *ORBIS* 16, No. 1 (Spring 1972): 257–75.

76. The NIE of 1958 and 1959 are summarized in JCS 1899/523, 20 October 1959, CCS 3340, "Strategic Air and ICBM Operations," 10 September 1959, JCS, NARS.

77. See for example Estimates of Sino-Soviet Capabilities World-Wide, 59–63, and Assessment of Dimensions of Soviet ICBM Threat to Security of US, 30 September 1957, "McConnell Report," Box 6, White Papers, LC.

78. For a good analysis of the basis of the NIE of December 1958, see Memorandum, Lawrence C. McQuade to Paul Nitze, "But Where Did the Missile Gap Go?" 31 May 1963, "May 1963 Folder," NH Box 16, NSA, 5–9.

79. He wrote of the U-2 flights: "Intelligence gained from this source provided proof that the horrors of the alleged 'bomber gap' and the later 'missile gap' were nothing more than imaginative creation of irresponsibility" (Eisenhower, *Waging Peace*, 547).

80. Freedman, *U.S. Intelligence and the Soviet Strategic Threat*, 67–72.

81. Memorandum, Lawrence C. McQuade to Paul Nitze, "But Where Did the Missile Gap Go?" 31 May 1963, "May 1963 Folder," NH Box 16, NSA, 9–10.

82. For background and a summary of his statement, see Memorandum, McNamara to the President, "The Missile Gap Controversy," 4 March 1963, "Missile Gap 2/63–5/63 Folder," Box 298, Subject Series, NSF, JFKL.

83. See for example the skeptical reaction of George Kistiakowsky, the president's special assistant for science and technology, when he first heard of the intelligence reductions: "I hope this estimate is not a political effort to cut down on trouble with Congress" (George B. Kistiakowsky, *A Scientist at the White House: The Private Diary of President Eisenhower's Special Assistant for Science and Technology* [Cambridge: Harvard University Press, 1976], 219).

84. Power's speech is quoted in Aliano, *American Defense Policy*, 122. See *New York Times*, 20 January 1960, 1; John Prados, *The Soviet Estimate: U.S. Intelligence Analysis and Russian Military Strength* (New York: Dial Press, 1982), 91–94.

85. These were the words of Governor Adams in Adams, *Firsthand Report*, 415.

86. Bundy, *Danger and Survival*, 334–50; Peter, *Abschrecken und Ueberleben*, 220–21.

87. This was the general theme of the following three speeches: Eisenhower, Radio and Television Address to the American People on Science in National Security, 7 November 1957, Eisenhower PPS, 1957, 789–99; Eisenhower, Annual Message to the Congress on the State of the Union, 9 January 1958, Eisenhower PPS, 1958, 2–15; Eisenhower, Radio and Television Address to the American

People on the Eve of South American Trip, 21 February 1960, Eisenhower PPS, 1960, 202–7.

88. Bundy, *Danger and Survival*, 340.

89. When the president assured the public that the United States was still superior in the nuclear field, he implied that to a certain degree superiority was important.

90. Both quotations from Memorandum of NSC meeting, 12 December 1957, FRUS, 1955–1957, 19: 704–9.

91. Eisenhower, *Waging Peace*, 205–35.

92. While American strategists tended to see deterrence primarily as a function of capabilities, the Europeans, especially the French, knew it to be a function of will *and* capabilities. See Steinbruner, who gives a detailed overview of the development of nuclear sharing proposals in the second half of the 1950s and the early 1960s in *The Cybernetic Theory of Decision*, 164–71.

93. Telegram from the Ambassador in Germany to the Department of State, 19 November 1957, FRUS, 1955–1957, 4: 186–87.

94. Letter from Macmillan to Eisenhower, 10 October 1957, FRUS, 1955–1957, 27: 785–86; Telegram from the Ambassador in Germany to the Department of State, 19 November 1957, FRUS, 1955–1957, 4: 186–87.

95. Steinbruner, *The Cybernetic Theory of Decision*, 153–54.

96. Memorandum of a Conversation, 23 November 1957, FRUS, 1955–1957, 4: 190–93; Memorandum of a Conversation, 21 November 1957, ibid., 193–206; Memorandum of a Conversation, 24 November 1957, ibid., 206–9.

97. Letter, Secretary of State to Chancellor Adenauer, 24 November 1957, FRUS, 1955–1957, 4: 210–11.

98. Letter, Macmillan to Eisenhower, n.d., FRUS, 1955–1957, 27: 788–89.

99. Record of a Meeting in the State Department, 17 October 1957, FRUS, 1955–1957, 27: 789–91.

100. Memorandum of a Conference with the President, 22 October 1957, FRUS, 1955–1957, 27: 800–801.

101. Memorandum of a Conversation, 23 October 1957, FRUS, 1955–1957, 27: 813–14.

102. Memorandum of Conversation, 25 October 1957, FRUS, 1955–1957, 27: 835–36.

103. Earlier, General Norstad had summarized the report as providing an unequivocal "yes" to the question of whether NATO still needed conventional forces in the nuclear age. The SACEUR underlined the importance of shield forces by pointing out that they provided an essential alternative to the employment of the ultimate nuclear capability. If NATO had only token shield forces, it would invite local aggression. See Telegram from the Political Adviser to the Chief of the U.S. Mission to the NATO to the Department of State, 2 October 1957, FRUS, 1955–1957, 4: 170–71.

104. All quotations from Memorandum of a Conversation, 24 October 1957, FRUS, 1955–1957, 4: 172–81.

105. Memorandum of NSC meeting, 12 December 1957, FRUS, 1955–1957, 4: 214–17. See Memorandum, Dulles to Eisenhower, 21 October 1957, FRUS, 1955–1957, 27: 796–800. The McMahon Act was amended in 1958, permitting exchange of information on the design and production of warheads and the transfer of fissionable materials. Such exchanges and transfers were allowed only with countries that had made "substantial progress" on their own. For the time being only the British qualified for such information. See Bundy, *Danger and Survival*, 471.

106. Steinbruner, *The Cybernetic Theory of Decision*, 173–91; Kelleher, *Germany and the Politics of Nuclear Weapons*, 122–55.

107. President Eisenhower tried in vain to get a postponement of the British decision in a last-minute call to Macmillan. See Letter, Dulles to Eisenhower, 5 March 1957, FRUS, 1955–1957, 27: 694–95; Memorandum of a Telephone Conversation between President Eisenhower and Prime Minister Macmillan, 5 March 1957, ibid., 695–96; Letter, Prime Minister Macmillan to President Eisenhower, 5 March 1957, ibid., 696–97.

108. On the impact of the Suez crisis on the development of nuclear sharing proposals, see Steinbruner, *The Cybernetic Theory of Decision*, 173–74; Bundy, *Danger and Survival*, 474–75.

109. Position Paper Prepared in the Bureau of European Affairs, 13 February 1957, FRUS, 1955–1957, 27: 693–94.

110. For Macmillan's outline and President Eisenhower's reaction, see Memorandum of Conversation, 22 March 1957, FRUS, 1955–1957, 27: 748–52.

111. Memorandum of a Conversation, 22 March 1957, FRUS, 1955–1957, 27: 746–47. During the discussions of the issue in the NSC, both Admiral Radford and Admiral Strauss made it clear that the United States at that point should not be in a hurry to change the law. They argued that the protection of classified information on the construction of nuclear weapons would not be adequately safeguarded by the allies. See Memorandum of NSC meeting, 11 April 1957, FRUS, 1955–1957, 19: 473–74; Memorandum of NSC meeting, 27 May 1957, ibid., 498–99.

112. In a meeting with his advisers in Bermuda, President Eisenhower "very emphatically" pointed out "that he did not want to make a commitment to production until we have a successful missile" (Memorandum of a Conference with the President, 22 March 1957, FRUS, 1955–1957, 27: 733–36).

113. Telegram from the U.S. Delegation at the NAC Heads of Government Meeting to the Department of State, 19 December 1957, FRUS, 1955–1957, 4: 255.

114. Telegram from the U.S. Delegation at the NATO Heads of Government Meeting to the Department of State, 17 December 1957, FRUS, 1955–1957, 4: 232–42. See Memorandum of a Conversation, 14 December 1957, ibid., 230–31; Telegram from the U.S. Delegation at the NATO Heads of Government Meeting to the Department of State, 19 December 1957, ibid., 253–56.

115. One treatment of the French effort regarding nuclear weapons is Bundy,

Danger and Survival, 472–87; for a more detailed outline of the same issue, see Lawrence Scheinman, *Atomic Energy Policy in France under the Fourth Republic* (Princeton: Princeton University Press, 1965); Wilfrid L. Kohl, *French Nuclear Diplomacy* (Princeton: Princeton University Press, 1971).

116. For the views of the president, see Memorandum of a Meeting with the President, 21 March 1960, NNP 1945–91, No. 00631, NSA; Memorandum of a Conference with the President, 8 August 1960, NNP 1945–91, No. 00662, NSA; Memorandum of Conference with the President, 13 September 1960, NNP 1945–91, No. 00676, NSA; Eisenhower, *Waging Peace*, 219.

117. Steinbruner, *The Cybernetic Theory of Decision*, 179–88; Kelleher, *Germany and the Politics of Nuclear Weapons*, 140–41. The report of the committee led to the installation of permissive action links (PALs), which made a presidential decision the precondition for activation of the weapons. On the development of the PALs, see Peter Stein and Peter Feaver, *Assuring Control of Nuclear Weapons: The Evolution of Permissive Action Links* (Lanham, Md.: University Press of America, 1987).

118. Trachtenberg, *History and Strategy*, 185–91.

119. Steinbruner, *The Cybernetic Theory of Decision*, 188–91.

Chapter 7

1. This view is advanced by many students of the period, although in varying degrees. See Bundy, *Danger and Survival*, 334–57; Aliano, *American Defense Policy*, 24–70; Greenstein, *The Hidden-Hand Presidency*, 46–48, 96–97. John Lewis Gaddis made a similar assessment in his outstanding study *The Strategies of Containment*, 164–97. For a convincing outline of Eisenhower's beliefs regarding nuclear matter, see Immerman, "Confessions of an Eisenhower Revisionist."

2. The history of test ban negotiations goes back to an early initiative of Jawaharlal Nehru of India, who called for the end of testing in the aftermath of the explosion of the U.S. *Bravo* test device on 22 February 1954. The test had exposed the twenty-three members of a Japanese fishing vessel to high radiation levels. On the negotiations of a nuclear test ban during the 1950s, see Hewlett and Holl, *Atoms for Peace and War*, 172–566; Eisenhower, *Waging Peace*, 466–84; Bundy, *Danger and Survival*, 328–34.

3. For a broader analysis of the Berlin crisis, see chapter 9.

4. On this point, see Bundy, *Danger and Survival*, 323; Stromseth, *The Origins of Flexible Response*, 21–22; Kistiakowsky, *A Scientist at the White House*, 399–401. John Foster Dulles and Robert Bowie, on the other hand, increasingly, but unsuccessfully, pushed for less emphasis on massive retaliation and a more rapid buildup of local defenses, particularly against the background of the Berlin crisis. The emphasis on massive retaliation had led the United States into a vicious circle, as Dulles pointed out in a talk with the president: "So long as the strategic concept contemplated this, our arsenal of weapons had to be adapted primarily

for that purpose and so long as our arsenal of weapons was adequate only for that kind of a response, we were compelled to rely on that kind of response" (Memorandum of Conversation, 1 April 1958, WHMS, "Meetings with the President, 1 Jan.–30 June 1958," DPEL). Dulles later noted, "the alternative [to massive retaliation] may not in fact prevent the war from becoming general nuclear war, but may prevent neutralism [of allied countries]" (Memorandum from Dulles to Eisenhower, 7 May 1958, NNP 1945–91, No. 00413, NSA).

5. For this insight, I am indebted to Aaron Friedberg, who points out the importance of internal factors of the American state (like its openness to interest group pressures and the content of American ideology) in the development of its particular form of a strategy of deterrence. See L. Friedberg, "Why Didn't the United States Become a Garrison State?" *International Security* 16, No. 4 (Spring 1992): 109–42. See also Gaddis, "Nuclear Weapons," 15–32.

6. J. C. Hopkins and Sheldon A. Goldberg, *The Development of the Strategic Air Command, 1946–1986* (Offutt Air Force Base: Neb.: Office of the Historian, Headquarters SAC, 1986), 89; Ball, *Politics and Force Levels*, 43–53, 116; Memorandum, Thomas S. Gates to the Special Assistant to the President for National Security Affairs, "Scope of Operational Capability of the Polaris Program," 10 January 1961, "NSC Meeting Minutes, 474th Meeting of NSC," 12 January 1961, NSC, NARS.

7. Thomas B. Cochran, William M. Arkin, and Milton M. Hoenig, *U.S. Nuclear Forces and Capabilities*, vol. 1, *Nuclear Weapons Databook* (Cambridge: Ballinger Publishing Company, 1984), 12–15.

8. For the development of U.S. nuclear war plans and the origins of SIOP-62, Rosenberg remains by far the best source. See Rosenberg, "The Origins of Overkill." See also Andreas Wenger, "Kontinuität und Wandel in der amerikanischen Nuklearstrategie: Präsident Eisenhowers Strategie der massiven Vergeltung und die nuklearstrategische Neuevaluation der Administration Kennedy," *Zürcher Beiträge zur Sicherheitspolitik und Konfliktforschung* 19 (Zürich: Center for Security Studies and Conflict Research, 1991), 53–65.

9. Arleigh Burke, CNO Personal Letter No. 5 to Retired Flag Officers, "Pertinent Information, Summary of Major Strategic Considerations for the 1960–1970 Era," 30 July 1958, enclosure to Letter, General Thomas S. Power to Air Force Chief of Staff, 9 May 1959, "SAC Folder," Box 27, White Papers, LC. See Wenger, "Kontinuität und Wandel in der amerikanischen Nuklearstrategie," 40–44.

10. For evolution of the no-cities approach, see Wenger, "Kontinuität und Wandel in der amerikanischen Nuklearstrategie," 44–52; Herbert Goldhamer and Andrew W. Marshall, "The Deterrence and Strategy of Total War, 1959–1961: A Method of Analysis," *RAND Memorandum RM-2301* (Santa Monica: The RAND Corporation, 1959); George A. Reed, *U.S. Defense Policy: U.S. Air Force Doctrine and Strategic Nuclear Weapons Systems, 1958–1964: The Case of the Minuteman ICBM*, Ph.D. diss. (Ann Arbor, Mich.: University Microfilms, 1986), 131–56; Alfred Goldberg, "A Brief Survey of the Evolution of Ideas about Counter-

force," *RAND Memorandum RM-5431-PR* (Santa Monica: The RAND Corporation, 1967).

11. This body of strategic thought is most closely associated with the writings of Bernard Brodie and Thomas Schelling. Brodie, *The Absolute Weapon*; Brodie, *Strategy in the Missile Age;* Schelling, *The Strategy of Conflict;* Schelling, *Arms and Influence.* The evolution of their thinking is outlined in Trachtenberg, *History and Strategy*, 3–46. See John Baylis and John Garnett, eds., *Makers of Nuclear Strategy* (London: Pinter Publishers, 1991), 19–56, 120–35.

12. Eisenhower, Farewell Radio and Television Address to the American People, 17 January 1961, Eisenhower PPS, 1960–1961, 1035–39. See also Eisenhower, *Waging Peace*, 614–16.

13. Both quotations from Kistiakowsky, *A Scientist at the White House*, 416, 414.

14. The best account of Eisenhower's reaction to the SIOP-62 is Rosenberg, "The Origins of Overkill," 4–8.

15. Eisenhower, Farewell Radio and Television Address to the American People, 17 January 1961, Eisenhower PPS, 1960–1961, 1035–40.

Chapter 8

1. For the relations between Kennedy and these persons before and after the election, see Ball, *Politics and Force Levels*, 15–40; Kaplan, *The Wizards of Armageddon*, 248–384; Bernard Brodie, "A Review of William W. Kaufmann's 'The McNamara Strategy,' " *RAND Paper P-3077* (Santa Monica: The RAND Corporation, 1965), 11–12.

2. Samuelson report, "Prospects and Policies for the American Economy," 6 January 1961, "Economy-Samuelson Report Folder," Box 1071, Pre-Presidential File, John F. Kennedy Papers, JFKL. See Sorensen, *Kennedy*, 266.

3. Kennedy initiated a complete reappraisal of the nation's security policy in his first State of the Union Message. See Kennedy, Annual Message to the Congress on the State of the Union, 30 January 1961, Kennedy PPS, 1961, 19–28. He noted his opposition to a defense budget ceiling two months later: "Our arms must be adequate to meet our commitments and insure security, without being bound by arbitrary budget ceilings. This nation can afford to be strong" (Kennedy, Special Message to the Congress on the Defense Budget, 28 March 1961, Kennedy PPS, 1961, 229–40).

4. McNamara described his vision of leadership in February 1961: "He [the manager] can either act as a judge or as a leader. In the former case, he sits and waits until subordinates bring to him problems for solution, or alternatives for choice. In the latter case, he immerses himself in the operations of the business or the governmental activity, examines the problems, the objectives, the alternative courses of action, chooses among them, and leads the organization to their accomplishment. In the one case it's a passive role; in the other case, an active role" (Interview, McNamara, 17 February 1961, Public Statements of Robert S.

McNamara, Vol. I, 1961, HOSD, Pentagon, 63). For a highly readable account of McNamara's complicated personality, see Deborah Shapley, *Promise and Power: The Life and Times of Robert S. McNamara* (Boston: Little, Brown and Company, 1993).

5. For recommendations of this sort, see the results of the Rockefeller Report, the Wheeler Committee Report, and the Symington Committee Report: Symington Report, Senate Armed Services Committee, Military Procurement Authorization, Fiscal Year 1962, 277–81; Alain C. Enthoven and K. Wayne Smith, *How Much Is Enough? Shaping the Defense Program, 1961–1969* (New York: Harper & Row Publishers, 1971), 11; Joint Chiefs of Staff Special Historical Study, *Role and Functions of the Joint Chiefs of Staff: A Chronology* (Washington, D.C.: Historical Division, Joint Secretariat, Joint Chiefs of Staff, 1987), 95–121. For a brilliant summary of these problems, see Memorandum, David E. Bell to McGeorge Bundy and Robert S. McNamara, 30 January 1961, "January 1961 Folder," NH Box 12, NSA.

6. Joint Chiefs of Staff Special Historical Study, *Role and Functions of the JCS*, 5–120.

7. The four task forces, which provided the base of the defense policy reappraisal, were led by civilians from McNamara's personal staff. This was part of a conscious decision of the incoming administration to limit the influence of the JCS. See Memorandum, Bundy to Kennedy, 30 January 1961, "NSC Meetings No. 475 2/1/61 Folder," Box 313, Meetings and Memoranda Series, NSF, JFKL; Memorandum, Brigadier General George S. Brown to the Secretary of the Army et al., "Operation Analysis Reports and Studies," 12 April 1961, "April 1961 Folder," NH Box 12, NSA; Memorandum, McNamara to Chairman, JCS, "Task Force Reports," 10 February 1961, in JCS 2101/408, 13 February 1961, CCS 3001, "Basic National Security Policy, 10 February 1961," JCS, NARS.

8. Kennedy, *The Strategy of Peace*, 37–38; Memorandum for the President, "Report on Implications for the U.S. Foreign and Defense Policy of Recent Intelligence Estimates," 23 August 1962, "August 1962 Folder," NH Box 14, NSA.

9. Memorandum, Walt W. Rostow to the President, 26 June 1961, "June 1961 Folder," NH Box 13, NSA.

10. For positive signals regarding Soviet-U.S. relations during the transition, see Letter, Averell W. Harriman to John F. Kennedy, 12 November 1960, and Letter, Harriman to Kennedy, 15 November 1960, both in "USSR General, 2/15/61–2/19/61 Folder," Box 176, Countries Series, NSF, JFKL; Memorandum, McGeorge Bundy, "Notes on Discussion of the Thinking of the Soviet Leadership," 13 February 1961, "USSR Security 1/61–5/61 Folder 105a," Countries Series, POF, JFKL.

11. David E. Bell, Handwritten Notes of the 496th NSC Meeting, 18 January 1962, "Executive Branch Memoranda Folder," Box 14, David E. Bell Papers, WHSF, JFKL.

12. Since November 1960, the relations between the Soviet Union and China were dramatically deteriorating, a fact that was not fully appreciated by the in-

coming administration. For the background of Khrushchev's speech, see Beschloss, *The Crisis Years*, 38–61.

13. Kennedy, *The Strategy of Peace*, 184.

14. Memorandum, Bundy to the President, "Policies Previously Approved in NSC Which Need Review," 30 January 1961, "NSC Meetings No. 475 2/1/6/1 Folder," Box 313, Meetings and Memoranda Series, NSF, JFKL.

15. AEC 867/49, "Atomic Energy Commission Weapons Custody and Use," 25 April 1961, History Division, U.S. Department of Energy, Washington, 1.

16. On McNamara's visit: Memorandum, RBA to General White, 25 January 1961, "January 1961 Folder," NH Box 12, NSA; Kaplan, *The Wizards of Armageddon*, 270–72.

17. Briefing for the president by the chairman of the JCS, in "The JCS Single Integrated Operational Plan 1962," 13 September 1961, enclosed to JCS 2056/281, 13 September 1961, CCS 3105, "Joint Planning, 13 September 1961," JCS, NARS. Printed and analyzed in Scott D. Sagan, "SIOP-62: The Nuclear War Plan Briefing to President Kennedy," *International Security* 12, No. 1 (Summer 1987): 22–51. For the reaction of the president, see Walt W. Rostow, *The Diffusion of Power: An Essay in Recent History* (New York: The Macmillan Company, 1972), 172–73.

18. Quoted in Stromseth, *The Origins of Flexible Response*, 27.

19. Memorandum, Rostow to Rusk, "Nuclear Weapons: The Dilemma and Thoughts on Its Resolution," 6 January 1961, "Rostow, Nov. 1960–Feb. 1961 Folder," Box 64, Staff Memoranda, POF, JFKL, 3.

20. A member of Bundy's staff informed the president on the result of the Bowie report. See Memorandum, Robert Komer to the President, "Your Meeting with Mr. Acheson on March 7th," 6 March 1961, "Staff Memoranda, Robert W. Komer 1/1/61–3/14/61 Folder," Box 321, Meetings and Memoranda Series, NSF, JFKL.

21. Former Secretary of State Dean Acheson chaired a group directed to come up with NATO policy recommendations. The group submitted its report in March, the recommendations of which were officially endorsed in National Security Memorandum No. 40. See "A Review of North Atlantic Problems for the Future," March 1961, "NATO Acheson Report 3/61 Folder," Box 220, NSF, JFKL; NSAM No. 40, "To Members of the NSC from McGeorge Bundy," 24 April 1961, "Vice Presidential Security File," Box 4, NSC-1961, Lyndon B. Johnson Library (further quoted as NSAM No. 40).

22. For Kennedy's decision to install PALs, see Peter Douglas Feaver, *Guarding the Guardians: Civilian Control of Nuclear Weapons in the United States* (Ithaca: Cornell University Press, 1985), 191–98.

23. Stromseth, *The Origins of Flexible Response*, 88–89.

24. Remarks by McNamara, NATO Ministerial Meeting, 5 May 1962, Restricted Session, "May 1962 Folder," NH Box 14, NSA, 15 (further quoted as McNamara, Athens address).

25. While members of the administration recognized the necessity of guide-

lines for the use of tactical nuclear weapons, a major study was not initiated until May 1962. Only in 1964, the first Draft Presidential Memorandum on the role of tactical nuclear forces in NATO strategy was finished. See Memorandum, Gilpatric to Bundy, "Nuclear Weapons," March 1961, "Nuclear Test Ban 4/59–6/61 Folder," Box 53, The Papers of Theodore C. Sorensen, WHSF, JFKL; Memorandum, McNamara to the Chairman, JCS, "A Study of Requirements for Tactical Nuclear Weapons," 23 May 1962, "Tactical Nuclear Weapons Vol. I Folder," Box 33, Maxwell D. Taylor Papers, NWCL; McNamara, Draft Memorandum for the President, "The Role of Tactical Nuclear Forces in NATO Strategy," 15 January 1965, FOIA/DOD.

26. Memorandum, Rusk to the Ambassador to France, No. 4470, 5 May 1961, "France-General 5/1/61–5/10/61 Folder," Box 70, Countries Series, NSF, JFKL.

27. NSAM No. 40, 9.

28. McNamara, Athens address, 11–13. For a comparable outline of the argument, see Albert Wohlstetter, "Nuclear Sharing: NATO and the N + 1 Country," *Foreign Affairs* 19, No. 3 (April 1961): 355–87.

29. For a detailed analysis of the rising tensions in Anglo-American nuclear relations, see Ian Clark, *Nuclear Diplomacy and the Special Relationship: Britain's Deterrent and America, 1957–1962* (Oxford: Claredon Press, 1994), 297–337.

30. John F. Kennedy, Address before the Canadian Parliament in Ottawa, 17 May 1961, Kennedy PPS, 1961, 382–87.

31. Legge, "Theater Nuclear Weapons," 14.

32. The Secretary of Defense noted that a full first-strike capability would be achieved "if our forces were so large and so effective, in relation to those of the Soviet Union, that we would be able to attack and reduce Soviet retaliatory power to the point at which it could not cause severe damage to U.S. population and industry" (McNamara, Draft Memorandum for the President, 23 September 1961, "Recommended Long Range Nuclear Delivery Force 1963–1967," FOIA/DOD, 4 [further quoted as DPM-61]).

33. Report of Senator Kennedy's National Security Policy Committee, n.d., "Kennedy Group on National Security, Aug.–Dec. 1960 Folder," Defense Department Series, Box 8, Roswell Gilpatric Papers, WHSF, JFKL (further quoted as Nitze report). See also Paul H. Nitze, "Power and Policy Problems in the Defense of the West," Draft #3, 22 April 1960, ibid.; Memorandum, Rostow to Kennedy, "Action Teams: Military and Foreign Policy," 17 November 1960, "Rostow 1960 Folder," Box 64, Staff Memoranda, POF, JFKL.

34. Nitze report, A-2.

35. Senate Armed Services Committee, Military Procurement Authorization, Fiscal Year 1962, 4. See McNamara, Remarks: Annual Luncheon, Associated Press, New York, 24 April 1961, Public Statements of Robert S. McNamara, Vol. 2, 1961, HOSD, Pentagon, 528.

36. This is explained by Henry S. Rowen, "Formulating Strategic Doctrine," in *Essays on Arms Control and National Security*, ed. Bernard F. Halloran (Washington, D.C.: U.S. Arms Control and Disarmament Agency, 1986), 55–89.

37. Letter, Thomas White to Thomas Power, 1 February 1961, "February 1961 Folder," NH Box 12, NSA; Letter, Royal B. Allison to General Hester, 23 February 1961, ibid.

38. John F. Kennedy, Special Message to the Congress on the Defense Budget, 28 March 1961, Kennedy PPS, 1961, 229–40, 299 (further quoted as Budget Message, 28 March 1961).

39. By individual missile program, this meant: + 160 Polaris missiles, − 18 Titan ICBMs, and + 60 Minuteman ICBMs. The best analysis of the fiscal year 1962 defense budget decisions remains Ball, *Politics and Force Levels*, 107–26.

40. Budget Message, 28 March 1961, 230, 233. A first draft by McGeorge Bundy was even more explicit in this regard: "We are not aiming to create forces whose objective is a preventive or preemptive war, or any other kind of massive first strike against another nation" (Memorandum, McGeorge Bundy to Theodore Sorensen, "Defense Message," 13 March 1961, "Defense 3/61 Folder," Box 273, NSF, JFKL).

41. The task force, together with three additional groups, was set up at the beginning of February and became the basis for the fiscal year 1962 defense budget amendments. See Memorandum, McNamara to Chairman, JCS, "Task Force Reports," 10 February 1961, in JCS 2101/408, 13 February 1961, CCS 3001, "Basic National Security Policy," 10 February 1961, JCS, NARS.

42. Walt W. Rostow, "Basic National Security Policy," S/P Draft, 26 March 1962, "March 1962 Folder," NH Box 14, NSA, 49.

43. DPM-61, 5.

44. McNamara defined such a posture as "one in which, after a Soviet attack, we would have a capability to retaliate, and with a high degree of assurance be able to destroy most of Soviet urban society, but in which we would not have a capability to counter-attack against Soviet military forces" (DPM-61, 4).

45. WSEG Report No. 50, "Evaluation of Strategic Offensive Weapons Systems," 27 December 1960, "WSEG Report No. 50 12/27/60 Folder," NH Box 11, NSA, 17 (further quoted as WSEG-50 report). See WSEG-50 report, Appendix E to Enclosure A, "The Feasibility of Achievement of Counterforce Objectives," 63–83.

46. WSEG-50 report, 21–22.

47. Both quotations from Memorandum for the Record, George W. Rathjens, "The General Balance of Strategic Forces and Their Relation to the Fiscal Year 1962 Budget," 21 September 1960, "Missiles (July–December 1960) (6) Folder," Box 12, Office of the Special Assistant for Science and Technology, 1957–1961, White House Office, DDEL. See Ball, *Politics and Force Levels*, 36.

48. On this point, see Kaplan, *The Wizards of Armageddon*, 258; Ball, *Politics and Force Levels*, 36–38; Memoranda, Robert H. Johnson to McGeorge Bundy, "The Fiscal Year 1962 Budget—Issues Relating to the U.S. Military Program," 27 and 30 January 1961, "Department of Defense 1/61 Folder," Box 273, Department and Agencies Series, NSF, JFKL.

49. General Noel F. Parrish, who had war gamed the no-cities counterforce

strategy for the air force, wrote to General White: "Nevertheless, the budget and the message represent an uneasy compromise between the advocates of 'finite' deterrence who surround the President and certain advocates of counterforce who are close to Mr. McNamara. Generally speaking, advocates of counterforce wrote the message while advocates of 'finite' deterrence dominated the budget decisions" (Letter, Brigadier General Parrish to General White, "Post-Missile Gap and Other Implications of the Current Budget," AFXAC, 7 April 1961, "April 1961 Folder," NH Box 12, NSA. See also Enthoven and Smith, *How Much Is Enough*, 170–71).

50. DPM-61, 4.

51. See chapters 9 and 10.

52. Kennedy read and agreed with the theses outlined in General Taylor's *The Uncertain Trumpet* and Liddell Hart's *Deterrent and Defense*. See Taylor, *General Maxwell Taylor*, 8, 219–29; Futrell, *A History of Basic Thinking in the USAF*, 317.

53. Nitze report, A-3.

54. "A Review of North Atlantic Problems for the Future," March 1961, "NATO Acheson Report 3/61 Folder," Box 220, NSF, JFKL, 51.

55. The pause concept was originally proposed by SACEUR General Norstad in 1960. See Stromseth, *The Origins of Flexible Response*, 31.

56. Letter, Arleigh Burke to Dean Acheson, 20 March 1961, CCS 9050/3070, "NATO (10 March 1961) Sec. 2," JCS, NARS; Memorandum, Nitze to the Sec-Def, "General Norstad's Comments on NATO Policy," 6 April 1961, ibid.; Memorandum, Chairman of the JCS to the Secretary of Defense, 7 March 1961, CCS 9050/3070, "NATO (11 February 1961) Sec. 1," JCS, NARS.

57. On this point, see McNamara, "The Military Role of Nuclear Weapons," 59–81; William W. Kaufmann, *The McNamara Strategy* (New York: Harper & Row Publishers, 1964), 102–34; Stromseth, *The Origins of Flexible Response*, 56–58.

58. For a detailed description of these studies, see Enthoven and Smith, *How Much Is Enough*, 117–64.

59. McNamara, Athens address, 16–22. Although Germany had formed one additional division and France had redrawn two divisions from Algeria due to the Berlin crisis, NATO was still one and two-thirds French and three and one-third German divisions short of the MC 26/4 force goals. See Memorandum, R. M. Miner to L. J. Legere, "Estimate of European NATO Buildup over the Next Year," 12 February 1962, "Strategic Balance V Folder," Box 33, Maxwell D. Taylor Papers, NWCL.

60. Memorandum, McNamara to Chairman, JCS, "Task Force Reports," 10 February 1961, in JCS 2101/408, 13 February 1961, CCS 3001, "Basic National Security Policy," 10 February 1961, JCS, NARS. See Paul H. Nitze, *From Hiroshima to Glasnost: At the Center of Decision* (New York: Grove Weidenfeld, 1989), 244–45.

61. Budget Message, 28 March 1961, 236–37.

62. For the reaction of the Europeans, see Stromseth, *The Origins of Flexible Response*, 96–175.

63. For a good survey of the critical European reaction to the Ann Arbor

speech, see Summary Analysis of Secretary McNamara's Speech, Ann Arbor, and the Press Reaction Thereto, n.d., Office of the Secretary of Defense, Pentagon. Brodie warned advocates of a conventional option for NATO that the United States would lose a lot of political credit in its relations with the Europeans because of such a policy. See Bernard Brodie, "A Comment on the Hoag Doctrine: RAND Internal Working Document (1962)," in *Writings on Strategy, 1961–1969, and Retrospectives*, ed. Marc Trachtenberg (New York: Garland, 1988), 95–110.

64. See chapter 7.

65. For a description of the briefing, based on interviews, see Kaplan, *The Wizards of Armageddon*, 260–62; Ball, *Politics and Force Levels*, 34. For the impact of Kaufmann's briefing, see Wenger, "Kontinuität und Wandel in der amerikanischen Nuklearstrategie," 47–52.

66. DPM-61, 4.

67. McNamara, "Remarks at the Commencement Exercises of the University of Michigan in Ann Arbor," 16 June 1962, "June 1962 Folder," NH Box 14, NSA, 2 (further quoted as McNamara, Ann Arbor speech).

68. McNamara, Ann Arbor speech, 10.

69. After describing the advantages of the no-cities counterforce option in terms of damage limitation, McNamara noted in his Athens address that perhaps "the most important implication of these observations is that nuclear superiority has important meanings" McNamara, Athens address, 5.

70. For a broader discussion of the symbolic aspects of nuclear policy see chapter 10.

71. Roswell Gilpatric, Speech Delivered to the Business Council, 21 October 1961, quoted in Memorandum, Adam Yarmolinsky to Theodore Sorensen, "Missile Gap Controversy," 3 May 1962, "May 1962 Folder," NH Box 14, NSA; Paul Nitze, Remarks to the Institute for Strategic Studies, London, 7 December 1961, "December 1961 Folder," NH Box 13, NSA; Robert S. McNamara, Remarks in Atlanta, Georgia, 11 November 1961, "November 1961 Folder," NH Box 13, NSA.

72. Minutes of National Security Meeting, 19 December 1961, "December 1961 Folder," NH Box 13, NSA.

73. The strategy, however, was not helpful to justify the necessity of a conventional buildup. And this was exactly the point where the European doubts about the credibility of the U.S. nuclear guarantee had started. With respect to this policy goal, McNamara emphasized—to some extent turning around the above mentioned argument—that all would suffer in a major war despite U.S. nuclear superiority. Moreover, while the Soviets would be deterred from escalating a conflict to the nuclear level, it was more probable that the alliance had to make the decision to go nuclear. See McNamara, Athens address, 13.

74. For a more detailed analysis of the erosion of the missile gap, see chapter 10.

75. On this point, see chapter 12.

76. McNamara, 19 January 1962, Senate Armed Services Committee, Military Procurement Authorization, Fiscal Year 1963, 16.

77. McNamara, 25 January 1962, House Appropriations Committee, Department of Defense Appropriations, Fiscal Year 1963, 249–50.

78. For the soft configuration of the Soviet ICBM and bomber force, see Berman and Baker, *Soviet Strategic Forces*, 45–50; Kurt Gottfried and Bruce C. Blair, eds., *Crisis Stability and Nuclear War* (New York: Oxford University Press, 1988), 128–30.

79. This line of thought is confirmed in the writings of the most important Soviet strategist of the nuclear age, Marshal V. D. Sokolovskii. See V. D. Sokolovskii, "The Nature of Modern War: Soviet Military Strategy (1962)," in *Nuclear Strategy, Arms Control, and the Future*, edited by Edward Haley, David Keithly, and Jack Merritt (Boulder: Westview Press, 1985), 138–46. For an assessment of Sokolovskii as a strategist, see Neil MacFarlane, "V. D. Sokolovskii," in *Makers of Nuclear Strategy*, ed. John Baylis and John Garnett (London: Pinter Publishers, 1991), 179–98.

80. McNamara, DOD Press Conference, Pentagon, 17 November 1961, Public Statements of Robert S. McNamara, Vol. 3, 1961, HOSD, Pentagon, 1470. See House Appropriations Committee, Department of Defense Appropriations, Fiscal Year 1963, 250.

81. Alain C. Enthoven, "1963 Nuclear Strategy Revisited," in *Ethics and Nuclear Strategy*, ed. H. Ford and F. Winters (New York: Orbis Books, 1977), 76.

82. Memorandum, General Lemnitzer to Robert S. McNamara, CM-190-61, " 'Doctrine' on Thermonuclear Attack," 18 April 1961, "April 1961 Folder," NH Box 12, NSA. The memorandum was written in answer to one of McNamara's famous "96 Trombones," which were part of the new administration's reappraisal of national security policy. See Memorandum, McNamara to the Secretaries of the Military Departments et al., "Assignment of Projects within the Department of Defense," 8 March 1961, in JCS 2101/413, 10 March 1961, CCS 5000, "Functional Organ," 8 March 1961, Sec. I, JCS, NARS.

83. History and Research Division, Headquarters, Strategic Air Command, "History of the Joint Strategic Target Planning Staff: Preparations of the SIOP-63," partially declassified, FOIA/DOD, fn. 10, 43.

84. For a good description of the SIOP-63, see Rowen, "Formulating Strategic Doctrine," 72–83; Desmond Ball, "The Development of the SIOP, 1960–1983," in *Strategic Nuclear Targeting*, ed. D. Ball and J. Richelson (Ithaca, N.Y.: Cornell University Press, 1986), 62–70.

85. General Power, the director of the Joint Strategic Target Planning Staff, informed the JCS that the guidelines for the SIOP–63 could not be met with respect to fallout: "It was not possible to comply with the constraints policy as regards expected dose levels from fallout at all the monitor points without reducing expected damage levels unacceptably" (Letter, General Power to JCS, "SIOP–63," 19 June 1962, in JCS 2056/332, CCS 3105, "Joint Planning," 8 March 1961, Sec. IV, JCS, NARS). See also Memorandum, Admiral Riley to

Chairman of the JCS, DJSM-824-62, "Briefing of the SIOP-63," 9 July 1962, CCS 3105, "Joint Planning," 8 March 1961, Sec. IV, JCS, NARS.

86. Memorandum, McNamara to the President, "Resumption of Atmospheric Nuclear Testing," 1 February 1962, "February 1962 Folder," NH Box 14, NSA.

87. Memorandum, Rear Admiral Wellings to the Chairman, JCS, DJSM-692-61, " 'War Game' of the Command and Control Aspects of the Implementation of SIOP-62," 12 June 1961, CCS 3511, "Training etc.," 21 April 1961, JCS, NARS; Memorandum, Secretary of the Air Force to SecDef, "Strengthening the National Military Command System, Project X," 18 October 1961, CCS 4930, "Command Facilities," 12 August 1961, Sec. IIA, JCS, NARS.

88. The new command system included airborne and hardened underground command posts. See McNamara, Senate Appropriations Committee, Department of Defense Appropriations, Fiscal Year 1963, 23–25. See Futrell, *A History of Basic Thinking in the USAF*, 394–95.

89. For a broader outline of this point see chapter 9.

90. Berman and Baker, *Soviet Strategic Forces*, 48–49.

91. "Briefing for the President by the Chairman, Joint Chiefs of Staff on the Joint Chiefs of Staff Single Integrated Operational Plan 1962 (SIOP-62)," 13 September 1961, "September 1961 Folder," NH Box 13, NSA, 18.

92. McNamara, Address to the Fellows of the American Bar Foundation, Chicago, 17 February 1962, "February 1962 Folder," NH Box 14, NSA, 5 (further quoted as McNamara, Address to the Fellows of the American Bar Foundation).

93. McNamara, Address to the Fellows of the American Bar Foundation, 7.

94. Interview, Roswell Gilpatric, 30 June 1970, OHI, JFKL, 84. See also Nitze, *From Hiroshima to Glasnost*, 250–52.

95. McNamara, Address to the Fellows of the American Bar Foundation, 7.

Chapter 9

1. The American perception of the Berlin crisis is closely related to the U.S. outlook on the Cold War generally, as outlined in chapter 8. There are numerous sources explaining the general view: Scope Paper, President's Meeting with Khrushchev, Vienna, 3–4 June 1961, 23 May 1961, BC 1958–62, No. 02050, NSA; Report by Dean Acheson, 28 June 1961, FRUS, 1961–1963, 14: 138–59 (further quoted as Acheson Berlin report).

2. Trachtenberg, *History and Strategy*, 180–91. New analyses of Khrushchev's reasons for unleashing the crisis based on Soviet and East German sources support Trachtenberg's thesis: Hope M. Harrison, "Ulbricht and the Concrete 'Rose': New Archival Evidence on the Dynamics of Soviet-East German Relations and the Berlin Crisis, 1958–1961," *Cold War International History Project Working Paper* No. 5, Washington, D.C.: Woodrow Wilson International Center for Scholars, May 1993; Vladislav M. Zubok, "Khrushchev and the Berlin Crisis, 1958–1962," *Cold War International History Project Working Paper* No. 6, Washington,

D.C.: Woodrow Wilson International Center for Scholars, May 1993. Other extremely helpful accounts on the Berlin crisis include William Burr, "U.S. Policy and the Berlin Crisis: An Overview," in *The Berlin Crisis, 1958–1962: Guide and Index*, edited by Thomas S. Blanton, Malcolm Byrne, Margarita S. Studemeister, and Lisa Thompson, vol. I (Alexandria, Va.: The National Security Archive, 1991), 31–47; Bundy, *Danger and Survival*, 358–90. For earlier accounts, see Jack Schick, *The Berlin Crisis, 1958–1962* (Philadelphia: University of Pennsylvania Press, 1971); Robert M. Slusser, *The Berlin Crisis of 1961: Soviet-American Relations and the Struggle for Power in the Kremlin, June–November 1961* (Baltimore: The Johns Hopkins University Press, 1973).

3. Memorandum, Mr. Timmons to Mr. Merchant, 25 November 1958, BC 1958–62, No. 00398, NSA; Letter from Paris to Secretary of State, 20 December 1958, BC 1958–62, No. 00544, NSA; Letter, Secretary Dulles to Embassy Paris, 22 December 1958, BC 1958–62, No. 00546, NSA.

4. For Thompson's views, see Burr, "U.S. Policy and the Berlin Crisis," 34; Trachtenberg, *History and Strategy*, 191.

5. When German defense minister Strauss urged quick delivery of nuclear warheads for the fighter-bomber unit, the State Department saw no political objection to proceeding in this matter. Memorandum, Acting Secretary Robert Murphy to the President, "NATO Atomic Stockpile in Germany," 24 December 1958, BC 1958–62, No. 00556, NSA; Telegram, Bonn to the Secretary of State, 16 February 1959, BC 1958–62, No. 00780, NSA; Memorandum for the Record, Department of State, 27 February 1959, BC 1958–62, No. 00837, NSA.

6. For a good review of different Soviet purposes in provoking the Berlin crisis: Hannes Adomeit, *Soviet Risk-Taking and Crisis Behavior: A Theoretical and Empirical Analysis* (London: George Allen & Unwin, 1982).

7. For an overview of these incidents, see Department of State, Bureau of Public Affairs, Top Secret History, Crisis over Berlin: American Policy Concerning the Soviet Threats to Berlin, 11/58–12/62, 1 October 1966, BC 1958–62, No. 02933, NSA, 1–2 (further quoted as Department of State Berlin History); Burr, "U.S. Policy and the Berlin Crisis," 33. For a recent assessment see William Burr, "Avoiding the Slippery Slope: The Eisenhower Administration and the Berlin Crisis, November 1958–January 1959," *Diplomatic History* 18, No. 2 (Spring 1994): 177–206.

8. Note from the Soviet Foreign Ministry to the American Ambassador at Moscow, Regarding Berlin, 27 November 1958, DG, 348–63; Address by Premier Khrushchev at a Soviet-Polish Meeting, "On Germany and Berlin," 10 November 1958, DG, 339–43.

9. Memorandum of Conference with the President, 6 March 1959, BC 1958–62, No. 00907, NSA.

10. Memorandum of Conversation with the French Ambassador et al., 3 February 1959, BC 1958–62, No. 00705, NSA.

11. Memorandum of Telephone Conversation with Secretary Dulles, 6 March 1959, BC 1958–62, No. 00899, NSA.

12. Memorandum of Conference with the President, 6 March 1959, BC 1958–62, No. 00907, NSA; Memorandum of Conversation with the President, 31 March 1959, BC 1958–62, No. 01088, NSA.

13. Memorandum for Mr. Herter, 6 March 1959, BC 1958–62, No. 00905, NSA.

14. Memorandum of Conversation, Adenauer, Dulles, et al., 8 February 1959, BC 1958–62, No. 00741, NSA.

15. Informal Notes on Meeting with the President, 5 March 1959, BC 1958–62, No. 00884, NSA; Burr, "U.S. Policy and the Berlin Crisis," 36; Eisenhower, *Waging Peace*, 340. The importance of these measures is underscored by President Eisenhower's anger over DeGaulle's decision not to allow the stationing of nuclear warheads for U.S. aircraft in France. On receiving the French decision, he wondered "whether or not this was likely to signal the beginning of the break-up of NATO" (Memorandum of Conversation with the President, 2 May 1959, BC 1958–62, No. 01247, NSA). It is of interest to note that confidence in the effectiveness of these measures decreased over time. The fact that the Soviets seemed unaffected led to calls for additional and more impressive measures of this sort. See Memorandum, T. Merchant to the Secretary, 8 July 1959, BC 1958–62, No. 01498, NSA; Letter, Deputy Undersecretary Murphy to General Nathan F. Twining, 7 July 1959, BC 1958–62, No. 01517, NSA.

16. Memorandum of Conference with the President, 9 March 1959, BC 1958–62, No. 00920, NSA; Memorandum of Conference with the President, 6 March 1959, BC 1958–62, No. 00907, NSA.

17. Memorandum for the Files, 27 February 1959, BC 1958–62, No. 00841, NSA; Memorandum of Meeting with the President, 3 March 1959, BC 1958–62, No. 00867, NSA.

18. For the best insight into the original contingency plans, particularly as put forward by the JCS: Department of State Berlin History, 97–101.

19. Scope Paper, Macmillan Talks, 19–23 March 1959, 17 March 1959, BC 1958–62, No. 00984, NSA.

20. Synopsis of State and Intelligence Material Reported to the President, 21 January 1959, BC 1958–62, No. 00652, NSA.

21. The best outline of the development of western contingency plans is Department of State Berlin History, 101–18. See Burr, "U.S. Policy and the Berlin Crisis," 35.

22. Memorandum for the President, "Berlin Contingency Planning," 4 March 1959, BC 1958–62, No. 00872, NSA.

23. Informal Notes on Meeting in President's Office, 5 March 1959, BC 1958–62, No. 00884, NSA.

24. Both quotations from Memorandum of Telephone Conversation with Secretary Dulles, 6 March 1959, BC 1958–62, No. 00899, NSA.

25. Memorandum of Meeting with the President, 28 April 1959, 30 April 1959, BC 1958–62, No. 01240, NSA.

26. Quoted in Department of State Berlin History, 110.

27. Memorandum for the National Security Council, "Studies of Military and Non-Military Counter-Measures in the Berlin Crisis," 28 April 1959, BC 1958–62, No. 01228, NSA.

28. The British view with respect to the Berlin crisis is well documented: Memorandum of Telephone Conversation with the President, 22 November 1958, BC 1958–62, No. 00364, NSA; Telephone Calls, 27 November 1958, BC 1958–62, No. 00419, NSA; Telegram from London to the Secretary of State, 25 April 1959, BC 1958–62, No. 01220, NSA; Telegram from London to the Secretary of State, 5 May 1959, BC 1958–62, No. 01252, NSA.

29. Memorandum of Conference with the President, 20 March 1959, BC 1958–62, No. 01032, NSA. See Memorandum of Conversation, 20 March 1959, BC 1958–62, No. 01015, NSA.

30. Memorandum of Telephone Conversation with Secretary Dulles, 6 March 1959, BC 1958–62, No. 00899, NSA.

31. Memorandum of Conference with the President, 19 June 1959, BC 1958–62, No. 01442, NSA.

32. Conversation with Chancellor Adenauer, 27 May 1959, BC 1958–62, No. 01309, NSA.

33. Letter, Moscow to the Secretary of State, "Conversation Harriman and Khrushchev," 25 June 1959, BC 1958–62, No. 01461, NSA. See Memorandum of Conversation, "Harriman-Khrushchev Conversations," 10 July 1959, BC 1958–62, No. 01509, NSA; Summary of Discussion between Vice President Nixon and Khrushchev on 26 July 1959, 27 July 1959, BC 1958–62, No. 01576, NSA; Soviet Note to the U.S. Government on Modernization of Armaments of U.S. Allies, 21 April 1959, BC 1958–62, No. 011093, NSA.

34. All quotations from Memorandum of NSC meeting, 2 May 1958, BC 1958–62, No. 00115, NSA. Dulles added at this point of the discussion that he would go to Europe and perform the "ritual act" of stating "that an attack on Berlin would be considered by us to be an attack on the United States" without knowing "whether he himself quite believed this or, indeed, whether his audience would believe it." In response, Eisenhower expressed surprise over Dulles's view, noting that if the United States did not "respond in this fashion to a Soviet attack on Berlin, we would first lose the city itself and, shortly after, all of Western Europe" (Ibid., 12).

35. Memorandum of Conference with the President, 19 August 1960, BC 1958–62, No. 01944, NSA. See Memorandum of NSC Meeting, 22 January 1959, BC 1958–62, No. 00655, NSA.

36. Secretary Herter informed the U.S. embassies in all NATO capitals that they should react to European doubts about the credibility of the U.S. security guarantee in the face of growing Soviet nuclear capability by emphasizing U.S. determination to honor its NATO commitments while at the same time avoiding any comment on the specific nature of U.S. military response. See Telegram, Secretary Herter to all NATO Capitals, 10 July 1959, BC 1958–62, No. 01506, NSA.

37. In August 1960, Robert Bowie discussed the findings of his report on the future of NATO with President Eisenhower. Bowie, on this occasion, again pointed to the psychological and political need for increased conventional forces if the alliance did not want to end up deterring itself. Eisenhower now admitted that "perhaps there has been a gap in his own thinking regarding this question" (Memorandum of Conference with the President, 19 August 1960, BC 1958–62, No. 01944, NSA).

38. Trachtenberg gives an excellent and well-documented overview of the discussions within the western alliance. See Trachtenberg, *History and Strategy*, 195–215.

39. Memorandum of Conference with the President, 13 July 1959, BC 1958–62, No. 01526, NSA. For further insight into the discussions leading to the Camp David talks, see Memorandum of Conference with the President, 16 June 1959, BC 1958–62, No. 01442, NSA; Memorandum of Telephone Conversation with the President, 8 July 1959, BC 1958–62, No. 01500, NSA.

40. See the exchange between the two heads of state: Memorandum of Conversation, 15 September 1959, BC 1958–62, No. 01654, NSA; Memorandum of Conversation, 27 September 1959, BC 1958–62, No. 01672, NSA.

41. Memorandum of Conference with the President, 19 June 1959, BC 1958–62, No. 01442, NSA.

42. Memorandum of Meeting with the President, 1 October 1959, BC 1958–62, No. 01681, NSA.

43. Both quotations from Memorandum of Conference with the President, 15 March 1960, BC 1958–62, No. 01846, NSA.

44. Trachtenberg, *History and Strategy*, 207.

45. The Eisenhower administration suspected that Khrushchev had used the U-2 incident in order to scuttle the summit conference. Serious domestic opposition from the military hard-liners seemed to have forced Khrushchev to take this cheap way out. See Memorandum of NSC meeting, 24 May 1960, BC 1958–62, No. 01915, NSA; Minutes of Cabinet meeting, 26 May 1960, BC 1958–62, No. 01917, NSA.

46. A few days before Kennedy's inauguration, a State Department paper noted that while it would be difficult to find a new approach to Berlin, thought "should be given to the possibility of other deterrents than the pure threat of ultimate thermonuclear war" (State Department Paper, "The Berlin Problem in 1961," 10 January 1961, BC 1958–62, No. 01982, NSA).

47. McGeorge Bundy presents the differences in the two administrations' approaches to the Berlin problem. See Bundy, *Danger and Survival*, 371–78.

48. The quotation is from a letter from Harriman to Kennedy. See Letter, Harriman to Kennedy, 15 November 1960, BC 1958–62, No. 01966, NSA.

49. Letter, Harriman to Kennedy, 15 November 1960, BC 1958–62, No. 01966, NSA; Letter, Stevenson to Kennedy, 22 November 1960, BC 1958–62, No. 01967, NSA.

50. Notes on Discussion of the Thinking of the Soviet Leadership, 11 Febru-

ary 1961, BC 1958–62, No. 01994, NSA. Kennedy's advisers remained skeptical about the show of Soviet fears regarding a nuclear-armed Germany. They counseled that "if Soviet concern over Germany's relation to atomic weapons is real, it is also an example of the duality of Soviet thinking: the German question is not only a real worry, but an excellent crowbar with which to pry at the seams of the Atlantic alliance" (Ibid.).

51. For the crisis in Laos, see Sorensen, *Kennedy*, 706–17; Schlesinger, *A Thousand Days*, 323–40; David K. Hall, "The Laos Crisis, 1960–1961," in *The Limits of Coercive Diplomacy: Laos, Cuba, Vietnam*, ed. Alexander George, David Hall, and William E. Simons (Boston: Little, Brown & Company, 1971), 36–85; Ushy Mahajani, "President Kennedy and U.S. Policy in Laos, 1961–1963," *Journal of Southeast Asian Studies* 2, No. 2 (September 1971): 87–99.

52. For the impact of the speech on President Kennedy see chapter 8.

53. John F. Kennedy, Annual Message to the Congress on the State of the Union, 30 January 1961, Kennedy PPS, 1961, 19–28. Sorensen has noted that the president himself inserted the words regarding imminent danger into a first draft of the address. See Sorensen, *Kennedy*, 325. See Sorensen's long list of foreign policy crisis in the first eight months of Kennedy's presidency (Ibid.).

54. For the German reaction to Kennedy's speech, see Memorandum of Conversation between Ambassador Grewe and the Undersecretary, 2 February 1991, FRUS, 1961–1963, 14: 5–6; Memorandum of Conversation between Foreign Minister Heinrich von Brentano and President Kennedy, 17 February 1961, ibid., 8–11; State Department Berlin History, Part 5, 2.

55. The spiral of East-West miscommunications during the first few months of Kennedy's presidency has found a dramatized account in Beschloss, *The Crisis Years*, 1–117.

56. Robert Kennedy and General Maxwell D. Taylor were directed to inquire into the causes of the debacle. Taylor soon became military representative of the president (starting his job on 1 July). President Kennedy's confidence in the Joint Chiefs of Staff was seriously undermined. The following interviews give an excellent insight into the depth of the frustration of the Kennedy administration after the ill-fated invasion: Interview, Maxwell D. Taylor, 12 April 1964, 7–20; Interview, Robert F. Kennedy, 1 March 1964, Vol. I, 50–61; Interview, Roswell Gilpatric, 5 May 1970, 10–15; Interview, Adam Yarmolinsky, 28 November 1964, 79; Interview, Theodore C. Sorensen, 26 March 1964, 20–25, all in OHI, JFKL.

57. Letter, Stewart Alsop to Martin Sommers, 22 May 1961, "Jan.–May 1961 Saturday Evening Post Folder," Box 30, The Papers of Stewart Alsop, LC.

58. For an account of the conversation, see Record of Conversation between Prime Minister Macmillan and President Kennedy, 5 June 1961, FRUS, 1961–1963, 14: 98–102. See also Position Paper Prepared in the Department of State, 25 May 1961, ibid., 71–75.

59. Even before Vienna, the western leaders agreed that because of the pressure on Khrushchev to achieve the appearance of success, the situation might become even more dangerous than in 1958–59. For this sort of argument, see

the discussions at the NATO ministerial meeting in May. The issue is expressed with particular forcefulness by Ambassador Thompson. See Memorandum of Conversation, NATO Ministerial Meeting, 10 May 1961, Rusk Memos Folder, NSA; Telegram, Thompson to the Secretary of State, 27 May 1961, FRUS, 1961–1963, 14: 77–78; Telegram, Thompson to the Department of State, 24 May 1961, ibid., 63–70; Telegram, Thompson to the Department of State, 4 February 1961, ibid., 6–7.

60. Aide-Mémoire from the Soviet Union to the Federal Republic of Germany, "Concerning a German Peace Treaty and Related Matters," 17 February 1961, DG, 635–41.

61. According to Beschloss, the Soviets raised the idea first in one of the secret meetings between Robert Kennedy and Georgi Bolshakov, a Soviet military intelligence agent with direct access to Khrushchev. See Beschloss, *The Crisis Years*, 152–81.

62. Khrushchev's verbal threat was confirmed in an Aide-Mémoire that the Soviet delegation handed to the Americans at the meeting. See Aide-Mémoire from the Soviet Union to the United States, Handed by Premier Khrushchev to President Kennedy at Vienna, 4 June 1961, DG, 642–46.

63. Khrushchev's Vienna performance and particularly his emotional tone stand in remarkable contrast to his matter-of-factness at the Camp David meeting with President Eisenhower.

64. All quotations from Memorandum of Conversation, 3 June 1961, BC 1958–62, No. 02075, NSA.

65. Memorandum of Conversation, 4 June 1961, BC 1958–62, No. 02077, NSA. See the abbreviated version of the conversation in FRUS, 1961–1963, 14: 87–98.

66. See Michael Beschloss's description of Kennedy's reaction to the sober exchange with Khrushchev. Beschloss compiles interesting interview material. Beschloss brings the meeting's atmosphere of tension, threat, and danger alive. He concludes that the event had a big influence on the president. The balance of self-confidence seems to have moved in favor of Khrushchev. See Beschloss, *The Crisis Years*, 182–236. For a different analysis of the meeting's impact, see Schlesinger, *A Thousand Days*, 343–78.

67. Report to the Nation by President Kennedy Following His Visit to Paris, Vienna, and London, 6 June 1961, DG, 646–51.

68. For European reactions to the shift in U.S. defense policy, see Telegram, Bonn to the Secretary of State, 8 March 1961, BC 1958–62, No. 02003, NSA; Memorandum for the Record, "Mr. Nitze's Meeting with NATO Secretary General Stikker," 27 June 1961, BC 1958–62, No. 02110, NSA; Current Intelligence Summary, 6 July 1961, BC 1958–62, No. 02139, NSA. European fears were heightened by rumors that the new administration was moving against further allocation of IRBMs to NATO countries. In fact, the Acheson report stressed the vulnerability of the IRBM bases in Turkey, Britain, and Italy, their provocative first-strike appearance, and their diminishing military importance in view of the

expanded U.S. strategic missile programs. See Memorandum, Undersecretary of State Bowles to the President, 7 April 1961, BC 1958–62, No. 02028, NSA; Memorandum for the Record, "Discussion of NATO Strategy," 25 May 1961, BC 1958–62, No. 02054, NSA.

69. Dean Acheson, "Wishing Won't Hold Berlin," *Saturday Evening Post,* 7 March 1959, 32–33, 85–86. For a good description of Acheson's views and role see Bundy, who portrays him as "a man with a mission" in early 1961, in *Danger and Survival,* 372–78.

70. For a discussion of Acheson's NATO report, the findings of which were officially endorsed in NSC Memorandum No. 40, see chapter 8.

71. In McGeorge Bundy's White House staff, Henry Kissinger was already working on the issue. See Memorandum, Bundy to the President, 27 March 1961, "Bundy, McGeorge 2/61–4/61 Folder," Box 62, Staff Memoranda, POF, JFKL.

72. In fact, McGeorge Bundy and the president were so impressed by Acheson's preliminary findings that they asked him to present his views at the meeting of Kennedy and Macmillan on 5 April. See Memorandum, Bundy to the President, 4 April 1961, "April 1961 Folder," NH Box 12, NSA; and Memorandum of Conversation between Macmillan and Kennedy, 6 April 1961, FRUS, 1961–1963, 14: 41–44. See also State Department Berlin History, Part 5, 14–18.

73. These two assumptions were widely accepted within the Kennedy administration from the beginning. What Acheson did was to state them with great clarity and force. Moreover, he integrated them into a framework for a complex, multistep politicomilitary strategy. For an earlier articulation of the same assumptions, see State Department Paper, "The Berlin Problem in 1961," 10 January 1961, BC 1958–62, No. 01982, NSA; Paper Prepared in the Department of State, undated, FRUS, 1961–1963, 14: 33–34.

74. Memorandum, Bundy to the President, 27 March 1961, "Bundy, McGeorge 2/61–4/61 Folder," Box 62, Staff Memoranda, POF, JFKL.

75. All quotations from Memorandum, Acheson to the President, 3 April 1961, "April 1961 Folder," NH Box 12, NSA.

76. It is possible that Acheson was influenced by Thomas Schelling. Marc Trachtenberg has located an unpublished paper by Schelling in Acheson's working files for his NATO report that stressed the same theme. Schelling wrote that "a main consequence of limited war, and main reason for engaging in it, is to raise the risk of general war." See Trachtenberg, *History and Strategy,* 217.

77. National Security Action Memorandum No. 41, "Military Planning for a Possible Berlin Crisis," 25 April 1961, NSC, NARS.

78. These studies were to determine the likely military course and the effects of (1) the use of substantial nonnuclear ground forces to open ground access to Berlin and (2) a substantial nonnuclear effort to reopen and maintain air access to Berlin; and (3) the military actions (such as blockade) undertaken in areas other than Central Europe to apply pressure on the Soviet Union for the reopening of access to Berlin. The studies are still classified and their results can

only be inferred from other source materials like Memorandum, Arleigh Burke to the SecDef, JCSM-187-61, 18 April 1961, "Germany-Berlin General Folder," Box 81, Countries Series, NSF, JFKL.

79. Memorandum, McNamara to the President, "Military Planning for a Possible Berlin Crisis," 5 May 1961, FRUS, 1961–1963, 14: 61–63. From the declassified sources available it becomes clear that the JCS's warning that the "Soviets cannot identify a precise level of violence short of which Western response would be non-nuclear and beyond which it would be nuclear" convinced the secretary of defense that substantial rather than limited nonnuclear action must be planned to reopen ground access. See Memorandum, Arleigh Burke to the SecDef, JCSM-187-61, 18 April 1961, "Germany-Berlin General Folder," Box 81, Countries Series, NSF, JFKL. McNamara advised the president to make sure that the attempt to reopen access to Berlin could not be stopped by East German forces alone. See State Department Berlin History, Part 5, 10–12.

80. A briefing paper for Kennedy's meeting with DeGaulle on 31 May–2 June 1961 emphasized the logic of U.S. thinking with particular clarity: "Thus, the threat of nuclear war is more credible if it appears that we will first create a substantial level of non-nuclear violence, over Berlin or any other issue, than if we merely threaten to initiate general nuclear war *ab initio*" (Memorandum, "DeGaulle's View on Conventional Force and Berlin," 26 May 1961, "France: Security Folder," Box 116a, Countries Series, POF, JFKL. For the bilateral talks, see Memorandum of Conversation between Macmillan and Kennedy, 6 April 1961, FRUS, 1961–1963, 14: 41–44; Memorandum of Conversation between Adenauer and Kennedy, 13 April 1961, ibid., 45–51; Memorandum of Conversation between DeGaulle and Kennedy, 31 May 1961, ibid., 80–83.

81. Report to the Nation by President Kennedy Following His Visit to Paris, Vienna, and London, 6 June 1961, DG, 646–51.

82. Address by Premier Khrushchev at Moscow, "Concerning the German Problem and Disarmament," 21 June 1961, DG, 663–66; Address by Premier Khrushchev at Moscow, "Concerning His Meeting at Vienna with President Kennedy," 15 June 1961, DG, 660–63.

83. Futrell, *A History of Basic Thinking in the USAF,* 337; Department of State Berlin History, Part 6, 4–5.

84. For interpretations of the Acheson report relying upon the declassification of its full text see: Trachtenberg, *History and Strategy,* 215–31; Beschloss, *The Crisis Years,* 242–61. For earlier standard accounts, see Sorensen, *Kennedy,* 584; Schlesinger, *A Thousand Days,* 381–83.

85. Report by Dean Acheson, 28 June 1961, FRUS, 1961–1963, 14: 138–59 (further quoted as Acheson Berlin report).

86. It should be noted that a thorough analysis of *why* Khrushchev was forcing the issue is missing from the report. Acheson's analysis assumed that the Soviets dared at all to voice such a threat due to their growing nuclear power. A paper of the Policy Planning Staff, for example, indicates other reasons: "It seems evident that Khrushchev has reached a point in time where he can no longer

tolerate the rearmament of the Federal Republic without a solution to the larger problem of assured Soviet control over the GDR" (Polk, James H., "A New Approach to the Issue of Berlin," 26 June 1961, "Berlin Overflow Folder," Box 34, Maxwell D. Taylor Papers, NWCL).

87. In a later memorandum, Acheson made the point with even greater clarity: "Khrushchev was now going further than the USSR had ventured since 1948, because he believed that the U.S.A. would not use nuclear weapons to stop him, and could not do so otherwise" (Memorandum, Acheson to Rusk, "Berlin—A Political Program," 1 August 1961, "Germany-Berlin General Folder," Box 82, Countries Series, NSF, JFKL).

88. Acheson criticized Eisenhower's Berlin contingency planning for assuming that nuclear weapons would be used without regard to Soviet perceptions. "This would really amount to preemptive war with nothing being done first to increase credibility," he noted to a group of advisers, and added, "It would involve the use of nuclear weapons without getting the benefit of their deterrent effect" (Record of Meeting of the Interdepartmental Coordinating Group on Berlin Contingency Planning, 16 June 1961, FRUS, 1961–1963, 14: 119–24).

89. Both quotations: Acheson Berlin report, 155. Walt Rostow underscored the same basic idea in a memorandum to the president pointing out that "we must make Mr. Khrushchev share the burden of making sacrifices to avoid nuclear war. This means we must be prepared to increase the risk of war on his side of the line as well as facing it on ours" (Memorandum, Rostow to the President, 26 June 1961, "Germany-Berlin General Folder," Box 81, Countries Series, NSF, JFKL).

90. The report did not spell out that Europe's greater vulnerability to Soviet nuclear attack was an important factor in the different appraisals of danger and advantages. In an earlier meeting, Acheson counseled to "proceed not by asking them [the allies], if they would be afraid if we said 'boo!'. We should, instead, say 'boo!' and see how far they jump" (Record of the Interdepartmental Coordinating Group on Berlin Contingency Planning, 16 June 1961, FRUS, 1961–1963, 14: 119–124, 122).

91. Acheson Berlin report, 157.

92. Memorandum for the Record, 29 June 1961, FRUS, 1961–1963, 14: 160–62; National Security Action Memorandum No. 58, 30 June 1961, ibid., 162–65.

93. Memorandum, Kaysen to Bundy, "Berlin Crisis and Civil Defense," 7 July 1961, "Germany-Berlin General Folder," Box 81, Countries Series, NSF, JFKL.

94. Chairman of the JCS, General Lemnitzer, to the President, CM-242-61, "Supply Levels in Berlin," 14 June 1961, "June 1961 Folder," NH Box 13, NSA.

95. Memorandum, Kaysen to Bundy, 3 July 1961, "Germany-Berlin General Folder," Box 81, Countries Series, NSF, JFKL. See Memorandum to the Record by Kaysen, "Conversation with General Taylor," 3 July 1961, Staff Memoranda, "Carl Kaysen 6/61–8/61 Folder," Box 320, Meetings and Memoranda Series, NSF, JFKL.

96. Covering Note on Henry Kissinger's Memo on Berlin, McGeorge Bundy, 7 July 1961, "July 1961 Folder," NH Box 13, NSA. See Memorandum, Lawrence Legere to General Taylor, "Matters for Discussion with General Lemnitzer on 11 July" 10 July 1961, "Berlin File-Col. Legere's Inactive Folder," Box 34, Maxwell D. Taylor Papers, NWCL.

97. Memorandum of NSC Discussion, 13 July 1961, FRUS, 1961–1963, 14: 192–94.

98. Memorandum, Schlesinger to Kennedy, 7 July 1961, FRUS, 1961–1963, 14: 173–176; Memorandum, Taylor to Kennedy, 12 July 1961, ibid., 186.

99. General Taylor favored a third alternative in which the declaration of national emergency would be announced in as low a key as possible. See Memorandum, Taylor to the President, 19 July 1961, "Berlin File-Col. Legere's Inactive," Box 34, Maxwell D. Taylor Papers, NWCL.

100. The issue of national emergency was discussed in the context of four choices for a military buildup over Berlin. The four alternatives and their discussion in the NSC meeting and a smaller follow-on meeting of the president with his top advisers are discussed in Memorandum of NSC Discussion, 13 July 1961, FRUS, 1961–1963, 14: 192–94. Memorandum, Bundy to the President et al., "Military Choices in Berlin Planning," 13 July 1961, "July 1961 Germany-Berlin General 7/13/61 Folder," Box 81, Countries Series, NSF, JFKL; "Some Pros and Cons of the Four Broad Choices," 13 July 1961, BC 1958–62, No. 02167, NSA; White House Paper, "Military Choices in Berlin Planning," n.d., BC 1958–62, No. 02168, NSA; "The military build-up: 'Low key' or 'high pressure?' " 17 July 1961, "July 1961 Folder," NH Box 13, NSA.

101. Memorandum, Kissinger to Bundy, "Negotiations," 14 July 1961, "Germany-Berlin General 7/14/61 Folder," Box 81, Countries Series, NSF, JFKL. See Memorandum, Thompson to the Secretary of State, "The Berlin Question," 19 June 1961, BC 1958–62, No. 02093, NSA; Schlesinger, *A Thousand Days*, 385–90.

102. Memorandum, Bundy to Sorensen, 22 July 1961, "Germany-Berlin General Folder," Box 81, Countries Series, NSF, JFKL.

103. Memorandum of Meeting on Berlin, 17 July 1961, FRUS, 1961–1963, 14: 209–12; Memorandum of Meeting on Berlin, 18 July 1961, ibid., 215–16; Memorandum, Bundy to Kennedy, 19 July 1961, ibid., 216–18.

104. Memorandum of NSC Meeting, 19 July 1961, FRUS, 1961–1963, 14: 219–22. Theodore Sorensen wrote an impressive summary of the argument against declaring an emergency using Acheson's own words to point out that actions that would be considered provocative should be avoided. Further, he referred to the paragraph of Acheson's report that stated that the more drastic preparations would be more impressive at a later stage as the crisis deepened. See Memorandum, Sorensen to the President, "The Decision on Berlin," 17 July 1961, BC 1958–62, No. 02184, NSA. See Trachtenberg, *History and Strategy*, 218.

105. National Security Action Memorandum No. 62, 24 July 1961, FRUS, 1961–1963, 14: 225–26.

106. Outgoing Telegram, Department of State, Letter from the President to Prime Minister Macmillan, 20 July 1961, "July 1961 Folder," NH Box 13, NSA.

107. Report to the Nation on the Berlin Crisis by President Kennedy, 25 July 1961, DG, 694–701. McGeorge Bundy sent a memorandum to Kennedy's speech writer, Theodore Sorensen, emphasizing that Henry Kissinger had made a similar point: "Because our buildup is mainly conventional, it seems to him [Kissinger] important to make clear our resolution on Berlin is not limited to such forces" (Memorandum, Bundy to Sorensen, 22 July 1961, "Germany-Berlin General Folder," Box 81, Countries Series, NSF, JFKL. See also Sorensen, *Kennedy*, 653–55; Bundy, *Danger and Survival*, 377).

108. One of the most memorable passages came only minutes into the address: "I hear it said that West Berlin is militarily untenable. And so was Bastogne. And so, in fact, was Stalingrad. Any dangerous spot is tenable if men—brave men—will make it so. We do not want to fight, but we have fought before. And others in earlier times have made the same dangerous mistake of assuming that the West was too selfish and too soft and too divided to resist invasions of freedom in other lands" (Report to the Nation on the Berlin Crisis by President Kennedy, 25 July 1961, DG, 695).

109. Report to the Nation on the Berlin Crisis by President Kennedy, 25 July 1961, DG, 699.

110. Information about military preparations leaked to the press before Kennedy made his speech. This may or may not have been a deliberate attempt by the government to enhance the credibility of the buildup. For a discussion of the evidence in this matter, see Trachtenberg, *History and Strategy*, 223–24; Beschloss, *The Crisis Years*, 244.

111. Documentary evidence substantiating this theory is scarce. On 25 October 1961, the NAC approved a directive to the NATO military authorities concerning Berlin contingency planning. SACEUR General Norstad pointed out in a subsequent talk with the British Minister of Defense that if he forwarded his military plans back to the NAC, they "would become known to the Russians, because of certain security weaknesses in the NATO Council" (Points of Interest Made by General Norstad during Lunch at Lancaster House on 1 November 1961, BC 1958–62, No. 02614, NSA). In December 1961, the secretary general of NATO decided not to have Norstad present his contingency plans before the NATO ministerial meeting, following British and French recommendations and rejecting Secretary Rusk's proposal. See Memorandum for the President, Chairman of the JCS Lemnitzer to the President, "27th Meeting, NATO Military Committee in Chief of Staff Session," 20 December 1961, BC 1958–62, No. 02652, NSA. Trachtenberg bases his case on a written exchange between himself and Secretary Rusk in 1984. See Trachtenberg, *History and Strategy*, 223–24.

112. See Burr, "U.S. Policy and the Berlin Crisis," 38–39; Nitze, *From Hiroshima to Glasnost*, 203.

113. Thomas C. Schelling, "Nuclear Strategy in the Berlin Crisis," 5 July 1961, FRUS, 1961–1963, 14: 170–72. Marc Trachtenberg explains the origins of the paper and has published it in a collection of U.S. sources. See Trachtenberg, *History and Strategy*, 224; Thomas C. Schelling, "Nuclear Strategy in the Berlin

Crisis," in *Writings on Strategy, 1961–1969, and Retrospectives,* ed. Marc Trachtenberg (New York: Garland Pub., 1988), 9–13.

114. Memorandum, Bundy to the President, 21 July 1961, BC 1958–62, No. 02209, NSA.

115. Both Kaplan and Trachtenberg give an account of these efforts. See Kaplan, *The Wizards of Armageddon,* 296–301; Trachtenberg, *History and Strategy,* 225. The initiation of the project is confirmed. See Memorandum, Kaysen to Bundy, 3 July 1961, "Germany–Berlin General Folder," Box 81, Countries Series, NSF, JFKL.

116. Memorandum, McNamara to the Chairman, JCS, 27 July 1961, BC 1958–62, No. 02227, NSA; Memorandum, Lawrence Legere to General Taylor, "Meeting of the Berlin Steering Group," 15 August 1961, BC 1958–62, No. 02311, NSA; Memorandum from Taylor to the White House, "Guidance for Berlin Contingency Planning," 17 August 1961, BC 1958–62, No. 02338, NSA.

117. For an early statement of general principles, see Memorandum, McNamara to the Chairman, JCS, 27 July 1961, BC 1958–62, No. 02227, NSA. Rusk and McNamara further pressed the American view in a Four-Power ambassadorial group meeting on 26 August. On this occasion, the secretary of defense noted that the administration was "so disturbed at the gaps in our planning that the US was now doing NATO planning" (Memorandum of Conversation, Four-Power Ambassadorial Group Meeting, 26 August 1961, Rusk Memos Folder, NSA). See also Department of State Berlin History, Part 6, 115–19.

118. For the reaction of the Europeans, see the memorandum of the conversation of the Quadripartite Ministerial Meeting in Berlin on 6 August 1961. Whereas the French representative noted that a probe by more than one division was "synonymous with the beginning of war," the British representative expressed reservations over concepts such as the "discreet use of nuclear weapons" (Memorandum of Conversation, "Second Quadripartite Ministerial Meeting on Berlin and Germany," 6 August 1961, FRUS, 1961–1963, 14: 299–303. See also Memorandum, Lawrence Legere to General Taylor, "Meeting of the Berlin Steering Group," 15 August 1961, BC 1958–62, No. 02311, NSA; U.K. Chiefs of Staff Committee, "The Berlin Situation," 27 September 1961, BC 1958–62, No. 02506, NSA).

119. In Washington, the JCS were split on the issue. Whereas the air force and the navy opposed a large-scale conventional buildup, the army thought such a step desirable. See Memorandum of Meeting, 20 October 1961, FRUS, 1961–1963, 14: 517–19.

120. Memorandum of Conversation, 4 October 1961, BC 1958–62, No. 02528, NSA. For additional insight into General Norstad's views, see Memorandum, McNamara to the President, "Military Build-up and Possible Action in Europe," Appendix A, 18 September 1961, BC 1958–62, No. 02484, NSA; Memorandum, Lawrence Legere to General Taylor, "General Norstad's Views," 28 September 1961, "Fldr. 109 Norstad Folder," Box 37, Maxwell D. Taylor Papers, NWCL.

121. For the role of Nitze, see Memorandum, Lawrence Legere to General

Taylor, "Meeting of the Berlin Steering Group," 15 August 1961, BC 1958–62, No. 02311, NSA; Burr, "U.S. Policy and the Berlin Crisis," 38; Nitze, *From Hiroshima to Glasnost,* 196–208.

122. Other secondary sources supplement our knowledge of the substance of NSAM 109. Of particular importance is the outline provided in J. C. Ausland's briefing for the president on Berlin contingency plans as held in August 1962. See John C. Ausland, "Briefing for President Kennedy on Berlin," 2 August 1962, BC 1958–62, No. 02842, NSA.

123. Letter, Kennedy to Norstad, including NSAM 109: "U.S. Policy on Military Actions in a Berlin Conflict," 20 October 1961, FRUS, 1961–1963, 14: 520–23 (further quoted as Kennedy-Norstad letter, 20 October 1961).

124. With respect to the employment of nuclear weapons, no priority was given to either of the three listed options. Kennedy noted that nuclear weapons should be used "starting with one of the following courses of action but continuing through C below [general nuclear war] if necessary" (Kennedy-Norstad letter, 20 October 1961). Ausland's briefing of August 1962 makes clear that it was not out of the question that the nuclear phase "could begin by direct recourse to general war" (John C. Ausland, "Briefing for President Kennedy on Berlin," 2 August 1962, BC 1958–62, No. 02842, NSA). President Kennedy had inquired at a meeting on 10 October whether there was much likelihood that the selective or tactical use of nuclear weapons could be undertaken without leading to general war. Secretary Rusk argued that the consequences of a general war were so very grave that the other options should be undertaken even though they might lead very quickly to general war. Paul Nitze proposed, by contrast, initiating a strategic strike in order to obtain the advantage of going first. Nitze added that with such a strike the United States "could in some real sense be victorious in the series of nuclear exchanges." Nitze was immediately challenged by Secretary McNamara who felt that "neither side could be sure of winning by striking first" (Minutes of Meeting, 10 October 1961, FRUS, 1961–1963, 14: 487–89). See Nitze, *From Hiroshima to Glasnost,* 204, and McNamara's statement in his Athens address.

125. All quotations from Kennedy-Norstad letter, 20 October 1961. After the president had conferred with the JCS on the employment of nuclear weapons in Europe in January 1962, he asked General Norstad to specify how many weapons of what yield he planned to employ, and against what targets. See Memorandum, Lt. General Wheeler to Kaysen, "Alert Procedures," 23 January 1962, "Fldr. 109 Norstad Folder," Box 37, Maxwell D. Taylor Papers, NWCL; Letter, Lemnitzer to Norstad, 18 January 1962, BC 1958–62, No. 02691, NSA.

126. Kennedy-Norstad letter, 20 October 1961.

127. Memorandum for the Record, "Meeting with General Norstad," 7 November 1961, BC 1958–62, No. 02619, NSA; Memorandum Prepared in the Department of State, 9 November 1961, FRUS, 1961–1963, 14: 557–61. See also Memorandum, Lawrence Legere to Bundy, "Differences among NATO allies on Broad Strategy," 24 October 1961, BC 1958–62, No. 02582, NSA.

128. Memorandum, Rusk and McNamara to the President, "General Norstad's Letter of 16 November," 1 December 1961, BC 1958–62, No. 02638, NSA. General Taylor agreed that Norstad's views were inconsistent with established U.S. policy. See Memorandum, Taylor to the President, 4 December 1961, BC 1958–62, No. 02640, NSA.

129. Memorandum for the Record by Legere, 5 December 1961, BC 1958–62, No. 02643, NSA.

130. John C. Ausland, "Briefing for President Kennedy on Berlin," 2 August 1962, BC 1958–62, No. 02842, NSA. See also Burr, "U.S. Policy and the Berlin Crisis," 39. There is some evidence that the Germans preferred to move directly from extended conventional ground action to a preemptive strike without going through intervening stages of demonstrative or tactical use of nuclear weapons out of fear to become the nuclear battlefield. Memorandum of Conversation between Ambassador Grewe and Secretary Rusk, 22 October 1961, Rusk Memos Folder, NSA. Memorandum of Conversation between Ambassador Grewe and the President, 24 October 1961, FRUS, 1961–1963, 14: 527–32.

131. Khrushchev's proposal of negotiations later in the year demonstrated to the Kennedy administration the deterrent impact of Kennedy's announcement of a large military buildup in his speech on 25 July. See Memorandum from Bohlen to Rusk, 3 October 1961, FRUS, 1961–1963, 14: 464–67. See chapter 10.

132. Among the better known analyses of the Berlin wall crisis are: Honoré Catudal, *Kennedy and the Berlin Wall: A Case Study in U.S. Decision Making* (Berlin: Verlag, 1980); Norman Gelb, *The Berlin Wall: Kennedy, Khrushchev and a Showdown in the Heart of Europe* (New York: Times Books, 1986); Trachtenberg, *History and Strategy*, 219–22; Bundy, *Danger and Survival*, 366–71.

133. McCloy to the Secretary of State, 29 July 1961, FRUS, 1961–1963, 14: 235; McCloy to the Secretary of State, 28 July 1961, ibid., 231–34.

134. Department of State to Finletter, 1 August 1961, BC 1958–62, No. 02245, NSA. See Department of State Berlin History, Part 6, 70–71.

135. All quotations from Address by Premier Khrushchev at Meeting with Rumanian Government Delegation, Moscow, 11 August 1961, DG, 716–21.

136. Khrushchev's Moscow speech of 7 August, *New York Times*, 8 August 1961, 8.

137. Telegram, Salinger to the President, 8 August 1961, BC 1958–62, No. 02276, NSA.

138. Address by Premier Khrushchev at Meeting with Rumanian Government Delegation, Moscow, 11 August 1961, DG, 716–21.

139. Current Intelligence Weekly Summary by the CIA, 17 August 1961, BC 1958–62, No. 02328, NSA. See Department of State Berlin History, Part 6, 77–81.

140. Department of State Berlin History, Part 6, 83.

141. Trachtenberg, *History and Strategy*, 221.

142. Minutes of Meeting of the Berlin Steering Group, 15 August 1961, FRUS, 1961–1963, 14: 333–34. Bundy advised the president not to take reprisals for the

border closing: "1) [T]his is something they have always had the power to do; 2) it is something they were bound to do sooner or later, unless they could control the exits from West Berlin to the West; 3) since it was bound to happen, it is as well to have it happen early, as *their* doing and *their* responsibility" (Memorandum, Bundy to the President, "Berlin Negotiations and Possible Reprisals," 14 August 1961, ibid., 330–31).

143. Legere expressed his relief over the border closing in even more unmistakable terms: "I forget who it was who said: 'If God did not exist, we should have to invent him' but the same line applies to the way these controls have shut off the refugees. 99% of these refugees have not been seeking legitimate political asylum or freedom from real oppression; they have been seeking a better shake economically" (Memorandum, Legere to Taylor, "Meeting of the Berlin Steering Group," 15 August 1961, BC 1958–62, No. 02311, NSA). There is evidence that both Acheson and Norstad believed that force should have been used to oppose the erection of the wall. See Trachtenberg, *History and Strategy*, 222. But this was clearly not the prevailing view at the time. See Bundy, *Danger and Survival*, 367.

144. Both Ambassador Thompson and Department of State German affairs officer John Ausland at some point forecasted such a contingency. See Telegram, Thompson to Department of State, 16 March 1961, FRUS, 1961–1963, 14: 30–33; Trachtenberg, *History and Strategy*, 221; Burr, "U.S. Policy and the Berlin Crisis," 39. See also the comments of Schlesinger and Rostow: Schlesinger, *A Thousand Days*, 394; Rostow, *The Diffusion of Power*, 231.

145. Catudal, *Kennedy and the Berlin Wall Crisis*, 200–203. See also Bundy, *Danger and Survival*, 366–370.

146. Statement of Secretary of State Rusk, "Concerning Travel Restrictions in Berlin," 13 August 1961, DG, 725–26. On 15 August the three western commandants in Berlin handed a letter of protest to their Soviet counterpart, and on 17 August notes of protest by the three western allies reached the Soviet foreign ministry. See Note from the American, British, and French Commandants at Berlin to the Soviet Commandant, 15 August 1961; Note from the American Embassy at Moscow to the Soviet Foreign Ministry, "Concerning Violation of the Quadripartite Status of Berlin," 17 August 1961, both in DG, 726–27.

147. Telegram, Berlin to the Secretary of State, 16 August 1961, FRUS, 1961–1963, 14: 339–41; Letter, Willy Brandt to Kennedy, 16 August 1961, ibid., 345–46; Current Intelligence Weekly Summary by the CIA, 17 August 1961, BC 1958–62, No. 02328, NSA.

148. Telegram, Rusk to Quadripartite Embassies, 17 August 1961, BC 1958–62, No. 02330, NSA; Record of Meeting of the Berlin Steering Group, 17 August 1961, FRUS, 1961–1963, 14: 347–49.

149. See Kennedy's letter of instruction to the vice president and his letter to Brandt: Letter, Kennedy to Johnson, 18 August 1961, BC 1958–62, No. 02351, NSA; Letter, Kennedy to Brandt, 18 August 1961, FRUS, 1961–1963, 14: 351–53. For several statements of Lyndon Johnson during his Berlin visit, see DG, 740–53.

150. Memorandum for the President, Bundy to the President, 18 August 1961, BC 1958–62, No. 02415, NSA. See State Department Berlin History, Part 6, 98.

151. Briefing Memorandum on Berlin, August 1961, BC 1958–62, No. 02333, NSA; Henry Owen to Bundy, 17 August 1961, BC 1958–62, No. 02336, NSA. It was the president himself who raised the question of a general defense buildup acceleration in two memoranda to the secretary of defense. See Memorandum, Kennedy to McNamara, 14 August 1961, BC 1958–62, No. 02301, NSA; Memorandum, Kennedy to McNamara, 14 August 1961, "August 1961 Folder," NH Box 13, NSA. McNamara requested the armed services to study what could be done in order to accelerate the readiness date for a capability to deploy six additional divisions to Europe from 1 January 1962 to 15 November 1961. See Memorandum, McNamara to Services Secretariats, August 1961, BC 1958–62, No. 02345, NSA. However, the secretary of defense reported back to the president that on such short notice there was really not too much that could be done: The U.S. bomber force was already large, the first 150 Minuteman ICBMs had been under construction *before* the development program was completed, and a new civil defense organization was being built up. See Memorandum, McNamara to the President, 16 August 1961; Memorandum, McNamara to the President, 17 August 1961; Memorandum, McNamara to the President, "Civil Defense," 16 August 1961, all in "August 1961 Folder," NH Box 13, NSA. Trachtenberg interprets these actions as indications that the Kennedy government perceived the wall episode to be a "serious escalation of the crisis" (Trachtenberg, *History and Strategy*, 221). I argue that the confidence crisis in Germany, rather than the border closing per se, inspired the Kennedy administration to action.

152. See the above quoted exchange among the president, Rusk, McNamara, and Nitze in Minutes of Meeting, 10 October 1961, FRUS, 1961–1963, 14: 487–89.

153. News Conference Statements by President Kennedy, "Concerning Berlin and the Appointment of General Clay," 30 August 1961, DG, 764.

154. Both quotations from Letter, Alsop to Martin Sommer, 5 July 1961, "June-August 1961 Saturday Evening Post Folder," Box 30, The Papers of Stewart Alsop, LC.

155. Memorandum, Kaysen to Bundy, 7 July 1961, "July 1961 Folder," NH Box 13, NSA; Letter, Kaysen to Bundy, 7 July 1961, Box W-4, The Papers of Arthur M. Schlesinger, WHSF, JFKL.

156. The exchange between Kennedy and Acheson came in the summer of 1961 with only one other witness present, namely McGeorge Bundy. For the latter's account see Bundy, *Danger and Survival*, 375.

157. Bundy has pointed to an article by Acheson in the *Saturday Evening Post* in 1959, in which the former secretary of state had called the option of local defeat without escalation to the nuclear level a course of "wisdom and restraint" (Acheson, "Wishing Won't Hold Berlin," 86; Bundy, *Danger and Survival*, 375–76; Douglas Brinkley, *Dean Acheson: The Cold War Years, 1953–71* [New Haven: Yale University Press, 1992], 134–53. For Nitze's views, see the interview

material in Trachtenberg, *History and Strategy*, 226; Nitze, *From Hiroshima to Glasnost*, 196–97; Kaplan, *The Wizards of Armageddon*, 291–306).

158. McNamara, "The Military Role of Nuclear Weapons," 79. See Bundy, *Danger and Survival*, 376.

159. Memorandum of Conversation, "Tripartite Meeting on Berlin and Germany," 5 August 1961, FRUS, 1961–1963, 14: 269–80, 272. Chancellor Adenauer made a comparable point in a talk with Dean Acheson in November 1961. When Acheson asked Adenauer whether he thought Khrushchev believed that the West would use nuclear weapons over Berlin, the chancellor answered that "while we must not use these weapons, we must not tell Khrushchev we would not do so" (Memorandum of Conversation, 21 November 1961, BC 1958–62, No. 02632, NSA).

160. Telegram, Thompson to the Secretary of State, 27 May 1961, FRUS, 1961–1963, 14: 77–78.

161. Both quotations from Memorandum of Conversation, 12 December 1961, Rusk Memos Folder, NSA.

162. Memorandum of Conversation, 21 November 1961, BC 1958–62, No. 02632, NSA.

163. On the occasion of these bilateral talks, British Foreign Secretary Lord Home proposed that the western presence in Berlin acquire a treaty-based legitimacy. See Memorandum of Conversation between Macmillan and Kennedy, 5 April 1961, FRUS, 1961–1963, 14: 36–40; Memorandum, Hillenbrand to Kohler, 25 April 1961, ibid., 57–61.

164. On 15 August Lawrence Legere noted to General Taylor that "Acheson's first plan steamrolled everything and everyone; it just about became the policy of the United States *faute de mieux*" (Memorandum, Legere to Taylor, "Meeting of Berlin Steering Group," 15 August 1961, BC 1958–62, No. 02311, NSA).

165. Memorandum, Bundy to the President, 29 May 1961, BC 1958–62, No. 02063, NSA. For background see Memorandum, Raskin to Bundy, "Negotiable Position on the Berlin Question," 1 June 1961, BC 1958–62, No. 02071, NSA.

166. Memorandum of NSC Meeting, 23 June 1961, FRUS, 1961–1963, 14: 160–62. See also Memorandum of Meeting on Berlin, 17 July 1961, ibid., 209–12.

167. One further reason for the slow progress on the substance of negotiations was that it was somewhat unclear where Secretary Rusk stood on this matter. See Paper Prepared by Secretary Rusk, 17 July 1961, FRUS, 1961–1963, 14: 207–09; Paper Prepared in the Department of State, undated, ibid., 236–41.

168. Minutes of Meeting of Inter-Departmental Coordination Group on Berlin, 26 July 1961, FRUS, 1961–1963, 14: 227–30. For a broader outline of Acheson's view regarding a political program, see Report by Dean Acheson, "Berlin: A Political Program," undated, ibid., 245–59.

169. Memorandum of Conversation, "Ministerial Consultations on Berlin," 5 August 1961, FRUS, 1961–1963, 14: 269–80. Rusk had discussed in a meeting with the president on 3 August the possibility of Ambassador Thompson making an early, quiet approach to Khrushchev. See Record of Meeting between the president, Rusk, and Owen, 3 August 1961, ibid., 264–67.

170. All quotations from Memorandum of Conversation, "Ministerial Consultations on Berlin," 5 August 1961, FRUS, 1961–1963, 14: 269–80.

171. The definitive French rejection of the U.S. proposal came in the quadripartite meeting on 6 August. See Memorandum of Conversation, "Ministerial Consultations on Berlin," 6 August 1961, FRUS, 1961–1963, 14: 291–98.

172. Memorandum of Conversation, "Ministerial Consultations on Berlin," 5 August 1961, FRUS, 1961–1963, 14: 269–80.

173. All quotations from Memorandum of Conversation, "Ministerial Consultations on Berlin," 6 August 1961, FRUS, 1961–1963, 14: 291–98.

174. Memorandum of Conversation between DeGaulle and Rusk, 8 August 1961, FRUS, 1961–1963, 14: 312–16. The main explanation for DeGaulle's uncompromising position was his fundamental conviction that Khrushchev did not want war any more than the West. At their meeting in Paris on 31 May DeGaulle told Kennedy that Soviet failure to act in spite of Khrushchev's assertion that his prestige was involved indicated that the Soviet leader did not want war. The French president pointed to the fact that the Soviet Union needed commercial relations with the West. For a summary of the conversation, see Department of State Berlin History, Part 5, 32–35.

175. Memorandum of Conversation, 10 August 1961, Rusk Memos Folder, NSA. Adenauer finally agreed to negotiations and the American proposal of timing.

176. Memorandum of Conversation between Rusk and Ambassador Alphand, 24 August 1961, Rusk Memos Folder, NSA.

177. Letter, Kennedy to Adenauer, 4 September 1961, FRUS, 1961–1963, 14: 389–91.

178. Memorandum of Conversation between the Secretary and Ambassador Alphand, 27 August 1961, Rusk Memos Folder, NSA; Memorandum of Conversation between the Secretary and Ambassador Alphand, 26 August 1961, Rusk Memos Folder, NSA.

179. Statement of President Kennedy at the Conclusion of the Visit of President Sukarno and President Keita, 13 September 1961, DG, 795.

180. Both quotations from Memorandum, Bundy to the President, "Issues to Be Settled with General Clay," 28 August 1961, BC 1958–62, No. 02415, NSA.

181. Memorandum, Bundy to Taylor, Rostow, Kissinger, and Owen, 10 August 1961, "Germany-Berlin General Folder," Box 82, Countries Series, NSF, JFKL.

182. See Kissinger's feedback to Bundy on the day after the meeting in Memorandum, Kissinger to Bundy, 11 August 1961, "Germany-Berlin General Folder," Box 82, Countries Series, NSF, JFKL.

183. Memorandum, Bundy to the President, "Berlin Negotiating Papers for Hyannisport," 11 August 1961, BC 1958–62, No. 02284, NSA.

184. Memorandum, Bundy to the President, "Berlin Negotiations and Possible Reprisals," 14 August 1961, FRUS, 1961–1963, 14: 330–31; Editorial note, ibid., 267–68; Memorandum, Bundy to the President, "What to say about Berlin negotiations this afternoon," 15 August 1961, BC 1958–62, No. 02312, NSA.

185. Letter with attached Memorandum, Kaysen to Bundy, 22 August 1961, "Staff Memoranda Carl Kaysen 6/61–8/61," Box 320, Meetings and Memoranda Series, NSF, JFKL. Around the same time, Averell Harriman wrote to the president that he believed Khrushchev to be seriously concerned about the remilitarization of Germany and concluded that "it is of very great importance to the security of the United States to prevent Germany from having independent nuclear capability" (Letter, Harriman to Kennedy, 1 September 1961, BC 1958–62, No. 02430, NSA).

186. Kaysen assumed that the growing nuclear striking power allowed Khrushchev to exploit his greater flexibility and control over the Warsaw Pact in contrast to the imperfectly united NATO powers and the advantages provided by the geography of Berlin. Moreover, he pointed to pressures on the Soviet leader from Soviet and Chinese hard-liners. See Letter with attached Memorandum, Kaysen to Bundy, 22 August 1961, "Staff Memoranda Carl Kaysen 6/61–8/61," Box 320, Meetings and Memoranda Series, NSF, JFKL.

187. Memorandum, Kissinger to Bundy, 18 August 1961, "Germany-Berlin General Folder," Box 82, Countries Series, NSF, JFKL. Marc Raskin had emphasized in a memorandum to Bundy at the beginning of June that if the West wanted West German participation in western defense, it had to accept "the more or less permanent partition of Germany, which implies the recognition of the East German state and acceptance of the *status quo* in Eastern Europe. In that case," he had added, "it would be unrealistic to expect West Berlin to remain as a Western controlled island of freedom in the heart of the East German state" (Memorandum, Raskin to Bundy, "Negotiable Positions on the Berlin Question," 1 June 1961, BC 1958–62, No. 02071, NSA).

188. All quotations from Memorandum, Kissinger to Bundy, 18 August 1961, "Germany-Berlin General Folder," Box 82, Countries Series, NSF, JFKL.

189. Memorandum, Kennedy to Rusk, 21 August 1961, FRUS, 1961–1963, 14: 359–60.

190. Memorandum of Conversation, "Quadripartite Foreign Ministers Meeting," 16 September 1961, Rusk Memos Folder, NSA.

191. Memorandum, Kennedy to Rusk, 21 August 1961, FRUS, 1961–1963, 14: 359–60.

192. Memorandum, Kennedy to Rusk, 12 September 1961, FRUS, 1961–1963, 14: 402–3; Memorandum, Bundy to Kennedy, 20 September 1961, ibid., 429–31.

193. For the announcement, see Statement by the Soviet Foreign Ministry, 14 September 1961, DG, 795–96. The Department of State Intelligence service had already interpreted a speech by Khrushchev on 8 September as a qualified pitch for negotiations. See Memorandum, Roger Hilsman to the Secretary of State, "Khrushchev on Berlin Settlement," 11 September 1961, BC 1958–62, No. 02462, NSA.

194. All quotations from Memorandum of Conversation, 21 September 1961, Rusk Memos Folder, NSA. For an even stronger Soviet attack on German militarism, see: Statement by Soviet Foreign Minister Gromyko at the United Nations General Assembly, 26 September 1961, DG, 812–23.

195. All quotations from: Memorandum of Conversation, 21 September 1961, Rusk Memos Folder, NSA. Secretary Rusk's guidelines for the talk are more explicit on this point: "President Kennedy has said that if the Soviet Union has genuine concern about the general security situation in Central Europe, these are questions which can be discussed and on which some headway might be made" (Memorandum, Rusk to the President, 20 September 1961, BC 1958–62, No. 02491, NSA).

196. Rusk expanded on the same issues in two further meetings with Gromyko on 28 September and 2 October. See Telegram, Department of State to the Embassy in France, 28 September 1961, FRUS, 1961–1963, 14: 439–41; Telegram, Department of State to the Embassy in France, 2 October 1961, ibid., 456–60.

197. Memorandum, Kennedy to Rusk, "Berlin Negotiations," 12 September 1961, BC 1958–62, No. 02464, NSA.

198. All quotations from Address by President Kennedy to the United Nations General Assembly, 25 September 1961, DG, 803–11.

199. Memorandum of Conversation, "Meeting of Ambassadorial Group," 3 October 1961, Rusk Memos Folder, NSA; Memorandum of Conversation, "Quadripartite Foreign Ministers Meeting," 12 December 1961, Rusk Memos Folder, NSA. On 21 August Bundy informed the president that they had received information that during a meeting of Warsaw Pact members in Moscow in early August 1961 the Polish delegation had succeeded in convincing Khrushchev not to set a deadline for an East German peace treaty and resolution of the Berlin problem. See McGeorge Bundy to Godfrey McHugh, 21 August 1961, BC 1958–62, No. 02404, NSA.

200. All quotations from Memorandum of Conversation, "Meeting of Ambassadorial Group," 3 October 1961, Rusk Memos Folder, NSA. When Rusk was asked later in the same meeting if he could imagine a Berlin arrangement without broader discussion of the issue of European security, he deliberately avoided the question.

201. Memorandum, Bundy to Kennedy, 2 October 1961, FRUS, 1961–1963, 14: 460–61.

202. All quotations from Memorandum of Conversation between Kennedy and Gromyko, 6 October 1961, FRUS, 1961–1963, 14: 468–80.

203. Memorandum, Bundy to the President, "Issues to be Settled with General Clay," 28 August 1961, BC 1958–62, No. 02415, NSA. Kaysen had warned of domestic opposition to Kennedy's "appeasement." Memorandum, Kaysen to Bundy, 22 August 1961, "Staff Memoranda Carl Kaysen 6/61–8/61 Folder," Box 320, Meetings and Memoranda Series, NSF, JFKL.

204. For the reactions of von Brentano as perceived by Secretary Rusk, see Memorandum of Conversation, "Quadripartite Foreign Ministers Meeting," 16 September 1961, Rusk Memos Folder, NSA; Memorandum of Conversation between the Secretary and British Foreign Secretary Lord Home, 17 September 1961, Rusk Memos Folder, NSA.

205. Memorandum of Conversation, "Meeting of Ambassadorial Group," 3 October 1961, Rusk Memos Folder, NSA.

206. All quotations from Memorandum of Conversation between Ambassador Grewe and the Secretary, 4 October 1961, Rusk Memos Folder, NSA. "Any serious damage to the idea of reunification," the Ambassador later said, "would give the Soviets added security, increase their self-confidence, and widen their freedom of action" (Ibid., see also Memorandum of Conversation between Acheson and Grewe, 11 October 1961, FRUS, 1961–1963, 14: 490–92).

207. All quotations from Letter, Kennedy to Adenauer, 13 October 1961, FRUS, 1961–1963, 14: 493–97. Rusk had told Grewe that the United States "envisaged a proposal whereby the US would say to the Soviets that it would keep no more than 5 divisions in other NATO countries if the Soviets kept no more than 5 divisions in other Warsaw Pact countries" (Memorandum of Conversation between Ambassador Grewe and the Secretary of State, 4 October 1961, Rusk Memos Folder, NSA).

208. All quotations from Letter, Kennedy to Adenauer, 13 October 1961, FRUS, 1961–1963, 14: 493–97.

209. Memorandum of Conversation between Ambassador Grewe and Secretary Rusk, 22 October 1961, Rusk Memos Folder, NSA. See Memorandum of Conversation between Grewe and Kennedy, 24 October 1961, FRUS, 1961–1963, 14: 527–32.

210. On this point see the sources quoted in Burr, "U.S. Policy and the Berlin Crisis," 40.

211. Letter, Khrushchev to Kennedy, 9 November 1961, FRUS, 1961–1963, 14: 567–80.

212. On NATO disunity in the fall of 1961, see Nitze, *From Hiroshima to Glasnost*, 196–97; Bundy, *Danger and Survival*, 382.

213. President Kennedy decided to plan a careful approach to Adenauer. Memorandum, Kennedy to Rusk, "Berlin Negotiations," 12 September 1961, BC 1958–62, No. 02464, NSA. Also, Bundy suggested that the president should bring in as personal adviser either Acheson or Bowie, because both had enormous influence in Germany. With respect to Acheson, he noted that the former secretary of state was at least interested in parallel peace treaties and "likes the negotiating position that is emerging at the staff level" (Memorandum, Bundy to Kennedy, "On Adenauer's Visit," 24 October 1961, BC 1958–62, No. 02583, NSA). Trachtenberg emphasizes the issue of Acheson's disappointment with Kennedy's negotiating approach as a tool to show how far the Kennedy administration was prepared to go to accommodate the Soviet Union. See Trachtenberg, *History and Strategy*, 230–31. Kissinger suggested that President Kennedy was the key to winning and holding Chancellor Adenauer's confidence. Memorandum, Bundy to Kennedy, 20 November 1961, FRUS, 1961–1963, 14: 588–89.

214. Memorandum of Conversation between Adenauer and Kennedy, 20 November 1961, FRUS, 1961–1963, 14: 590–95, 592.

215. Memorandum of Conversation between Sir David O. Gore (U.K.), Dean Rusk, et al., 24 November 1961, Rusk Memos Folder, NSA; Memorandum of Conversation between Ambassador Grewe and Secretary Rusk, 22 October 1961, Rusk Memos Folder, NSA.

216. On the 1954 declaration see chapter 4.

217. Adenauer stressed that the declaration "had never been made with any reference to the Soviet Union" and that it did not mention the stockpiling in Germany of weapons made by others. See Memorandum of Conversation between Adenauer and Kennedy, 22 November 1961, FRUS, 1961–1963, 14: 620–32; Memorandum of Conversation between Adenauer and Kennedy, 21 November 1961, ibid., 614–18.

218. Memorandum of Conversation, "Quadripartite Foreign Ministers Meeting," 11 December 1961, FRUS, 1961–1963, 14: 650–59.

219. Memorandum of Conversation, "Quadripartite Foreign Ministers Meeting," 12 December 1961, FRUS, 1961–1963, 14: 672–78.

220. For the agreed formula of compromise, see Memorandum of Telephone Conversation between Kennedy and DeGaulle, 12 December 1961, FRUS, 1961–1963, 14: 679–81.

221. Telegram, Rusk to Thompson, 29 December 1961, FRUS, 1961–1963, 14: 714–15.

222. Memorandum of Conversation between Macmillan and Kennedy, 22 December 1961, FRUS, 1961–1963, 14: 701–04. George F. Kennan, at that time ambassador to Yugoslavia, wrote to Thompson that there was "something badly wrong with the diplomacy which gives to our allies the power to tell us with whom and when we may have the privilege of normal diplomatic discussion about matters which are not only of mutual interest but of greatest importance to world peace" (Letter, Kennan to Thompson, 26 December 1961, ibid., 705–8).

223. Memorandum, Kennedy to Rusk, 15 January 1962, FRUS, 1961–1963, 14: 759–60.

224. For background on the Bolshakov–Robert Kennedy meetings, see Beschloss, *The Crisis Years*, 152–57. The first contact is confirmed in Letter, Khrushchev to Robert Kennedy, 18 January 1962, FRUS, 1961–1963, 14: 763–66.

225. All quotations from Letter, Kennedy to Khrushchev, 15 February 1962, FRUS, 1961–1963, 14: 819–22. See also Memorandum of Conversation between Adzhubei, Bolshakov, and Kennedy, 31 January 1962, ibid., 780–84.

226. Nitze, *From Hiroshima to Glasnost*, 206. The Americans did only consult with the British before presenting the new proposals to the Soviets. See Memorandum of Conversation, "British American Bilateral Talks," 11 March 1962, Rusk Memos Folder, NSA.

227. Quoted in Burr, "U.S. Policy and the Berlin Crisis," 40, who gives the best account of the development of the talks in 1962. See Memorandum of Conversation between Governing Mayor Brandt and Secretary Rusk, 21 June 1962, Rusk Memos Folder, NSA. Nitze, *From Hiroshima to Glasnost*, 206–7.

228. Memorandum of Conversation between Governing Mayor Brandt and Secretary Rusk, 21 June 1962, Rusk Memos Folder, NSA.

229. The impact of the Cuban crisis on the political atmosphere over the Berlin question is confirmed in Bundy, *Danger and Survival*, 362; Nitze, *From Hiroshima to Glasnost*, 207; Trachtenberg, *History and Strategy*, 231; Burr, "U.S. Policy and the Berlin Crisis," 40–41.

230. The basis of the 1971 Berlin agreement was German acceptance of the boundaries set by World War II (Oder-Neisse line) in exchange for Soviet guarantees of western access to West Berlin. See Bundy, *Danger and Survival*, 385–90.

231. With respect to these broader questions, Trachtenberg's analysis of the meaning of the Berlin crisis is extremely helpful and stimulating. See *History and Strategy*, 231–34.

232. General DeGaulle was the champion of independence from the U.S. guarantee, noting in a letter to Kennedy on 11 January 1962: "Even if the adversary is armed so as to be able to kill you 10 times, the fact that one could kill just once or even simply tear his arms off could after all, make him think" (Letter, DeGaulle to Kennedy, 11 January 1962, BC 1958–62, No. 02676, NSA).

233. For a good study on the German perspective of the MLF, see Christoph Hoppe, *Zwischen Teilhabe und Mitsprache: Die Nuklearfrage in der Allianzpolitik Deutschlands 1959–1966* (Baden-Baden: Nomos Verlagsgesellschaft, 1993).

234. Secretary Rusk noted in bilateral talks with the British in March 1962 that "it seems likely that they [the Soviets] consider that they are stuck with public positions." In the same meeting, Ambassador Thompson noted that Khrushchev's recent speech to the Central Committee Plenum indicated that the conflict with the Chinese would continue. He added, "it seemed possible that the big Soviet loan to Ulbricht might be a sort of sop to him in lieu of positive action with respect to the peace treaty and status of West Berlin" (Memorandum of Conversation, "British-American Bilateral Talks," 11 March 1962, Rusk Memos Folder, NSA).

235. For a broader discussion of the connection between the Berlin crisis and U.S. claims of nuclear superiority see chapter 10.

Chapter 10

1. For a theoretically elegant and convincing outline of the signaling and symbolic character of nuclear politics, see Jervis, *The Meaning of the Nuclear Revolution*, 174–225.

2. Eisenhower, Annual Message to the Congress on the State of the Union, 12 January 1961, Eisenhower PPS, 1960–1961, 912–30.

3. For a detailed account of McNamara's blunder, see Ball, *Politics and Force Levels*, 88–92; Memorandum, Adam Yarmolinsky to Theodore Sorensen, "Missile Gap Controversy," 3 May 1962, "May 1962 Folder," NH Box 14, NSA.

4. On 4 March 1963, Bundy demanded—in connection with a reappraisal of the missile gap history—more information material from Yarmolinsky "on

the immediate period when we [were] sure there was no missile gap—Dec 60–Feb 61" (Memorandum, Bundy to Yarmolinsky, 4 March 1963, "May 1963 Folder," NH Box 15, NSA). See also Ball, *Politics and Force Levels*, 92–100; McGeorge Bundy, "The Presidency and Peace," *Foreign Affairs* 42, No. 3 (April 1964): 353–65; Jerome Wiesner, "Arms Control: Current Prospects and Problems," *Bulletin of the Atomic Scientists* 26, No. 3 (May 1970): 6–8; Herbert York, *Race to Oblivion: A Participant's View of the Arms Race* (New York: Simon & Schuster, 1970), 57, 147; Schlesinger, *A Thousand Days*, 498–500.

5. Memorandum, Lawrence C. McQuade to Paul Nitze, "But Where Did the Missile Gap Go?" 31 May 1963, "May 1963 Folder," NH Box 16, NSA, 15. The memorandum is the best available governmental study of the missile gap history.

6. The satellites for the first time allowed a comprehensive mapping of Soviet strategic forces, which was completed by September 1961. See Freedman, *U.S. Intelligence and the Soviet Strategic Threat*, 77; Ball, *Politics and Force Levels*, 100–102.

7. Memorandum, C. P. Cabell to General Taylor, "Current Status of Soviet and Satellite Military Forces and Indications of Military Intentions," 6 September 1961, "September 1961 Folder," NH Box 13, NSA. The Soviet Union, moreover, focused on the development and production of IRBMs. This subtracted additional resources from the Soviet ICBM programs. See Memorandum, Lawrence C. McQuade to Paul Nitze, "But Where Did the Missile Gap Go?" 31 May 1963, "May 1963 Folder," NH Box 16, NSA, 16–18.

8. Hopkins and Goldberg, *The Development of the Strategic Air Command*, 96; Ball, *Politics and Force Levels*, 50–51.

9. Quoted in Memorandum, Yarmolinsky to Sorensen, "Missile Gap Controversy," 3 May 1962, "May 1962 Folder," NH Box 14, NSA. Bundy notes that Gilpatric's address was encouraged by the president and cleared in separate meetings with Secretary Rusk, Secretary McNamara, and himself. He proceeds to underline the point that the speech was intended for reassurance. See Bundy, *Danger and Survival*, 381–82.

10. The speech led to several news articles in *Newsweek, Business Week, U.S. News and World Report*, and *New York Times*, all emphasizing the nonexistence of a missile gap. For a summary of the articles, see Memorandum, Yarmolinsky to Sorensen, "Missile Gap Controversy," 3 May 1962, "May 1962 Folder," NH Box 14, NSA.

11. All quotations from McNamara, Remarks in Atlanta, Georgia, 11 November 1961, "November 1961 Folder," NH Box 13, NSA. On the occasion of two press conferences at about the same time, McNamara combined boasts of U.S. nuclear superiority with reassurance of U.S. willingness to use nuclear weapons in the defense of West Berlin. In response to a query as to whether the secretary of defense was implying that the United States would use nuclear weapons in connection with the Berlin situation, McNamara replied: "We will use nuclear weapons whenever we feel it necessary to protect our vital interests. Our nuclear stockpile is several times that of the Soviet Union and we will use either tactical

weapons or strategic weapons in whatever quantities wherever, whenever it's necessary to protect this nation and its interests" (McNamara, Interview on "JFK
Report" Television Program, Washington, 28 September 1961, Public Statements of Robert S. McNamara, Vol. 3, 1961, HOSD, Pentagon, 1443). See also
McNamara, Interview with the Hearst Headline Panel, New York, 29 October
1961, ibid., 1450).

12. McNamara, Athens address, 5.

13. For a detailed analysis of the Kennedy-Adenauer talks, see chapter 9.

14. Nitze, Remarks to the Institute of Strategic Studies, London, 11 December 1961, "December 1961 Folder," NH Box 13, NSA.

15. Minutes of National Security Council Meeting, 19 December 1961, "December 1961 Folder," NH Box 13, NSA.

16. Telegram, Embassy in Germany to the Department of State, 17 February
1961, FRUS, 1961–1963, 14: 824–27.

17. Memorandum of Conversation between Grewe and Kennedy, 19 February
1962, FRUS, 1961–1963, 14: 830–34.

18. Bundy, *Danger and Survival*, 382.

19. Quoted in Bundy, *Danger and Survival*, 382.

20. Roger Hilsman, *To Move a Nation: The Politics of Foreign Policy in the Administration of John F. Kennedy* (Garden City, N.Y.: Doubleday & Company, 1967), 163.
For interpretations of Gilpatric's speech that rely heavily on Hilsman's account,
see Ball, *Politics and Force Levels*, 97–98; Beschloss, *The Crisis Years*, 328–32.

21. For an analysis of the speech and Khrushchev's reaction, see chapter 9.

22. Letter, Khrushchev to Kennedy, 29 September 1961, FRUS, 1961–1963,
14: 444–55. As early as 10 September, Cyrus Sulzberger, a columnist for the
New York Times had delivered a message from Khrushchev to Kennedy in which
Khrushchev proposed some sort of informal contact. See editorial note, ibid.,
401–2.

23. Letter, Kennedy to Khrushchev, 16 October 1961, FRUS, 1961–1963, 14:
502–8. Office of the Secretary of Defense, Historical Office, History of the Strategic Arms Competition, 1945–1972, Part 2, March 1981, BC 1958–62, No.
02944, NSA. See Burr, "U.S. Policy and the Berlin Crisis," 38. For an alternative
explanation of the letters, see Beschloss, *The Crisis Years*, 319–26.

24. Letter, Thompson to Kennan, 20 October 1961, BC 1958–62, No. 02570,
NSA. It is interesting to see Thompson making this case, as he had been convinced in the spring of 1961 that Khrushchev would at least go ahead and sign
the peace treaty and, at one point, had judged the chances of war to be close to
50–50. See Memorandum, Thompson to the Secretary of State, 27 May 1961,
BC 1958–62, No. 02061, NSA. Thompson had now to explain why Khrushchev
did not sign the peace treaty after all.

25. Address by Premier Khrushchev at Meeting with Rumanian Government
Delegation, Moscow, 11 August 1961, DG, 716–21, 718–19. See Address by Premier Khrushchev at Moscow, Concerning His Meeting at Vienna with President
Kennedy, 15 June 1961, DG, 660–63. For a comparable argument in a different
context, see Trachtenberg, *History and Strategy*, 220–21.

26. In early January 1962, Khrushchev complained in a letter to Robert Kennedy that the West seemed to stick to a policy "from the position of strength." He then emphasized that Kennedy had himself said that the balance of power was equal. See Message to Attorney General Kennedy, 18 January 1961, FRUS, 1961–1963, 14: 763–66.

27. All quotations from Memorandum, McNamara to the President, "US and Soviet Military Buildup and Probable Effects on Berlin Situation," 21 June 1962, BC 1958–62, No. 02816, NSA.

28. The five-year defense plan was one of the tools of the Planning-Programming-Budgeting System (PPBS), which was developed by Charles Hitch and - McNamara in 1961. The PPBS was applauded at that time for the clarity and logic it brought to the military planning and budgeting process. Budget Director Bell, for example, praised McNamara's achievement in a letter to the president calling the PPBS "literally revolutionary" (Memorandum, Bell to the President, "Fiscal Year 1963 Defense Budget Issues," 13 November 1961, "November 1961 Folder," NH Box 13, NSA). Chairman of the House Armed Services Committee Carl Vinson noted "that never before has a Secretary of Defense covered the panorama of military activities in such detail" (House Armed Services Committee, Department of Defense Appropriations, Fiscal Year 1963, 3158). However, Desmond Ball has later shown that the PPBS allowed rationalization of budget decisions that were decidedly more political than the administration was prepared to admit at the time. See Ball, *Politics and Force Levels*, 127–42. For the PPBS see Enthoven and Smith, *How Much Is Enough*, 31–72; Michael D. Hobkirk, *The Politics of Defense Budgeting: A Study of Organization and Resource Allocation in the United Kingdom and the United States* (Washington: National Defense University Press, 1983), 29–35.

29. The numbers are readily accessible in a summary memorandum from Kaysen to the President: Memorandum, Kaysen to the President, 9 December 1961, "December 1961 Folder," NH Box 13, NSA. The Defense Department expanded the total program number of Minuteman ICBMs to 1,100 in December 1961 in order to compensate for the elimination of the mobile Minuteman version from the program. See Memorandum, McNamara to the President, 7 December 1961, "December 1961 Folder," NH Box 13, NSA. For the secretary of defense's original proposal, see DPM-61; Memorandum, McNamara to the President, "Recommended DoD Defense Fiscal Year 63 Budget and 1963–67 Program," 6 October 1961, "October 1961 Folder," NH Box 13, NSA.

30. Memorandum, Bell to the President, "Fiscal Year 1963 Defense Budget Issues," 13 November 1961, "November 1961 Folder," NH Box 13, NSA.

31. Memorandum, Taylor to Bell, "Excesses and Deficiencies on the SecDef Proposed Budget for Fiscal Year 63," 21 November 1961, "November 1961 Folder," NH Box 13, NSA. Pointing to the questionable balance between strategic and conventional forces, Carl Kaysen rhetorically asked if McNamara's proposal was "the New Look which corresponds to the President's program?" (Memorandum, Kaysen to Bundy, "Secretary McNamara's Memorandum on the

Defense Budget dated 6 October 1961," 13 November 1961, "DoD Defense Budget Fiscal Year 1963 Folder," Box 275, Department and Agencies Series, NSF, JFKL).

32. Others who also thought that the proposed expansion of the strategic forces was too large included General Taylor, David Bell, and McGeorge Bundy. See Memorandum, Taylor to Bell, "Excesses and Deficiencies on the SecDef Proposed Budget for Fiscal Year 63," 21 November 1961, "November 1961 Folder," NH Box 13, NSA. Memorandum, Bell to the President, "Fiscal Year 1963 Defense Budget Issues," 13 November 1961, "November 1961 Folder," NH Box 13, NSA.

33. Memorandum, Kaysen to Bundy, "Secretary McNamara's Memorandum on the Defense Budget dated 6 October 1961," 13 November 1961, "DoD Defense Budget Fiscal Year 1963 Folder," Box 275, Department and Agencies Series, NSF, JFKL. For confirmation of Kaysen's argument, see the estimates as presented in DPM-61, 11 and appendix I; Memorandum, Lawrence C. McQuade to Paul Nitze, "But Where Did the Missile Gap Go?" 31 May 1963, "May 1963 Folder," NH Box 16, NSA, 9a.

34. Memorandum, Kaysen to the President, 9 December 1961, "December 1961 Folder," NH Box 13, NSA.

35. All quotations from Memorandum, Kaysen to the President, "Force Structure and Defense Budget," 22 November 1961, "November 1961 Folder," NH Box 13, NSA.

36. Memorandum, Kaysen to the President, "Force Structure and Defense Budget," 22 November 1961, "November 1961 Folder," NH Box 13, NSA. In December, the White House staff developed several proposals, which covered the middle ground between McNamara's numbers and Kaysen's numbers. See Memorandum, Kaysen to the President, 9 December 1961, "December 1961 Folder," NH Box 13, NSA.

37. Several memoranda suggest that Kaysen's view had an important influence on President Kennedy in December 1961. See Memorandum, Bundy to the President, 22 November 1961, "November 1961 Folder," NH Box 13, NSA; Memorandum, from the White House Staff to the President, 9 December 1961, "December 1961 Folder," NH Box 13, NSA.

38. Schlesinger, *A Thousand Days*, 500.

39. The production rate for the Minuteman missiles was somewhat reduced, leaving the total number of authorized Minuteman ICBMs at eight hundred under the fiscal year 1963 defense budget. See Ball, *Politics and Force Levels*, 127–35, whose account still is the most detailed analysis of the fiscal year 1963 defense budget decisions.

40. For the decisions of March see chapter 8.

41. Ball, *Politics and Force Levels*, 173–78, 234–40.

42. Memorandum, Bell to the President, "Fiscal Year 1963 Defense Budget Issues," 13 November 1961, "November 1961 Folder," NH Box 13, NSA. A White House outline for a talk of the president to the NSC on the future direc-

tion of national security affairs on 18 January 1962 noted that sentiment in Congress "for more missiles and more nuclear weapons is pretty strong—I don't think such sentiment can be rationally defended, but there it is. The totals we have set are all we need—with a comfortable margin of safety. To be honest with you, we would probably be safe with less" (White House, "Outline for Talk to NSC, 18 January 1962," 17 January 1962, "NSC Meetings 1962 No. 496 1/18/62 Folder," Box 313, Meetings and Memoranda Series, NSF, JFKL). For the presidential presentation as held, see Summary of the President's Remarks to the National Security Council, 18 January 1962, ibid.

43. Ball, *Politics and Force Levels*, 240–52. See Schlesinger, *A Thousand Days*, 499–501; Bundy, *Danger and Survival*, 547.

44. For a detailed list of the different cost estimates, see Memorandum, McNamara to the President, "Recommended Department of Defense Fiscal Year 63 Budget and 1963–67 Program," 6 October 1961, "October 1961 Folder," NH Box 13, NSA. See Memorandum, McNamara to the President, 7 December 1961, "December 1961 Folder," NH Box 13, NSA.

45. DPM-61, 3.

46. Memorandum, McNamara to the President, "Recommended Department of Defense Fiscal Year 63 Budget and 1963–67 Program," 6 October 1961, "October 1961 Folder," NH Box 13, NSA. However, it was first of all the air force that criticized the suggested strategic force as far too small. See Memorandum, JCS to the SecDef, JCSM-848-61, "DoD Budget for Fiscal Year 1963," 7 December 1961, CCS 7000, "General," 9 October 1961, JCS, NARS. McNamara had to realize that the no-cities counterforce strategy, which he was using for political purposes, readily lent itself as a basis for large force requirements. See chapter 12.

47. Acheson Berlin report, 146. The argument was taken up in a presidential briefing paper for the NSC meeting of 13 July: "It would be useful to convince the Soviets that a Berlin crisis would lead to a *permanent* increase in the DOD budget, such as followed the Korean war" (Memorandum, "Briefing for Tuesday NSC Meeting," 12 July 1961, BC 1958–62, No. 02161, NSA).

48. For an analysis of Kennedy's speech and Khrushchev's reaction thereto see chapter 9.

49. For this line of argument, see Memorandum by Raymond L. Garthoff, Sent by Executive Secretary Battle to Carl Kaysen through McGeorge Bundy, "The Interaction of Soviet and Western Military Postures," 13 October 1961, BC 1958–62, No. 02550, NSA; Memorandum, Kaysen to Bundy, "Secretary McNamara's Memorandum on the Defense Budget dated 6 October 1961," 13 November 1961, "DoD Defense Budget Fiscal Year 1963 Folder," Box 275, Department and Agencies Series, NSF, JFKL; Bundy, *Danger and Survival*, 384.

50. Memorandum, Kennedy to McNamara, 14 August 1961, BC 1958–62, No. 02301, NSA.

51. Memorandum, Taylor to the President, 4 September 1961, BC 1958–62, No. 02442, NSA; Department of State, Bureau of Intelligence and Research,

"Assessment of Current Soviet Intentions in the Berlin Crisis, August 28–September 4," 4 September 1961, BC 1958–62, No. 02439, NSA.

52. Memorandum, Taylor to the President, 4 September 1961, BC 1958–62, No. 02442, NSA. See Memorandum, Nitze to McNamara, 24 August 1961, quoted in Letter from Lemnitzer to Norstad, 28 August 1961, BC 1958–62, No. 02414, NSA.

53. It is not clear from the record available who else was participating in the meeting. General Taylor proposed that the president include chairman of the JCS Lemnitzer and, perhaps, Dean Acheson. Memorandum, Taylor to the President, 4 September 1961, BC 1958–62, No. 02442, NSA.

54. Both quotations from Memorandum, Kennedy to Rusk and McNamara, 8 September 1961, FRUS, 1961–1963, 14: 398–99.

55. It is unclear whether Kennedy received a separate reply of Secretary Rusk or if the secretary of state just concurred with McNamara's memorandum.

56. All quotations from Memorandum, McNamara to the President, "Military Build-up and Possible Action in Europe," 18 September 1961, BC 1958–62, No. 02484, NSA.

57. Memorandum, McNamara to Kennedy, "Military Build-up and Possible Action in Europe," Appendix A, 18 September 1961, BC 1958–62, No. 02484, NSA. For a broader outline of Norstad's views see chapter 9. The same arguments were used in 1958 when the Eisenhower administration discussed how best to reassure the Europeans about U.S. resolve. While Chairman of the JCS Twining had argued that increased emphasis on conventional forces would devalue the nuclear deterrent, John Foster Dulles had pointed out that unless the allies did not possess some kind of local defense, the United States would lose them even before the war started. See part 2, chapter 6.

58. All quotations from Memorandum, Kissinger to Bundy, 3 October 1961, BC 1958–62, No. 02523, NSA. For earlier statements of Kissinger in this regard, see Memorandum, Kissinger to Bundy, "Some Additional Observations Regarding the Call-up of Reserves; Military and Disarmament Planning," 8 September 1961, BC 1958–62, No. 02454, NSA; Memorandum, Kissinger to the President, "Major Defense Options," 22 March 1961, BC 1958–62, No. 02014, NSA.

59. Memorandum, McNamara to the President, "Military Build-up and Possible Action in Europe," 18 September 1961, BC 1958–62, No. 02484, NSA. See Memorandum, Taylor to the President, 18 September 1961, BC 1958–62, No. 02488, NSA.

60. Memorandum for the Record by General Taylor, "Meeting with the President on the Military Build-up and Possible Action in Europe," 18 September 1961, FRUS, 1961–1963, 14: 428–29. When the president indicated that he thought the two divisions should be transformed as quickly as possible into regular army divisions, McNamara replied that he was "not sure that the permanent establishment needs two additional divisions" pointing to a probable fiscal year 1963 defense budget in the order of $64 billion (Ibid.).

61. On 28 September, the Kennedy administration revealed the temporary

reinforcement of the U.S. Air Force Europe by over two hundred fighter aircraft. See Memorandum by Raymond L. Garthoff, Sent by Executive Secretary Battle to Carl Kaysen through McGeorge Bundy, "The Interaction of Soviet and Western Military Postures," 13 October 1961, BC 1958–62, No. 02550, NSA. See Burr, "U.S. Policy and the Berlin Crisis," 38.

62. All quotations from Memorandum of Conversation between Rusk and Gromyko, "Germany and Berlin, Disarmament, Red China," 21 September 1961, Rusk Memos Folder, NSA.

63. On 19 July 1962, President Kennedy met Ambassador Dobrynin to discuss the Berlin matter. Kennedy used the occasion to stress "that Soviet-created tensions in Berlin had caused increases in Western rearmament and that any new crisis would have a similar effect." He noted further the "disagreement which the United States has with its Allies on the diffusion of nuclear weapons, and said that Soviet-created tensions could only increase the danger of results which the Soviet Government would not like" (Memorandum of Conversation between the President and Ambassador Dobrynin, 18 July 1962, BC 1958–62, No. 02820, NSA).

64. Memorandum, McNamara to the President, 22 June 1962, BC 1958–62, No. 02816, NSA.

65. In his memorandum on the interaction of Soviet and Western military postures, Raymond Garthoff underscored that allied unity was becoming the critical component. While he concluded that the military demonstrations by the United States probably had led the Soviet leaders to raise their estimate of U.S. determination, the readiness of the NATO allies to follow the U.S. lead in increasing military preparedness had not impressed the Soviets. Moreover, the Soviets probably believed that they were successful in their intimidation of the Europeans by demonstrating their nuclear and missile strength. See Memorandum by Raymond L. Garthoff, Sent by Executive Secretary Battle to Carl Kaysen through McGeorge Bundy, "The Interaction of Soviet and Western Military Postures," 13 October 1961, BC 1958–62, No. 02550, NSA.

66. Memorandum, Bell to the President, "Fiscal Year 1963 Defense Budget Issues," 13 November 1961, "November 1961 Folder," NH Box 13, NSA. See Memorandum, Taylor to Bell, "Excesses and Deficiencies on the SecDef Proposed Budget for Fiscal Year 63," 21 November 1961, "November 1961 Folder," NH Box 13, NSA.

67. Memorandum, Kaysen to Bundy, "Secretary McNamara's Memorandum on the Defense Budget dated 6 October 1961," 13 November 1961, "DoD Defense Budget Fiscal Year 1963 Folder," Box 275, Department and Agencies Series, NSF, JFKL. Kaysen furthermore noted that the reduction "may make it significantly more difficult for us to convince our Allies to increase their conventional war capabilities in NATO" (Ibid.).

68. Desmond Ball has noted that the Minuteman numbers were reconsidered in late December and that the decisions were finalized in a meeting between the president, the secretary of defense, and the JCS. See *Politics and Force Levels*, 135.

69. Senate Armed Services Committee, Military Procurement Authorization, Fiscal Year 1963, 14–16; Senate Appropriations Committee, Statement of Secretary of Defense McNamara on Department of Defense Appropriations, Fiscal Year 1963, 13–15.

70. See Ball, *Politics and Force Levels*, 127–42.

71. See chapter 9.

72. The question of where the missile gap had gone was brought up during the congressional hearings by Senator Symington. Symington inquired why the fact that the intelligence estimates were reduced by 96.5 percent over the last nineteen months did not show up in broader changes of the defense budget. Senate Armed Services Committee, Military Procurement Authorization, Fiscal Year 1963, 49–50; Stuart Symington, "Where the Missile Gap Went," *The Reporter* 26, No. 4 (15 February 1962): 21–23. Symington's question triggered the first inquiry of the Kennedy administration into the history of the missile gap. See Memorandum, Evelyn Lincoln to McGeorge Bundy, 11 February 1962, "February 1962 Folder," NH Box 15, NSA.

73. Department of State, Bureau of Intelligence and Research, "Assessment of Current Soviet Intentions in the Berlin Crisis: August 28–September 4," 4 September 1961, "Folder V," Box 34, The Papers of Maxwell D. Taylor, NWCL.

74. For an overview of these developments, see Glenn T. Seaborg, *Kennedy, Khrushchev, and the Test Ban*, with the assistance of Benjamin S. Loeb (Berkeley: University of California Press, 1981), 14–68. Seaborg was chairman of the AEC from 1961 to 1971. His book is the most comprehensive history of the test ban. See Schlesinger, *A Thousand Days*, 450–505.

75. Other distinguished members of this group were William Baker, Hans A. Bethe, Norris E. Bradbury, James B. Fisk, John S. Foster, George B. Kistiakowsky, Frank Press, Louis H. Roddis, John W. Tukey, Walter H. Zinn, and Spurgeon M. Keeny. See Report of the Ad Hoc Panel on Nuclear Testing, 21 July 1961, "July 1961 Folder," NH Box 13, NSA (further quoted as Panofsky report).

76. All quotations from Panofsky report. With respect to improvements of tactical nuclear weapons resulting from further testing, the panel found it difficult "to evaluate the potential value of nuclear warhead improvements to either the U.S. or the USSR since there is no established doctrine on the use of tactical weapons."

77. Panofsky report.

78. Memorandum, JCS to the SecDef, "Comments of JCS on Report of the Ad Hoc Panel on Nuclear Testing," 2 August 1961, "Nuclear Weapons Panofsky Panel 8/4/61–9/5/61 Folder," Box 302, Subject Series, NSF, JFKL. Due to time constraints, the secretary of defense did not comment on the report and the JCS position. Instead, he asked the director of defense research and engineering, Harold Brown, to answer for him. Brown forwarded a memorandum that gave only half-hearted support to the position of the JCS to the White House. See Letter, Harold Brown to Jerome Wiesner, 3 August 1961, "August 1961 Folder," NH Box 13, NSA.

79. Memorandum, Kennedy to Taylor, 7 August 1961, "Nuclear Weapons Panofsky Panel 8/4/61–9/5/61 Folder," Box 302, Subject Series, NSF, JFKL. For additional critique of the JCS position see Memorandum, Bundy to the President, "The NSC Meeting on Nuclear Tests," 8 August 1961, "August 1961 Folder," NH Box 13, NSA; Letter, Allen Dulles to Jerome Wiesner, 3 August 1961, "August 1961 Folder," NH Box 13, NSA. Arthur Schlesinger described the JCS paper as "assertive, ambiguous, semiliterate and generally unimpressive" (Schlesinger, *A Thousand Days*, 456).

80. Memorandum, Taylor to the President, "Report of Ad Hoc Panel on Nuclear Testing," 7 August 1961, "Nuclear Weapons Panofsky Panel 8/4/61–9/5/61 Folder," Box 302, Subject Series, NSF, JFKL.

81. Both quotations from Memorandum, Bundy to the President, "The NSC Meeting on Nuclear Tests," 8 August 1961, "August 1961 Folder," NH Box 13, NSA.

82. For a summary of the NSC discussions see Seaborg, *Kennedy, Khrushchev, and the Test Ban*, 74–78; Schlesinger, *A Thousand Days*, 457–58.

83. Bundy, "The Presidency and Peace," 353–65. For additional description of President Kennedy's angry reaction see Sorensen, *Kennedy*, 619; Schlesinger, *A Thousand Days*, 459.

84. Seaborg, *Kennedy, Khrushchev, and the Test Ban*, 81–84.

85. For the origin of the proposal see Seaborg, *Kennedy, Khrushchev, and the Test Ban*, 85–86; Schlesinger, *A Thousand Days*, 458–61.

86. Quoted in Schlesinger, *A Thousand Days*, 482–83.

87. All quotations from Seaborg, *Kennedy, Khrushchev, and the Test Ban*, 87–91.

88. The timing of Khrushchev's announcement suggests that the Soviet test program was not only thought to enhance the Soviet position regarding Berlin, but may also have helped the Soviet leader to mollify his domestic critics. For background regarding Soviet domestic policy tension at the Twenty-Second Party Congress, see Beschloss, *The Crisis Years*, 317–53.

89. Quoted in Seaborg, *Kennedy, Khrushchev, and the Test Ban*, 112.

90. Statement by the President with Respect to Nuclear Testing, 2 November 1961, "November 1961 Folder," NH Box 13, NSA. Only General LeMay seems to have insisted on the immediate resumption of proof testing at that time. See Memorandum, Bundy to the President, "Nuclear Testing and NSC Meeting," 1 November 1961, "November 1961 Folder," NH Box 13, NSA. For the NSC meeting which finalized the decision see NSC Action No. 2440, Record of Actions of the NSC, "Nuclear Testing," 2 November 1961, "November 1961 Folder," NH Box 13, NSA.

91. All quotations from Statement by the President with Respect to Nuclear Testing, 2 November 1961, "November 1961 Folder," NH Box 13, NSA. On 30 November, the assistant secretary of defense for international security affairs, Paul Nitze, asked the JCS to study the question of whether "the military and strategic implications of Soviet nuclear advances [were] such as to undermine the future confidence of our Allies in US nuclear superiority, and if so, what

steps should the US consider taking to deal with the situation" (Memorandum, Assistant Secretary of Defense [ISA] to the JCS, "Implications of Soviet Nuclear Advances," 30 November 1961, in JCS 2101/448, 5 December 1961, CCS 2210, "Enemy Capabilities," 30 November 1961, Sec. I, JCS, NARS).

92. The following sentence of Kennedy's press announcement summarized the message of Gilpatric's speech: "The United States does not find it necessary to explode 50 megaton nuclear devices to confirm that we have many times more nuclear power than any other nation on earth and that these capabilities are deployed so as to survive any sneak attack and thus enable us to devastate any nation which initiates a nuclear attack on the United States" (Statement by the President with Respect to Nuclear Testing, 2 November 1961, "November 1961 Folder," NH Box 13, NSA). The connection of the two issues is particularly obvious in McNamara's speech of 11 November; see McNamara, Remarks in Atlanta, Georgia, 11 November 1961, "November 1961 Folder," NH Box 13, NSA.

93. Memorandum, Assistant Secretary of Defense (ISA) to the JCS, "Implications of Soviet Nuclear Advances," 30 November 1961, in JCS 2101/448, 5 December 1961, CCS 2210, "Enemy Capabilities," 30 November 1961, Sec. I, JCS, NARS.

94. For a summary of the meeting's discussion, see Seaborg, *Kennedy, Khrushchev, and the Test Ban*, 119–21.

95. British Prime Minister Macmillan met with President Kennedy on 21 and 22 December in Bermuda in order to discuss the future of disarmament and the testing issue. For a summary of the discussions see Seaborg, *Kennedy, Khrushchev, and the Test Ban*, 125–31.

96. For a summary of the views of no-testers like Wiesner, Schlesinger, and Stevenson, see Selected Atmospheric Testing Issues and Positions Taken Thereon, 10 January 1962, "Nuclear Testing II Folder," Box 32, Maxwell D. Taylor Papers, NWCL; Seaborg, *Kennedy, Khrushchev, and the Test Ban*, 137.

97. For the importance of McNamara's argument, see Schlesinger, *A Thousand Days*, 486–88; Seaborg, *Kennedy, Khrushchev, and the Test Ban*, 103–5.

98. An early draft of his memorandum to the president admitted that further "improvements in the efficiency of strategic and tactical weapons did not appear in themselves likely to lead to major changes in the military balance" (Draft Memorandum, SecDef to the President, "The US-USSR Military Balance with and without a Test Ban," n.d., "January 1962 Folder," NH Box 14, NSA).

99. Memorandum, McNamara to the President, "Resumption of Atmospheric Nuclear Testing," 1 February 1962, "February 1962 Folder," NH Box 14, NSA; Draft Memorandum, SecDef to the President, "The US-USSR Military Balance with and without a Test Ban," n.d., "January 1962 Folder," NH Box 14, NSA. McNamara's argumentation resembled a report to the president by the chairman of the AEC. Seaborg noted that increasingly "much of the future effort of each side will be directed at measures designed to prevent the delivery of enemy weapons while at the same time preserving the deliverability of one's own weap-

ons in spite of the enemy's preventive measures" (Seaborg, *Kennedy, Khrushchev, and the Test Ban*, 123–24).

100. Memorandum, Chairman of the JCS Lemnitzer to the President, JCSM-127-62, "JCS Views on Resumption of Nuclear Testing," 16 February 1962, "February 1962 Folder," NH Box 14, NSA. See Memorandum, W.Y.S. to General Taylor, "JCS Views of Atmospheric Testing," 14 February 1962, "Nuclear Testing II Folder," Box 32, Maxwell D. Taylor Papers, NWCL.

101. Memorandum, JCS to SecDef, 22 December 1961, in Selected Atmospheric Testing Issues and Positions Taken Thereon, 10 January 1962, "Nuclear Testing II Folder," Box 32, Maxwell D. Taylor Papers, NWCL.

102. This argument contradicted McNamara's above-mentioned claim that the military defense of the nation required further atmospheric testing. See Draft Memorandum, SecDef to the President, "The US-USSR Military Balance with and without a Test Ban," n.d., "January 1962 Folder," NH Box 14, NSA.

103. Memorandum, McNamara to the President, "The Diffusion of Nuclear Weapons with and without a Test Ban Agreement," 12 February 1962, "February 1962 Folder," NH Box 15, NSA.

104. Selected Atmospheric Testing Issues and Positions Taken Thereon, 10 January 1962, "Nuclear Testing II Folder," Box 32, Maxwell D. Taylor Papers, NWCL.

105. Seaborg, *Kennedy, Khrushchev, and the Test Ban*, 136–38. For the position of Secretary Rusk see Memorandum, Rusk to Kennedy, "Atmospheric Nuclear Testing," 20 February 1962, "February 1962 Folder," NH Box 14, NSA.

106. Selected Atmospheric Testing Issues and Positions Taken Thereon, 10 January 1962, "Nuclear Testing II Folder," Box 32, Maxwell D. Taylor Papers, NWCL.

107. Kennedy, Radio and Television Address to the American People, "Nuclear Testing and Disarmament," 2 March 1962, Kennedy PPS, 1962, 186–92.

108. The president finalized the decision on the test series at an NSC meeting on 18 April: NSC Action No. 2450, Record of Actions of the NSC, "Nuclear Atmospheric Test Series 1962," 18 April 1962, "April 1962 Folder," NH Box 14, NSA.

109. Seaborg, *Kennedy, Khrushchev, and the Test Ban*, 157. Seaborg gives the best account of the problems and successes of the American test series, Ibid., 150–58.

110. Quoted in Seaborg, *Kennedy, Khrushchev, and the Test Ban*, 137.

111. Such considerations had had considerable impact on the formulation of Eisenhower's New Look as outlined in the JCS's approach to military strategy in a time of growing Soviet nuclear capabilities in 1953. See chapter 1.

112. For the Kennedy administration's reappraisal of NATO strategy as outlined in the Acheson report and NSAM No. 40, see chapter 8.

113. For a broader outline of this argument see chapter 9.

114. All quotations from McNamara, Interview on "Today" Program of WRC-TV and NBC-TV with John Chancellor and Martin Agronsky, Washington, 26 February 1962, Public Statements of Robert S. McNamara, Vol. 2, 1962, HOSD, Pentagon, 890–93.

115. For a broader outline of these arguments see chapter 8.

116. All quotations from McNamara, Athens address. At this point McNamara went on to quote studies that forecasted, for a general nuclear war in 1966, 25 million deaths for the United States and somewhat fewer for Europe if the attacks were limited to military targets. If urban-industrial targets were attacked, however, the United States might incur 75 million deaths and Europe would face the prospect of losing 115 million people.

117. All quotations from McNamara, Athens address. Because of limited numbers of nuclear warheads and technological limitations of delivery vehicles (low accuracy of bombers), both British and French national nuclear forces could only be used in a counter-city strike.

118. All quotations from McNamara, Athens address. Compare McNamara's skeptical assessment of these contingencies with Paul Nitze's comment that he proposed moving from conventional warfare directly to a strategic strike in connection with the discussion of Berlin contingency planning. See chapter 9.

119. McNamara referred to the success of the conventional buildup during the Berlin crisis in support of his argument. The buildup, so the argument ran, had given the Soviets second thoughts. See chapter 9.

120. Adam Yarmolinsky and Daniel Ellsberg helped McNamara prepare the speech for Ann Arbor. See Ball, *Politics and Force Levels*, 197; Kaplan, *The Wizards of Armageddon*, 285. On 31 May McNamara asked Secretary of State Rusk for comments on a draft of the address. See Memorandum, McNamara to Rusk, 31 May 1962, "May 1962 Folder," NH Box 14, NSA. For the full text see McNamara, Remarks at the Commencement Exercises of the University of Michigan in Ann Arbor, 16 June 1962, "June 1962 Folder," NH Box 14, NSA.

121. Memorandum, Bundy to the President, 1 June 1962, "June 1962 Folder," NH Box 14, NSA.

122. Memorandum, Bundy to the President, 7 June 1962, "DoD 6/62 Folder," Box 274, Department and Agencies Series, NSF, JFKL.

123. Former French premier Debré was ordered by DeGaulle to lay down a counterbarrage against McNamara's claims. In addition, the chief foreign editor of *Le Monde* explained the French strategic viewpoint in a series of articles. See Summary Analysis of Secretary McNamara's Speech, Ann Arbor, and Press Reaction Thereto, n.d., Office of the Secretary of Defense, Pentagon. Telegram, Randolph A. Kidder, Counselor of Embassy in Paris, to State Department, "Articles of *Le Monde's* Foreign Editor on the Current Difficulties within the Atlantic Alliance," 21 June 1962, "June 1962 Folder," NH Box 14, NSA.

124. Memorandum for the Record, Nils A. Lennartson, "British Reaction to McNamara's Ann Arbor Speech," 18 June 1962; Memorandum, Lennartson to McNamara, 19 June 1962; Telegram, London to the Secretary of State, 19 June 1962, all in "June 1962 Folder," NH Box 14, NSA.

125. McNamara, Response to Question Reference to British Nuclear Forces in Ann Arbor Speech, n.d.; Telegram, from Paris to the Secretary of State, 26 June 1962, both in "June 1962 Folder," NH Box 14, NSA.

126. Telegram from Paris to Paul Nitze and Charles Hitch, "French Strategic Viewpoints," 7 April 1962, "April 1962 Folder," NH Box 14, NSA.

127. Of particular annoyance for the Kennedy administration was that Henry Kissinger at the same time published an article that noted that the United States should support a modest French nuclear force program at this stage as the best means to bring about the creation of a European Atomic Force and thus resolve current differences with the French. See Henry A. Kissinger, "The Unsolved Problems of European Defense," *Foreign Affairs* 40, No. 4 (July 1962): 515–41.

128. McNamara, Athens address.

129. For a fascinating outline of the inner conflicts of defense policymakers and the argument that war-fighting strategies satisfy certain psychological needs, see Kull, *Minds at War.*

130. McNamara, Address to the Fellows of the American Bar Foundation, 5.

131. See part 2, chapter 6.

Chapter 11

1. For a broader analysis of his memorandum to the president see chapter 10.

2. On 22 January 1963, President Kennedy addressed the NSC to express his personal attitude toward a range of national security policy issues. Looking back on the Cuban missile crisis, he noted that for both the United States and the Soviet Union the big problem of the time was "to protect our interests and prevent a nuclear war" (Notes on Remarks by President Kennedy before the NSC, 22 January 1963, CMC 1962, No. 02869, NSA).

3. Robert Kennedy, *Thirteen Days: A Memoir of the Cuban Missile Crisis* (New York: W.W. Norton, 1969). See Schlesinger, *A Thousand Days*, 794–819; Sorensen, *Kennedy*, 737–93; Hilsman, *To Move a Nation*, 159–232.

4. Allison, *Essence of Decision.*

5. Schlesinger, *A Thousand Days*, 841.

6. James G. Blight and David A. Welch, *On the Brink: Americans and Soviets Reexamine the Cuban Missile Crisis* (New York: Hill and Wang, 1989); Bruce J. Allyn, James G. Blight, and David A. Welch, eds., *Back to the Brink: Proceedings of the Moscow Conference on the Cuban Missile Crisis, January 27–28, 1989,* CSIA Occasional Paper No. 9 (Boston: University Press of America, 1992); James G. Blight, *The Shattered Crystal Ball: Fear and Learning in the Cuban Missile Crisis* (Lanham, Md.: Rowman and Littlefield, 1990); Bruce J. Allyn, James G. Blight, and David A. Welch, *Cuba on the Brink: Fidel Castro, the Missile Crisis and the Collapse of Communism* (New York: Pantheon, 1993); Bruce J. Allyn, James G. Blight, and David A. Welch, "Essence of Revision: Moscow, Havana and the Cuban Missile Crisis," *International Security* 14, No. 3 (Winter 1989/1990): 136–72. For an extensive bibliography of writings on the Cuban missile crisis see Laurence Chang, *The*

Cuban Missile Crisis, 1962: Guide and Index, vol. I (Alexandria, Va.: The National Security Archive, 1990), 155–72.

7. The National Security Adviser had been informed by a CIA representative the day before. Bundy, however, had decided not to rob the president of a night of quiet sleep, because the intelligence information could not be presented until morning and a hastily arranged meeting would jeopardize security. See Bundy's memorandum to the president of 4 March 1963, in which he justified his decision, in *Danger and Survival*, 684–85. Bundy's account of the missile crisis is one of the best available. It is the advantage of his work that he touches on all the relevant questions with the experience and firsthand knowledge of a participant in the crisis. At the same time he is in full command of all the relevant scholarly work on the matter. Finally, his chapter on the Cuban missile crisis is well structured and easily readable.

8. John F. Kennedy, Radio and Television Report to the American People on the Soviet Arms Buildup in Cuba, 22 October 1962, Kennedy PPS, 1962, 806–9.

9. In reality, the risk of escalation of the conflict to the nuclear level might well have been greater during the Berlin crisis in 1961.

10. This outline of the history of the Cuban missile crisis is based on the excellent chronology of events in the National Security Archive Documents Reader. The reader compiles a useful selection of key documents of the crisis that are drawn from the archive's extensive microfiche collection. See Laurence Chang and Peter Kornbluh, eds., *The Cuban Missile Crisis, 1962: A National Security Archive Documents Reader* (New York: The New Press, 1992). See the shorter chronology in Blight and Welch, *On the Brink*, 373–83.

11. Bundy, *Danger and Survival*, 392.

12. At the January 1992 Havana conference, Castro made it clear that he had opposed Khrushchev's decision to deploy the missiles secretly. It had been his view that the deployment should have been done openly, because it was legal under international law. See Arthur Schlesinger, Jr., "Four Days with Fidel: A Havana Diary," *New York Review of Books*, 16 March 1992, 24. See also Blight, Allyn, and Welch, *Cuba on the Brink*.

13. A briefing paper for the president's press conference of 13 September 1962, noted that the "Congressional head of steam on this is the most serious that we have had. . . . The immediate hazard is that the Administration may appear to be weak and indecisive" (Memorandum on Cuba for the Press Conference, 13 September 1962, CMC 1962, No. 00407, NSA). For the position of Keating see Senator Kenneth Keating's Speech to U.S. Senate, 9 October 1962, in David L. Larson, *The "Cuban Crisis" of 1962: Selected Documents, Chronology and Bibliography*, 2d ed. (Lanham, Md.: University Press of America, 1986), 55.

14. Kennedy, *Thirteen Days*, 2–4; Elie Abel, *The Missile Crisis* (New York: Batam Books, 1966), 8. Dobrynin was the only one who gave such explicit assurances. The other Soviet statements were always phrased in terms of avoidance of offensive weapons. At the Moscow conference it became clear that Dobrynin did not

know about the missiles until Dean Rusk told him one hour before President Kennedy announced it publicly in his speech on 22 October. Rusk recalls that he saw Dobrynin age "ten years in front of my eyes" (Blight and Welch, *On the Brink*, 185, 256–57; Allyn, Blight, and Welch, "Essence of Revision," 155).

15. Quoted in Arnold L. Horelick and Myron Rush, *Strategic Power and Soviet Foreign Policy* (Chicago: The University of Chicago Press, 1966), 145.

16. Quoted in Beschloss, *The Crisis Years*, 456. See Raymond L. Garthoff, *Reflections on the Cuban Missile Crisis*, rev. ed. (Washington, D.C.: The Brookings Institution), 47–48.

17. President Kennedy's Statement on Soviet Military Shipments to Cuba, Press Conference, 4 September 1962, CMC 1962, No. 00340, NSA.

18. John F. Kennedy, The President's News Conference of 13 September 1962, Kennedy PPS, 1962, 674–81, 674–75.

19. Joint Resolution of Congress on Cuba, 20/26 September 1962, in Larson, *The "Cuban Crisis" of 1962*, 33. The vote in the House was 386 to 7 and in the Senate 86 to 1 in favor of the resolution.

20. Bundy takes issue with criticism that Kennedy announced the naval quarantine before making an attempt to settle the crisis by diplomatic means. I agree with his point that this critique overlooks that Kennedy's decision reflected a strong national conviction. See Bundy, *Danger and Survival*, 407–13. For such critique see Ronald Steel, "Endgame: *Thirteen Days* by Robert Kennedy," *New York Review of Books*, 13 March 1969, 15–22.

21. Kennedy, *Thirteen Days*, 45.

22. Marc Trachtenberg, ed., "White House Tapes and Minutes of the Cuban Missile Crisis, Off-the-Record Meeting on Cuba, 16 October 1962, 11:50 a.m.–12:57 p.m.," *International Security* 10, No. 1 (Summer 1985): 170–94.

23. McCone's views and the debate about his opinion within the administration is well documented in a series of recently declassified CIA documents. See Mary S. McAuliffe, ed., *CIA Documents on the Cuban Missile Crisis, 1962* (Washington, D.C.: History Staff, CIA, 1992), 1–138 (further quoted as CIA Documents Reader).

24. Memorandum, Schlesinger to Bundy, 22 August 1962, CMC 1962, No. 00288, NSA.

25. John McCone, Memorandum of Discussion with Mr. McGeorge Bundy, 5 October 1962, reprinted in CIA Documents Reader, 115–17.

26. Horelick and Rush, *Strategic Power and Soviet Foreign Policy*, 126–40; Garthoff, *Reflections on the Cuban Missile Crisis*, 8–11; Allison, *Essence of Decision*, 237–44; Hilsman, *To Move a Nation*, 200–202; Herbert S. Dinerstein, *The Making of a Missile Crisis: October 1962* (Baltimore: The Johns Hopkins University Press, 1976), 150–83.

27. On this occasion Khrushchev stated that the sole purpose of the missile deployment in Cuba had been to deter an American invasion. For an analysis of the speech see Ronald R. Pope, ed., *Soviet Views on the Cuban Missile Crisis: Myth and Reality in Foreign Policy Analysis* (Lanham, Md.: University Press of America, 1982), 83.

28. For an excellent summary of Soviet motives for the deployment taking account of the new information, see Allyn, Blight, and Welch, "Essence of Revision," 138–44; Blight and Welch, *On the Brink*, 116–17; 293–97.

29. Nikita Khrushchev, *Khrushchev Remembers*, trans. and ed. by Strobe Talbott (Boston: Little, Brown & Company, 1970), 493.

30. Allyn, Blight, and Welch, "Essence of Revision," 147–53.

31. Khrushchev, *Khrushchev Remembers*, 493. See Nikita Khrushchev, *Khrushchev Remembers: The Last Testament*, trans. and ed. by Strobe Talbott (Boston: Little, Brown & Company, 1974), 511.

32. Khrushchev, *Khrushchev Remembers*, 492. For further background on the Bay of Pigs see chapter 9.

33. Brigadier General Edward Lansdale, The Cuban Project, 20 February 1962, in Chang and Kornbluh, *The Cuban Missile Crisis*, 23–37.

34. Special Group Augmented, Guidelines for Operation Mongoose, 14 March 1962, in Chang and Kornbluh, *The Cuban Missile Crisis*, 38–39. For further details on Operation Mongoose see the document collection of the NSA.

35. For more details see Chang and Kornbluh, *The Cuban Missile Crisis*, 5–6.

36. Garthoff, *Reflections on the Cuban Missile Crisis*, 8; Khrushchev, *Khrushchev Remembers: The Last Testament*, 510.

37. Allyn, Blight, and Welch, "Essence of Revision," 138–41; Garthoff, *Reflections on the Cuban Missile Crisis*, 8–11.

38. Khrushchev, *Khrushchev Remembers*, 494. Allyn, Blight, and Welch correctly pointed out that different Soviet individuals understood the deployment differently. For a summary of who said what, see Allyn, Blight, and Welch, "Essence of Revision," 141–44.

39. On 16 November 1961, Radio Moscow had stated that Roswell Gilpatric's address of 21 October was not "the speech of a single wild general or politician who has lost his equilibrium but a clearly organized campaign whose aim, judging by everything, is to intimidate the Soviet Union and exacerbate still further the international situation" (Radio Moscow Home Service Commentary, 16 November 1961, quoted in Horelick and Rush, *Strategic Power and Soviet Foreign Policy*, 85).

40. See chapter 9.

41. Allyn, Blight, and Welch, "Essence of Revision," 143–44.

42. Khrushchev, *Khrushchev Remembers*, 494.

43. Bundy, *Danger and Survival*, 416.

44. Trachtenberg, "Off-the-Record Meeting on Cuba, 16 October." See Allyn, Blight, and Welch, "Essence of Revision," 146; Memorandum on Cuba for the Press Conference, 13 September 1962, CMC 1962, No. 00407, NSA.

45. Bundy, *Danger and Survival*, 418.

46. Raymond L. Garthoff, *Intelligence Assessment and Policymaking: A Decision Point in the Kennedy Administration* (Washington, D.C.: The Brookings Institution, 1984), 27.

47. Trachtenberg, "Off-the-Record Meeting on Cuba, 16 October 1962, 6:30–7:55 p.m.," 185.

48. Memorandum by Raymond Garthoff, "The Military Significance of the Soviet Missile Bases in Cuba," 27 October 1962, quoted in Garthoff, *Reflections on the Cuban Missile Crisis*, 202–3. For a retrospective look at his own assessment see Garthoff, *Intelligence Assessment and Policymaking*, 27–34.

49. Trachtenberg, "Off-the-Record Meeting on Cuba, 16 October 1962, 6:30–7:55 p.m.," 177.

50. Trachtenberg, "Off-the-Record Meeting on Cuba, 16 October 1962, 11:50 a.m.–12:57 p.m.," 171.

51. Trachtenberg, "Off-the-Record Meeting on Cuba, 16 October 1962, 11:50 a.m.–12:57 p.m.," 181. Kennedy's first reaction was paralleled by others (for example, John McCloy and Charles Bohlen) as the circle of those informed was growing. See Elie Abel, *The Missile Crisis* (New York: Bantam Books, 1966), 44–45; Bundy, *Danger and Survival*, 398.

52. Kennedy, Television and Radio Interview, 17 December 1962, Kennedy PPS, 1962, 898, 901. On 22 January 1963, Kennedy addressed the NSC and underscored the factor of time for his decision to implement a quarantine. Addressing the Soviet options, he noted that if "they had only to act in an hour or two, their actions would have been spasmodic and might have resulted in nuclear war" (Notes on Remarks by President Kennedy before the NSC, 22 January 1963, CMC 1962, No. 02869, NSA).

53. Allyn, Blight, and Welch, "Essence of Revision," 155–56; Blight and Welch, *On the Brink*, 305–7.

54. Trachtenberg, "Off-the-Record Meeting on Cuba, 16 October 1962, 6:30–7:55 p.m.," 193.

55. For further discussion of the role of these individuals, see Bundy, *Danger and Survival*, 398–400, who in particular underscores the influence of Robert Lovett's call for moderation in the president's decision. Regarding the role of Robert Kennedy see Kennedy, *Thirteen Days*, 37. For a less favorable assessment of Robert Kennedy's moderation see Trachtenberg, "White House Tapes and Minutes of the Cuban Missile Crisis: Introduction to Documents," 166–67.

56. For the position of Dean Acheson as expressed on Wednesday and Thursday, 17 and 18 October, see McCone, Memorandum for the File of Meeting on 17 October, 19 October 1962, in CIA Documents Reader, 169–73; Memorandum of Conversation in the Conference Room of Undersecretary of State, 19 October 1962, CMC 1962, No. 00699, NSA. Kennedy, *Thirteen Days*, 38–39. For another argument in favor of an air strike, see Douglas Dillon to the President, 17 October 1962, CMC 1962, No. 00647, NSA.

57. For the development of McGeorge Bundy's thinking, see Bundy, *Danger and Survival*, 400–401.

58. Memorandum of Conversation in the Conference Room of the Undersecretary of State, 19 October 1962, CMC 1962, No. 00699, NSA.

59. Memorandum of Conversation in the Conference Room of the Undersecretary of State, 19 October 1962, CMC 1962, No. 00699, NSA. During the first meeting of the ExComm on 16 October, Robert Kennedy wrote a note saying:

"I now know how Tojo felt when he was planning Pearl Harbor" (Kennedy, *Thirteen Days*, 31). On the question of whether the note was passed to the president see Bundy, *Danger and Survival*, 398.

60. Position of George W. Ball, 18 October 1962, in Chang and Kornbluh, *The Cuban Missile Crisis*, 121–22.

61. McCone, Memorandum for the File of Meeting on 18 October 1962, 11:00 a.m., in CIA Documents Reader, 183–84. On the occasion of the last briefing on an air strike on 21 October 1962, Robert Kennedy noted that this action "would lead to unpredictable military responses by the Soviet Union which could be so serious as to lead to general nuclear war" (Notes on 21 October 1962 Meeting with the President, 21 October 1962, CMC 1962, No. 00738, NSA).

62. See McNamara's statements in Trachtenberg, "Off-the-Record Meeting on Cuba, 16 October 1962, 6:30–7:55 p.m.," 182–83; McCone, Memorandum for the File of Meeting on 18 October 1962, 11:00 a.m., in CIA Documents Reader, 184.

63. Memorandum of Meeting in Conference Room of the Undersecretary of State, 19 October 1962, CMC 1962, No. 00699, NSA. See Bundy, *Danger and Survival*, 398.

64. Memorandum by Theodore Sorensen, 20 October 1962, CMC 1962, No. 00722, NSA.

65. Memorandum by Theodore Sorensen, 20 October 1962, CMC 1962, No. 00722, NSA. With the benefit of hindsight, McGeorge Bundy pointed to two further advantages of the blockade. Part of the reason that the Soviets turned out to be very reluctant to challenge the blockade was that they wanted to protect their highly secret and sensitive cargo. Second, a blockade was far easier to control than an air attack. See Bundy, *Danger and Survival*, 420–23.

66. Kennedy, *Thirteen Days*, 21.

67. For the development of the debate on Friday, see Memorandum of Conversation in the Conference Room of the Undersecretary of State, 19 October 1962, CMC 1962, No. 00699, NSA.

68. Bundy, *Danger and Survival*, 401; Kennedy, *Thirteen Days*, 23.

69. Both quotations from Notes on 21 October 1962 Meeting with the President, 21 October 1962, CMC 1962, No. 00738, NSA. See McCone, Memorandum of Meeting with the President, 21 October 1962, in CIA Documents Reader, 241–42.

70. Bundy, *Danger and Survival*, 403–4.

71. All quotations from John F. Kennedy, Radio and Television Report to the American People on the Soviet Arms Buildup in Cuba, 22 October 1962, Kennedy PPS, 1962, 806–9.

72. Bundy, *Danger and Survival*, 398.

73. Kennedy, *Thirteen Days*, 30; Cable from Joint Chiefs of Staff, announcing DEFCON 3 military alert, 23 October 1962, in Chang and Kornbluh, *The Cuban Missile Crisis*, 155.

74. See Chronology, in Chang and Kornbluh, *The Cuban Missile Crisis*, 365–66.

75. General Power, the commander-in-chief of the SAC, decided on his own authority to transmit the order to raise SAC's alert posture using nonencrypted messages. He apparently thought it important to impress the Soviets with SAC's readiness. For the best assessment of the episode, see Garthoff, *Reflections on the Cuban Missile Crisis*, 63–64.

76. On the immense tension that marked this meeting of the ExComm, see Kennedy, *Thirteen Days*, 43–50.

77. McGeorge Bundy, Executive Committee Record of Action, 24 October 1962, 10:00 a.m., 24 October 1962, in Chang and Kornbluh, *The Cuban Missile Crisis*, 165–66.

78. Dean Rusk, *As I Saw It, by Dean Rusk As Told to Richard Rusk*, edited by Daniel S. Papp (New York: Penguin Books, 1990), 237.

79. Roy Medvedev, *All Stalin's Men*, trans. by Harold Shukman (New York: Doubleday, 1985), 52. Blight and Welch now record that Mikoyan confirmed Medvedev's account to be factual. See Blight and Welch, *On the Brink*, 306–7.

80. McGeorge Bundy, Executive Committee Record of Action, 25 October 1962, 10:00 a.m., 25 October, in Chang and Kornbluh, *The Cuban Missile Crisis*, 167–68; John McCone, Memorandum for the File, "Executive Committee Meeting 10/25/62—10:00 a.m.," in CIA Documents Reader, 305–7.

81. Supplement 6 to Joint Evaluation of Soviet Missile Threat in Cuba, 26 October 1962, in CIA Documents Reader, 313–14.

82. Bromley Smith, Summary Record of NSC Executive Committee Meeting, 26 October 1962, 10:00 a.m., in Chang and Kornbluh, *The Cuban Missile Crisis*, 177–83. See the memorandum of discussion at the ExComm meeting of the previous evening: Bromley Smith, Summary Record of NSC Executive Committee Meeting, 25 October 1962, 5:00 p.m., CMC 1962, No. 01337, NSA.

83. John Scali's Notes of First Meeting with Soviet Embassy Counselor and KGB Officer Alexandr Fomin, 26 October 1962, in Chang and Kornbluh, *The Cuban Missile Crisis*, 184.

84. Letter, Khrushchev to Kennedy, 26 October 1961, CMC 1962, No. 01388, NSA.

85. For a detailed assessment of the matter, see Garthoff, *Reflections on the Cuban Missile Crisis*, 80–81; Allyn, Blight, and Welch, "Essence of Revision," 156–57.

86. For Khrushchev's second proposal see Khrushchev Communiqué to Kennedy, 27 October 1962, in Chang and Kornbluh, *The Cuban Missile Crisis*, 197–99.

87. For such speculation see McGeorge Bundy, transcriber, "October 27, 1962: Transcripts of the Meetings of the ExComm," ed. James G. Blight, *International Security* 12, No. 3 (Winter 1987–88): 30–92 (further quoted as Bundy, "October 27 transcripts").

88. Supplement 7 to Joint Evaluation of Soviet Missile Threat in Cuba, 27

October 1962, in CIA Documents Reader, 323–25; Central Intelligence Agency Memorandum, The Crisis, USSR/Cuba, 27 October 1962, in CIA Documents Reader, 327–29.

89. David A. Welch and James G. Blight, "The Eleventh Hour of the Cuban Missile Crisis: An Introduction to the ExComm Transcripts," *International Security* 12, No. 3 (Winter 1987–88): 5–29.

90. Kennedy, *Thirteen Days*, 93.

91. Chronology, in Chang and Kornbluh, *The Cuban Missile Crisis*, 376.

92. General Burchinal, not a friend of McNamara, reported that the secretary of defense "turned absolutely white" when the message reached him and "yelled hysterically, 'This means war with the Soviet Union' " (John B. Schmidt and Jude Straser, Interview of General David A. Burchinal, 11 April 1975, United States Air Force Oral History Program, CMC 1962, No. 03268, NSA). Roger Hilsman noted that President Kennedy's laconic reaction to the incident was a short laugh that broke the tension and the remark, "There is always someone who doesn't get the word" (Hilsman describes the episode in Letter, Hilsman to Mrs. Kennedy, 6 March 1964, CMC 1962, No. 03190, NSA).

93. For the impact of the shoot-down of the U-2 on the debate in the Ex-Comm, see McGeorge Bundy, "October 27 transcripts," 63–72. Welch and Blight have stressed that the account of many former ExComm members that the shoot-down was the turning point in the crisis does not stand up to a close reading of the transcripts. They argue that the sense of urgency had already been there *before* the incident became known. Also, despite the shoot-down, the ExComm quickly turned its attention to the primary problem of how to respond to Khrushchev's second proposal. See Welch and Blight, "The Eleventh Hour of the Cuban Missile Crisis," 19–20.

94. See for example McNamara's remarks on 19 October: Memorandum of Conversation in Conference Room of the Undersecretary of State, 19 October 1962, CMC 1962, No. 00699, NSA.

95. Bundy, "October 27 transcripts," 34–44. The view was perpetuated by the account of Robert Kennedy in *Thirteen Days*, 83–88.

96. Bundy, *Danger and Survival*, 429. In this connection, Dean Rusk wrote an interesting letter to James G. Blight recording his account of the matter:

In any event, President Kennedy asked me to take up with the Turkish government the matter of withdrawing these missiles. On May 1, 1961, I attended a meeting of the Foreign Ministers of CENTO held in Ankara. . . . After dinner I had a walk in the garden with Mr. Selim Sarper, the Foreign Minister of Turkey, and took up with him the matter of withdrawing the Jupiters from Turkey. He expressed considerable concern on two grounds. First, he said that the Turkish government had just gotten approval in its parliament for the Turkish costs of the Jupiter missiles and that it would be very embarrassing for them to go right back and tell the Parliament that the Jupiters were being withdrawn. Second, he said that it would be very damaging to the morale of Turkey if the Jupiters were to be withdrawn before Polaris submarines became available in the Mediterranean but these submarines would not become available until the spring of 1963. Upon returning to Washington, I went over these Turkish points with President Kennedy, and he accepted the idea of some delay in removing the Jupiters. (Letter, Rusk to Blight, 25 February 1987, CMC 1962, No. 03322, NSA.)

97. There is a possibility that the president's feelings were so strong on this matter because he had hinted secretly to the Soviet government (through Robert Kennedy to Anatoly Dobrynin) on 26 October that he would agree to such a deal.

98. Bundy, "October 27 transcripts," 50; also 36.

99. Bundy, "October 27 transcripts," 59; see also 54.

100. Bundy, "October 27 transcripts," 83.

101. Bundy, "October 27 transcripts," 39.

102. See the remarks of John F. Kennedy in Bundy, "October 27 transcripts," 37, 48, 59.

103. Bundy, "October 27 transcripts," 59. For the importance of Thompson's statement, who lately has become the unsung hero of the crisis, see Bundy, "October 27 transcripts," 57; Bundy, *Danger and Survival*, 430–31.

104. Sorensen and Robert Kennedy drafted the letter, which was sent the same evening. For the letter see President Kennedy's letter to Premier Khrushchev, 27 October 1962, in Chang and Kornbluh, *The Cuban Missile Crisis*, 223–25.

105. For an excellent account of the meeting see Bundy, *Danger and Survival*, 432–34; Kennedy, *Thirteen Days*, 98–102; Allison, *Essence of Decision*, 225.

106. Bundy, "October 27 transcripts," 79.

107. Bundy, "October 27 transcripts," 92. Other members of the ExComm have also recorded that they left the last meeting less than optimistic. See Kennedy, *Thirteen Days*, 87; Sorensen, *Kennedy*, 715–16.

108. Letter, Rusk to Blight, 25 February 1987, CMC 1962, No. 03322, NSA.

109. Bundy, *Danger and Survival*, 435.

110. Chang and Kornbluh, *The Cuban Missile Crisis*, 84.

111. For this point see Bundy, *Danger and Survival*, 436–38; Blight, Comments in Bundy, "October 27 transcripts," 83–85.

112. For a broader account of the episode see Allyn, Blight, and Welch, "Essence of Revision," 165.

113. On Soviet intelligence reports, see Garthoff, *Reflections on the Cuban Missile Crisis*, 92–93.

114. Both quotations from Prime Minister Fidel Castro's Letter to Premier Khrushchev, 26 October 1962, in Chang and Kornbluh, *The Cuban Missile Crisis*, 189. Castro explained his thinking at the 1992 Havana conference. See Schlesinger, "Four Days with Fidel," 24. See also Blight, Allyn, and Welch, *Cuba on the Brink*.

115. For background on Castro's letter and its impact on the Soviet Chairman, see Garthoff, *Reflections on the Cuban Missile Crisis*, 91–92; and Allyn, Blight, and Welch, "Essence of Revision," 166–68. For Khrushchev's own account, see Nikita Khrushchev, *Khrushchev Remembers: The Glasnost Tapes*, trans. and ed. by Jer-

rold L. Schecter with Vyacheslav V. Luchkov (Boston: Little, Brown & Company, 1990), 177.

116. See Khrushchev's comment on the matter in his letter of 28 October: Premier Khrushchev's Communiqué to President Kennedy, 28 October 1962, in Chang and Kornbluh, *The Cuban Missile Crisis*, 226–29.

117. See the presentation of the evidence in Allyn, Blight, and Welch, "Essence of Revision," 159–63; Garthoff, *Reflections on the Cuban Missile Crisis*, 91.

118. In his memoirs, Khrushchev indicates that Castro gave the order to shoot down the American U-2. However, Sergei Khrushchev, the son of the Soviet leader, has insisted that his father knew at the time that Soviets had shot down the plane. See Khrushchev, *Khrushchev Remembers*, 499; and Allyn, Blight, and Welch, "Essence of Revision," 162.

119. All quotations from John Scali, "I Was the Secret Go-Between in the Cuban Crisis," *Family Weekly*, 25 October 1964, 4–5, 12–14. See also Bundy, *Danger and Survival*, 438–39; Garthoff, *Reflections on the Cuban Missile Crisis*, 90; Allyn, Blight, and Welch, "Essence of Revision," 166.

120. This was in fact the standard line of Khrushchev's defense of the whole affair: Khrushchev's Report on the International Situation, 12 December 1962, reprinted in Pope, *Soviet Views on the Cuban Missile Crisis*, 71–107; Khrushchev, *Khrushchev Remembers*, 500.

121. For this argument see Garthoff, *Reflections on the Cuban Missile Crisis*, 91.

122. At the Moscow conference, Andrei Gromyko underscored the importance of the Turkish missiles and stressed that the Soviet government regarded their removal as part of the general agreement. See Allyn, Blight, and Welch, "Essence of Revision," 164.

123. For further analysis see Allyn, Blight, and Welch, "Essence of Revision," 157–59; Garthoff, *Reflections on the Cuban Missile Crisis*, 87.

124. Robert Kennedy, on the other hand, wrote that he told Dobrynin that "we had to have a commitment by tomorrow that those bases would be removed. I was not giving them an ultimatum, but a statement of fact" (*Thirteen Days*, 86).

125. With respect to this issue, Robert Kennedy wrote that he informed Dobrynin that President Kennedy "had ordered their removal some time ago, and it was our judgment that, within a short time after this crisis was over those missiles would be gone" (*Thirteen Days*, 87).

126. Rusk et al., "The Lessons of the Cuban Missile Crisis," 85.

127. Bundy, *Danger and Survival*, 453–58; Welch and Blight, "The Eleventh Hour of the Cuban Missile Crisis," 27–28.

128. See McNamara's foreword in Chang and Kornbluh, *The Cuban Missile Crisis*, xi–xiii. For a different account see Mark Kramer, "Tactical Nuclear Weapons, Soviet Command Authority, and the Cuban Missile Crisis," *Cold War International History Project BULLETIN* 3 (Fall 1993): 40–46.

129. An important next step for the historiography of the Cuban crisis is to check the recollections of the Soviet and Cuban participants against Cuban and Soviet documents.

130. Rusk et al., "The Lessons of the Cuban Missile Crisis," 85. For additional evidence see Trachtenberg, *History and Strategy*, 235–36, whose assessment of the impact of the nuclear balance on American policy during the Cuban crisis is excellent. As we will see, however, his analysis of the Soviet case is less convincing. Trachtenberg's article originally appeared in Marc Trachtenberg, "The Influence of Nuclear Weapons in the Cuban Missile Crisis," *International Security* 10, No. 1 (Summer 1985): 137–63.

131. Taylor, "The Legitimate Claims of National Security," 582.

132. Blight and Welch, *On the Brink*, 150. See Nitze, *From Hiroshima to Glasnost*, 227. For a similar point see Trachtenberg, *History and Strategy*, 253–58; Garthoff, *Intelligence Assessment and Policymaking*, 34. It is interesting that with time passing the belief that U.S. strategic superiority influenced the outcome of the crisis seems to have lost support. For earlier arguments to this end see Henry A. Kissinger, "Reflections on Cuba," *Reporter*, 22 November 1963, 21–24; Albert Wohlstetter and Roberta Wohlstetter, "Controlling the Risks in Cuba," *Adelphi Papers* 17 (April 1965); Power, *Design for Survival*, 154.

133. Trachtenberg, "Off-the-Record Meeting on Cuba, 16 October 1962, 6:30–7:55 p.m.," 187.

134. Letter, Kennedy to Khrushchev, 22 October 1962, CMC 1962, No. 00844, NSA.

135. All quotations from Trachtenberg, "Off-the-Record Meeting on Cuba, 16 October 1962, 6:30–7:55 p.m.," 184–93.

136. On this point see Garthoff, *Intelligence Assessment and Policymaking*, 27–28.

137. Kennedy, Television and Radio Interview: "After Two Years—A Conversation with the President," 17 December 1962, Kennedy PPS, 1962, 889–904.

138. Nitze, for example, has argued that "Soviet MR/IRBMs in Cuba could materially hasten the loss of our nuclear superiority, a loss we could ill afford because of our relative weakness in conventional capabilities in much of the world" (Nitze, *From Hiroshima to Glasnost*, 221–27). See also Dean Rusk's assessment of the view of McCone on 16 October: Trachtenberg, "Off-the-Record Meeting Cuba, 16 October 1962, 11:50–12:57 p.m.," 177.

139. Trachtenberg, "Off-the-Record Meeting on Cuba, 16 October 1962, 11:50 a.m.–12:57 p.m.," 174.

140. See General Taylor's presentation of the view of the JCS at the beginning of the afternoon session in Trachtenberg, "Off-the-Record Meeting on the Cuban Missile Crisis, 16 October 1962, 6:30–7:55 p.m.," 181–82.

141. Trachtenberg, "Off-the-Record Meeting on Cuba, 16 October 1962, 6:30–7:55 p.m.," 182.

142. Trachtenberg, "Off-the-Record Meeting on Cuba, 16 October 1962, 6:30–7:55 p.m.," 194. Marc Trachtenberg has pointed to the fact that this kind of reasoning "tends to draw one to the extremes: either a full-scale surprise attack or no direct military action at all, but not the brandishing of threats to coerce an adversary" (*History and Strategy*, 250).

143. Trachtenberg, "Off-the-Record Meeting on Cuba, 16 October 1962, 11:50

a.m.–12:57 p.m.," 176. President Kennedy at some point also doubted that the Soviets would retaliate with nuclear weapons "because obviously why would the Soviets permit nuclear war to begin under that sort of half-assed way?" (Ibid., 180).

144. Trachtenberg, "Off-the-Record Meeting on Cuba, 16 October 1962, 11:50 a.m.–12:57 p.m.," 188.

145. Trachtenberg, "Off-the-Record Meeting on Cuba, 16 October 1962, 11:50 a.m.–12:57 p.m.," 176.

146. It is worth noting that Stevenson, who favored a political solution involving negotiation over a Turkey-Cuba missile trade, was also primarily motivated by fear of escalation: He wrote to the president: "I know your dilemma is to strike before the Cuban sites are operational or to risk waiting until a proper groundwork of justification can be prepared. The national security must come first. But the means adopted have such incalculable consequences that I feel you should have made it clear that the existence of nuclear missile bases anywhere is negotiable before we start anything" (Letter, Stevenson to Kennedy, 17 October 1962, CMC 1962, No. 00652, NSA).

147. Memorandum by Theodore Sorensen, 20 October 1962, CMC 1962, No. 00722, NSA.

148. Notes on 21 October 1962 Meeting with the President, 21 October 1962, CMC 1962, No. 00738, NSA.

149. All quotations from Bundy, "October 27 transcripts," 54–55.

150. Nitze, *From Hiroshima to Glasnost*, 221–25.

151. The best argumentation in this regard that I have seen is Richard K. Betts, *Nuclear Blackmail and Nuclear Balance* (Washington, D.C.: The Brookings Institution, 1987), 109–23.

152. Gromyko, Mikoyan, and Burlatsky all deny such allegations. See Blight and Welch, *On the Brink*, 296–97; Allyn, Blight, and Welch, "Essence of Revision," 138–39.

153. Moscow, however, put the armed forces of the Warsaw Pact on alert on 23 October, the Cuban armed forces were fully mobilized and on their highest alert, and work on the missiles sites in Cuba was rapidly progressing throughout the crisis. See Chang and Kornbluh, *The Cuban Missile Crisis*, 368–69.

154. Trachtenberg, *History and Strategy*, 259.

155. The quotation is from Charles E. Bohlen, *Witness to History, 1929–1969* (New York: W.W. Norton, 1973), 495–96. See also Trachtenberg, *History and Strategy*, 257.

156. On the technical limitations of the Soviet missile systems see Berman and Baker, *Soviet Strategic Forces*, 88. Trachtenberg acknowledges such a consideration in *History and Strategy*, 255.

157. According to the American editor Norman Cousins, Khrushchev indicated to him in a conversation only a few months after the crisis that there indeed had been differences in opinion between himself and the military. Cousins quoted the Soviet chairman as follows: "When I asked the military advisers

if they could assure me that holding fast would not result in the death of five hundred million human beings, they looked at me as though I was out of my mind or, what was worse, a traitor. . . . So I said myself: To hell with these maniacs. If I can get the United States to assure me that it will not attempt to overthrow the Cuban government, I will remove the missiles" ("The Cuban Missile Crisis: An Anniversary," *Saturday Review*, 15 October 1977, 4).

158. Khrushchev, *Khrushchev Remembers*, 497.

159. All quotations from Letter, Khrushchev to Kennedy, 26 October 1962, CMC 1962, No. 01388, NSA.

160. Letter, Kennedy to Khrushchev, 22 October 1962; Letter, Kennedy to Khrushchev, 23 October 1962; Letter, Khrushchev to Kennedy, 26 October 1962; Letter, Khrushchev to Kennedy, 17 October 1962; Letter, Kennedy to Khrushchev, 28 October 1962, all in Chang and Kornbluh, *The Cuban Missile Crisis*, 148–49, 161–62, 185–88, 197–99, 230–31.

161. Bundy, *Danger and Survival*, 453.

Chapter 12

1. Letter, Kennedy to Khrushchev, 28 October 1962, in Chang and Kornbluh, *The Cuban Missile Crisis*, 230–32.

2. The need for, and the approach to, diplomatic initiatives is discussed in Memorandum by Raymond Garthoff, "The Khrushchev Proposal for a Turkey-Cuba Tradeoff," 27 October 1962, CMC 1962, No. 01518, NSA; Memorandum by Raymond Garthoff, "Significance of the Soviet Backdown for Future US Policy," 29 October 1962, CMC 1962, No. 01651, NSA; Memorandum, Kaysen to Bundy, "Summits and All That," 31 October 1962, CMC 1962, No. 00154, NSA.

3. For the impact of the Cuban missile crisis on the president's national security policy priorities and his new strength with respect to the domestic policy environment, see Bundy, *Danger and Survival*, 460; Schlesinger, *A Thousand Days*, 893; Sorensen, *Kennedy*, 800–04; Rusk, *As I Saw It*, 246–59.

4. With respect to the long term, it is unclear how much the Cuban missile crisis was a cause for Khrushchev's fall from power in October 1964.

5. All quotations from Khrushchev's Report on the International Situation, 12 December 1962, reprinted in Pope, *Soviet Views on the Cuban Missile Crisis*, 71–107. See Khrushchev's explanation in his memoirs, *Khrushchev Remembers*, 488–505.

6. Letter, Khrushchev to Kennedy, 28 October 1962, in Chang and Kornbluh, *The Cuban Missile Crisis*, 226–29.

7. Khrushchev wrote that "with the elimination of the Cuban crisis we relieved mankind of the direct menace of combat use of lethal nuclear weapons that impended over the world. Can't we solve a far simpler question—that of cessation of experimental explosions of nuclear weapons in the peaceful condi-

tions?" (Letter, Khrushchev to Kennedy, 19 December 1962, in Chang and Kornbluh, *The Cuban Missile Crisis*, 393).

8. Seaborg has explained the origins of the misunderstanding in detail. See Seaborg, *Kennedy, Khrushchev, and the Test Ban*, 178–81.

9. See Letter, Khrushchev to Kennedy, 30 October 1962; Letter Khrushchev to Kennedy, 10 December 1962, both in Chang and Kornbluh, *The Cuban Missile Crisis*, 382, 393. See also Memorandum of Conversation between Dean Rusk and Anastas Mikoyan, 30 November 1962, Rusk Memos Folder, NSA.

10. See Seaborg, *Kennedy, Khrushchev, and the Test Ban*, 206–7; Sorensen, *Kennedy*, 803.

11. John F. Kennedy, Commencement Address at American University in Washington, 10 June 1963, Kennedy PPS, 1963, 459–64.

12. The history of the LTBT is told in detail by Seaborg, *Kennedy, Khrushchev, and the Test Ban*, 162–261; Bundy, *Danger and Survival*, 460–61.

13. The experience of the LTBT undoubtedly contributed to the signing of other agreements such as the Treaty on the Non-Proliferation of Nuclear Weapons (NPT) in 1969 and the first strategic arms limitations agreements (SALT I and SALT II). See Garthoff, *Reflections on the Cuban Missile Crisis*, 135; and Seaborg, *Kennedy, Khrushchev, and the Test Ban*, 285–92.

14. On the Outer Space treaty see Raymond Garthoff, "Banning the Bomb in Outer Space," *International Security* 5, No. 3 (Winter 1980/81): 25–40. For the text of the treaty see Seaborg, *Kennedy, Khrushchev, and the Test Ban*, 302–5. For a more detailed account of the détente of 1963, see Amitai Etzioni, "Das Kennedy-Experiment," in *Friedensforschung*, ed. Ekkehart Krippendorff (Köln: Kiepenheuer & Witsch, 1968), 393–412.

15. All quotations from John F. Kennedy, Commencement Address at American University in Washington, 10 June 1963, Kennedy PPS, 1963, 459–64. According to Sorensen, Kennedy took great care to put forward a fundamentally new emphasis with regard to U.S.–Soviet relations. The effect of the speech on Khrushchev appears to have been profound. The address, for example, was published in its entirety in the Soviet press. See Sorensen, *Kennedy*, 807–10; and Seaborg, *Kennedy, Khrushchev, and the Test Ban*, 211–18.

16. It is interesting to note in this connection that the end of the Cold War evolved in a time of high tensions between East and West. It seems that fear of nuclear war was heavily involved in Soviet and American decisions between 1983 and 1990. At a recent conference at Princeton University on the end of the Cold War (25–27 February 1993, moderated by Fred I. Greenstein and Don Oberdorfer) both former Soviet foreign minister Aleksandr Bessmertnykh and former U.S. secretary of state George Shultz emphasized the importance of the accident in the Soviet nuclear power plant in Chernobyl for the end of the Cold War. Like the Cuban missile crisis, Chernobyl highlighted the nuclear danger and pointed out what a world would look like after a nuclear exchange. The most thorough account of the end of the Cold War I have seen so far is Don Oberdorfer, *The Turn: From the Cold War to a New Era: The United States and the Soviet Union, 1983–1990* (New York: Simon and Schuster, 1992).

17. For General Burchinal's comments on the missile crisis, see chapter 11.

18. Robert McNamara, Memorandum for the President, "Recommended Fiscal Year 1964–Fiscal Year 1968 Strategic Retaliatory Forces," 21 November 1962, FOIA/DOD, 6 (further quoted as DPM-62). McNamara noted that under a no-cities counterforce strategy "we would be counting on our ability to destroy their will, not their ability, to destroy our cities." In case the Soviets struck first, he added, this was a desirable option to have. However, he stressed "it would be foolish to count on it working to the point that it would form the basis for a belief that we could strike first without retaliation" (Ibid., 9).

19. Robert McNamara, Memorandum for the President, "Recommended 1966–1970 Programs for Strategic Offensive Forces, Continental Air and Missile Defense Forces, and Civil Defense," 3 December 1964, FOIA/DOD, 5 (further quoted as DPM-63).

20. Kull, *Minds at War*, 128–41.

21. DPM-63, I-5. In December 1964, McNamara reduced the required levels of destruction somewhat to "25 percent of its population (55 million people) and more than two-thirds of its industrial capacity." Robert McNamara, Memorandum for the President, "Recommended Fiscal Year 1966–1970 Programs for Strategic Offensive Forces, Continental Air and Missile Defense Forces, and Civil Defense," 3 December 1964, FOIA/DOD, 4 (further quoted as DPM-64).

22. Draft Presidential Memorandum on Strategic Offensive and Defense Forces, 9 January 1969, FOIA/DOD, 5 (further quoted as DPM-1969). Already in 1965 McNamara had pointed out that "it would be virtually impossible for us to be able to ensure anything approaching perfect protection for our population, no matter how large the general nuclear war force we were to provide, even if we were to strike first." Successive additional capacity for damage limitation would have diminishing marginal value and the Soviets could offset the American efforts at substantially less cost. See Robert McNamara, Memorandum for the President, "Recommended Fiscal Year 1967–71 Strategic Offensive and Defensive Forces," 1 November 1965, FOIA/DOD, 4–5.

23. DPM-1969, 2.

24. For further discussion of the development of the SIOP, see Ball, "Development of the SIOP, 1960–1983," 69–70.

25. Robert McNamara, Memorandum for the President, "Strategic Offensive and Defensive Forces," 15 January 1968, FOIA/DOD, 6.

26. John F. Kennedy, Address in New York City before the General Assembly of the United Nations, 25 September 1961, Kennedy PPS, 1961, 618–26.

Bibliography

I list here only the writings that have been of use to the making of this book. This bibliography indicates the range of reading upon which I have formed my ideas and includes all the material that is quoted in the notes.

Abbreviations of Archival Sources

DDEL: Dwight D. Eisenhower Library, Abilene, Kansas.
    AWF   Papers of Dwight D. Eisenhower as President (Ann Whitman File)
    A   Administration Series
    OSANSA   Office of the Special Assistant for National Security Affairs
    NSC   National Security Council Series
    PP   Policy Papers Subseries
    S   Subject Series
DPP: John Foster Dulles Papers, 1889–1959, Seeley G. Mudd Library, Princeton University.
DPEL: John Foster Dulles Papers, 1951–1959, Seeley G. Mudd Library, Princeton University.
    GCMS   General Correspondence and Memoranda Series
    SS   Subject Series
    TTS   Telephone Transcript Series
    WHMS   White House Memoranda Series
FOIA/DOD: Freedom of Information Act, Office of the Secretary of Defense, the Pentagon, Washington, D.C.
JFDOHC: John Foster Dulles Oral History Collection, Seeley G. Mudd Library, Princeton University.
JFKL: John F. Kennedy Library, Boston, Massachusetts.
    Kennedy, John Fitzgerald, Pre-Presidential Papers, 1947–1961

POF   Kennedy, John Fitzgerald, President's Office Files, 1961–1963
Countries Series
Department and Agencies Series
Staff Memoranda Series

NSF   Kennedy, John Fitzgerald, National Security Files, 1961–1963
Countries Series
Department and Agencies Series
Meetings and Memoranda Series
Subject Series

WHSF   Kennedy, John Fitzgerald, White House Staff Files, 1961–1963
Bell, David, 1947–1980
Gilpatric, Roswell, 1956–1967
Schlesinger, Arthur M., Jr., 1939–1983
Sorensen, Theodore, 1953–1964

OHI   Oral History Interviews

LC: Library of Congress, Washington, D.C.
   Nathan F. Twining Papers
   Thomas D. White Papers
   Joseph and Stewart Alsop Papers

NARS: National Archives and Record Service, Washington, D.C.
JCS   Papers of the Joint Chiefs of Staff, Record Group 218, Modern
Military Branch

NSC   Records of the National Security Council, Record Group 273,
Diplomatic Branch

NSA: National Security Archive, Washington, D.C.
NH Box: Nuclear History Box, No. 11-16. Most of these documents are
by now included in the microfiche collections.

NNP 1945–91: U.S. Nuclear Nonproliferation Policy, 1945–1991, microfiche
collection

BC 1958–62: Berlin Crisis, 1958–1962, microfiche collection

CMC 1962:   Cuban Missile Crisis, 1962, microfiche collection

Rusk Memos Folder: Recently released material that is not yet included in the
microfiche collections.

NWCL: National War College Library, Washington, D.C.
   Maxwell D. Taylor Papers
   Lyman L. Lemnitzer Papers

Published Sources

Bundy, McGeorge, transcriber. "October 27, 1962: Transcripts of the Meetings
of the ExComm." Edited by James G. Blight. *International Security* 12, No. 3
(Winter 1987–88): 30–92.

Burr, William, project director. *The Berlin Crisis, 1958–1962: Guide and Index.* Edited by Thomas S. Blanton, Malcolm Byrne, Margarita S. Studemeister, and Lisa Thompson. Alexandria, Va.: The National Security Archive, 1991.

Chang, Laurence, ed. *The Cuban Missile Crisis, 1962: Guide and Index.* Alexandria, Va.: The National Security Archive, 1990.

Chang, Laurence, and Peter Kornbluh, eds. *The Cuban Missile Crisis, 1962: A National Security Archive Documents Reader.* New York: The New Press, 1992.

Declassified Documents Collection. Available on microfiche at a number of university libraries and from the Center for Research Libraries in Chicago. (DDC)

Eisenhower, Dwight D. *Public Papers of the Presidents of the United States (PPS), 1953–1961.* Washington, D.C.: GPO, 1954–1962.

Foran, Virginia I., project director. *U.S. Non-Proliferation Policy, 1945–1991: Guide and Index.* Edited by Thomas S. Blanton, Malcolm Byrne, Margarita S. Studemeister, and Lisa Thompson. Alexandria, Va.: The National Security Archive, 1991.

Foreign Relations of the United States (FRUS), followed by the year. Compiled by the Office of the Historian, U.S. Department of State. These volumes constitute the official record of U.S. foreign policy. All published by the Government Printing Office (GPO), Washington, D.C.

FRUS, 1946, 6: Eastern Europe; Soviet Union

FRUS, 1948, 1: General; United Nations, Part 1 and 2

FRUS, 1950, 1: National Security Affairs; Foreign Economic Policy

FRUS, 1952–1954, 2: National Security Affairs (in two parts)

FRUS, 1952–1954, 5: Western European Security

FRUS, 1952–1954, 6: Western Europe and Canada

FRUS, 1952–1954, 8: Eastern Europe; Soviet Union

FRUS, 1952–1954, 14: China and Japan

FRUS, 1952–1954, 15: Korea (in two parts)

FRUS, 1952–1954, 16: The Geneva Conference

FRUS, 1955–1957, 2: China

FRUS, 1955–1957, 3: China

FRUS, 1955–1957, 4: Western European Security and Integration

FRUS, 1955–1957, 19: National Security

FRUS, 1955–1957, 27: Western Europe and Canada

FRUS, 1961–1963, 14: Berlin Crisis, 1961–1962

Kennedy, John F. *Public Papers of the Presidents of the United States (PPS), 1961–1963.* Washington, D.C.: GPO, 1962–1964.

McAuliffe, Mary S. *CIA Documents on the Cuban Missile Crisis, 1962.* Washington, D.C.: History Staff, CIA, 1992.

Sagan, Scott D. "SIOP-62: The Nuclear War Plan Briefing to President Kennedy." *International Security* 12, No. 1 (Summer 1987): 41–52.

Schelling, Thomas C. "Nuclear Strategy in the Berlin Crisis." In *Writings on Strategy, 1961–1969, and Retrospectives,* ed. Marc Trachtenberg. New York: Garland Pub., 1988.

Trachtenberg, Marc, ed. "White House Tapes and Minutes of the Cuban Missile Crisis, Off-the-Record Meeting on Cuba, October 16, 1962." *International Security* 10, No. 1 (Summer 1985): 170–94.

United States Senate, Committee on Foreign Relations. *Documents on Germany, 1944–1961.* Washington, D.C.: GPO, 1961. (DG)

Wampler, Robert A. *Nuclear Weapons and the Atlantic Alliance: A Guide to U.S. Sources.* Produced for the Nuclear History Program. College Park, Md.: Center for International Studies, 1989.

Books and Articles

Abel, Elie. *The Missile Crisis.* New York: Bantam Books, 1966.

Acheson, Dean. *Present at the Creation: My Years in the State Department.* New York: W.W. Norton & Company, 1969.

———. "Wishing Won't Hold Berlin." *Saturday Evening Post,* 7 March 1959, 32–33, 85–86.

Adams, Sherman. *Firsthand Report: The Inside Story of the Eisenhower Administration.* New York: Harper & Brothers, 1961.

Adomeit, Hannes. *Soviet Risk-Taking and Crisis Behavior: A Theoretical and Empirical Analysis.* London: George Allen & Unwin, 1982.

Aliano, Richard A. *American Defense Policy from Eisenhower to Kennedy: The Politics of Changing Military Requirements, 1957–1961.* Athens: Ohio University Press, 1975.

Allison, Graham T. *Essence of Decision: Explaining the Cuban Missile Crisis.* Boston: Little, Brown & Company, 1971.

Allyn, Bruce J., James G. Blight, and David A. Welch. *Back to the Brink: Proceedings of the Moscow Conference on the Cuban Missile Crisis, January 27–28, 1989.* CSIA Occasional Paper No. 9. Boston: University Press of America, 1992.

———. *Cuba on the Brink: Fidel Castro, the Missile Crisis and the Collapse of Communism.* With the assistance of David Lewis. New York: Pantheon, 1993.

———. "Essence of Revision: Moscow, Havana and the Cuban Missile Crisis." *International Security* 14, No. 3 (Winter 1989/90): 136–72.

Alsop, Joseph. "After Ike, the Deluge." *Washington Post,* 7 October 1959, A17.

Alsop, Joseph, and Stewart Alsop. *The Reporter's Trade.* New York: Reynal & Company, 1958.

Alsop, Stewart. "Our Gamble with Destiny." *Saturday Evening Post,* 16 May 1959, 23, 114–18.

Anders, Roger M. "Essay on Sources." In *Atoms for Peace and War, 1953–1961,* ed. Richard G. Hewlett and Jack M. Holl, 657–74. Berkeley: University of California Press, 1989.

Axelrod, Robert. *The Evolution of Cooperation.* New York: Basic Books, 1984.

Ball, Desmond. "The Development of the SIOP, 1960–1983." In *Strategic Nuclear*

Targeting, ed. Desmond Ball and Jeffrey Richelson. Ithaca, N.Y.: Cornell University Press, 1986.

———. *Politics and Force Levels: The Strategic Missile Program of the Kennedy Administration*. Berkeley: University of California Press, 1980.

Ball, Desmond, and Jeffrey Richelson, eds. *Strategic Nuclear Targeting*. Ithaca: Cornell University Press, 1986.

Baylis, John, and John Garnett, eds. *Makers of Nuclear Strategy*. London: Pinter Publishers, 1991.

Berman, Robert P., and John C. Baker. *Soviet Strategic Forces: Requirements and Responses*. Washington, D.C.: The Brookings Institution, 1982.

Bernstein, Barton J. "The Quest for Security: American Foreign Policy and International Control of the Atomic Bomb, 1942–1946." *The Journal of American History* 60, No. 4 (March 1974): 1003–44.

Beschloss, Michael R. *The Crisis Years: Kennedy and Khrushchev, 1961–1963*. New York: HarperCollins Publishers, 1991.

Betts, Richard K. *Nuclear Blackmail and Nuclear Balance*. Washington, D.C.: The Brookings Institution, 1987.

Blackett, P. M. S. *Fear, War, and the Bomb: The Military and Political Consequences of Atomic Energy*. New York: Whittlesey House, McGraw-Hill Book Company, 1949.

Blight, James G. "The New Psychology of War and Peace." *International Security* 11, No. 3 (Winter 1986–87): 175–86.

———. *The Shattered Crystal Ball: Fear and Learning in the Cuban Missile Crisis*. Savage, Md.: Rowman and Littlefield, 1990.

Blight, James G., and David A. Welch. *On the Brink: Americans and Soviets Reexamine the Cuban Missile Crisis*. New York: Hill and Wang, 1989.

Bobbitt, Philip, Lawrence Freedman, and Gregory F. Treverton, eds. *U.S. Nuclear Strategy: A Reader*. London: Macmillan, 1989.

Bohlen, Charles E. *Witness to History, 1929–1969*. New York: W.W. Norton, 1973.

Borden, William Liscum. *There Will Be No Time*. New York: Macmillan, 1946.

Bottome, Edgar M. *The Missile Gap: A Study of the Formulation of Military and Political Policy*. Rutherford, N.J.: Fairleigh Dickinson University Press, 1971.

Bowie, Robert R. "Eisenhower, Atomic Weapons and Atoms for Peace." In *Atoms for Peace: An Analysis after Thirty Years*, ed. Joseph F. Pilat, Robert E. Pendley, and Charles K. Ebinger. Boulder: Westview Press, 1985.

Brands, H. W., Jr. "Testing Massive Retaliation: Credibility and Crisis Management in the Taiwan Strait." *International Security* 12 (Spring 1988): 124–51.

Brinkley, Douglas. *Dean Acheson: The Cold War Years, 1953–1971*. New Haven: Yale University Press, 1992.

Brodie, Bernard. *The Absolute Weapon: Atomic Power and World Order*. New York: Harcourt, Brace & Company, 1946; reprint ed., Freeport, N.Y.: Books for Libraries Press, 1972.

———. "A Comment on the Hoag Doctrine: RAND Internal Working Document (1962)." In *Writings on Strategy, 1961–1969, and Retrospectives*, ed. Marc Trachtenberg. New York: Garland Pub., 1988.

———. "Nuclear Weapons: Strategic or Tactical?" *Foreign Affairs* 32, No. 2 (January 1954): 217–28.

———. "A Review of William W. Kaufmann's 'The McNamara Strategy.' " *RAND Paper P-3077*. Santa Monica: The RAND Corporation, 1965.

———. *Strategy in the Missile Age*. Princeton: Princeton University Press, 1959.

———. "Unlimited Weapons and Limited War." *The Reporter* 11, No. 9 (18 November 1954): 16–21.

Bundy, McGeorge. *Danger and Survival: Choices about the Bomb in the First Fifty Years*. New York: Vintage Books, 1988.

———. "Early Thoughts on Controlling the Nuclear Arms Race: A Report to the Secretary of State, January 1953." *International Security* 7 (Fall 1982): 3–27.

———. "The Presidency and Peace." *Foreign Affairs* 42, No. 3 (April 1964): 353–65.

Burr, William. "Avoiding the Slippery Slope: The Eisenhower Administration and the Berlin Crisis, November 1958–January 1959." *Diplomatic History* 18, No. 2 (Spring 1994): 177–206.

———. "U.S. Policy and the Berlin Crisis: An Overview." In *The Berlin Crisis, 1958–1962: Guide and Index*, ed. Thomas S. Blanton, Malcolm Byrne, Margarita S. Studemeister, and Lisa Thompson. Alexandria, Va.: The National Security Archive, 1992.

Catudal, Honoré. *Kennedy and the Berlin Wall: A Case Study in U.S. Decision Making*. Berlin: Verlag, 1980.

Challener, Richard D. "John Foster Dulles: The Certainty/Uncertainty Principle." *Zürcher Beiträge zur Sicherheitspolitik und Konfliktforschung* 10 (1989). Zurich: Center for Security Studies, 1989.

Clark, Ian. *Nuclear Diplomacy and the Special Relationship: Britain's Deterrent and America, 1957–1962*. Oxford: Clarendon Press, 1994.

Clausewitz, Carl von. *On War*. Ed. and trans. Michael Howard and Peter Paret. Princeton: Princeton University Press, 1976.

Cochran, Thomas B., William M. Arkin, and Milton M. Hoenig. *U.S. Nuclear Forces and Capabilities*. Vol. I, Nuclear Weapons Databook. Cambridge: Ballinger Publishing Company, 1984.

Cotter, Cornelius, ed. *Political Science Annual* 6 (1975). Indianapolis: Bobbs-Merrill, 1975.

Cousins, Norman. "The Cuban Missile Crisis: An Anniversary." *Saturday Review*, 15 October 1977, 4.

Cutler, Robert. *No Time for Rest*. Boston: Little, Brown & Company, 1966.

Dinerstein, Herbert S. *The Making of a Missile Crisis: October 1962*. Baltimore: The Johns Hopkins University Press, 1976.

Dingman, Roger. "Atomic Diplomacy during the Korean War." *International Security* 13, No. 3 (Winter 1988–89): 50–91.

Divine, Robert A. *Foreign Policy and U.S. Presidential Elections, 1952–1960*. New York: New Viewpoints, 1974.

Dulles, John Foster. "Address before the American Society of Newspapers Editors, April 18, 1953." *Department of State Bulletin*, 27 April 1953, 603–8.

————. "The Evolution of Foreign Policy." *Department of State Bulletin*, 25 January 1954, 107–10.

————. "Policy for Security and Peace." *Foreign Affairs* 32, No. 3 (April 1954): 353–64.

————. "A Policy of Boldness." *Life* 32, 19 May 1952, 146–60.

Eden, Lynn. "The End of U.S. Cold War History? A Review Essay." *International Security* 18, No. 1 (Summer 1993): 174–207.

Eisenhower, Dwight D. *The White House Years: Mandate for Change, 1953–1956.* New York: Doubleday & Company, 1963.

————. *The White House Years: Waging Peace, 1956–1961.* New York: Doubleday & Company, 1965.

Enthoven, Alain C. "1963 Nuclear Strategy Revisited." In *Ethics and Nuclear Strategy*, ed. Harold Ford and Francis Winters. New York: Orbis Books, 1977.

Enthoven, Alain C., and K. Wayne Smith. *How Much Is Enough? Shaping the Defense Program, 1961–1969.* New York: Harper & Row Publishers, 1971.

Etzioni, Amitai. "Das Kennedy-Experiment." In *Friedensforschung*, ed. Ekkehart Krippendorff. Köln: Kiepenheuer & Witsch, 1968.

Feaver, Peter Douglas. *Guarding the Guardians: Civilian Control of Nuclear Weapons in the United States.* Ithaca, N.Y.: Cornell University Press, 1992.

Foot, Rosemary J. "Nuclear Coercion and the Ending of the Korean Conflict." *International Security* 13, No. 3 (Winter 1988–89): 92–112.

————. *The Wrong War: American Policy and the Dimensions of the Korean Conflict, 1950–1953.* Ithaca, N.Y.: Cornell University Press, 1985.

Ford, Harold, and Francis X. Winters, eds. *Ethics and Nuclear Strategy?* New York: Orbis Books, 1977.

Freedman, Lawrence. *The Evolution of Nuclear Strategy.* New York: St. Martin's Press, 1981.

————. *U.S. Intelligence and the Soviet Strategic Threat.* 2d ed. London: The Macmillan Press, 1986.

Friedberg, Aaron L. "Why Didn't the United States Become a Garrison State?" *International Security* 16, No. 4 (Spring 1992): 109–42.

Futrell, Robert Frank. *Ideas, Concepts, Doctrine: A History of Basic Thinking in the United States Air Force, 1907–1964.* 2d ed. Maxwell Air Force Base, Ala.: Air University, 1974.

Gaddis, John Lewis. "Expanding the Data Base: Historians, Political Scientists, and the Enrichment of Security Studies." *International Security* 12, No. 1 (Summer 1987): 3–21.

————. "International Relations Theory and the End of the Cold War." *International Security* 17, No. 3 (Winter 1992–93): 5–58.

————. "The Long Peace: Elements of Stability in the Postwar International System." *International Security* 10, No. 4 (Spring 1986): 99–142.

————. *The Long Peace: Inquiries into the History of the Cold War.* New York: Oxford University Press, 1987.

————. "Nuclear Weapons, the End of the Cold War, and the Future of the

International System." In *Nuclear Weapons in the Changing World*, ed. Patrick J. Garrity and Steven A. Maaranen. New York: Plenum Press, 1992.

———. *Strategies of Containment: A Critical Appraisal of Postwar American National Security Policy*. New York: Oxford University Press, 1982.

———. "The Unexpected John Foster Dulles: Nuclear Weapons, Communism, and the Russians." In *John Foster Dulles and the Diplomacy of the Cold War*, ed. Richard H. Immerman. Princeton: Princeton University Press, 1990.

Gaddis, John Lewis, and Paul H. Nitze. "NSC-68 and the Soviet Threat Reconsidered." *International Security* 4, No. 1 (Spring 1980): 164–76.

Garrity, Patrick J., and Steven A. Maaranen, eds. *Nuclear Weapons in the Changing World: Perspectives from Europe, Asia, and North America*. New York: Plenum Press, 1992.

Garthoff, Raymond L. "Banning the Bomb in Outer Space." *International Security* 5, No. 3 (Winter 1980–81): 25–40.

———. *Intelligence Assessment and Policymaking: A Decision Point in the Kennedy Administration*. Washington, D.C.: The Brookings Institution, 1984.

———. *Reflections on the Cuban Missile Crisis*. Rev. ed. Washington, D.C.: The Brookings Institution, 1989.

Gelb, Norman. *The Berlin Wall: Kennedy, Khrushchev and a Showdown in the Heart of Europe*. New York: Times Books, 1986.

George, Alexander, and Richard Smoke. *Deterrence in American Foreign Policy: Theory and Practice*. New York: Columbia University Press, 1974.

George, Alexander, David K. Hall, and William E. Simons, eds. *The Limits of Coercive Diplomacy: Laos, Cuba, Vietnam*. Boston: Little, Brown & Company, 1971.

Gilpin, Robert. *War and Change in World Politics*. New York: Cambridge University Press, 1981.

Goldberg, Alfred. "A Brief Survey of the Evolution of Ideas about Counterforce." *RAND Memorandum RM-5431-PR*. Santa Monica: The RAND Corporation, 1967.

Goldhamer, Herbert, and Andrew W. Marshall. "The Deterrence and Strategy of Total War, 1959–1961: A Method of Analysis." *RAND Memorandum RM-2301*. Santa Monica: The RAND Corporation, 1959.

Goodpaster, Andrew. "Presidential Transitions and Foreign Policy: Eisenhower and Kennedy." In *Papers on Presidential Transitions and Foreign Policy*. Vol. 5, Reflections of Five Public Officials, ed. Kenneth W. Thompson. Lanham, Md.: University Press of America, 1987.

Gottfried, Kurt, and Bruce G. Blair, eds. *Crisis Stability and Nuclear War*. New York: Oxford University Press, 1988.

Grabbe, Hans-Jürgen. "Konrad Adenauer, John Foster Dulles, and West German–American Relations." In *John Foster Dulles and the Diplomacy of the Cold War*, ed. Richard H. Immerman. Princeton: Princeton University Press, 1990.

Gray, Colin S. " 'Gap' Prediction and America's Defense: Arms Race Behavior in the Eisenhower Years." *Orbis* 16, No. 1 (Spring 1972): 257–75.

————. "Nuclear Strategy: The Case for a Theory of Victory." *International Security* 4, No. 1 (Summer 1970): 54–87.

Greenstein, Fred I. "Coming to Terms with Kennedy." *Reviews in American History* 20 (1992): 96–104.

————. "Eisenhower As an Activist President: A New Look at the Evidence." *Political Science Quarterly* 94 (Winter 1979–80): 575–99.

————. *The Hidden-Hand Presidency: Eisenhower As Leader.* New York: Basic Books, 1982.

Haley, P. Edward, David M. Keithly, and Jack Merritt, eds. *Nuclear Strategy, Arms Control, and the Future.* Boulder: Westview Press, 1985.

Hall, David K. "The Laos Crisis, 1960–1961." In *The Limits of Coercive Diplomacy: Laos, Cuba, Vietnam,* ed. Alexander George, David Hall, and William E. Simons. Boston: Little, Brown & Company, 1971.

Halloran, Bernard F., ed. *Essays on Arms Control and National Security.* Washington: U.S. Arms Control and Disarmament Agency, 1986.

Halperin, Morton H. *Bureaucratic Politics and Foreign Policy.* Washington, D.C.: The Brookings Institution, 1974.

Harrison, Hope M. "Ulbricht and the Concrete 'Rose': New Archival Evidence on the Dynamics of Soviet–East German Relations and the Berlin Crisis, 1958–1961," *Cold War International History Project Working Paper* No. 5, Washington, D.C.: Woodrow Wilson International Center for Scholars, May 1993.

Herring, George C. " 'A Good Stout Effort': John Foster Dulles and the Indochina Crisis, 1954–1955." In *John Foster Dulles and the Diplomacy of the Cold War,* ed. Richard H. Immerman. Princeton: Princeton University Press, 1990.

Herring, George C., and Richard H. Immerman. "Eisenhower, Dulles, and Dienbienphu: 'The Day We Didn't Go to War' Revisited." *Journal of American History* 71, No. 2 (September 1984): 343–63.

Hewlett, Richard G., and Francis Duncan. *Atomic Shield, 1947–1952.* Vol. 2, A History of the U.S. Atomic Energy Commission. University Park, Pa.: Pennsylvania State University Press, 1969.

Hewlett, Richard G., and Jack M. Holl. *Atoms for Peace and War, 1953–1961: Eisenhower and the Atomic Energy Commission.* Berkeley: University of California Press, 1989.

Hilsman, Roger. *To Move a Nation: The Politics of Foreign Policy in the Administration of John F. Kennedy.* Garden City, N.Y.: Doubleday & Company, 1967.

Hobkirk, Michael D. *The Politics of Defense Budgeting: A Study of Organization and Resource Allocation in the United Kingdom and the United States.* Washington: National Defense University Press, 1983.

Holsti, Ole, and Alexander George. "The Effects of Stress on the Performance of Foreign Policy-Makers." In *Political Science Annual* 6 (1975), ed. Cornelius Cotter. Indianapolis: Bobbs-Merrill, 1975.

Hopkins, J. C., and Sheldon A. Goldberg. *The Development of the Strategic Air Command, 1946–1986.* Offutt Air Force Base, Neb.: Office of the Historian, Headquarters SAC, 1986.

Hoppe, Christoph. *Zwischen Teilhabe und Mitsprache: Die Nuklearfrage in der Allianz-politik Deutschlands, 1959–1966.* Baden-Baden: Nomos Verlagsgesellschaft, 1993.

Horelick, Arnold L., and Myron Rush. *Strategic Power and Soviet Foreign Policy.* Chicago: The University of Chicago Press, 1966.

Hughes, Emmet J. *The Ordeal of Power: A Political Memoir of the Eisenhower Years.* New York: Athenaeum, 1963.

Immerman, Richard H. "Confessions of an Eisenhower Revisionist: An Agonizing Reappraisal." *Diplomatic History* 14, No. 3 (Summer 1990): 319–42.

———. "Eisenhower and Dulles: Who Made the Decisions?" *Political Psychology* 1 (Autumn 1979): 21–38.

———, ed. *John Foster Dulles and the Diplomacy of the Cold War.* Princeton: Princeton University Press, 1990.

———. "The United States and the Geneva Conference of 1954: A New Look." *Diplomatic History* 14, No. 1 (Winter 1990): 43–66.

Jackson, Robert. *Air War over Korea.* London: Allan, 1973.

Jervis, Robert. *The Illogic of American Nuclear Strategy.* Ithaca, N.Y.: Cornell University Press, 1984.

———. *The Logic of Images in International Relations.* Princeton: Princeton University Press, 1970.

———. *The Meaning of the Nuclear Revolution: Statecraft and the Prospect of Armageddon.* Ithaca, N.Y.: Cornell University Press, 1989.

———. *Perceptions and Misperceptions in International Politics.* Princeton: Princeton University Press, 1976.

Jervis, Robert, Richard Ned Lebow, and Janice Gross Stein. *Psychology and Deterrence.* Baltimore: Johns Hopkins University Press, 1985.

Joint Chiefs of Staff Special Historical Study. *Role and Functions of the Joint Chiefs of Staff: A Chronology.* Washington, D.C.: Historical Division, Joint Secretariat, Joint Chiefs of Staff, 1987.

Kaplan, Fred. *The Wizards of Armageddon.* New York: Simon and Schuster, 1983.

Kaplan, Lawrence S. *NATO and the United States: The Enduring Alliance.* Boston: Twayne Publishers, 1988.

Kaufmann, William W. *The McNamara Strategy.* New York: Harper & Row Publishers, 1964.

———, ed. *Military Policy and National Security.* Princeton: Princeton University Press, 1956.

———. "The Requirements of Deterrence." In *U.S. Nuclear Strategy: A Reader,* ed. Philip Bobbitt, Lawrence Freedman, and Gregory F. Treverton. London: Macmillan, 1989.

Kaysen, Carl. "Is War Obsolete? A Review Essay." *International Security* 14, No. 4 (Spring 1990): 42–64.

Kelleher, Catherine McArdle. *Germany and the Politics of Nuclear Weapons.* New York: Columbia University Press, 1975.

Kennan, George F. "The Sources of Soviet Conduct." *Foreign Affairs* 25, No. 4 (July 1947): 566–82.

Kennedy, John F. "A Democrat Looks at Foreign Policy." *Foreign Affairs* 36, No. 1 (October 1957): 44–59.

———. *The Strategy of Peace.* Ed. by Allan Nevins. New York: Harper & Brothers, 1960.

Kennedy, Robert. *Thirteen Days: A Memoir of the Cuban Missile Crisis.* New York: W.W. Norton, 1969.

Khrushchev, Nikita. *Khrushchev Remembers.* Trans. and ed. Strobe Talbott. Boston: Little, Brown and Company, 1970.

———. *Khrushchev Remembers: The Glasnost Tapes.* Trans. and ed. Jerrold L. Schecter with Vyacheslav V. Luchkov. Boston: Little, Brown and Company, 1990.

———. *Khrushchev Remembers: The Last Testament.* Trans. and ed. Strobe Talbott. Boston: Little, Brown and Company, 1974.

Kiefer, Edward C. "President Dwight D. Eisenhower and the End of the Korean War." *Diplomatic History* 10, No. 3 (Summer 1986): 267–89.

Killian, James R., Jr. *Sputnik, Scientists, and Eisenhower: A Memoir of the First Special Assistant to the President for Science and Technology.* Cambridge: MIT Press, 1977.

Kinnard, Douglas. *President Eisenhower and Strategy Management: A Study in Defense Politics.* Lexington: University Press of Kentucky, 1977.

Kissinger, Henry A. *The Necessity for Choice: Prospects of American Foreign Policy.* New York: Harper & Brothers, 1961.

———. *Nuclear Weapons and Foreign Policy.* New York: Published for the Council on Foreign Relations by Harper & Brothers, 1957.

———. "Reflections on Cuba." *Reporter,* 22 November 1963, 21–24.

———. "The Unsolved Problems of European Defense." *Foreign Affairs* 40, No. 4 (July 1962): 515–41.

Kistiakowsky, George B. *A Scientist at the White House: The Private Diary of President Eisenhower's Special Assistant for Science and Technology.* Cambridge: Harvard University Press, 1976.

Kohl, Wilfrid L. *French Nuclear Diplomacy.* Princeton: Princeton University Press, 1971.

Kramer, Mark. "Tactical Nuclear Weapons, Soviet Command Authority, and the Cuban Missile Crisis." *Cold War International History Project Bulletin* 3 (Fall 1993): 40–46.

Krippendorff, Ekkehart, ed. *Friedensforschung.* Köln: Kiepenheuer & Witsch, 1968.

Kull, Steven. *Minds at War: Nuclear Reality and the Inner Conflicts of Defense Policymakers.* New York: Basic Books, 1988.

Larson, David L. *The "Cuban Crisis" of 1962: Selected Documents, Chronology and Bibliography.* 2d ed. Lanham: University Press of America, 1986.

Legge, J. Michael. "Theater Nuclear Weapons and the NATO Strategy of Flexible Response." *RAND Report R-2964-FF.* Santa Monica: The RAND Corporation, 1983.

LeMay, Curtis E. *Mission with LeMay: My Story.* With the assistance of K. MacKinlay. New York: Doubleday, 1965.

Levering, Ralph B. *The Public and American Foreign Policy, 1918–1978.* New York: Morrow, 1978.

Liddell Hart, B. H. *Deterrent or Defense: A Fresh Look at the West's Military Position.* New York: Praeger, 1960.

―――. *The Revolution in Warfare.* New Haven: Yale University Press, 1946.

Lilienthal, David E. *The Atomic Energy Years, 1945–1950.* Vol. 2, The Journals of David E. Lilienthal. New York: Harper & Row, 1964.

―――. *The Venturesome Years, 1950–1955.* Vol. 3, The Journals of David E. Lilienthal. New York: Harper & Row, 1966.

Louis, Roger W. "Dulles, Suez, and the British." In *John Foster Dulles and the Diplomacy of the Cold War,* ed. Richard H. Immerman. Princeton: Princeton University Press, 1990.

MacFarlane, Neil. "V. D. Sokolovskii." In *Makers of Nuclear Strategy,* ed. John Baylis and John Garnett. London: Pinter Publishers, 1991.

Mahajani, Ushy. "President Kennedy and U.S. Policy in Laos, 1961–1963." *Journal of Southeast Asian Studies* II, No. 2 (September 1971): 87–99.

Mandelbaum, Michael. *The Nuclear Revolution: International Politics before and after Hiroshima.* New York: Cambridge University Press, 1981.

McNamara, Robert S. "The Military Role of Nuclear Weapons: Perceptions and Misperceptions." *Foreign Affairs* 62, No. 1 (Fall 1983): 59–81.

Medvedev, Roy. *All Stalin's Men.* Trans. Harold Shukman. New York: Doubleday, 1985.

Mueller, John. "The Essential Irrelevance of Nuclear Weapons: Stability in the Postwar World." *International Security* 13, No. 2 (Fall 1988): 55–79.

―――. *Retreat from Doomsday: The Obsolescence of Major War.* New York: Basic Books, 1989.

Nitze, Paul H. "Atoms, Strategy and Policy." *Foreign Affairs* 34, No. 2 (January 1956): 187–98.

―――. *From Hiroshima to Glasnost: At the Center of Decision.* New York: Grove Weidenfeld, 1989.

Nye, Joseph S. "Nuclear Learning and U.S.-Soviet Security Regimes." *International Organization* 41 (Summer 1987): 371–402.

Oberdorfer, Don. *The Turn: From the Cold War to a New Era: The United States and the Soviet Union, 1983–1990.* New York: Simon and Schuster, 1992.

Oppenheimer, Robert. "Atomic Weapons and American Policy," *Foreign Affairs* 31 (July 1953): 525–35.

Osgood, Robert E. *Limited War: The Challenge to American Security.* Chicago: University of Chicago Press, 1957.

―――. *NATO: The Entangling Alliance.* Chicago: University of Chicago Press, 1962.

Peter, Thomas. *Abschrecken und Ueberleben im Nuklearzeitalter: Präsident Eisenhowers Sicherheitspolitik des "New Look."* Ph.D. diss. Grüsch: Verlag Rüegger, 1990.

Pope, Ronald R., ed. *Soviet Views on the Cuban Missile Crisis: Myth and Reality in Foreign Policy Analysis.* Lanham, Md.: University Press of America, 1982.

Power, Thomas S. *Design for Survival.* New York: Coward-McCann, 1965.

Prados, John. *The Sky Would Fall: Operation Vulture: The U.S. Bombing Mission in Indochina, 1954.* New York: The Dial Press, 1983.

———. *The Soviet Estimate: U.S. Intelligence Analysis and Russian Military Strength.* New York: Dial Press, 1982.

" 'Project Solarium': A Collective Oral History." John Foster Dulles Centennial Conference. Speakers: General Andrew J. Goodpaster, Robert R. Bowie, Ambassador George F. Kennan. Princeton: Princeton University, 27 February 1988.

Pruessen, Ronald W. "John Foster Dulles and the Predicaments of Power." In *John Foster Dulles and the Diplomacy of the Cold War,* ed. Richard H. Immerman. Princeton: Princeton University Press, 1990.

———. *John Foster Dulles: The Road to Power.* New York: Free Press, 1982.

Rabinowitch, Eugene. "The Hydrogen Bomb and the Great Unsolved Problems." *Bulletin of the Atomic Scientists* 10 (May 1954): 146–47, 168.

Rearden, Steven L. *The Evolution of American Strategic Doctrine: Paul H. Nitze and the Soviet Challenge.* Boulder: Westview Press, 1984.

Reed, George A. *U.S. Defense Policy: U.S. Air Force Doctrine and Strategic Nuclear Weapons Systems, 1958–1964: The Case of the Minuteman ICBM.* Ph.D. diss. Ann Arbor, Mich.: University Microfilms, 1986.

Rees, David. *Korea: The Limited War.* New York: St. Martin's Press, 1964.

Richardson, Robert C., III. "NATO Nuclear Strategy: A Look Back." *Strategic Review* 9, No. 2 (Spring 1981): 35–43.

Ridgway, Matthew B. *Soldier: The Memoirs of Matthew B. Ridgway.* New York: Harper, 1956.

Rosenberg, David Alan. "American Atomic Strategy and the Hydrogen Bomb Decision." *Journal of American History* 66 (June 1979): 62–78.

———. "The Origins of Overkill: Nuclear Weapons and American Strategy, 1945–1960." *International Security* 7, No. 4 (Spring 1983): 3–71.

———. "Reality and Responsibility: Power and Process in Making of United States Nuclear Strategy, 1945–1968." *Journal of Strategic Studies* 9, No. 1 (March 1986): 35–52.

———. "U.S. Nuclear Stockpile, 1945–1960." *Bulletin of the Atomic Scientists* 38, No. 3 (May 1982): 25–30.

———. "U.S. Nuclear Strategy: Theory vs. Practice." *Bulletin of the Atomic Scientists* 43, No. 2 (March 1987): 20–26.

Rostow, Walt W. *The Diffusion of Power: An Essay in Recent History.* New York: The Macmillan Company, 1972.

Rowen, Henry S. "Formulating Strategic Doctrine." In *Essays on Arms Control and National Security,* ed. Bernard F. Halloran. Washington, D.C.: U.S. Arms Control and Disarmament Agency, 1986.

Rusk, Dean. *As I Saw It, by Dean Rusk As Told to Richard Rusk.* Ed. Daniel S. Papp. New York: Penguin Books, 1990.

Rusk, Dean, Robert McNamara, George W. Ball, Roswell L. Gilpatric, Theodore Sorensen, and McGeorge Bundy. "The Lessons of the Cuban Missile Crisis." *Time,* 27 September 1982, 85–86.

Sapolsky, Harvey M. *The Polaris System Development: Bureaucratic and Programmatic Success in Government.* Cambridge: Harvard University Press, 1972.

Scali, John. "I Was the Secret Go-Between in the Cuban Crisis." *Family Weekly,* 25 October 1964, 4–5, 12–14.

Scheinman, Lawrence. *Atomic Energy Policy in France under the Fourth Republic.* Princeton: Princeton University Press, 1965.

Schelling, Thomas C. *Arms and Influence.* New Haven: Yale University Press, 1966.

———. "Nuclear Strategy in the Berlin Crisis." In *Writings on Strategy, 1961–1969, and Retrospectives,* ed. Marc Trachtenberg. New York: Garland Pub., 1988.

———. *The Strategy of Conflict.* Cambridge: Harvard University Press, 1960.

Schick, Jack. *The Berlin Crisis, 1958–1962.* Philadelphia: University of Pennsylvania Press, 1971.

Schilling, Warner R., Paul Y. Hammond, and Glenn H. Snyder. *Strategy, Politics, and Defense Budgets.* New York: Columbia University Press, 1966.

Schlesinger, Arthur M., Jr. "Four Days with Fidel: A Havana Diary." *New York Review of Books,* 16 March 1992, 24.

———. *A Thousand Days: John F. Kennedy in the White House.* Cambridge: The Riverside Press, 1965.

Schlesinger, James R. "Atoms for Peace Revisited." In *Atoms for Peace: An Analysis after Thirty Years,* ed. Joseph F. Pilat, Robert E. Pendley, and Charles K. Ebinger. Boulder: Westview Press, 1985.

Schöttli, Thomas U. *USA und EVG: Truman, Eisenhower und die Europa-Armee.* Ph.D. diss. Bern: Lang Verlag, 1994.

Schwartz, David N. *NATO's Nuclear Dilemmas.* Washington, D.C.: The Brookings Institution, 1983.

Seaborg, Glenn T. *Kennedy, Khrushchev, and the Test Ban.* With the assistance of Benjamin S. Loeb. Berkeley: University of California Press, 1981.

Seabury, Paul, ed. *The Balance of Power.* San Francisco: Chandler, 1965.

Shapley, Deborah. *Promise and Power: The Life and Times of Robert S. McNamara.* Boston: Little, Brown and Company, 1993.

Shepley, James. "How Dulles Averted War." *Life,* 16 January 1956, 70–72.

Slusser, Robert M. *The Berlin Crisis of 1961: Soviet-American Relations and the Struggle for Power in the Kremlin, June-November 1961.* Baltimore: The Johns Hopkins University Press, 1973.

Snyder, Glenn. "The Balance of Power and the Balance of Terror." In *The Balance of Power,* ed. Paul Seabury. San Francisco: Chandler, 1965.

———. "The 'New Look' of 1953." In *Strategy, Politics, and Defense Budgets,* ed. Warner R. Schilling, Paul Y. Hammond, and Glenn H. Snyder. New York: Columbia University Press, 1966.

Sokolovskii, V. D. "The Nature of Modern War: Soviet Military Strategy (1962)." In *Nuclear Strategy, Arms Control, and the Future,* ed. Edward Haley, David Keithly, and Jack Merritt. Boulder: Westview Press, 1985.

Sorensen, Theodore C. *Kennedy.* London: Pan Books Ltd., 1965.

Spillmann, Kurt R. *Aggressive USA? Amerikanische Sicherheitspolitik, 1945–1985*. Stuttgart: Klett-Cotta, 1985.

Stassen, Harold, and Marshall Houts. *Eisenhower: Turning the World toward Peace*. St. Paul: Merrill/Magnus Publishing Corporation, 1990.

Steel, Ronald. "Endgame: *Thirteen Days* by Robert Kennedy." *New York Review of Books*, 13 March 1969, 15–22.

Stein, Peter, and Peter Feaver. *Assuring Control of Nuclear Weapons: The Evolution of Permissive Action Links*. Lanham, Md.: University Press of America, 1987.

Steinbruner, John D. *The Cybernetic Theory of Decision: New Dimensions of Political Analysis*. Princeton: Princeton University Press, 1974.

Steininger, Rolf. "John Foster Dulles, the European Defense Community and the German Question." In *John Foster Dulles and the Diplomacy of the Cold War*, ed. Richard H. Immerman. Princeton: Princeton University Press, 1990.

Strauss, Lewis L. *Men and Decision*. Garden City, N.Y.: Doubleday & Company, 1962.

Stromseth, Jane E. *The Origins of Flexible Response: NATO's Debate over Strategy in the 1960s*. New York: St. Martin's Press, 1988.

Symington, Stuart. "Where the Missile Gap Went." *The Reporter* 26, No. 4 (15 February 1962): 21–23.

Taylor, John M. *General Maxwell Taylor: The Sword and the Pen*. New York: Doubleday, 1989.

Taylor, Maxwell D. "The Legitimate Claims of National Security." *Foreign Affairs* 52, No. 3 (April 1974): 577–94.

———. *The Uncertain Trumpet*. New York: Harper, 1960.

Trachtenberg, Marc. *History and Strategy*. Princeton: Princeton University Press, 1991.

———. "The Influence of Nuclear Weapons in the Cuban Missile Crisis." *International Security* 10, No. 1 (Summer 1985): 137–63.

———, ed. *Writings on Strategy, 1961–1969, and Retrospectives*. Vol. 4, The Development of American Strategic Thought. New York: Garland Pub., 1988.

Waltz, Kenneth. "The Spread of Nuclear Weapons: More May Be Better." *Adelphi Papers* 171. London: The International Institute for Strategic Studies, 1981.

Wampler, Robert Allen. *Ambiguous Legacy: The United States, Great Britain and the Foundations of NATO Strategy, 1948–1957*. Ph.D. diss. Ann Arbor, Mich.: University Microfilms, 1991.

Watson, Robert J., *The Joint Chiefs of Staff and National Policy, 1953–1954*. Vol. 5, *History of the Joint Chiefs of Staff*. Washington, D.C.: Historical Division, Joint Chiefs of Staff, 1986.

Welch, David A., and James G. Blight. "The Eleventh Hour of the Cuban Missile Crisis: An Introduction to the ExComm Transcripts." *International Security* 12, No. 3 (Winter 1987–88): 5–29.

Wells, Samuel F., Jr. "The Origins of Massive Retaliation." *Political Science Quarterly* 96, No. 1 (Spring 1981): 31–52.

———. "Sounding the Tocsin: NSC-68 and the Soviet Threat." *International Security* 4, No. 2 (Fall 1979): 116–58.

Wenger, Andreas. "Kontinuität und Wandel in der amerikanischen Nuklearstrategie: Präsident Eisenhowers Strategie der massiven Vergeltung und die nuklearstrategische Neuevaluation der Administration Kennedy." *Zürcher Beiträge zur Sicherheitspolitik und Konfliktforschung* 19 (1991). Zürich: Center for Security Studies, 1991.

White, Theodore H. *The Making of the President 1960.* New York: Athenaeum, 1961.

Wiesner, Jerome. "Arms Control: Current Prospects and Problems." *Bulletin of the Atomic Scientists* 26, No. 3 (May 1970): 6–8.

Wohlstetter, Albert. "The Delicate Balance of Terror." *Foreign Affairs* 37, No. 3 (January 1959): 211–34.

———. "Nuclear Sharing: NATO and the N + 1 Country." *Foreign Affairs* 19, No. 3 (April 1961): 355–87.

Wohlstetter, Albert, and Roberta Wohlstetter. "Controlling the Risks in Cuba." *Adelphi Papers* 17 (April 1965). London: The International Institute for Strategic Studies, 1965.

Wohlstetter, A. J., F. S. Hoffman, R. J. Lutz, and H. S. Rowen. "Selection and Use of Strategic Air Bases." *RAND Report R-266.* Santa Monica: The RAND Corporation, 1962.

York, Herbert. *Race to Oblivion: A Participant's View of the Arms Race.* New York: Simon and Schuster, 1970.

Zubok, Vladislav M. "Khrushchev and the Berlin Crisis, 1958–1962," *Cold War International History Project Working Paper,* No. 6. Washington, D.C.: Woodrow Wilson International Center for Scholars, May 1993.

Index

About the Author

Andreas Wenger is deputy director of the Center for Security Studies and Conflict Research at the Swiss Federal Institute of Technology Zurich. He has been a student of nuclear learning since 1991, when he started to write on John F. Kennedy's foreign policy during the Berlin crisis. The major work on this book was done from 1992 to 1994 as a visiting fellow of the Woodrow Wilson School and the Center of International Studies at Princeton University.